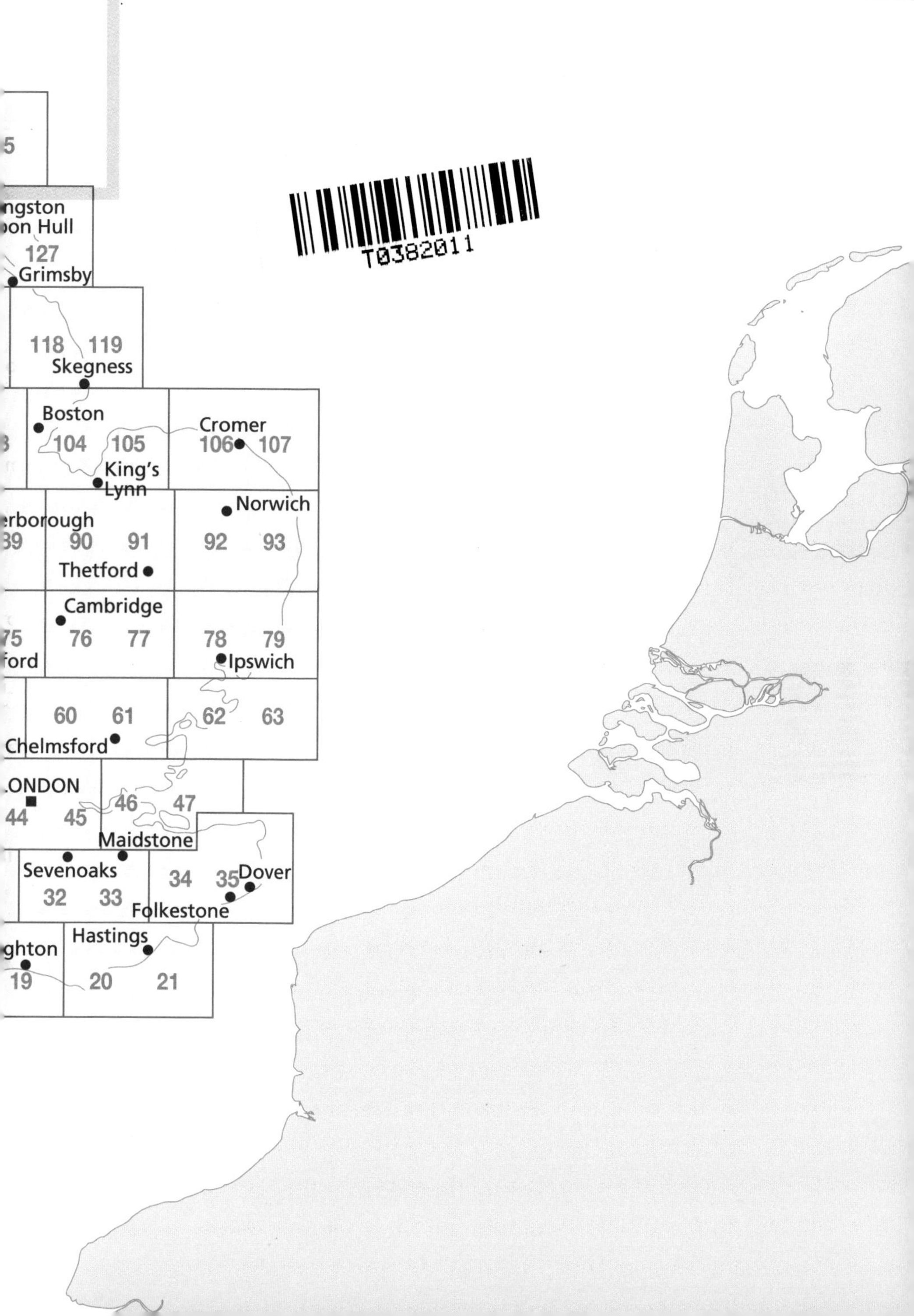

5

ngston
on Hull
127
●Grimsby

118 \ 119
Skegness●

Boston
●
104 \ 105
King's
●Lynn

Cromer
106● ●107

erborough
●
39 \ 90 \ 91
Thetford ●

Norwich
●
92 \ 93

Cambridge
●
●75 \ 76 \ 77
ford

78 \ 79
●Ipswich

60 \ 61
Chelmsford●

62 \ 63

●ONDON
■
44 \ 46 \ 47
45
Maidstone●

Sevenoaks
●
32 \ 33

34 \ 35●Dover
●
Folkestone

ghton \ Hastings●
19 \ 20 \ 21

Mileage chart

The mileage chart shows distances in miles between two towns along AA-recommended routes. Using motorways and other main roads this is normally the fastest route, though not necessarily the shortest.

The journey times are shown in hours and minutes. These times should be used as a guide only and do not allow for unforeseen traffic delays, rest breaks or fuel stops.

For example, the 377 miles (607 km) journey between Glasgow and Norwich should take approximately 7 hours 18 minutes.

Journey times

Distances in miles (one mile equals 1.6093 km)

AA

2024
Driver's Atlas
BRITAIN

Scale 1:250,000
or 3.95 miles to 1 inch

20th edition June 2023 © AA Media Limited 2023

All cartography in this atlas edited, designed and produced by the Mapping Services Department of AA Media Limited (A05841).

This atlas contains Ordnance Survey data © Crown copyright and database right 2023. Contains public sector information licensed under the Open Government Licence v3.0. Ireland mapping and Mileage chart and journey times contains data available from openstreetmap.org © under the Open Database License found at opendatacommons.org

Published by AA Media Limited, whose registered office is Grove House, Lutyens Close, Basingstoke, Hampshire RG24 8AG, UK. Registered number 06112600

ISBN: 978 0 7495 8335 4 (flexibound)

A CIP catalogue record for this book is available from The British Library.

Disclaimer: The contents of this atlas are believed to be correct at the time of the latest revision, it will not contain any subsequent amended, new or temporary information including diversions and traffic control or enforcement systems. The publishers cannot be held responsible or liable for any loss or damage occasioned to any person acting or refraining from action as a result of any use or reliance on material in this atlas, nor for any errors, omissions or changes in such material. This does not affect your statutory rights.

The publishers would welcome information to correct any errors or omissions and to keep this atlas up to date. Please write to the Atlas Editor, AA Media Limited, Grove House, Lutyens Close, Basingstoke, Hampshire, RG24 8AG, UK. **E-mail:** *roadatlasfeedback@aamediagroup.co.uk*

Acknowledgements: AA Media Limited would like to thank the following for information used in the creation of this atlas: Cadw, English Heritage, Forestry Commission, Historic Scotland, National Trust and National Trust for Scotland, RSPB, The Wildlife Trust, Scottish Natural Heritage, Natural England, The Countryside Council for Wales. Award winning beaches from 'Blue Flag' and 'Keep Scotland Beautiful' (summer 2022 data): for latest information visit *www.blueflag.org* and *www.keepscotlandbeautiful.org* Ireland mapping: Republic of Ireland census 2016 © Central Statistics Office and Northern Ireland census 2016 © NISRA (population data); Logainm.ie (placenames); Roads Service and Transport Infrastructure Ireland.
Printed by Oriental Press, Dubai.

* The UK's most up-to-date atlases based on a comparison of 2023 UK Road Atlases available on the market in November 2022.

Contents

Map pages south	**inside front cover**
Mileage chart and journey times	**endpaper**
Route planner	**II–VII**
Motorways	**VIII–X**
Restricted junctions	VIII–IX
Smart motorways	X
Atlas symbols	**1**
Road maps 1:250,000 scale	**2–237**
Channel Islands 1:150,000 scale	236
Isle of Man 1:317,000 scale	237
Orkney Islands 1:636,000 scale	234
Shetland Islands 1:636,000 scale	235
Western Isles 1:700,000 scale	232–233
Index to place names	**238–318**
County, administrative area map	238–239
Place name index	240–318
Ireland	**endpaper**
Map pages north	**inside back cover**

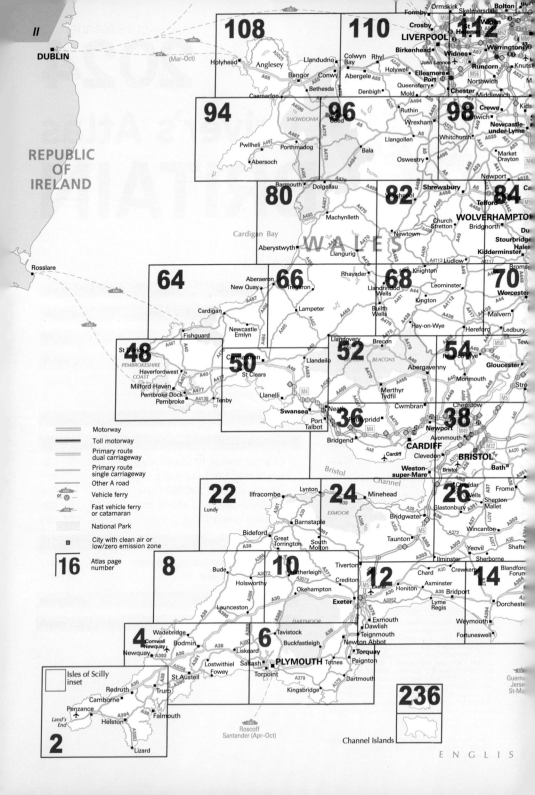

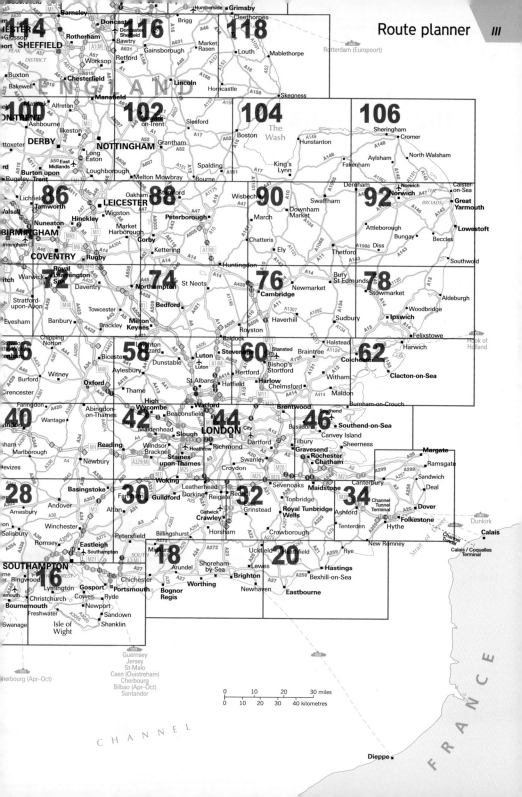

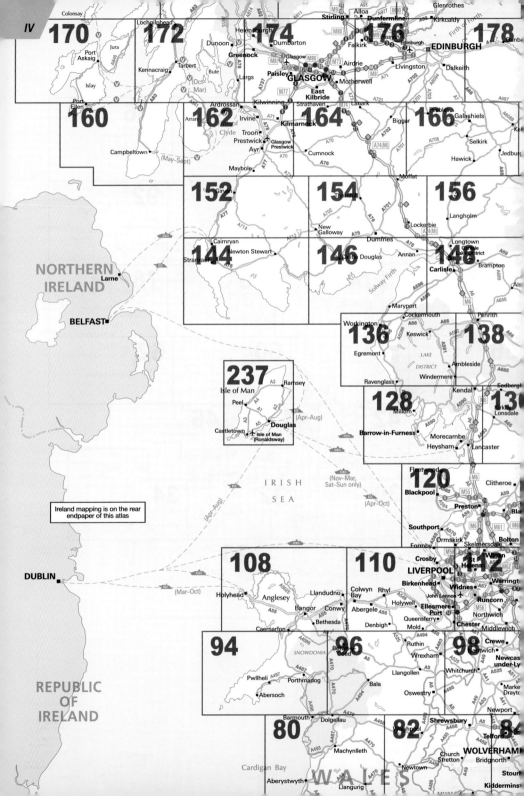

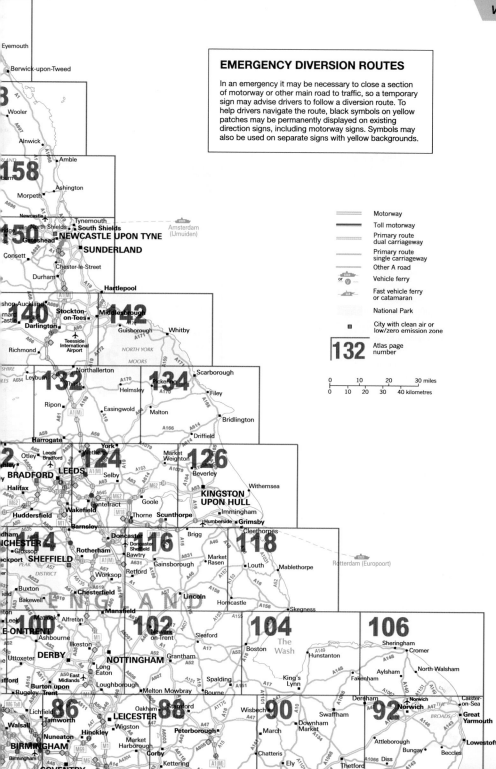

EMERGENCY DIVERSION ROUTES

In an emergency it may be necessary to close a section of motorway or other main road to traffic, so a temporary sign may advise drivers to follow a diversion route. To help drivers navigate the route, black symbols on yellow patches may be permanently displayed on existing direction signs, including motorway signs. Symbols may also be used on separate signs with yellow backgrounds.

Motorway
Toll motorway
Primary route
dual carriageway
Primary route
single carriageway
Other A road
Vehicle ferry
Fast vehicle ferry
or catamaran
National Park
City with clean air or
low/zero emission zone

132 Atlas page
number

| 0 | 10 | 20 | 30 miles |
| 0 | 10 | 20 | 30 | 40 kilometres |

FERRY OPERATORS

Hebrides and west coast Scotland
calmac.co.uk
skyeferry.co.uk
western-ferries.co.uk

Orkney and Shetland
northlinkferries.co.uk
pentlandferries.co.uk
orkneyferries.co.uk
shetland.gov.uk/ferries

Isle of Man
steam-packet.com

Ireland
irishferries.com
poferries.com
stenaline.co.uk

North Sea (Scandinavia and Benelux)
dfdsseaways.co.uk
poferries.com

Isle of Wight
wightlink.co.uk
redfunnel.co.uk

Channel Islands
condorferries.co.uk

France and Belgium
brittany-ferries.co.uk
condorferries.co.uk
eurotunnel.com
dfdsseaways.co.uk
poferries.com

Northern Spain
brittany-ferries.co.uk

═══	Motorway
═══	Toll motorway
▪▪▪▪	Primary route dual carriageway
──	Primary route single carriageway
──	Other A road
or Ⓥ	Vehicle ferry
	Fast vehicle ferry or catamaran
	National Park
▪	City with clean air or low/zero emission zone
192	Atlas page number

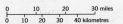

0 10 20 30 miles
0 10 20 30 40 kilometres

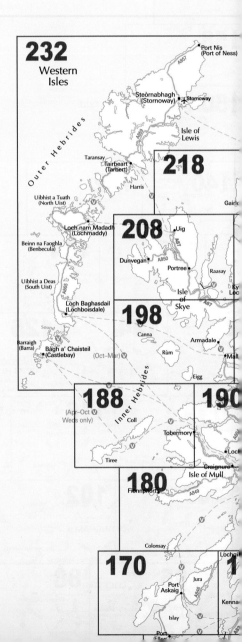

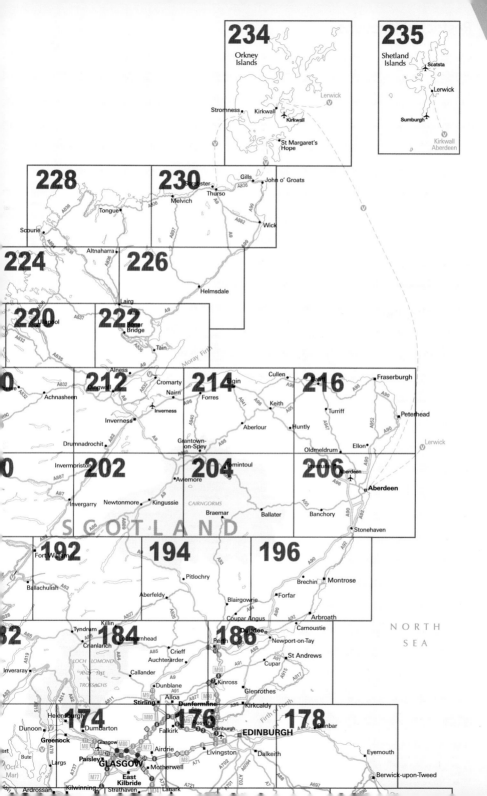

VIII Restricted junctions

Motorway and primary route junctions which have access or exit restrictions are shown on the map pages thus:

M1 London - Leeds

Junction	Northbound	Southbound
2	Access only from A1 *(northbound)*	Exit only to A1 *(southbound)*
4	Access only from A41 *(northbound)*	Exit only to A41 *(northbound)*
6A	Access only from M25 *(no link from A405)*	Exit only to M25 *(no link from A405)*
7	Access only from A414	Exit only to A414
17	Exit only to M45	Access only from M45
19	Exit only to M6 *(northbound)*	Exit only to A14 *(southbound)*
21A	Exit only, no access	Access only, no exit
24A	Access only, no exit	Access only from A50 *(eastbound)*
35A	Exit only, no access	Access only, no exit
43	Exit only to M621	Access only from M621
48	Exit only to A1(M) *(northbound)*	Access only from A1(M) *(southbound)*

M2 Rochester - Faversham

Junction	Westbound	Eastbound
1	No exit to A2 *(eastbound)*	No access from A2 *(westbound)*

M3 Sunbury - Southampton

Junction	Northeastbound	Southwestbound
8	Access only from A303, no exit	Exit only to A303, no access
10	Exit only, no access	Access only, no exit
14	Access only from M27 only, no exit	No access to M27 *(westbound)*

M4 London - South Wales

Junction	Westbound	Eastbound
1	Access only from A4 *(westbound)*	Exit only to A4 *(eastbound)*
2	Access only from A4 *(westbound)*	Access only from A4 *(eastbound)*
21	Exit only to M48	Access only from M48
23	Access only from M48	Exit only to M48
25	Exit only, no access	Access only, no exit
25A	Exit only, no access	Access only, no exit
29	Exit only to A48(M)	Access only from A48(M)
38	Exit only, no access	No restriction
39	Access only, no exit	No access or exit
42	Exit only to A483	Access only from A483

M5 Birmingham - Exeter

Junction	Northeastbound	Southwestbound
10	Access only, no exit	Exit only, no access
11A	Access only from A417 *(westbound)*	Exit only to A417 *(eastbound)*
18A	Exit only to M49	Access only from M49
18	Exit only, no access	Access only, no exit

M6 Toll Motorway

Junction	Northwestbound	Southeastbound
T1	Access only, no exit	No access or exit
T2	No access or exit	Exit only, no access
T5	Access only, no exit	Exit only to A5148 *(northbound)*, no access
T7	Exit only, no access	Access only, no exit
T8	Exit only, no access	Access only, no exit

M6 Rugby - Carlisle

Junction	Northbound	Southbound
3A	Exit only to M6 Toll	Access only from M6 Toll
4	Exit only to M42 *(southbound)* & A446	Exit only to A446
4A	Access only from M42 *(southbound)*	Exit only to M42
5	Exit only, no access	Access only, no exit
10A	Exit only to M54	Access only from M54
11A	Access only from M6 Toll	Exit only to M6 Toll
with M56 (jct 20A)	No restriction	Access only from M56 *(eastbound)*
20	Exit only to M56 *(westbound)*	Access only from M56 *(eastbound)*
24	Access only, no exit	Exit only, no access
25	Access only, no exit	Access only, no exit
30	Access only from M61	Exit only to M61
31A	Access only, no exit	
45	Exit only, no access	Access only, no exit

M8 Edinburgh - Bishopton

Junction	Westbound	Eastbound
6	Exit only, no access	Access only, no exit
6A	Access only, no exit	Exit only, no access
7	Access only, no exit	Exit only, no access
7A	Exit only, no access	Access only from A725 *(northbound)*, no exit
8	No access from M73 *(southbound)* or from A8 *(eastbound)* & A89	No exit to M73 *(northbound)* or to A8 *(westbound)* & A89
9	Access only, no exit	Exit only, no access
13	Access only from M80 *(southbound)*	Exit only to M80 *(northbound)*
14	Access only, no exit	Exit only, no access
16	Exit only to A804	Access only from A879
17	Exit only to A82	No restriction
18	Access only from A82 *(eastbound)*	Exit only to A814
19	No access from A814 *(westbound)*	Exit only to A814 *(westbound)*
20	Exit only, no access	Access only, no exit
21	Access only, no exit	Exit only to A8
22	Exit only to M77 *(southbound)*	Access only from M77 *(northbound)*
23	Exit only to B768	Access only from B768
25	No access or exit from or to A8	No access or exit from or to A8
25A	Exit only, no access	Access only, no exit
28	Exit only, no access	Access only, no exit
28A	Exit only to A737	Access only from A737
29A	Exit only to A8	Access only, no exit

M9 Edinburgh - Dunblane

Junction	Northwestbound	Southeastbound
2	Access only, no exit	Exit only, no access
3	Access only, no exit	Exit only, no access
6	Access only, no exit	Exit only to A905
8	Exit only to M876 *(southwestbound)*	Access only from M876 *(northeastbound)*

M11 London - Cambridge

Junction	Northbound	Southbound
4	Access only from A406 *(eastbound)*	Exit only to A406
5	Access only, no exit	Access only, no exit
8A	Access only, no exit	No direct access, use jct 8
9	Exit only to A11	Access only from A11
13	Exit only, no access	Access only, no exit
14	Exit only, no access	Access only, no exit

M20 Swanley - Folkestone

Junction	Northwestbound	Southeastbound
2	Staggered junction; follow signs - access only	Staggered junction; follow signs - exit only
3	Exit only to M26 *(westbound)*	Access only from M26 *(eastbound)*
5	Access only from A20	For access follow signs - exit only to A20
6	No restriction	For exit follow signs
10	Access only, no exit	Exit only, no access
11A	Exit only, no access	Access only, no exit

M23 Hooley - Crawley

Junction	Northbound	Southbound
7	Exit only to A23 *(northbound)*	Access only from A23 *(southbound)*
10A	Access only, no exit	Exit only, no access

M25 London Orbital

Junction	Clockwise	Anticlockwise
1B	No direct access, use slip road to jct 2 Exit only	Access only, no exit
5	No exit to M26 *(eastbound)*	No access from M26
19	Exit only, no access	Access only, no exit
21	Access only from M1 *(southbound)* Exit only to M1 *(northbound)*	Access only from M1 *(southbound)* Exit only to M1 *(northbound)*
31	No exit (use slip road via jct 30), access only	No access (use slip road via jct 30), exit only

M26 Sevenoaks - Wrotham

Junction	Westbound	Eastbound
with M25 (jct 5)	Exit only to clockwise M25 *(westbound)*	Access only from anticlockwise M25 *(eastbound)*
with M20 (jct 3)	Access only from M20 *(northwestbound)*	Exit only to M20 *(southeastbound)*

M27 Cadnam - Portsmouth

Junction	Westbound	Eastbound
4	Staggered junction; follow signs - access only from M3 *(southbound)*. Exit only to M3 *(northbound)*	Staggered junction; follow signs - access only from M3 *(southbound)*. Exit only to M3 *(northbound)*
10	Exit only, no access	Access only, no exit
12	Staggered junction; follow signs - exit only to M275 *(southbound)*	Staggered junction; follow signs - access only from M275 *(northbound)*

M40 London - Birmingham

Junction	Northwestbound	Southeastbound
3	Exit only, no access	Access only, no exit
7	Exit only, no access	Access only, no exit
8	Exit only to M40/A40	Access only from M40/A40
13	Exit only, no access	Access only, no exit
14	Access only, no exit	Exit only, no access
16	Access only, no exit	Exit only, no access

M42 Bromsgrove - Measham

Junction	Northeastbound	Southwestbound
1	Access only, no exit	Exit only, no access
7	Exit only to M6 *(northwestbound)*	Access only from M6 *(northwestbound)*
7A	Exit only to M6 *(southbound)*	No access or exit
8	Access only from M6 *(southbound)*	Exit only to M6 *(northwestbound)*

M45 Coventry - M1

Junction	Westbound	Eastbound
Dunchurch (unnumbered)	Access only from A45	Exit only, no access
with M1 (jct 17)	Access only from M1 *(northbound)*	Exit only to M1 *(southbound)*

M48 Chepstow

Junction	Westbound	Eastbound
21	Access only from M4 *(westbound)*	Exit only to M4 *(eastbound)*
23	No exit to M4 *(eastbound)*	No Access from M4 *(westbound)*

M53 Mersey Tunnel - Chester

Junction	Northbound	Southbound
11	Access only from M56 *(westbound)* Exit only to M56 *(eastbound)*	Access only from M56 *(westbound)* Exit only to M56 *(eastbound)*

M54 Telford - Birmingham

Junction	Westbound	Eastbound
with M6 (jct 10A)	Access only from M6 *(northbound)*	Exit only to M6 *(southbound)*

M56 Chester - Manchester

Junction	Westbound	Eastbound
1	Access only from M60 *(westbound)*	Exit only to M60 *(eastbound)* & A34 *(northbound)*
2	Exit only, no access	Access only, no exit
3	Access only, no exit	Exit only, no access
4	Exit only, no access	Access only, no exit
7	Exit only, no access	No restriction
8	Access only, no exit	No access or exit
9	No exit to M6 *(southbound)*	No access from M6 *(northbound)*
15	Exit only to M53	Access only from M53
16	No access or exit	No restriction

M57 Liverpool Outer Ring Road

Junction	Northbound	Southeastbound
3	Access only, no exit	Exit only, no access
5	Access only from A580 (westbound)	Exit only, no access

M60 Manchester Orbital

Junction	Clockwise	Anticlockwise
2	Access only, no exit	Access only, no exit
3	No access from M56	Access only from A34 (northbound)
4	Access only from A34 (northbound). Exit only to M56	Access only from M56 (eastbound). Exit only to A34 (southbound)
5	Access and exit only from and to A5103 (northbound)	Access and exit only from and to A5103 (southbound)
7	No direct access, use slip road to jct 8. Exit only to A56	Access only from A56. No exit, use jct 8
14	Access from A580 (eastbound)	Exit only to A580 (westbound)
16	Access only, no exit	Exit only, no access
20	Exit only, no access	Access only, no exit
22	No restriction	Exit only, no access
25	Exit only, no access	No restriction
26	No restriction	Exit only, no access
27	Access only, no exit	Access only, no access

M61 Manchester - Preston

Junction	Northwestbound	Southeastbound
3	No access or exit	Exit only, no access
with M6 (jct 30)	Exit only to M6 (northbound)	Access only from M6 (southbound)

M62 Liverpool - Kingston upon Hull

Junction	Westbound	Eastbound
23	Access only, no exit	Exit only, no access
32A	No access to A1(M) (southbound)	No restriction

M65 Preston - Colne

Junction	Northeastbound	Southwestbound
9	Exit only, no access	Access only, no exit
11	Access only, no exit	Exit only, no access

M66 Bury

Junction	Northbound	Southbound
with A56	Access only from A56 (northbound)	Access only from A56 (southbound)
1	Exit only, no access	Access only, no exit

M67 Hyde Bypass

Junction	Westbound	Eastbound
1A	Access only, no exit	Exit only, no access
2	Exit only, no access	Access only, no exit

M69 Coventry - Leicester

Junction	Northbound	Southbound
2	Access only, no exit	Exit only, no access

M73 East of Glasgow

Junction	Northbound	Southbound
1	No exit to A74 & A721	No exit to A74 & A721
2	No access from or exit to A89. No access from (eastbound)	No access from or exit to A89. No exit to M8 (westbound)

M74 and A74(M) Glasgow - Gretna

Junction	Northbound	Southbound
3	Exit only, no access	Access only, no exit
3A	Access only, no exit	Exit only, no access
4	No access from A74 & A721	Access only, no exit to A74 & A721
7	Access only, no exit	Exit only, no access
9	No access or exit	Exit only, no access
10	No restriction	Access only, no exit
11	Access only, no exit	Access only, no exit
12	Exit only, no access	Access only, no exit
18	Exit only, no access	Access only, no exit

M77 Glasgow - Kilmarnock

Junction	Northbound	Southbound
with M8 (jct 22)	No exit to M8 (westbound)	No access from M8 (eastbound)
4	Access only, no exit	Exit only, no access
6	Access only, no exit	Exit only, no access
7	Access only, no exit	No restriction
8	Exit only, no access	Exit only, no access

M80 Glasgow - Stirling

Junction	Northbound	Southbound
4A	Exit only, no access	Access only, no exit
6A	Access only, no exit	Exit only, no access
8	Exit only to M876 (northeastbound)	Access only from M876 (southwestbound)

M90 Edinburgh - Perth

Junction	Northbound	Southbound
1	No exit, access only	Exit only to A90
2A	Exit only to A92 (eastbound)	Access only from A92 (westbound)
7	Access only, no exit	Exit only, no access
8	Exit only, no access	Access only, no exit
10	No access from A912. No exit to A912 (southbound)	No access from A912 (northbound). No exit to A912

M180 Doncaster - Grimsby

Junction	Westbound	Eastbound
1	Access only, no exit	Exit only, no access

M606 Bradford Spur

Junction	Northbound	Southbound
2	Access only, no access	No restriction

M621 Leeds - M1

Junction	Clockwise	Anticlockwise
2A	Access only, no exit	Exit only, no access
4	No exit or access	No restriction
5	Access only, no exit	Exit only, no access
6	Exit only, no access	Access only, no exit
with M1 (jct 43)	Exit only to M1 (southbound)	Access only from M1 (northbound)

M876 Bonnybridge - Kincardine Bridge

Junction	Northeastbound	Southwestbound
with M80 (jct 5)	Access only from M80 (northeastbound)	Exit only to M80 (southwestbound)
with M9 (jct 8)	Exit only to M9 (eastbound)	Access only from M9 (westbound)

A1(M) South Mimms - Baldock

Junction	Northbound	Southbound
2	Exit only, no access	Access only, no exit
3	No restriction	Access only, no access
5	Access only, no exit	No access or exit

A1(M) Pontefract - Bedale

Junction	Northbound	Southbound
41	No access to M62 (eastbound)	No restriction
43	Access only from M1 (northbound)	Exit only to M1 (southbound)

A1(M) Scotch Corner - Newcastle upon Tyne

Junction	Northbound	Southbound
57	Exit only to A66(M) (eastbound)	Access only from A66(M) (westbound)
65	No access. Exit only to A194(M) & A1 (northbound)	No exit. Access only from A194(M) & A1 (southbound)

A3(M) Horndean - Havant

Junction	Northbound	Southbound
1	Access only from A3	Exit only to A3
4	Exit only, no access	Access only, no exit

A38(M) Birmingham, Victoria Road (Park Circus)

Junction	Northbound	Southbound
with B4132	No exit	No access

A48(M) Cardiff Spur

Junction	Westbound	Eastbound
29	Access only from M4 (westbound)	Exit only to M4 (eastbound)
29A	Exit only to A48 (westbound)	Access only from A48 (eastbound)

A57(M) Manchester, Brook Street (A34)

Junction	Westbound	Eastbound
with A34	No exit	No access

A58(M) Leeds, Park Lane and Westgate

Junction	Northbound	Southbound
with A58	No restriction	No access

A64(M) Leeds, Clay Pit Lane (A58)

Junction	Westbound	Eastbound
with A58	No exit (to Clay Pit Lane)	No access (from Clay Pit Lane)

A66(M) Darlington Spur

Junction	Westbound	Eastbound
with A1(M) (jct 57)	Exit only to A1(M) (southbound)	Access only from A1(M) (northbound)

A74(M) Gretna - Abington

Junction	Northbound	Southbound
18	Exit only, no access	Access only, no exit

A194(M) Newcastle upon Tyne

Junction	Northbound	Southbound
with A1(M) (jct 65)	Access only from A1(M) (northbound)	Exit only to A1(M) (southbound)

A12 M25 - Ipswich

Junction	Northeastbound	Southwestbound
13	Access only, no exit	No restriction
14	Exit only, no access	Access only, no exit
20A	Exit only, no access	Access only, no exit
20B	Access only, no exit	Exit only, no access
21	No restriction	Access only, no exit
23	Exit only, no access	Access only, no exit
24	Exit only, no access	Access only, no exit
27	Exit only, no access	Access only, no exit
Dedham & Stratford St Mary (unnumbered)	Exit only	Access only

A14 M1 - Felixstowe

Junction	Westbound	Eastbound
with M1/M6 (jct19)	Exit only to M6 and M1 (northbound)	Access only from M6 and M1 (southbound)
4	Exit only, no access	Access only, no exit
21	Access only, no exit	Exit only, no access
22	Exit only, no access	Access only from A1 (southbound)
23	Access only, no exit	Access only, no exit
26	No restriction	Access only, no exit
34	Access only, no exit	Exit only, no access
36	Exit only to A11, access only from A1303	Access only from A11
38	Access only from A11	Exit only to A11
39	Exit only, no access	Access only, no exit
61	Access only, no exit	Exit only, no access

A55 Holyhead - Chester

Junction	Westbound	Eastbound
8A	Exit only, no access	Access only, no exit
23A	Access only, no exit	Exit only, no access
24A	Exit only, no access	No access or exit
27A	No restriction	No access or exit
33A	Exit only, no access	Access only, no exit
33B	Exit only, no access	Access only, no exit
36A	Exit only to A5104	Access only from A5104

Smart motorways

Since Britain's first motorway (the Preston Bypass) opened in 1958, motorways have changed significantly. A vast increase in car journeys over the last 64 years has meant that motorways quickly filled to capacity. To combat this, the recent development of **smart motorways** uses technology to monitor and actively manage traffic flow and congestion.

Various active traffic management methods are used:

- Traffic flow is monitored using CCTV
- Speed limits are changed to smooth traffic flow and reduce stop-start driving
- Capacity of the motorway can be increased by either temporarily or permanently opening the hard shoulder to traffic
- Warning signs and messages alert drivers to hazards and traffic jams ahead
- Lanes can be closed in the case of an accident or emergency by displaying a red X sign
- Emergency refuge areas are located regularly along the motorway where there is no hard shoulder available

Smart motorways can be classified into three different types as shown below. Since January 2022, plans for the opening of further schemes have been put on hold. The table lists smart motorways in operation and the colour-coded text indicates the type of smart motorway.

CONTROLLED MOTORWAY	Variable speed limits without hard shoulder (the hard shoulder is used in emergencies only)
HARD SHOULDER RUNNING	Variable speed limits with part-time hard shoulder (the hard shoulder is open to traffic at busy times when signs permit)
ALL LANE RUNNING	Variable speed limits with hard shoulder as permanent running lane (there is no hard shoulder); this is standard for all new smart motorway schemes since 2013

SMART MOTORWAY SECTIONS	
M1	J6A–10, J10–13, J13–19, J23A–25, J25–28, J28–31, J31–32, J32–35A, J39–42
M3	J2–4A
M4	J3–12, J19–20, J24–28
M5	J4A–6, J15–17
M6	J2–4, J4–10A, J10A–15, J16–19, J21A–26
M9	J1–1A
M20	J3–5, J4–7
M23	J8–10
M25	J2–3, J5–6, J6–23, J23–27, J27–30
M27	J4–11
M42	J3A–7, J7–9
M56	J6–8
M60	J8–18
M62	J10–12, J18–20, J25–26, J26–28, J28–29, J29–30
M90	M9 J1A–M90 J3

Quick tips

- Never drive in a lane closed by a red X
- Keep to the speed limit shown on the gantries
- A solid white line indicates the hard shoulder – do not drive in it unless directed

- A broken white line indicates a normal running lane
- Exit the smart motorway where possible if your vehicle is in difficulty. In an emergency, move onto the hard shoulder where there is one, or the nearest emergency refuge area
- Put on your hazard lights if you break down

M4	Motorway with number
Toll	Toll motorway with toll station
5	Restricted motorway junctions
Fleet Todhills	Motorway service area, rest area
	Motorway and junction under construction
A3	Primary route single/dual carriageway
	Primary route junction with and without number
3	Restricted primary route junctions
	Primary route service area
BATH	Primary route destination
A1123	Other A road single/dual carriageway
B2070	B road single/dual carriageway
	Minor road more than 4 metres wide, less than 4 metres wide
	Roundabout
	Interchange/junction
	Narrow primary/other A/B road with passing places (Scotland)
	Road under construction
	Road tunnel
Toll	Road toll, steep gradient (arrows point downhill)
5	Distance in miles between symbols
	Railway line, in tunnel
	Railway station, tram stop, level crossing
	Preserved or tourist railway
628 637 Lecht Summit	Height in metres, mountain pass
	Snow gates (on main routes)
or	Vehicle ferry (all year, seasonal)
	Fast vehicle ferry or catamaran
or	Passenger ferry (all year, seasonal)
	Airport (major/minor), heliport

F	International freight terminal
H	24-hour Accident & Emergency hospital
C	Crematorium
P·R	Park and Ride (at least 6 days per week)
	City, town, village or other built-up area
	National boundary, county or administrative boundary
	Scenic route
i i	Tourist Information Centre (all year, seasonal)
V	Visitor or heritage centre
	Caravan site (AA inspected)
	Camping site (AA inspected)
	Caravan & camping site (AA inspected)
	Abbey, cathedral or priory
	Ruined abbey, cathedral or priory
	Castle, historic house or building
	Museum or art gallery, industrial interest
	Aqueduct or viaduct
	Garden, arboretum
	Vineyard, brewery or distillery
	Country park, theme park
	Showground
	Farm or animal centre
	Zoological or wildlife collection
	Bird collection, aquarium
	RSPB site
	National Nature Reserve (England, Scotland, Wales)
	Local nature reserve, Wildlife Trust reserve
	Forest drive
	National trail

	City with clean air zone, low/zero emission zone
	Picnic site, hill-fort
	Waterfall, viewpoint
	Prehistoric monument, Roman antiquity
1066	Battle site with year
	Preserved or tourist railway
	Cave or cavern
	Windmill, monument or memorial
	Beach (award winning)
	Lighthouse
	Golf course
	Football stadium
	County cricket ground
	Rugby Union national stadium
	International athletics stadium
	Horse racing, show jumping
	Air show venue, motor-racing circuit
	Ski slope (natural, artificial)
	National Trust site (England & Wales, Scotland)
	English Heritage site
	Historic Scotland site
	Cadw (Welsh heritage) site
	Major shopping centre, other place of interest
	Attraction within urban area
	World Heritage Site (UNESCO)
	National Park and National Scenic Area (Scotland)
	Forest Park
	Heritage coast

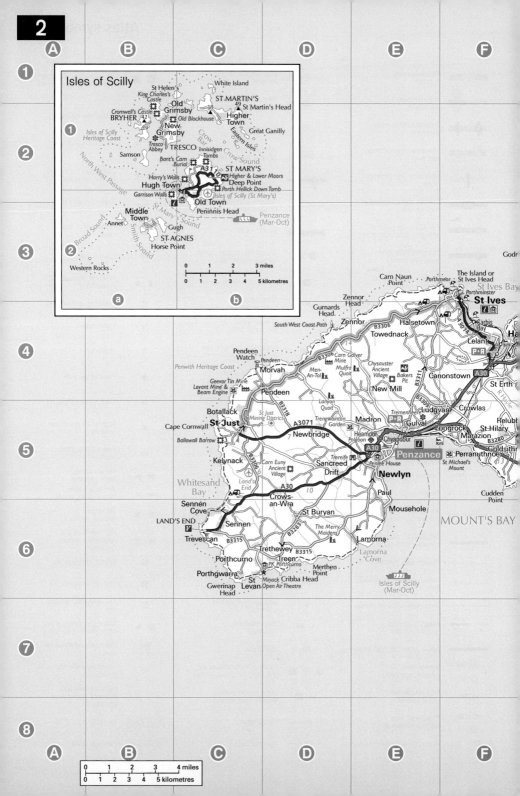

A B C D E F

1 2 3 4 5 6 7 8

Isles of Scilly

White Island

St Helen's
King Charles's
Castle
Cromwell's Castle
BRYHER 42
Old Blockhouse
Old
Grimsby
New
Grimsby
Isles of Scilly
Heritage Coast
Tresco
Abbey
TRESCO
Samson
Bant's Carn
Burial
Harry's Walls
Hugh Town
Garrison Walls
Middle
Town
Annet
Gugh
ST. AGNES
Horse Point
Western Rocks

ST.MARTIN'S
St Martin's Head
18
Higher
Town
49
Great Ganilly
Eastern Isles
Crow Bar
Crow Sound
Innisidgen
Tombs
ST MARY'S
Higher & Lower Moors
Deep Point
Porth Hellick Down Tomb
Old Town
Isles of Scilly (St Mary's)
Peninnis Head
Penzance
(Mar-Oct)

Isles of Scilly
North West Passage
St Mary's Sound
Broad Sound
Smith Sound

0   1   2   3 miles
0 1 2 3 4 5 kilometres

a b

Godr

The Island or
St Ives Head
Porthmeor
St Ives Bay
Porthminster
St Ives
Carn Naun
Point
Carbis
Bay
Ha
Zennor
Head
Gurnards
Head
Zennor
Towednack
Halsetown
South West Coast Path
Lelant
P·R
Carn Galver
Mine
B3306
Chysauster
Ancient
Village
Bakers
Pit
Canonstown
A30
Pendeen
Watch
Pendeen
Morvah
Men-
An-Tol
Mulfra
Quoit
New Mill
St Erth
Geevor Tin Mine
Levant Mine &
Beam Engine
Pendeen
Lanyon
Quoit
Trengwainton
Garden
Madron
P·R
Tremenheere
Ludgvan
Crowlas
Penwith Heritage Coast
Botallack
St Just
Mining District
A3071
Gulval
Longrock
Relubl
St Hilary
Cape Cornwall
St Just
Newbridge
Heamoor
Poltair
Chyandour
Marazion
B3280
Goldsithn
Ballowall Barrow
Kelynack
Carn Euny
Ancient
Village
Sancreed
Drift
Trereife
Penlee House
Penzance
Newlyn
St Michael's
Mount
Perranuthnoe
3
Whitesand
Bay
Land's
End
10
A30
Crows-
an-Wra
St Buryan
Paul
Mousehole
MOUNT'S BAY
Cudden
Point
Sennen
Cove
LAND'S END
Sennen
Trevescan
The Merry
Maidens
Lamorna
Porthcurno
Trethewey
Treen
Lamorna
Cove
B3315
B3315
Porthgwarra
St
Levan
PK Porthcurno
Cribba Head
Minack
Open Air Theatre
Merthen
Point
Isles of Scilly
(Mar-Oct)
Gwennap
Head

0   1   2   3 miles
0 1 2 3 4 5 kilometres

A B C D E F

A   B   C   D   E   F

1

2

3   Higher Sh

Lower Sh

4

5   Dizzard Point
St
Gennys
Crackington Haven
Cambeak   Ce

Sweets

6   Witchcraft   15   B3263
& Magic   Wa

Pentire Point Widemouth   Marsh
Heritage Coast   Tresparrett

Boscastle
Trevalga

Castle   B3263   Lesnewth
TINTAGEL HEAD
Tintagel   Trethevey
Bossiney   Tre
Old Post Office
Penhallic Point   Trewarmett   Davidstow
Treknow
Vale of Avalon   Cornwall
B3314   at War

7   South West Coast Path   Delabole   Pengelly
Westdowns   Camelford
Rumps   Varley   Port Isaac   Lanteglos   Crowdy
Point   Head   Bay   Trewalder   Reservoi
Port Quin   Kellan   Helstone
Bay   Head   Port-Gaverne
Pentire Point   Port   Port   St Teath
Quin   Isaac   Treveighan   419
8   Padstow Bay   BROWN
Bee-Centre   Pendoggett   WILLY
Hayle Bay   Trelights   St Teath   Michaelstow
Stepper Point   Polzeath   Churchtown

A   B   4   C   B3314   D   A39   E   F   3 O
Trevose   St Endellic   elill
Heritage Coast   Trequite   St Breward
TREVOSE HEAD   St Minver   St Tudy   Jamaica
0 1 2 3 4 miles
Dinas   0 1 2 3 4 5 kilometres   St Kew
Head   St Kew
Highway

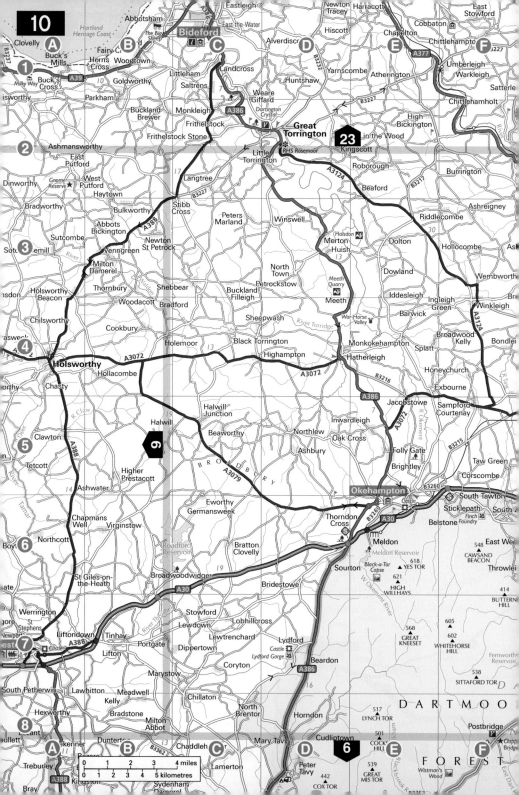

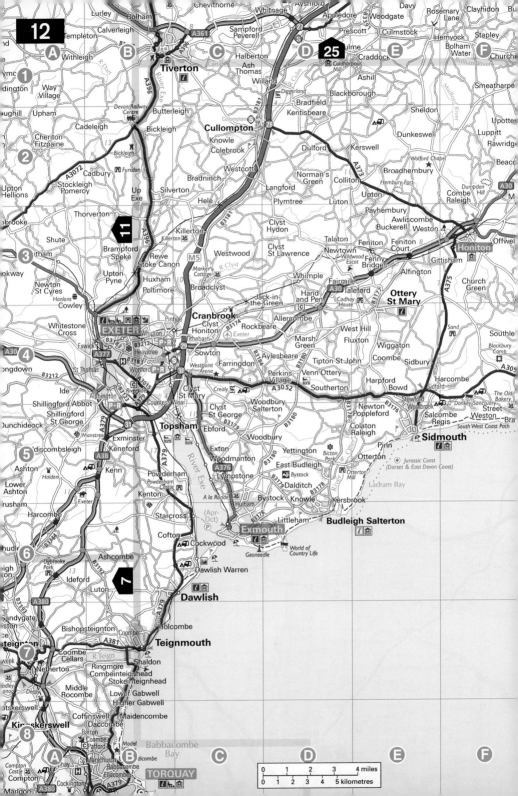

G H J K L M

27 **28**

16

1
2
3
4
5
6
7
8

Waldron
Iwerne Minster
Shrot Iwerne
Farnham
Gussage St Andrew
Chettle
Boveridge
Cranborne
Alderholt
North Gorley
South Gorley
Ibsley Common
Rockford Common

Tarrant Gunville
Gussage St Michael
Jimbone St Giles
Borne Manor
Cranborne
B3078
Ibsley
Stuckton

Tarrant Hinton
A354
Long Crichel
Gussage All Saints
Church & Earthworks
Edmondsham
Romford
Dorset Heavy Horse Farm Park
Verwood
B3081
Woodlands
Horton
Mannington
Three Legged Cross
Ringwood
Paulner
Burle Stree
Liberty's Owl, Raptor & Reptile Centre

Tarrant Launceston
Tarrant Monkton
Manswood
Moor Crichel
B3078
Holt
St Leonards
A31
Avon-Heath
Kingston Great Common
Bur

Royal Signals
Tarrant Rawston
Witchampton
Hinton Martell
Holt Heath
West Moors
FOXBURY HILL
Bisterne
Sandford
Thorr Hill

rum
St Mary
Charlton on the Hill
Hall & Woodhouse
Charlton Marshall
Tarrant Rushton
Tarrant Keyneston
Badbury Rings
Ferndown
Knoll
Hampreston
Leigh Park
Longham
Dudsbury
West Parley
Hurn
Bournemouth
Aviation
A338
Avon
Ripley
Bransgore
Burton

Thorncombe
Tarrant Crawford
Shapwick
Kingston Lacy
Hillbutts
Abbott Street
Pamphill
Wimborne Minster
A31
Merley
Cudnell
Ensbury
Red Hill
Adventure Wonderland
Throop
B3073
Somerford
Highcli
Walkfc cliffe
Christchurch

Spetisbury
A350
White Mill
Sturminster Marshall
Corfe Mullen
A349
Bearwood
West Howe
Kinson
East Howe
Moordown
Winton
A3060
Wick
Mudeford
Christchu
Christchu

Winterborne Zelston
Morden
East Morden
B3075
Lytchett Matravers
Broadstone
Canford Heath
Upton Heath
Wallisdown
Talbot Village
A3049
Iford
Castle
Boscombe
Southbourne
Hengistbury Head
HENGISTBURY H

A35
West Morden
Farmer Palmers
Organford
Lytchett Minster
Upton
B3074
Newtown
Branksome
B3065
Pokesdown
Tuckton
BOURNEMOUTH

WAREHAM FOREST
Morden Bog
Hamworthy
Lower Hamworthy
Parkstone
Westbourne
Branksome Park
Lilliput
POOLE
Canford Cliffs

Sandford
Northport
Arne
Poole Harbour
Brownsea Island
Sandbanks
Toll
POOLE BAY

Binnegar
Stoborough
Wareham
Ridge
Stoborough Heath
Hartland Moor
The Blue Pool
Purbeck Heritage Coast
Studland Bay
Studland Beach
V

East Stoke
West Holme
ISLE OF PURBECK
Dorset Adventure
Studland
THE FORELAND Old Harry
Cherbourg (Apr-Oct)

orth
B3070
Purbeck Hills
Church Knowle
Corfe Castle
Swanage Railway
B3351
Ulwell
New Swanage
Ballard Point
Swanage Bay
Guernsey Jersey St-Malo

Purbeck Marine
Kimmeridge
B3069
Kingston
Harman's Cross
Herston
Swanage
Langton Matravers
Durlston
DURLSTON HEAD
Anvil Point

Kimmeridge Bay
South West Coast Path
Worth Matravers
Chapman's Pool
Jurassic Coast (Dorset & East Devon Coast)
ST ALDHELM'S OR ST ALBAN'S HEAD

G H J K L M

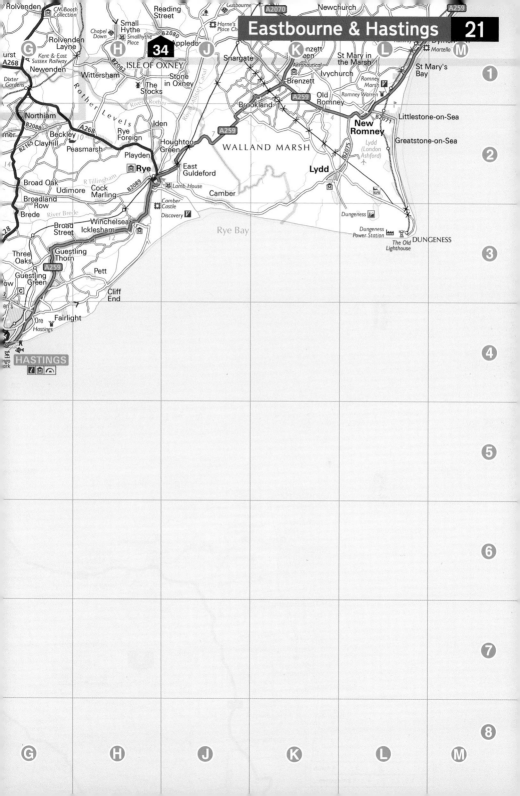

Rolvenden
CM Booth Collection
Reading Street
Gusbourne
Newchurch
A2070
A259

G
Chapel Down
Small Hythe
Smallhythe Place
Horne's Place Chl
H
34
B2080
Appledore
J
Snargate
Aeronautical
K
nzett een
St Mary in the Marsh
Ivychurch
L
M
Martello
A259

Rolvenden Layne
A268
Newenden
ISLE OF OXNEY
Wittersham
Stone in Oxney
Brenzett
Old Romney
Romney Marsh
Romney Warren
St Mary's Bay
1

Dixter Gardens
Kent & East Sussex Railway
The Stocks
Brookland
A259
New Romney
B2071
Littlestone-on-Sea
Greatstone-on-Sea

Northiam
B2088
A268
Iden
Rye Foreign
Houghton Green
WALLAND MARSH
B2075
Lydd (London Ashford)
2

Beckley
Clayhill
Peasmarsh
Playden
East Guldeford
Lydd

B2165
Broad Oak
Udimore
Cock Marling
B2089
Rye
Lamb House
Camber
Dungeness
Dungeness Power Station
3

Broadland Row
Brede
River Brede
Broad Street
Winchelsea
Icklesham
Camber Castle
Discovery
Rye Bay
The Old Lighthouse
DUNGENESS

Three Oaks
Guestling Thorn
A259
Pett
4

Guestling Green
Fairlight
Ore
Hastings
Cliff End

HASTINGS

5

6

7

8

G
H
J
K
L
M

A B C D E F

1

2

North West
Point

*Lundy
Heritage Coast* LUNDY

3 142 ▲ Bideford (Apr-Oct)
Ilfracombe (Apr-Oct)

Marine
Reserve
Shutter Point Surf Point

Bag
Po

Croyd

4

BARNSTAPLE

5 OR

BIDEFORD BAY **Westwa**

HARTLAND POINT *Shipload
Bay*
Titchberry Abbotsh

Damehole
Point *Hartland Abbey
& Gardens* Clovelly *The
S*

Stoke Ford
Fairy Cross

6 Hartland Quay Hartland B3248 Buck's
Mills Horns
Cross Woodtown

*Speke's Mill
Mouth* 4 B3237 *Milky Way* A39 Goldworthy
Milford Buck's
Cross 10

*Docton
Mill* Philham Woolfardisworthy Parkham
Buckla
Brev

Hardisworthy F

Welcombe

7 Darracott Meddon Ashmansworthy

Gooseham 16 **9** East
Putford

Morwenstow Dinworthy *Gnome
Reserve* ★ West
Putford

Higher Sharpnose Point Bradworthy Haytown

*South West
Coast Path* Shop Bulkworthy
Woodford A39

Lower Sharpnose Point *Tamar
Lakes* Sutcombe Abbots
Bickington

8 Steeple Point Kilkhampton Sutcom ll *River* Ne
St

A3

Cbb Milton
Damerel

Venr

A

B C D E Thornbury F

0   1   2   3   4 miles
0 1 2 3 4 5 kilometres

Northcott Poughill A39 Dunsdon Holsworthy

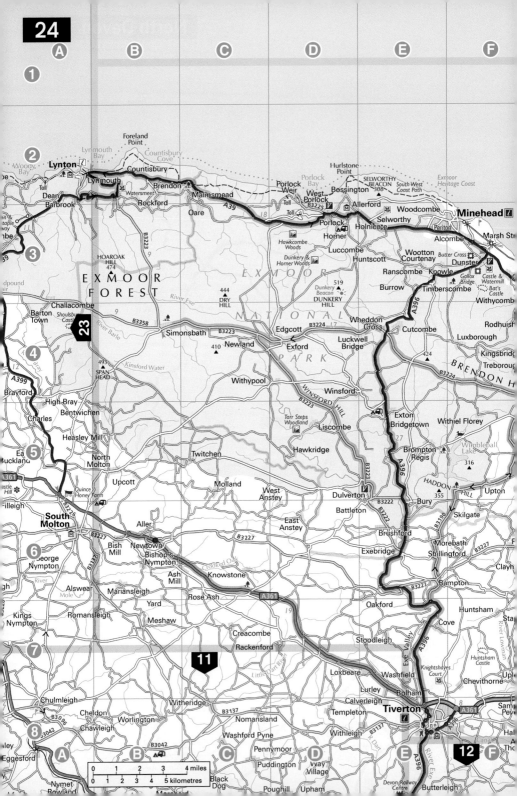

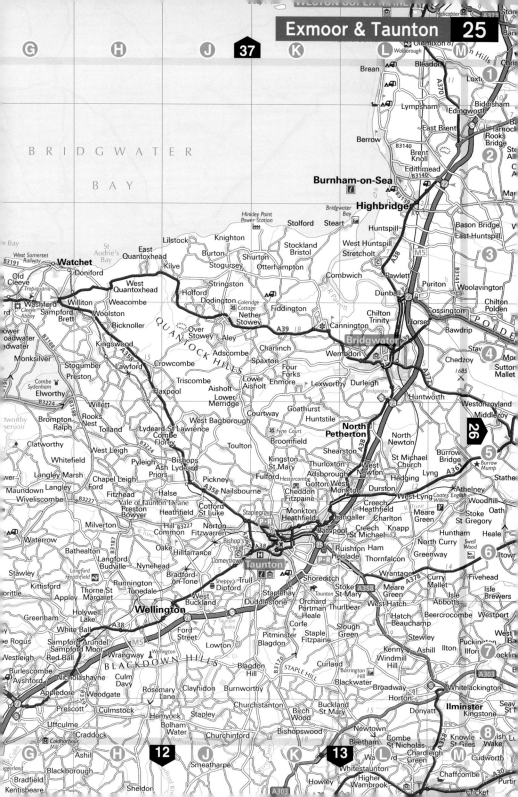

G   H   J   **37**   K   L   M

WESTON SUPER MARE
Helicopter
Oldmixon
Walborough
Loxto
Brean
Bleadon
Biddisham
Lympsham
Edingworth
East Brent
Berrow
Rooks
Bridge
Brent
Knoll
Edithmead
B3140
Burnham-on-Sea
Bason Bridge
East-Huntspill
Highbridge
Huntspill
West Huntspill
Stretcholt
Chilton
Polden

B R I D G W A T E R

B A Y

Knighton
Stolford
Steart
Lilstock
Stockland
Bristol
Burton
Shurton
Combwich
Pawlett
Dunball
Puriton
Woolavington
Cossington
POLDE

West Somerset
Railway
Watchet
Doniford
St Audrie's
Bay
East
Quantoxhead
Kilve
Stringston
Otterhampton
Hinkley Point
Power Station
Old Cleeve
Washford
Williton
West
Quantoxhead
Holford
Dodington
Fiddington
Chilton
Trinity
Horsey
Bawdrip

Tropiquaria
Cleeve Abbey
Sampford
Brett
Woolston
Weacombe
Nether
Stowey
Coleridge
Cottage
A39
Cannington
Wembdon
Bridgwater
Stav
Chedzoy
Sutton
Mallet

Monksilver
Bicknoller
Over
Stowey
Aley
Charlinch
Spaxton
Four
Forks
Enmore
Lexworthy
Durleigh
Huntworth
Westonzoyland
Middlezoy

Stogumber
Preston
Kingswood
Crowcombe
Adscombe
Lower
Aisholt
Goathurst
Huntstile
North
Petherton
North
Newton
Burrow
Bridge

Elworthy
Combe
Sydenham
Lawford
Triscombe
Aisholt
Lower
Merridge
Courtway
West Bagborough
Broomfield
Fyne Court
Shearston
St Michael
Church
Burrow
Mump
Athelney
Stathe

Brompton
Ralph
Willett
Rooks
Nest
Tolland
Lydeard St Lawrence
Combe
Florey
Toulton
Kingston
St Mary
Fulford
Thurloxton
Adsborough
West
Newton
Lyng
Woodhill
Oath
Stoke
St Gregory

Clatworthy
West Leigh
Pyleigh
Bishops
Lydeard
Pickney
Hestercombe
Gotton
West
Monkton
Durston
West-Lyng
Coates
Willow
Meare
Green
Huntham
Heale

Whitefield
Langley Marsh
Chapel Leigh
Ford
Fitzhead
Halse
Nailsbourne
Cheddon
Fitzpaine
Monkton
Heathfield
Langaller
Creech
Heathfield
Charlton
Knapp
North Curry
Swell
Wood

Maundown
Langley
Wiveliscombe
Milverton
Cotford
St Luke
Staplegrove
Creech
St Michael
Greenway

Waterrow
Bathealton
Milverton
Preston
Bowyer
Heathfield
Norton
Fitzwarren
Bishop's
Hull
Bathpool
Ruishton
Henlade
Thornfalcon
Wrantage
Curry
Mallet
Fivehead

Stawley
Langford
Budville
Nynehead
Oake
Hillfarrance
Comeytrowe
Trull
Taunton
Staplehay
Shoreditch
Stoke
St Mary
Meare
Green
Isle
Brewers

Kittisford
Appley
Thorne St
Margaret
Runnington
Bradford-
on-Tone
West
Buckland
Dipford
Duddlestone
Orchard
Portman
Heale
Thurlbear
West Hatch
Hatch
Beauchamp
Westport

Greenham
Holywell
Lake
Wellington
Ford
Street
Lowton
Corfe
Pitminster
Blagdon
Staple
Fitzpaine
Slough
Green
Stewley
Puckington

Sampford Arundel
Sampford Moor
Red Ball
Wrangway
Curland
Barrington
Hill
Blackwater
Kenny
Windmill
Hill
Ashill
Ilton
Ilfor

Burlescombe
Nicholashayne
Culm
Davy
BLACKDOWN HILLS
Blagdon
Hill
Broadway
Horton
Donyatt
Ilminster
Kingstone

Appledore
Prescott
Woodgate
Culmstock
Rosemary
Lane
Clayhidon
Burnworthy
Churchstanton
Birch
Wood
Buckland
St Mary
Whitelackington

Ashford
Uffculme
Craddock
Hemyock
Bolham
Water
Stapley
Bishopswood
Combe
St Nicholas
Knowle
St Giles
Wake
Cudworth

Coldharbour
Mill
Ashill
Churchinford
Newtown
Beetham
Chardleigh
Green
Chaffcombe

Bradfield
Kentisbeare
Blackborough
Sheldon
Smeatharpe
Howley
Higher
Wambrook
Whitestaunton
Wa

G   **12**   H   J   K   **13**   L   M

A303

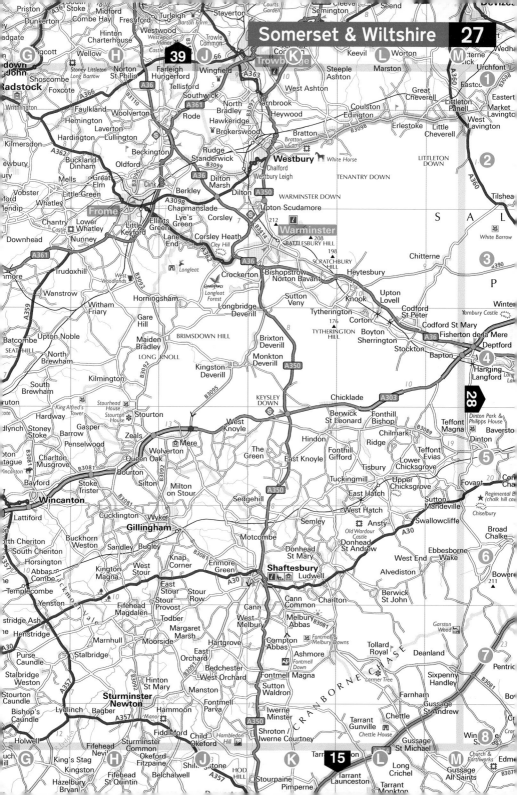

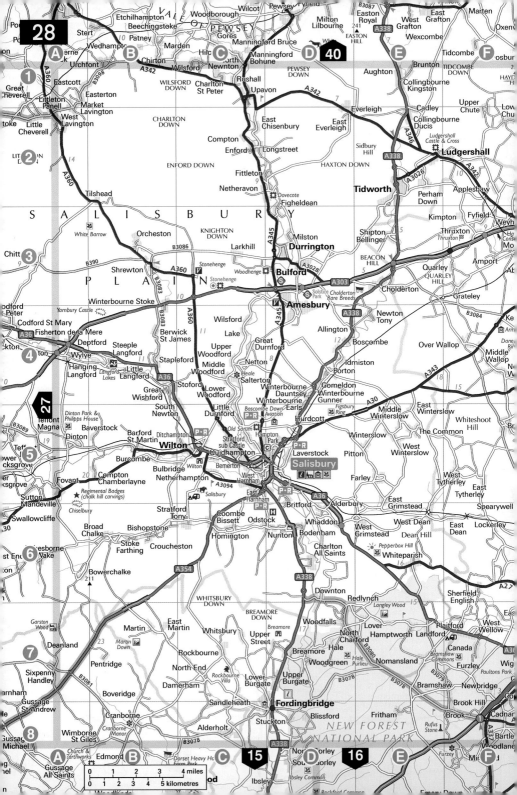

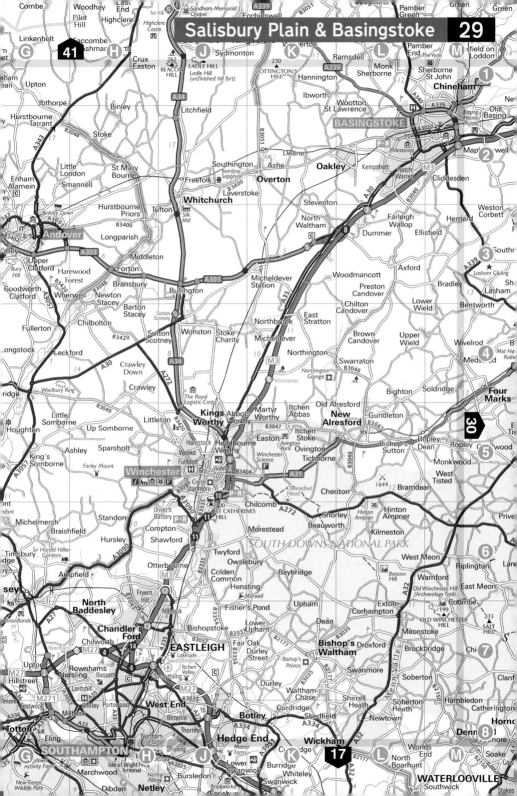

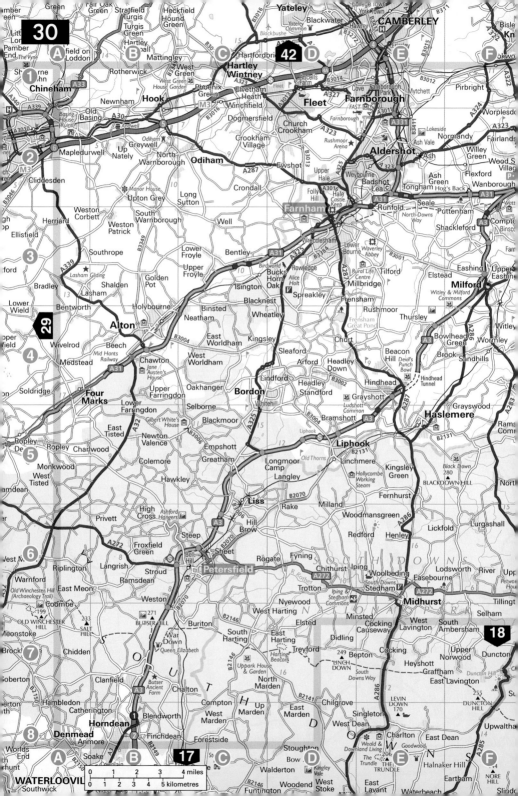

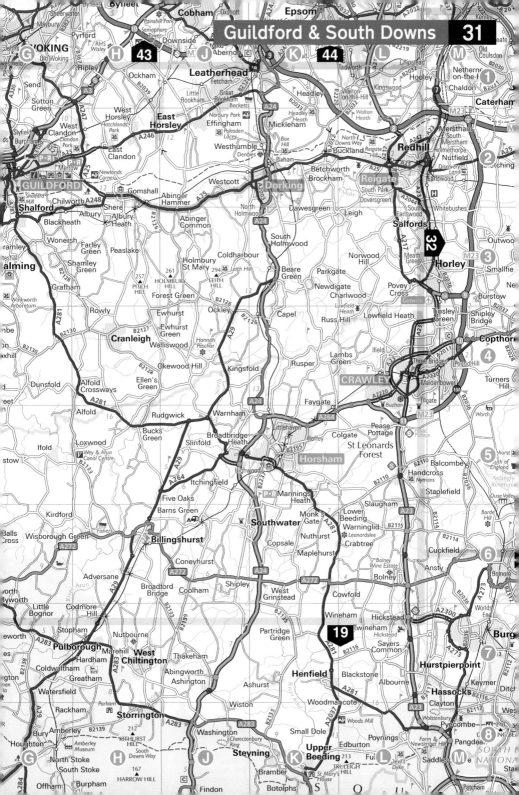

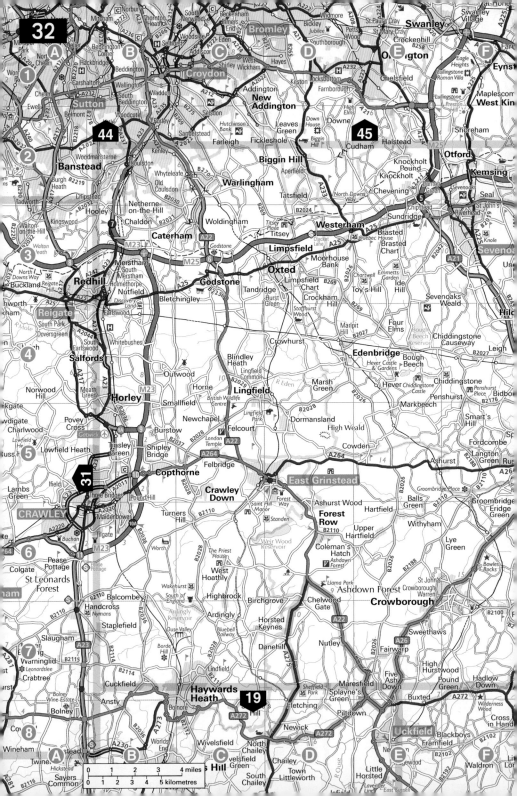

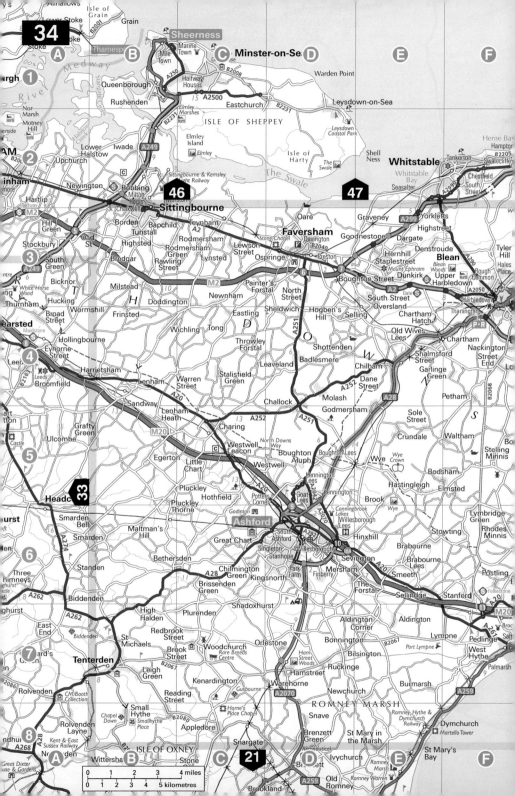

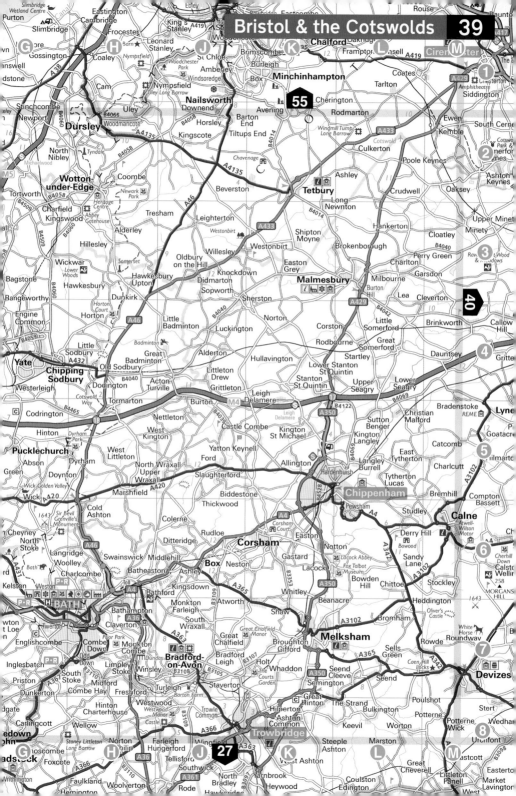

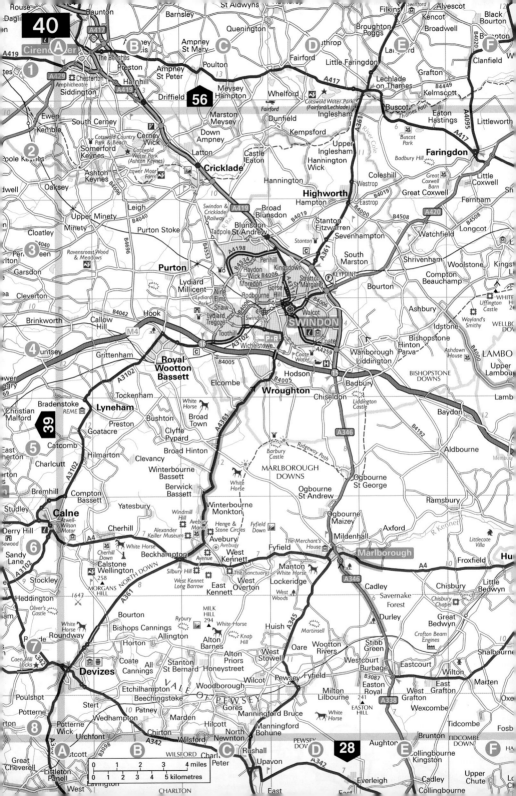

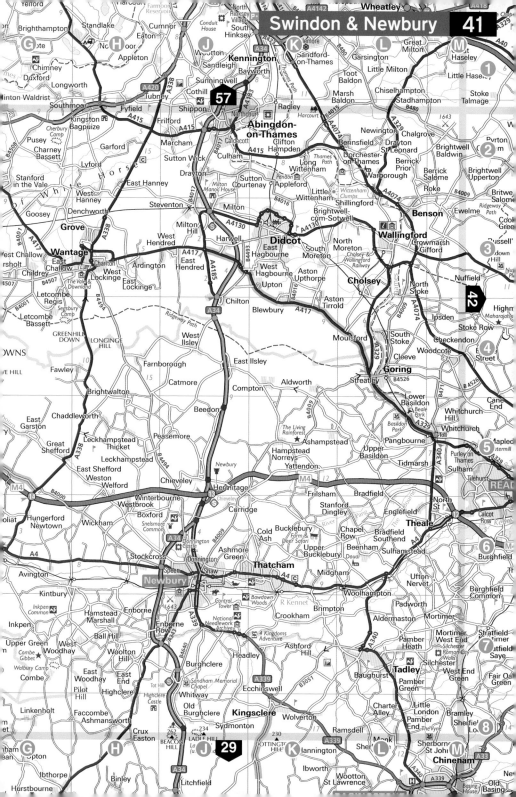

62

Dengie

ham

nster

G

Holliwell
Point

Crouch

Foulness
Point

Courtsend

Churchend

FOULNESS
ISLAND

H

J

K

L

M

1

2

3

4

r-on-Sea

Warden Point

Leysdown-on-Sea

B2231

Leysdown
Coastal Park

PEY

Isle of
Harty

The
Swale

Shell
Ness

The Swale

Oare

Faversham

ne Chapel

Davington
B2040

Preston

bringe

's

North
Street

Sheldwich

Selling

Hogben's
Hill

South Street
Overstand

Chartham
Hatch

Old Wives
Lees

Boughton Street

Dunkirk

Upper
Harbledown

Harbledown

34

ley

A299

Yorkletts

Highstreet

Dargate

Hernhill

Staplestreet

Mount Ephraim

Denstroude

Blean

Blean
Woods

Goodnestone

Whitstable
Bay

Seasalter

A299

Tankerton

Swalecliffe

Chestfield

South
Street

B2205

Greenhill

Rough
Common

Hales
Place

Tyler
Hill

Broad
Oak

Wildwood

East
Blean

35

Herne

Broomfield

Herne Bay

Seaside

Herne Bay

Hampton

Beltinge

Reculver Towers
& Roman Fort

Reculver

Bishopstone

A299

6

Boyden
Gate

Hoath

Upstreet

Marsden

Westbere

Sarre

Chislet

St Nicholas-
at-Wade

A28

A253

West
Stourmouth

Stodmarsh

35

Whitstable

Shalmsford
Street
End

Garlinge
Green

Chilham

Dane
Street

Chartham

Thanington

Hackington

A2

P·R

Bridge

Lower Hardres

Bishopsbourne

K

Howletts

Canterbury

Littlebourne

Bramling

Bekesbourne

Patrixbourne

Adisham

Aylesham

North Downs
Way

Ickham

Wickhambreaux

Seaton

Wingham

A257

Staple

Goodnestone

Nonington

Chillenden

Ra.

L

Stodmarsh

Preston

Elmstone

Durlock

Wingham

Marshborough

Hoaden

Ash

A257

Woodnesboro

Statenborough

Eastry

M

East Stourmouth

Westmarsh

Cop
Street

R Stour

Minnis Bay

Birchington

Acol

B2190

Monkton

A299

Mar

St Mildred's Bay

Westgate-
on-Sea

35

Westl

MA

ISLE OF
NET

Durlock

Minster

A2046

Great Mong

Bettesnanger

Stone
Cross

Richborou
Amphith

7

8

1

2

3

4

5

6

7

8

A251

aveland

Badlesmere

Shottenden

North
Street

Sturry

Stourmouth

Fordwich

Town Hall

Sturry

Faversham

B2040

Old
Wives
Lees

A290

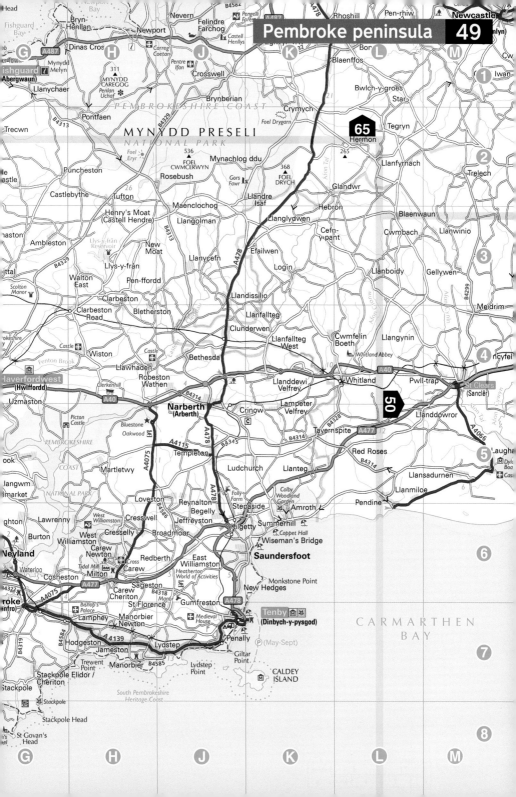

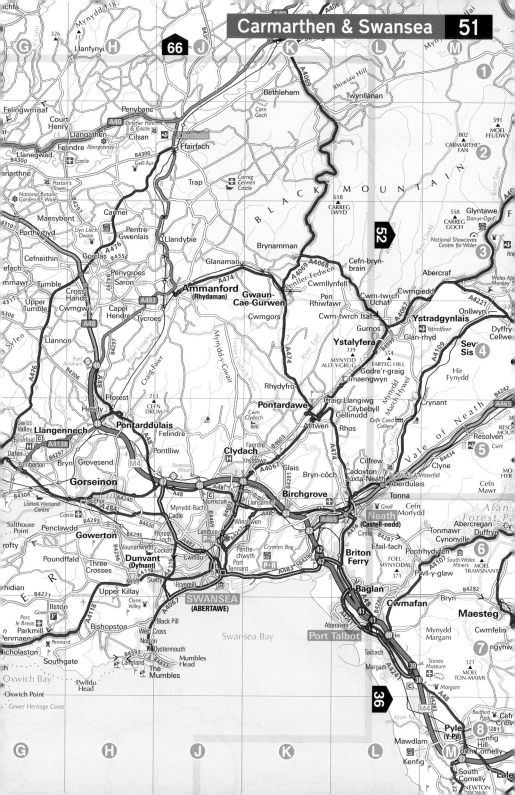

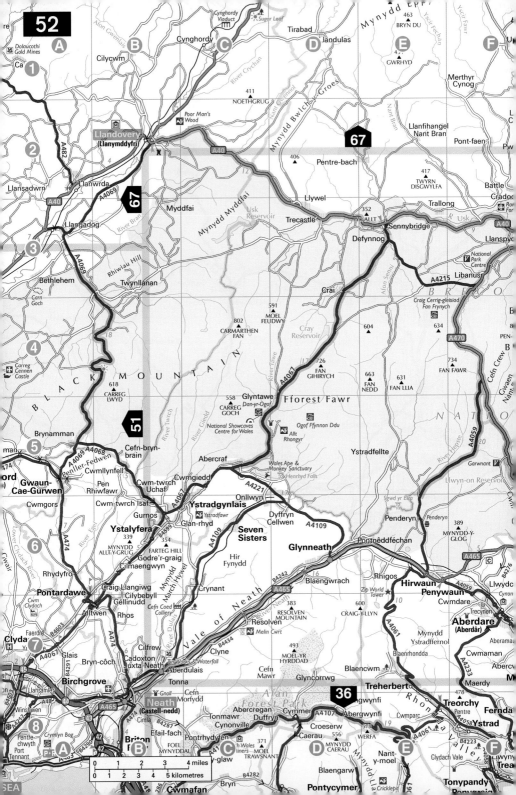

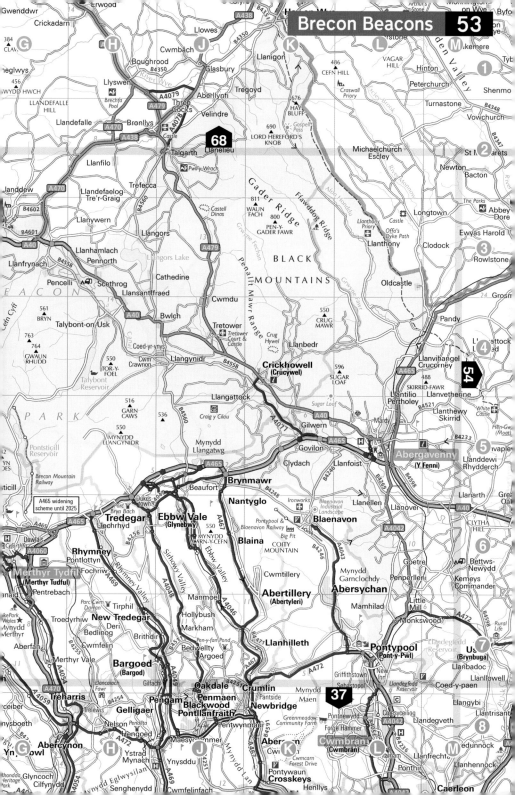

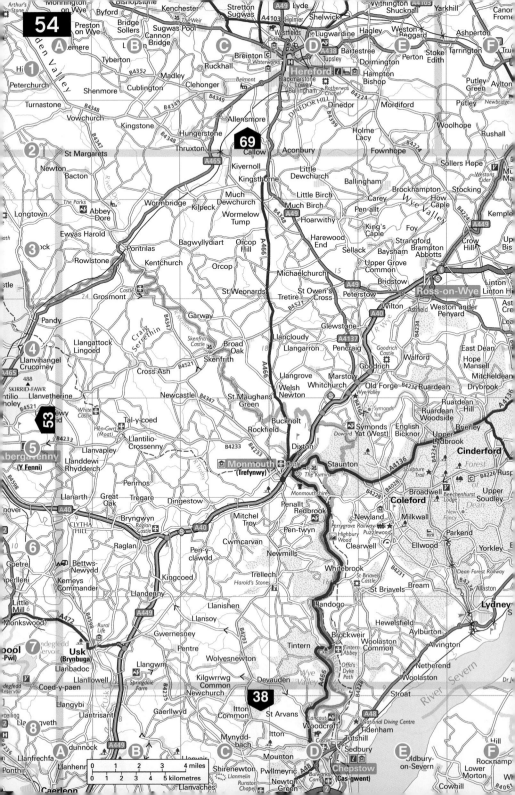

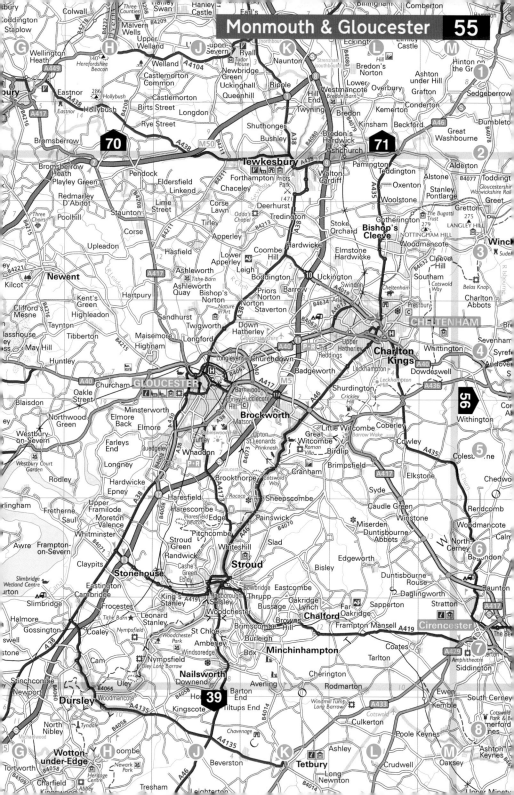

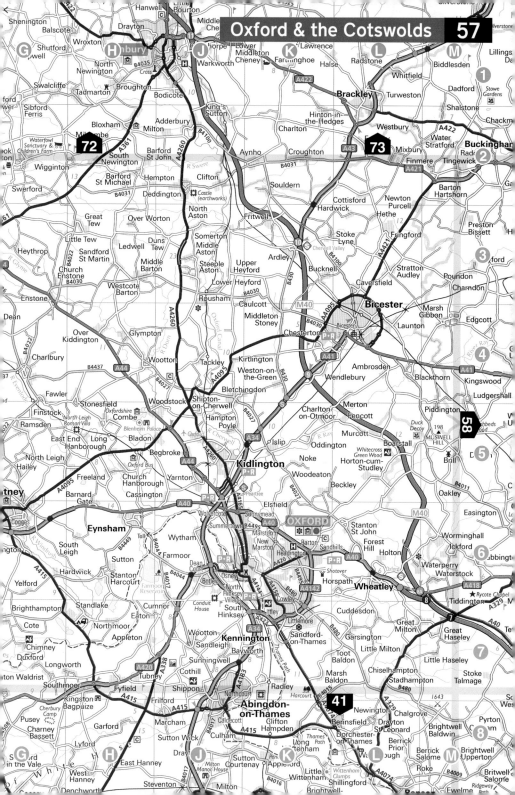

Oxford & the Cotswolds   57

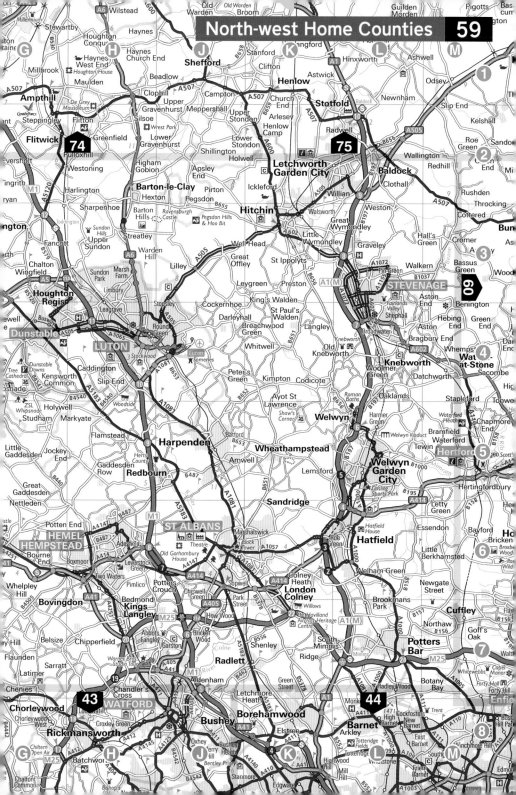

North-west Home Counties 59

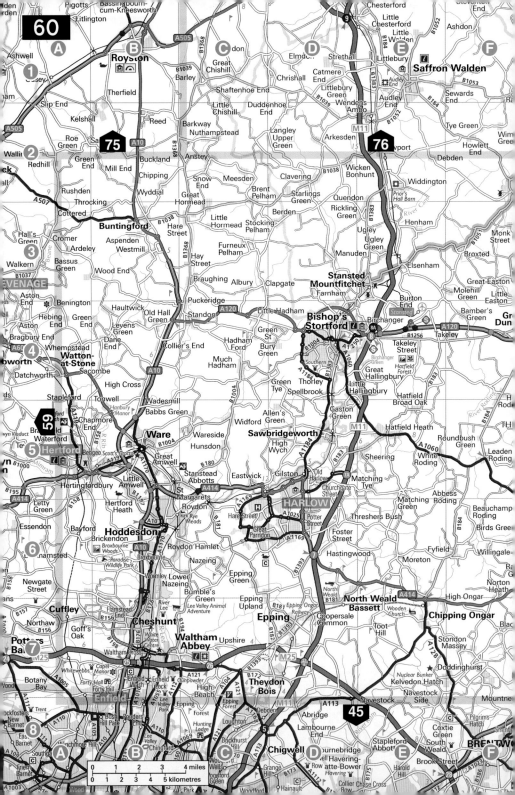

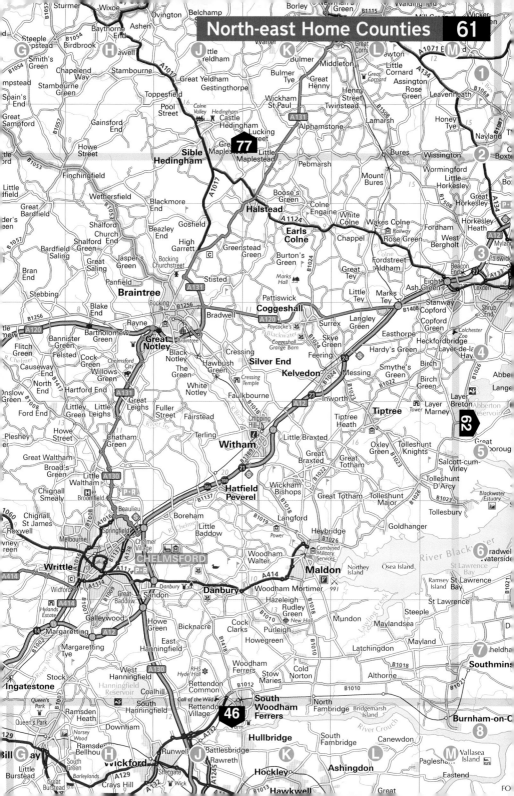

Hemley
Alderton
Hollesley
Bay
Bawdsey
Falkenham
imley
Mary
Old
Felixstowe

Felixstowe
79

Landguard Fort
andguard
oint

Hook of Holland

G H J K L M

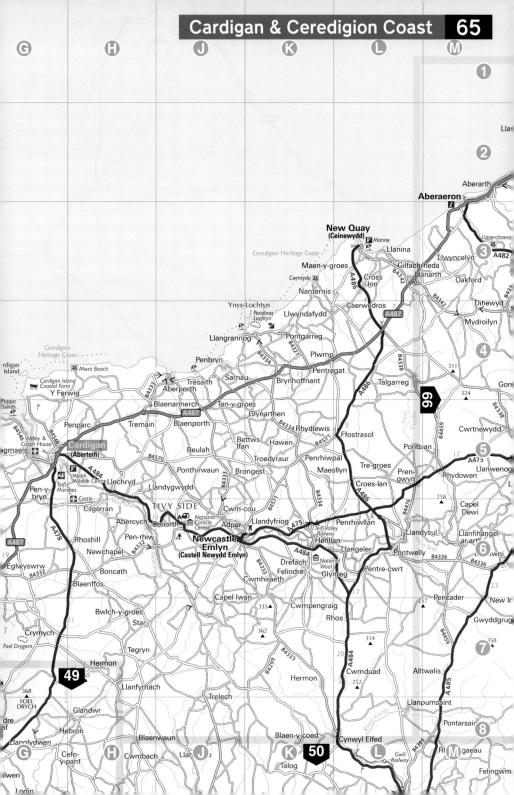

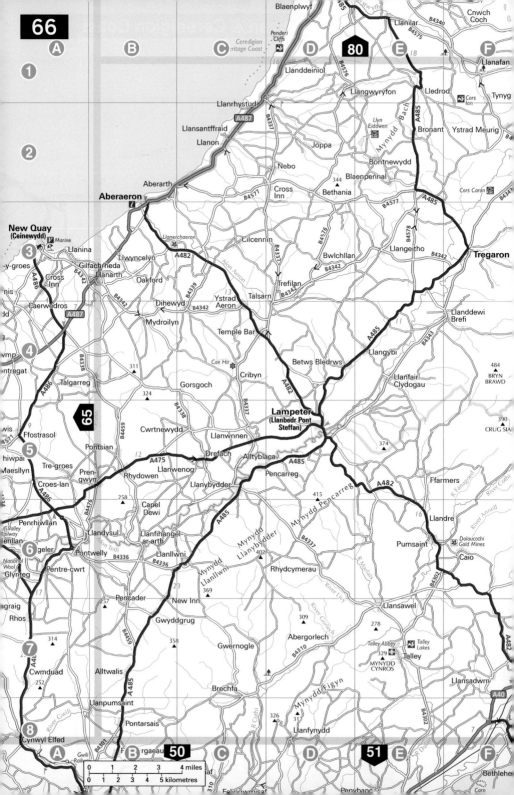

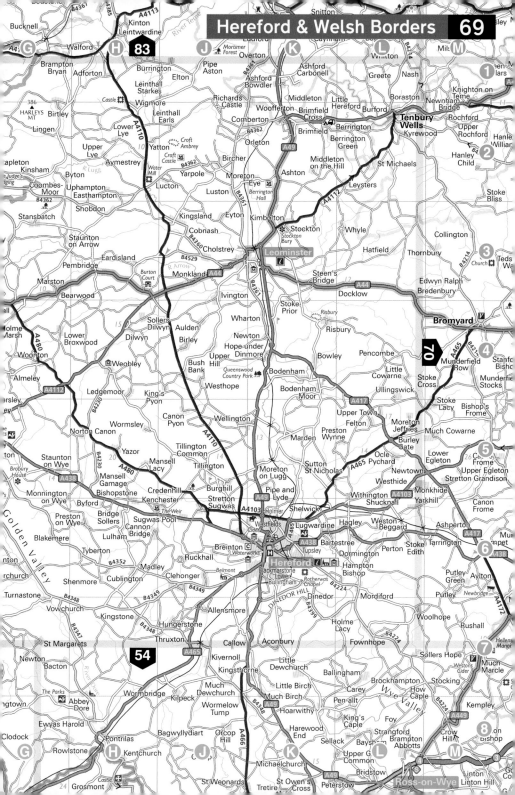

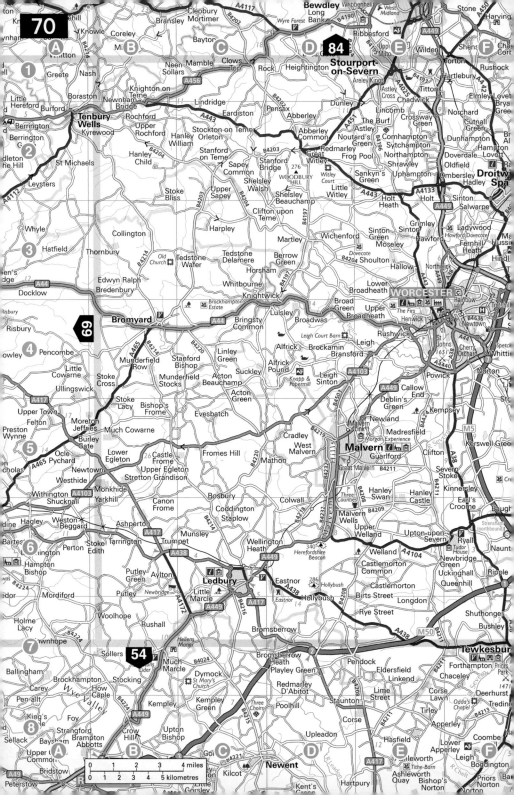

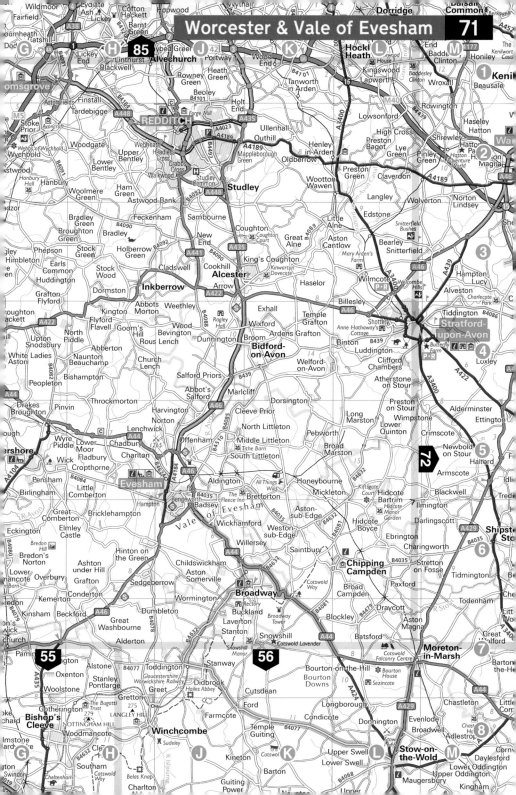

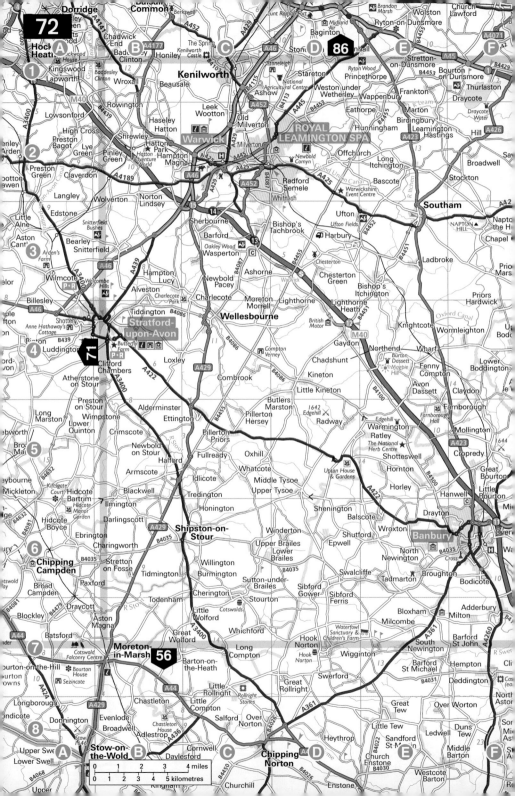

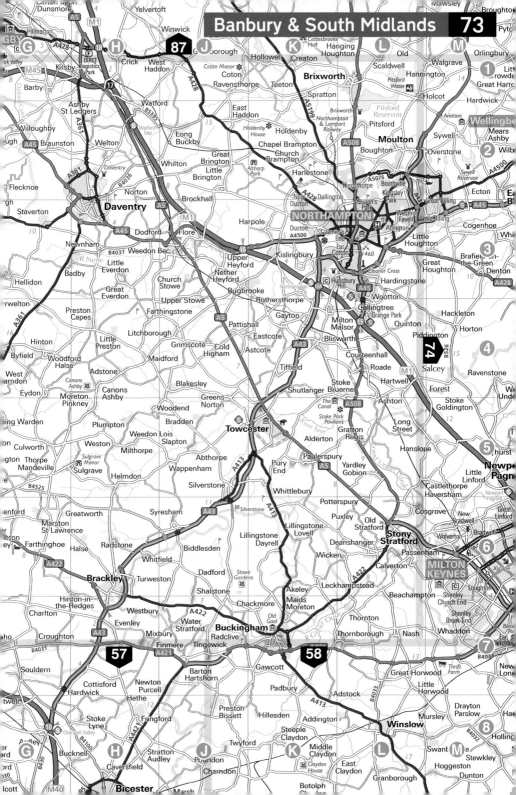

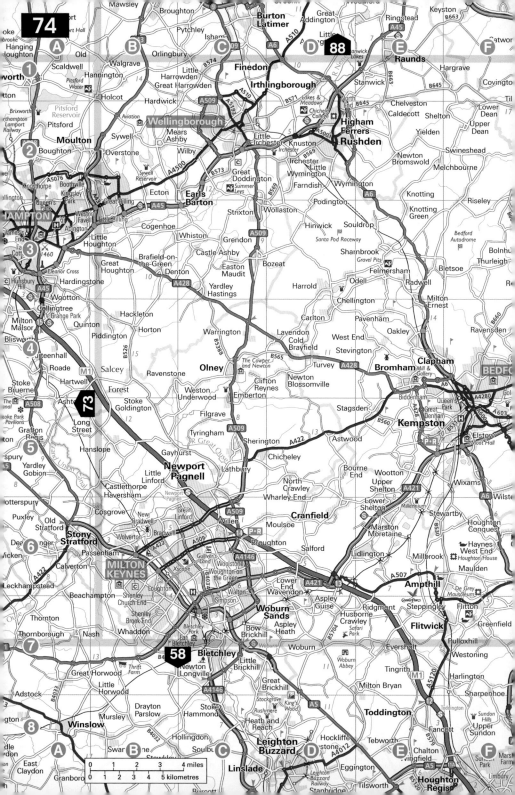

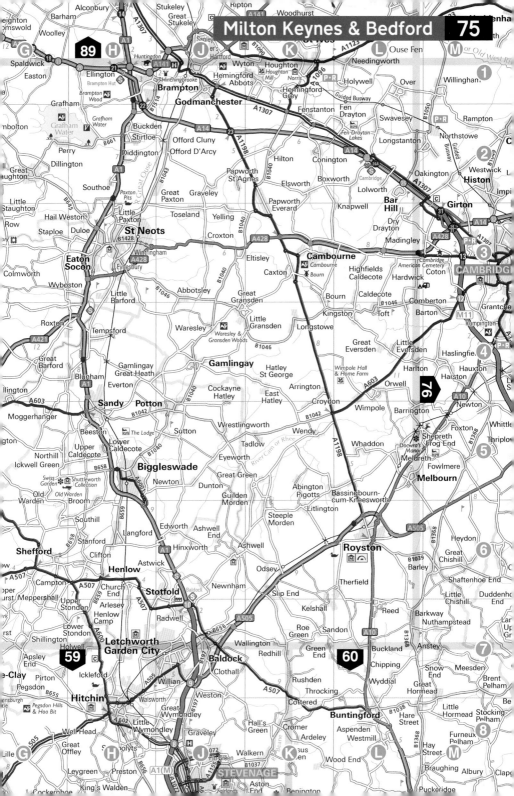

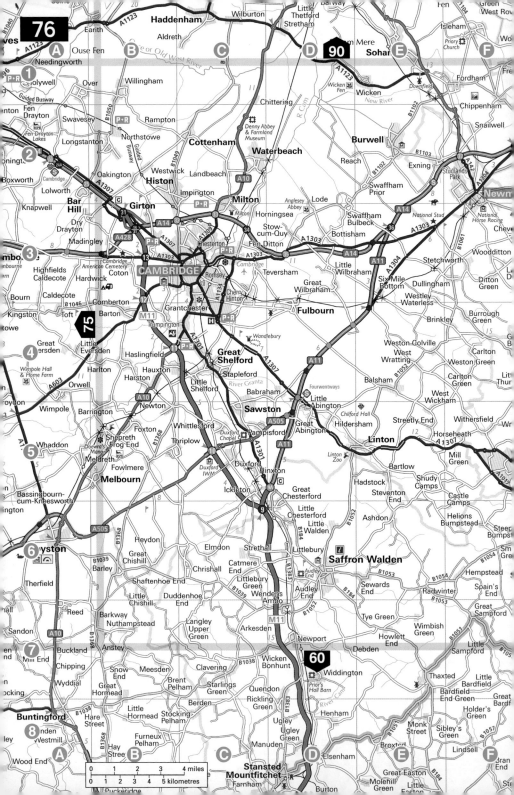

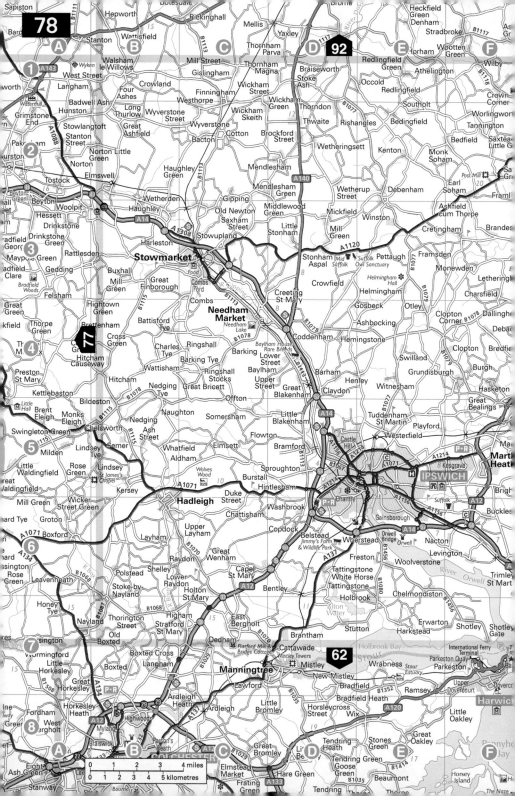

G H J 93 K L M

Cratfield Cookley Wenhaston Reedbeds **Southwold**
Huntingfield Blackheath Blythburgh Southwold Pier
B1117 Walpole Thorington Walberswick
Bramfield A144 B1387
Laxfield Hevenoingham Dunwich Forest Suffolk Coast
Ubbeston Green Darsham Westleton Heath Dunwich
ee Westleton Dunwich Heath
Peasenhall Sibton B1122 Middleton Minsmere
A1120 Yoxford Middleton Moor
Badingham Bruisyard Theberton Eastbridge
ngton Bruisyard Street A12 Carlton Mères Leiston Abbey
Cransford Rendham Kelsale Power Station
Swefling Carlton Saxmundham B1119 Knodishall Thorpe Ness
orth Green Great Glemham Benhall Street Benhall Green Sternfield **Leiston** Aldringham Thorpeness
Stratford St Andrew Friday Street B1121 Knodishall Common B1353
ham Hacheston Farnham Friston North Warren
on Snape A1094 B1122
Marlesford Little Glemham Snape Street Snape Maltings Snape
Blaxhall B1069 **Aldeburgh**
ee Campsea Ash Tunstall Tunstall Forest Aldeburgh Bay
Rendlesham Tunstall B1078
Ufford Chillesford Sudbourne
A1152 B1084
Eyke B1084 Butley Orford
Bromeswell 12 Castle Orford Ness
ridge Rendlesham Forest Orford Ness
Sutton Heath Capel St Andrew
Sutton Boyton Orfordness-Havergate
ingfield Shottisham Hollesley Suffolk Heritage Coast
B1083
North Weir Point
urne Hollesley Bay
emley Alderton
Bawdsey
Falkenham
nley Mary
Old Felixstowe
Felixstowe
anguard Fort
ndguard int
Hook of Holland

G H J K L M

1 2 3 4 5 6 7 8

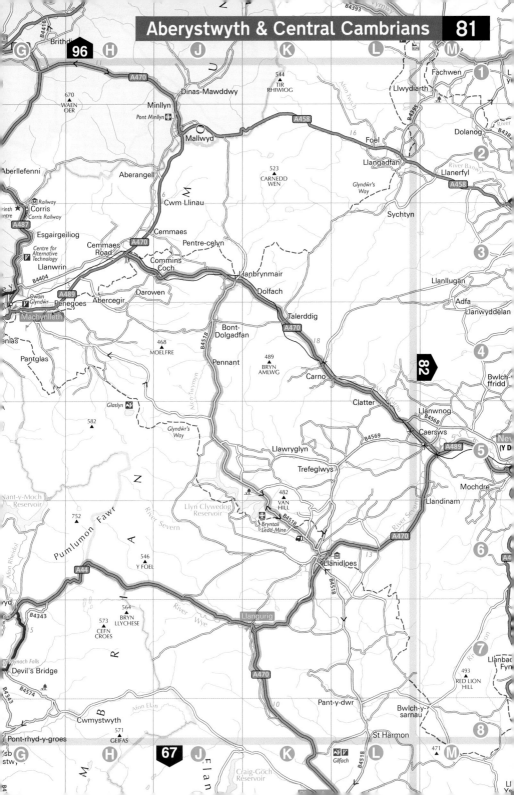

96

G   H   J   K   L   M

B4416
Brithdi
A470
670
WAEN
OER
Dinas-Mawddwy
Minllyn
Pont Minllyn
Mallwyd
544
TIR
RHIWIOG
A458
16
Foel
Fachwen
Llwydiarth
B4395
Dolanog
B4382
Llangadfan
Llanerfyl
A458
River Banwy
Carnedd
Wen
523
CARNEDD
WEN
Glyndŵr's
Way
Sychtyn
Aberllefenni
Aberangell
Cwm Llinau
Railway
Corris
Corris Railway
A487
Esgairgeiliog
Centre for
Alternative
Technology
Llanwrin
B4404
Owain
Glyndŵr
Penegoes
Machynlleth
Cemmaes
Cemmaes
Road
A470
Pentre-celyn
Commins
Coch
Darowen
Abercegir
Llanbrynmair
Dolfach
Talerddig
A470
18
Llanllugan
Adfa
Llanwyddelan
82
Bont-
Dolgadfan
468
MOELFRE
Pennant
489
BRYN
AMLWG
Carno
Clatter
Bwlch-
ffridd
Llanwnog
B4568
Caersws
A489
New
(Y D
Pantglas
Glaslyn
582
Glyndŵr's
Way
Llawryglyn
Trefeglwys
482
VAN
HILL
Mochdre
Llandinam
Nant-y-Moch
Reservoir
752
Pumlumon Fawr
Llyn Clywedog
Reservoir
Bryntail
Lead Mine
B4518
River Severn
A470
13
546
Y FOEL
A44
Llanidloes
B4518
564
BRYN
LLYCHESE
573
CEFN
CROES
River Wye
Llangurig
Red Lion
Hill
493
RED LION
HILL
B4343
Mynach Falls
Devil's Bridge
B4574
B4343
Cwmystwyth
A470
Pant-y-dwr
Bwlch-y-
sarnau
Pont-rhyd-y-groes
571
GEIFAS
67
Gilfach
St Harmon
471
M

G   H   J   K   L   M

1
2
3
4
5
6
7
8

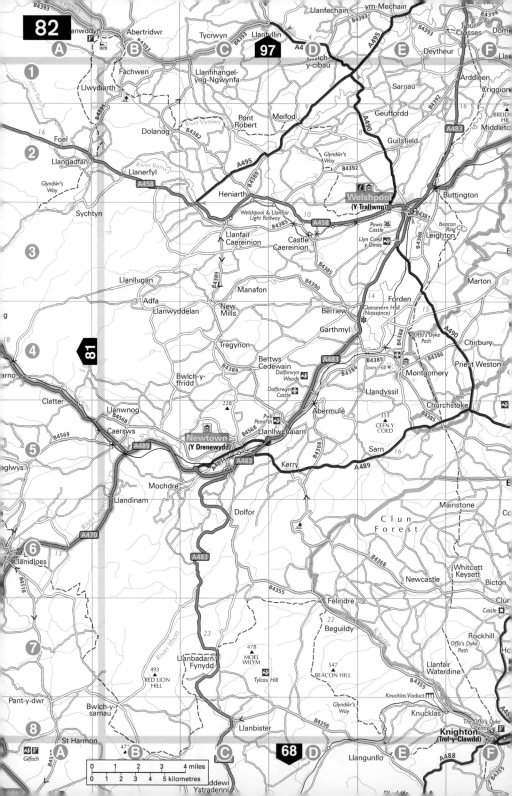

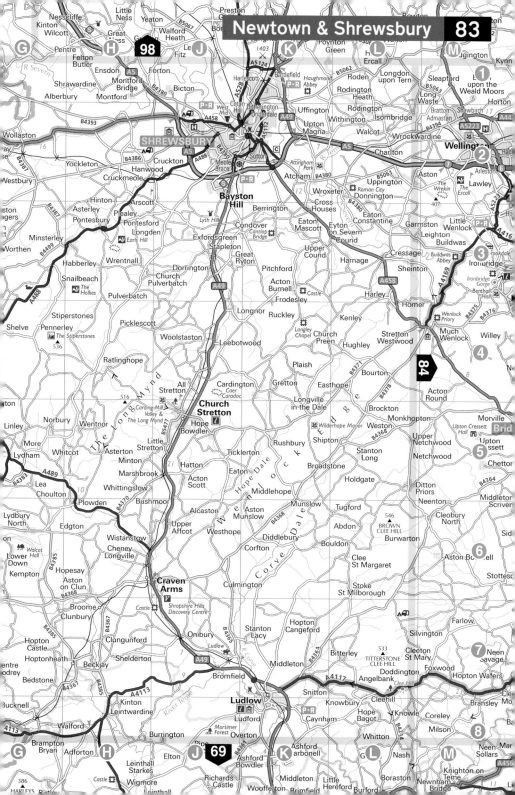

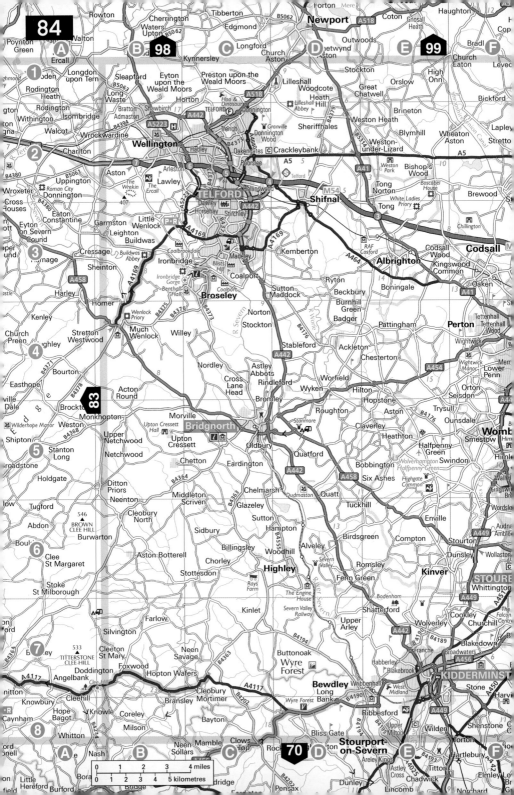

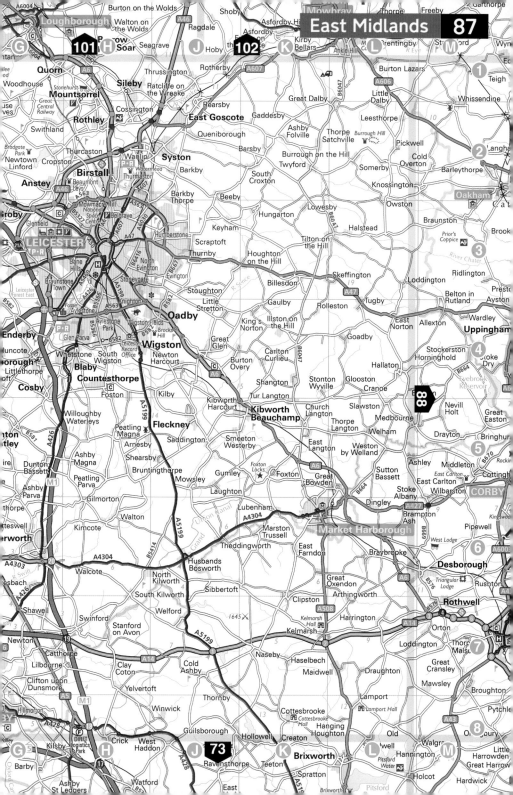

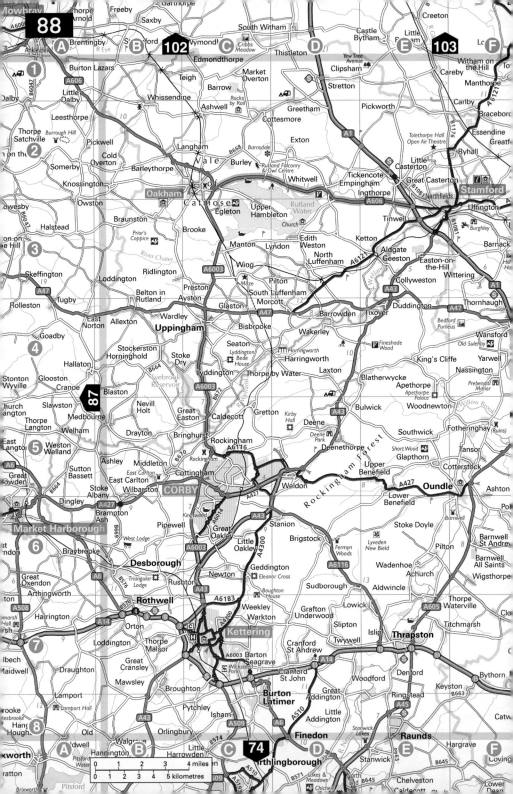

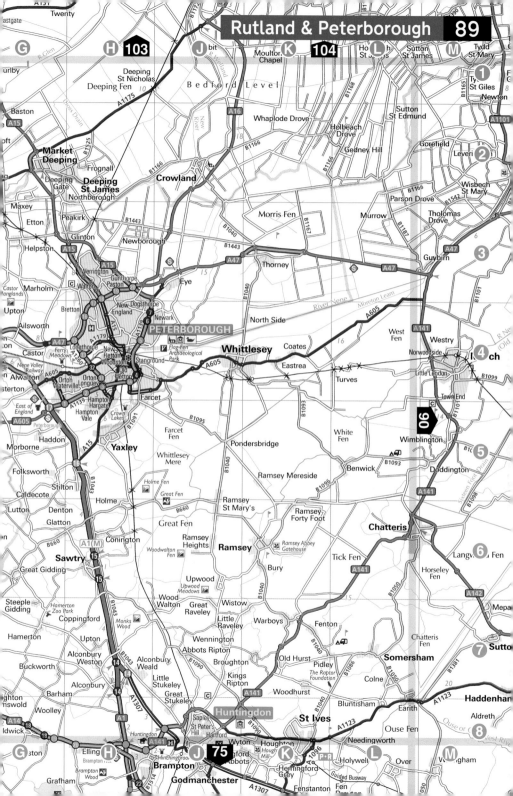

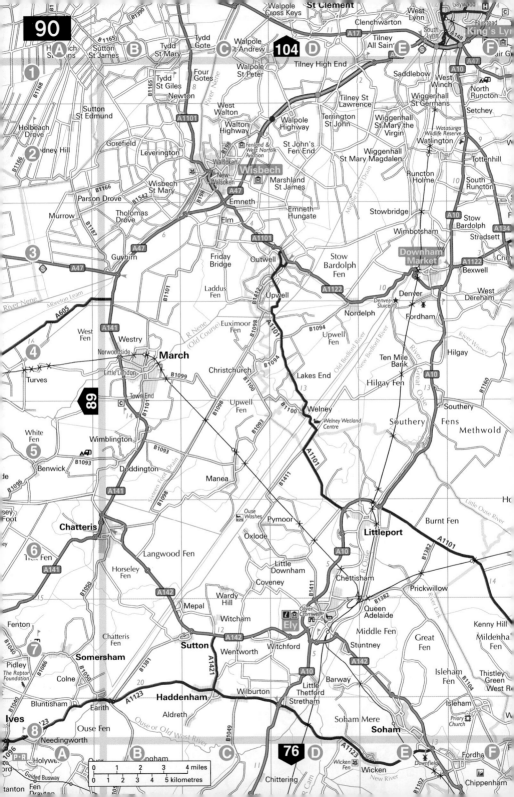

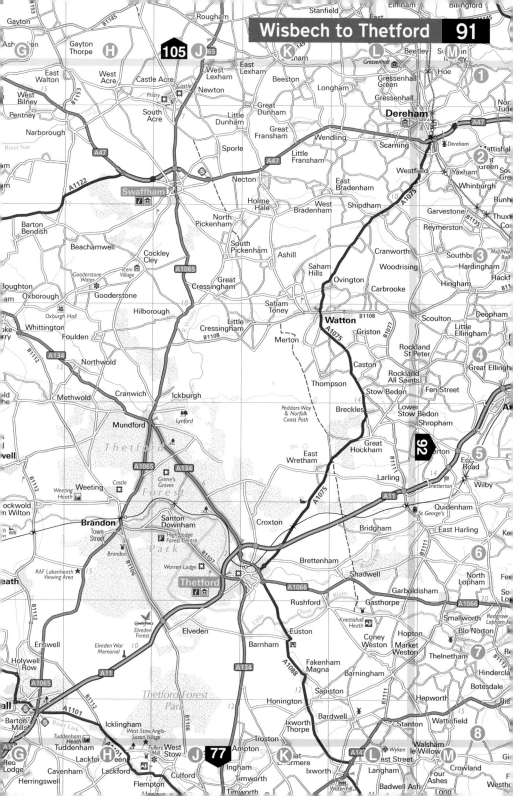

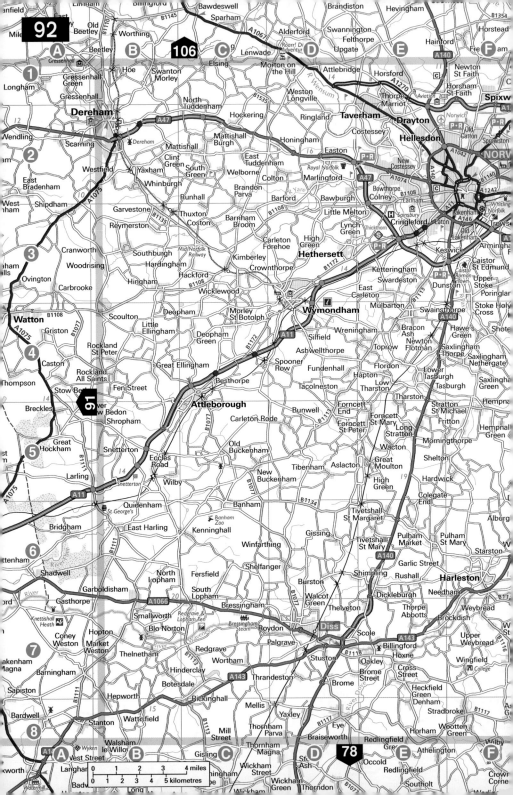

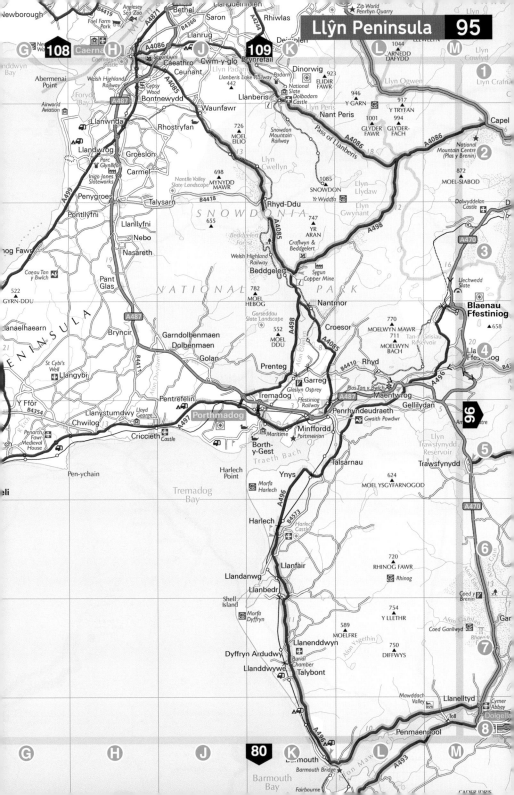

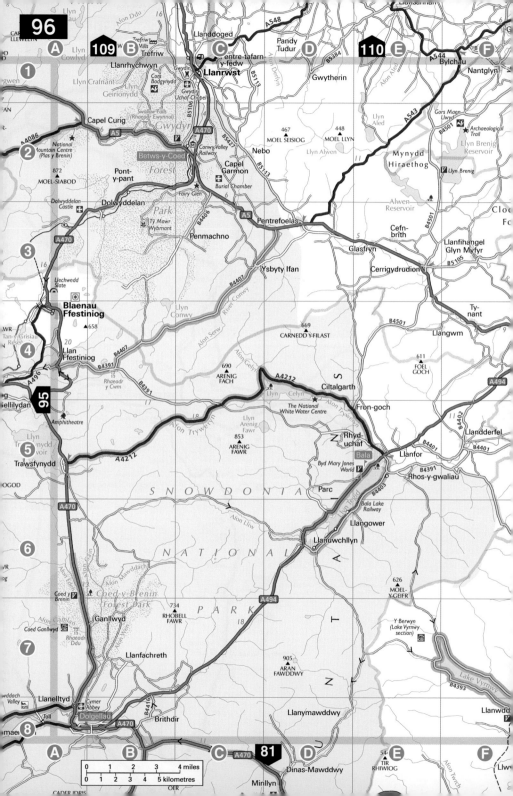

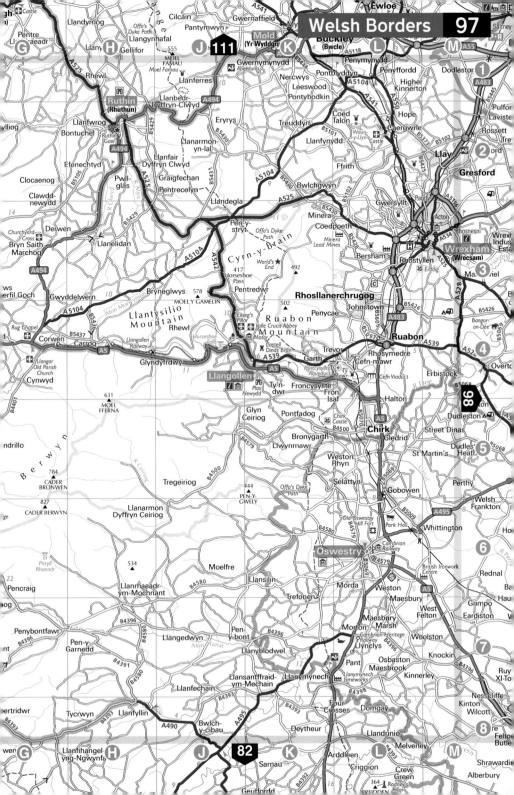

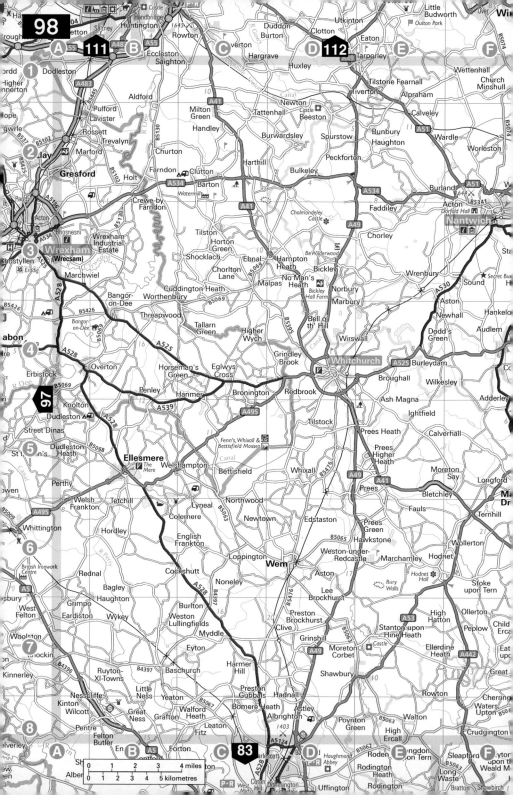

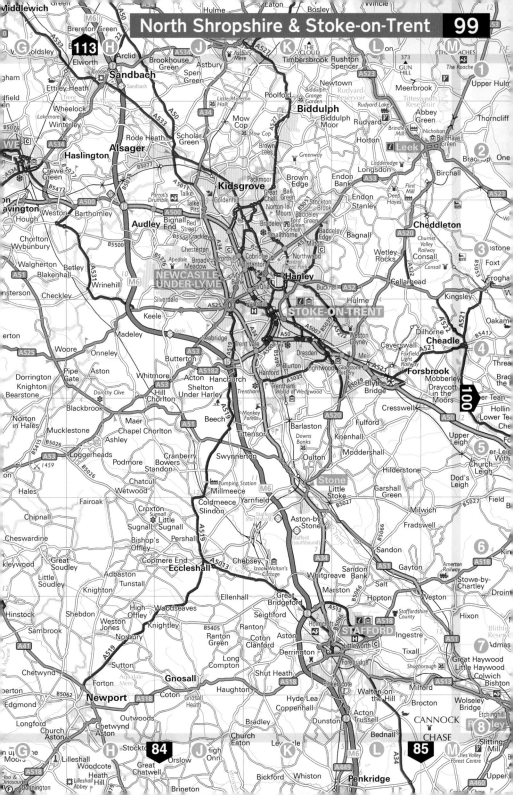

G H 117 J K Woodhall Spa L 118 M

Potterhanworth
Nocton
B1202
B1178
B1188
Kirkstead
Kirkby on Bain
Wood Enderby
Revesby
East Kirkby
1
Metheringham
Blankney
B1189
Martin
B1191
Timberland Delph
B1192
Tattershall Thorpe
Tumby
Mareham le Fen
A155
A153
Scopwick
Kirkby Green
B1191
Timberland
Tattershall
Tattershall College
Coningsby
Tumby Woodside
New Bolingbroke
ARK Wildlife & Dinosaur Park
2
Ashby de la Launde
Thorpe Tilney
Walcott
B1189
Dogdyke
Hawthorn Hill
Battle of Britain Memorial Flight
New York
Tattershall Castle
West
Fen
Northlar
B1183
A15
B1429
Digby
Dorrington
Billinghay
Chapel Hill
Scrub Hill
Bloxholm
North Kyme
Holland Fen
Gipsey Bridge
Frithville
B1184
Sibsey Trader Windmill
B1183
Ruskington
A153
Anwick
South Kyme
R Witham
B1392
Langrick
Fishtoft Drove
3
B1184
Cranwell
Leasingham
B1209
Evedon
Ewerby
B1395
Anton's Gowt
Witham Way
H
Cranwell Aviation
North Raceby
Holdingham
A17
Kirkby la Thorpe
Howell
East Heckington
Holland Fen
Boston
C
South Raceby
Sleaford
Asgarby
A17
A1121
A52
4
caster
A15
Quarrington
Heckington
Great Hale
Heckington
Little Hale
Helpringham
Swineshead
B1395
104
A57
B1395
A16
Fram
Silk Willoughby
Burton Pedwardine
Scredington
Bicker
Kirton
Swaby
Aswarby
Spanby
Swineshead
Wigtoft
Sutterton
Skeldyke
5
Heydour
Aisby
Aunsby
Osbournby
Swaton
Northorpe
Donington
B1181
A17
Burtoft
Algarkirk
Dembleby
Newton
Walcot
Threekingham
A52
Quadring Eaudike
B1391
Fosdyke
Haceby
Braceby
Pickworth
Horbling
Billingborough
Quadring
A152
A16
Sapperton
Humby
Folkingham
A15
Pointon
Westhorpe
Gosberton
6
Lenton
Ingoldsby
Laughton
Aslackby
Dowsby
B1397
Risegate
Surfleet
C
B1356
Moulton Seas End
B1135
A17
Sarace
Irnham
Rippingale
B1177
Dunsby
R Glen
Pinchbeck Engine
Holbe Clou
Corby Glen
A151
Kirkby Underwood
Hacconby
B1180
Pinchbeck
Weston
Moulton
A151
7
B1357
Grimsthorpe Castle
Hanthorpe
Elsthorpe
Grimsthorpe
Morton
Dyke
B1180
Springfield
Mill Green
B1165
Whapl
Swinstead
Edenham
A15
Bourne
B1193
Eastgate
A151
Twenty
Spalding
A151
Pulney
Romany
B1172
Moulton Chapel
8
Creeton
Little Bytham
R Glen
Lound
Witham on the Hill
A151
Cowbit
R Welland
A16
G Careby H J Thurlby K 89 L M
Manthorpe
Carlby
A6121
Deeping Fen
A1175
Bedford Level

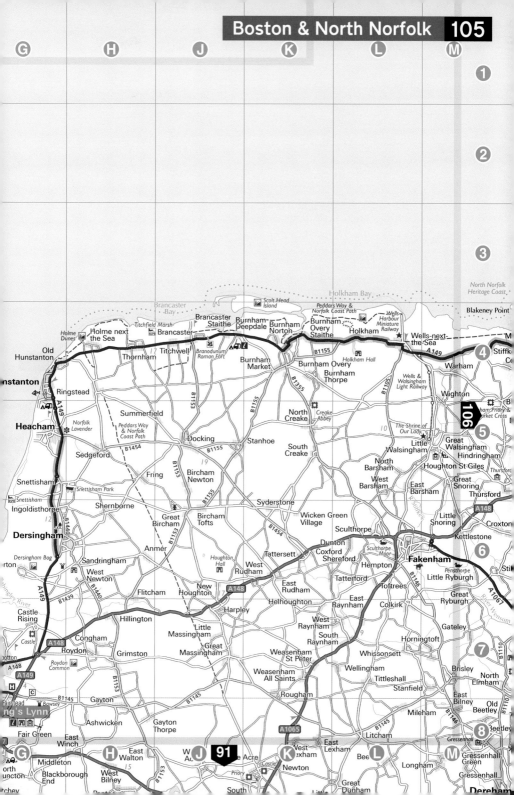

G H J K L M

1

2

3

4

110

Great Orme
Heritage Coast

GREAT ORME'S HEAD

Great Orme
Tramway

Toll

Little Ormes He

Penrhyn

5

Llandudno

Llandrillo-
yn-Rhôs

RM

Conwy
Bay

Deganwy

Welsh

Dulas
Bay

RNLI Moelfre
Seawatch Centre

Moelfre

Llanallgo

Benllech

Cors Goch
rgoch

Red Wharf
Bay

Pentraeth

Red Wharf Bay

Llanddona

Puffin Island

Penmon Priory

Toll

Black Point

Llangoed

Hafoty Medieval
House

Beaumaris
Castle

Gaol

Courthouse

Beaumaris

Llansadwrn

Llandegfan

Dwygyfylchi

Capelulo

Penmaenmawr

Conwy

Conwy
Castle

15A

Llandudno
Junction

Llansanffraid
Glan Conwy

Bry
y-M

A470

6

nydd

Plas Cadnant

fairpwllgwyngyll

Bryn
Celli Ddu

Menai
Bridge
(Porthaethwy)

Penrhyn
Castle

Bangor

Llandygai

Penrhyn
Column

Y Felinheli

Britannia
Bridge

Pont
Newydd

Glasinfryn

Greenwood
Family Park

Pentir

Bethel

Seion

Llanddeiniolen

Saron

Llanrug

Rhiwlas

Deiniolen

B4366

Caeathro

Cwm-y-glo

Brynrefail

Llanberis Lake

Waunfawr

Llanberis

Llansadwrn

Spinnies

Abergwyngregyn

Coedydd
Aber

Aber Falls

Afon Anafon

Aber

Llanfairfechan

Rowen

Ty'n-y-Groes

Henryd

Graig

Tal-y-Cafn

Eglwysbach

SNOWDONIA

610
TAL-Y-FAN

Talybont

Llanbedr-y-Cennin

Tal-y-Bont

Adventure Parc
Snowdonia

Dolgarrog

Afon Dulyn

NATIONAL

PARK

Afon Ddu

Vale of Conwy

7

Llanddoged

8

rwst

tafarn-
y-fedw

Trefriw
Woollen Mills

Trefriw

Swallow Falls

Gwydir
Uchaf Chapel

Gwydir
Castle

Tal-y-
bont

Llanllechid

Rachub

Tregarth

Bethesda

Zip World
Penrhyn Quarry

Penrhyn
Slate Landscape

Moel
Winion

580

Y Drosgl

757

Foel-Fras

942

Afon Caseg

Carnedd
Llewelyn

1062

Carnedd
Dafydd

1044

Elidir
Fawr

Llyn
Eigiau

Llyn
Cowlyd

Llyn
Crafnant

Llyn
Geirionydd

G H 95 J K L 96 M

National
Slate
Museum

Dolbadarn
Castle

923

442

946

Y Garn

917

Y Tryfan

Llyn Ogwen

Llyn Padarn

Nant Peris

Llyn Peris

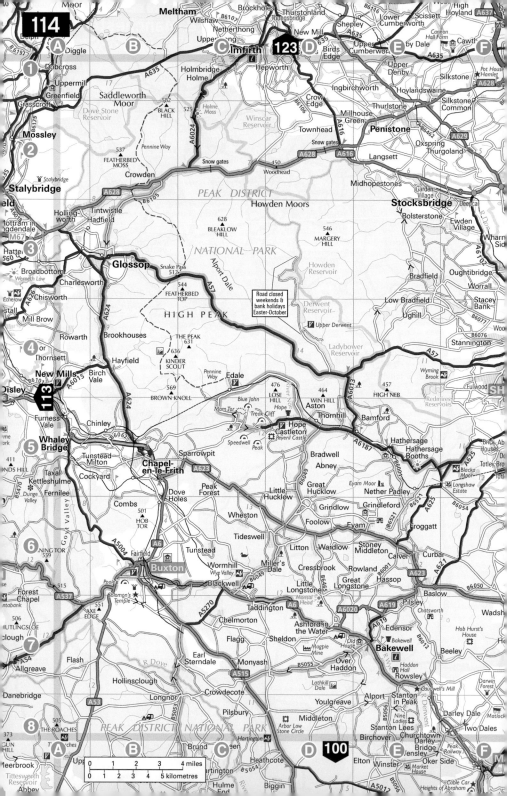

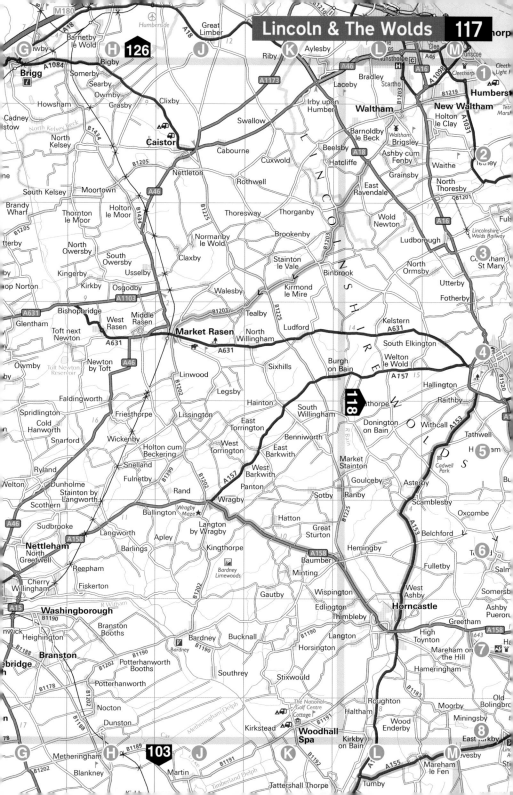

G   H   J   K   L   M

1

2

3

4

5

6

7

8

rpe Dunes

ddlethorpe
Helen

Seal Sanctuary &
Wildlife Centre

Mablethorpe

A52

Trusthorpe

A1111

Sutton on Sea

Sandilands

h

A52

Markby

Huttoft

urlby

B1449

Anderby

On Your Marques
Model Car

sthorpe

Mumby

rworth

Chapel Point

1B

ughby

Hogsthorpe

**Chapel
St Leonards**

Sloothby

Habertoft

Addlethorpe

Fantasy Island

Ingoldmells

Ingoldmells
Point

A52

Lincolnshire Coast
Light Railway

Burgh le Marsh

A158

Natureland Seal
Sanctuary

Village Church
Farm

Skegness

the Marsh

G   **104**   H   J   K   L   M

Croft

pe St Peter

Wainfleet
Haven

Wainfleet

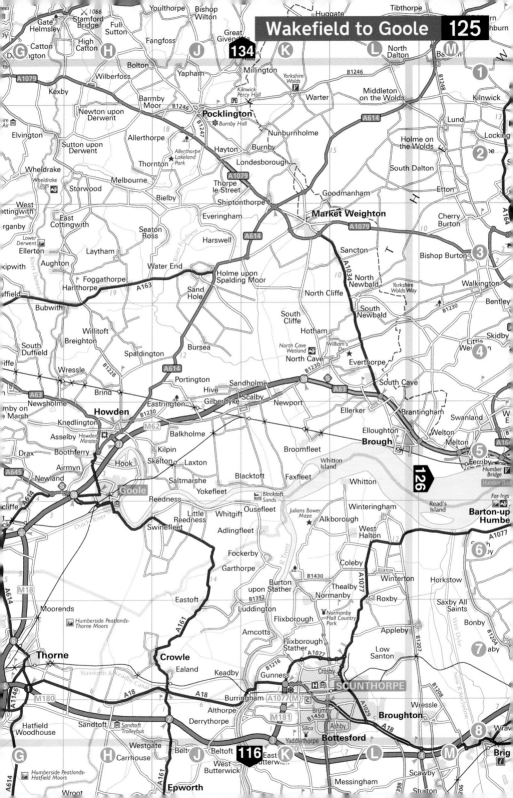

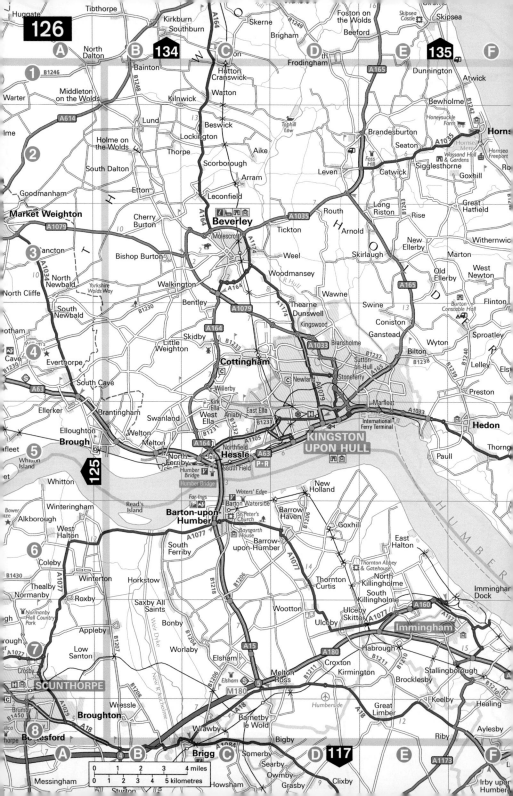

G   H   J   K   L   M

1
2
3

borough

4

Hilston
vstwick
Tunstall
ton
sea   Roos
Rimswell
B1242
Owthorne
alsham   Withernsea
B1362
Lighthouse
ngham
Hollym   5
ham   Winestead   Holmpton
A1033
Patrington   RAF
Patrington   Holmpton
Haven   Bunker
Welwick
Weeton   B1445   Easington   6
Skeffling
Spurn
Heritage
Coast
Kilnsea
Spurn Point
7
U A R Y
GRIMSBY   Spurn
Heritage Coast
Cleethorpes   SPURN HEAD
Old
Clee   Rotterdam (Europoort)
A46
anstthorpe   Thrunscoe
e
rtho   Cleethorpes Coast
m   Cleethorpes   Railway   **118** J   K   L   M   8
A16
G   H
carthо
B1219
Humberston
New Waltham   Tetney
Marshes

128

A   B   C   D   E   F

1

136   137

2

3

4

5

6

7

8

A   B   C   D   E   F

Seascale
Hallsenna Moor
Drigg   Holmrook
Eskdale
652
HARTER
FELL   Seath Ta

Ravenglass
& Eskdale
Railway
Ravenglass
Muncaster Castle,
Hawk & Owl Centre
Roman
Bath
House   A595
Devoke
Water
Hall
Dunnerdale   Seathwa

Waberthwaite   573
WHITFELL   Ulpha

LAKE   DISTRICT
NATIONAL
Broughton
Mills   A593

Hycemoor   Bootle   PARK
Selker Bay   Swinside
Stone Circle   Broughton-in-Fu

600
BLACK
COMBE   A595   Lady
Hall   Foxfield   Griz
Gutterby Spa   Whitbeck
The Green

The Hill   Kirkby-in-
Beck
Whicham
Silecroft   Soutergate
Kirksanton   A5093   Millom   A595
Hodbarrow   Ireleth   12

Haverigg   Askam
in Furness
Haverigg
Point   Lindal in
Furness
Sandscale Haws   South Lakes
Safari Zoo

North Walney   Dalton-   Li
in-Furness   Urs
BARROW-
IN-FURNESS   Hawcoat   Newton   St
with
Furness
Abbey   Bow
Bridge   Dendron
Vickerstown   A590   Barrow
Island   A5087

ISLE OF
WALNEY   Ramp
Sheep
Island   Piel
Castle
Piel Islan
Hilpsford Point   South
Walney   Piel Bar

0   1   2   3   4 miles
0   1   2   3   4   5 kilometres

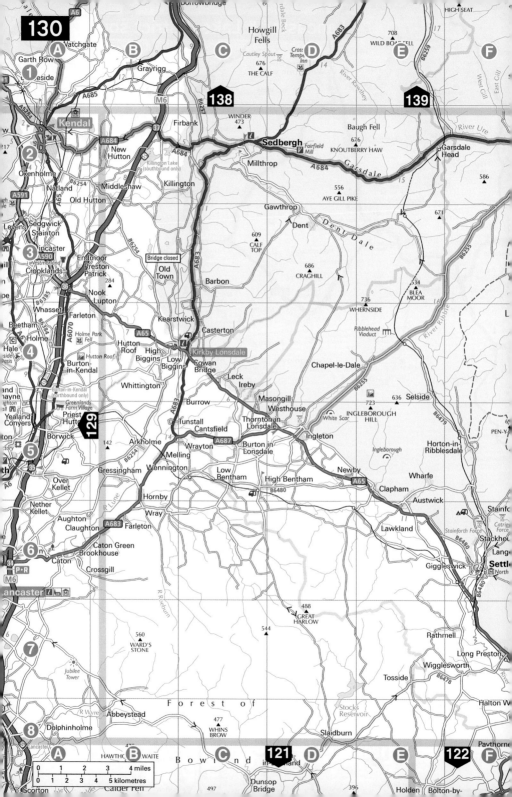

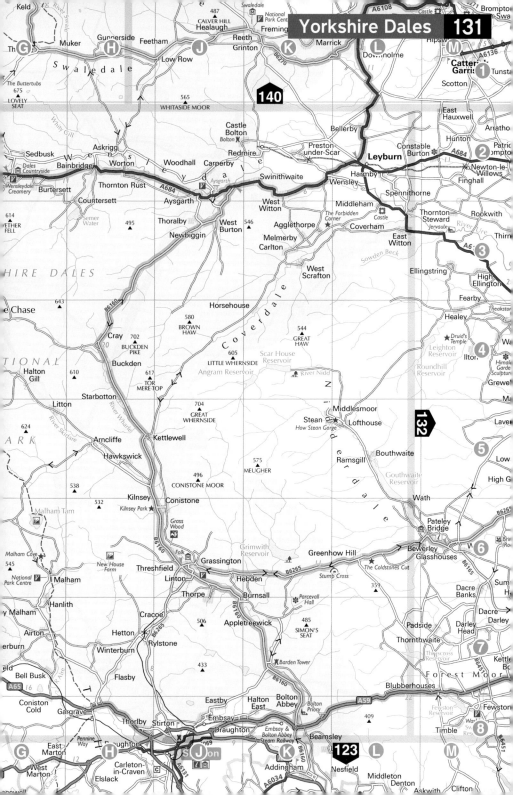

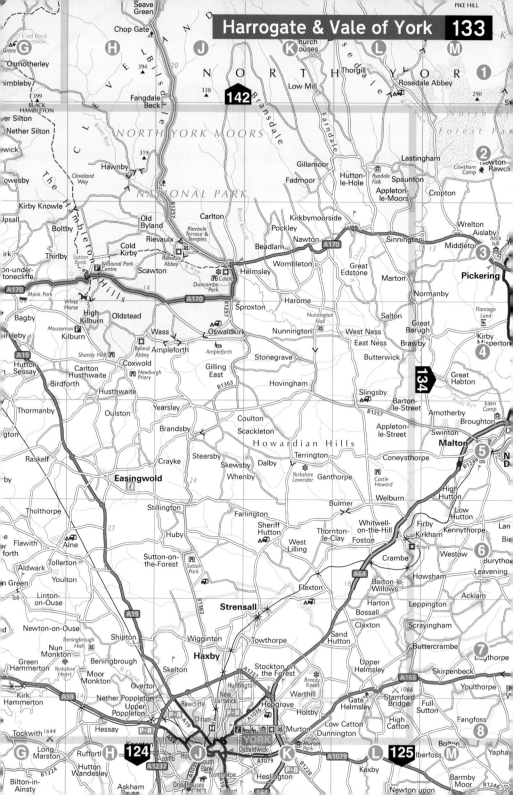

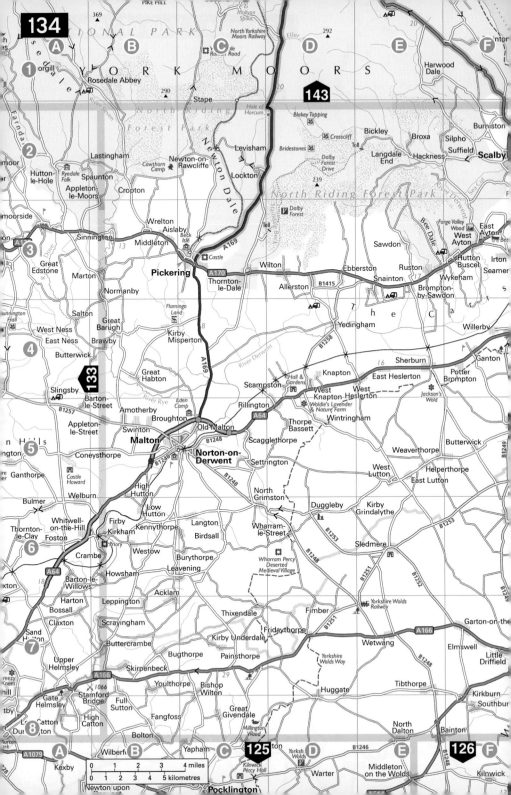

G H J K L M

1

2

Point

d Way

th Bay Railway

Castle

Scarborough

er's Mount

165 P·R 'Osgodby Cayton Bay

field

B1261

ayton The Wyke

Fair Collection

Lebberston Filey Brigg A1039

Gristhorpe **Filey**

Bird Garden & Animal Park

Muston

A1039

Hunmanby Filey Bay

Fordon Reighton Flamborough Head Heritage Coast

Wold Newton Speeton Thornwick Bay

B1229 Bempton Cliffs North Landing

Burton Fleming Buckton Bempton

Grindale A165 Flamborough Cliffs

B1259 Flamborough Selwicks Bay

FLAMBOROUGH HEAD

B1255 Hall & Gardens

Sewerby

B1253 Bondville Model Village

Rudston Monolith Boynton **Bridlington**

Bessingby BRIDLINGTON BAY

Carnaby Hilderthorpe

Haisthorpe A1038

Kilham Thornholme World of Rock

Burton Agnes Bridlington Animal

Parva A165

Lowthorpe Hareham

A614 Fraisthorpe

Nafferton Gransmoor

Great Kelk Lissett Barmston

Wansford B1242

Gembling Ulrome

Foston on the Wolds Skipsea Castle Skipsea

kerne B1249 Beeford

Brigham

North Frodingham

A165 **126** Dunning

8

G H J K L M

Atwick

Bewholme

Honeysuckle

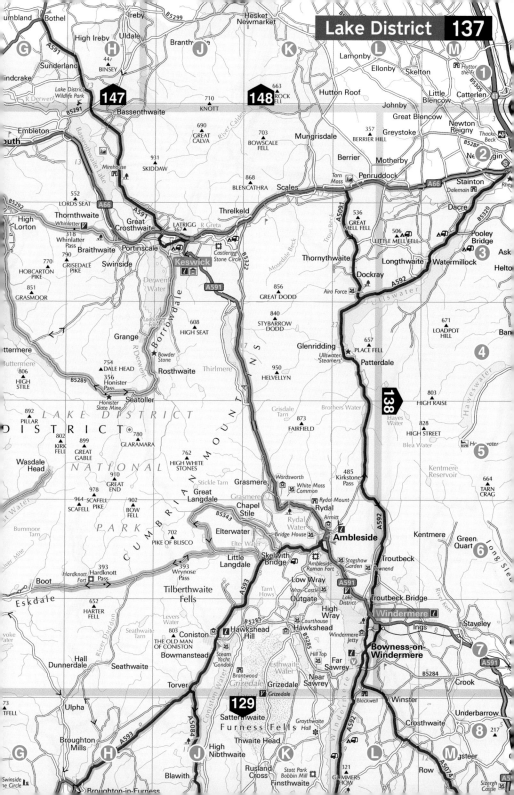

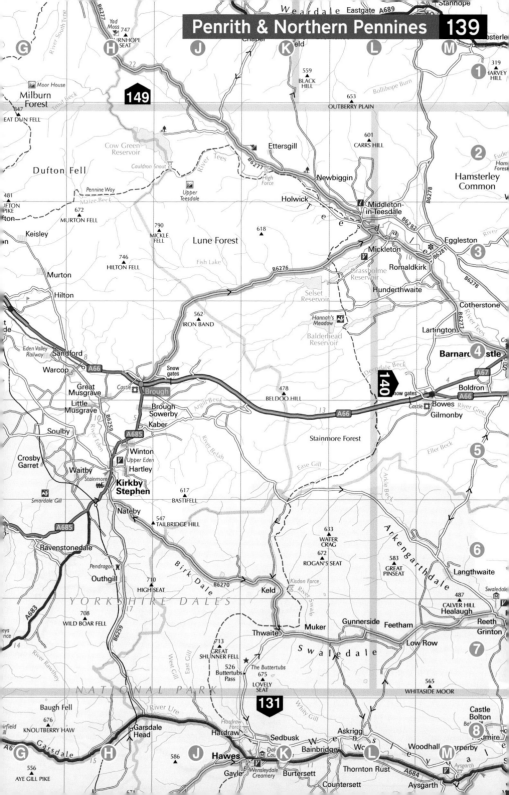

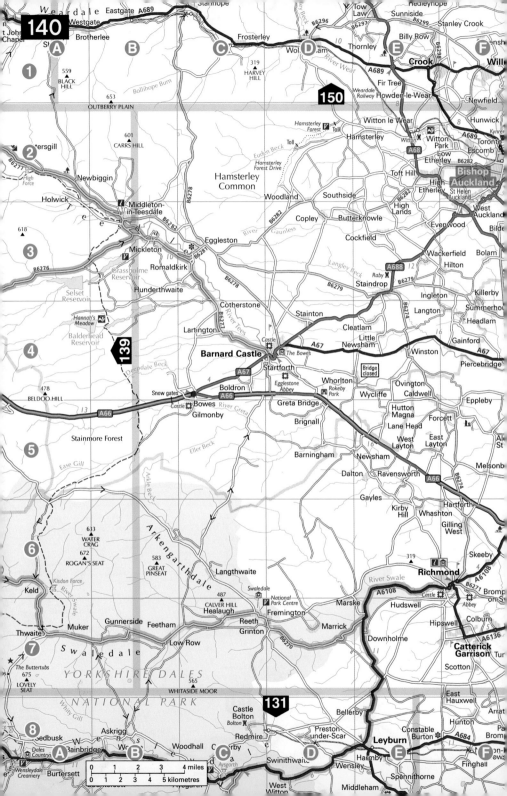

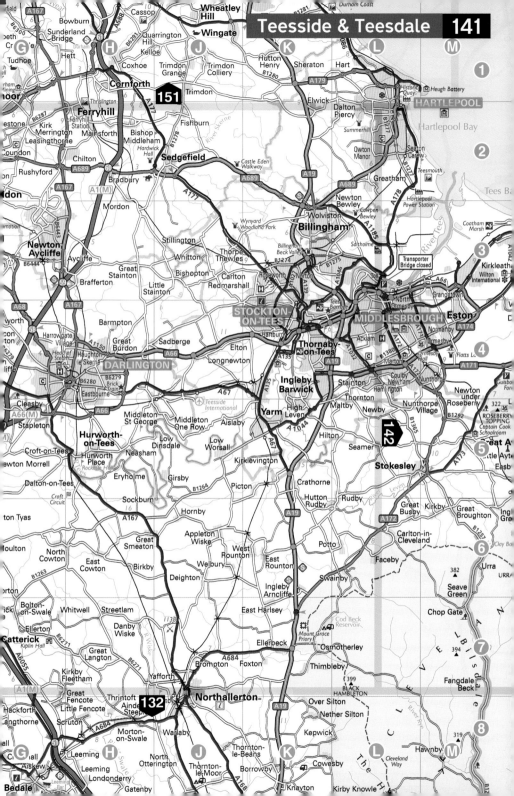

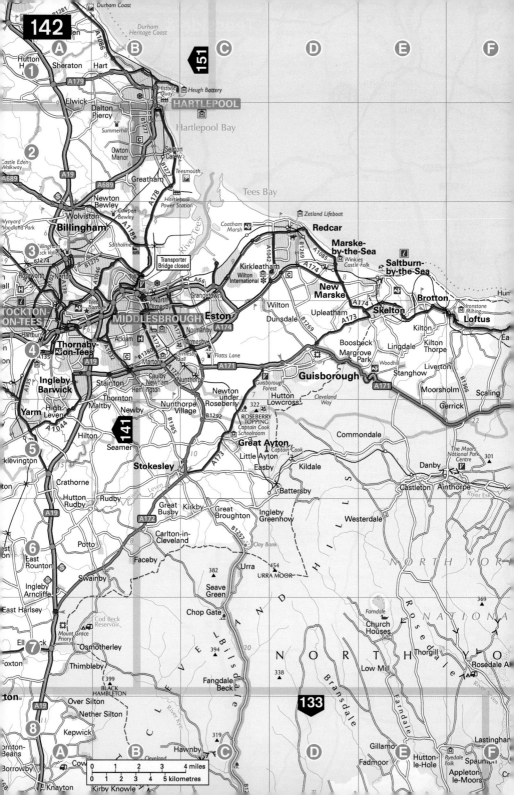

Staithes
Captain Cook & Staithes
well
Runswick Bay
North Yorkshire and Cleveland Heritage Coast
Runswick
Goldsborough
Ellerby
Overdale Wyke
Lythe
A174
Sandsend Wyke
Sandsend
Hickleby
West Barnby
East Barnby
Whitby
Abbey
Saltwick Bay
Dunsley
Newholm
Ugthorpe
Ruswarp
B1410
Stainsacre
Aislaby
Briggswath
Sneaton
High Hawsker
A171
Sleights
Ugglebarnby
Egton
Iburndale
Ness Point or North Cheek
Esk Dale
Grosmont
A169
B1447
Robin Hood's Bay
Bridge
Blue Bank
Old Coastguard
Fylingthorpe
Robin Hood's Bay
B1416
Old Peak or South Cheek
Falling Foss
A171
Ravenscar
Goathland
Mallyan Spout
North Yorkshire Moors Railway
Eller Beck
292
R - K
Staintondale
Wheeldale Roman Road
Hayburn Wyke
O R S
M O O R S
Harwood Dale
Cloughton Wyke
Stape
Hole of Horcum
Cloughton
Blakey Topping
134
Burniston
A165
Cromer Point
Levisham
Bickley
Crosscliff
Silpho
Cleveland Way
Broxa
Bridestones
Toll
Langdale End
Suffield
Scalby
Dalby Forest Drive
Hackness
Newby
th Bay Railway
Lockton
239
River Derwent
Castle
Newton-on-Ra e
Sea Cut
Falsgrave
C
North Riding Forest Park
Scarborough

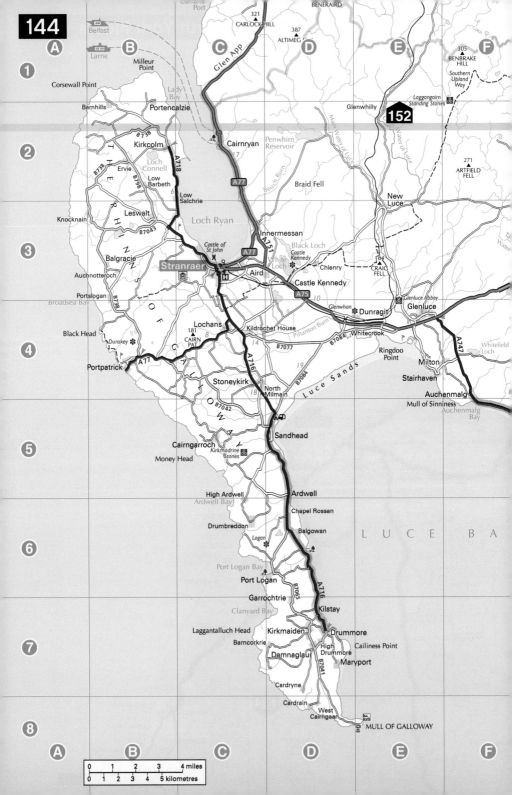

153

146

Creebank
Glentrool
Bargrennan
716
LAMACHAN
HILL
675
LA J L
654
MILLF
Galloway
Deer Range
Wild Goat Park
Murray's
Raiders' Road
Forest Drive
325
CAIRN
EDWARD
440
GARLICK
HILL
402
ROUND
FELL
471
FELL OF FLEET
Loch
Ochiltree
Loch
Knowe
Wood of Cree

GALLOWAY

Carseriggan
Challoch
Minnigaff
Loch
Grannoch
Loch
Fleet
208
AUCHENCLOY HILL
Skerrow
Barfad
214
CULVENNAN
FELL
Newton
Stewart
Creebridge
Kirroughtree
710
CAIRNSMORE
OF FLEET
335
WHITE TOP
OF CULREACH
Shennanton
Palnure
Big Water of Fleet
Cairnsmore of Fleet
367
BENGR
Craighlaw
Kirkcowan
Baltersan
Gem Rock
Upper
Ruscoe
Carstramon
Wood
Mill on
the Fleet
Gatehouse
of Fleet
Littletor
Clugston
Causeway
End
Creetown
Fleet
Valley
Anwoth
Cardoness
Castle
Fell
Loch
Torhouse
Stone Circle
Wigtown
Kirkmabreck
455
CAIRNHARROW
Cairnholy
Chambered Cairns
Girthon
THE
Bladnoch
Kirwaugh
Carsluith
Carsluith
Castle
Lennox
Plunton
MACHARS
Braehead
Ravenshall
Point
Mossyard
Fleet
Bay
Margrie
Culshabbin
Kirkinner
Orchardton
Bay
Islands
of Fleet
Kirkandrews
Barrachan
Whauphill
Little
Aities
Culscadden
Wigtown Bay
Borness
Elrig
Druchtag
Motte
Sorbie
Pouton
Garlieston
Crugglton
Bay
Ringdoo Point
Mochrum
Drumtroddan
Cup & Ring
Drumtroddan
Standing Stones
Drummoddie
Broughton
Mains
Galloway House
Port William
Big Balcraig
'Wren's Egg'
Standing Stones
Priory
Barsalloch Fort
Monreith
Whithorn
Story
Whithorn
Barsalloch Point
Rispain
Camp
Point of Leg
Portyerrock
St Ninian's
Cave
Kidsdale
Isle of Whithorn
St Ninian's
Chapel
(ruin)
Cutcloy
BURROW HEAD

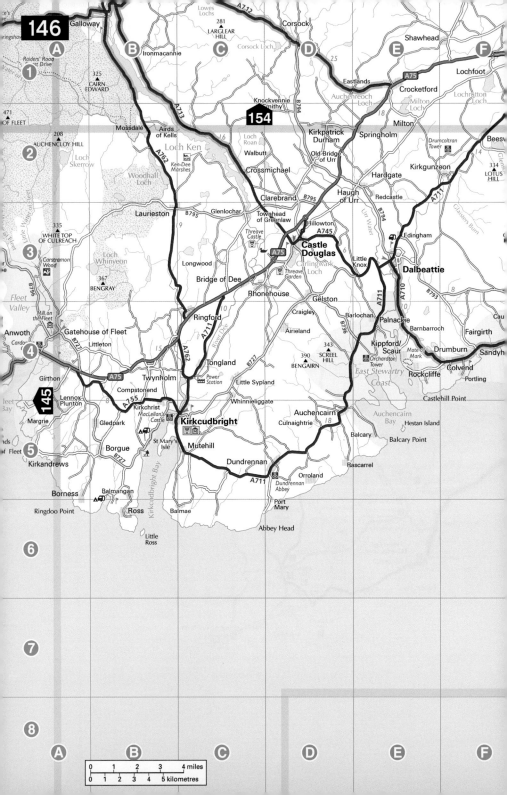

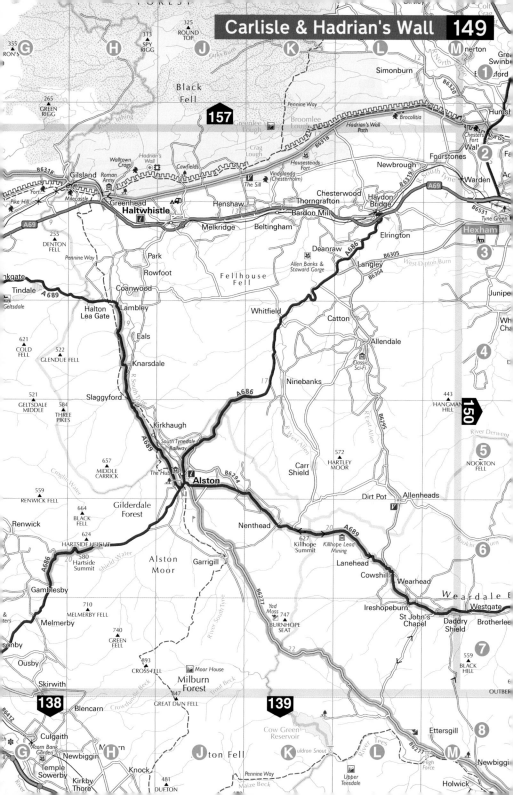

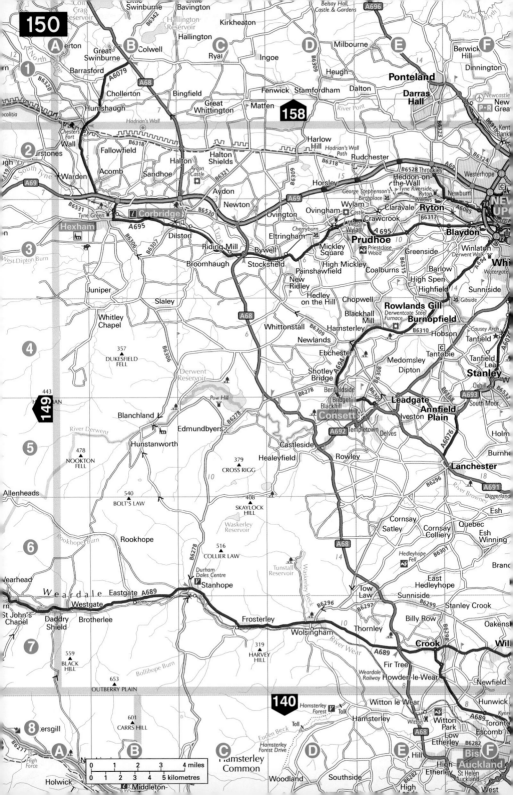

Nev Cumn

New Galloway

St Jo Town

Blawqu

1
2
3
4
5
6
7
8

G H J K L M

163
164
154
145

Minishant
Dalrymple
River Doon
B730
Rank
B742
Grimmet
G
B77
A77
Maybole
Kirkmichael
Patna
Kilmein Hill 429
Waterside
Scottish Industrial
464 BENBEOCH
K
High Pennyvenie
Burnton
L
M
ybank
B742
B741
B
Loch Spallander Reservoir
treehill
itreehill
Keirs Hill 306
Burnton
Dalmellington
ILL
Loch Finlas
Threave
B7045
Crosshill
B741
Straiton
Mossdale 536
Carsphairn Forest
697 WINDY STANDARD
fton Reservoir
Maratz Hill 320
Ness Glen
Loch Doon
Drumjohn
Bow Burn
796 CAIRNSMORE OF CARSPHAIRN
Dalquhairn
nockeen
Balloch
Garleffin Fell 429
Linfern Loch
Tallaminnock
Loch Bradan
523 CRAIGLEE
Loch Doon Castle
Carrick Forest Drive
Loch Recar
Cairnhorn Burn
622
Carsphairn
Water
R R R I C K
549 POLMADDIE HILL
768 SHALLOCH ON MINNOCH
Loch Macaterick
695 MEAUL
Polmaddy Burn
Kendoon Loch
vehead
B729
Galloway
781 KIRRIEREOCH HILL
813 CORSERINE
The Glenkens
346 GARWALL HILL
842 MERRICK
Loch Moan
Loch Enoch
716 MILFIRE
Loch Dungeon
Forest Park
Loch Neidricken
Silver Flowe
Knocksheen
Garroch
River Cree
Glen Trool Lodge
Bruce
Loch Trool
Loch Dee
380 BENNAN
A762
A714
Glentrool
22
Creebank
Glentrool Bargrennan
716 LAMACHAN HILL
675 LARG HILL
654 MILLFORE
Clatteringshaws Loch
Bruce's Stone
Clatteringshaws
New Galloway
lamford
Loch Dornal
Knowe
B7027
440 GARLICK HILL
Wild Goat Park
Murray's
Galloway Deer Range
A712
402 ROUND FELL
471 FELL OF FLEET
Black Water o
Raiders' Road Forest Drive
325 CAIRN EDWARD
Loch Ochiltree
Wood of Cree
G A L L O W A Y
145
Loch nnoch
Loch Fleet
208 AUCHENCLOY HILL
Loch Skerrow
Carseriggan
Challoch
710 CAIRNSMORE OF FLEET
Barfad
214 NNAN LL
G
Minnigaff
Kirroughtree
L
M
Newton Stewart
H
B7079
J
dge
K
Big Water o
Cairnsmore of Fleet
335 WHITE TOP OF CULREACH
Shennanton
A714
Palnure
Little Water of Fleet

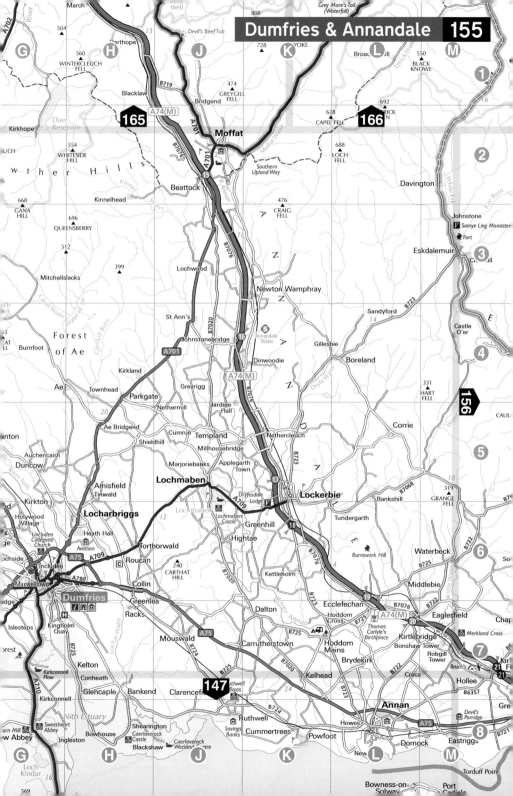

165 A74(M)

166

Moffat

Beattock

156

147

Lochmaben

Locharbriggs

Dumfries

Lockerbie

Annan

Place names and features

March, Well, Devil's Beef Tub, Grey Mare's Tail (Waterfall), YOKE, Broad..., BLACK KNOWE

WINTERCLEUCH FELL, Harthope, GREYGILL FELL, CAPEL FELL, ...RICK...

Kirkhope, Daer Reservoir, Blacklaw, Blackwood, Bridgend, Davington

WHITESIDE HILL, w t h e r H i l l s, Kinnelhead, Southern Upland Way

Kinnelhead, CRAIG FELL, Johnstone, Samye Ling Monaster..., Fort

GANA HILL, QUEENSBERRY, Lochwood, Eskdalemuir, ...Hill

Mitchellslacks, Newton Wamphray, Sandyford, Castle O'er

St Ann's, Annandale Water, Gillesbie, Boreland

Forest of Ae, Burnfoot, Johnstonebridge, Dinwoodie, HART FELL, CAUL...

Kirkland, Greyrigg, Jardine Hall, Corrie

Ae, Townhead, Parkgate, Nethermill, Templand, Nethercleuch

Ae Bridgend, Shieldhill, Cumrue, Millhousebridge, Applegarth Town

Auchencairn, Duncow, Amisfield, Tinwald, Marjoriebanks, Lochmaben, Bankshill, GRANGE FELL

Kirkton, Holywood Village, Lincluden Collegiate Church, Heath Hall, Dryfesdale Lodge, Lochmaben Castle, Greenhill, Tundergarth, Waterbeck

Aviation, Torthorwald, Hightae, Burnswark Hill, Middlebie

Maxwelltown, Roucan, Collin, Kettleholm, CARTHAT HILL

Lincluden, Greenlea, Racks, Dalton, Ecclefechan, Eaglesfield, Merkland Cross

Islesteps, Kingholm Quay, Mouswald, Carrutherstown, Hoddom Cross, Thomas Carlyle's Birthplace, Kirtlebridge, Bonshaw Tower, Robgill Tower, Bruce's...

Kinmount, Hoddom Mains, Brydekirk, Kelhead, Creca, Hollee

Kirkconnell Flow, Kelton, Conheath, Bankend, Clarencefield, Ruthwell Cross, Devil's Porridge

Glencaple, Sweetheart Abbey, Shearington, Caerlaverock Castle, Ruthwell Savings Banks, Cummertrees, Powfoot, Annan, Dornock, Eastriggs

...orn Mill, ...w Abbey, Ingleston, Bowhouse, Blackshaw, Caerlaverock Wetland Centre, New..., Howes, Torduff Point

Loch Kindar, Nith Estuary, Bowness-on-Solway, Port...

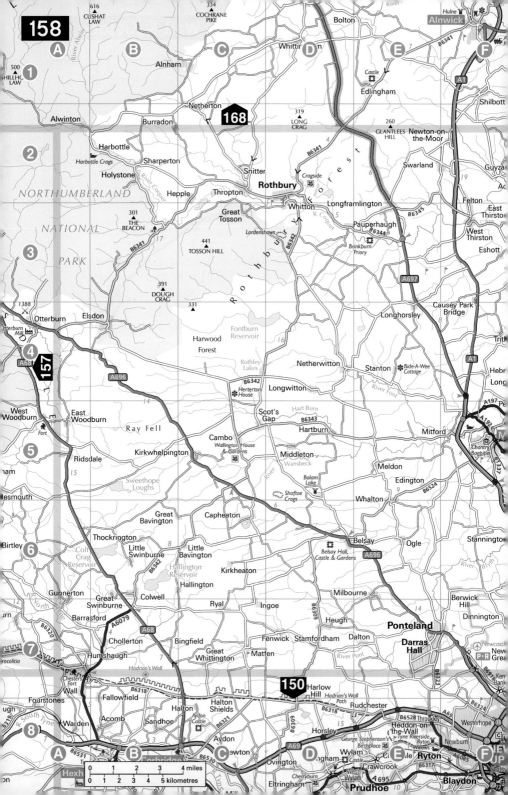

G   H   J   K   L   M

1

esbury

Seaton Point

Alnmouth

Alnmouth
Bay

169

Warkworth

Amble

Coquet Island

2

er Hill

High
Hauxley

Togston

Broomhill

Druridge Bay

3

hill
Row

Druridge
Bay

Widdrington

North Northumberland
Heritage Coast

Widdrington
Station

Cresswell

4

A1068

ham

Ellington

Lynemouth

A189 Woodhorn   Beacon Point

QE2

shington

A197

Hirst

**Newbiggin-
by-the-Sea**

Wansbeck
Riverside

thal

B1334

5

A1147

edlington

A193 C

Cowpen

Blyth

331

B1331

A1068

A189

Newsham

A192

South
Newsham

6

A1061

nlington

A192

New
Hartley

Seaton

Seaton
Sluice

Seaton
Hall

A190

**Seaton
Delaval**

B1326

St Mary's

A19

B1322

A192

Earsdon

A1148

Dudley
ideopen

A1056

**Whitley
Bay**

Killingworth

Shiremoor

Monkseaton

Cullercoats

7

Forest Hall

A191

New
York

A193

P·R

Rising
Sun

Tynemouth

A189

**North
Shields**

Tynemouth Priory
& Castle

151

Amsterdam
(IJmuiden)

P·R

Longbenton

Gosforth

A1058

Willington

Int. Ferry
Terminal

Tyne Tunnel

**SOUTH
SHIELDS**

Jesmond

Wallsend

Heaton

A184

Jarrow

Electronic Toll

Westoe

A183

Marsden
Bay

8

Walker

B1313

Souter Ligh
& The Leas

Byker

Hebburn

Monkton

Marsden

Whitburn Coastal Park

A184

Felling

Cleadon
Park

Cleadon

Souter Point

Whitburn

G   H   J   K   L   M

BEINN SHOLUM 346

Eilean a' Chùirn

Rubha Mòr

tra

Port Ellen

A846

Ardbeg

Rubha na Gainmhich

Port Ellen - Kennacraig

Lagavulin

Laphroaig

Texa

ISLAY

THE OA

165 MAOL BUIDHE

Lower Killeyan

Risabus

Kinnabus

American

Loch Kinnabus

MULL OF OA

Ballycastle (Apr-Sept)

Rubha nan Leacan

Kilnaughton Bay

Ear

K

0 1 2 3 4 miles
0 1 2 3 4 5 kilometres

GIGHA

Rhunahaorine
Point

CRUACH MHIC
GOUGAIN

264
CNOC AN
SAMHLAID

Ardminish

G

Achamore

H

Rhunahaorine

Tayinloan

J

172

K

Cour

L

M

1

North Arr

Cara

Grogport

Barmollack

Pinrmill

Penrioch

Loch
Tanna

A83

354
CRUACH
NAN GABHAR

Muasdale

Whitefarland

715
BEINN
BHARRAIN

2

Glen Torsa

Imachar

Balliekine

Glenacardoch
Point

Belloch

Carradale Village

Bridgend

Carradale

Port Righ

2

Glenbarr

454
BEINN AN TUIRC

Dippen

Waterfoot

Torrisdale

Carradale
Point

162

A R R

Cleongart

319

408
BORD
MOR

Saddell

Machrie
Bay

Tormore

Auchagallon
Stone Circle Machrie

3

Bellochantuy Bay

Bellochantuy

396
SGREADAN
HILL

Saddell
Bay

Machrie Moor
Stone Circles

Moss Farm Road
Stone Circle

Lussa
Loch

Tangy Loch

Ugadale

Torbeg

Drumadoon
Point

BEIN

Balmichael

Shiskine

Glen Lussa

Peninver

Ardnacross
Bay

Blackwaterfoot

Kilpatrick

4

Kilpatrick Dun

Kilkenzie

A83

Kilmichael

Drumadoon
Bay

Brown Head

Machrihanish
Bay

Campbeltown

Corriecravie

Sliddery

Torr a' Chaisteal Fort

Lag

Machrihanish

B842

Campbeltown
Loch

Island Davaar

5

Drumlemble

B843

Stewarton

Kildalloig

Kilkerran

Campbeltown-Ardrossan
(May-Sept)

385
THE
STATE

352
BEINN GHUILEAN

Kildalloig

Achinhoan

446
CNOC
MOY

Ballycastle
(Apr-Sept)

Dalsmeran

Ru Stafnish

6

A LICE

Stone Glen

B842

Cattadale

Polliwilline Bay

Macharioch

Carskey

Southend

7

Dunaverty

Carskey Bay

Borgadalemore
Point

Sound of Sanda

Sheep Island

Sanda Island

G

H

J

K

L

M

8

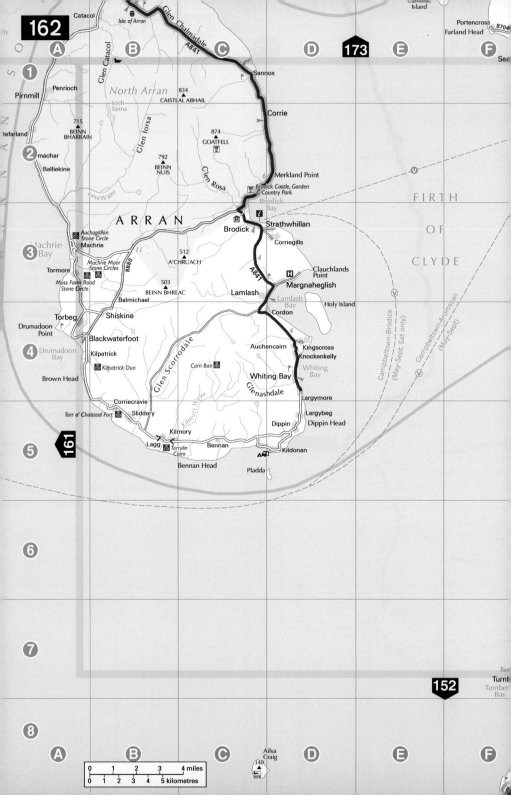

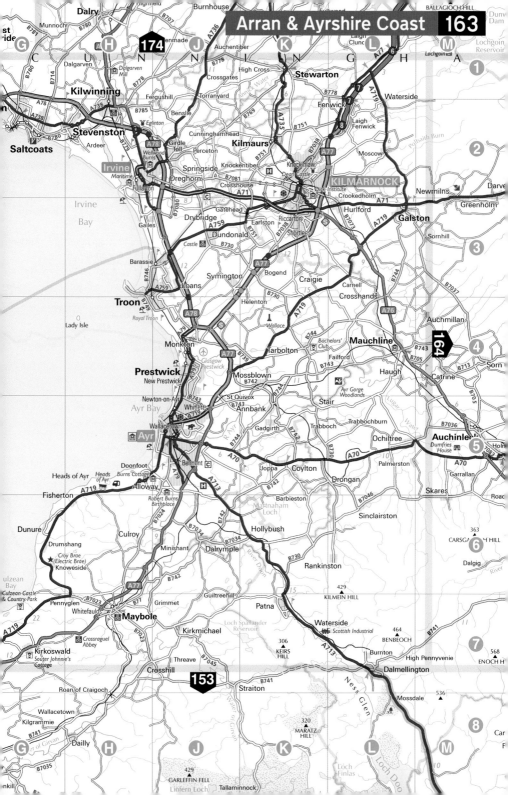

174

153

164

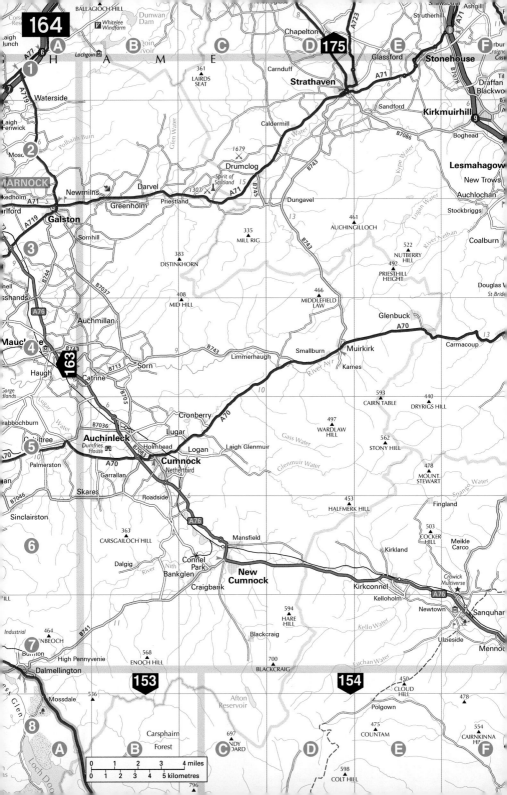

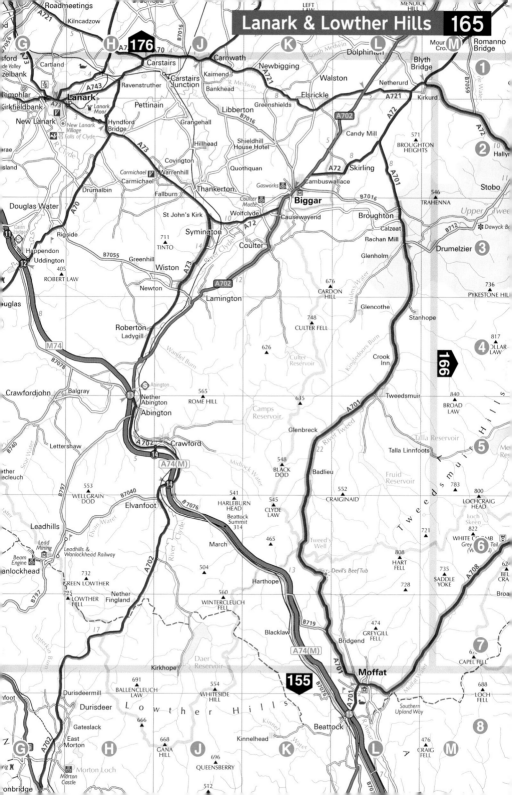

G **H** **J** **K** **L** **M**

1

Causeway
flooded at
high tide

HOLY ISLAND

Holy
Island
Lindisfarne
Castle
Lindisfarne
Priory
Castle Point
Guile Point

2

Longstone
FARNE
ISLANDS
Staple
Sound
Inner
Sound
North Northumberland
Heritage Coast

Budle
Bay
Bamburgh
B1342
Belford
B1340
Bamburgh
B6349
Grace
Darling

3

Seahouses
North Sunderland
Lucker
B1341
Warenford
Beadnell
Swinhoe
B1340
Beadnell
Bay
A1
Newstead
Chathill
Tughall
Ellingham
Preston
High Newton-by-the-Sea

4

Cattle
Ros Castle
Preston
Tower
Christon
Bank
Embleton &
Newton Links
267
CATERAN
HILL
North
Charlton
Fallodon
Embleton
Embleton
Bay
B6346
B6341
South
Charlton
Dunstanburgh
Castle

5

ewick
Eglingham
Rock
Rennington
Dunstan
Craster
B6341
Stamford
Howick
Hall
Cullernose Point
Beanley
B1340
Howick

River Aln
Longhoughton
B6341
Denwick
Boulmer
Hulne
Bolton
Alnwick
Aln Valley
Railway
Lesbury
Seaton Point

6

Castle
Edlingham
A1
Alnmouth
Alnmouth
Bay

7

Shilbottle
A1068
260
GLANTLEES
HILL
Newton-on-
the-Moor
Warkworth Castle
& Hermitage
Warkworth
159
Amble
Coquet Island
Swarland
Gloster Hill
Guyzance
High
Hauxley
Acklington
Togston
Felton
Broomhill

8

L...mlington
B63.
B6344
South
Broomhill
Red Row
Druridge Bay
Pauperhaugh
West
Thirston
Brinkburn...
Eshott

G **H** **J** **K** **L** **M**

Ⓐ   Ⓑ   Ⓒ   Ⓓ   Ⓔ   Ⓕ 1

① ② ③ ④ ⑤ ⑥ ⑦ ⑧

Dubh

Nave Island

Ardnave
Point

Gor

Tòn Mhòr

Kilnave

Eilean Mòr

Sanaigmore

Loch
Gruinart

Rubha Lamanais

Loch
Gorr

Lecht Gruinart

Gleann Mòr

Saligo Bay

B8018

B8017

Gruinart

Loch
Gorm

G'eann Mòr

Coul Point

B8018

Sunderland

A847

Machir
Bay

Kilchoman

Bruichladdich

Loch
Indaal

ISLAY

Bowmore

Kilchiaran Bay

Islay Life

Port
Charlotte

231
▲
BEINN TART A'MHILL

River

Lossit Bay

RHINNS

Nerabus

Laggan
Point

Duich R.

Rubha na
Faing

A847

Portnahaven

Port Wemyss

Laggan

Bay

Orsay

RHINNS
POINT

Rubha Mòr

Kint

165
▲
MAOL BU

THE

Lower
Killeyan

Ris

0   1   2   3   4 miles
0   1   2   3   4   5 kilometres

Glendebadel Bay
364

Scalasaig
Machrins
B8086
B8087
B8085

181

J U R A

Corpach Bay

466
BEINN
BHREAC

Glen Grundale

Lussa River

Ardlussa

Lussa Point
Lussagiven

Rubha
Bàn

ORONSAY
Eilean
Ghaoideamal

453
RAINBERG MÒR

Shian
Bay

A846

Colonsay-Port Askaig

Loch
Righ Mòr

Keills Chapel

Rubh' an t-Sàilein

Loch Tarbert

Danna
Island

Rubha a' Mhàil

St Cormac's
Chapel

Kilmory Knap
Chapel

Rubha
Bholsa

363
SGARBH
BREAC

506
SCRINADLE

Jura Forest

398
BEINN
TARSUINN

Kilmory Bay

Point Knap

Bunnahabhain

316
GUIR-
BHEINN

Loch a'
Chnuic Bhric

784
BEINN
AN OIR
734

Paps of Jura

24

Knockrome
Ardfernal

Kilberry
Sculpture
Stone

Port
Askaig

Finlaggan

Keills

Feolin Ferry

560
GLAS BHEINN

Jura

Keils

Kilberry Head
Keppoch Point
Tire

Loch
Finlaggan

Ballygrant

A846
8

Loch
Ballygrant

Loch
Lossit

529
DUBH
BHEINN

Craighouse

342
BRAT
BHEINN

Small
Isles

Rubha na
Caillich

Loch

266
BEINNE
DUBH

Cabrach

ISLAND

Am Fraoch
Eilean

Brosdale
Island

Rubha na Tràille

429
SGÒRR NAM
FAOILEANN
471

McArthur's
Head

Port Askaig - Kennacraig

ISLAY

490
BEINN BHEIGEIR

Rubha Liath
Ardtalla

454
BEINN URARAIDH
Loch Uraraidh

Claggain
Bay

Kinerara

Kintour

Ardmore
Point

Kildalton
Cross

Tarbert

GIGHA

346
BEINN SHOLUM

Eilean
a' Chùirn

Ardminish

Rhunahaorine
Point

Achamore

Port
A846
Lagavulin
Laphroaig
Texa

Arr

Rubha na
Gainn

Port Ellen - Kennacraig

160

Tayinloan

Cara

172

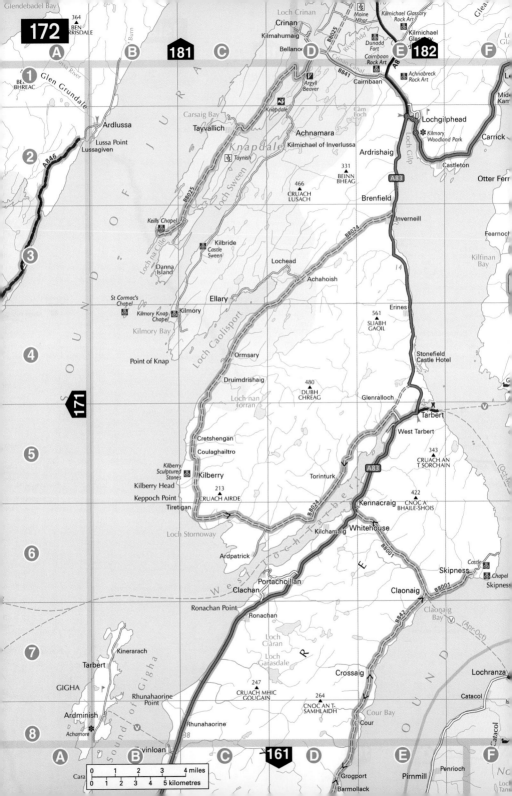

Arddarroch
702 BEINN E Eden
713 GI
655 NN SUINN

G B8000
Barnacarry
505 CRUACH AN LOCHAIN
A886
H
182
Loch Eck
J
643
618 BEINN BHEAG
Sligrachan
K
183 CREACHAN MOR
L
A814
Whistlefield
M
BEINN AORACH
Garelochhead
Snow gates
Greenfield
1
Glen Fruin

Dunans Castle
River Ruel
742 BEINN MHOR
Argyll Forest Park
Rockville
B872
B833
Glen Fruin
435 CRUACH CHUILCEACHAN
re
Glenmassen
643 CLACH BHEINN
664 BEINN RUADH
Ardentinny
Coulport
Shandon
2
Benmore
548 STRONCHULLIN HILL
Clynder
B833
Rhu
Hill House
Glen Massen
Benmore
Loch Long
Garelochhead

432 CRUACH NAN CUILEAN
601 SGORACH MOR
Rashfield
Ardbeg
Blairmore
Cove
Rosneath
Kilmodan Sculptured Stones
Loch Tarsan
Kilmun A880
Glendaruel
B836
Clachaig
Kilmun
Strone
Kilcreggan
Holy Loch
Stronafian
Glen Lean
606
Glenkin
Sandbank
Hunter's Quay
Kilcreggan

454 BEINN BHREAC
611 CRUACH NAN CAPULL
Ardnadam
Gourock
Ardh
3
Glenstriven
503 BISHOP'S SEAT
Dunoon
P
Ashton
GREEN
A770
Levan
Larkfield
Braeside
A78
505 BEINN BHREAC
Castle House
Cloch Point
Chrisswell
Ardentraive
Ardhallow
Lunderston Bay
Loch Thom
P·R
Colintraive
Altgaltraig
391 KILMARNOCK HILL
Ardgowan
Greenock Cut
G
Port Driseach
Rhubodach
Knockdow
322 BEINN RUADH
Inverkip
Shielhill
Garvock
Cairncur
4
Tighnabruaich
Kames
BUTE
Kilbride
267 KAMES HILL
Ardmaleish
Knockdow
Innellan
Wemyss Bay
Upper Skelmorlie
174
41 REUCH HILL
Clyde Muirshiel Regional Park
illhouse
Blair's Ferry
207 CNOC NA CARRAIGE
Kildavanan
St Colmac
Port Bannatyne
Ardyne Point
Toward
Skelmorlie
Kildavaig
Ettrick Bay
Ardbeg
Toward Quay
522 HILL OF STAKE
5
Ardlamont
Kyles of Bute
Castle
Bogany Point
Knock Castle
Ardlamont Point
Rothesay
St Mary's Chapel (ruin)
Ascog
Quarter
Routenburn
6
Skelmorlie Aisle
Vikingar!
483 IRISH LAW
Ballianlay
Straad
A844
Ardencraig
Kerrycroy
Loch Ascog
Largs
A760
Meikle Kilmory
Loch Fad
B881
A78
Inchmarnock
Midpark
Mount Stuart
Bruchag
GREAT CUMBRAE ISLAND
B896
Kelburn Castle
Kilbirn
7
Ardscalpsie Point
Kingarth
B896
Fairlie
371 COCK LAW
Glenga
B881
Kilchattan Bay
Millport
B896
Strayanan Bay
Kilchattan
Kilchattan Bay
Camphill Reservoir
Sound of Bute
St Blane's Church
Fairlie Roads
Hunterston Power Station
Dalry
Drakemyre
B780
of Arran
Garrochty
Little Cumbrae Island
Portencross
Farland Head
8
37
Garroch Head
Seamill
WEST KILBRIDE
Munnoch
B780
Da
Chalmadale
A841
G
Sanno
H
162
J
K
Seamill
B7047
L
marven
M
Kilwinning
834 EAL ABHAIL
Corrie
Ardrossan

Clyde
Fir

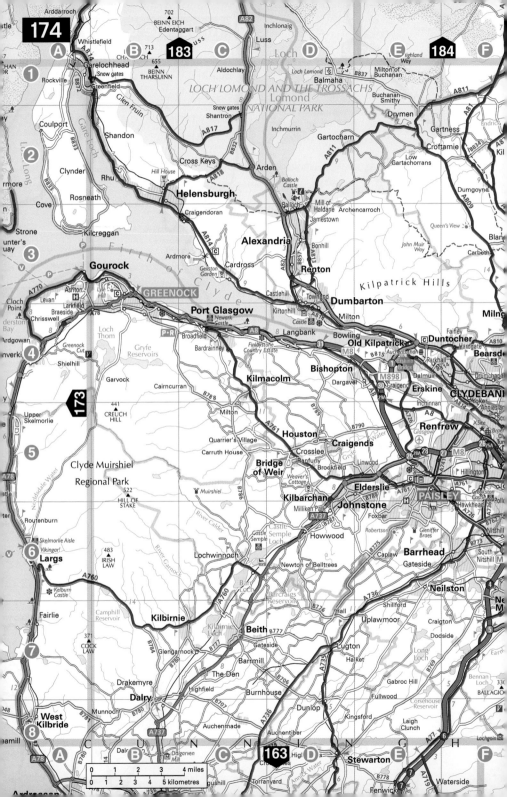

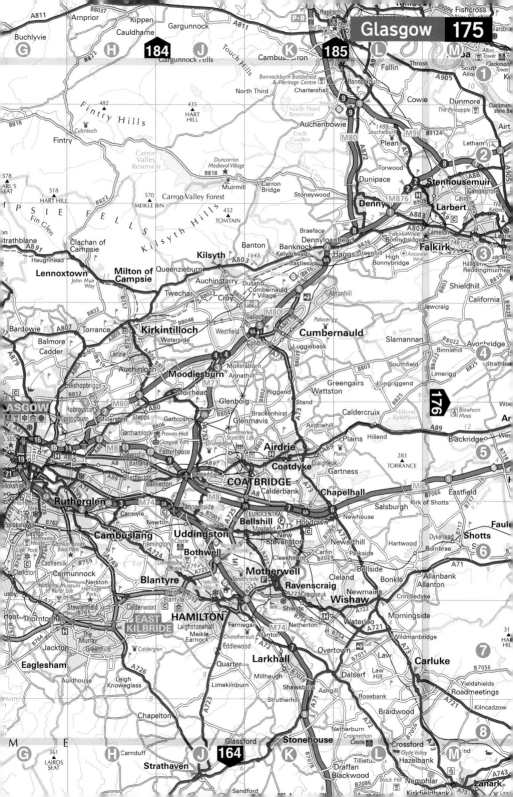

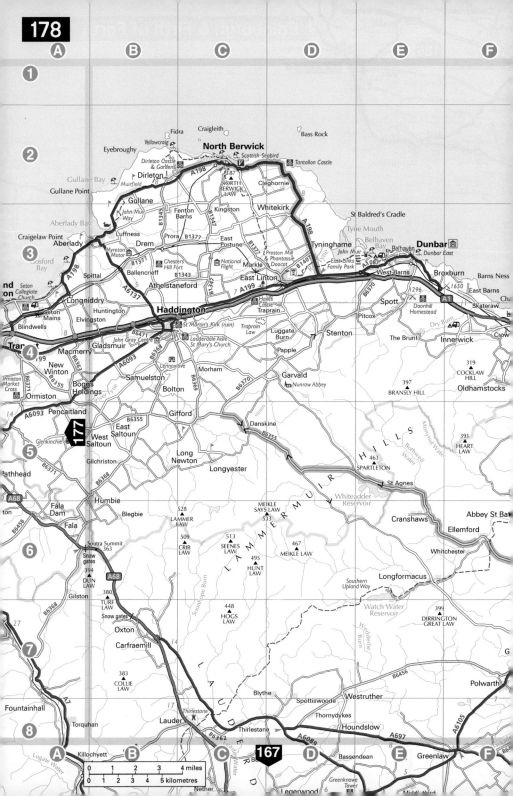

Bac Mòr or Dutchman's Cap

A **B** **C** eag **D** **189** **E** **F**

1

Staffa

Fingal's

Little Colonsay

Inch Kenneth
Inchkenneth Chapel
(ruin)

Loch na Keal
Isle of Mull

2

491
▲
CREACH BHEINN

Fossil Tree ★

Burg

3

IONA

Iona Abbey
& Nunnery

Baile Mòr
MacLean's Cross

Fionnphort

St Columba
Exhibition
Centre

Rubha nan Cearc

Kintra

Aridhglas

A849

Bunessan

Loch Assapol

Lo

ROSS OF MULL

4

Soa Island

Erraid

Uisken

Ardchiavaig

'Rubh'
Ardalanish

Re
B

5

Torran Rocks

6

Eilean
Dubh

7

Kiloran Bay

143
▲
CARNAN
EOIN

Ru

COLONSAY

Kiloran

Kilchattan

Scalasaig

B8086

B8087

Machrins

Colonsay

B8085

8

A **B** **C** **D** **171** **E** **F**

0 1 2 3 4 miles
0 1 2 3 4 5 kilometres

Gar

Oronsay

Dubh Eilean

Rubha
Bàn

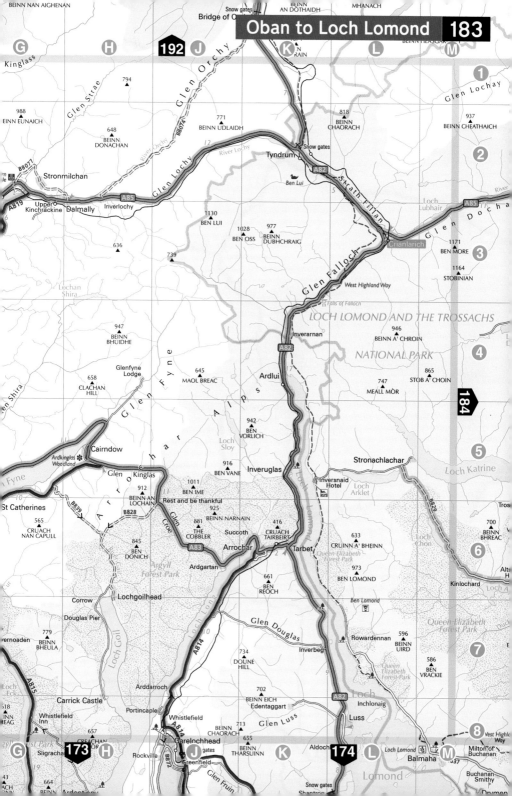

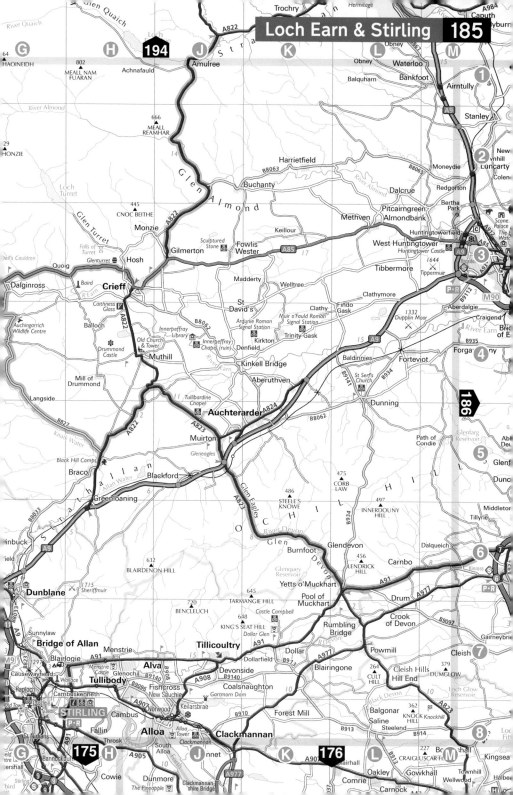

Arr
Grishipoll
Clabhach
Hogh Bay   Ballyhaugh
Totronald
Coll   Acha
Arileod   Uig
Feall
Bay

Bàgh a' Chaisteil
(Castlebay)
ⓥ
(Apr-Oct. Weds only)

Calgary Point
Crossapol
Bay
Rubha
Fàsachd

Loch Breachacha

Gunna
Rubha Dubh

Caoles   ⓥ
Rubha Port   B8069
Bhiosd   Clachan   Ruaig
Mòr
Balephetrish
Bay
Loch
Bhasapoll   B8068
Hough   Gott
Bay   Cornaigmore   Kenovay   Bay
Ballevullin
Tiree
Kilkenneth
Scarinish
Moss   Heylipoll   B8065
Middleton   TIREE
B8068
Barrapoll   B8065
Hynish Bay
Loch a'   B8067   Balemartine
Phuill
Mannal
Rinn
Thorbhais   Hynish
Balephuil Bay

0   1   2   3   4 miles
0 1 2 3 4 5 kilometres

G 747 BINNEIN SHUAS **202** H J K Snow gates 94 L CÀRN NA CAIM M **1** Loch an Dùn

1049 GEAL CHÀRN

896 MEALL CRUAIDH 769 CREAGAN MÒR

Loch Pattack

1088 BEINN A' CHLACHAIR

926 GLAS MHEALL MÒR **2**

1034 CÀRN DEARG

975 A' MHARCONAICH 459 Drumochter Summit

1101 BEINN EIBHINN

1008 BEINN UDLAMAIN 991 SGAIRNEACH MHÒR Dalnaspidal

1145 BEN ALDER

Loch Garry 20 Snow gates Dalnacardoch **3**

844 MEALL A' BHEALAICH

Loch Con

Glen Garry

952 SGÒR GAIBHRE

Loch Errochty Trinafour B847

864 BEINN PHARIAGAIN

626 SRÒN A CHLAONAIDH 841 BEINN MHOLACH

892 BEINN A' CHUALLAICH Glen 511 TORR DUBH **4**

194 Tay For

nnoch ation Bridge of Ericht Killichonan 16 Kinloch Rannoch Drumchastle Dunalastair B846 R Tummel Tummel Bridge

Dunan B846 Finnart Loch Rannoch Inverhadden Tempar Dunalastair Water

Loch Eigheach Bridge of Gaur Carie Camghouran

Tay Forest Park 1081 SCHIEHALLION **5**

Loch Rannoch and Glen Lyon

931 MEALL BUIDHE 745 MEALL A' MHUIC 1042 CÀRN MAIRG

860 CAM CHREAG 824 BEINN DEARG 1027 CÀRN GORM

B846 Còsh Kei **6** urn

Loch an Daimh Glen Lyon River Lyon Fortingall Fortingall Yew ★ Tay Forest Park

Bridge of Balgie Fearnan Kenmore

924 MEALL A' CHOIRE LEITH 1116 MEALL GARBH 1000 MEALL GREIGH The Scottish Crannog Centre

Pubil 780 MEALL LUAIDHE Acharn **7**

908 BEINN NAN OIGHREAG 1214 BEN LAWERS Leckbuie 713 BEINN BHREAC

1038 MEALL GHAORDIE Lochan na Làirige Lawers A827 25 Loch Tay

Ben Lawers Milton Morenish 864 SRÒN A' CHA **8**

G en Lochay H River Lochay Falls of Lochay J **184** renish K Milton Morenish L M

Mor ch Longhouse Finlarig Ardeo N

Killin

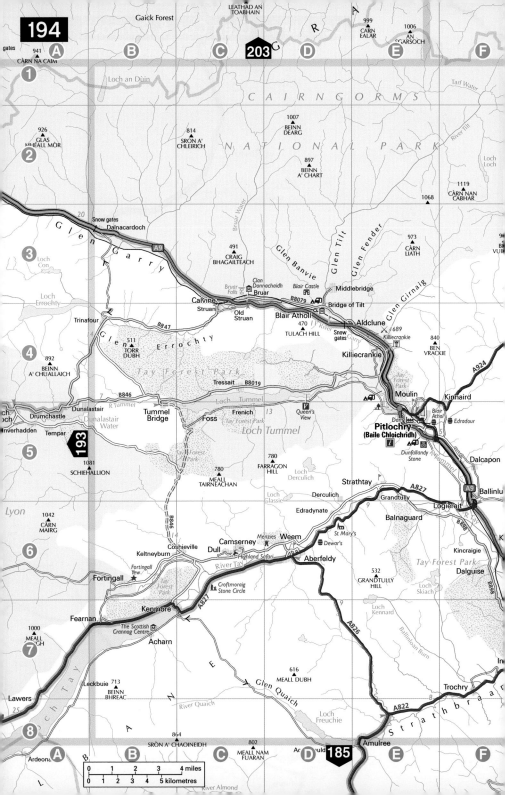

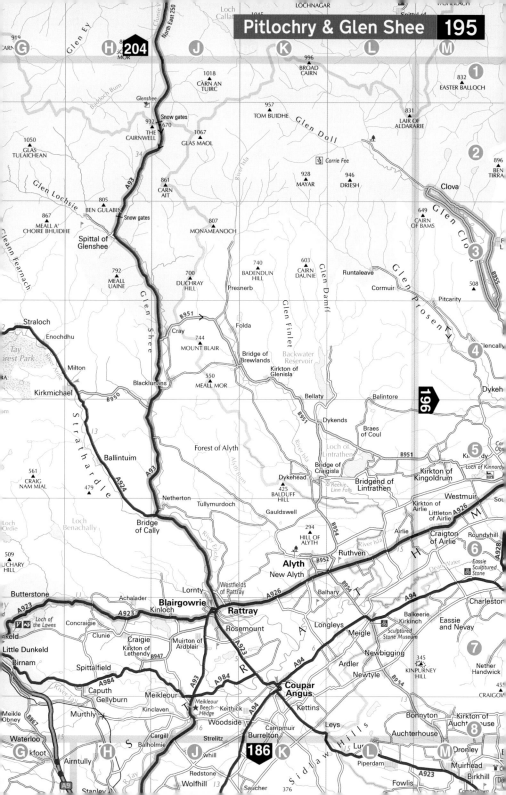

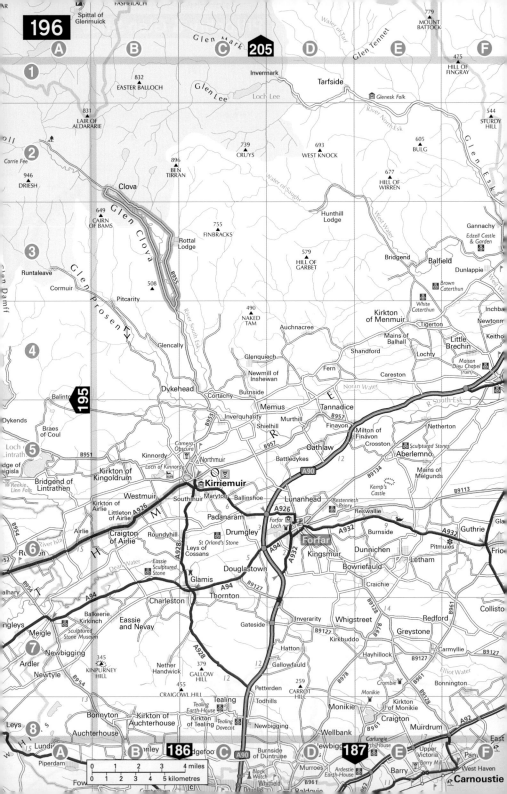

Talisker
Bay
Talisker

Glen Eynort
Minginish
Glen Eynort

208

en
Brittle
Forest

147
BEINN
BHREAC

Gr

Loch Eynort

434
AN CRÙACHIN
Glenbrittle
Bualintur

Loch Brittle

Rubha an Dùnain

Loch Baghasdail
(Lochboisdale)

C U

CANNA
210
CÀRN A' GHAILL
A'Chill
Canna
Harbour

Garrisdale Point

Sanday

Kilmory
Bay

Rubha
Shamhnan
Insir

Sound of Canna

302
MULLACH
MÓR

A' Bhrìdeanach

570
ORVAL

Loc
Kinloch

Oigh-sgeir

RÙM

810
ASKIVAL

Harris
Bay

763
SGÙRR NAN
GILLEAN

The Small Isles

Rubha nam
Meirleach

Sound

Eilean
nan Each

189

M

Port

0   1   2   3   4 miles
0 1 2 3 4 5 kilometres

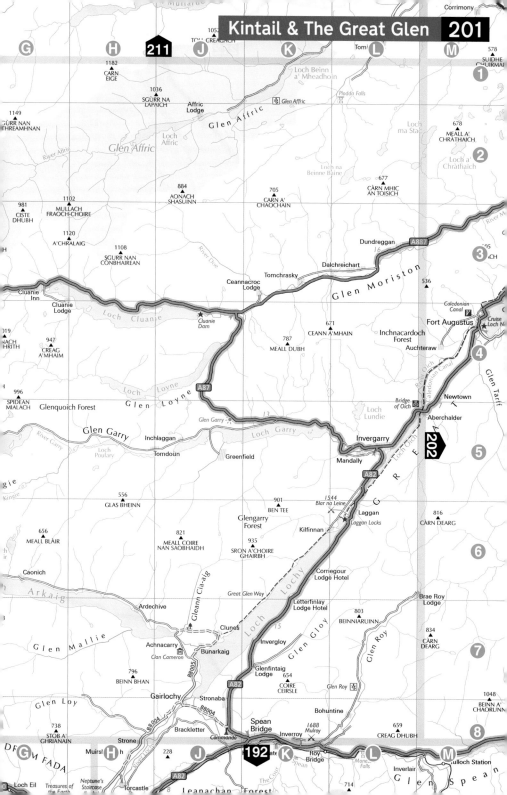

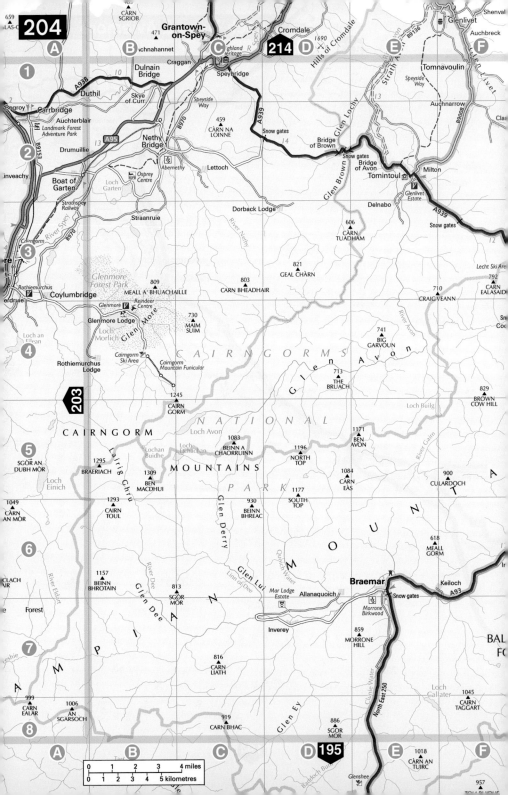

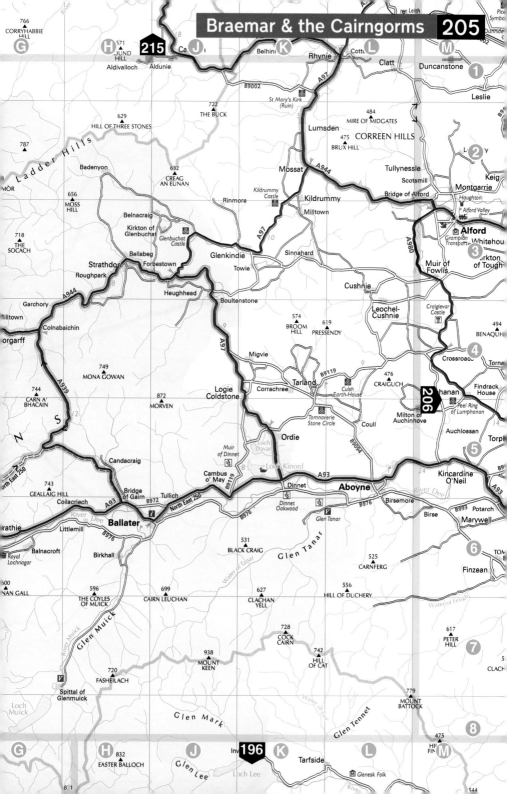

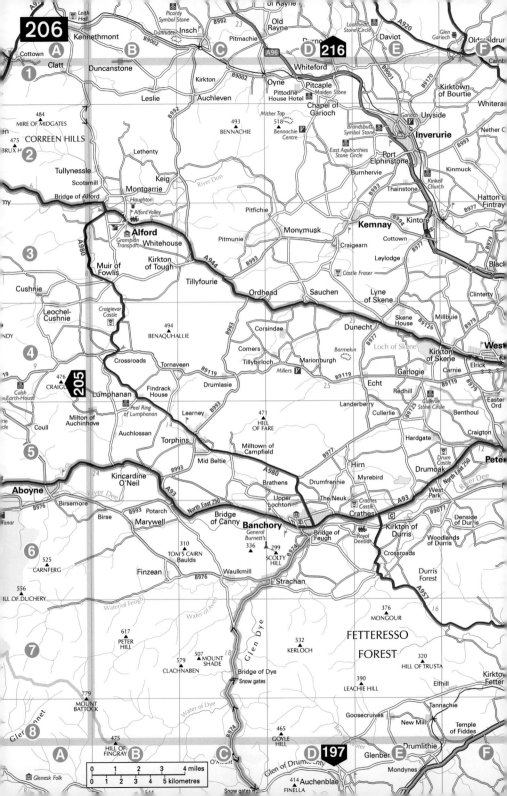

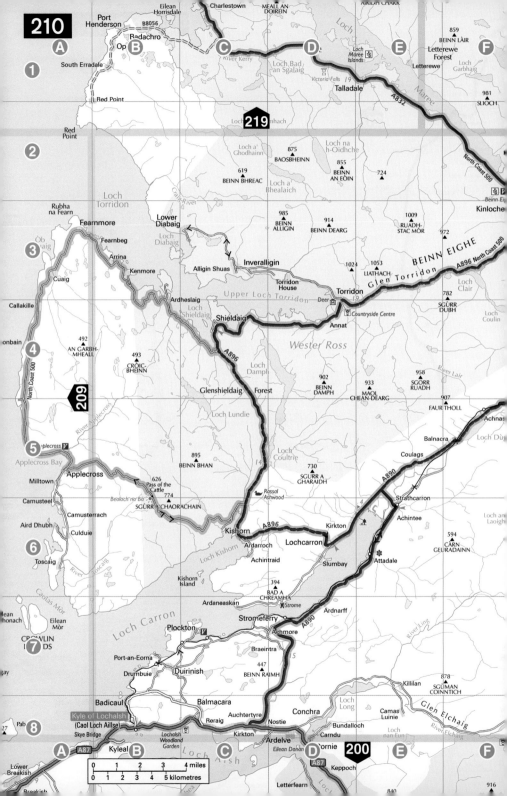

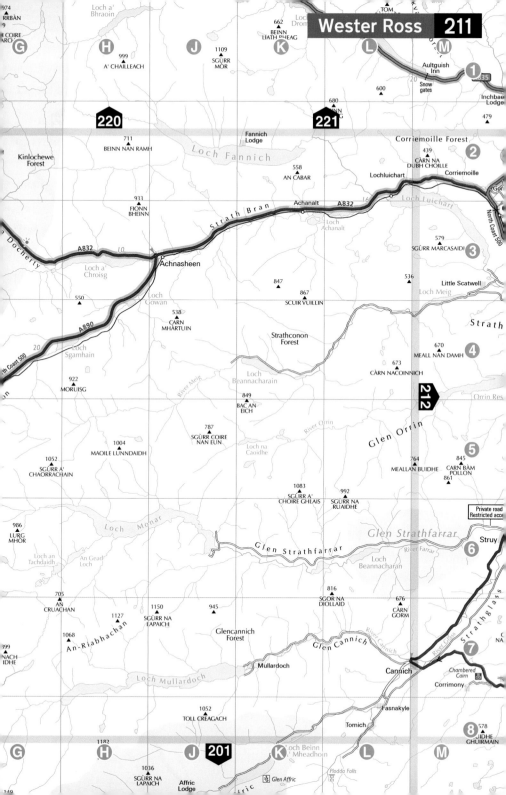

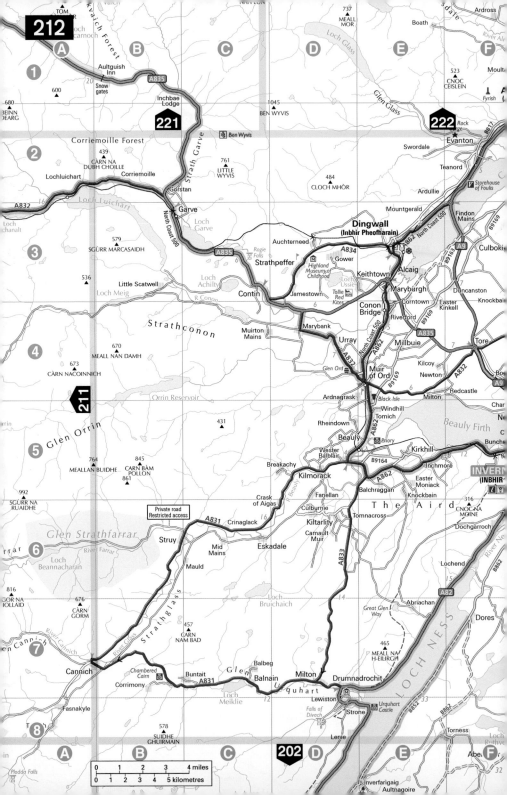

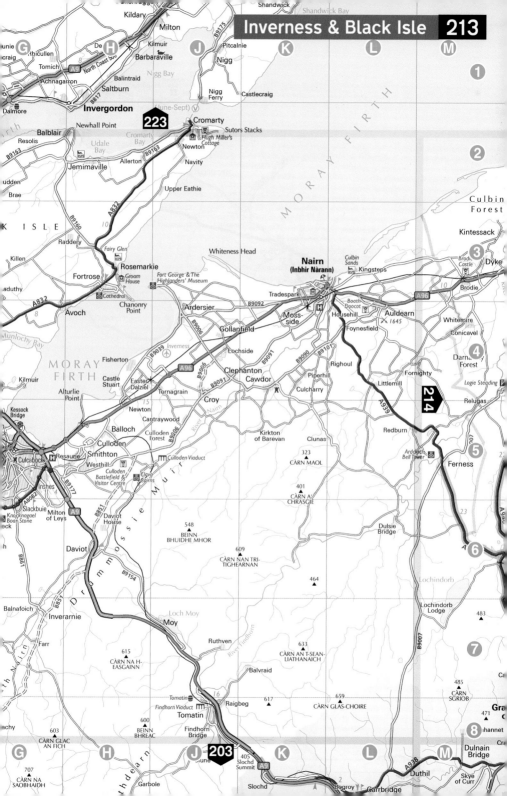

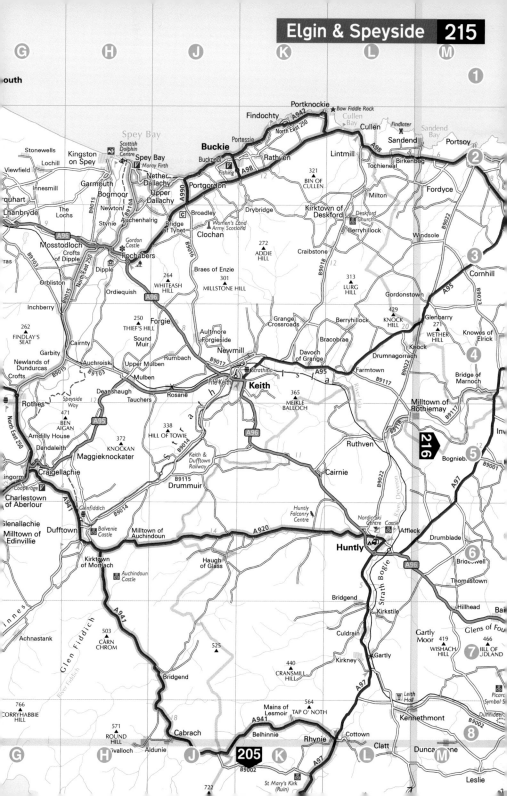

G H J K L M

1
2
3
4
5
6
7
8

Rosehearty
Pittulie
Castle, Lighthouse & Museum
Sandhaven
Kinnaird Head
Craigiefold
Pitsligo
Peathill
Fraserburgh
B9031
Fraserburgh Bay
Percyhorner
Pitblae
Cairnbulg
Inverallochy
Aberdour Bay
Coburby
North East 250
Maggie's Hoosie
B9031
B9031
Mid Ardlaw
Whitelinks Bay
New dour
Boyndlie
B9032
St Combs
A90
Tyrie
A98
Memsie
10
B9093
Memsie Cairn
Rathen
ew sligo
A981
Newburgh
Lonmay
Crofts of Savoch
12
Loch of Strathbeg
Rattray Head
234 WAUGHTON HILL
Crimond
anykelly
Strichen
12
Blackhill
B9093
New Leeds
A952
North East 250
18
5
B9093
Leys
St Fergus
Scotstown Head
Denhead
Backfolds
Kirktown
A90
Fetterangus
Rora
A981
A950
6
Deer Abbey
Dunshillock
River Ugie
Inverugie
ew eer
Maud
B9106
Aden
Mintlaw
Longside
Buchanhaven
Peterhead
Railway
B9029
Old Deer
A950
Inverquhomery
H
Peterhead
Arbuthnot
B9029
Blackhill of Clackriach
9
Peterhead Bay
Drymuir
Bulwark
Stuartfield
A948
Millbreck
Nether Kinmundy
Hillhead of Cocklaw
Prison
Invernettie
Nethermuir
Clola
B9030
Knaven
Kinnadie
Blackhill
Boddam
Stirling
Auchnagatt
Kinknockie
Lendrum Terrace
Buchan Ness
irnorrie rownhill
12
Inkhorn
Coldwells
Ardallie
A952
Longhaven
A90
ick han
Arthrath
Muirtack
Hatton
Auchiries
Bullers of Buchan
North Haven
14
Slains
Toll of Birness
17
Cruden Bay
B9005
Ythanbank
Bogbrae
Chapel Hill
Bay of Cruden
Auchedly
Birness
North East 250
B9975
Altar Tomb of William Forbes
Whinnyfold
The Skares
Ythsie
Kinharrachie
20
Artrochie
Ellon
P·R
dden rden
Esslemont
A920
Kirkton of Logie Buchan
Kirktown of Slains
Collieston
Pitmedden
Logierieve
B9005
6
Forvie
Housieside
B90
G H J **207** K L M
Ud rea
Udny Station
A90
Newburgh
and
Foveran
Pettymuk
Cultercullen

A B C D E F

1

2

3

4

5

6

7

8

Loch Shell

SOUND OF SHIANT

Loch Rollum

SHIANT ISLANDS

Fladda-chùain

Eilean Trodday

Rubha Hunish

Duntulm

Kilmaluag

A855

Skye Museum of Island Life

Flodigarry

Eilean Flodigarry

Lùb Score

Poldorais

An Tairbeart (Tarbert)

Borneskitaig

Kilmuir

Heribusta

Kilvaxter

542

MEALL NA SUIREAMACH

Digg

Staffin Bay

Staffin Island

Balgown

Brogaig

Linicro

Stenscholl

Staffin

Loch nam Madadh (Lochmaddy)

208

Totscore

464

BIODA BUIDHE

Trotternish

Kilt Rock

Ellishader

209

Idrigill

River Rha

Maligar

Marishader

Valtos

Rubha nam Brathairean

River Conon

611

BEINN EDRA

Garros

Culnaknock

Uig (Uige)

Fairy Glen

Uig Bay

Earl

Le

D

Tote

A855

Loch Sni

A B C D E F

0 1 2 3 4 miles
0 1 2 3 4 5 kilometres

608

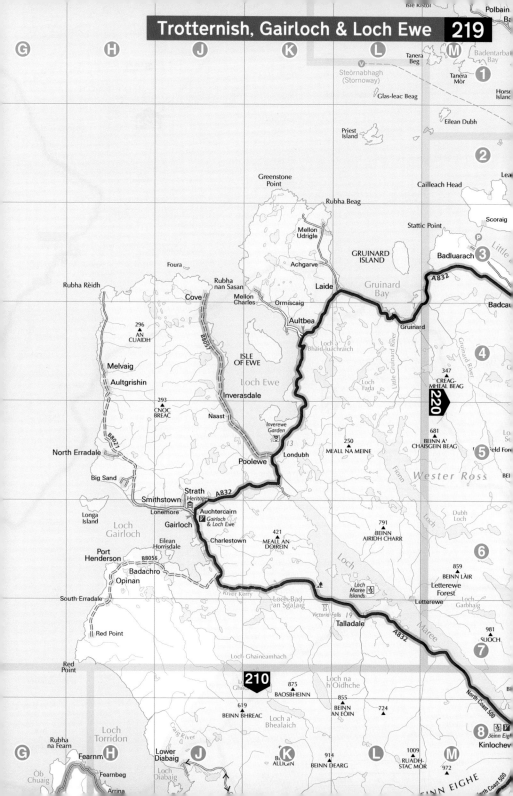

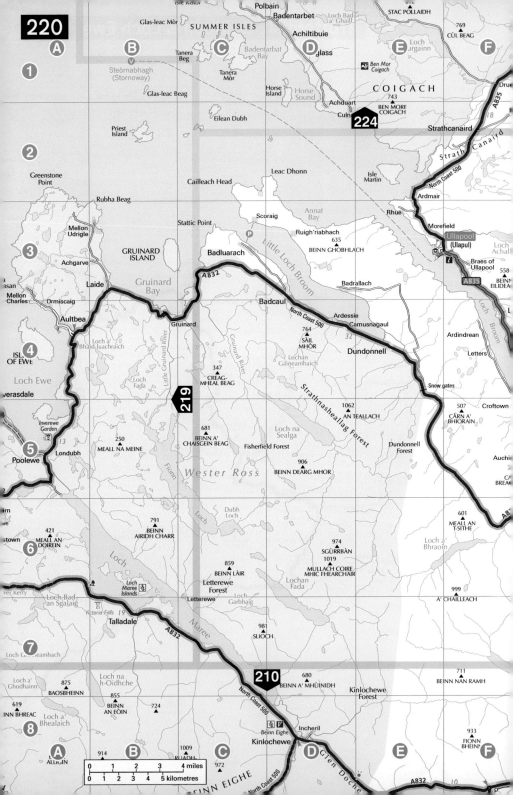

G   H   J   K   L   M

1
2
3
4
5
6
7
8

227

COB
BHEINN

Lothbeg

Strath

River Brora

Dalreavoch

Loch
Horn

520
BEN
HORN

Loch
Bro—

Dalchalm

Clynelish

Brora

Golspie Burn

378
CAGAR
FEOSAIG

Backies

A9

Doll

446
BEN LUNDIE

383
BEN BHRAGGIE

Rhives

Dunrobin
Castle

Carn
Liath

North Coast 500

Golspie

rboll

Cambusavie

Loch
Fleet

Littleferry

adninish

Skelbo

Skelbo Street

Fourpenny

Birichin

B9168

Embo

Embo Street

Pitgrudy

Royal Dornoch

Evelix

A949

more

A9

Camore

Historylinks

Dornoch

Carnegie
Courthouse

Cuthill

Dornoch
Point

Innis Mhor

Tarbat Ness

Wilkhaven

Dornoch
Firth Bridge

Dornoch Firth

Portmahomack

Tarbat Discovery
Centre

Morangie

Glenmorangie

Inver

B9165

Rockfield

84

Lower Arboll

Tain
(Baile Dhubhthaich)

Toulvaddie

Lochslin

Loch
Eye

Rhynie

Hill of
Fearn

Balmuchy

B9165

Newfield

Hilton of Cadboll
Chapel (ruin)

6

Fearn

B9165

Tullich

Hilton of Cadboll

allchraggan

Arabella

Balintore

Kildary

Shandwick

Shandwick Bay

Milton

Ankerville

Kilmuir

B9175

Pitcalnie

Barbaraville

Nigg

Nigg Bay

intraid

rn

Nigg Ferry

Castlecraig

on

(June-Sept)

Cromarty

Sutors Stacks

Hugh Miller's
Cottage

Newton

B9163

Navity

213

214

Burghead B

Findhorn

Hemp

Allerton

Upper Eathie

MORAY FIRTH

Culbin
Forest

Findhorn
Bay

Kincorth
House

8

Cromarty
Bay

Whiteness Head

G   H   J   K   L   M

Kintessack

Sueno's Stone

Grange Hall

Nairn

Culbin

Brodie

Falconer

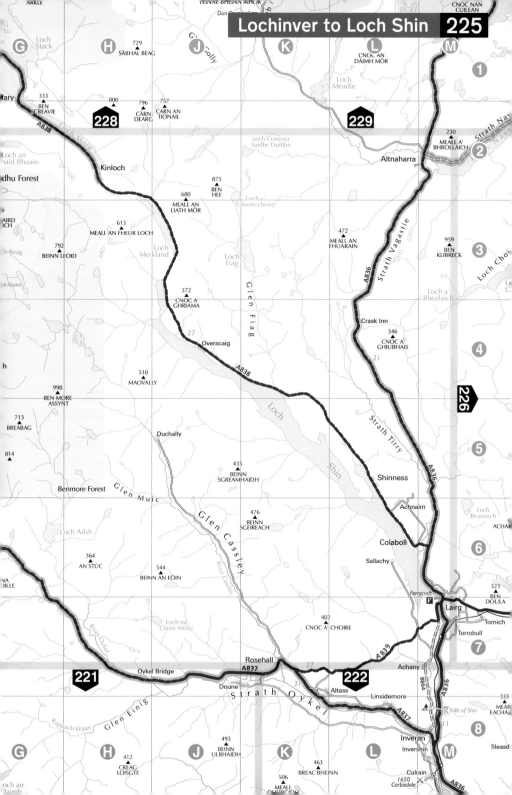

G   H   J   K   L   M

1

Altnabreac Station

CNOC NAN GALL

Rumsdale Water

Strathmore W

Dalnawillan Lodge

Loch an Thulachan

Loch More

Loch Sand

Achavanich

Loch Rangag

Loch ↗ nster

STEMSTER HILL
248

248

Grey Ca of Cam

230

348
▲
BEN ALISKY

226
▲
COIRE NA BEINNE

287
▲
BEN-A-CHIELT

231

Upper Lybster

Roste

Hi

Glutt Lodge

264
▲
CNOCAN CONACHREAG

Swiney

2

Mi

NOCKFIN HEIGHTS

Houstry

Land-hallow

Forse

Invershore

Lybster

Occu

Lybster Bay

317
▲
CNOC LOCH MHADADH

Dunbeath Water

Smerral

Latheronwheel

Clan Gunn

Latheron

437
▲
C COIRE FEÀRNA

Berriedale Water

484
▲
MAIDEN PAP

Braemore

Knockally

Janetstown

A9

Laidhay Croft

3

518
▲
CNOC AN EIREANNAICH

705
▲
MORVEN

Snow gates

Dunbeath
Heritage

Dunbeath Bay

Ramscraigs

626
▲
SCARABEN

Borgue

554
▲
CREAG SCALABSDALE

Langwell Forest

Newport

20

4

dge

416
▲
N BEINN UBHAIN

401
▲
CNOC NA MAOILE

Langwell House

Berriedale

A897

North Coast 500

Torrish

an

River Helmsdale

404
▲
CREAG THORARAIDH

A9

Badbea Historic Village

Ord of Caithness

5

N AIN

591
▲
BEINN MHEALAICH

Navidale

Timespan

West Helmsdale

Gartymore

Snow gates

East Helmsdale

Helmsdale

Portgower

Glen Loth

Lothmore

6

othbeg

m

7

8

G   H   J   K   L   M

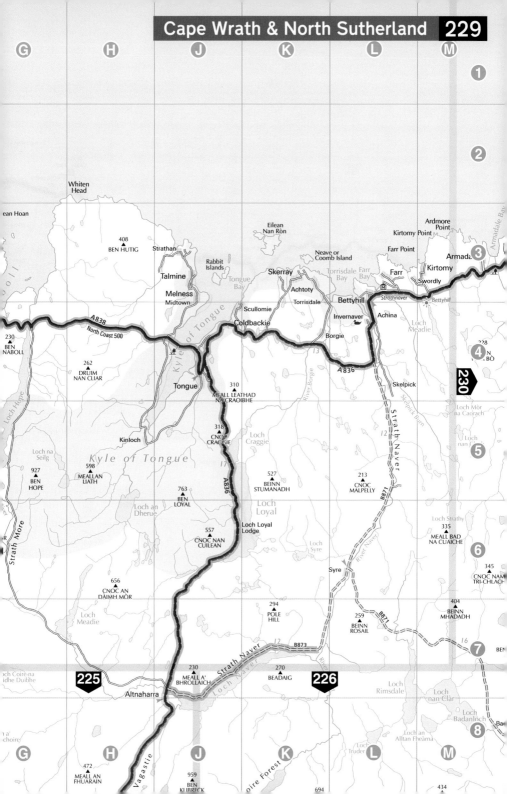

G · H · J · K · L · M

1
2
3
4
5
6
7
8

Whiten Head

ean Hoan

408
BEN HUTIG

Strathan

Talmine

Rabbit Islands

Eilean Nan Ròn

Neave or Coomb Island

Torrisdale Farr Bay

Ardmore Point

Kirtomy Point

Farr Point

Armada

Kirtomy

Melness

Midtown

Skerray

Achtoty

Torrisdale

Scullomie

Coldbackie

Bettyhill

Strathnaver

Farr

Swordly

Bettyhill

A838

North Coast 500

Kyle of Tongue

Invernaver

Achina

Loch Meadie

230
BEN NABOLL

262
DRUIM NAN CLIAR

Tongue

Borgie

A836

13

River Borgie

Skelpick

Skelpick Burn

228
N BÒ

230

Loch Mòr na Caorach

310
MEALL LEATHAD NA CRAOIBHE

Kinloch

Loch na Seilg

Kyle of Tongue

927
BEN HOPE

598
MEALLAN LIATH

318
CNOC CRAGGIE

Loch Craggie

17

A836

527
BEINN STUMANADH

213
CNOC MALPELLY

B871

Strath Naver

River Naver

12

nan C

Loch Strathy

335
MEALL BAD NA CUAICHE

763
BEN LOYAL

Loch an Dherue

Loch Loyal

Strath More

557
CNOC NAN CUILEAN

Loch Loyal Lodge

Loch Syre

Syre

345
CNOC NAM TRI-CHLACH

404
BEINN MHADADH

656
CNOC AN DÀIMH MÒR

Loch Meadie

294
POLE HILL

259
BEINN ROSAIL

B871

16

BEN

225

230
MEALL A' BHROLLAICH

Strath Naver

12

B873

270
BEADAIG

226

Loch Rimsdale

Loch nan Clàr

Loch Badanlòch

Ba

8

Altnaharra

och Coire-na idhe Duibhe

a' hoire

472
MEALL AN FHUARAIN

Vagastie

959
BEN KLIBRECK

oire Forest

Loch Truderi

Loch nan Clàr

Loch Alltan Fhearnà

694

434

G · H · J · K · L · M

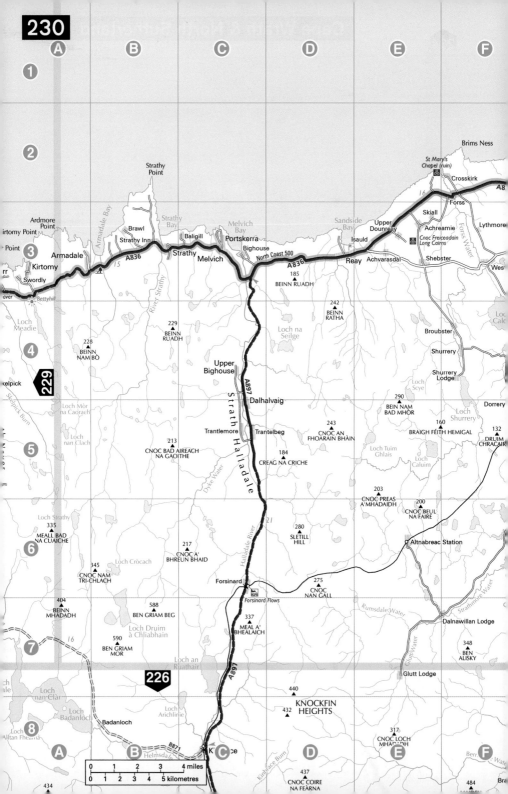

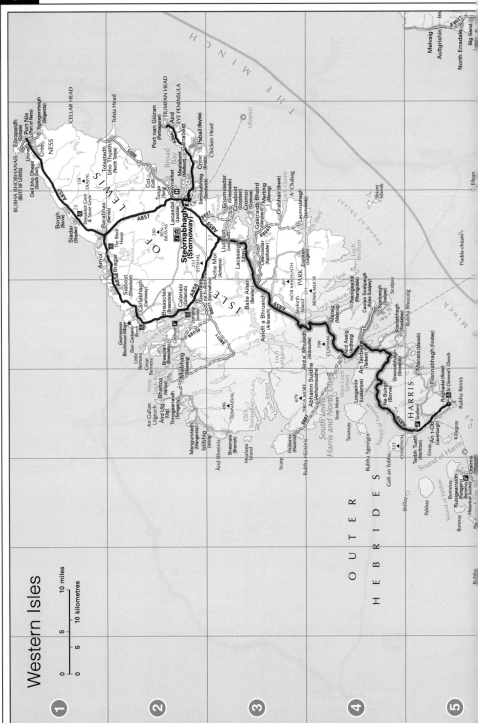

Western Isles

10 miles

10 kilometres

THE MINCH

Melvaig
Autgrishin
North Erradale
Big Sand

Ullapool

Sound of Shiant

Shiant Islands

Eilean

Minch

Flodda-chuain

CELLAR HEAD

Spiogarstagh
(Skigersta)
Port Nis
(Port of Ness)
Eòropaidh
(Eoropie)
RUBHA RHOBHANAS
(BUT OF LEWIS)
Dell bho Dheas
(South Dell)
Lional
Cros
NESS
Siadar
(Shader)
Borgh
(Borve)
A857
Barabhas
(Barvas)
A857
A858
Bragar
Arnol
Siabost
(Shawbost)
The Black
House
Steinacleit Cairn
& Stone Circle
DIABAL
158
28

Tolsta Head

Tolastadh
bho Thuath
(North Tolsta)
Great River
Col
(Coll)
Tunga
(Tong)
280
ISLE
OF
LEWIS
Carlabhagh
(Carloway)
Doune Broch
Breascleit
(Breasclete)
A858
Calanais
(Callanais)
Steinacleit
Dun Carloway
Broch
Garenin
Blackhouse Village
Little
Bernera
Great
Bernera

Port nan Giùran
(Portnaguran)
TIUMPAN HEAD
Aird
EYE PENINSULA
Pabail
(Bayble)
Broad
Bay
Bac
Sandwick
Cnoc
(Knock)
Chicken Head

Meall
Newmarket
bho Tuath
Meabost
(Melbost)
Lacasdal
(Laxdale)
Steòrnabhagh
(Stornoway)
BEN
BRAVAS
Griomsiadar
(Grimshader)
Crosbost
(Crossbost)
Sanndabhaig
(Sandwick)
A866
A857
Acha Mor
(Achmore)
Liurbost
(Laxay)
37
233
Airidh na h-Aibhne
(Arivruaich)
A858
Baile Ailein
(Balallan)
Cearsiadar
(Kershader)
Gearraidh Bhaird
(Garynahine)
Grabhair
(Gravir)
Marbhig
(Marvig)
Crosnasg
(Crossbost)
A' Chabag
Cromore
Loch Shell
Loch
Brollum

PARK
401
MOR MHONADH
799
BEINN MHOR
Seaforth
Island
Loch Seaforth
Loch Claidh
Mòraig
(Maraig)
Reinigeadal
(Rhenigidale)
Caolas Sgalpaigh
(Kyles Scalpay)
Sgalpaigh
(Scalpay)
Rubha Bhocaig

OUTER

HEBRIDES

Mangurstadh
(Mangersta)
Àird Uig
(Uig)
Aird Bhreinis
Timsgearraidh
(Timsgarry)
Islibhig
(Islivig)
Breanais
(Brenish)
An Callan
Bhaltos
(Valtos)
Uigeach
(Uig)
Bhaltos
(Valtos)
Miabhaig
(Miavaig)
Bearnais
(Bernera)
Mealista
Island
Scarp
TEANNAVAL
496
Loch Resort
Loch
Langavat
TARGA MÒRE
West Loch
Roag
Loch
Tealasdal
Aird a' Mhulaidh
(Ardvourlie)
Abhainn Suidhe
(Amhuinnsuidhe)
CLISHAM
Aird Asaig
(Ardhasaig)
An Tairbeart
(Tarbert)
Losgaintir
(Luskentyre)
TARGA MÒRE
679
Bun Abhainn Eadarra
(Bunavoneadar)
Rubha Sgeirigh
Scadabhagh
(Scadabay)
Greosabhagh
(Grosebay)
HARRIS
Màraig
(Manish)
Flionnsabhagh (Finsbay)
Ne Buirgh
(Borve)
Sgarasta Mhòr
(Scarista)
Seilebost
Roghadal (Rodel)
St Clement's Church
Rubha Reinis
24

Harris and North Uist
South Uist
Sound of Taransay

Taransay
Losgaintir
(Luskentyre)
Tasabh Tuath
(Northton)
CHAIPAVAL
365
Ensay
(Easaigh)
Àn t-Ob
(Leverburgh)
Killegray
Otalmís
Gob an Tobha

Sound of Harris

Rubha
Shillay
Pabbay
Shìlebhig
Boreray
Bernera
Beag
Ruaigearraidh
(Ruisgarry)
Berneray
Historical
Society

Roghadal

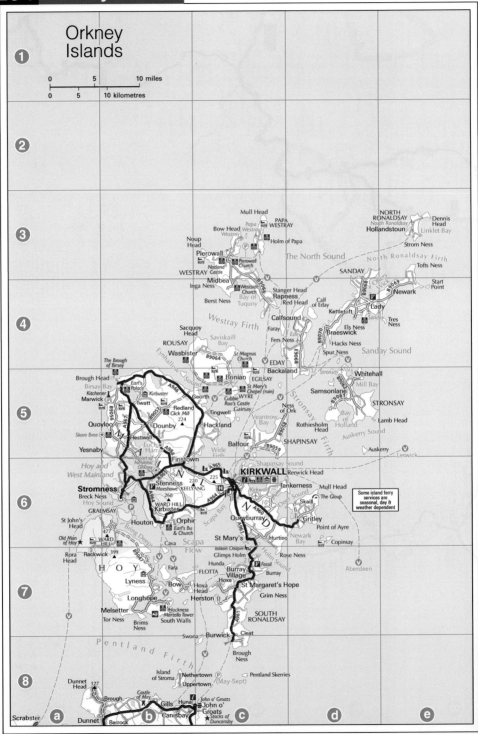

Orkney
Islands

0   5   10 miles
0   5   10 kilometres

Mull Head
Bow Head   PAPA
Westray   WESTRAY
Papa *Westray*
Holm of Papa

NORTH
RONALDSAY
North Ronaldsay   Dennis
Hollandstoun   Head
Linklet Bay
Strom Ness

Noup
Head
Pierowall
Pierowall
Natland   Pierowall
Castle   Church
WESTRAY
Midbea
Inga Ness   Westside
Church
Berst Ness   Bay of
Tuquoy

The North Sound
North Ronaldsay Firth

SANDAY

Tofts Ness

Stanger Head   Start
Rapness   Red Head   Newark   Point
Calf
of Eday   Lady
Calfsound   Kettletoft   Tres
Faray   Eday   Ness
Fers Ness   Els Ness   Braeswick
Hacks Ness
Spur Ness

Sacquoy
Head
Saviskaill
ROUSAY   Bay
Wasbister   St Magnus
Church
The Brough
of Birsay
Brough Head
Birsay Bay   Earl's
Kitchener   Palace
Marwick   Kirbuster
Twatt

Sanday Sound

EDAY
Backaland   *Stronsay*   Whitehall
Mill Bay
Brinian   EGILSAY
St Mary's   Samsonlane
Chapel (ruin)
WYRE   STRONSAY
Cubbie   Bay
Roo's Castle   of
Gairsay   Holland   Lamb Head

Redland
Click Mill
Quoyloo   224   Ness
of Ork
Skara Brae   Dounby   Hackland
Hestwall   Tingwall
Yesnaby   Loch of   Balfour
Harray   SHAPINSAY
Finstown   Wide
Firth
Hoy and   *Heart of*
West Mainland   *Neolithic*
Orkney

Veantrow
Bay
Rothiesholm
Head   Auskerry Sound
Auskerry
Lerwick

Shapinsay Sound
KIRKWALL   Rerwick Head
Stenness   220   223
Maeshowe   222   Mull Head
Stromness   KEELYANG   Tankerness   The Gloup
268
Breck Ness   WARD HILL
Hoy Sound   Kirbister   Skaill
GRAEMSAY
St John's
Head   Houton
Old Man   Orphir
of Hoy   WARD   Earl's Bu
477   HILL   & Church
Rora   Rackwick   St Mary's
Head   399   Cava
HOY   Flow   Italian Chapel
Glimps Holm
Lyness   Fara   Hunda
FLOTTA   Burray
Bow   Village
Longhope   Hoxa   Hoxa   Burray
Head   Herston   St Margaret's Hope
Melsetter   Hacknesg   Grim Ness
Tor Ness   Martello Tower
Brims   South Walls   SOUTH
Ness   Swona   RONALDSAY
Burwick   Cleat
Brough
Ness

Some island ferry
services are
seasonal, day &
weather dependent

Queybarray
Gritley
Point of Ayre
Hurtiso
Newark
Bay   Copinsay
Rose Ness
Aberdeen

Pentland Firth

Dunnet
Head   127
Island   Nethertown
Brough   of Stroma
Castle   Uppertown   (May–Sept)   Pentland Skerries
of Mey
Gills   Huna
Scrabster   Canisbay   John o'
Dunnet   Groats
Barrock   John o' Groats
Stacks of
Duncansby

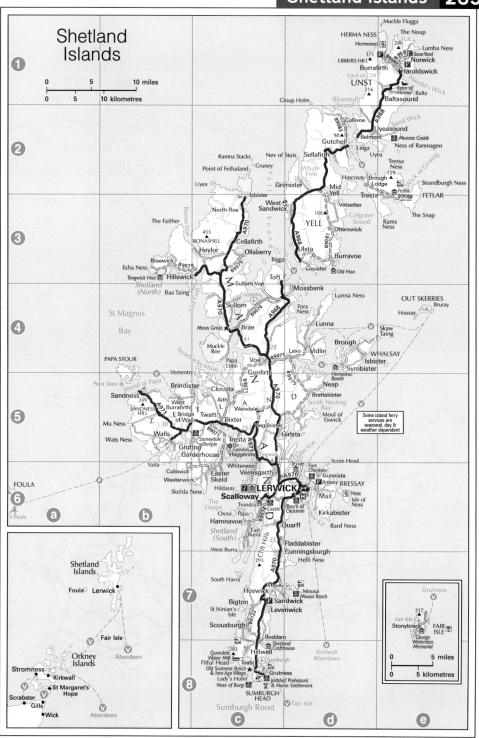

Shetland Islands

0   5   10 miles

0   5   10 kilometres

Muckle Flugga
The Noup
HERMA NESS
Hermaness
280
Lamba Ness
171
Saxa Vord
Norwick
LIBBERS HILL
Burrafirth
Haroldswick
UNST
Loch of Cliff
Harold's Wick
216
Keen of Hamar
Balta
Baltasound

Gloup Holm
Bluemull Sound

Cullivoe
Uyeasound
Sand Wick

Ramna Stacks
Nev of Stuis
Gruney
98
Belmont
Muness Castle
Point of Fethaland
Linga
Ness of Ramnageo
Uyea
Uyea
Hascosay
Brough Lodge
Tressa Ness
159
Strandburgh Ness
Isbister
Grimister
Mid Yell
Tresta
FETLAR
B9088
West Sandwick
Vatsetter
North Roe
188
The Snap
The Faither
YELL
Colgrave Sound
Rams Ness
453
RONASHILL
Collafirth
Otterswick
Heylor
Ollaberry
Braewick
Bigga
Ulsta
Burravoe
Esha Ness
Hillswick
Copister
Old Haa
Tangwick Haa
Shetland (North)
Sullom Voe
Toft
Baa Taing
Mossbank
Lunna Ness
OUT SKERRIES
Bruray
Sullom
Fora Ness
Housay
St Magnus
Mavis Grind
Brae
Lunna
Skaw Taing
Bay
Muckle Roe
Papa Little
Voe
Vidlin
Brough
WHALSAY
Isbister
PAPA STOUR
Vementry
Gonfirth
Neap
Symbister
Papa Stour
Brindister
Clousta
Brettabister
Sandness
249
West Burrafirth
Aith
Weisdale
South Nesting Bay
SANDNESS HILL
E Bridge of Walls
Twatt
Bixter
Moul of Eswick
Mu Ness
Walls
Tresta
Aeglibister
Girlsta
Some island ferry services are seasonal, day & weather dependent
Wats Ness
Gruting
Staneydale Temple
Da Gairdins
Haggersta
Gardenhouse
Vaila
Whiteness
Score Head
Culswick
Easter Skeld
Veensgarth
Fort Charlotte
Gunnista
FOULA
Westerwick
Hildasay
A970
Bressay
BRESSAY
Skelda Ness
Scalloway
LERWICK
Mail
Noss
Isle of Noss
Foula
Trondra
Papa
Broch of Clickimin
Kirkabister
Oxna
Hamnavoe
East Burra
Quarff
Bard Ness
Shetland (South)
Fladdabister
West Burra
Cunningsburgh
Helli Ness
293
Cliff Hills
South Havra
Stove
Mousa
Shetland Islands
Hoswick
Mousa Broch
Foula
Lerwick
Bigton
Sandwick
St Ninian's Isle
Levenwick
Scousburgh
Fair Isle
Boddam
Stonybreck
FAIR ISLE
Orkney Islands
Quendale
283
Shetland Crofthouse
George Waterston Memorial
Water Mill
Fitful Head
Hillwell
Toab
Stromness
Old Scatness Broch
Grutness
0   5 miles
Kirkwall
St Margaret's Hope
& Iron Age Village
Jarlshof Prehistoric
Lady's Holm
& Norse Settlement
0   5 kilometres
Scrabster
Gills
Ness of Burgi
SUMBURGH HEAD
Wick
Aberdeen
Sumburgh Roost
Fair Isle

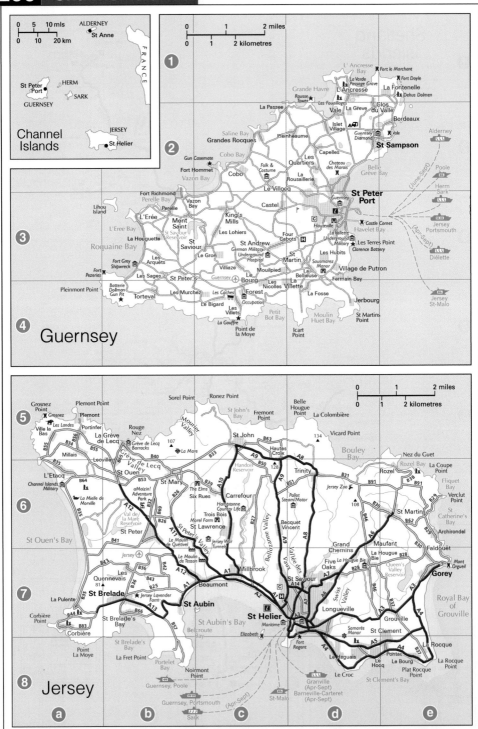

Guernsey

Jersey

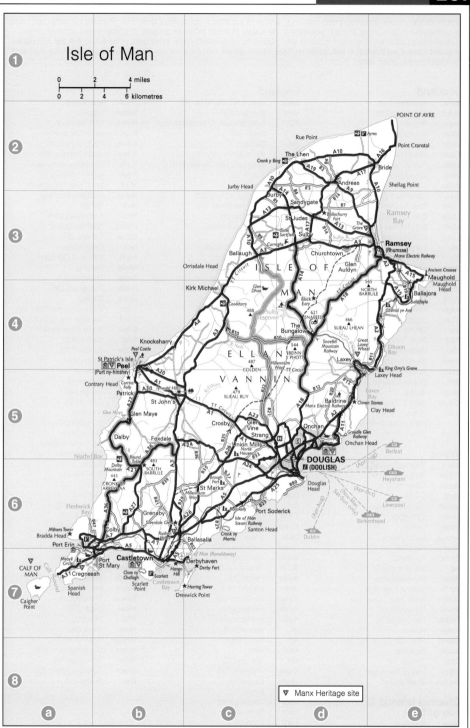

Isle of Man

```
0        2        4 miles
|--------|--------|
0    2      4     6 kilometres
```

POINT OF AYRE

Rue Point

The Lhen

Cronk y Bing

A10

Jurby Head

A19

Bride

Point Cranstal

A17

Andreas

Shellag Point

Jurby

Sandygate

St Judes

Ballachurry
Fort

The
Grove

Ramsey
Bay

Close
Sartfield

Sulby

Curraghs

Sulby R.

Ramsey
(Rhumsaa)

Manx Electric Railway

Ballaugh

Churchtown

Orrisdale Head

ISLE OF

Glen
Auldyn

Ancient Crosses

Maughold

Kirk Michael

Cooildarry

Glen
Dhoo

MAN

Block
Eary

565
NORTH
BARRULE

Maughold
Head

Ballajora

Bollafayle

488

Sulby
Reservoir

621
SNAEFELL

466
SLIEAU LHEAN

Cashtal yn Ard

Knocksharry

Peel Castle

The
Bungalow

R. Neb

B10

Snaefell
Mountain
Railway

Great
Laxey
Wheel

Dhoon
Bay

St Patrick's Isle

Peel
(Purt ny-hinshey)

A20

ELLAN

544
BEINN
Y PHOTT

Laxey

King Orry's Grave

Laxey Head

Contrary Head

Corrins
Folly

A1

487
COLDEN

Millennium
Way

TT Circuit

Patrick

A30

Tynwald Hill

VANNIN

479
SLIEAU RUY

Laxey
Bay

Glen Maye

Glen Maye

St John's

TT Circuit

A7

A23

Crosby

Glen
Vine

Baldrine

Cloven Stones

Manx Electric Railway

Clay Head

Dalby

Foxdale

Strang

Onchan

Groudle Glen
Railway

Belfast

Niarbyl Bay

Dalby
Mountain

Round
Table

483
SOUTH
BARRULE

Union Mills

Norse
Houses

Onchan Head

Heysham

CRONK
ARREY

443

St Marks

Broom
Fort

DOUGLAS
(DOOLISH)

Douglas
Head

Liverpool

Fleshwick
Bay

Grenaby

Millennium
Way

A24

Port Soderick

Isle of Man
Steam Railway

Santon Head

Birkenhead

Milners Tower

Bradda Head

Colby

Silverdale Glen

Rushen
Abbey

Cronk ny
Merriu

Dublin

Port Erin

Meayll
Circle

Port
St Mary

Ballasalla

Isle of Man (Ronaldsway)

A5

Castletown

Derbyhaven

Derby Fort

CALF OF
MAN

A31

Cregneash

Close ny
Chollagh

Hango
Hill

Spanish
Head

Scarlett
Point

Scarlett

Castletown
Bay

Herring Tower

Caigher
Point

Dreswick Point

▽ Manx Heritage site

This index lists places appearing in the main map section of the atlas in alphabetical order. The reference following each name gives the atlas page number and grid reference of the square in which the place appears. The map shows counties, unitary authorities and administrative areas, together with a list of the abbreviated name forms used in the index. The top 100 places of tourist interest are indexed in red, World Heritage sites in green, motorway service areas in blue, airports in blue italic and National Parks in green italic.

Scotland

Abers	Aberdeenshire
Ag & B	Argyll and Bute
Angus	Angus
Border	Scottish Borders
C Aber	City of Aberdeen
C Dund	City of Dundee
C Edin	City of Edinburgh
C Glas	City of Glasgow
Clacks	Clackmannanshire (1)
D & G	Dumfries & Galloway
E Ayrs	East Ayrshire
E Duns	East Dunbartonshire (2)
E Loth	East Lothian
E Rens	East Renfrewshire (3)
Falk	Falkirk
Fife	Fife
Highld	Highland
Inver	Inverclyde (4)
Mdloth	Midlothian (5)
Moray	Moray
N Ayrs	North Ayrshire
N Lans	North Lanarkshire (6)
Ork	Orkney Islands
P & K	Perth & Kinross
Rens	Renfrewshire (7)
S Ayrs	South Ayrshire
S Lans	South Lanarkshire
Shet	Shetland Islands
Stirlg	Stirling
W Duns	West Dunbartonshire (8)
W Isls	Western Isles
	(Na h-Eileanan an Iar)
W Loth	West Lothian

Wales

Blae G	Blaenau Gwent (9)
Brdgnd	Bridgend (10)
Caerph	Caerphilly (11)
Cardif	Cardiff
Carmth	Carmarthenshire
Cerdgn	Ceredigion
Conwy	Conwy
Denbgs	Denbighshire
Flints	Flintshire
Gwynd	Gwynedd
IoA	Isle of Anglesey
Mons	Monmouthshire
Myr Td	Merthyr Tydfil (12)
Neath	Neath Port Talbot (13)
Newpt	Newport (14)
Pembks	Pembrokeshire
Powys	Powys
Rhondd	Rhondda Cynon Taf (15)
Swans	Swansea
Torfn	Torfaen (16)
V Glam	Vale of Glamorgan (17)
Wrexhm	Wrexham

Channel Islands & Isle of Man

Guern	Guernsey
Jersey	Jersey
IoM	Isle of Man

England

BaNES	Bath & N E Somerset (18)
Barns	Barnsley (19)
BCP	Bournemouth, Christchurch and Poole (20)
Bed	Bedford
Birm	Birmingham
Bl w D	Blackburn with Darwen (21)
Bolton	Bolton (22)
Bpool	Blackpool
Br & H	Brighton & Hove (23)
Br For	Bracknell Forest (24)
Bristl	City of Bristol
Bucks	Buckinghamshire
Bury	Bury (25)
C Beds	Central Bedfordshire
C Brad	City of Bradford
C Derb	City of Derby
C KuH	City of Kingston upon Hull
C Leic	City of Leicester
C Nott	City of Nottingham
C Pete	City of Peterborough
C Plym	City of Plymouth
C Port	City of Portsmouth
C Sotn	City of Southampton
C Stke	City of Stoke-on-Trent
C York	City of York
Calder	Calderdale (26)
Cambs	Cambridgeshire
Ches E	Cheshire East
Ches W	Cheshire West and Chester
Cnwll	Cornwall
Covtry	Coventry
Cumb	Cumbria
Darltn	Darlington (27)
Derbys	Derbyshire
Devon	Devon
Donc	Doncaster (28)
Dorset	Dorset
Dudley	Dudley (29)
Dur	Durham
E R Yk	East Riding of Yorkshire
E Susx	East Sussex
Essex	Essex
Gatesd	Gateshead (30)
Gloucs	Gloucestershire
Gt Lon	Greater London
Halton	Halton (31)
Hants	Hampshire
Hartpl	Hartlepool (32)
Herefs	Herefordshire
Herts	Hertfordshire
IoS	Isles of Scilly
IoW	Isle of Wight
Kent	Kent
Kirk	Kirklees (33)
Knows	Knowsley (34)
Lancs	Lancashire
Leeds	Leeds
Leics	Leicestershire
Lincs	Lincolnshire
Lpool	Liverpool
Luton	Luton
M Keyn	Milton Keynes

Manch	Manchester
Medway	Medway
Middsb	Middlesbrough
N Linc	North Lincolnshire
N Som	North Somerset
N Tyne	North Tyneside (35)
N u Ty	Newcastle upon Tyne
N York	North Yorkshire
NE Lin	North East Lincolnshire
Nhants	Northamptonshire
Norfk	Norfolk
Notts	Nottinghamshire
Nthumb	Northumberland
Oldham	Oldham (36)
Oxon	Oxfordshire
R & Cl	Redcar & Cleveland
Readg	Reading
Rochdl	Rochdale (37)
Rothm	Rotherham (38)
Rutlnd	Rutland
S Glos	South Gloucestershire (39)
S on T	Stockton-on-Tees (40)
S Tyne	South Tyneside (41)
Salfd	Salford (42)
Sandw	Sandwell (43)
Sefton	Sefton (44)
Sheff	Sheffield
Shrops	Shropshire
Slough	Slough (45)
Solhll	Solihull (46)
Somset	Somerset
St Hel	St Helens (47)
Staffs	Staffordshire
Sthend	Southend-on-Sea
Stockp	Stockport (48)
Suffk	Suffolk
Sundld	Sunderland
Surrey	Surrey
Swindn	Swindon
Tamesd	Tameside (49)
Thurr	Thurrock (50)
Torbay	Torbay
Traffd	Trafford (51)
W & M	Windsor & Maidenhead (52)
W Berk	West Berkshire
W Susx	West Sussex
Wakefd	Wakefield (53)
Warrtn	Warrington (54)
Warwks	Warwickshire
Wigan	Wigan (55)
Wilts	Wiltshire
Wirral	Wirral (56)
Wokham	Wokingham (57)
Wolves	Wolverhampton (58)
Worcs	Worcestershire
Wrekin	Telford & Wrekin (59)
Wsall	Walsall (60)

ORKNEY
ISLANDS

SHETLAND
ISLANDS

WESTERN ISLES (Na h-Eileanan an Iar)

HIGHLAND

MORAY

S C O T L A N D

ABERDEENSHIRE
Aberdeen

ANGUS

PERTH &
KINROSS
Dundee

ARGYLL
AND BUTE

STIRLING

FIFE

1

8   FALK   Edinburgh
4   2
W   E LOTH
Glasgow   6   LOTH
7   5
3

NORTH
AYRSHIRE

S LANS

E AYRS

SCOTTISH
BORDERS

S AYRS

DUMFRIES &
GALLOWAY

NORTHUMBERLAND

Newcastle
upon Tyne   35
41
30
Sunderland

CUMBRIA

DURHAM   32
27 40 R & CL
Middlesbrough

IoM

NORTH YORKSHIRE

Blackpool   LANCASHIRE   Bradford   York   EAST RIDING
OF YORKSHIRE
Leeds   Kingston
upon Hull
21   26
22 25 37 36   33   53
55   N LINC   NE
44   47 42   49   19   28   LIN
Liverpool 34 54 51 Manchester   38
56   31   48   Sheffield

IoA

CONWY   FLINTS   CHES
W   CHES
E   DERBYS   NOTTS   LINCOLNSHIRE
DENBGS
Stoke-on-
WREXHAM   Trent   Derby   Nottingham

GWYNEDD

STAFFS

LEICS   RUTLAND
Leicester   Peterborough   NORFOLK

59

SHROPSHIRE   58 60   Birmingham
29 43   Coventry
46   NHANTS   CAMBS

POWYS   WORCS   WARWKS   Milton
Keynes   BED   SUFFOLK

CERDGN   HEREFS   BEDS Luton

W A L E S   E N G L A N D

PEMBKS   CARMTH   MONS   GLOUCS   OXON   BUCKS   HERTS   ESSEX

12 9
13   16   Southend-
15 11   on-Sea
Swansea   10   14   Bristol   Reading   GREATER
17   N   39   Swindon   52 45   LONDON   50   MEDWAY
Cardiff   SOM   18   W BERK   57 24   SURREY
Plymouth   WILTSHIRE   KENT

SOMERSET   HAMPSHIRE   W SUSX   E SUSX

DEVON   DORSET   Southampton   23
20   Portsmouth

CORNWALL   IoW
Plymouth   Torbay   CHANNEL   Guernsey
ISLANDS
Jersey

IoS

A

Abbas Combe
Somset.................27 G6
Abberley Worcs...............70 D2
Abberley Common
Worcs.......................70 D2
Abberton Essex...........62 B4
Abberton Worcs...........71 H4
Abbess Roding Essex....60 F5
Abbeydale Sheff..........114 E6
Abbey Dore Herefs........54 B3
Abbey Green Staffs........99 L2
Abbey St Bathans
Border....................178 F6
Abbeystead Lancs.......130 B8
Abbeytown Cumb........147 L5
Abbey Village Lancs.....121 J6
Abbey Wood Gt Lon......45 J4
Abbotrule Border........167 J6
Abbots Bickington
Devon........................9 K3
Abbots Bromley
Staffs.....................100 B7
Abbotsbury Dorset........14 B5
Abbots Deuglie
P & K.......................186 B5
Abbotsham Devon........22 F6
Abbotskerswell
Devon........................7 K3
Abbots Langley
Herts........................59 H7
Abbots Leigh N Som.....38 D5
Abbotsley Cambs..........75 J3
Abbots Morton
Worcs........................71 H4
Abbots Ripton Cambs....89 J7
Abbot's Salford
Warwks......................71 J4
Abbots Worthy Hants....29 J5
Abbotts Ann Hants........29 G3
Abbott Street Dorset.....15 J3
Abdon Shrops...............83 L6
Aberaeron Cerdgn..........66 B3
Aberaman Rhondd........52 F7
Aberangell Gwynd.........81 J2
Aberarder Highld.........202 F1
Aberargie P & K...........186 B4
Aberarth Cerdgn...........66 B2
Aberavon Neath............51 L7
Abercanaid Myr Td.......53 G7
Abercarn Caerph...........37 K2
Abercastle Pembks........64 B7
Abercegir Powys...........81 H3
Aberchalder Highld......202 B5
Aberchirder Abers........216 C4
Abercorn W Loth.........176 E3
Abercraf Powys.............52 C5
Abercregan Neath.........36 D2
Abercwmboi Rhondd.....52 F7
Abercych Pembks...........65 H6
Abercynon Rhondd........37 G2
Aberdalgie P & K.........185 M4
Aberdare Rhondd..........52 F7
Aberdaron Gwynd.........94 C7
Aberdeen C Aber.........207 H4
Aberdeen Airport
C Aber....................207 G3
Aberdour Fife.............177 G2
Aberdulais Neath..........52 B7
Aberdyfi Gwynd............80 E4
Aberedw Powys............68 C5
Abereiddy Pembks.........48 D2
Abererch Gwynd............95 G5
Aberfan Myr Td............53 G7
Aberfeldy P & K..........194 D6
Aberffraw IoA.............108 D7
Aberford Leeds...........124 C3
Aberfoyle Stirlg..........184 C7
Abergavenny Mons........53 L5
Abergele Conwy...........110 C6
Abergorlech Carmth.......66 D7
Abergwesyn Powys.........67 J4
Abergwili Carmth...........50 F2
Abergwynfi Neath.........36 D2
Abergwyngregyn
Gwynd......................109 J6

Abergynolwyn Gwynd.....80 F3
Aberkenfig Brdgnd........36 D4
Aberlady E Loth..........178 B3
Aberlemno Angus.........196 E5
Aberllefenni Gwynd.......81 G2
Aberllynfi Powys...........68 D6
Aberlour,
Charlestown of
Moray.....................215 G5
Abermule Powys............82 D5
Abernant Carmth...........50 D2
Abernant Rhondd..........52 F7
Abernethy P & K..........186 C4
Abernyte P & K............186 D2
Aberporth Cerdgn..........65 J4
Abersoch Gwynd............94 E6
Abersychan Torfn.........53 K7
Aberthin V Glam............36 F5
Abertillery Blae G........53 K7
Abertridwr Caerph.........37 H3
Abertridwr Powys..........97 G8
Aberuthven P & K.........185 K4
Aberystwyth Cerdgn.......80 D6
Abingdon-on-
Thames Oxon............41 J2
Abinger Common
Surrey.......................31 J3
Abinger Hammer
Surrey.......................31 H2
Abington Nhants...........73 L3
Abington S Lans..........165 H5
Abington Pigotts
Cambs........................75 K5
Abington Services
S Lans.....................165 H4
Abingworth W Susx........18 F3
Ab Kettleby Leics........102 B7
Ablington Gloucs..........56 C6
Abney Derbys..............114 D5
Aboyne Abers.............205 L5
Abhainn Suidhe
W Isls......................232 d4
Abram Wigan..............112 E2
Abriachan Highld........212 E7
Abridge Essex...............45 J2
Abronhill N Lans.........175 K3
Abson S Glos...............39 G5
Abthorpe Nhants...........73 J5
Aby Lincs.................118 F5
Acaster Malbis
C York.....................124 E2
Acaster Selby N York...124 E3
Accrington Lancs.........121 L5
Acha Ag & B...............188 F5
Achahoish Ag & B........172 D3
Achalader P & K..........195 H7
Achaleven Ag & B........182 D1
Acha Mor W Isls..........232 f3
Achanalt Highld.........211 K3
Achandunie Highld.......222 E6
Achany Highld............222 D2
Acharacle Highld.........190 D3
Acharn Highld.............190 E6
Acharn P & K.............194 B7
Achavanich Highld........231 H6
Achduart Highld..........224 C7
Achfary Highld............228 D7
Achgarve Highld.........219 K3
A'Chill Highld............198 D4
Achiltibuie Highld........224 C6
Achina Highld.............229 L4
Achinhoan Ag & B.......161 J6
Achintee Highld...........210 E6
Achintraid Highld.........210 C6
Achlyness Highld.........228 C5
Achmelvich Highld.......224 C4
Achmore Highld..........210 D7
Achmore W Isls..........232 f3
Achnacarnin Highld......224 C3
Achnacarry Highld........201 J7
Achnacloich Highld......199 J4
Achnaconeran
Highld.....................202 C2
Achnacroish Ag & B.....191 G7
Achnadrish Ag & B.......189 L6
Achnafauld P & K..........185 J1
Achnagarron Highld......222 F7
Achnaha Highld...........189 L3

Achnahaird Highld........224 B5
Achnahannet Highld......214 B8
Achnairn Highld..........225 L6
Achnalea Highld..........191 G4
Achnamara Ag & B........172 D2
Achnasheen Highld......211 J3
Achnashellach
Highld.....................210 F5
Achnastank Moray........215 G7
Achosnich Highld.........189 K3
Achranich Highld.........190 E6
Achreamie Highld........230 E3
Achriabhach Highld......192 B3
Achriesgill Highld........228 C5
Achtoty Highld............229 K3
Achurch Nhants............88 E6
Achvaich Highld..........222 F3
Achvarasdal Highld.......230 E3
Ackergill Highld..........231 L5
Acklam Middsb............141 L4
Acklam N York............134 B7
Ackleton Shrops............84 D4
Acklington Nthumb.......159 G2
Ackton Wakefd...........124 C6
Ackworth Moor Top
Wakefd....................124 C7
Acle Norfk...................93 J2
Acock's Green Birm.......85 K6
Acol Kent....................35 J2
Acomb C York............124 E1
Acomb Nthumb...........150 B2
Aconbury Herefs...........54 D2
Acton Ches E...............98 F2
Acton Gt Lon...............44 D4
Acton Staffs.................99 J4
Acton Suffk..................77 K5
Acton Wrexhm..............97 M3
Acton Beauchamp
Herefs........................70 C4
Acton Bridge
Ches W....................112 E6
Acton Burnell Shrops.....83 K3
Acton Green Herefs........70 C4
Acton Round Shrops........84 B4
Acton Scott Shrops........83 J5
Acton Trussell Staffs.....99 L8
Acton Turville S Glos.....39 J4
Adbaston Staffs............99 H6
Adber Dorset................26 E7
Adbolton Notts...........101 L5
Adderbury Oxon...........72 F7
Adderley Shrops............98 F4
Addiewell W Loth.........176 D5
Addingham C Brad.......123 G1
Addington Bucks...........58 C3
Addington Gt Lon..........45 G7
Addington Kent.............33 H2
Addiscombe Gt Lon........45 G6
Addlestone Surrey.........43 H7
Addlethorpe Lincs.......119 H7
Adeyfield Herts............59 H6
Adfa Powys...................82 B4
Adforton Herefs............69 H1
Adisham Kent................35 G4
Adlestrop Gloucs..........56 E3
Adlingfleet E R Yk........125 K6
Adlington Lancs..........121 J7
Admaston Staffs.........100 B7
Admaston Wrekin..........84 B2
Adpar Cerdgn................65 J6
Adsborough Somset.......25 L5
Adscombe Somset..........25 J4
Adstock Bucks..............58 C3
Adstone Nhants............73 H4
Adswood Stockp..........113 K4
Adversane W Susx.........31 H6
Advie Highld..............214 D7
Adwick le Street
Donc......................124 E8
Adwick upon
Dearne Donc...........115 J2
Ae D & G...................155 H4
Ae Bridgend D & G.......155 H5
Afan Forest Park
Neath........................36 D2
Affleck Abers.............216 B6
Affpuddle Dorset..........14 F4
Affric Lodge Highld......201 J2

Afon-wen Flints..........110 F6
Afton IoW....................16 D5
Agglethorpe N York.....131 K3
Aigburth Lpool...........111 L4
Aike E R Yk...............126 C2
Aiketgate Cumb...........148 E5
Aikton Cumb...............148 B4
Ailsworth C Pete...........89 G4
Ainderby Quernhow
N York.....................132 E4
Ainderby Steeple
N York.....................132 E2
Aingers Green Essex......62 D4
Ainsdale Sefton..........120 D7
Ainstable Cumb...........148 F5
Ainsworth Bury...........121 L8
Ainthorpe N York........142 E5
Aintree Sefton............111 L2
Ainville W Loth...........176 F5
Aird Ag & B................181 M7
Aird D & G.................144 D3
Aird Highld................199 J5
Aird W Isls................232 g2
Aird a' Mhulaidh
W Isls......................232 e3
Aird Asaig W Isls........232 e4
Aird Dhubh Highld......209 L6
Airdeny Ag & B...........182 E2
Airdrie N Lans...........175 K5
Airdriehill N Lans.......175 K5
Airds of Kells D & G....154 B7
Aird Uig W Isls..........232 d2
Airidh a bhruaich
W Isls......................232 e3
Airieland D & G...........146 D4
Airlie Angus..............195 L6
Airmyn E R Yk............125 H5
Airntully P & K...........186 A1
Airor Highld..............199 L4
Airth Falk..................176 B2
Airton N York.............131 G7
Aisby Lincs................103 G5
Aisby Lincs................116 E3
Aish Devon....................7 G4
Aish Devon....................7 J4
Aisholt Somset.............25 J4
Aiskew N York............132 D2
Aislaby N York...........134 B3
Aislaby N York...........143 H5
Aislaby S on T............141 J5
Aisthorpe Lincs..........116 F5
Aith Shet..................235 c5
Akeld Nthumb............168 E4
Akeley Bucks................73 K6
Albaston Cnwll..............6 B2
Alberbury Shrops..........83 G1
Albourne W Susx...........19 H3
Albrighton Shrops.........84 E3
Albrighton Shrops.........98 C8
Alburgh Norfk...............92 F6
Albury Herts.................60 C3
Albury Surrey................31 H2
Albury Heath Surrey......31 H3
Alcaig Highld.............212 E3
Alcaston Shrops............83 J6
Alcester Warwks...........71 K3
Alciston E Susx.............20 B5
Alcombe Somset...........24 F3
Alconbury Cambs..........89 H7
Alconbury Weald
Cambs.......................89 H7
Alconbury Weston
Cambs.......................89 H7
Aldborough N York......132 F6
Aldborough Norfk.......106 E5
Aldbourne Wilts...........40 E5
Aldbrough E R Yk.......127 G3
Aldbrough St John
N York.....................140 F5
Aldbury Herts...............58 F5
Aldcliffe Lancs...........129 K7
Aldclune P & K...........194 E4
Aldeburgh Suffk...........79 K3
Aldeby Norfk................93 J5
Aldenham Herts............43 J2
Alderbury Wilts.............28 D6
Alderford Norfk..........106 D8
Alderholt Dorset...........28 C8

Alderley Gloucs 39 H3
Alderley Edge
  Ches E 113 J5
Aldermans Green
  Covtry 86 D6
Aldermaston W Berk 41 L7
Alderminster Warwks ... 72 B5
Aldershot Hants 30 E2
Alderton Gloucs 55 M2
Alderton Nhants 73 K5
Alderton Suffk 79 H6
Alderton Wilts 39 J4
Aldfield N York 132 D5
Aldford Ches W 98 B2
Aldgate Rutlnd 88 E3
Aldham Essex 61 L3
Aldham Suffk 78 C5
Aldingbourne W Susx 18 C5
Aldingham Cumb 129 G5
Aldington Kent 34 E7
Aldington Worcs 71 J5
Aldington Corner
  Kent 34 E7
Aldivalloch Moray 205 H1
Aldochlay Ag & B 174 C1
Aldreth Cambs 90 C8
Aldridge Wsall 85 J4
Aldringham Suffk 79 J3
Aldsworth Gloucs 56 D6
Aldunie Moray 215 H8
Aldwark Derbys 100 E2
Aldwark N York 133 G6
Aldwick W Susx 18 C6
Aldwincle Nhants 88 E6
Aldworth W Berk 41 K4
Alexandria W Duns 174 D3
Aley Somset 25 J4
Alfington Devon 12 E3
Alfold Surrey 31 H5
Alfold Crossways
  Surrey 31 H4
Alford Abers 206 B3
Alford Lincs 118 F6
Alford Somset 26 E5
Alfreton Derbys 101 H2
Alfrick Worcs 70 D4
Alfrick Pound Worcs ... 70 D4
Alfriston E Susx 20 B5
Algarkirk Lincs 103 M5
Alhampton Somset 26 F4
Alkborough N Linc 125 K6
Alkham Kent 35 H6
Alkmonton Derbys 100 D5
Allaleigh Devon 7 J5
Allanaquoich Abers 204 D6
Allanbank N Lans 175 L6
Allanton Border 179 H7
Allanton N Lans 175 L6
Allanton S Lans 175 K7
Allaston Gloucs 54 F6
Allbrook Hants 29 J7
All Cannings Wilts 40 B7
Allendale Nthumb 149 L4
Allenheads Nthumb 149 L4
Allen's Green Herts 60 D5
Allensmore Herefs 69 J7
Allenton C Derb 101 G6
Aller Devon 24 B6
Aller Somset 26 B5
Allerby Cumb 147 L6
Allercombe Devon 12 D4
Allerford Somset 24 D3
Allerston N York 134 D3
Allerthorpe E R Yk 125 J2
Allerton C Brad 123 G4
Allerton Highld 213 H2
Allerton Lpool 111 L4
Allerton Bywater
  Leeds 124 C5
Allerton Mauleverer
  N York 132 F7
Allesley Covtry 86 C7
Allestree C Derb 101 G5
Allexton Leics 88 B4
Allgreave Ches E 113 L7
Allhallows Medway 46 D4
Alligin Shuas Highld 210 C3

Allington Dorset 13 L4
Allington Lincs 102 E4
Allington Wilts 28 D4
Allington Wilts 39 K5
Allington Wilts 40 B7
Allithwaite Cumb 129 J4
Alloa Clacks 185 J8
Allonby Cumb 147 J6
Alloway S Ayrs 163 J5
Allowenshay Somset 26 B8
All Stretton Shrops 83 J4
Alltchaorunn Highld ... 192 C6
Alltsigh Highld 202 C2
Alltwalis Carmth 66 B7
Alltwen Neath 51 K5
Alltyblaca Cerdgn 66 C5
Almeley Herefs 69 G4
Almington Staffs 99 G5
Almodington W Susx 18 C5
Almondbank P & K 185 M3
Almondbury Kirk 123 H7
Almondsbury S Glos 38 E4
Alne N York 133 G6
Alness Highld 222 E7
Alnham Nthumb 168 E7
Alnmouth Nthumb 169 J7
Alnwick Nthumb 169 J6
Alperton Gt Lon 44 D4
Alphamstone Essex 77 K7
Alpheton Suffk 77 K4
Alphington Devon 11 L6
Alport Derbys 114 E8
Alpraham Ches E 98 E1
Alresford Essex 62 C4
Alrewas Staffs 85 L1
Alsager Ches E 99 H2
Alsop en le Dale
  Derbys 100 D2
Alston Cumb 149 J5
Alston Devon 13 H2
Alstone Gloucs 55 M2
Alstonefield Staffs 100 C2
Alston Sutton Somset .. 26 B2
Alswear Devon 23 L6
Altandhu Highld 224 B6
Altarnun Cnwll 9 G8
Altass Highld 222 C2
Altcreich Ag & B 190 D8
Altgaltraig Ag & B 173 H4
Althorne Essex 61 L7
Althorpe N Linc 125 K8
Altnabreac Station
  Highld 230 E6
Altnaharra Highld 225 M2
Altofts Wakefd 124 B5
Alton Derbys 115 G8
Alton Hants 30 B4
Alton Staffs 100 B4
Alton Barnes Wilts 40 C7
Alton Pancras Dorset ... 14 D3
Alton Priors Wilts 40 C7
Alton Towers Staffs ... 100 B4
Altrincham Traffd 113 H4
Altskeith Hotel Stirlg .. 184 B6
Alva Clacks 185 J7
Alvanley Ches W 112 D6
Alvaston C Derb 101 H5
Alvechurch Worcs 85 J8
Alvecote Warwks 86 B3
Alvediston Wilts 27 L6
Alveley Shrops 84 D6
Alverdiscott Devon 23 H6
Alverstoke Hants 17 H3
Alverstone IoW 17 H5
Alverthorpe Wakefd ... 123 L6
Alverton Notts 102 C4
Alves Moray 214 E3
Alvescot Oxon 56 F6
Alveston S Glos 38 F3
Alveston Warwks 72 B3
Alvingham Lincs 118 E4
Alvington Gloucs 54 E7
Alwalton C Pete 89 G4
Alweston Dorset 26 F8
Alwinton Nthumb 168 D7
Alwoodley Leeds 123 K3
Alyth P & K 195 K6
Am Bàgh a Tuath
  W Isls 233 b9

Ambergate Derbys 101 G3
Amberley Gloucs 55 J7
Amberley W Susx 18 D3
Amble Nthumb 159 G2
Amblecote Dudley 84 F6
Ambler Thorn C Brad .. 123 G5
Ambleside Cumb 137 K6
Ambleston Pembks 49 G3
Ambrosden Oxon 57 L4
Amcotts N Linc 125 K7
Amersham Bucks 42 F2
Amersham
  Common Bucks 42 F2
Amersham Old
  Town Bucks 42 F2
Amersham on the
  Hill Bucks 58 F7
Amesbury Wilts 28 D3
Amhuinnsuidhe
  W Isls 232 d4
Amington Staffs 86 B3
Amisfield D & G 155 H5
Amlwch IoA 108 F3
Ammanford Carmth 51 J3
Amotherby N York 134 B5
Ampfield Hants 29 H6
Ampleforth N York 133 J4
Ampney Crucis
  Gloucs 56 B7
Ampney St Mary
  Gloucs 56 C7
Ampney St Peter
  Gloucs 56 B7
Amport Hants 28 F3
Ampthill C Beds 74 F6
Ampton Suffk 77 J1
Amroth Pembks 49 K6
Amulree P & K 185 J1
Amwell Herts 59 K5
Anaheilt Highld 191 G4
Ancaster Lincs 103 G4
Ancells Farm Hants 30 D1
Ancroft Nthumb 168 E1
Ancrum Border 167 K4
Anderby Lincs 119 G6
Anderson Dorset 15 H4
Andover Hants 29 G3
Andoversford Gloucs ... 56 A4
Andreas IoM 237 d2
Anerley Gt Lon 45 G6
Anfield Lpool 111 K3
Angarrack Cnwll 3 G4
Angelbank Shrops 83 L7
Angle Pembks 48 E6
Anglesey IoA 108 E5
Anglesey Abbey
  Cambs 76 D3
Angmering W Susx 18 E5
Angram N York 124 D2
Ankerville Highld 223 H6
Ankle Hill Leics 102 C8
Anlaby E R Yk 126 C5
Anmer Norfk 105 H6
Anmore Hants 17 J1
Anna Valley Hants 29 G3
Annbank S Ayrs 163 K5
Anne Hathaway's
  Cottage Warwks 71 L4
Annfield Plain Dur 150 F5
Anniesland C Glas 174 F5
Ansdell Lancs 120 D5
Ansford Somset 26 F5
Ansley Warwks 86 C5
Anslow Staffs 100 E7
Anslow Gate Staffs ... 100 D7
Anstey Herts 60 C2
Anstey Leics 87 G2
Anstruther Fife 187 J6
Ansty W Susx 19 J2
Ansty Warwks 86 E6
Ansty Wilts 27 L6
An Tairbeart W Isls 232 e4
Anthorn Cumb 147 L4

Antingham Norfk 106 F5
An t-Ob W Isls 232 d5
Antonine Wall 175 L3
Anton's Gowt Lincs ... 103 M3
Antony Cnwll 6 B5
Antrobus Ches W 112 F5
Anwick Lincs 103 J3
Anwoth D & G 145 M4
Aperfield Gt Lon 32 D2
Apethorpe Nhants 88 E4
Apley Lincs 117 J6
Apperknowle Derbys .. 115 G5
Apperley Gloucs 55 K3
Appin Ag & B 191 J6
Appleby N Linc 126 B7
Appleby-in-
  Westmorland
  Cumb 139 G3
Appleby Magna Leics ... 86 C2
Appleby Parva Leics 86 C2
Applecross Highld 209 L5
Appledore Devon 23 G5
Appledore Devon 25 G8
Appledore Kent 34 C8
Appleford Oxon 41 K2
Applegarth Town
  D & G 155 J5
Appleshaw Hants 28 F2
Appleton Halton 112 D4
Appleton Oxon 57 H7
Appleton Warrtn 112 F5
Appleton-le-Moors
  N York 133 L3
Appleton-le-Street
  N York 134 B5
Appleton Roebuck
  N York 124 E3
Appleton Thorn
  Warrtn 112 F5
Appleton Wiske
  N York 141 J6
Appletreehall Border .. 167 H6
Appletreewick
  N York 131 K7
Appley Somset 25 G6
Apse Heath IoW 17 G5
Apsley End C Beds 59 J2
Apuldram W Susx 18 A5
Arabella Highld 223 H6
Arbirlot Angus 196 F7
Arborfield Wokham 42 C6
Arborfield Cross
  Wokham 42 C6
Arbourthorne Sheff ... 115 G4
Arbroath Angus 197 G7
Arbuthnott Abers 197 K2
Archddu Carmth 50 F5
Archdeacon Newton
  Darltn 141 G4
Archencarroch
  W Duns 174 D3
Archiestown Moray ... 214 F5
Archirondel Jersey 236 e6
Arclid Ches E 99 H1
Ardallie Abers 217 J6
Ardanaiseig Hotel
  Ag & B 182 F3
Ardaneaskan Highld .. 210 C7
Ardarroch Highld 210 C6
Ardbeg Ag & B 160 D1
Ardbeg Ag & B 173 J5
Ardbeg Ag & B 173 K2
Ardcharnich Highld ... 220 F4
Ardchiavaig Ag & B ... 180 E4
Ardchonnel Ag & B ... 182 D5
Ardchronie Highld 222 E4
Ardchullarie More
  Stirlg 184 D5
Arddarroch Ag & B 183 J7
Arddleen Powys 82 F1
Ard Dorch Highld 209 J8
Ardechive Highld 201 H7
Ardeer N Ayrs 163 H2
Ardeley Herts 60 A3
Ardelve Highld 210 D8
Arden Ag & B 174 C2
Ardens Grafton
  Warwks 71 K4

Ardentallen Ag & B...... 182 B3
Ardentinny Ag & B...... 173 L2
Ardentraive Ag & B...... 173 H4
Ardeonaig Stirlg...... 184 E1
Ardersier Highld...... 213 J4
Ardessie Highld...... 220 D4
Ardfern Ag & B...... 182 A6
Ardfernal Ag & B...... 171 K4
Ardgartan Ag & B...... 183 J6
Ardgay Highld...... 222 D4
Ardgour Highld...... 191 K4
Ardgowan Inver...... 173 L4
Ardhallow Ag & B...... 173 K4
Ardhasig W Isls...... 232 e4
Ardheslaig Highld...... 210 B3
Ardindrean Highld...... 220 F4
Ardingly W Susx...... 32 C7
Ardington Oxon...... 41 H3
Ardlamont Ag & B...... 173 G5
Ardleigh Essex...... 62 C3
Ardleigh Heath
Essex...... 62 C2
Ardler P & K...... 195 L7
Ardley Oxon...... 57 K3
Ardlui Ag & B...... 183 K4
Ardlussa Ag & B...... 172 B2
Ardmair Highld...... 220 E2
Ardmaleish Ag & B...... 173 J5
Ardminish Ag & B...... 172 B8
Ardmolich Highld...... 190 E3
Ardmore Ag & B...... 174 C3
Ardmore Highld...... 222 F4
Ardnadam Ag & B...... 173 K3
Ardnagrask Highld...... 212 E4
Ardnamurchan
Highld...... 190 B3
Ardnarff Highld...... 210 D7
Ardnastang Highld...... 190 F4
Ardpatrick Ag & B...... 172 C6
Ardrishaig Ag & B...... 172 E2
Ardross Highld...... 222 E6
Ardrossan N Ayrs...... 163 G2
Ardslignish Highld...... 190 B4
Ardtalla Ag & B...... 171 J7
Ardtoe Highld...... 190 C3
Arduaine Ag & B...... 182 A5
Ardullie Highld...... 212 E2
Ardvasar Highld...... 199 K5
Ardvorlich P & K...... 184 D3
Ardvourlie W Isls...... 232 e3
Ardwell D & G...... 144 D5
Ardwick Manch...... 113 J3
Areley Kings Worcs...... 70 E1
Arevegaig Highld...... 190 D3
Arford Hants...... 30 D4
Argoed Caerph...... 53 J7
Argyll Forest Park
Ag & B...... 183 J6
Aribruach W Isls...... 232 e3
Aridhglas Ag & B...... 180 D3
Arileod Ag & B...... 188 F5
Arinagour Ag & B...... 189 G5
Ariogan Ag & B...... 182 C3
Arisaig Highld...... 199 K7
Arisaig House Highld...... 199 L7
Arkendale N York...... 132 F7
Arkesden Essex...... 76 C7
Arkholme Lancs...... 130 B5
Arkleton D & G...... 156 C4
Arkley Gt Lon...... 44 E2
Arksey Donc...... 115 L1
Arkwright Town
Derbys...... 115 H7
Arle Gloucs...... 55 L4
Arlecdon Cumb...... 136 E4
Arlesey C Beds...... 75 H7
Arleston Wrekin...... 84 B2
Arley Ches E...... 112 F5
Arlingham Gloucs...... 55 G6
Arlington Devon...... 23 K4
Arlington E Susx...... 20 B4
Armadale Highld...... 199 K5
Armadale Highld...... 230 A3
Armadale W Loth...... 176 C5
Armathwaite Cumb...... 148 E5
Arminghall Norfk...... 92 F3
Armitage Staffs...... 85 J1
Armley Leeds...... 123 K4

Armscote Warwks...... 72 B5
Armthorpe Donc...... 115 L1
Arnabost Ag & B...... 188 F4
Arncliffe N York...... 131 H5
Arncroach Fife...... 187 H6
Arndilly House
Moray...... 215 G5
Arne Dorset...... 15 H5
Arnesby Leics...... 87 H5
Arngask P & K...... 186 B5
Arnisdale Highld...... 200 C3
Arnish Highld...... 209 J5
Arniston Mdloth...... 177 K6
Arnol W Isls...... 232 f1
Arnold E R Yk...... 126 E3
Arnold Notts...... 101 L4
Arnprior Stirlg...... 184 D7
Arnside Cumb...... 129 K4
Aros Ag & B...... 190 B7
Arrad Foot Cumb...... 129 G4
Arram E R Yk...... 126 C2
Arran N Ayrs...... 162 B3
Arrathorne N York...... 132 C2
Arreton IoW...... 17 G5
Arrina Highld...... 210 B3
Arrington Cambs...... 75 K4
Arrochar Ag & B...... 183 K6
Arrow Warwks...... 71 J3
Arscott Shrops...... 83 J2
Artafallie Highld...... 212 F4
Arthington Leeds...... 123 K2
Arthingworth
Nhants...... 87 L7
Arthrath Abers...... 217 H6
Artrochie Abers...... 217 J7
Arundel W Susx...... 18 D4
Asby Cumb...... 136 E3
Ascog Ag & B...... 173 J5
Ascot W & M...... 42 F6
Ascott-under-
Wychwood Oxon...... 56 F4
Asenby N York...... 132 F4
Asfordby Leics...... 102 B8
Asfordby Hill Leics...... 102 B8
Asgarby Lincs...... 103 J4
Ash Kent...... 35 H3
Ash Kent...... 45 L6
Ash Somset...... 26 C7
Ash Surrey...... 30 E2
Ashampstead W Berk...... 41 K5
Ashbocking Suffk...... 78 E4
Ashbourne Derbys...... 100 D3
Ashbrittle Somset...... 25 G6
Ashburton Devon...... 7 H2
Ashbury Devon...... 10 D5
Ashbury Oxon...... 40 E4
Ashby N Linc...... 125 L8
Ashby by Partney
Lincs...... 118 F7
Ashby cum Fenby
NE Lin...... 118 C2
Ashby de la Launde
Lincs...... 103 H2
Ashby-de-la-Zouch
Leics...... 86 D1
Ashby Folville Leics...... 87 K2
Ashby Magna Leics...... 87 H5
Ashby Parva Leics...... 87 G5
Ashby Puerorum
Lincs...... 118 D7
Ashby St Ledgers
Nhants...... 73 H2
Ashby St Mary
Norfk...... 93 G3
Ashchurch Gloucs...... 55 L2
Ashcombe Devon...... 11 L8
Ashcombe N Som...... 37 M7
Ashcott Somset...... 26 C4
Ashdon Essex...... 76 E6
Ashdown Forest
E Susx...... 32 E6
Ashe Hants...... 29 K2
Asheldham Essex...... 62 A7
Ashen Essex...... 77 H6
Ashendon Bucks...... 58 B5
Asheridge Bucks...... 58 F6
Ashfield Herefs...... 54 E4
Ashfield Stirlg...... 185 G6

Ashfield cum
Thorpe Suffk...... 78 E3
Ashfield Green Suffk...... 92 F8
Ashford Devon...... 7 G6
Ashford Devon...... 23 H4
Ashford Kent...... 34 D6
Ashford Surrey...... 43 H6
Ashford Bowdler
Shrops...... 69 K1
Ashford Carbonell
Shrops...... 69 K1
Ashford Hill Hants...... 41 K7
Ashford in the
Water Derbys...... 114 D7
Ashgill S Lans...... 175 K7
Ash Green Surrey...... 30 E2
Ash Green Warwks...... 86 D6
Ashill Devon...... 12 E1
Ashill Norfk...... 91 K3
Ashill Somset...... 25 L7
Ashingdon Essex...... 46 E2
Ashington Nthumb...... 159 G5
Ashington Somset...... 26 E6
Ashington W Susx...... 18 F3
Ashkirk Border...... 167 G5
Ashleworth Gloucs...... 55 J3
Ashleworth Quay
Gloucs...... 55 J3
Ashley Cambs...... 77 G3
Ashley Ches E...... 113 H5
Ashley Devon...... 10 F3
Ashley Gloucs...... 39 L2
Ashley Hants...... 16 B4
Ashley Hants...... 29 G5
Ashley Kent...... 35 J5
Ashley Nhants...... 87 L5
Ashley Staffs...... 99 H5
Ashley Wilts...... 39 J4
Ashley Green Bucks...... 58 F6
Ash Magna Shrops...... 98 E4
Ashmansworth
Hants...... 41 H8
Ashmansworthy
Devon...... 22 E7
Ash Mill Devon...... 24 C6
Ashmore Dorset...... 27 K7
Ashmore Green
W Berk...... 41 J6
Ashorne Warwks...... 72 C3
Ashover Derbys...... 115 G8
Ashow Warwks...... 72 C1
Ashperton Herefs...... 70 B6
Ashprington Devon...... 7 J4
Ash Priors Somset...... 25 J5
Ashreigney Devon...... 10 F3
Ash Street Suffk...... 78 B5
Ashtead Surrey...... 44 D8
Ash Thomas Devon...... 12 C1
Ashton Cnwll...... 3 G5
Ashton Devon...... 11 K7
Ashton Herefs...... 69 K2
Ashton Inver...... 173 L3
Ashton Nhants...... 73 L5
Ashton Nhants...... 88 F5
Ashton Common
Wilts...... 39 K8
Ashton Hayes
Ches W...... 112 D7
Ashton-in-
Makerfield Wigan...... 112 E2
Ashton Keynes Wilts...... 40 B2
Ashton-on-Ribble
Lancs...... 121 G4
Ashton under Hill
Worcs...... 71 H6
Ashton-under-Lyne
Tamesd...... 113 L2
Ashton Vale Bristl...... 38 E6
Ashurst Hants...... 16 D1
Ashurst Kent...... 32 F5
Ashurst Lancs...... 121 G8
Ashurst W Susx...... 19 G3
Ashurst Wood
W Susx...... 32 D6
Ash Vale Surrey...... 30 E2
Ashwater Devon...... 9 K5
Ashwell Herts...... 75 J6
Ashwell Rutlnd...... 88 C2

Ashwell End Herts...... 75 J6
Ashwellthorpe Norfk...... 92 D4
Ashwick Somset...... 26 F2
Ashwicken Norfk...... 105 H8
Askam in Furness
Cumb...... 128 F4
Askern Donc...... 124 E7
Askerswell Dorset...... 14 A4
Askett Bucks...... 58 D6
Askham Cumb...... 138 D3
Askham Notts...... 116 C6
Askham Bryan
C York...... 124 E2
Askham Richard
C York...... 124 E2
Asknish Ag & B...... 172 F1
Askrigg N York...... 131 H2
Askwith N York...... 123 H2
Aslackby Lincs...... 103 H6
Aslacton Norfk...... 92 D5
Aslockton Notts...... 102 C4
Aspatria Cumb...... 147 K6
Aspenden Herts...... 60 B3
Aspley Guise C Beds...... 74 D7
Aspley Heath C Beds...... 74 D7
Aspull Wigan...... 121 J8
Asselby E R Yk...... 125 H5
Assington Suffk...... 77 L6
Assington Green
Suffk...... 77 H4
Astbury Ches E...... 99 J1
Astcote Nhants...... 73 J4
Asterby Lincs...... 118 C5
Asterley Shrops...... 83 H3
Asterton Shrops...... 83 H5
Asthall Oxon...... 56 F5
Asthall Leigh Oxon...... 56 F5
Astle Highld...... 223 G3
Astley Shrops...... 98 D8
Astley Warwks...... 86 C5
Astley Wigan...... 113 G2
Astley Worcs...... 70 D2
Astley Abbots Shrops...... 84 C4
Astley Bridge
Bolton...... 121 K7
Astley Cross Worcs...... 70 E1
Aston Birm...... 85 J5
Aston Ches E...... 98 E3
Aston Ches W...... 112 E5
Aston Derbys...... 114 D5
Aston Flints...... 111 J7
Aston Herts...... 59 L4
Aston Oxon...... 57 G7
Aston Rothm...... 115 J4
Aston Shrops...... 84 E5
Aston Shrops...... 98 D6
Aston Staffs...... 99 H4
Aston Staffs...... 99 K7
Aston Wokham...... 42 C4
Aston Wrekin...... 84 B2
Aston Abbotts Bucks...... 58 D4
Aston Botterell
Shrops...... 84 B6
Aston-by-Stone
Staffs...... 99 K6
Aston Cantlow
Warwks...... 71 K3
Aston Clinton Bucks...... 58 E5
Aston Crews Herefs...... 54 F4
Aston End Herts...... 59 L3
Aston Fields Worcs...... 71 G1
Aston Flamville L
eics...... 86 F5
Aston Ingham Herefs...... 55 G4
Aston le Walls
Nhants...... 72 F4
Aston Magna Gloucs...... 71 L7
Aston Munslow
Shrops...... 83 K6
Aston on Clun
Shrops...... 83 H6
Aston Pigott Shrops...... 83 G3
Aston Rogers Shrops...... 83 G3
Aston Rowant Oxon...... 58 D7
Aston Somerville
Worcs...... 71 J6
Aston-sub-Edge
Gloucs...... 71 K6

Aston Tirrold Oxon.........41 K3
Aston-upon-Trent
  Derbys............ 101 H6
Aston Upthorpe
  Oxon............41 K3
Astwick C Beds.............75 J6
Astwood M Keyn.............74 D5
Astwood Worcs.............71 G2
Astwood Bank Worcs.....71 J3
Aswarby Lincs.............103 H4
Aswardby Lincs............118 E7
Atcham Shrops.............83 K2
Athelhampton Dorset....14 E4
Athelington Suffk.........78 E1
Athelney Somset.........25 M5
Athelstaneford
  E Loth............ 178 C3
Atherington Devon.........23 J6
Atherstone Warwks......86 C4
Atherstone on Stour
  Warwks............72 B4
Atherton Wigan.......... 113 G2
Atlow Derbys............. 100 E3
Attadale Highld.......... 210 E6
Atterby Lincs............. 117 G3
Attercliffe Sheff..........115 G4
Atterton Leics.............86 D4
Attingham Park
  Shrops............83 K2
Attleborough Norfk...92 C4
Attleborough
  Warwks............86 D5
Attlebridge Norfk.........92 D1
Attleton Green Suffk....77 G4
Atwick E R Yk.............126 F1
Atworth Wilts..............39 J7
Aubourn Lincs............. 116 F8
Auchbreck Moray....... 214 F8
Auchedly Abers.......... 217 G7
Auchenblae Abers.... 197 H1
Auchenbowie Stirlg....175 L2
Auchencairn D & G.... 146 D5
Auchencairn D & G.... 155 G5
Auchencairn N Ayrs.... 162 D4
Auchencrow Border..... 179 H6
Auchendinny
  Mdloth............ 177 H6
Auchengray S Lans.... 176 D7
Auchenhalrig Moray.... 215 J3
Auchenheath S Lans.... 164 F2
Auchenhessnane
  D & G............ 154 E3
Auchenlochan
  Ag & B............ 173 G4
Auchenmade N Ayrs.... 174 C8
Auchenmalg D & G..... 144 F4
Auchentiber N Ayrs.... 174 C8
Auchindrain Ag & B.... 182 E6
Auchindrean Highld.... 221 G5
Auchininna Abers...... 216 C5
Auchinleck E Ayrs...... 164 B5
Auchinloch N Lans..... 175 H4
Auchinstarry N Lans....175 J3
Auchintore Highld....... 191 L2
Auchiries Abers.......... 217 K6
Auchlean Highld....... 203 K5
Auchlee Abers.......... 207 G6
Auchleven Abers...... 206 C1
Auchlochan S Lans.... 164 F3
Auchlossan Abers...... 206 B5
Auchlyne Stirlg......... 184 B2
Auchmillan E Ayrs.... 164 A4
Auchmithie Angus.... 197 G7
Auchmuirbridge
  Fife............ 186 C6
Auchnacree Angus....... 196 D4
Auchnagatt Abers...... 217 H6
Auchnarrow Moray.... 204 F2
Auchnotteroch
  D & G............ 144 B3
Auchroisk Moray....... 215 H4
Auchterarder P & K.... 185 K5
Auchteraw Highld...... 202 B4
Auchterblair Highld.... 203 L2
Auchtercairn Highld.... 219 J6
Auchterderran Fife.... 186 C7
Auchterhouse Angus.... 196 B8
Auchterless Abers...... 216 D6

Auchtermuchty Fife.... 186 D5
Auchterneed Highld..... 212 D3
Auchtertool Fife......... 177 H1
Auchtertyre Highld..... 210 C8
Auchtubh Stirlg......... 184 C4
Auckengill Highld...... 231 L3
Auckley Donc........... 115 M2
Audenshaw Tamesd..... 113 K3
Audlem Ches E..........98 F4
Audley Staffs.............99 J3
Audley End Essex......76 D6
Audley End House
  & Gardens Essex......76 D6
Audnam Dudley.........84 F6
Aughton E R Yk........ 125 G3
Aughton Lancs.......... 111 L1
Aughton Lancs.......... 129 L6
Aughton Rothm........ 115 J4
Aughton Wilts.........28 E1
Aughton Park Lancs.... 112 B1
Auldearn Highld........ 213 L4
Aulden Herefs..........69 J4
Auldgirth D & G........ 154 F5
Auldhouse S Lans...... 175 H7
Ault a' chruinn
  Highld............ 200 E2
Aultbea Highld......... 219 K4
Aultgrishin Highld..... 219 H4
Aultguish Inn
  Highld............ 221 J7
Ault Hucknall
  Derbys............ 115 J7
Aultmore Moray........ 215 J4
Aultnagoire Highld..... 202 E2
Aultnamain Highld..... 222 F5
Aunsby Lincs........... 103 H5
Aust S Glos............38 E3
Austerfield Donc...... 116 A3
Austrey Warwks........86 C3
Austwick N York........ 130 E5
Authorpe Lincs........ 118 E5
Avebury Wilts...........40 C6
Aveley Thurr...........45 L4
Avening Gloucs.........39 K2
Averham Notts......... 102 C2
Aveton Gifford
  Devon............7 G6
Aviemore Highld....... 203 L3
Avington W Berk......41 G6
Avoch Highld.......... 213 G4
Avon Hants............15 L3
Avonbridge Falk...... 176 B4
Avon Dassett
  Warwks............72 E4
Avonmouth Bristl.....38 D5
Avonwick Devon.......7 G4
Awbridge Hants.......28 F6
Awliscombe Devon....12 E3
Awre Gloucs...........55 H6
Awsworth Notts....... 101 J4
Axbridge Somset......26 B1
Axford Hants..........29 L3
Axford Wilts..........40 E6
Axminster Devon......13 H3
Axmouth Devon........13 G4
Aycliffe Dur.......... 141 G3
Aydon Nthumb......... 150 C2
Aylburton Gloucs......54 E7
Aylesbeare Devon......12 D4
Aylesbury Bucks......58 D5
Aylesby NE Lin........ 126 F8
Aylesford Kent........33 J2
Aylesham Kent........35 H4
Aylestone C Leic......87 H4
Aylestone Park
  C Leic............87 H4
Aylmerton Norfk....... 106 E5
Aylsham Norfk........ 106 E6
Aylton Herefs........70 B6
Aylworth Gloucs......56 C4
Aymestrey Herefs.....69 H2
Aynho Nhants........57 K2
Ayot St Lawrence
  Herts............59 K5
Ayr S Ayrs............ 163 J5
Aysgarth N York....... 131 J2
Ayshford Devon........25 G7

Ayside Cumb........... 129 J3
Ayston Rutlnd..........88 C4
Ayton Border.......... 179 J6
Azerley N York......... 132 C5

B

Babbacombe Torbay........7 L3
Babbs Green Herts.......60 C5
Babcary Somset.........26 E5
Babraham Cambs........76 D4
Babworth Notts......... 116 B5
Backaland Ork.......... 234 d4
Backfolds Abers........ 217 J4
Backford Ches W........ 111 L6
Backies Highld......... 223 H2
Back of Keppoch
  Highld............ 199 K7
Backwell N Som.........38 C6
Baconsthorpe Norfk.... 106 D5
Bacton Herefs..........54 A2
Bacton Norfk........... 107 H5
Bacton Suffk...........78 C2
Bacup Lancs........... 122 C6
Badachro Highld....... 219 J6
Badanloch Highld...... 226 E2
Badbury Swindn........40 D4
Badby Nhants..........73 H3
Badcall Highld......... 228 C4
Badcaul Highld......... 220 D3
Baddeley Edge
  C Stke............99 K3
Baddeley Green
  C Stke............99 K3
Baddesley Clinton
  Warwks............86 B8
Baddesley Ensor
  Warwks............86 C4
Baddidarrach Highld... 224 D4
Baddinsgill Border..... 176 F7
Badenscoth Abers...... 216 D6
Badentarbet Highld.... 224 B6
Badenyon Abers........ 205 H2
Badger Shrops.........84 D4
Badgeworth Gloucs......55 K4
Badgworth Somset......26 B2
Badicaul Highld........ 210 B8
Badingham Suffk.......79 G2
Badlesmere Kent.......34 D4
Badlieu Border........ 165 K5
Badlipster Highld...... 231 J5
Badluarch Highld...... 220 C3
Badninish Highld...... 223 G3
Badrallach Highld..... 220 D3
Badsey Worcs..........71 J5
Badshot Lea Surrey....30 E2
Badsworth Wakefd..... 124 C7
Badwell Ash Suffk.....78 B2
Bagber Dorset.........27 H8
Bagby N York.......... 133 G4
Bag Enderby Lincs..... 118 E6
Bagendon Gloucs.......56 A6
Bàgh a' Chaisteil
  W Isls............ 233 b9
Bagillt Flints......... 111 H6
Baginton Warwks.......86 D8
Baglan Neath..........51 L6
Bagley Shrops.........98 B6
Bagley Somset.........26 C3
Bagnall Staffs.........99 L3
Bagshot Surrey........42 E7
Bagstone S Glos.......39 G3
Bagworth Leics........86 F2
Bagwyllydiart Herefs...54 C3
Baildon C Brad........ 123 H3
Baildon Green
  C Brad............ 123 H3
Baile Ailein W Isls.... 232 f3
Baile a' Mhanaich
  W Isls............ 233 b6
Baile Mòr Ag & B...... 180 D3
Baillieston C Glas.... 175 J5
Bainbridge N York..... 131 H2
Bainshole Abers....... 216 D7
Bainton C Pete.........89 G3
Bainton E R Yk........ 126 B1

Baintown Fife......... 186 F6
Bairnkine Border...... 167 K6
Bakewell Derbys....... 114 E7
Bala Gwynd............96 E5
Balallan W Isls........ 232 f3
Balbeg Highld......... 212 C7
Balbeggie P & K...... 186 C2
Balblair Highld........ 213 G2
Balby Donc............ 115 K2
Balcary D & G......... 146 E5
Balchraggan Highld.... 212 E5
Balchrick Highld...... 228 B4
Balcombe W Susx........32 B6
Balcomie Links Fife.... 187 K5
Baldersby N York....... 132 E4
Baldersby St James
  N York............ 132 E4
Balderstone Lancs...... 121 J4
Balderton Notts........ 102 D3
Baldinnie Fife........ 187 G5
Baldinnies P & K...... 185 L4
Baldock Herts..........75 J6
Baldock Services
  Herts............75 J6
Baldovie C Dund....... 187 G2
Baldrine IoM.......... 237 d5
Baldslow E Susx........20 F3
Bale Norfk............ 106 B5
Baledgarno P & K...... 186 D2
Balemartine Ag & B.... 188 C7
Balerno C Edin........ 177 G5
Balfarg Fife.......... 186 D6
Balfield Angus........ 196 E3
Balfour Ork........... 234 c5
Balfron Stirlg........ 174 F1
Balgaveny Abers....... 216 C6
Balgonar Fife......... 185 L8
Balgowan D & G........ 144 D6
Balgowan Highld....... 202 F6
Balgown Highld........ 218 B7
Balgracie D & G....... 144 B3
Balgray S Lans........ 165 H5
Balham Gt Lon..........44 F5
Balhary P & K......... 195 L6
Balholmie P & K....... 186 B1
Baligill Highld....... 230 C3
Balintore Angus....... 195 L5
Balintore Highld...... 223 J6
Balintraid Highld..... 223 G7
Balivanich W Isls..... 233 b6
Balkeerie Angus....... 196 B7
Balkholme E R Yk...... 125 J5
Ballachulish Highld... 191 L5
Ballajora IoM......... 237 e4
Ballantrae S Ayrs..... 152 C5
Ballasalla IoM........ 237 b6
Ballater Abers........ 205 J6
Ballaugh IoM.......... 237 c3
Ballchraggan Highld... 223 G6
Ballencrieff E Loth... 178 B3
Ballevullin Ag & B.... 188 B6
Ball Green C Stke......99 K3
Ball Haye Green
  Staffs............99 M2
Ball Hill Hants.......41 H7
Ballianlay Ag & B..... 173 H6
Ballidon Derbys....... 100 D2
Balliekine N Ayrs..... 161 L2
Balliemore Ag & B..... 182 F7
Balligmorrie S Ayrs... 152 F4
Ballimore Stirlg...... 184 C4
Ballindalloch Moray... 214 E7
Ballindean P & K...... 186 D2
Ballinger Common
  Bucks............58 E7
Ballingham Herefs......54 E2
Ballingry Fife........ 186 C2
Ballinluig P & K...... 194 F5
Ballinshoe Angus...... 196 C5
Ballintuim P & K...... 195 H5
Balloch Highld........ 213 H5
Balloch N Lans........ 175 K4
Balloch P & K......... 185 H4
Balloch W Duns........ 174 D3
Balls Cross W Susx.....31 G6
Balls Green E Susx.....32 E5
Ballygown Ag & B...... 189 K7

Ballygrant Ag & B 171 G5
Ballyhaugh Ag & B...... 188 F5
Balmacara Highld 210 C8
Balmaclellan D & G...... 154 B6
Balmae D & G 146 C6
Balmaha Stirlg............. 174 D1
Balmalcolm Fife........... 186 E5
Balmangan D & G........ 146 B5
Balmedie Abers 207 H2
Balmerino Fife............. 186 F3
Balmichael N Ayrs 162 B3
Balmore E Duns........... 175 G4
Balmuchy Highld......... 223 J5
Balmule Fife 177 G2
Balmullo Fife............... 187 G4
Balnacoil Highld.......... 226 E6
Balnacra Highld........... 210 F5
Balnacroft Abers 205 G6
Balnafoich Highld 213 G7
Balnaguard P & K........ 194 E6
Balnahard Ag & B........ 180 F1
Balnain Highld 212 C7
Balnakeil Highld........... 228 F2
Balne N York............... 124 F6
Balquharn P & K.......... 185 L1
Balquhidder Stirlg....... 184 C3
Balsall Common
  Solhll 86 B7
Balsall Heath Birm......85 J6
Balscote Oxon............72 E6
Balsham Cambs...........76 E4
Baltasound Shet......... 235 e1
Baltersan D & G 145 J3
Balthangie Abers......... 216 F4
Baltonsborough
  Somset...................26 D4
Balvicar Ag & B........... 181 M4
Balvraid Highld............ 200 C3
Balvraid Highld............ 213 K7
Bamber Bridge
  Lancs 121 H5
Bamber's Green
  Essex.....................60 F4
Bamburgh Nthumb...... 169 H3
Bamburgh Castle
  Nthumb 169 H3
Bamford Derbys 114 E5
Bampton Cumb............ 138 D4
Bampton Devon............24 E6
Bampton Oxon............56 F7
Bampton Grange
  Cumb 138 D4
Banavie Highld............ 191 L2
Banbury Oxon.............72 F6
Bancffosfelen
  Carmth...................50 F3
Banchory Abers 206 D6
Banchory-Devenick
  Abers 207 G5
Bancycapel Carmth......50 E3
Bancyfelin Carmth........50 D2
Bandirran P & K.......... 186 C2
Banff Abers 216 D2
Bangor Gwynd 109 H6
Bangor-on-Dee
  Wrexhm..................98 B4
Bangors Cnwll 9 G5
Bangour Village
  W Loth................... 176 D4
Banham Norfk 92 C6
Bank Hants.................16 C2
Bankend D & G............ 147 H2
Bankfoot P & K............ 185 M1
Bankglen E Ayrs.......... 164 C6
Bankhead C Aber 207 G4
Bankhead S Lans 165 J1
Banknock Falk............ 175 K3
Banks Lancs 120 E6
Bankshill D & G........... 155 L5
Banningham Norfk...... 106 F6
Bannister Green
  Essex.....................61 H4
Bannockburn Stirlg 175 L1
Banstead Surrey...........44 E7
Bantham Devon.............. 6 F6
Banton N Lans 175 K3
Banwell N Som............38 B8
Bapchild Kent..............34 C3

Bapton Wilts 27 M4
Barabhas W Isls......... 232 f1
Barassie S Ayrs.......... 163 J3
Barbaraville Highld 223 G6
Barbieston S Ayrs....... 163 K5
Barbon Cumb.............. 130 C3
Barbrook Devon...........23 L2
Barby Nhants..............73 G1
Barcaldine Ag & B....... 191 J7
Barcombe E Susx........19 L3
Barcombe Cross
  E Susx...................19 L3
Barden Park Kent.........33 G4
Bardfield End Green
  Essex.....................61 G2
Bardfield Saling
  Essex.....................61 G3
Bardney Lincs 117 J7
Bardon Leics...............86 F2
Bardon Mill Nthumb.... 149 K3
Bardowie E Duns......... 175 G4
Bardrainney Inver....... 174 C4
Bardsea Cumb 129 G5
Bardsey Leeds 124 B2
Bardsey Island
  Gwynd....................94 B7
Bardwell Suffk............91 L8
Bare Lancs 129 K6
Barfad D & G 145 G2
Barford Norfk..............92 D3
Barford Warwks..........72 C3
Barford St John
  Oxon 57 H2
Barford St Martin
  Wilts 28 B5
Barford St Michael
  Oxon 57 H2
Barfrestone Kent.........35 H5
Bargeddie N Lans 175 J5
Bargoed Caerph 53 J7
Bargrennan D & G....... 153 H6
Barham Cambs............89 G7
Barham Kent...............35 G5
Barham Suffk..............78 D4
Bar Hill Cambs............75 L2
Barholm Lincs.............88 F2
Barkby Leics...............87 J2
Barkby Thorpe Leics....87 J2
Barkestone-le-Vale
  Leics 102 C5
Barkham Wokham........42 C6
Barking Gt Lon............45 H3
Barking Suffk..............78 C4
Barking Riverside
  Gt Lon 45 J4
Barkingside Gt Lon......45 H3
Barking Tye Suffk........78 C4
Barkisland Calder....... 122 F6
Barkla Shop Cnwll......... 3 J2
Barkston Lincs............ 102 F4
Barkston Ash N York... 124 D4
Barkway Herts............75 L7
Barlanark C Glas......... 175 H5
Barlaston Staffs..........99 K5
Barlavington W Susx....18 C3
Barlborough Derbys ... 115 J6
Barlby N York............. 124 F4
Barlestone Leics.........86 E3
Barley Herts...............76 B6
Barley Lancs............... 122 B3
Barleythorpe Rutlnd....88 B2
Barling Essex..............46 F3
Barlings Lincs............. 117 H6
Barlochan D & G......... 146 E4
Barlow Derbys............ 115 G6
Barlow Gatesd............ 150 E3
Barlow N York............. 124 F5
Barmby Moor E R Yk... 125 J2
Barmby on the
  Marsh E R Yk......... 125 G5
Barmollack Ag & B...... 161 K1
Barmouth Gwynd........80 E1
Barmpton Darltn........ 141 H4
Barmston E R Yk......... 135 J7
Barnacarry Ag & B...... 182 E8
Barnack C Pete............88 F3
Barnard Castle Dur.... 140 D4
Barnard Gate Oxon......57 H6

Barnardiston Suffk........77 G5
Barnbarroch D & G 146 E4
Barnburgh Donc 115 J2
Barnby Suffk...............93 K5
Barnby Dun Donc 124 F8
Barnby in the
  Willows Notts......... 102 E3
Barnby Moor Notts..... 116 A5
Barncorkrie D & G...... 144 D7
Barnes Gt Lon.............44 E5
Barnes Street Kent......33 H4
Barnet Gt Lon..............44 E2
Barnetby le Wold
  N Linc.................. 126 C8
Barney Norfk.............. 106 B6
Barnham Suffk............91 K7
Barnham W Susx........18 C5
Barnham Broom
  Norfk......................92 C3
Barnhead Angus 197 G5
Barnhill C Dund 187 H2
Barnhill Moray............ 214 E3
Barnhills D & G........... 152 B7
Barningham Dur 140 D5
Barningham Suffk........91 L7
Barnoldby le Beck
  NE Lin................... 118 C2
Barnoldswick Lancs.... 122 C2
Barns Green W Susx....31 J6
Barnsley Barns........... 115 G1
Barnsley Gloucs..........56 B6
Barnstaple Devon........23 J5
Barnston Essex............61 G4
Barnston Wirral.......... 111 J5
Barnstone Notts......... 102 B5
Barnt Green Worcs......85 H8
Barnton C Edin........... 177 G4
Barnton Ches W.......... 112 F6
Barnwell All Saints
  Nhants....................88 F6
Barnwell St Andrew
  Nhants....................88 F6
Barnwood Gloucs........55 K4
Barr S Ayrs................. 153 G4
Barra W Isls................ 233 b9
Barra Airport
  W Isls.................... 233 b9
Barrachan D & G........ 145 H5
Barraigh W Isls........... 233 b9
Barrananaoil Ag & B... 182 B6
Barrapoll Ag & B......... 188 B7
Barrasford Nthumb..... 158 A7
Barrhead E Rens......... 174 F6
Barrhill S Ayrs............ 152 F5
Barrington Cambs........76 B5
Barrington Somset.......26 B7
Barripper Cnwll............ 3 H4
Barrmill N Ayrs........... 174 C7
Barrock Highld............ 231 J2
Barrow Gloucs............55 K3
Barrow Lancs.............. 121 L3
Barrow Rutlnd.............88 C1
Barrow Somset............27 G5
Barrow Suffk...............77 H2
Barrowby Lincs........... 102 E5
Barrowden Rutlnd........88 D4
Barrowford Lancs....... 122 C3
Barrow Gurney
  N Som....................38 D6
Barrow Haven N Linc.. 126 E6
Barrow-in-Furness
  Cumb 128 E5
Barrow Island Cumb... 128 E5
Barrow-upon-
  Humber N Linc 126 D6
Barrow upon Soar
  Leics 101 L8
Barrow upon Trent
  Derbys.................. 101 G6
Barry Angus 187 J1
Barry V Glam..............37 H6
Barry Island V Glam....37 H6
Barsby Leics...............87 K2
Barsham Suffk............93 H5
Barston Solhll.............86 B7
Bartestree Herefs.......69 L6
Barthol Chapel
  Abers 216 F7

Bartholomew Green
  Essex.....................61 H4
Barthomley Ches E......99 H3
Bartley Hants.............28 F8
Bartley Green Birm......85 H6
Bartlow Cambs............76 E5
Barton Cambs.............76 B4
Barton Ches W............98 C2
Barton Gloucs.............56 C3
Barton Lancs.............. 120 E8
Barton Lancs.............. 121 G3
Barton N York............. 141 G5
Barton Oxon...............57 K6
Barton Torbay............... 7 K3
Barton Bendish
  Norfk......................91 G3
Barton End Gloucs.......39 J2
Barton Hartshorn
  Bucks.....................57 M2
Barton in Fabis Notts.. 101 K6
Barton in the Beans
  Leics 86 E3
Barton-le-Clay
  C Beds...................59 H2
Barton-le-Street
  N York 133 L5
Barton-le-Willows
  N York 133 L6
Barton Mills Suffk.......91 G8
Barton-on-Sea
  Hants......................16 B4
Barton-on-the-
  Heath Warwks........56 E2
Barton St David
  Somset...................26 D5
Barton Seagrave
  Nhants....................88 C7
Barton Stacey Hants....29 H3
Barton Town Devon.....23 L4
Barton Turf Norfk....... 107 H7
Barton-under-
  Needwood Staffs..... 100 D8
Barton-upon-
  Humber N Linc 126 C6
Barton Waterside
  N Linc................... 126 C6
Barvas W Isls............. 232 f1
Barway Cambs............90 D7
Barwell Leics..............86 F4
Barwick Devon............10 E4
Barwick Somset..........26 E8
Barwick in Elmet
  Leeds 124 B3
Bascote Warwks..........72 E2
Bashall Eaves Lancs ... 121 K2
Basildon Essex............46 B3
Basingstoke Hants......29 M2
Baslow Derbys............ 114 E6
Bason Bridge Somset...25 M3
Bassaleg Newpt..........37 L3
Bassendean Border.... 167 K1
Bassenthwaite Cumb... 137 H2
Bassett C Sotn............29 H7
Bassingbourn-cum-
  Kneesworth
  Cambs...................75 L5
Bassingham Lincs....... 102 E1
Bassingthorpe Lincs... 102 F6
Bassus Green Herts.....60 B3
Baston Lincs...............89 G2
Bastwick Norfk........... 107 J8
Batchworth Herts........43 H2
Batcombe Dorset.........14 C2
Batcombe Somset........27 G4
Batford Herts..............59 J5
Bath BaNES.................39 H7
Bath BaNES.................39 H7
Bathampton BaNES.....39 H7
Bathealton Somset......25 G6
Batheaston BaNES......39 H6
Bathford BaNES..........39 H6
Bathgate W Loth........ 176 D5
Bathley Notts............. 102 C2
Bathpool Cnwll............. 5 L2
Bathpool Somset.........25 K6
Bath Side Essex..........62 F2
Bathville W Loth......... 176 C5

Bathway Somset............26 E2
Batley Kirk......................123 J5
Batsford Gloucs...........71 L7
Battersby N York..........142 D5
Battersea Gt Lon............44 F4
Battisford Tye Suffk.......78 B4
Battle E Susx 20 F3
Battle Powys..................52 F2
Battledykes Angus....196 D5
Battlefield Shrops.........83 K1
Battlesbridge Essex.......46 C2
Battleton Somset...........24 E6
Baughton Worcs..........70 F6
Baughurst Hants............41 L7
Baulds Abers.............206 B6
Baulking Oxon..............40 F3
Baumber Lincs...........117 L6
Baunton Gloucs..........56 A6
Baverstock Wilts..........28 B5
Bawburgh Norfk..........92 D2
Bawdeswell Norfk......106 C7
Bawdrip Somset...........25 M4
Bawdsey Suffk.............79 H6
Bawtry Donc..............115 M3
Baxenden Lancs........122 B5
Baxterley Warwks........86 C4
Bay Highld 208 D4
Bayble W Isls.............232 g2
Baybridge Hants..........29 K6
Baycliff Cumb............129 G5
Baydon Wilts.................40 F5
Bayford Herts................60 A6
Bayford Somset...........27 G5
Bayhead W Isls.........233 b6
Baylham Suffk...............78 D4
Baysham Herefs...........54 E3
Bayston Hill Shrops......83 J2
Baythorne End Essex...77 G6
Bayton Worcs................84 C8
Bayworth Oxon.............57 J7
Beachampton Bucks.....73 L6
Beachamwell Norfk......91 H3
Beachy Head E Susx....20 C6
Beacon Devon...............12 F2
Beacon End Essex........61 M3
Beacon Hill Notts......102 D2
Beacon Hill Surrey.......30 E4
Beacon's Bottom
  Bucks...................42 C2
Beaconsfield Bucks.....42 F3
Beaconsfield
  Services Bucks.....42 F3
Beadlam N York.........133 K3
Beadlow C Beds..........75 G6
Beadnell Nthumb......169 J4
Beaford Devon.............10 E2
Beal N York................124 E5
Beal Nthumb..............169 G2
Bealsmill Cnwll..............6 A1
Beaminster Dorset........13 L3
Beamish Dur..............151 G4
Beamish - The
  Living Museum
  of the North Dur...150 F4
Beamsley N York........131 K8
Beanacre Wilts..............39 K7
Beanley Nthumb........169 G5
Beardon Devon.............10 D7
Beare Green Surrey......31 K3
Bearley Warwks............71 L3
Bearpark Dur..............151 G6
Bearsden E Duns........174 F4
Bearsted Kent...............33 K3
Bearstone Shrops.........99 G5
Bearwood BCP..............15 K3
Bearwood Birm............85 H6
Bearwood Herefs..........69 H4
Beattock D & G............155 J2
Beauchamp Roding
  Essex...................60 F6
Beauchief Sheff 115 G5
Beaufort Blae G............53 J5
Beaulieu Essex............61 H6
Beaulieu Hants.............16 E3
Beaulieu (National
  Motor Museum)
  Hants...................16 E2
Beauly Highld 212 E5

Beaumaris IoA............109 H6
Beaumaris Castle
  IoA.......................109 J6
Beaumont Cumb........148 C3
Beaumont Essex...........62 E3
Beaumont Jersey........236 c7
Beaumont Leys
  C Leic....................87 H2
Beausale Warwks..........72 B1
Beauworth Hants..........29 L6
Beaworthy Devon........10 C5
Beazley End Essex........61 H3
Bebington Wirral........111 K5
Beccles Suffk................93 J5
Becconsall Lancs........120 F6
Beckbury Shrops..........84 D3
Beckenham Gt Lon......45 G6
Beckermet Cumb.......136 E6
Beckfoot Cumb..........147 J5
Beckford Worcs............71 H7
Beckhampton Wilts......40 C6
Beckingham Lincs......102 E2
Beckingham Notts......116 C4
Beckington Somset......27 J2
Beckjay Shrops.............83 H7
Beckley E Susx.............21 G2
Beckley Oxon...............57 K5
Beck Row Suffk............91 G7
Beck Side Cumb.........128 F3
Beckton Gt Lon............45 H4
Beckwithshaw
  N York.................132 D8
Becontree Gt Lon.........45 J3
Becquet Vincent
  Jersey...................236 c6
Bedale N York............132 D2
Bedchester Dorset........27 J7
Beddau Rhondd............37 G4
Beddgelert Gwynd........95 K3
Beddingham E Susx......19 L4
Beddington Gt Lon........44 F6
Beddington Corner
  Gt Lon...................44 F6
Bedfield Suffk...............78 F2
Bedford Bed.................74 F5
Bedgrove Bucks...........58 D5
Bedhampton Hants.......17 K2
Bedingfield Suffk..........78 E2
Bedlam N York...........132 D7
Bedlington Nthumb....159 G5
Bedlinog Myr Td...........53 H7
Bedminster Bristl.........38 E6
Bedminster Down
  Bristl....................38 E6
Bedmond Herts.............59 J7
Bednall Staffs...............99 L8
Bedrule Border...........167 J5
Bedstone Shrops..........83 G7
Bedwas Caerph.............37 J3
Bedwellty Caerph.........53 J7
Bedworth Warwks........86 D6
Beeby Leics...................87 J2
Beech Hants..................30 B4
Beech Staffs..................99 J5
Beech Hill W Berk.........42 B7
Beechingstoke Wilts.....40 C8
Beedon W Berk.............41 J5
Beeford E R Yk...........135 H8
Beeley Derbys.............114 E7
Beelsby NE Lin...........117 K2
Beenham W Berk..........41 L6
Beer Devon..................13 G5
Beer Somset.................26 B5
Beercrocombe
  Somset.................25 L7
Beer Hackett Dorset.....14 B1
Beesands Devon.............7 J7
Beesby Lincs..............118 F5
Beeson Devon................7 J7
Beeston C Beds............75 H5
Beeston Ches W...........98 D2
Beeston Leeds............123 K4
Beeston Norfk..............91 K1
Beeston Notts.............101 K5
Beeston Regis Norfk ...106 E4
Beeswing D & G..........146 F2
Beetham Cumb...........129 K4
Beetham Somset...........25 L8

Beetley Norfk.............106 A8
Begbroke Oxon.............57 J5
Begelly Pembks.............49 J6
Beguildy Powys............82 D7
Beighton Norfk..............93 H2
Beighton Sheff...........115 H5
Beinn Na Faoghla
  W Isls..................233 c7
Beith N Ayrs...............174 C7
Bekesbourne Kent........35 G4
Belaugh Norfk.............107 G8
Belbroughton Worcs....85 G7
Belchalwell Dorset........14 E1
Belchamp Otten
  Essex...................77 J6
Belchamp St Paul
  Essex...................77 H6
Belchamp Walter
  Essex...................77 J6
Belchford Lincs...........118 D6
Belford Nthumb..........169 G3
Belgrave C Leic.............87 H3
Belhaven E Loth..........178 E3
Belhelvie Abers..........207 H2
Belhinnie Abers..........215 K8
Bellabeg Abers...........205 H3
Bellanoch Ag & B........182 A8
Bellaty Angus.............195 K4
Bell Busk N York.........131 G7
Belleau Lincs..............118 E5
Bell End Worcs..............85 G7
Bellerby N York...........131 L2
Belle Vue Cumb..........148 C4
Belle Vue Wakefd......123 L6
Bellfield S Lans...........164 F3
Bellfields Surrey...........31 G2
Bell Hill Hants...............30 C6
Bellingdon Bucks.........58 F6
Bellingham Nthumb....157 L5
Belloch Ag & B............161 H2
Bellochantuy Ag & B...161 H3
Bell o' th' Hill Ches W....98 D4
Bellshill N Lans...........175 J6
Bellside N Lans...........175 L6
Bellsquarry W Loth....176 E5
Bells Yew Green
  E Susx..................33 G6
Belluton BaNES............38 E7
Belmaduthie Highld....213 G3
Belmont Bl w D..........121 K7
Belmont Gt Lon............44 E7
Belmont S Ayrs...........163 J5
Belmont Shet.............235 d2
Belnacraig Abers........205 J3
Belper Derbys.............101 G3
Belsay Nthumb...........158 D6
Belses Border..............167 J4
Belsford Devon...............7 H4
Belsize Herts................59 G7
Belstead Suffk..............78 D6
Belstone Devon.............10 F6
Belthorn Bl w D..........121 L5
Beltinge Kent................47 K6
Beltingham Nthumb....149 K3
Beltoft N Linc.............116 D1
Belton Leics................101 H7
Belton Lincs...............102 F4
Belton N Linc..............116 C1
Belton Norfk.................93 K3
Belton House Lincs......102 F5
Belton in Rutland
  Rutlnd...................88 B3
Belvedere Gt Lon..........45 J4
Belvoir Leics...............102 D5
Bembridge IoW.............17 J5
Bemerton Wilts............28 C5
Bempton E R Yk.........135 J5
Benacre Suffk...............93 K6
Benbecula W Isls........233 c7
Benbecula Airport
  W Isls..................233 c6
Benbuie D & G...........154 C3
Benderloch Ag & B.....191 H8
Benenden Kent.............33 K6
Benfieldside Dur........150 D4
Benfleet Essex..............46 C3
Bengeo Herts................60 A5
Bengeworth Worcs.......71 J5

Benhall Green Suffk.......79 H3
Benhall Street Suffk......79 H3
Benholm Abers 197 K3
Beningbrough
  N York.................133 H7
Benington Herts............59 M4
Benington Lincs..........104 C3
Benllech IoA...............109 G5
Benmore Ag & B.........173 K2
Bennan N Ayrs...........162 C5
Ben Nevis Highld........192 B3
Benniworth Lincs.......117 K5
Benover Kent................33 J4
Ben Rhydding
  C Brad.................123 H2
Benslie N Ayrs............163 J2
Benson Oxon................41 L3
Benthoul C Aber.........206 F5
Bentley Donc..............115 K1
Bentley E R Yk...........126 C4
Bentley Hants...............30 C3
Bentley Suffk................78 D6
Bentley Warwks............86 C4
Bentpath D & G..........156 B4
Bentwichen Devon.......24 B5
Bentworth Hants..........30 A4
Benvie Angus.............186 E2
Benville Dorset.............14 A2
Benwick Cambs............89 L5
Beoley Worcs................71 J1
Beoraidbeg Highld 199 L6
Bepton W Susx.............18 B3
Berden Essex................60 D3
Berea Pembks...............48 D2
Bere Alston Devon..........6 C3
Bere Ferrers Devon.........6 C3
Bere Regis Dorset.........14 F4
Bergh Apton Norfk........93 G4
Berinsfield Oxon...........41 L2
Berkeley Gloucs............55 G7
Berkhamsted Herts......59 G6
Berkley Somset.............27 J2
Berkswell Solhll............86 B7
Bermondsey Gt Lon......45 G4
Bernera Highld...........200 C2
Bernisdale Highld......208 F4
Berrick Prior Oxon........41 L2
Berrick Salome Oxon....41 L2
Berriedale Highld.......227 K4
Berrier Cumb..............137 L2
Berriew Powys..............82 D4
Berrington Shrops........83 K3
Berrington Worcs..........69 L2
Berrington Green
  Worcs...................69 L2
Berrow Somset.............25 L2
Berrow Green Worcs....70 D3
Berryfields Bucks.........58 C5
Berryhillock Moray....215 L3
Berryhillock Moray....215 L4
Berrynarbor Devon.......23 J3
Berry Pomeroy
  Devon.....................7 J4
Bersham Wrexhm........97 L3
Bersted W Susx............18 C5
Bertha Park P & K.......186 A3
Berwick E Susx............20 B5
Berwick Bassett
  Wilts...................40 C5
Berwick Hill Nthumb...158 F6
Berwick St James
  Wilts...................28 B4
Berwick St John
  Wilts...................27 L6
Berwick St Leonard
  Wilts...................27 L5
Berwick-upon-
  Tweed Nthumb......179 K7
Bescar Lancs..............120 E7
Besford Worcs..............71 G5
Bessacarr Donc..........115 L2
Bessingby E R Yk.......135 J6
Bessingham Norfk.....106 E5
Besthorpe Norfk..........92 C4
Besthorpe Notts........116 D8
Bestwood Village
  Notts..................101 K3
Beswick E R Yk..........126 C2

Betchworth Surrey........31 K2
Bethania Cerdgn..........66 D2
Bethel Gwynd.............109 G7
Bethel IoA...............108 E7
Bethersden Kent..........34 C6
Bethesda Gwynd...........109 J7
Bethesda Gwynd...........109 J7
Bethesda Pembks..........49 J4
Bethlehem Carmth.........51 K1
Bethnal Green Gt Lon....45 G4
Betley Staffs............99 H3
Betsham Kent.............45 L5
Betteshanger Kent........35 J4
Bettiscombe Dorset.......13 K3
Bettisfield Wrexhm.......98 C5
Bettws Brdgnd............36 D3
Bettws Newpt.............37 L3
Bettws Cedewain
Powys....................82 C4
Bettws Ifan Cerdgn......65 J5
Bettws-Newydd
Mons.....................54 A6
Bettyhill Highld........229 L3
Betws Bledrws
Cerdgn...................66 D4
Betws Gwerfil Goch
Denbgs...................97 G3
Betws-y-Coed
Conwy....................96 C2
Betws-yn-Rhos
Conwy...................110 C6
Beulah Cerdgn............65 J5
Beulah Powys.............67 K4
Bevercotes Notts........116 B6
Beverley E R Yk.........126 C3
Beverston Gloucs.........39 K2
Bewcastle Cumb..........156 F7
Bewdley Worcs............84 D7
Bewerley N York.........132 B6
Bewholme E R Yk.........126 E1
Bexhill-on-Sea
E Susx...................20 E4
Bexley Gt Lon............45 J5
Bexleyheath Gt Lon......45 J5
Bexwell Norfk............90 F3
Beyton Suffk.............77 L2
Beyton Green Suffk......77 L2
Bhaltos W Isls..........232 d2
Bhatarsaigh W Isls.....233 b10
Bibury Gloucs............56 C6
Bicester Oxon............57 L4
Bickenhill Solhll.......85 L6
Bicker Lincs............103 L5
Bickerstaffe Lancs.....112 C2
Bickerton N York.......124 C1
Bickford Staffs.........84 F2
Bickington Devon.........7 J2
Bickington Devon.........23 H5
Bickleigh Devon..........6 D4
Bickleigh Devon.........12 B2
Bickley Ches W...........98 D3
Bickley Gt Lon...........45 H6
Bickley N York..........134 E2
Bicknacre Essex..........61 J7
Bicknoller Somset.......25 H4
Bicknor Kent.............33 L2
Bicton Shrops............82 F6
Bicton Shrops............83 J1
Bidborough Kent..........32 F5
Biddenden Kent...........33 L5
Biddenham Bed............74 E4
Biddestone Wilts.........39 K5
Biddisham Somset.........26 B2
Biddlesden Bucks.........73 J6
Biddulph Staffs..........99 K2
Biddulph Moor Staffs....99 K2
Bideford Devon...........23 G6
Bidford-on-Avon
Warwks...................71 K4
Bielby E R Yk...........125 J2
Bieldside C Aber........207 G5
Bierley IoW..............17 G6
Bierton Bucks............58 D5
Big Balcraig D & G.....145 H6
Bigbury Devon............6 F6
Bigbury-on-Sea
Devon.....................6 F6
Bigby Lincs............117 H1

Biggar S Lans..........165 K2
Biggin Derbys..........100 D2
Biggin Hill Gt Lon......32 D2
Biggleswade C Beds......75 H5
Bigholms D & G..........156 B6
Bighouse Highld........230 C3
Bighton Hants...........29 L4
Biglands Cumb..........148 A4
Bignall End Staffs......99 J3
Bignor W Susx...........18 D3
Bigrigg Cumb...........136 D5
Big Sand Highld........219 H5
Bigton Shet............235 c7
Bilborough C Nott......101 K4
Bilbrook Somset.........25 G3
Bilbrough N York.......124 E2
Bilbster Highld........231 K5
Bildershaw Dur.........140 F3
Bildeston Suffk.........78 B5
Billericay Essex........46 B2
Billesdon Leics.........87 K3
Billesley Warwks........71 K3
Billingborough Lincs...103 J3
Billinge St Hel........112 D2
Billingford Norfk.......92 E7
Billingford Norfk......106 B7
Billingham S on T......141 K3
Billinghay Lincs.......103 J2
Billingley Barns.......115 H1
Billingshurst W Susx....31 H6
Billingsley Shrops......84 C6
Billington C Beds.......58 F4
Billington Lancs.......121 L4
Billockby Norfk.........93 J2
Billy Row Dur..........150 E7
Bilsborrow Lancs.......121 G3
Bilsby Lincs...........119 G6
Bilsham W Susx..........18 D5
Bilsington Kent.........34 D7
Bilsthorpe Notts.......101 M1
Bilston Mdloth.........177 H5
Bilston Wolves..........85 G4
Bilstone Leics..........86 D3
Bilton E R Yk..........126 E4
Bilton N York..........132 D7
Bilton Warwks...........86 F8
Bilton-in-Ainsty
N York.................124 D1
Binbrook Lincs.........117 K3
Bincombe Dorset.........14 D5
Binegar Somset..........26 E2
Binfield Br For.........42 D6
Binfield Heath Oxon....42 C5
Bingfield Nthumb.......158 B7
Bingham Notts..........102 B4
Bingley C Brad.........123 G3
Binham Norfk...........106 B5
Binley Covtry...........86 E7
Binley Hants............29 H2
Binley Woods
Warwks...................86 E7
Binnegar Dorset.........15 G5
Binniehill Falk........176 B4
Binscombe Surrey........30 F3
Binstead IoW............17 H4
Binsted Hants...........30 C3
Binsted W Susx..........18 D4
Binton Warwks...........71 K4
Bintree Norfk..........106 B7
Birch Essex.............61 M4
Birchall Staffs.........99 M2
Bircham Newton
Norfk..................105 J5
Bircham Tofts Norfk...105 J6
Birchanger Essex........60 E4
Birchanger Green
Services Essex.........60 E4
Birch Cross Staffs....100 C6
Bircher Herefs..........69 J2
Birchfield Birm.........85 J5
Birch Green Essex......61 M4
Birchgrove Cardif.......37 J4
Birchgrove Swans........51 K5
Birchgrove W Susx.......32 D7
Birchington Kent........35 J2
Birchley Heath
Warwks...................86 C5
Birchover Derbys.......100 E1

Birch Services
Rochdl................122 C8
Birch Vale Derbys......114 A4
Birchwood Lincs........116 F7
Birch Wood Somset.......25 K8
Birchwood Warrtn.......112 F4
Bircotes Notts.........115 M3
Birdbrook Essex.........77 G6
Birdforth N York.......133 G4
Birdham W Susx..........17 M3
Birdingbury Warwks......72 E2
Birdlip Gloucs..........55 L5
Birdsall N York........134 C6
Birds Edge Kirk.........123 J8
Birds Green Essex.......60 F6
Birdsgreen Shrops.......84 D6
Birdsmoorgate
Dorset...................13 K3
Birdwell Barns.........115 G2
Birgham Border.........168 B2
Birichin Highld........223 G3
Birkby N York..........141 H6
Birkdale Sefton........120 D7
Birkenbog Abers........215 L2
Birkenhead Wirral......111 K4
Birkenhead
(Queensway)
Tunnel Lpool..........111 K4
Birkenhills Abers......216 E5
Birkenshaw Kirk........123 J5
Birkhall Abers.........205 H6
Birkhill Angus.........186 F1
Birkhill D & G.........166 B6
Birkin N York..........124 E5
Birley Herefs...........69 J4
Birley Carr Sheff......115 G3
Birling Kent............46 B7
Birlingham Worcs........71 G5
Birmingham Birm.........85 J6
Birmingham Airport
Solhll...................85 L6
Birnam P & K...........195 G7
Birness Abers..........217 J7
Birse Abers............206 B6
Birsemore Abers........205 L5
Birstall Kirk..........123 J5
Birstall Leics..........87 H2
Birstwith N York.......132 C7
Birtley Gatesd.........151 G4
Birtley Herefs..........69 G2
Birtley Nthumb.........157 L6
Birts Street Worcs......70 D7
Bisbrooke Rutlnd........88 C4
Biscathorpe Lincs.....118 C5
Bisham W & M............42 D4
Bishampton Worcs........71 H4
Bish Mill Devon.........24 B6
Bishop Auckland
Dur....................140 F2
Bishopbridge Lincs.....117 G4
Bishopbriggs E Duns...175 G4
Bishop Burton
E R Yk.................126 B3
Bishop Middleham
Dur....................141 H2
Bishopmill Moray.......214 D2
Bishop Monkton
N York.................132 E6
Bishop Norton Lincs...117 G3
Bishopsbourne Kent.....35 G4
Bishops Cannings
Wilts....................40 B7
Bishop's Castle
Shrops...................83 G5
Bishop's Caundle
Dorset...................27 G8
Bishop's Cleeve
Gloucs...................55 L3
Bishop's Frome
Herefs...................70 B5
Bishop's Green Essex....61 G4
Bishop's Hull Somset....25 J6
Bishop's Itchington
Warwks...................72 E3
Bishops Lydeard
Somset...................25 J5
Bishop's Norton
Gloucs...................55 J3

Bishop's Nympton
Devon....................24 B6
Bishop's Offley Staffs...99 H6
Bishop's Stortford
Herts....................60 D4
Bishop's Sutton
Hants....................29 L5
Bishop's Tachbrook
Warwks...................72 C3
Bishop's Tawton
Devon....................23 J5
Bishopsteignton
Devon.....................7 K2
Bishopstoke Hants.......29 J7
Bishopston Swans........51 H7
Bishopstone Bucks.......58 D6
Bishopstone E Susx......19 M5
Bishopstone Herefs......69 H5
Bishopstone Kent........47 K6
Bishopstone Swindn......40 E4
Bishopstone Wilts.......28 B6
Bishopstrow Wilts.......27 K3
Bishop Sutton BaNES.....38 D7
Bishop's Waltham
Hants....................29 K7
Bishopswood Somset......25 K8
Bishop's Wood Staffs...84 E2
Bishopsworth Bristl.....38 E6
Bishop Thornton
N York.................132 D6
Bishopthorpe C York...124 F2
Bishopton Darltn.......141 J3
Bishopton Rens.........174 E4
Bishop Wilton E R Yk..134 C7
Bishton Newpt...........38 B3
Bishton Staffs.........100 A7
Bisley Gloucs...........55 K6
Bisley Surrey...........42 F8
Bissoe Cnwll.............3 K3
Bisterne Hants..........15 L3
Bitchfield Lincs.......103 G6
Bittadon Devon..........23 J3
Bittaford Devon..........6 F4
Bitterley Shrops........83 L7
Bitterne C Sotn.........29 J8
Bitteswell Leics........87 G6
Bitton S Glos...........39 G6
Bix Oxon................42 B4
Bixter Shet............235 c5
Blaby Leics.............87 H4
Blackadder Border......179 H7
Blackawton Devon.........7 J5
Blackborough Devon.....12 E1
Blackborough End
Norfk....................90 F1
Black Bourton Oxon......56 F6
Blackboys E Susx........20 B2
Blackbrook Derbys......101 G3
Blackbrook St Hel......112 D3
Blackbrook Staffs.......99 H5
Blackburn Abers........206 F3
Blackburn Bl w D.......121 K5
Blackburn W Loth.......176 D5
Blackburn with
Darwen Services
Bl w D.................121 K5
Blackcraig E Ayrs.....164 C7
Black Crofts Ag & B...182 D1
Blackdog Abers.........207 H3
Black Dog Devon.........11 J3
Blackdown Dorset........13 K2
Blacker Hill Barns....115 G2
Blackfen Gt Lon.........45 J5
Blackfield Hants........16 E3
Blackford P & K........185 J5
Blackford Somset........26 B2
Blackford Somset........26 F8
Blackfordby Leics.....101 G8
Blackhall C Edin......177 H4
Blackhall Colliery
Dur....................151 K6
Blackhall Mill
Gatesd.................150 E4
Blackhaugh Border......166 F2
Blackheath Gt Lon.......45 G5
Blackheath Sandw........85 H6
Blackheath Suffk........93 J8
Blackheath Surrey.......31 G3

Blackhill Abers............ 217 K3
Blackhill Abers............ 217 K5
Blackhill Dur 150 D5
Blackhill of
 Clackriach Abers.... 217 H5
Blacklaw D & G 165 K7
Blackley Manch 113 J2
Blacklunans P & K....... 195 J4
Blackmarstone
 Herefs................... 69 K6
Blackmill Brdgnd 36 E3
Blackmoor Hants.......... 30 C5
Blackmoor N Som........ 38 C7
Blackmoorfoot Kirk.... 123 G7
Blackmore Essex........ 60 F7
Blackmore End
 Essex.................... 61 H2
Black Mountains 53 K3
Blackness Falk 176 E3
Blacknest Hants.......... 30 D3
Black Notley Essex 61 J4
Blacko Lancs 122 C3
Black Pill Swans 51 J7
Blackpool Bpool 120 D4
Blackpool Devon........... 7 K6
Blackpool Zoo Bpool... 120 D4
Blackridge W Loth 176 B5
Blackrod Bolton........... 121 J7
Blacksboat Moray....... 214 E6
Blackshaw D & G 147 J2
Blackshaw Head
 Calder 122 E5
Blackstone W Susx........ 19 H3
Black Street Suffk 93 K6
Blackthorn Oxon........... 57 L4
Blackthorpe Suffk 77 K2
Blacktoft E R Yk.......... 125 J5
Blacktop C Aber 207 G4
Black Torrington
 Devon.................... 10 C4
Blackwall Derbys........ 100 E3
Blackwall Tunnel
 Gt Lon................... 45 H4
Blackwater Cnwll.......... 3 J3
Blackwater Hants......... 42 D7
Blackwater IoW 17 G5
Blackwater Somset....... 25 K7
Blackwaterfoot
 N Ayrs.................. 162 A4
Blackwell Cumb 148 D4
Blackwell Derbys........ 101 H2
Blackwell Derbys........ 114 C6
Blackwell Warwks 72 B5
Blackwell Worcs.......... 71 H1
Blackwood Caerph 37 J2
Blackwood D & G 154 F5
Blackwood S Lans 164 F1
Blacon Ches W 111 L7
Bladnoch D & G.......... 145 J4
Bladon Oxon 57 J5
Blaenannerch Cerdgn... 65 H5
Blaenau Ffestiniog
 Gwynd 96 A4
Blaenau Ffestiniog
 Gwynd 96 A4
Blaenavon Torfn........... 53 K6
Blaenavon
 Industrial
 Landscape Torfn...... 53 K6
Blaencwm Rhondd....... 52 E7
Blaenffos Pembks 65 H6
Blaengarw Brdgnd........ 36 D2
Blaengwrach Neath........ 52 D6
Blaengwynfi Neath........ 36 D2
Blaenpennal Cerdgn 66 E2
Blaenplwyf Cerdgn....... 80 D7
Blaenporth Cerdgn....... 65 J5
Blaenrhondda
 Rhondd................. 52 E7
Blaenwaun Carmth........ 50 B1
Blaen-y-coed
 Carmth.................. 50 D1
Blagdon N Som............. 38 D8
Blagdon Somset.......... 25 K7
Blagdon Torbay............. 7 K4
Blagdon Hill Somset.... 25 K7
Blaich Highld............. 191 K2
Blain Highld.............. 190 D3

Blaina Blae G................ 53 J6
Blair Atholl P & K...... 194 D4
Blair Drummond
 Stirlg 184 F7
Blairgowrie P & K....... 195 J7
Blairhall Fife............. 176 D1
Blairingone P & K....... 185 K7
Blairlogie Stirlg.......... 185 H7
Blairmore Ag & B....... 173 L2
Blairmore Highld........ 228 C4
Blair's Ferry Ag & B..... 173 G4
Blaisdon Gloucs........... 55 G5
Blakebrook Worcs......... 84 E7
Blakedown Worcs.......... 84 F7
Blake End Essex.......... 61 H4
Blakemere Ches W 112 D7
Blakemere Herefs......... 69 G6
Blakenall Heath
 Wsall.................... 85 H3
Blakeney Gloucs........... 54 F6
Blakeney Norfk 106 B4
Blakenhall Ches E....... 99 G3
Blakenhall Wolves........ 85 G4
Blakesley Nhants.......... 73 J4
Blanchland Nthumb..... 150 B5
Blandford Forum
 Dorset.................. 15 G2
Blandford St Mary
 Dorset.................. 15 G2
Blanefield Stirlg.......... 174 F3
Blankney Lincs.......... 103 H1
Blantyre S Lans.......... 175 J6
Blàr a' Chaorainn
 Highld................. 191 L3
Blarghour Ag & B....... 182 E5
Blargie Highld........... 202 F6
Blarmachfoldach
 Highld................. 191 L3
Blaston Leics............. 88 B4
Blatherwycke Nhants..... 88 D4
Blawith Cumb 129 G2
Blawquhairn D & G..... 154 B5
Blaxhall Suffk............ 79 H3
Blaxton Donc 116 A2
Blaydon Gatesd......... 150 F3
Bleadney Somset......... 26 C3
Bleadon N Som........... 25 M1
Blean Kent............... 34 F3
Bleasby Notts........... 102 B3
Blebocraigs Fife........ 187 G4
Bleddfa Powys............ 68 E2
Bledington Gloucs......... 56 E4
Bledlow Bucks............ 58 C7
Bledlow Ridge Bucks ... 42 D2
Blegbie E Loth.......... 178 B6
Blencarn Cumb 138 F2
Blencogo Cumb......... 147 L5
Blendworth Hants........ 30 B8
Blenheim Palace
 Oxon.................... 57 H5
Blennerhasset Cumb... 147 L6
Bletchingdon Oxon....... 57 J4
Bletchingley Surrey...... 32 B3
Bletchley M Keyn......... 58 E2
Bletchley Shrops......... 98 F5
Bletchley Park
 Museum M Keyn..... 74 C7
Bletherston Pembks..... 49 H4
Bletsoe Bed.............. 74 E3
Blewbury Oxon........... 41 K4
Blickling Norfk 106 E6
Blidworth Notts......... 101 L2
Blidworth Bottoms
 Notts................... 101 L2
Blindcrake Cumb 147 K7
Blindley Heath
 Surrey................. 32 C4
Blindwells E Loth...... 177 L4
Blisland Cnwll.............. 5 H2
Blissford Hants........... 28 D8
Bliss Gate Worcs......... 84 D8
Blisworth Nhants........ 73 K4
Blithbury Staffs......... 100 B8
Blockley Gloucs.......... 71 L7
Blofield Norfk............ 93 G2
Blofield Heath Norfk ... 93 G2
Blo Norton Norfk........ 92 B7
Bloomfield Border...... 167 J4

Blore Staffs.............. 100 C3
Bloxham Oxon............ 72 E7
Bloxholm Lincs......... 103 H2
Bloxwich Wsall........... 85 H3
Bloxworth Dorset......... 15 G4
Blubberhouses
 N York................ 132 B7
Blue Anchor Somset..... 24 F3
Blue Bell Hill Kent 46 C7
Blue John Cavern
 Derbys................ 114 C5
Blundellsands Sefton.. 111 J2
Blundeston Suffk......... 93 L4
Blunham C Beds......... 75 H4
Blunsdon St
 Andrew Swindn...... 40 C3
Bluntington Worcs....... 84 F8
Bluntisham Cambs...... 89 L8
Blurton C Stke........... 99 K4
Blyborough Lincs....... 116 F3
Blyford Suffk............. 93 J7
Blymhill Staffs........... 84 E2
Blyth Notts............. 115 L4
Blyth Nthumb.......... 159 H5
Blyth Bridge Border.... 165 M1
Blythburgh Suffk......... 93 J7
Blythe Border........... 178 D7
Blythe Bridge Staffs..... 99 L4
Blyth Services Notts.... 115 L4
Blyton Lincs............ 116 D3
Boarhills Fife........... 187 J5
Boarhunt Hants.......... 17 H2
Boarstall Bucks.......... 57 L5
Boath Highld........... 222 D6
Boat of Garten
 Highld................ 203 L2
Bobbing Kent............ 46 E6
Bobbington Staffs....... 84 E5
Bocking Essex........... 61 J4
Bocking
 Churchstreet
 Essex.................. 61 J3
Boddam Abers.......... 217 L6
Boddam Shet........... 235 c7
Boddington Gloucs...... 55 K3
Bodedern IoA.......... 108 D5
Bodelwyddan Denbgs.. 110 D6
Bodenham Herefs........ 69 K4
Bodenham Wilts......... 28 D6
Bodenham Moor
 Herefs.................. 69 K4
Bodewryd IoA.......... 108 E4
Bodfari Denbgs......... 110 F7
Bodffordd IoA.......... 108 F6
Bodham Norfk.......... 106 D4
Bodiam E Susx........... 33 K7
Bodicote Oxon........... 72 F6
Bodinnick Cnwll........... 5 H5
Bodle Street Green
 E Susx................. 20 D3
Bodmin Cnwll............. 5 G3
Bodmin Moor Cnwll...... 5 J1
Bodsham Kent........... 34 E5
Boduan Gwynd........... 94 F5
Bodwen Cnwll.............. 5 H3
Bogallan Highld........ 212 F4
Bogbrae Abers.......... 217 J7
Bogend S Ayrs.......... 163 K3
Boggs Holdings
 E Loth................ 177 L4
Boghall Mdloth........ 177 H5
Boghall W Loth......... 176 D5
Boghead S Lans......... 164 F2
Bogmoor Moray....... 215 H2
Bogmuir Abers......... 197 G3
Bogniebrae Abers...... 216 B5
Bognor Regis W Susx... 18 C6
Bogroy Highld.......... 203 L2
Bogue D & G........... 154 B6
Bohortha Cnwll............ 3 L5
Bohuntine Highld...... 201 L8
Bolam Dur.............. 140 F3
Bolberry Devon............ 7 G7
Boldmere Birm........... 85 K5
Boldre Hants............. 16 C3
Boldron Dur............ 140 C4
Bole Notts.............. 116 C4
Bolehill Derbys......... 100 F2

Bolham Devon 24 E7
Bolham Water Devon ... 25 J8
Bolingey Cnwll............. 3 K1
Bollington Ches E 113 L6
Bolney W Susx............ 31 L6
Bolnhurst Bed............ 74 F3
Bolnore W Susx........... 19 J2
Bolshan Angus.......... 197 G6
Bolsover Derbys........ 115 J7
Bolsterstone Sheff...... 114 F3
Boltby N York........... 133 G3
Bolton Bolton........... 121 L8
Bolton Cumb............ 138 F3
Bolton E Loth.......... 178 B4
Bolton E R Yk.......... 125 J1
Bolton Nthumb......... 169 G6
Bolton Abbey N York.. 131 K8
Bolton-by-Bowland
 Lancs.................. 122 B1
Boltonfellend Cumb... 148 E2
Boltongate Cumb....... 147 M6
Bolton-le-Sands
 Lancs.................. 129 K6
Bolton Low Houses
 Cumb.................. 147 M6
Bolton-on-Swale
 N York................ 141 G7
Bolton Percy N York... 124 E3
Bolton upon Dearne
 Barns.................. 115 J2
Bolventor Cnwll............ 5 J1
Bomere Heath
 Shrops................. 98 C8
Bonar Bridge Highld... 222 E3
Bonawe Ag & B......... 182 E2
Bonby N Linc.......... 126 C7
Boncath Pembks......... 65 H6
Bonchester Bridge
 Border................ 167 J6
Bondleigh Devon......... 10 F4
Bonds Lancs............ 121 G2
Bo'ness Falk............ 176 D3
Boney Hay Staffs......... 85 J2
Bonhill W Duns........ 174 D3
Boningale Shrops........ 84 E3
Bonjedward Border..... 167 K5
Bonkle N Lans......... 175 L4
Bonnington Angus...... 196 F7
Bonnington Kent......... 34 E7
Bonnybank Fife......... 186 F6
Bonnybridge Falk...... 175 L3
Bonnykelly Abers...... 217 G4
Bonnyrigg Mdloth..... 177 J5
Bonnyton Angus....... 196 B6
Bonsall Derbys......... 100 F2
Bonshaw Tower
 D & G................. 155 M7
Bont-Dolgadfan
 Powys................. 81 J4
Bont-goch Cerdgn...... 80 F6
Bontnewydd Cerdgn.... 66 E2
Bontnewydd Gwynd.... 95 H1
Bontuchel Denbgs....... 97 G2
Bonvilston V Glam....... 37 G5
Boode Devon............. 23 H4
Booker Bucks............ 42 D3
Boon Border............ 167 J1
Boosbeck R & Cl....... 142 E4
Boose's Green Essex.... 61 K2
Boot Cumb.............. 137 G6
Booth Calder........... 122 F5
Boothby Graffoe
 Lincs.................. 103 G2
Boothby Pagnell
 Lincs.................. 102 F6
Boothferry E R Yk..... 125 H5
Boothstown Salfd...... 113 G2
Boothtown Calder..... 123 G5
Boothville Nhants........ 73 L2
Bootle Cumb........... 128 D2
Bootle Sefton.......... 111 K3
Boraston Shrops......... 70 B1
Bordeaux Guern...... 236 e2
Borden Kent............. 34 B3
Bordon Hants............ 30 D4
Boreham Essex........... 61 J6
Boreham Street
 E Susx................. 20 D4

Borehamwood Herts......44 D2
Boreland D & G............155 L4
Boreraig Highld............208 C4
Borgh W Isls................232 f1
Borgh W Isls................233 b9
Borgie Highld................229 K4
Borgue D & G..............146 B5
Borgue Highld...............227 K4
Borley Essex..................77 J6
Borneskitaig Highld......218 B7
Borness D & G.............146 A5
Boroughbridge
N York......................132 F6
Borough Green Kent......33 G2
Borrowash Derbys.........101 H5
Borrowby N York...........132 F2
Borrowdale Cumb.........137 J4
Borrowstoun Falk........176 D3
Borstal Medway..............46 B6
Borth Cerdgn.................80 E5
Borthwick Mdloth........177 K6
Borthwickbrae
Border......................166 F6
Borthwickshiels
Border......................166 F6
Borth-y-Gest Gwynd......95 K5
Borve Highld................209 G5
Borve W Isls................232 d4
Borve W Isls................232 f1
Borve W Isls................233 b9
Borwick Lancs..............129 L5
Bosbury Herefs..............70 C5
Boscastle Cnwll...............8 E6
Boscombe BCP...............15 L4
Boscombe Wilts.............28 D4
Bosham W Susx.............17 L2
Bosherston Pembks......49 G8
Bosley Ches E..............113 K7
Bossall N York.............133 L7
Bossiney Cnwll...............8 E6
Bossingham Kent...........34 F5
Bossington Somset........24 D2
Bostock Green
Ches W....................112 F7
Boston Lincs................104 B4
Boston Spa Leeds........124 C2
Boswinger Cnwll..............4 F7
Botallack Cnwll...............2 C5
Botany Bay Gt Lon.........59 M7
Botesdale Suffk.............92 C7
Bothal Nthumb............159 G5
Bothamsall Notts..........116 A6
Bothel Cumb................147 L6
Bothenhampton
Dorset.......................13 L4
Bothwell S Lans...........175 J6
Bothwell Services
(southbound)
S Lans......................175 J6
Botley Bucks.................59 G7
Botley Hants.................29 K8
Botley Oxon..................57 J6
Botolph Claydon
Bucks........................58 B3
Botolphs W Susx...........19 G4
Bottesford Leics...........102 D5
Bottesford N Linc........125 L8
Bottisham Cambs...........76 D3
Bottomcraig Fife..........186 F3
Bottoms Calder............122 D6
Botusfleming Cnwll.........6 B4
Botwnnog Gwynd...........94 E6
Bough Beech Kent..........32 E4
Boughrood Powys...........68 C6
Boughton Nhants...........73 L2
Boughton Norfk.............91 G3
Boughton Notts............116 B7
Boughton Aluph
Kent.........................34 D5
Boughton Green
Kent.........................33 K3
Boughton Lees Kent......34 D5
Boughton
Monchelsea Kent....33 K3
Boughton Street
Kent.........................34 E3
Bouldon Shrops.............83 K6
Boulmer Nthumb..........169 K6

Boultenstone Abers......205 J3
Boultham Lincs............116 F7
Bourn Cambs.................75 K3
Bournbrook Birm...........85 J6
Bourne Lincs................103 H7
Bournebridge Essex......45 J2
Bourne End Bucks..........42 E3
Bourne End C Beds........74 D5
Bourne End Herts..........59 G6
Bournemouth BCP..........15 K4
Bournemouth
Airport BCP...............15 L3
Bournes Green
Sthend......................46 E3
Bournheath Worcs..........85 G8
Bournmoor Dur............151 H5
Bournville Birm.............85 J7
Bourton Dorset..............27 H5
Bourton Oxon................40 E3
Bourton Shrops.............83 L4
Bourton Wilts................40 B7
Bourton on
Dunsmore
Warwks.....................72 E1
Bourton-on-the-
Hill Gloucs................56 D2
Bourton-on-the-
Water Gloucs............56 D4
Bousd Ag & B..............189 G4
Bouth Cumb................129 H3
Bouthwaite N York.......131 L5
Boveridge Dorset...........28 B7
Bovey Tracey Devon........7 J1
Bovingdon Herts............59 G7
Bow Devon....................11 G4
Bow Gt Lon...................45 G4
Bow Ork......................234 b7
Bow Brickhill M Keyn.....74 C7
Bowbridge Gloucs..........55 J6
Bowburn Dur...............151 H7
Bowcombe IoW...............16 F5
Bowd Devon....................12 E4
Bowden Border............167 H4
Bowden Hill Wilts..........39 L6
Bowdon Traffd.............113 H4
Bower Highld...............231 J3
Bowerchalke Wilts.........28 A6
Bowermadden
Highld.....................231 J3
Bowers Staffs...............99 J5
Bowers Gifford
Essex........................46 C3
Bowershall Fife............176 F1
Bower's Row Leeds......124 B5
Bowes Dur..................140 C4
Bowgreave Lancs.........121 G2
Bowhouse D & G.........147 H2
Bowland Border............167 G2
Bowley Herefs...............69 K4
Bowlhead Green
Surrey.......................30 E4
Bowling C Brad............123 H4
Bowling W Duns..........174 E4
Bowmanstead Cumb....137 J7
Bowmore Ag & B.........170 F6
Bowness-on-
Solway Cumb...........147 L3
Bowness-on-
Windermere
Cumb......................137 L7
Bow of Fife Fife...........186 E5
Bowriefauld Angus......196 E6
Bowsden Nthumb........168 E2
Bow Street Cerdgn........80 E6
Bowthorpe Norfk..........92 E2
Box Gloucs....................55 K7
Box Wilts......................39 J6
Boxford Suffk................77 L6
Boxford W Berk.............41 H6
Boxgrove W Susx...........18 B4
Boxley Kent...................33 K2
Boxmoor Herts..............59 H6
Boxted Essex.................62 B2
Boxted Suffk.................77 J4
Boxted Cross Essex........62 B2
Boxworth Cambs...........75 L2
Boyden Gate Kent..........47 L6
Boylestone Derbys........100 D5

Boyndie Abers..............216 C2
Boyndlie Abers............217 G2
Boynton E R Yk............135 H6
Boysack Angus.............197 G6
Boythorpe Derbys.........115 G7
Boyton Cnwll...................9 J6
Boyton Suffk.................79 H5
Boyton Wilts.................27 L4
Boyton Cross Essex........61 G6
Boyton End Suffk...........77 G5
Bozeat Nhants...............74 C3
Brabourne Kent.............34 E6
Brabourne Lees Kent.....34 E6
Brabstermire Highld.....231 K2
Bracadale Highld..........208 E6
Braceborough Lincs........88 F2
Bracebridge Heath
Lincs.......................117 G7
Bracebridge Low
Fields Lincs..............116 F7
Braceby Lincs...............103 G5
Bracewell Lancs...........122 C2
Brackenfield Derbys......101 G2
Brackenhirst N Lans.....175 K5
Brackla Brdgnd..............36 E4
Bracklesham W Susx......17 L3
Brackletter Highld........201 J8
Brackley Nhants.............73 H6
Bracknell Br For.............42 E6
Braco P & K.................185 H5
Bracobrae Moray..........215 L4
Bracon Ash Norfk..........92 E4
Bracora Highld.............199 L6
Bracorina Highld..........199 L6
Bradbourne Derbys......100 D3
Bradbury Dur...............141 H2
Bradden Nhants............73 J5
Bradeley C Stke.............99 K3
Bradenham Bucks..........42 D2
Bradenstoke Wilts.........39 M4
Bradfield Devon.............12 D1
Bradfield Essex.............62 D2
Bradfield Norfk............106 F5
Bradfield Sheff.............114 F3
Bradfield W Berk...........41 L6
Bradfield Combust
Suffk........................77 K3
Bradfield Green
Ches E.......................99 G2
Bradfield Heath
Essex........................62 D3
Bradfield St Clare
Suffk........................77 K3
Bradfield St George
Suffk........................77 K3
Bradfield Southend
W Berk......................41 L6
Bradford C Brad..........123 H4
Bradford Devon...............9 L4
Bradford Abbas
Dorset.......................26 E8
Bradford Leigh Wilts......39 J7
Bradford-on-Avon
Wilts.........................39 J7
Bradford-on-Tone
Somset.......................25 J6
Bradford Peverell
Dorset.......................14 C4
Bradiford Devon.............23 J5
Brading IoW...................17 H5
Bradley Derbys.............100 E4
Bradley Hants................29 M3
Bradley NE Lin..............118 C1
Bradley Staffs................99 K8
Bradley Wolves..............85 G4
Bradley Worcs................71 H3
Bradley Green Worcs......71 H3
Bradley in the
Moors Staffs............100 B4
Bradley Stoke S Glos......38 E4
Bradmore Notts............101 L6
Bradninch Devon...........12 C2
Bradnop Staffs.............100 A2
Bradpole Dorset.............13 L4
Bradshaw Calder..........123 G4
Bradstone Devon..............9 K8
Bradwall Green
Ches E......................113 H8

Bradwell Derbys...........114 D5
Bradwell Essex..............61 J4
Bradwell M Keyn...........74 B6
Bradwell Norfk..............93 K3
Bradwell-on-Sea
Essex........................62 B6
Bradwell Waterside
Essex........................62 B6
Bradworthy Devon..........9 J3
Brae Highld.................213 G2
Brae Shet...................235 c4
Braeface Falk..............175 K3
Braehead Angus...........197 H5
Braehead D & G...........145 J4
Braehead S Lans...........176 C7
Braeintra Highld..........210 D7
Braemar Abers.............204 E6
Braemore Highld..........221 G5
Braemore Highld..........227 J3
Brae Roy Lodge
Highld.....................201 L6
Braeside Inver.............173 L4
Braes of Coul Angus.....195 L5
Braes of Enzie
Moray......................215 J3
Braes of Ullapool
Highld.....................220 F3
Braeswick Ork.............234 d4
Braevallich Ag & B......182 D6
Braewick Shet.............235 b3
Brafferton Darltn.........141 H3
Brafferton N York........132 F5
Brafield-on-the-
Green Nhants...........74 B3
Bragar W Isls...............232 f2
Bragbury End Herts......59 L4
Braidwood S Lans........175 L8
Brailsford Derbys.........100 E4
Braintree Essex.............61 J4
Braiseworth Suffk.........78 D1
Braishfield Hants..........29 G6
Braiswick Essex.............62 B3
Braithwaite Cumb........137 H3
Braithwell Donc..........115 K3
Bramber W Susx............19 G4
Bramcote Warwks..........86 E5
Bramdean Hants...........29 L5
Bramerton Norfk...........93 G3
Bramfield Herts.............59 M5
Bramfield Suffk.............93 H8
Bramford Suffk.............78 D5
Bramhall Stockp..........113 K5
Bramham Leeds...........124 C2
Bramhope Leeds..........123 K2
Bramley Hants..............41 M8
Bramley Leeds.............123 K4
Bramley Rothm...........115 J3
Bramley Surrey.............31 G3
Bramling Kent...............35 G4
Brampford Speke
Devon.......................11 L5
Brampton Cambs...........75 J1
Brampton Cumb..........138 F3
Brampton Cumb..........148 F3
Brampton Lincs............116 D5
Brampton Norfk...........106 F7
Brampton Norfk...........115 H2
Brampton Suffk.............93 J6
Brampton Abbotts
Herefs.......................54 E3
Brampton Ash
Nhants.....................87 L6
Brampton Bryan
Herefs.......................83 G8
Brampton-en-le-
Morthen Rothm.....115 J4
Bramshall Staffs..........100 B6
Bramshaw Hants...........28 F7
Bramshott Hants...........30 D5
Bramwell Somset...........26 B5
Branault Highld...........190 B3
Brancaster Norfk..........105 J4
Brancaster Staithe
Norfk......................105 J4
Brancepeth Dur...........150 F7
Branchill Moray...........214 D4
Branderburgh
Moray......................214 F1

Brandesburton
E R Yk............... **126** E2
Brandeston Suffk............**78** F3
Brandiston Norfk....... **106** D7
Brandon Dur **151** G6
Brandon Lincs **102** E3
Brandon Suffk............**91** H6
Brandon Warwks.........**86** E7
Brandon Parva Norfk **92** C2
Brandsby N York........ **133** J5
Brandy Wharf Lincs **117** G3
Bran End Essex.........**61** G3
Branksome BCP...........**15** K4
Branksome Park
BCP........................**15** K4
Bransbury Hants.........**29** H3
Bransby Lincs **116** E5
Branscombe Devon....... **12** F5
Bransford Worcs.........**70** E4
Bransgore Hants.........**16** A3
Bransholme C KuH **126** D4
Bransley Shrops..........**84** B7
Branston Leics **102** D6
Branston Lincs **117** G7
Branston Staffs **100** E7
Branston Booths
Lincs **117** H7
Branstone IoW **17** G5
Brant Broughton
Lincs **102** E2
Brantham Suffk...........**78** D7
Branthwaite Cumb **136** E3
Branthwaite Cumb **148** B7
Brantingham E R Yk.... **125** L5
Branton Donc........... **115** M2
Branton Nthumb **168** F6
Branton Green
N York **132** F6
Branxton Nthumb **168** D2
Brassington Derbys **100** E2
Brasted Kent..............**32** E3
Brasted Chart Kent........**32** E3
Brathens Abers **206** D5
Bratoft Lincs **119** G8
Brattleby Lincs **116** F5
Bratton Wilts...............**27** K2
Bratton Wrekin **84** B2
Bratton Clovelly
Devon......................**10** C6
Bratton Fleming
Devon......................**23** K4
Bratton Seymour
Somset.....................**26** F5
Braughing Herts..........**60** C3
Braunston Nhants........**73** G2
Braunston Rutlnd..........**88** B3
Braunstone Town
Leics **87** G3
Braunton Devon **23** H4
Brawby N York **134** B4
Brawl Highld.............. **230** B3
Bray W & M...............**42** E4
Braybrooke Nhants........**87** L6
Brayford Devon **23** L4
Bray Shop Cnwll **5** M2
Brayton N York.......... **124** F4
Braywick W & M...........**42** E4
Breachwood Green
Herts.......................**59** J4
Breacleit W Isls.......... **232** e2
Breaclete W Isls **232** e2
Breadsall Derbys......... **101** G5
Breadstone Gloucs........**55** G7
Breage Cnwll **3** G5
Breakachy Highld........ **212** D5
Breakish Highld......... **199** L2
Brealangwell Lodge
Highld.................... **222** C3
Bream Gloucs.............**54** E6
Breamore Hants.........**28** D7
Brean Somset.............**25** L1
Breanais W Isls **232** d3
Brearton N York..........**32** E7
Breascleit W Isls **232** e2
Breasclete W Isls **232** e2
Breaston Derbys **101** J5
Brechfa Carmth...........**66** C7
Brechin Angus **196** F4

Breckles Norfk.............**91** L5
Brecon Powys..............**53** G3
Brecon Beacons
National Park **52** F3
Bredbury Stockp......... **113** L3
Brede E Susx...............**21** G3
Bredenbury Herefs.......**69** L3
Bredfield Suffk............**78** F4
Bredgar Kent...............**34** B3
Bredhurst Kent............**46** D7
Bredon Worcs..............**71** G6
Bredon's Hardwick
Worcs.....................**71** G7
Bredon's Norton
Worcs.....................**71** G6
Bredwardine Herefs......**69** G5
Breedon on the Hill
Leics..................... **101** H7
Breich W Loth............ **176** C6
Breightmet Bolton....... **121** L8
Breighton E R Yk........ **125** G4
Breinton Herefs...........**69** J6
Bremhill Wilts.............**39** L5
Brenchley Kent............**33** H5
Brendon Devon............**24** B2
Brenfield Ag & B **172** E2
Brenish W Isls **232** d3
Brent Cross Gt Lon.......**44** E3
Brent Eleigh Suffk........**77** L5
Brentford Gt Lon **44** D5
Brentingby Leics......... **102** C8
Brent Knoll Somset.......**25** M2
Brent Mill Devon **7** G4
Brent Pelham Herts **60** C2
Brentwood Essex.........**45** L2
Brenzett Kent..............**21** K1
Brenzett Green Kent......**34** D8
Brereton Staffs............**85** J1
Brereton Green
Ches E................... **113** H8
Bressay Shet............. **235** d6
Bressingham Norfk........**92** C7
Bretby Derbys............ **100** F7
Bretford Warwks..........**86** E7
Bretforton Worcs..........**71** K5
Bretherton Lancs......... **121** G6
Brettabister Shet........ **235** d5
Brettenham Norfk..........**91** L6
Brettenham Suffk..........**77** L4
Bretton C Pete............**89** H4
Bretton Flints............. **111** K8
Brewood Staffs............**84** F2
Briantspuddle Dorset.....**14** F4
Brickendon Herts.........**60** A6
Bricket Wood Herts.......**59** J2
Brick Houses Sheff...... **114** F5
Bricklehampton
Worcs.....................**71** H6
Bride IoM **237** e2
Bridekirk Cumb.......... **147** K7
Bridestowe Devon.........**10** D6
Brideswell Abers........ **216** B6
Bridford Devon **11** J7
Bridge Kent................**35** G4
Bridgefoot Angus........ **186** F1
Bridgehampton
Somset.....................**26** E6
Bridge Hewick
N York **132** E5
Bridgehill Dur **150** D5
Bridgemary Hants........**17** H2
Bridgend Abers.......... **215** L7
Bridgend Ag & B **161** K2
Bridgend Ag & B **171** G6
Bridgend Ag & B **182** B8
Bridgend Angus **196** E3
Bridgend Brdgnd.........**36** E4
Bridgend Cerdgn.........**65** G5
Bridgend D & G.......... **165** L7
Bridgend Devon **6** E6
Bridgend Fife **186** F5
Bridgend Moray......... **215** J7
Bridgend P & K.......... **186** B3
Bridgend W Loth........ **176** E3
Bridgend of
Lintrathen Angus.... **195** L5
Bridge of Alford
Abers.................... **206** B2

Bridge of Allan
Stirlg **185** G7
Bridge of Avon
Moray.................... **204** E2
Bridge of Avon
Moray.................... **214** E7
Bridge of Balgie
P & K **193** J6
Bridge of
Brewlands Angus ... **195** J4
Bridge of Brown
Highld.................... **204** D2
Bridge of Cally
P & K **195** J6
Bridge of Canny
Abers.................... **206** C6
Bridge of Craigisla
Angus **195** K5
Bridge of Dee D & G.... **146** C3
Bridge of Don
C Aber **207** H4
Bridge of Dun Angus... **197** G5
Bridge of Dye Abers.... **206** C7
Bridge of Earn
P & K **186** B4
Bridge of Ericht
P & K **193** H5
Bridge of Feugh
Abers.................... **206** D6
Bridge of Gairn
Abers.................... **205** H6
Bridge of Gaur
P & K **193** H5
Bridge of Marnoch
Abers.................... **216** B4
Bridge of Muchalls
Abers.................... **207** G6
Bridge of Orchy
Ag & B **192** E7
Bridge of Tilt P & K..... **194** D4
Bridge of Tynet
Moray.................... **215** J3
Bridge of Walls Shet.... **235** b5
Bridge of Weir Rens.... **174** D5
Bridgerule Devon **9** H4
Bridge Sollers
Herefs.....................**69** H6
Bridge Street Suffk.......**77** K5
Bridgetown Somset.......**24** E5
Bridge Trafford
Ches W.................. **112** C7
Bridgham Norfk...........**91** L6
Bridgnorth Shrops........**84** C5
Bridgwater Somset........**25** L4
Bridgwater Services
Somset.................. **25** L4
Bridlington E R Yk...... **135** J6
Bridport Dorset...........**13** L4
Bridstow Herefs...........**54** E3
Brierfield Lancs.......... **122** C3
Brierley Barns........... **124** C7
Brierley Gloucs............**54** F5
Brierley Hill Dudley......**85** G6
Brigg N Linc.............. **117** G1
Briggate Norfk........... **107** G6
Briggswath N York....... **143** H5
Brigham Cumb........... **136** F2
Brigham E R Yk.......... **135** G8
Brighouse Calder........ **123** H6
Brighstone IoW...........**16** E5
Brighthampton Oxon.....**57** G7
Brightley Devon...........**10** E5
Brightling E Susx.........**20** D2
Brightlingsea Essex......**62** D5
Brighton Br & H **19** J5
Brighton City
Airport W Susx...... **19** G5
Brighton le Sands
Sefton................... **111** J2
Brightons Falk........... **176** C3
Brightwalton W Berk.....**41** H5
Brightwell Suffk...........**78** F5
Brightwell Baldwin
Oxon........................**41** M2
Brightwell-cum-
Sotwell Oxon..........**41** L3
Brightwell
Upperton Oxon........**42** A2

Brignall Dur **140** D5
Brig o'Turk Stirlg **184** C6
Brigsley NE Lin.......... **118** C2
Brigsteer Cumb.......... **129** K2
Brigstock Nhants..........**88** D6
Brill Bucks.................**58** A5
Brill Cnwll **3** J5
Brilley Herefs..............**68** F5
Brimfield Herefs...........**69** K2
Brimfield Cross
Herefs.....................**69** K2
Brimington Derbys...... **115** H6
Brimley Devon **7** J1
Brimpsfield Gloucs........**55** L5
Brimpton W Berk..........**41** K7
Brimscombe Gloucs.......**55** K7
Brimstage Wirral **111** J5
Brincliffe Sheff........... **115** F4
Brind E R Yk.............. **125** H4
Brindister Shet........... **235** c5
Brindle Lancs............. **121** J5
Brineton Staffs............**84** E2
Bringhurst Leics..........**88** B5
Bringsty Common
Herefs.....................**70** C4
Brington Cambs..........**88** F7
Brinian Ork............... **234** c5
Briningham Norfk....... **106** C5
Brinkhill Lincs........... **118** E6
Brinkley Cambs............**76** F4
Brinklow Warwks.........**86** E7
Brinkworth Wilts..........**40** A4
Brinscall Lancs........... **121** J6
Brinsley Notts............ **101** J3
Brinsworth Rothm....... **115** H4
Brinton Norfk............. **106** C5
Brisley Norfk............. **105** M7
Brislington Bristl..........**38** F6
Brissenden Green
Kent........................**34** C6
Bristol Bristl...............**38** E5
Bristol Airport
N Som..................... **38** D7
Briston Norfk............. **106** C6
Britannia Lancs.......... **122** D6
Britford Wilts..............**28** D5
Brithdir Caerph............**53** J7
Brithdir Gwynd............**96** B8
British Legion
Village Kent..............**33** J2
Briton Ferry Neath........**51** L6
Britwell Salome
Oxon........................**42** A2
Brixham Torbay **7** L5
Brixton Devon **6** E5
Brixton Gt Lon.............**44** F5
Brixton Deverill Wilts....**27** K4
Brixworth Nhants.........**73** L1
Brize Norton Oxon........**56** F6
Brize Norton
Airport Oxon.......... **56** F6
Broad Alley Worcs........**70** F2
Broad Blunsdon
Swindn....................**40** D3
Broadbottom
Tamesd.................. **113** M3
Broadbridge W Susx......**17** M2
Broadbridge Heath
W Susx.....................**31** J5
Broad Campden
Gloucs.....................**71** L6
Broad Carr Calder....... **123** G6
Broad Chalke Wilts........**28** B6
Broadclyst Devon......... **12** C3
Broadfield Inver **174** C4
Broadford Highld........ **199** K2
Broadford Bridge
W Susx.....................**31** H6
Broadgairhill Border **166** C7
Broad Green Worcs........**70** D4
Broadhaugh Border **179** H7
Broad Haven Pembks......**48** E5
Broadheath Traffd **113** H4
Broadhembury
Devon...................... **12** E2
Broadhempston
Devon........................**7** J3
Broad Hinton Wilts........**40** C5

Broadland Row
E Susx 21 G2
Broadley Moray............ 215 J3
Broad Marston
Worcs..............................71 K5
Broadmayne Dorset.......14 D5
Broad Meadow
Staffs..............................99 J3
Broadmoor Pembks.......49 J6
Broadoak Dorset............13 K3
Broad Oak E Susx 20 C2
Broad Oak E Susx 21 G2
Broad Oak Herefs............54 C4
Broad Oak Staffs.............35 G3
Broad Oak St Hel 112 D3
Broadsands Torbay............ 7 K4
Broad's Green Essex....61 H5
Broadstairs Kent............35 K2
Broadstone BCP 15 J4
Broadstone Shrops...83 K5
Broad Street E Susx....21 H3
Broad Street Kent 33 L2
Broad Town Wilts...........40 C5
Broadwas Worcs............70 D4
Broadwater Herts...........59 L4
Broadwater W Susx......18 F5
Broadwaters Worcs......84 E7
Broadway Pembks........48 E5
Broadway Somset...........25 L7
Broadway Worcs.............71 K6
Broadwell Gloucs............54 E5
Broadwell Gloucs............56 D3
Broadwell Oxon 56 E6
Broadwell Warwks........72 F2
Broadwindsor Dorset.....13 K2
Broadwood Kelly
Devon..............................10 F4
Broadwoodwidger
Devon 9 K6
Brochel Highld.............. 209 J5
Brochroy Ag & B........ 182 E2
Brockamin Worcs...........70 D4
Brockbridge Hants..........29 L7
Brockdish Norfk...............92 E7
Brockenhurst Hants........16 C3
Brocketsbrae S Lans.... 164 F2
Brockford Street
Suffk................................78 D2
Brockhall Nhants.............73 J2
Brockhall Village
Lancs............................ 121 K3
Brockham Surrey............31 K2
Brockhampton
Gloucs.............................56 B4
Brockhampton Hants....17 K2
Brockhampton
Herefs.............................54 E2
Brockholes Kirk............123 H7
Brocklesby Lincs............126 E7
Brockley N Som.............38 C6
Brockley Suffk................77 J1
Brockley Green Suffk....77 G5
Brockley Green Suffk....77 J4
Brockmoor Dudley 84 F5
Brockton Shrops.............83 G3
Brockton Shrops.............83 G6
Brockton Shrops.............83 L5
Brockweir Gloucs............54 D7
Brockworth Gloucs..........55 K5
Brocton Staffs.................99 L8
Brodick N Ayrs...............162 C3
Brodie Moray..................214 B3
Brodsworth Donc........... 115 J1
Brogaig Highld...............218 C7
Brokenborough Wilts...39 K3
Broken Cross Ches E ... 113 K6
Brokerswood Wilts........27 J2
Bromborough Wirral... 111 K5
Brome Suffk...................92 D7
Brome Street Suffk........92 D7
Bromeswell Suffk............79 G4
Bromfield Cumb............. 147 L5
Bromfield Shrops.............83 J7
Bromham Bed................74 E4
Bromham Wilts...............39 L7
Bromley Dudley 85 G6
Bromley Gt Lon...............45 H6
Bromley Shrops..............84 D4

Bromley Cross Bolton.. 121 L7
Brompton Medway.........46 C6
Brompton N York 141 J7
Brompton-by-
Sawdon N York......134 E3
Brompton-on-
Swale N York...........140 F7
Brompton Ralph
Somset............................25 G5
Brompton Regis
Somset............................24 E5
Bromsberrow Gloucs....70 D7
Bromsberrow Heath
Gloucs.............................55 G2
Bromsgrove Worcs........71 G1
Bromyard Herefs............70 B4
Bronant Cerdgn..............66 E2
Brongest Cerdgn............65 K5
Bronington Wrexhm....98 C4
Bronllys Powys................68 D7
Bronwydd Carmth..........50 E2
Bronygarth Shrops..........97 K5
Brook Hants 28 F8
Brook IoW........................16 E5
Brook Kent......................34 E6
Brook Surrey....................30 F4
Brooke Norfk....................93 G4
Brooke Rutlnd.................88 B3
Brookenby Lincs 117 K3
Brookfield Rens..............174 D5
Brookhampton
Somset............................26 F5
Brook Hill Hants 28 F8
Brookhouse Lancs......... 129 L6
Brookhouse Rothm 115 K4
Brookhouse Green
Ches E.......................99 J1
Brookhouses Derbys ...114 B4
Brookland Kent................21 K1
Brooklands Traffd......... 113 H4
Brookmans Park
Herts...............................59 L7
Brook Street Essex.........45 L2
Brook Street Kent..........34 C7
Brookthorpe Gloucs...55 J5
Brookwood Surrey.........42 F8
Broom C Beds..................75 H6
Broom Rothm................. 115 H3
Broom Warwks................71 K4
Broome Norfk..................93 H5
Broome Shrops................83 H7
Broome Worcs.................84 F7
Broomedge Warrtn 113 G4
Broomfield Essex............61 H5
Broomfield Kent..............33 L3
Broomfield Kent..............47 K6
Broomfield Somset 25 K5
Broomfleet E R Yk........ 125 K5
Broomhaugh
Nthumb.......................150 C3
Broom Hill Barns.......... 115 H2
Broom Hill Notts............101 K3
Broomhill Nthumb 159 G2
Broompark Dur..............151 G6
Brora Highld...................226 F7
Broseley Shrops..............84 C3
Brotherlee Dur...............150 A7
Brotherton N York........ 124 D5
Brotton R & Cl............... 142 E4
Broubster Highld........... 230 F4
Brough Cumb................. 139 H4
Brough E R Yk............... 125 L5
Brough Highld................231 J2
Brough Notts..................102 D2
Brough Shet...................235 d4
Broughall Shrops............98 E4
Brough Lodge Shet 235 d2
Brough Sowerby
Cumb.......................... 139 H5
Broughton Border........ 165 L3
Broughton Cambs..........89 K7
Broughton Flints............ 111 K8
Broughton Hants...........28 F5
Broughton Lancs........... 121 G4
Broughton M Keyn........74 C6
Broughton N Linc......... 126 B8
Broughton N York.........122 D1
Broughton N York......... 134 B5

Broughton Nhants..........88 B7
Broughton Oxon 72 E6
Broughton Salfd 113 J2
Broughton V Glam.........36 E6
Broughton Astley
Leics................................87 G5
Broughton Gifford
Wilts.........................39 K7
Broughton Green
Worcs.......................71 G3
Broughton Hackett
Worcs.......................71 G4
Broughton-in-
Furness Cumb 128 F3
Broughton Mains
D & G.......................145 J6
Broughton Mills
Cumb.......................128 F2
Broughton Moor
Cumb.......................147 J7
Broughton Poggs
Oxon...........................56 E7
Broughty Ferry
C Dund 187 H2
Brown Candover
Hants.........................29 L4
Brown Edge Staffs 99 L4
Brownhill Abers.............217 G6
Brownhills Fife 187 H4
Brownhills Wsall.............85 J3
Brown Lees Staffs 99 K2
Brownsea Island
Dorset.......................15 J5
Brown's Green Birm...85 J5
Browns Hill Gloucs.........55 K7
Brownston Devon 7 G5
Broxa N York.................. 134 E2
Broxbourne Herts............60 B6
Broxburn E Loth 178 E3
Broxburn W Loth 176 E4
Broxted Essex.................60 F3
Bruan Highld..................231 K7
Bruar P & K................... 194 C3
Bruchag Ag & B 173 J6
Bruichladdich
Ag & B.......................170 E6
Bruisyard Suffk...............79 G2
Bruisyard Street
Suffk.........................79 G2
Brumby N Linc 125 K8
Brund Staffs...................100 C1
Brundall Norfk.................93 G2
Brundish Suffk................78 F1
Brundish Street
Suffk.........................78 F1
Brunery Highld 190 E3
Brunswick Village
N u Ty 159 G7
Brunthwaite C Brad 122 F2
Bruntingthorpe Leics...87 H5
Brunton Fife 186 E3
Brunton Wilts 28 E1
Brushford Devon............11 G4
Brushford Somset..........24 E6
Bruton Somset...............27 G4
Bryan's Green Worcs...70 F2
Bryanston Dorset...........15 G2
Brydekirk D & G............ 155 L7
Bryher IoS........................ 2 a1
Brympton Somset..........26 D7
Bryn Carmth...................51 G5
Bryn Neath.....................36 C3
Bryn Wigan 112 E2
Brynamman Carmth...51 K3
Brynberian Pembks....64 F7
Bryncir Gwynd 95 H4
Bryn-côch Neath............51 L5
Bryncroes Gwynd...........94 D6
Bryncrug Gwynd.............80 E3
Bryneglwys Denbgs...97 H3
Bryneglwys &
Abergynolwyn
Slate Landscape
Gwynd.......................80 F3
Brynford Flints................ 111 G6
Bryn Gates Wigan 112 E2
Bryngwran IoA 108 D6
Bryngwyn Mons.............54 B6

Bryngwyn Powys.............68 D5
Bryn-Henllan
Pembks.....................64 E6
Brynhoffnant Cerdgn...65 K4
Brynmawr Blae G.........53 J5
Bryn-mawr Gwynd.......94 D5
Brynmenyn Brdgnd.......36 D4
Brynmill Swans..............51 J6
Brynna Rhondd 36 F4
Brynrefail Gwynd.......... 109 H8
Brynsadler Rhondd.........37 G4
Bryn Saith Marchog
Denbgs......................97 G3
Brynsiencyn IoA 108 F7
Brynteg IoA 109 G5
Bryn-y-Maen Conwy... 110 B6
Bualintur Highld............ 198 F2
Bubbenhall Warwks...86 D8
Bubwith E R Yk............. 125 H4
Buccleuch Border.......... 166 E6
Buchanan Smithy
Stirlg.........................174 E1
Buchanhaven Abers....217 L5
Buchanty P & K............. 185 J2
Buchany Stirlg................ 184 F6
Buchlyvie Stirlg.............. 184 C8
Buckabank Cumb.......... 148 C5
Buckden Cambs..............75 H2
Buckden N York............. 131 H4
Buckenham Norfk...........93 H3
Buckerell Devon.............12 E3
Buckfast Devon 7 H3
Buckfastleigh Devon ... 7 H3
Buckhaven Fife.............. 186 F7
Buckholt Mons 54 D5
Buckhorn Weston
Dorset.......................27 H6
Buckhurst Hill Essex....45 H2
Buckie Moray................. 215 J2
Buckingham Bucks.........73 K7
Buckland Bucks..............58 E5
Buckland Devon 7 G6
Buckland Gloucs.............71 J7
Buckland Herts...............75 L7
Buckland Kent................35 J6
Buckland Oxon 41 G2
Buckland Surrey.............31 K2
Buckland Brewer
Devon.......................22 F7
Buckland Common
Bucks.........................58 F6
Buckland Dinham
Somset.......................27 H2
Buckland Filleigh
Devon.......................10 C3
Buckland in the
Moor Devon 7 G2
Buckland
Monachorum
Devon 6 D3
Buckland Newton
Dorset.......................14 D2
Buckland Ripers
Dorset.......................14 C6
Buckland St Mary
Somset.......................25 L8
Buckland-Tout-
Saints Devon............. 7 H6
Bucklebury W Berk.........41 K6
Bucklers Hard Hants....16 E3
Bucklesham Suffk...........78 F6
Buckley Flints 111 J8
Bucklow Hill Ches E.... 113 G5
Buckminster Leics 102 E7
Bucknall C Stke..............99 K3
Bucknall Lincs................ 117 H7
Bucknell Oxon 57 K3
Bucknell Shrops..............83 G8
Buckpool Moray............ 215 J2
Bucksburn C Aber.......... 207 G4
Buck's Cross Devon.......22 E6
Bucks Green W Susx....31 H5
Buckshaw Village
Lancs........................ 121 H6
Bucks Horn Oak
Hants.........................30 D3
Buck's Mills Devon 22 E6
Buckton E R Yk............. 135 J5

Buckton Nthumb 169 G2
Buckworth Cambs 89 G7
Budby Notts 115 L7
Bude Cnwll.................... 9 G4
Budge's Shop Cnwll........ 5 M4
Budleigh Salterton
Devon................12 D6
Budock Water Cnwll........ 3 K5
Buerton Ches E..............99 G4
Bugbrooke Nhants........73 J3
Bugle Cnwll 4 F4
Bugley Dorset...............27 H6
Bugthorpe E R Yk.........134 B7
Buildwas Shrops 84 B3
Builth Road Powys.......68 B4
Builth Wells Powys.......68 B4
Bulbridge Wilts............28 C5
Bulford Wilts................28 D3
Bulkeley Ches E.............98 D2
Bulkington Warwks......86 E6
Bulkington Wilts..........39 L8
Bulkworthy Devon......... 9 K3
Bullbrook Br For 42 E6
Bullington Hants 29 J3
Bullington Lincs 117 H6
Bulmer Essex...............77 J6
Bulmer N York............133 L6
Bulmer Tye Essex........77 J6
Bulphan Thurr.............45 M3
Bulwark Abers............217 H5
Bulwell C Nott............101 K4
Bulwick Nhants..........88 D5
Bumble's Green
Essex.................60 C6
Bunacaimb Highld......199 K7
Bunarkaig Highld.......201 J7
Bunbury Ches E............98 E2
Bunchrew Highld........212 F5
Bundalloch Highld......210 D8
Bunessan Ag & B.........180 E3
Bungay Suffk..............93 G5
Bunnahabhain
Ag & B............171 H4
Bunny Notts 101 L6
Buntait Highld............212 C7
Buntingford Herts.......60 B3
Bunwell Norfk..............92 D5
Burbage Leics..............86 F5
Burbage Wilts..............40 E7
Burchett's Green
W & M..............42 D4
Burcombe Wilts...........28 B5
Burcott Bucks 58 E4
Bures Essex..................77 K7
Burford Oxon...............56 E5
Burford Shrops 69 L2
Burg Ag & B 189 J7
Burgess Hill W Susx.....19 J2
Burgh Suffk..................78 F4
Burgh by Sands
Cumb................148 B3
Burgh Castle Norfk.....93 K3
Burghclere Hants.........41 J7
Burghead Moray.........214 D1
Burghfield W Berk.......42 A6
Burghfield Common
W Berk.............42 A6
Burgh Heath Surrey......44 E7
Burghill Herefs.............69 J5
Burgh Island Devon..... 6 F6
Burgh le Marsh
Lincs...............119 G7
Burgh next Aylsham
Norfk...............106 F7
Burgh on Bain
Lincs...............117 L4
Burgh St Margaret
Norfk................93 J2
Burgh St Peter
Norfk................93 K5
Burghwallis Donc.......124 E7
Burham Kent...............46 B7
Buriton Hants.............30 C7
Burland Ches E.............98 E2
Burlawn Cnwll.............. 4 F2
Burleigh Gloucs...........55 K7
Burlescombe Devon....25 G7
Burleston Dorset..........14 E4

Burley Hants 16 B2
Burley Rutlnd..............88 C2
Burleydam Ches E........98 E4
Burley Gate Herefs......69 L5
Burley in
Wharfedale
C Brad.............123 H2
Burley Street Hants......16 B2
Burley Wood Head
C Brad.............123 H2
Burlton Shrops.............98 C7
Burmarsh Kent............34 E7
Burmington Warwks....72 C6
Burn N York 124 F5
Burnage Manch..........113 K3
Burnaston Derbys......100 F6
Burnbrae N Lans........176 B6
Burnby E R Yk.............125 K2
Burneside Cumb.........138 D7
Burneston N York........132 D3
Burnett BaNES............38 F7
Burnfoot Border.........166 F6
Burnfoot Border.........167 H6
Burnfoot D & G...........155 G4
Burnfoot D & G...........156 C3
Burnfoot D & G...........156 C4
Burnfoot P & K...........185 K6
Burnham Bucks...........42 F4
Burnham Deepdale
Norfk...............105 J4
Burnham Market
Norfk...............105 K4
Burnham Norton
Norfk...............105 K4
Burnham-on-
Crouch Essex.......46 F2
Burnham-on-Sea
Somset.............25 L2
Burnham Overy
Norfk...............105 K4
Burnham Overy
Staithe Norfk....105 K4
Burnham Thorpe
Norfk...............105 K4
Burnhead D & G..........154 E3
Burnhervie Abers.......206 D2
Burnhill Green
Staffs................84 E4
Burnhope Dur............150 F5
Burnhouse N Ayrs.......174 D7
Burniston N York........134 F2
Burnley Lancs............122 C4
Burnmouth Border.....179 K6
Burn of Cambus
Stirlg...............184 F6
Burnopfield Dur........150 F4
Burnsall N York..........131 J7
Burnside Angus..........196 C4
Burnside Angus..........196 E5
Burnside Fife.............186 B5
Burnside Moray..........214 E1
Burnside W Loth........176 E3
Burnside of
Duntrune Angus......187 G1
Burntisland Fife.........177 H2
Burnton E Ayrs...........163 L7
Burntwood Staffs........85 J2
Burntwood Green
Staffs................85 J2
Burnt Yates N York....132 C7
Burnworthy Somset....25 J7
Burpham Surrey..........31 G2
Burpham W Susx.........18 E4
Burradon Nthumb......168 E7
Burrafirth Shet..........235 e1
Burravoe Shet...........235 d3
Burray Village Ork......234 c7
Burrells Cumb............138 E4
Burrelton P & K.........195 K8
Burridge Devon...........13 H2
Burridge Hants...........17 G1
Burrill N York.............132 C3
Burringham N Linc....125 K8
Burrington Devon......10 F2
Burrington Herefs......69 J1
Burrington N Som......38 C8
Burrough Green
Cambs..............76 F4

Burrough on the
Hill Leics.............87 L2
Burrow Lancs.............130 C4
Burrow Somset...........24 E3
Burrow Bridge
Somset.............26 A5
Burrowhill Surrey.......42 F7
Burry Green Swans......50 F7
Burry Port Carmth......50 F5
Burscough Lancs.......120 F7
Burscough Bridge
Lancs...............120 F7
Bursea E R Yk.............125 J4
Bursledon Hants..........16 F1
Burstall Suffk..............78 D5
Burstock Dorset..........13 K2
Burston Norfk..............92 D6
Burstow Surrey...........32 B5
Burstwick E R Yk........126 F5
Burtersett N York........131 G2
Burtholme Cumb.......148 F3
Burthorpe Green
Suffk................77 H2
Burtle Somset.............26 B3
Burtoft Lincs..............103 L5
Burton BCP................15 M4
Burton Ches W...........111 K6
Burton Ches W...........112 D8
Burton Pembks............49 G6
Burton Somset...........25 J3
Burton Wilts...............39 J4
Burton Agnes E R Yk...135 H6
Burton Bradstock
Dorset...............13 L4
Burton-by-Lincoln
Lincs...............116 F6
Burton Coggles
Lincs...............103 G7
Burton End Essex........60 E4
Burton Fleming
E R Yk.............135 G5
Burton Hastings
Warwks.............86 E5
Burton Hill Wilts.........39 L3
Burton-in-Kendal
Cumb................129 L4
Burton-in-Kendal
Services Cumb 129 L4
Burton in Lonsdale
N York..............130 C5
Burton Joyce Notts......101 M4
Burton Latimer
Nhants.............88 C8
Burton Lazars Leics.....87 L1
Burton Leonard
N York..............132 E6
Burton on the
Wolds Leics.......101 L7
Burton Overy Leics......87 J4
Burton Pedwardine
Lincs...............103 J4
Burton Pidsea
E R Yk.............127 G4
Burton Salmon
N York..............124 D5
Burton's Green Essex....61 K3
Burton upon
Stather N Linc....125 K6
Burton upon Trent
Staffs...............100 E7
Burton Waters Lincs....116 F6
Burtonwood Warrtn....112 E3
Burtonwood
Services Warrtn 112 E4
Burwardsley Ches W.....98 D2
Burwarton Shrops.......84 B6
Burwash E Susx...........33 H7
Burwash Common
E Susx................20 D2
Burwash Weald
E Susx................20 D2
Burwell Cambs............76 E2
Burwell Lincs.............118 E5
Burwen IoA................108 E3
Burwick Ork...............234 c8
Bury Bury..................122 B7
Bury Cambs...............89 K6
Bury Somset...............24 E6

Bury W Susx................18 D3
Bury Green Herts.........60 D4
Bury St Edmunds
Suffk................77 J2
Burythorpe N York.....134 C6
Busby E Rens.............175 G6
Buscot Oxon................40 E2
Bush Abers.................197 J4
Bush Bank Herefs........69 J4
Bushbury Wolves.........85 G3
Bushey Herts..............43 J2
Bushey Heath Herts.....43 J2
Bush Hill Park Gt Lon...45 G2
Bushley Worcs.............70 F7
Bushmoor Shrops........83 J6
Bushton Wilts..............40 B5
Bussage Gloucs...........55 K7
Butcombe N Som..........38 D7
Bute Ag & B...............173 H4
Butleigh Somset...........26 D5
Butleigh Wootton
Somset.............26 D4
Butlers Marston
Warwks.............72 D4
Butley Suffk................79 H4
Buttercrambe N York...133 L7
Butterdean Border......179 G5
Butterknowle Dur......140 E3
Butterleigh Devon......12 C2
Buttermere Cumb.......137 G4
Buttershaw C Brad......123 H5
Butterstone P & K......195 G7
Butterton Staffs..........99 J4
Butterton Staffs........100 B2
Butterwick Lincs........104 C4
Butterwick N York......133 L4
Butterwick N York......134 F5
Buttington Powys........82 E2
Buttonoak Shrops.......84 D7
Buxhall Suffk...............78 B3
Buxted E Susx..............20 A2
Buxton Derbys...........114 B6
Buxton Norfk.............106 F7
Buxton Heath Norfk....106 E7
Bwlch Powys...............53 J4
Bwlchgwyn Wrexhm....97 K2
Bwlchllan Cerdgn........66 D3
Bwlchtocyn Gwynd......94 E7
Bwlch-y-cibau
Powys................97 J8
Bwlch-y-ffridd
Powys................82 B4
Bwlch-y-groes
Pembks..............65 H7
Bwlch-y-sarnau
Powys................82 B8
Byers Green Dur.........150 F7
Byfield Nhants............73 G4
Byfleet Surrey.............43 H7
Byford Herefs.............69 H6
Byker N u Ty..............151 G3
Bylchau Conwy...........110 D8
Byley Ches W.............113 G7
Byram N York............124 D5
Byrness Nthumb.........157 K2
Bystock Devon............12 D5
Bythorn Cambs...........88 F7
Byton Herefs...............69 G2
Bywell Nthumb..........150 D3
Byworth W Susx..........31 G7

C

Cabourne Lincs.........117 J2
Cabrach Ag & B.........171 J5
Cabrach Moray..........215 J8
Cabus Lancs..............121 G2
Cadbury Devon...........11 L4
Cadbury World Birm...85 J7
Cadder E Duns...........175 H4
Caddington C Beds......59 H4
Caddonfoot Border....167 G3
Cadeby Donc..............115 K2
Cadeby Leics..............86 D3
Cadeleigh Devon.........11 L4
Cade Street E Susx.......20 C2

Cadgwith Cnwll 3 J7
Cadham Fife 186 D6
Cadishead Salfd 113 G3
Cadle Swans 51 J6
Cadley Lancs 121 G4
Cadley Wilts 28 E2
Cadley Wilts 40 E6
Cadmore End Bucks 42 C3
Cadnam Hants 28 F8
Cadney N Linc 117 G2
Cadoxton V Glam 37 H6
Cadoxton Juxta-
   Neath Neath 51 L5
Caeathro Gwynd 95 J1
Caenby Lincs 117 G4
Caerau Brdgnd 36 D2
Caerau Cardif 37 H5
Caer Farchell
   Pembks 48 D3
Caergeiliog IoA 108 D5
Caergwrle Flints 97 L2
Caerlanrig Border 156 D2
Caerleon Newpt 37 M3
Caernarfon Gwynd 108 F8
Caernarfon Castle
   Gwynd 108 F8
Caerphilly Caerph 37 J3
Caersws Powys 82 B5
Caerwedros Cerdgn 65 L4
Caerwent Mons 38 C3
Caerwys Flints 110 F6
Caio Carmth 66 F6
Cairinis W Isls 233 c6
Cairnbaan Ag & B 172 E1
Cairnbulg Abers 217 J2
Cairncross Border 179 J5
Cairncurran Inver 174 C4
Cairndow Ag & B 183 H5
Cairneyhill Fife 176 E2
Cairngarroch D & G 144 C5
Cairngorms
   National Park 204 C5
Cairn Lodge
   Services S Lans .. 165 G3
Cairnorrie Abers 217 G6
Cairnryan D & G 144 C2
Cairnty Moray 215 H4
Caister-on-Sea
   Norfk 93 L2
Caistor Lincs 117 J2
Caistor St Edmund
   Norfk 92 F3
Calanais W Isls 232 e2
Calbourne IoW 16 E5
Calcoed Flints 111 G6
Calcot Gloucs 56 C6
Calcot Row W Berk 42 A6
Calcots Moray 215 G2
Caldbeck Cumb 148 B6
Caldecote Cambs 75 L3
Caldecote Cambs 89 G5
Caldecott Nhants 74 E2
Caldecott Oxon 41 J2
Caldecott Rutlnd 88 C5
Calderbank N Lans 175 K5
Calder Bridge Cumb 136 E6
Caldercruix N Lans 175 L5
Calder Grove Wakefd .. 123 L6
Caldermill S Lans 164 D2
Calder Vale Lancs 121 G2
Calderwood S Lans 175 H7
Caldey Island
   Pembks 49 K7
Caldicot Mons 38 C3
Caldmore Wsall 85 H4
Caldwell N York 140 E5
Calf of Man IoM 237 a7
Calfsound Ork 234 d4
Calgary Ag & B 189 J6
Califer Moray 214 D3
California Falk 176 B3
California Norfk 93 K1
Calke Derbys 101 G7
Calke Abbey Derbys 101 G7
Callakille Highld 209 L4
Callander Stirlg 184 D5
Callanish W Isls 232 e2

Callestick Cnwll 3 K2
Calligarry Highld 199 K5
Callington Cnwll 6 A3
Callow Herefs 69 J7
Callow End Worcs 70 E4
Callow Hill Wilts 40 B4
Calmore Hants 29 G7
Calmsden Gloucs 56 B6
Calne Wilts 39 M6
Calshot Hants 16 F3
Calstock Cnwll 6 C3
Calstone Wellington
   Wilts 40 B6
Calthorpe Norfk 106 E6
Calthorpe Street
   Norfk 107 J7
Calthwaite Cumb 148 E6
Calton Staffs 100 C3
Calveley Ches E 98 E2
Calver Derbys 114 E6
Calverhall Shrops 98 E5
Calverleigh Devon 11 L3
Calverley Leeds 123 J3
Calverton M Keyn 73 L6
Calverton Notts 101 L3
Calvine P & K 194 C3
Calzeat Border 165 L3
Cam Gloucs 55 H7
Camasachoirce
   Highld 190 F4
Camasine Highld 190 F4
Camas Luinie Highld .. 210 E8
Camastianavaig
   Highld 209 H6
Camault Muir Highld ... 212 D6
Camber E Susx 21 J2
Camberley Surrey 42 E7
Camberwell Gt Lon 44 F5
Camblesforth N York .. 124 F5
Cambo Nthumb 158 C5
Camborne Cnwll 3 H4
Camborne &
   Redruth Mining
   District Cnwll 3 H4
Cambourne Cambs 75 K3
Cambridge Cambs 76 C3
Cambridge Gloucs 55 H7
Cambridge Airport
   Cambs 76 C3
Cambrose Cnwll 3 H3
Cambus Clacks 185 H8
Cambusavie Highld 223 G3
Cambusbarron
   Stirlg 185 G8
Cambuskenneth
   Stirlg 185 G8
Cambuslang S Lans 175 H6
Cambus o' May
   Abers 205 J5
Cambuswallace
   S Lans 165 K2
Camden Town Gt Lon ... 44 F4
Cameley BaNES 38 E8
Camelford Cnwll 8 E7
Camelon Falk 176 B3
Camerory Highld 214 C7
Camerton BaNES 39 G8
Camerton Cumb 136 E2
Camghouran P & K 193 J5
Camieston Border 167 J4
Cammachmore
   Abers 207 G6
Cammeringham
   Lincs 116 F5
Camore Highld 223 G4
Campbeltown
   Ag & B 161 J5
Campbeltown
   Airport Ag & B 161 H5
Cample D & G 154 F4
Campmuir P & K 195 K8
Camps W Loth 176 E5
Campsall Donc 124 E7
Campsea Ash Suffk 79 G4
Campton C Beds 75 G6
Camptown Border 167 K6
Camrose Pembks 48 F4
Camserney P & K 194 C6

Camusnagaul Highld ... 191 L2
Camusnagaul Highld ... 220 D4
Camusteel Highld 209 L6
Camusterrach
   Highld 209 L6
Canada Hants 28 F7
Candacraig Abers 205 H5
Candlesby Lincs 118 F7
Candy Mill Border 165 L2
Cane End Oxon 42 B4
Canewdon Essex 46 E2
Canford Cliffs BCP 15 K5
Canford Heath BCP 15 J4
Canisbay Highld 231 L2
Canley Covtry 86 C7
Cann Dorset 27 K7
Canna Highld 198 C4
Cann Common
   Dorset 27 K7
Cannich Highld 211 L7
Cannington Somset 25 K4
Canning Town Gt Lon ... 45 H4
Cannock Staffs 85 H2
Cannock Chase
   Staffs 99 M8
Cannon Bridge
   Herefs 69 H6
Canonbie D & G 156 C6
Canon Frome Herefs 70 B5
Canon Pyon Herefs 69 J5
Canons Ashby
   Nhants 73 H4
Canonstown Cnwll 2 F4
Canterbury Kent 34 F3
Canterbury
   Cathedral Kent 34 F3
Cantley Norfk 93 H3
Canton Cardif 37 J5
Cantraywood Highld ... 213 J5
Cantsfield Lancs 130 C5
Canvey Island Essex 46 D4
Canwick Lincs 117 G7
Canworthy Water
   Cnwll 9 G6
Caol Highld 191 L2
Caolas Scalpaigh
   W Isls 232 e4
Caoles Ag & B 188 D6
Caonich Highld 201 G6
Capel Kent 33 H4
Capel Surrey 31 K4
Capel Bangor Cerdgn ... 80 E7
Capel Coch IoA 108 F5
Capel Curig Conwy 96 A2
Capel Dewi Carmth 50 F2
Capel Dewi Cerdgn 66 B6
Capel-Dewi Cerdgn 80 E6
Capel Garmon Conwy 96 C2
Capel Hendre Carmth ... 51 H4
Capel Iwan Carmth 65 J7
Capel-le-Ferne Kent ... 35 H6
Capelles Guern 236 d2
Capel Parc IoA 108 F4
Capel St Andrew
   Suffk 79 H5
Capel St Mary Suffk ... 78 C6
Capel Seion Cerdgn 80 E7
Capelulo Conwy 109 L6
Capenhurst Ches W 111 K6
Cape Wrath Highld 228 D1
Capheaton Nthumb 158 C6
Caplaw E Rens 174 E6
Cappercleuch
   Border 166 C5
Capton Devon 7 J5
Caputh P & K 195 H7
Caradon Mining
   District Cnwll 5 L2
Carbeth Stirlg 174 F3
Carbis Bay Cnwll 2 F4
Carbost Highld 208 F5
Carbost Highld 208 F7
Carbrook Sheff 115 G4
Carbrooke Norfk 91 L3
Car Colston Notts 102 B4
Carcroft Donc 124 E8
Cardenden Fife 186 C7
Cardhu Moray 214 F5

Cardiff Cardif 37 J5
Cardiff Airport
   V Glam 37 G6
Cardiff Gate
   Services Cardif 37 K4
Cardiff West
   Services Cardif 37 H4
Cardigan Cerdgn 65 G5
Cardington Bed 74 F5
Cardington Shrops 83 K4
Cardinham Cnwll 5 H3
Cardrain D & G 144 D8
Cardrona Border 166 D2
Cardross Ag & B 174 C3
Cardryne D & G 144 D7
Cardurnock Cumb 147 L3
Careby Lincs 88 E1
Careston Angus 196 E4
Carew Pembks 49 H6
Carew Cheriton
   Pembks 49 H6
Carew Newton
   Pembks 49 H6
Carey Herefs 54 E2
Carfin N Lans 175 K6
Carfraemill Border 178 B7
Cargate Green Norfk 93 H2
Cargenbridge D & G 155 G7
Cargill P & K 195 J8
Cargo Cumb 148 C3
Cargreen Cnwll 6 C4
Carham Nthumb 168 B2
Carhampton Somset 24 F3
Carharrack Cnwll 3 J3
Carie P & K 193 K5
Carinish W Isls 233 c6
Carisbrooke IoW 16 F5
Cark Cumb 129 H4
Carkeel Cnwll 6 B4
Càrlabhagh W Isls 232 e2
Carlbury Darltn 140 F4
Carlby Lincs 88 F2
Carleen Cnwll 3 G5
Carleton Forehoe
   Norfk 92 C3
Carleton-in-Craven
   N York 122 E1
Carleton Rode Norfk ... 92 D5
Carleton St Peter
   Norfk 93 H3
Carlincraig Abers 216 D5
Carlingcott BaNES 39 G8
Carlisle Cumb 148 D4
Carlisle Lake
   District Airport
   Cumb 148 E3
Carlops Border 177 G6
Carloway W Isls 232 e2
Carlton Barns 124 B7
Carlton Bed 74 D4
Carlton Cambs 76 F4
Carlton Leeds 123 L5
Carlton Leics 86 E3
Carlton N York 124 F5
Carlton N York 131 K3
Carlton N York 133 J3
Carlton Notts 101 L4
Carlton S on T 141 J3
Carlton Suffk 79 H2
Carlton Colville Suffk ... 93 K5
Carlton Curlieu Leics ... 87 K4
Carlton Green Cambs ... 76 F4
Carlton Husthwaite
   N York 133 G4
Carlton-in-
   Cleveland N York 142 B6
Carlton in Lindrick
   Notts 115 L5
Carlton-le-
   Moorland Lincs 102 E2
Carlton Miniott
   N York 132 F4
Carlton-on-Trent
   Notts 116 D8
Carlton Scroop
   Lincs 102 F4
Carluke S Lans 175 L7
Carmacoup S Lans 164 F4

Carmarthen Carmth 50 E2
Carmel Carmth 51 H3
Carmel Flints 111 G6
Carmel Gwynd 95 H2
Carmichael S Lans 165 H2
Carmunnock C Glas 175 G6
Carmyle C Glas 175 H6
Carmyllie Angus.........196 E7
Carnaby E R Yk 135 H6
Carnbee Fife.............187 J6
Carnbo P & K 185 L6
Carn Brea Cnwll 3 H3
Carnbrogie Abers........216 F8
Carndu Highld............210 D8
Carnduff S Lans 164 D1
Carnell E Ayrs 163 L3
Carnforth Lancs 129 K5
Carn-gorm Highld 200 E2
Carnhell Green Cnwll......3 G4
Carnie Abers.............206 F4
Carnkie Cnwll 3 H4
Carnkie Cnwll 3 J4
Carno Powys.............81 K4
Carnock Fife............176 E1
Carnon Downs Cnwll.......4 C7
Carnousie Abers.........216 C4
Carnoustie Angus........187 J1
Carnwath S Lans 165 J1
Carol Green Solhll........86 C7
Carperby N York........131 J2
Carradale Ag & B 161 K2
Carradale Village
  Ag & B.................161 K2
Carrbridge Highld........203 L2
Carrefour Jersey.........236 c6
Carreglefn IoA............108 E4
Carr Gate Wakefd.......123 L5
Carrhouse N Linc 116 C1
Carrick Ag & B 172 F2
Carrick Castle
  Ag & B.................183 H8
Carriden Falk............176 D3
Carrington Mdloth.......177 J6
Carrington Traffd........113 H3
Carrog Denbgs..........97 H4
Carron Falk..............176 B2
Carron Moray............214 F6
Carronbridge D & G.....154 F3
Carron Bridge Stirlg....175 K2
Carronshore Falk 176 B2
Carr Shield Nthumb.....149 K5
Carrutherstown
  D & G..................155 J7
Carruth House Inver....174 C5
Carrville Dur.............151 H6
Carsaig Ag & B.........181 H3
Carseriggan D & G......145 G2
Carsethorn D & G.......147 H3
Carshalton Gt Lon.........44 F6
Carsington Derbys.......100 E2
Carskey Ag & B.........161 H7
Carsluith D & G.........145 K4
Carsphairn D & G 153 L4
Carstairs S Lans 165 H1
Carstairs Junction
  S Lans.................165 J1
Carterton Oxon 56 F6
Carthew Cnwll..............4 F5
Carthorpe N York.......132 D3
Cartland S Lans 165 G1
Cartmel Cumb...........129 H4
Carway Carmth 50 F4
Cashe's Green Gloucs...55 J6
Cassington Oxon 57 J5
Cassop Dur.............151 J7
Castel Guern............236 c3
Casterton Cumb 130 C4
Castle Acre Norfk.........91 J1
Castle Ashby Nhants.....74 C3
Castlebay W Isls.........233 b9
Castle Bolton N York...131 J2
Castle Bromwich
  Solhll..................85 K5
Castle Bytham Lincs...103 G8
Castlebythe Pembks.....49 H2
Castle Caereinion
  Powys..................82 D3
Castle Camps Cambs...76 F6

Castle Carrock
  Cumb..................148 F4
Castlecary N Lans.......175 K3
Castle Cary Somset.......26 F5
Castle Combe Wilts.......39 J5
Castlecraig Highld.......223 H7
Castle Donington
  Leics..................101 H6
Castle Douglas
  D & G..................146 D3
Castle Eaton Swindn......40 C2
Castle Eden Dur.........151 K7
Castleford Wakefd......124 C5
Castle Frome Herefs 70 C5
Castle Gresley
  Derbys.................100 F8
Castle Hedingham
  Essex..................77 H7
Castlehill Border..........166 C3
Castlehill Highld..........231 H2
Castle Hill Suffk.........78 D5
Castlehill W Duns.......174 D3
Castle Howard
  N York.................133 L5
Castle Kennedy
  D & G..................144 D3
Castle Lachlan
  Ag & B.................182 E7
Castlemartin Pembks.....48 F7
Castlemilk C Glas 175 G6
Castlemorton Worcs......70 E6
Castlemorton
  Common Worcs 70 E6
Castle O'er D & G........156 A4
Castle Rising Norfk......105 G2
Castleside Dur..........150 D5
Castle Stuart Highld....213 H4
Castlethorpe M Keyn 74 B5
Castleton Ag & B........172 E2
Castleton Border.........156 E4
Castleton Derbys.........114 D5
Castleton N York........142 E5
Castleton Newpt.........37 K4
Castleton Rochdl........122 D7
Castletown Highld.......231 H3
Castletown IoM.........237 b7
Castletown Sundld......151 J4
Castley N York.........123 K2
Caston Norfk.............91 L4
Castor C Pete............89 G4
Catacol N Ayrs.........172 F7
Catcliffe Rothm.........115 H4
Catcomb Wilts............40 A5
Catcott Somset...........26 B4
Caterham Surrey.........32 C3
Catfield Norfk...........107 H7
Catford Gt Lon...........45 G5
Catforth Lancs...........121 G4
Cathcart C Glas 175 G6
Cathedine Powys.........53 H3
Catherington Hants......30 B8
Catherston
  Leweston Dorset 13 J4
Catisfield Hants..........17 G2
Catlodge Highld.........202 F6
Catmere End Essex......76 C6
Catmore W Berk..........41 J4
Caton Lancs.............129 L6
Caton Green Lancs......129 L6
Catrine E Ayrs...........164 B4
Catsfield E Susx..........20 E3
Catsgore Somset..........26 D6
Catshill Worcs............85 G8
Cattadale Ag & B........161 H7
Cattal N York...........133 G8
Cattawade Suffk.........62 D2
Catterall Lancs...........121 G3
Catterick N York........141 G7
Catterick Bridge
  N York.................141 G7
Catterick Garrison
  N York.................140 F7
Catterlen Cumb.........148 E7
Catterline Abers.........197 L2
Catterton N York........124 D2
Catteshall Surrey.........31 G3
Catthorpe Leics..........87 G7
Cattistock Dorset.........14 B3

Catton N York...........132 E4
Catton Nthumb..........149 L4
Catwick E R Yk.........126 E2
Catworth Cambs 88 F8
Caudle Green Gloucs....55 L6
Caulcott Oxon............57 K3
Cauldcots Angus........197 G6
Cauldhame Stirlg........184 E8
Cauldmill Border 167 H6
Cauldon Staffs..........100 B3
Cauldwell Derbys..........86 B1
Caulkerbush D & G......147 G4
Caulside D & G..........156 D6
Caundle Marsh
  Dorset..................27 G8
Caunton Notts..........102 C1
Causeway Bank D & G...145 J3
Causeway End Essex......61 G4
Causewayend S Lans...165 K3
Causewayhead Stirlg...185 G7
Causeyend Abers........207 H2
Causey Park Bridge
  Nthumb.................158 F3
Cavendish Suffk..........77 J5
Cavenham Suffk..........77 H1
Caversfield Oxon.........57 L3
Caversham Readg.........42 B5
Caverswall Staffs.........99 L4
Caverton Mill Border ...167 M4
Cawdor Highld..........213 K4
Cawood N York..........124 E3
Cawsand Cnwll.............6 C5
Cawston Norfk..........106 D7
Cawthorne Barns........123 K8
Caxton Cambs...........75 K3
Caynham Shrops.........83 K8
Caythorpe Lincs.........102 F3
Caythorpe Notts.........102 B4
Cayton N York..........135 G3
Ceannabeinne
  Highld.................228 F3
Ceann a Bhaigh
  W Isls.................233 b6
Ceannacroc Lodge
  Highld.................201 K3
Cearsiadar W Isls.......232 f3
Cefn Newpt.............37 L3
Cefn-brith Conwy.........96 E3
Cefn-bryn-brain
  Carmth.................51 L3
Cefn-coed-y-
  cymmer Myr Td......53 G6
Cefn Cribwr Brdgnd......36 D4
Cefneithin Carmth......51 G3
Cefngorwydd Powys......67 J5
Cefn-mawr Wrexhm......97 L4
Cefn-y-pant Carmth......49 K3
Cellardyke Fife.........187 J6
Cellarhead Staffs.........99 L3
Cemaes IoA............108 E3
Cemmaes Powys.........81 H3
Cemmaes Road
  Powys..................81 H3
Cenarth Cerdgn..........65 J6
Ceres Fife..............186 F5
Cerne Abbas Dorset......14 C3
Cerney Wick Gloucs......40 B2
Cerrigydrudion
  Conwy..................96 E3
Ceunant Gwynd..........95 J1
Chaceley Gloucs.........55 J2
Chacewater Cnwll..........3 K3
Chackmore Bucks.........73 K7
Chacombe Nhants.........72 F5
Chadbury Worcs..........71 H5
Chadderton Oldham......113 K1
Chaddesden C Derb...101 G5
Chaddesley Corbett
  Worcs..................84 F8
Chaddlehanger
  Devon..................6 C1
Chaddleworth
  W Berk.................41 H5
Chadlington Oxon.........57 G4
Chadshunt Warwks......72 D4
Chadwell Leics..........102 C7
Chadwell Heath
  Gt Lon.................45 J3

Chadwell St Mary
  Thurr..................45 M4
Chadwick Worcs.........70 E2
Chadwick End Solhll......86 B8
Chaffcombe Somset......13 J1
Chafford Hundred
  Thurr..................45 L4
Chagford Devon.........11 G7
Chailey E Susx.........19 K2
Chainhurst Kent.........33 J4
Chaldon Surrey.........32 B3
Chaldon Herring
  Dorset..................14 E5
Chale IoW..............16 F6
Chale Green IoW.........16 F6
Chalfont Common
  Bucks..................43 G3
Chalfont St Giles
  Bucks..................43 G2
Chalfont St Peter
  Bucks..................43 G3
Chalford Gloucs.........55 K7
Chalford Wilts..........27 K2
Chalgrove Oxon.........41 M2
Chalk Kent..............46 A5
Chalkwell Kent..........34 B2
Challacombe Devon......23 L3
Challoch D & G.........145 H2
Challock Kent...........34 D5
Chalton C Beds.........59 G3
Chalton Hants..........30 B7
Chalvey Slough.........42 F4
Chalvington E Susx......20 B4
Chandler's Cross
  Herts..................43 H2
Chandler's Ford
  Hants..................29 H7
Channel Tunnel
  Terminal Kent 35 G6
Chantry Somset.........27 G3
Chantry Suffk..........78 D5
Chapel Fife............186 D8
Chapel Allerton
  Leeds..................123 L3
Chapel Allerton
  Somset.................26 B2
Chapel Amble Cnwll......4 F2
Chapel Brampton
  Nhants.................73 K2
Chapel Chorlton
  Staffs..................99 J5
Chapelend Way
  Essex..................77 G6
Chapel-en-le-Frith
  Derbys.................114 B5
Chapel Green
  Warwks.................72 F3
Chapel Haddlesey
  N York.................124 E5
Chapelhall N Lans 175 K5
Chapel Hill Abers......217 K7
Chapel Hill Lincs........103 K2
Chapel Hill N York......123 L2
Chapelhope Border......166 C5
Chapelknowe D & G....156 B7
Chapel Lawn Shrops.....82 F7
Chapel-le-Dale
  N York.................130 E4
Chapel Leigh
  Somset.................25 H5
Chapel of Garioch
  Abers..................206 D1
Chapel Rossan
  D & G..................144 D6
Chapel Row W Berk......41 L6
Chapel St Leonards
  Lincs..................119 H6
Chapel Stile Cumb......137 K6
Chapelton Abers.........207 G6
Chapelton Angus........197 G6
Chapelton Devon.........23 J6
Chapelton S Lans.......175 J8
Chapeltown Bl w D......121 L7
Chapeltown Moray......204 F2
Chapeltown Sheff......115 G3
Chapmanslade Wilts...27 J2
Chapmans Well
  Devon..................9 J6

Chapmore End Herts 60 B5
Chappel Essex 61 L3
Chard Somset 13 H2
Chard Junction
  Somset 13 J2
Chardleigh Green
  Somset 13 H1
Chardstock Devon 13 H2
Charfield S Glos 39 G3
Charing Kent 34 C5
Charingworth Gloucs 71 L6
Charlbury Oxon 57 G4
Charlcombe BaNES 39 H6
Charlcutt Wilts 39 M5
Charlecote Warwks 72 C3
Charlemont Sandw 85 H5
Charles Devon 23 L5
Charleston Angus 196 C7
Charlestown C Aber 207 H5
Charlestown C Brad 123 H3
Charlestown Calder 122 E5
Charlestown Cnwll 5 G5
Charlestown Cnwll 5 G5
Charlestown Fife 176 E2
Charlestown Highld 213 G5
Charlestown Highld 219 J6
Charlestown Salfd 113 J2
Charlestown of
  Aberlour Moray 215 G5
Charles Tye Suffk 78 B4
Charlesworth Derbys 114 A3
Charlinch Somset 25 K4
Charlottetown Fife 186 E5
Charlton Gt Lon 45 H4
Charlton Nhants 73 G7
Charlton Nthumb 157 K5
Charlton Oxon 41 H3
Charlton Somset 25 L6
Charlton Somset 27 G2
Charlton W Susx 18 B3
Charlton Wilts 27 K6
Charlton Wilts 39 L3
Charlton Worcs 71 H5
Charlton Wrekin 83 L2
Charlton Abbots
  Gloucs 56 B3
Charlton Adam
  Somset 26 D5
Charlton All Saints
  Wilts 28 D6
Charlton Down
  Dorset 14 D4
Charlton
  Horethorne
  Somset 26 F6
Charlton Kings
  Gloucs 55 L4
Charlton Mackrell
  Somset 26 D5
Charlton Marshall
  Dorset 15 G2
Charlton Musgrove
  Somset 27 G5
Charlton-on-
  Otmoor Oxon 57 K5
Charlton on the Hill
  Dorset 15 G2
Charlton St Peter
  Wilts 28 C1
Charlwood Hants 30 A5
Charlwood Surrey 31 L3
Charminster Dorset 14 D4
Charmouth Dorset 13 J4
Charndon Bucks 58 A3
Charney Bassett
  Oxon 41 G2
Charnock Richard
  Lancs 121 H7
Charnock Richard
  Services Lancs 121 H7
Charsfield Suffk 78 F3
Charter Alley Hants 41 L8
Charterhall Border 179 G8
Charterhouse Somset ... 26 D1
Chartershall Stirlg 175 K1
Chartham Kent 34 E4
Chartham Hatch
  Kent 34 E4

Chartridge Bucks 58 F7
Chart Sutton Kent 33 K4
Charvil Wokham 42 C5
Charwelton Nhants 73 G4
Chase Cross Gt Lon 45 K2
Chase Terrace Staffs 85 J2
Chasetown Staffs 85 J2
Chastleton Oxon 56 E3
Chasty Devon 9 J4
Chatburn Lancs 121 L2
Chatcull Staffs 99 H5
Chatham Medway 46 C6
Chatham Green
  Essex 61 H5
Chathill Nthumb 169 J4
Chatsworth Derbys 114 E7
Chattenden Medway 46 C5
Chatteris Cambs 90 B6
Chatterton Lancs 122 B6
Chattisham Suffk 78 C6
Chatto Border 168 B5
Chatton Nthumb 168 F4
Chawleigh Devon 11 G3
Chawton Hants 30 B4
Cheadle Staffs 100 A4
Cheadle Stockp 113 K4
Cheadle Heath
  Stockp 113 K4
Cheadle Hulme
  Stockp 113 K4
Cheam Gt Lon 44 E7
Chearsley Bucks 58 B6
Chebsey Staffs 99 J6
Checkendon Oxon 42 A4
Checkley Ches E 99 G4
Checkley Staffs 100 B5
Chedburgh Suffk 77 H3
Cheddar Somset 26 C2
Cheddington Bucks 58 F4
Cheddleton Staffs 99 L3
Cheddon Fitzpaine
  Somset 25 K6
Chedgrave Norfk 93 H4
Chedington Dorset 13 L2
Chediston Suffk 93 H7
Chedworth Gloucs 56 B5
Chedzoy Somset 25 M4
Cheetham Hill
  Manch 113 J2
Cheldon Devon 11 H3
Chelford Ches E 113 J6
Chellaston C Derb 101 G6
Chellington Bed 74 D4
Chelmarsh Shrops 84 C5
Chelmer Village
  Essex 61 H6
Chelmondiston Suffk ... 78 E6
Chelmorton Derbys 114 C7
Chelmsford Essex 61 H6
Chelmsley Wood
  Solhll 85 L6
Chelsea Gt Lon 44 F4
Chelsfield Gt Lon 45 J7
Chelsworth Suffk 77 L5
Cheltenham Gloucs 55 L4
Chelveston Nhants 74 E1
Chelvey N Som 38 C6
Chelwood BaNES 38 F7
Chelwood Gate
  E Susx 32 D6
Cheney Longville
  Shrops 83 H6
Chenies Bucks 43 G2
Chepstow Mons 38 D2
Cherhill Wilts 40 B6
Cherington Gloucs 55 K7
Cherington Warwks 72 C6
Cheriton Hants 29 L5
Cheriton Kent 35 G7
Cheriton Pembks 49 G7
Cheriton Swans 50 F6
Cheriton Bishop
  Devon 11 H6
Cheriton Fitzpaine
  Devon 11 K4
Cherrington Wrekin 98 F8
Cherry Burton
  E R Yk 126 B3

Cherry Hinton Cambs 76 C3
Cherry Orchard
  Worcs 70 F4
Cherry Willingham
  Lincs 117 G6
Chertsey Surrey 43 H6
Cherwell Valley
  Services Oxon 57 K3
Cheselbourne Dorset 14 E3
Chesham Bucks 58 F7
Chesham Bury 122 B7
Chesham Bois Bucks 58 F7
Cheshunt Herts 60 B7
Chesil Beach Dorset 14 B6
Cheslyn Hay Staffs 85 H3
Chessetts Wood
  Warwks 85 L8
Chessington Gt Lon 44 D7
Chessington World
  of Adventures
  Gt Lon 44 D7
Chester Ches W 112 B7
Chesterblade Somset ... 26 F3
Chesterfield Derbys 115 G7
Chesterfield Staffs 85 K3
Chesterhill Mdloth 177 K5
Chester-le-Street
  Dur 151 G5
Chester Moor Dur 151 G5
Chesters Border 167 J5
Chesters Border 167 K7
Chester Services
  Ches W 112 C6
Chesterton Cambs 76 C3
Chesterton Cambs 89 G4
Chesterton Gloucs 56 A7
Chesterton Oxon 57 K4
Chesterton Shrops 84 D4
Chesterton Staffs 99 J3
Chesterton Green
  Warwks 72 D3
Chesterwood
  Nthumb 149 L2
Chester Zoo Ches W ... 112 B7
Chestfield Kent 47 J6
Cheston Devon 7 G4
Cheswardine Shrops 99 G6
Cheswick Nthumb 168 F1
Chetnole Dorset 14 B2
Chettisham Cambs 90 D6
Chettle Dorset 27 L8
Chetton Shrops 84 B5
Chetwynd Wrekin 99 G7
Chetwynd Aston
  Wrekin 99 H8
Cheveley Cambs 76 F3
Chevening Kent 32 E2
Chevington Suffk 77 H3
Cheviot Hills 168 A7
Chevithorne Devon 24 F7
Chew Magna BaNES 38 E7
Chew Stoke BaNES 38 E7
Chewton Keynsham
  BaNES 38 F6
Chewton Mendip
  Somset 26 E2
Chicheley M Keyn 74 C5
Chichester W Susx 18 B5
Chickerell Dorset 14 C6
Chicklade Wilts 27 K4
Chidden Hants 30 A7
Chiddingfold Surrey 30 F4
Chiddingly E Susx 20 B3
Chiddingstone Kent 32 E4
Chiddingstone
  Causeway Kent 32 F4
Chideock Dorset 13 K4
Chidham W Susx 17 L2
Chidswell Kirk 123 K6
Chieveley W Berk 41 J5
Chieveley Services
  W Berk 41 J6
Chignall St James
  Essex 61 G6
Chignall Smealy
  Essex 61 G5
Chigwell Essex 45 H2
Chigwell Row Essex 45 J2

Chilbolton Hants 29 H4
Chilcomb Hants 29 J5
Chilcombe Dorset 13 M4
Chilcompton Somset 26 F2
Chilcote Leics 86 C2
Childer Thornton
  Ches W 111 K6
Child Okeford Dorset 27 J8
Childrey Oxon 41 G3
Child's Ercall Shrops 98 F7
Childswickham
  Worcs 71 J6
Childwall Lpool 112 B4
Chilfrome Dorset 14 B3
Chilgrove W Susx 18 A3
Chilham Kent 34 E4
Chillaton Devon 10 C8
Chillenden Kent 35 H4
Chillerton IoW 16 F5
Chillesford Suffk 79 H4
Chillington Devon 7 J7
Chillington Somset 13 K1
Chilmark Wilts 27 L5
Chilmington Green
  Kent 34 C6
Chilson Oxon 56 F4
Chilsworthy Cnwll 6 B2
Chilsworthy Devon 9 J4
Chiltern Hills 42 C2
Chilthorne Domer
  Somset 26 D7
Chilton Bucks 58 B5
Chilton Dur 141 H2
Chilton Oxon 41 J4
Chilton Candover
  Hants 29 L4
Chilton Cantelo
  Somset 26 E6
Chilton Foliat Wilts 40 F6
Chilton Polden
  Somset 26 B4
Chilton Street Suffk 77 H5
Chilton Trinity
  Somset 25 L4
Chilwell Notts 101 K5
Chilworth Hants 29 H7
Chilworth Surrey 31 G3
Chimney Oxon 57 G7
Chineham Hants 30 A1
Chingford Gt Lon 45 G2
Chinley Derbys 114 B5
Chinnor Oxon 58 C7
Chipnall Shrops 99 G6
Chippenham Cambs 76 F1
Chippenham Wilts 39 L5
Chipperfield Herts 59 H7
Chipping Herts 60 B2
Chipping Lancs 121 J2
Chipping Campden
  Gloucs 71 L6
Chipping Hill Essex 61 K5
Chipping Norton
  Oxon 56 F3
Chipping Ongar
  Essex 60 E7
Chipping Sodbury
  S Glos 39 G4
Chipping Warden
  Nhants 72 F5
Chipstable Somset 25 G6
Chipstead Kent 32 E3
Chipstead Surrey 32 B2
Chirbury Shrops 82 F4
Chirk Wrexhm 97 L5
Chirnside Border 179 H6
Chirnsidebridge
  Border 179 H7
Chirton Wilts 40 B8
Chisbury Wilts 40 F6
Chiselborough
  Somset 26 C8
Chiseldon Swindn 40 D4
Chiselhampton Oxon 57 L7
Chiserley Calder 122 F5
Chisholme Border 166 F6
Chislehurst Gt Lon 45 H6
Chislet Kent 47 L6
Chiswell Green Herts 59 J7

Chiswick Gt Lon 44 E4
Chisworth Derbys 113 M3
Chithurst W Susx 30 D6
Chittering Cambs 76 C1
Chitterne Wilts 27 M3
Chittlehamholt
Devon 23 K7
Chittlehampton
Devon 23 K6
Chittoe Wilts 39 L6
Chivelstone Devon 7 H7
Chivenor Devon 23 H4
Chlenry D & G 144 D3
Chobham Surrey 42 F7
Cholderton Wilts 28 E3
Cholesbury Bucks 58 F6
Chollerton Nthumb 158 B7
Cholsey Oxon 41 L3
Cholstrey Herefs 69 J3
Chop Gate N York 142 C7
Choppington
Nthumb 159 G5
Chopwell Gatesd 150 E4
Chorley Ches E 98 E3
Chorley Lancs 121 H6
Chorley Shrops 84 C6
Chorleywood Herts 43 G2
Chorleywood West
Herts 43 G2
Chorlton Ches E 99 G3
Chorlton-cum-
Hardy Manch 113 J3
Chorlton Lane
Ches W 98 C3
Choulton Shrops 83 H5
Chrishall Essex 76 C6
Chrisswell Inver 173 L4
Christchurch BCP 15 M4
Christchurch Cambs 90 C4
Christchurch Newpt 37 M3
Christian Malford
Wilts 39 L5
Christon N Som 38 B8
Christon Bank
Nthumb 169 J5
Christow Devon 11 J7
Chudleigh Devon 11 K8
Chudleigh Knighton
Devon 7 J1
Chulmleigh Devon 11 G3
Church Lancs 121 L5
Churcham Gloucs 55 H4
Church Aston
Wrekin 99 H8
Church Brampton
Nhants 73 K2
Church Broughton
Derbys 100 D5
Church Cove Cnwll 3 J8
Church Crookham
Hants 30 D2
Churchdown Gloucs 55 K4
Church Eaton Staffs 99 J8
Church Green Devon ... 12 F3
Church Hanborough
Oxon 57 H5
Church Houses
N York 142 F7
Churchill Devon 13 H3
Churchill N Som 38 C7
Churchill Oxon 56 F3
Churchill Worcs 71 G4
Churchill Worcs 84 F7
Churchinford
Somset 25 K8
Church Knowle
Dorset 15 H6

Church Langton
Leics 87 K5
Church Lawford
Warwks 86 F7
Church Leigh Staffs 100 A5
Church Lench Worcs 71 H4
Church Mayfield
Staffs 100 D4
Church Minshull
Ches E 98 F1
Church Norton
W Susx 18 B6
Churchover Warwks ... 87 G7
Church Preen Shrops ... 83 K4
Church Pulverbatch
Shrops 83 H3
Churchstanton
Somset 25 J8
Churchstoke Powys 82 F5
Churchstow Devon 7 G6
Church Stowe
Nhants 73 J3
Church Street Kent 46 B5
Church Stretton
Shrops 83 J5
Churchtown Cnwll 5 H1
Churchtown Derbys ... 114 E8
Churchtown IoM 237 d3
Churchtown Lancs 121 G2
Church Village
Rhondd 37 H3
Church Warsop
Notts 115 K7
Churston Ferrers
Torbay 7 K5
Churt Surrey 30 D4
Churton Ches W 98 B2
Churwell Leeds 123 K5
Chwilog Gwynd 95 G5
Chyandour Cnwll 2 E5
Cilcain Flints 111 G7
Cilcennin Cerdgn 66 C3
Cilfrew Neath 52 B7
Cilfynydd Rhondd 37 G3
Cilgerran Pembks 65 H6
Cilmaengwyn Neath 51 L4
Cilmery Powys 67 L4
Cilsan Carmth 51 H2
Ciltalgarth Gwynd 96 D4
Cilycwm Carmth 67 G6
Cimla Neath 36 B2
Cinderford Gloucs 54 F5
Cinder Hill Wolves 85 G5
Cippenham Slough 42 F4
Cirencester Gloucs 56 A7
City Gt Lon 45 G4
City Airport Gt Lon 45 H4
Clabhach Ag & B 188 F5
Clachaig Ag & B 173 J3
Clachaig Inn Highld 192 B5
Clachan Ag & B 172 C6
Clachan Ag & B 182 A4
Clachan Ag & B 182 F6
Clachan Ag & B 191 G7
Clachan Highld 209 H6
Clachan-a-Luib
W Isls 233 c6
Clachan Mor Ag & B ... 188 C6
Clachan na Luib
W Isls 233 c6
Clachan of Campsie
E Duns 175 G3
Clachan-Seil Ag & B .. 181 M4
Clachnaharry Highld .. 213 G5
Clachtoll Highld 224 C3
Clacket Lane
Services Surrey 32 D3
Clackmannan
Clacks 185 J8
Clackmannanshire
Bridge Fife 176 C2
Clackmarras Moray 214 F3
Clacton-on-Sea
Essex 62 G5
Cladich Ag & B 182 F3
Cladswell Worcs 71 J3
Claggan Highld 190 E6
Claigan Highld 208 C4

Clanfield Hants 30 B7
Clanfield Oxon 56 F7
Clanville Hants 28 F2
Clanville Somset 26 F5
Claonaig Ag & B 172 E6
Clapgate Herts 60 C3
Clapham Bed 74 F4
Clapham Gt Lon 44 F5
Clapham N York 130 C5
Clapham W Susx 18 F4
Clapton Somset 13 K2
Clapton Somset 26 F2
Clapton-in-
Gordano N Som 38 C5
Clapton-on-the-
Hill Gloucs 56 D4
Claravale Gatesd 150 E3
Clarbeston Pembks 49 H3
Clarbeston Road
Pembks 49 H4
Clarborough Notts 116 B5
Clare Suffk 77 H5
Clarebrand D & G 146 D2
Clarencefield D & G ... 147 J2
Clarilaw Border 167 H5
Clarkston E Rens 175 G6
Clashmore Highld 223 G4
Clashmore Highld 224 C3
Clashnessie Highld 224 C3
Clashnoir Moray 204 F2
Clathy P & K 185 K4
Clathymore P & K 185 L3
Clatt Abers 205 L1
Clatter Powys 81 L5
Clatworthy Somset 25 G5
Claughton Lancs 121 G3
Claughton Lancs 130 B6
Claughton Wirral 111 J4
Claverdon Warwks 71 L2
Claverham N Som 38 C6
Clavering Essex 60 D2
Claverley Shrops 84 E5
Claverton BaNES 39 H7
Clawdd-coch V Glam .. 37 G5
Clawdd-newydd
Denbgs 97 G3
Clawton Devon 9 J5
Claxby Lincs 117 J3
Claxton N York 133 L7
Claxton Norfk 93 H3
Claybrooke Magna
Leics 86 F5
Clay Coton Nhants 87 H7
Clay Cross Derbys 115 H8
Claydon Oxon 72 F4
Claydon Suffk 78 D5
Claygate D & G 156 D6
Claygate Kent 33 J4
Claygate Surrey 44 D7
Clayhall Gt Lon 45 H3
Clayhanger Devon 24 F6
Clayhidon Devon 25 J7
Clayhill E Susx 21 G2
Clayock Highld 231 H4
Claypits Gloucs 55 H6
Claypole Lincs 102 D3
Clayton C Brad 123 G4
Clayton Donc 124 C8
Clayton W Susx 19 J3
Clayton-le-Moors
Lancs 121 L4
Clayton-le-Woods
Lancs 121 H6
Clayton West Kirk 123 K7
Clayworth Notts 116 B4
Cleadale Highld 199 G7
Cleadon S Tyne 151 J3
Cleadon Park S Tyne . 151 J3
Clearbrook Devon 6 D3
Clearwell Gloucs 54 E6
Cleasby N York 141 G5
Cleat Ork 234 d8
Cleatlam Dur 140 E4
Cleator Cumb 136 D4
Cleator Moor Cumb .. 136 E4
Cleckheaton Kirk 123 J5
Cleehill Shrops 83 L7
Cleekhimin N Lans 175 K6

Clee St Margaret
Shrops 83 L6
Cleethorpes NE Lin 127 H8
Cleeton St Mary
Shrops 84 B7
Cleeve N Som 38 C7
Cleeve Oxon 41 L4
Cleeve Hill Gloucs 55 M3
Cleeve Prior Worcs 71 J5
Cleghornie E Loth 178 D2
Clehonger Herefs 69 J6
Cleish P & K 186 A7
Cleland N Lans 175 L6
Clenamacrie Ag & B .. 182 C2
Clenchwarton Norfk .. 104 F7
Clenerty Abers 216 E3
Clent Worcs 85 G7
Cleobury Mortimer
Shrops 84 C7
Cleobury North
Shrops 84 B6
Cleongart Ag & B 161 H3
Clephanton Highld 213 J4
Clerkhill D & G 156 A3
Cleuch-head D & G ... 154 E3
Clevancy Wilts 40 B5
Clevedon N Som 38 B6
Cleveleys Lancs 120 D2
Cleverton Wilts 39 L4
Clewer Somset 26 C2
Cley next the Sea
Norfk 106 C4
Cliburn Cumb 138 E3
Cliddesden Hants 29 M2
Cliffe Medway 46 C5
Cliffe N York 125 G4
Cliff End E Susx 21 H3
Cliffe Woods Medway . 46 C5
Clifford Herefs 68 E5
Clifford Leeds 124 C2
Clifford Chambers
Warwks 71 L4
Clifford's Mesne
Gloucs 55 G4
Clifton Bristl 38 E5
Clifton C Beds 75 H6
Clifton N York 101 K5
Clifton C York 133 J8
Clifton Calder 123 H6
Clifton Cumb 138 D2
Clifton Derbys 100 D4
Clifton Devon 23 J3
Clifton Donc 115 K3
Clifton Lancs 120 F4
Clifton N York 123 J2
Clifton Oxon 57 J2
Clifton Worcs 70 F5
Clifton Campville
Staffs 86 B2
Clifton Hampden
Oxon 41 K2
Clifton Reynes
M Keyn 74 C4
Clifton upon
Dunsmore
Warwks 87 G7
Clifton upon Teme
Worcs 70 C3
Cliftonville Kent 35 K1
Climping W Susx 18 D5
Clink Somset 27 H2
Clint N York 132 D7
Clinterty C Aber 206 F3
Clint Green Norfk 92 B2
Clintmains Border 167 J3
Clippesby Norfk 93 J2
Clipsham Rutlnd 88 D1
Clipston Nhants 87 K7
Clipston Notts 101 M5
Clipstone C Beds 58 F3
Clipstone Notts 115 L8
Clitheroe Lancs 121 L3
Clive Shrops 98 D7
Cliveden Bucks 42 E4
Clixby Lincs 117 J2
Cloatley Wilts 39 M3
Clocaenog Denbgs 97 G2
Clochan Moray 215 J3

Clodock Herefs 53 L3
Clola Abers............. 217 J5
Clophill C Beds............74 F6
Clopton Nhants............88 F7
Clopton Suffk............78 F4
Clopton Corner Suffk....78 F4
Clos du Valle Guern...... 236 d2
Closeburn D & G........ 154 F4
Closeburnmill D & G ... 154 F3
Closworth Somset 14 B1
Clothall Herts............59 L2
Clotton Ches W........... 112 D8
Clough Foot Calder.... 122 D5
Clough Head Calder 123 G6
Cloughton N York 143 K7
Clousta Shet 235 c5
Clova Angus............ 196 B2
Clovelly Devon............22 E6
Clovenfords Border.... 167 G3
Clovulin Highld........ 191 K4
Clowne Derbys 115 J6
Clows Top Worcs..........70 C1
Cluanie Inn Highld.... 201 G3
Cluanie Lodge
  Highld................ 201 G3
Clugston D & G........ 145 H4
Clun Shrops 82 F7
Clunas Highld............ 213 K5
Clunbury Shrops 83 G7
Clunderwen Carmth......49 J4
Clune Highld............ 203 J1
Clunes Highld............ 201 J7
Clungunford Shrops......83 H7
Clunie P & K............ 195 H7
Clunton Shrops............83 G7
Cluny Fife 186 D7
Clutton BaNES............38 F8
Clutton Ches W............98 C2
Clutton Hill BaNES........38 F8
Clydach Mons............53 K5
Clydach Swans 51 K5
Clydach Vale Rhondd......36 F2
Clydebank W Duns 174 F4
Clyffe Pypard Wilts......40 B5
Clynder Ag & B 174 A2
Clyne Neath............52 C7
Clynnog Fawr Gwynd 95 G3
Clyro Powys............68 E5
Clyst Honiton Devon......12 C4
Clyst Hydon Devon 12 D3
Clyst St George
  Devon................12 C5
Clyst St Lawrence
  Devon................12 D3
Clyst St Mary Devon 12 C4
Cnoc W Isls............ 232 g2
Cnwch Coch Cerdgn 80 F8
Coad's Green Cnwll........5 L1
Coalburn S Lans........ 164 F3
Coalburns Gatesd...... 150 E3
Coaley Gloucs............55 H7
Coalhill Essex 61 J7
Coalpit Heath S Glos 38 F4
Coal Pool Wsall............85 H4
Coalport Wrekin............84 C3
Coalsnaughton
  Clacks................ 185 J7
Coaltown of
  Balgonie Fife 186 E7
Coaltown of
  Wemyss Fife........ 186 E7
Coalville Leics 86 E2
Coanwood Nthumb...... 149 H3
Coat Somset............26 C7
Coatbridge N Lans...... 175 J5
Coatdyke N Lans........ 175 K5
Coate Swindn 40 D4
Coate Wilts............40 B7
Coates Cambs............89 K4
Coates Gloucs............55 L7
Coates Lincs............ 116 E5
Coates W Susx 18 D3
Cobbaton Devon............23 K6
Coberley Gloucs............55 L5
Cobham Kent............46 A6
Cobham Surrey............43 J7
Cobham Services
  Surrey................43 J8

Cobnash Herefs 69 J3
Cobo Guern 236 c2
Cobridge C Stke............99 K3
Coburby Abers............ 217 H2
Cockayne Hatley
  C Beds................75 J5
Cock Bridge Abers...... 205 G4
Cockburnspath
  Border................ 179 G4
Cock Clarks Essex..........61 K7
Cockenzie and Port
  Seton E Loth........ 177 L4
Cockerham Lancs........ 120 F1
Cockermouth Cumb.... 136 F2
Cockernhoe Herts..........59 J4
Cockett Swans............51 J6
Cockfield Dur............ 140 E3
Cockfield Suffk............77 K4
Cockfosters Gt Lon......44 F2
Cock Green Essex............61 H4
Cocking W Susx 18 B3
Cocking Causeway
  W Susx................18 B2
Cockington Torbay 7 K3
Cocklake Somset............26 C2
Cockley Cley Norfk........91 H3
Cock Marling E Susx......21 H2
Cockpole Green
  Wokham................42 D4
Cockshutt Shrops..........98 B6
Cockthorpe Norfk...... 106 B4
Cockwood Devon............12 C6
Cockyard Derbys........ 114 B5
Coddenham Suffk........78 D4
Coddington Herefs........70 C6
Coddington Notts...... 102 D2
Codford St Mary
  Wilts................27 L4
Codford St Peter
  Wilts................27 L4
Codicote Herts............59 K4
Codmore Hill W Susx......31 H7
Codnor Derbys............ 101 H3
Codrington S Glos........39 G5
Codsall Staffs............84 F3
Codsall Wood Staffs......84 F3
Coedpoeth Wrexhm........97 L3
Coed Talon Flints............97 L2
Coed-y-paen Mons......53 M7
Coed-yr-ynys Powys......53 J4
Coffinswell Devon............7 K3
Cofton Devon............12 C6
Cofton Hackett
  Worcs................85 H7
Cogan V Glam 37 J6
Cogenhoe Nhants........74 B3
Cogges Oxon............57 G6
Coggeshall Essex............61 K4
Coignafearn Highld.... 203 H2
Coilacriech Abers...... 205 H6
Coilantogle Stirlg...... 184 D6
Coillore Highld........ 208 E6
Coity Brdgnd............36 E4
Col W Isls............ 232 g2
Colaboll Highld........ 225 L6
Colan Cnwll................4 D4
Colaton Raleigh
  Devon................12 D5
Colbost Highld........ 208 C5
Colburn N York............ 140 F7
Colby Cumb............ 138 F3
Colby IoM............ 237 b6
Colchester Essex............62 B3
Colchester Zoo
  Essex................62 A4
Cold Ash W Berk............41 K6
Cold Ashby Nhants........87 J7
Cold Ashton S Glos........39 H6
Cold Aston Gloucs........56 C4
Coldbackie Highld...... 229 J4
Cold Brayfield
  M Keyn................74 D4
Coldean Br & H............19 J4
Coldeast Devon............7 J2
Colden Calder............ 122 E5
Colden Common
  Hants................29 J6
Cold Hanworth Lincs... 117 G5

Coldharbour Surrey........31 J3
Cold Higham Nhants 73 J4
Coldingham Border 179 J5
Cold Kirby N York........ 133 H3
Coldmeece Staffs..........99 J6
Cold Norton Essex..........61 K7
Cold Overton Leics........88 B2
Coldred Kent............35 H5
Coldridge Devon............11 G4
Coldstream Border...... 168 C2
Coldwaltham W Susx......18 D3
Coldwells Abers........ 217 H6
Cole Somset............26 F5
Colebatch Shrops..........83 G6
Colebrook Devon............12 C2
Colebrooke Devon............11 H5
Coleby Lincs............ 102 F1
Coleby N Linc............ 125 L6
Coleford Devon............11 H5
Coleford Gloucs............54 E6
Coleford Somset 27 G2
Colegate End Norfk......92 E6
Colehill Dorset............15 J3
Coleman's Hatch
  E Susx................32 D6
Colemere Shrops..........98 B6
Colemore Hants............30 B5
Colenden P & K............ 186 B2
Colerne Wilts............39 J6
Colesbourne Gloucs......56 A5
Coleshill Bucks............42 F2
Coleshill Oxon............40 E2
Coleshill Warwks........85 L5
Coley BaNES............26 E1
Colgate W Susx............31 L5
Colinsburgh Fife...... 187 H6
Colinton C Edin........ 177 H5
Colintraive Ag & B...... 173 H4
Colkirk Norfk............ 105 L7
Coll Ag & B............ 189 G5
Coll W Isls............ 232 g2
Collace P & K............ 186 C2
Collafirth Shet............ 235 c3
Coll Airport Ag & B 188 F5
Collaton Devon..............7 G7
Collaton St Mary
  Torbay................7 K4
College of Roseisle
  Moray................ 214 E2
College Town Br For 42 D7
Collessie Fife............ 186 E5
Collier Row Gt Lon........45 J2
Collier's End Herts........60 B4
Collier Street Kent........33 J4
Collieston Abers........ 217 K8
Collin D & G............ 155 H6
Collingbourne
  Ducis Wilts........28 E2
Collingbourne
  Kingston Wilts......28 E1
Collingham Leeds...... 124 B3
Collingham Notts...... 102 D1
Collington Herefs..........70 B3
Collingtree Nhants........73 L4
Collins Green Warrtn... 112 E3
Colliston Angus........ 196 F7
Colliton Devon............12 E2
Collyweston Nhants......88 E3
Colmonell S Ayrs...... 152 D5
Colmworth Bed............75 G3
Colnabaichin Abers.... 205 G4
Colnbrook Slough..........43 G5
Colne Cambs............89 L7
Colne Lancs............ 122 D3
Colne Engaine Essex......61 K3
Colney Norfk............92 E3
Colney Heath Herts......59 K6
Coln Rogers Gloucs......56 B6
Coln St Aldwyns
  Gloucs................56 C6
Coln St Dennis
  Gloucs................56 B5
Colonsay Ag & B........ 180 E7
Colonsay Airport
  Ag & B............ 180 E8
Colpy Abers............ 216 C7
Colquhar Border 166 E2
Colsterworth Lincs...... 102 F7

Colston Bassett
  Notts................ 102 B5
Coltfield Moray 214 D2
Coltishall Norfk............ 106 F8
Colton Cumb............ 129 G3
Colton Leeds............ 124 B4
Colton N York............ 124 E2
Colton Norfk............92 D2
Colton Staffs............ 100 B7
Colt's Hill Kent............33 H4
Colvend D & G............ 146 F4
Colwall Herefs............70 D6
Colwell Nthumb............ 158 B6
Colwich Staffs............ 100 A7
Colwinston V Glam........36 E5
Colworth W Susx............18 C5
Colwyn Bay Conwy...... 110 B5
Colyford Devon............13 G4
Colyton Devon............13 G4
Combe Oxon............57 H5
Combe W Berk............41 G4
Combe Down BaNES......39 H7
Combe Fishacre
  Devon................7 J3
Combe Florey
  Somset................25 J5
Combe Hay BaNES........39 G7
Combeinteignhead
  Devon................7 K2
Combe Martin Devon 23 J3
Combe Raleigh
  Devon................12 F3
Comberbach Ches W... 112 F6
Comberford Staffs........85 L3
Comberton Cambs........75 L4
Comberton Herefs........69 K2
Combe St Nicholas
  Somset................13 H1
Combrook Warwks........72 C4
Combs Derbys............ 114 B6
Combs Suffk............78 C3
Combs Ford Suffk........78 C3
Combwich Somset..........25 K3
Comers Abers............ 206 D4
Comeytrowe Somset......25 J6
Comhampton Worcs......70 E2
Commins Coch
  Powys................81 J3
Commondale N York.... 142 E5
Common End Cumb..... 136 D3
Common Moor Cnwll 5 K2
Compstall Stockp........ 113 L4
Compstonend D & G... 146 B4
Compton Devon..............7 K3
Compton Hants............29 J6
Compton Staffs............84 E6
Compton Surrey............30 F3
Compton W Berk............41 K4
Compton W Susx............30 C7
Compton Wilts............28 C2
Compton Abbas
  Dorset................27 K7
Compton Abdale
  Gloucs................56 B6
Compton Bassett
  Wilts................40 B6
Compton
  Beauchamp Oxon......40 F3
Compton Bishop
  Somset................26 B1
Compton
  Chamberlayne
  Wilts................28 B5
Compton Dando
  BaNES................38 F7
Compton Dundon
  Somset................26 C5
Compton Durville
  Somset................26 B7
Compton Greenfield
  S Glos................38 E4
Compton Martin
  BaNES................38 D8
Compton
  Pauncefoot
  Somset................26 F6
Compton Valence
  Dorset................14 B4

Comrie Fife 176 D1
Comrie P & K 185 G3
Conaglen House
  Highld 191 K3
Concha Highld 210 D8
Concraigie P & K 195 H7
Conderton Worcs 71 G6
Condicote Gloucs 56 D3
Condorrat N Lans 175 K4
Condover Shrops 83 J3
Coney Hill Gloucs 55 J4
Coneyhurst W Susx 31 J6
Coneysthorpe N York 133 L5
Coney Weston Suffk 91 L7
Congerstone Leics 86 D3
Congham Norfk 105 H7
Congleton Ches E 113 J8
Congresbury N Som 38 C7
Conheath D & G 147 H2
Conicavel Moray 214 B4
Coningsby Lincs 103 L2
Conington Cambs 75 K2
Conington Cambs 89 H6
Conisbrough Donc 115 K2
Conisholme Lincs 118 E3
Coniston Cumb 137 J7
Coniston E R Yk 126 E4
Coniston Cold
  N York 131 G8
Conistone N York 131 J6
Connah's Quay Flints 111 J7
Connel Ag & B 182 C1
Connel Park E Ayrs 164 C6
Connor Downs Cnwll 3 K4
Conon Bridge Highld 212 E4
Cononley N York 122 E2
Consall Staffs 99 M3
Consett Dur 150 E5
Constable Burton
  N York 132 B2
Constable Lee Lancs 122 B5
Constantine Cnwll 3 J5
Constantine Bay
  Cnwll 4 D2
Contin Highld 212 C3
Conwy Conwy 109 L6
Conwy Castle Conwy 109 L6
Conyer's Green Suffk 77 K2
Cooden E Susx 20 E4
Cookbury Devon 9 K4
Cookham W & M 42 E4
Cookham Dean
  W & M 42 E4
Cookham Rise
  W & M 42 E4
Cookhill Worcs 71 J3
Cookley Suffk 93 H7
Cookley Worcs 84 E7
Cookley Green Oxon 42 B3
Cookney Abers 207 G6
Cook's Green Essex 62 E4
Cooks Green Suffk 77 L4
Cooksmill Green
  Essex 61 G6
Coolham W Susx 31 J6
Cooling Medway 46 C5
Coombe Cnwll 4 E5
Coombe Devon 7 L2
Coombe Devon 12 E4
Coombe Gloucs 39 H2
Coombe Hants 30 A7
Coombe Bissett
  Wilts 28 C6
Coombe Cellars
  Devon 7 K2
Coombe Hill Gloucs 55 K3
Coombe Keynes
  Dorset 14 F5
Coombe Pafford
  Torbay 7 L3
Coombes W Susx 19 G4
Coombes-Moor
  Herefs 69 G2
Coombeswood
  Dudley 85 H6
Coopersale
  Common Essex 60 D7
Copdock Suffk 78 D6

Copford Essex 61 M4
Copford Green
  Essex 61 L4
Copgrove N York 132 E6
Copister Shet 235 d3
Cople Bed 75 G5
Copley Dur 140 D3
Copmanthorpe
  C York 124 E2
Copmere End Staffs 99 J6
Copp Lancs 120 F3
Coppenhall Staffs 99 K8
Copperhouse Cnwll 2 F4
Coppingford Cambs 89 H7
Copplestone Devon 11 H4
Coppull Lancs 121 H7
Copsale W Susx 31 K6
Copster Green Lancs 121 K4
Copston Magna
  Warwks 86 F5
Cop Street Kent 35 J3
Copt Hewick N York 132 E5
Copthorne W Susx 32 B5
Copt Oak Leics 86 F2
Copythorne Hants 28 F8
Corbets Tey Gt Lon 45 K3
Corbière Jersey 236 a7
Corbridge Nthumb 150 C3
Corby Nhants 88 C5
Corby Glen Lincs 103 G7
Cordon N Ayrs 162 D4
Coreley Shrops 84 B8
Corfe Somset 25 K7
Corfe Castle Dorset 15 H6
Corfe Mullen Dorset 15 J3
Corfton Shrops 83 J6
Corgarff Abers 205 G4
Corhampton Hants 29 L7
Corlae D & G 154 B3
Corley Warwks 86 C6
Corley Services
  Warwks 86 C6
Cormuir Angus 195 L3
Cornard Tye Suffk 77 K6
Cornforth Dur 151 H7
Cornhill Abers 216 B3
Cornhill-on-Tweed
  Nthumb 168 C2
Cornholme Calder 122 D5
Cornoigmore Ag & B 188 C6
Cornsay Dur 150 E6
Cornsay Colliery Dur 150 F6
Corntown Highld 212 D3
Corntown V Glam 36 E5
Cornwall Airport
  Newquay Cnwll 4 D3
Cornwell Oxon 56 F3
Cornwood Devon 6 E4
Cornworthy Devon 7 J5
Corpach Highld 191 L2
Corpusty Norfk 106 D6
Corrachree Abers 205 K4
Corran Highld 191 K4
Corran Highld 200 C4
Corrie D & G 155 L5
Corrie N Ayrs 162 C2
Corriecravie N Ayrs 162 B5
Corriegills N Ayrs 162 D3
Corriegour Lodge
  Hotel Highld 201 K6
Corriemoille Highld 212 B2
Corrimony Highld 212 B7
Corringham Lincs 116 E4
Corringham Thurr 46 B4
Corris Gwynd 81 G2
Corris Uchaf Gwynd 81 G2
Corrow Ag & B 183 H7
Corry Highld 199 K1
Corscombe Devon 10 F5
Corscombe Dorset 13 M2
Corse Gloucs 55 H3
Corse Lawn Gloucs 55 J2
Corsham Wilts 39 K6
Corsindae Abers 206 D4
Corsley Wilts 27 J3
Corsley Heath Wilts 27 J3
Corsock D & G 154 D6
Corston BaNES 39 G7

Corston Wilts 39 L4
Corstorphine C Edin 177 G4
Cortachy Angus 196 C4
Corton Suffk 93 L4
Corton Wilts 27 L4
Corton Denham
  Somset 26 F6
Coruanan Highld 191 L3
Corwen Denbgs 97 G4
Coryton Devon 10 C7
Coryton Thurr 46 C4
Cosby Leics 87 G4
Coseley Dudley 85 G5
Cosgrove Nhants 73 L6
Cosham C Port 17 J2
Cosheston Pembks 49 G6
Coshieville P & K 194 C6
Cossall Notts 101 J4
Cossington Leics 87 H2
Cossington Somset 26 A4
Costessey Norfk 92 E2
Costock Notts 101 L7
Coston Leics 102 D7
Coston Norfk 92 C3
Cote Oxon 57 G7
Cotebrook Ches W 112 E7
Cotehill Cumb 148 E5
Cotes Leics 101 K7
Cotesbach Leics 87 G6
Cotford St Luke
  Somset 25 J6
Cotgrave Notts 101 M5
Cothal Abers 207 G3
Cotham Notts 102 C3
Cotherstone Dur 140 C4
Cothill Oxon 57 J7
Cotleigh Devon 13 G3
Cotmanhay Derbys 101 J4
Coton Cambs 76 B3
Coton Nhants 73 J1
Coton Staffs 99 J7
Coton Clanford
  Staffs 99 K7
Coton Hill Shrops 83 J2
Coton in the Elms
  Derbys 86 B1
Cotswold Airport
  Wilts 39 L2
Cotswolds 55 M6
Cotswold Wildlife
  Park & Gardens
  Oxon 56 E6
Cott Devon 7 H4
Cottam Lancs 121 G4
Cottam Notts 116 D5
Cottenham Cambs 76 C2
Cottered Herts 60 A3
Cotteridge Birm 85 J7
Cotterstock Nhants 88 F5
Cottesbrooke Nhants 87 K8
Cottesmore Rutlnd 88 C2
Cottingham E R Yk 126 C4
Cottingham Nhants 88 B5
Cottingley C Brad 123 G3
Cottisford Oxon 57 L2
Cotton Suffk 78 C2
Cottown Abers 206 E3
Cottown Abers 215 L8
Cottown of Gight
  Abers 216 F6
Cotts Devon 6 C3
Coughton Warwks 71 J3
Coulaghailtrop Ag & B 172 C5
Coulags Highld 210 E5
Coulby Newham
  Middsb 142 B4
Coull Abers 205 L5
Coulport Ag & B 173 L2
Coulsdon Gt Lon 32 B2
Coulston Wilts 27 L2
Coulter S Lans 165 K3
Coulton N York 133 K5
Coultra Fife 186 F3
Cound Shrops 83 L3
Coundon Dur 141 G2
Countersett N York 131 H2
Countess Wear
  Devon 12 B4

Countesswells
  C Aber 207 G4
Countesthorpe Leics 87 H4
Countisbury Devon 24 B2
Coupar Angus P & K 195 K7
Coupland Nthumb 168 D3
Cour Ag & B 172 D8
Courteachan Highld 199 L6
Courteenhall Nhants 73 L4
Court Henry Carmth 51 H2
Courtsend Essex 47 G2
Courtway Somset 25 J5
Cousland Mdloth 177 K5
Cousley Wood E Susx 33 H6
Cove Ag & B 173 L2
Cove Border 179 G4
Cove Devon 24 E7
Cove Hants 30 E1
Cove Highld 219 J3
Cove Bay C Aber 207 H5
Covehithe Suffk 93 L6
Coven Staffs 85 G3
Coveney Cambs 90 C6
Covenham St
  Bartholomew
  Lincs 118 D3
Covenham St Mary
  Lincs 118 D3
Coventry Covtry 86 D7
Coverack Cnwll 3 K7
Coverack Bridges
  Cnwll 3 H5
Coverham N York 131 L3
Covington Cambs 74 F1
Covington S Lans 165 J2
Cowan Bridge Lancs 130 C4
Cowbeech E Susx 20 C3
Cowbit Lincs 103 L8
Cowbridge V Glam 36 F5
Cowden Kent 32 E5
Cowdenbeath Fife 177 G1
Cowers Lane Derbys 100 F3
Cowes IoW 16 F3
Cowesby N York 133 G2
Cowfold W Susx 31 K6
Cowhill S Glos 38 E3
Cowie Stirlg 175 L1
Cowley Devon 11 K5
Cowley Gloucs 55 L5
Cowley Gt Lon 43 H4
Cowley Oxon 57 K7
Cowling Lancs 121 H6
Cowling N York 122 E2
Cowling N York 132 C3
Cowlinge Suffk 77 G4
Cowpen Nthumb 159 H5
Cowplain Hants 17 K1
Cowshill Dur 149 L6
Cowslip Green
  N Som 38 C7
Cowthorpe N York 132 F8
Coxbank Ches E 98 F4
Coxbench Derbys 101 G4
Coxford Cnwll 8 F5
Coxford Norfk 105 K6
Coxheath Kent 33 J3
Coxhoe Dur 151 H7
Coxley Somset 26 D3
Coxley Wick Somset 26 D3
Coxtie Green Essex 45 K2
Coxwold N York 133 H4
Coychurch Brdgnd 36 E4
Coylton S Ayrs 163 K5
Coylumbridge Highld 203 L3
Coytrahen Brdgnd 36 D4
Crabbs Cross Worcs 71 J2
Crabtree W Susx 31 K6
Crackenthorpe
  Cumb 138 F3
Crackington Haven
  Cnwll 8 F5
Crackley Staffs 99 J3
Cracklybank Shrops 84 D2
Cracoe N York 131 J7
Craddock Devon 25 G8
Cradley Dudley 85 G6
Cradley Herefs 70 D5
Cradley Heath Sandw 85 G6

Cradoc Powys 52 F2
Crafthole Cnwll 6 B5
Craggan Highld.............204 C1
Cragganmore Moray ... 214 E6
Craghead Dur.............150 F5
Cragside Nthumb 158 D2
Crai Powys.................52 D3
Craibstone Moray 215 L3
Craichie Angus 196 E6
Craig Angus 197 H5
Craig Highld.............211 G4
Craigbank E Ayrs 164 C6
Craigburn Border 177 H7
Craigcleuch D & G 156 C5
Craigdam Abers 216 F7
Craigdhu Ag & B 182 B6
Craigearn Abers 206 D3
Craigellachie Moray 215 G5
Craigend P & K..........186 B4
Craigend Rens.............174 E4
Craigendoran Ag & B 174 C3
Craigends Rens.............174 D5
Craighlaw D & G 145 G3
Craighouse Ag & B 171 K5
Craigie P & K.............195 H7
Craigie S Ayrs 163 K3
Craigiefold Abers 217 H2
Craigley D & G 146 D4
Craig Llangiwg Neath.....................51 K4
Craiglockhart C Edin 177 H4
Craigmillar C Edin 177 J4
Craigneston D & G 154 D5
Craigneuk N Lans 175 K5
Craigneuk N Lans 175 K6
Craignure Ag & B 190 E8
Craigo Angus 197 H4
Craigrothie Fife 186 F5
Craigruie Stirlg 184 B4
Craigton Angus 196 E8
Craigton C Aber 206 F5
Craigton E Rens 174 F7
Craigton of Airlie Angus.................196 B6
Craik Border.............166 E2
Crail Fife.............187 K5
Crailing Border.............167 L4
Craiselound N Linc 116 C2
Crakehall N York 132 C2
Crambe N York 133 L6
Cramlington Nthumb ... 159 G6
Cramond C Edin 177 G3
Cramond Bridge C Edin.............177 G4
Cranage Ches E.............113 H7
Cranberry Staffs.............99 J5
Cranborne Dorset...........28 B8
Cranbourne Br For.........42 F5
Cranbrook Devon...........12 C4
Cranbrook Kent 33 K6
Cranfield C Beds.............74 D6
Cranford Gt Lon.............43 J5
Cranford St Andrew Nhants.....................88 D7
Cranford St John Nhants.....................88 D7
Cranham Gloucs.............55 K5
Crank St Hel 112 D2
Cranleigh Surrey...........31 H4
Cranmore Somset...........26 F3
Cranoe Leics 87 L4
Cransford Suffk.............79 G2
Cranshaws Border.........178 E6
Crantock Cnwll 4 C4
Cranwell Lincs.............103 G3
Cranwich Norfk.............91 H4
Cranworth Norfk.............92 B3
Craobh Haven Ag & B 182 A6
Crarae Ag & B.............182 E7
Crask Inn Highld.............225 L4
Crask of Aigas Highld.....................212 D6
Craster Nthumb 169 K5
Cratfield Suffk.............93 G7
Crathes Abers 206 E6
Crathie Abers 205 G6

Crathie Highld.............202 E6
Crathorne N York 141 K5
Craven Arms Shrops........83 H6
Crawcrook Gatesd.........150 E3
Crawford S Lans.............165 J5
Crawfordjohn S Lans ... 165 G5
Crawley Hants 29 H4
Crawley Oxon.............57 G5
Crawley W Susx.............31 L4
Crawley Down W Susx.....................32 C5
Crawton Abers.............197 L1
Cray N York.............131 H4
Cray P & K.............195 J4
Crayford Gt Lon.............45 K5
Crayke N York.............133 H5
Crays Hill Essex.............46 B2
Creacombe Devon.........24 C7
Creagan Inn Ag & B.........191 J7
Creag Ghoraidh W Isls.....................233 c7
Creagorry W Isls.............233 c7
Creaguaineach Lodge Highld.............192 E3
Creaton Nhants.............73 K1
Creca D & G.............155 M7
Credenhill Herefs.............69 J5
Crediton Devon.............11 J5
Creebank D & G.............153 H6
Creebridge D & G.............145 J2
Creech Heathfield Somset.....................25 L6
Creech St Michael Somset.....................25 L6
Creed Cnwll 4 E6
Creekmouth Gt Lon.........45 J4
Creeting St Mary Suffk.....................78 D3
Creeton Lincs.............103 G8
Creetown D & G 145 K3
Cregneash IoM.............237 a7
Creich Fife.............186 E3
Creigiau Cardif.............37 G4
Cremyll Cnwll................ 6 C5
Cressage Shrops.............83 L3
Cressbrook Derbys.............114 D6
Cresselly Pembks.............49 H6
Cressex Bucks.............42 D3
Cressing Essex.............61 J4
Cresswell Nthumb 159 H4
Cresswell Pembks.............49 H6
Cresswell Staffs.............99 L5
Creswell Derbys.............115 K6
Cretingham Suffk.............78 F3
Cretshengan Ag & B.........172 C5
Crewe Ches E.............99 G2
Crewe-by-Farndon Ches W.............98 B2
Crewe Green Ches E.............99 G2
Crewkerne Somset.............13 K1
Crewton C Derb.............101 G5
Crianlarich Stirlg.............183 L3
Cribyn Cerdgn.............66 C4
Criccieth Gwynd.............95 J5
Crich Derbys.............101 G2
Crichton Mdloth 177 K6
Crick Nhants.............87 H8
Crickadarn Powys.............68 C6
Cricket St Thomas Somset.............13 J2
Crickhowell Powys.............53 K4
Cricklade Wilts.............40 C3
Cricklewood Gt Lon.............44 E3
Crieff P & K.............185 H3
Criggion Powys.............82 F1
Crigglestone Wakefd.............123 L7
Crimond Abers.............217 K3
Crimplesham Norfk.............90 F3
Crimscote Warwks.............72 B5
Crinaglack Highld.............212 C6
Crinan Ag & B.............182 A8
Crindledyke N Lans.............175 L6
Cringleford Norfk.............92 E3
Crinow Pembks.............49 J5
Croachy Highld.............213 G8
Crockenhill Kent.............45 J6
Crocker End Oxon.............42 B3

Crockernwell Devon 11 H6
Crockerton Wilts.............27 K3
Crocketford D & G.............154 E7
Crockham Hill Kent.........32 D3
Croeserw Neath.............36 D2
Croes-goch Pembks.........48 D2
Croes-lan Cerdgn.............65 L5
Croesor Gwynd.............95 L4
Croesyceiliog Carmth.........50 E3
Croesyceiliog Torfn.............37 L2
Croft Leics.............87 G4
Croft Lincs.............104 E1
Croft Warrtn.............112 F3
Croftamie Stirlg.............174 E2
Crofton Wakefd.............124 B6
Croft-on-Tees N York.............141 H5
Croftown Highld.............220 F5
Crofts Moray.............215 G4
Crofts Bank Traffd.............113 H3
Crofts of Dipple Moray.............215 H3
Crofts of Haddo Abers.............216 F6
Crofts of Savoch Abers.............217 K3
Crofty Swans.............51 G6
Croggan Ag & B.............181 L3
Croglin Cumb.............148 F5
Croick Highld.............222 B3
Cromarty Highld.............223 H7
Crombie Fife.............176 E2
Cromdale Highld.............214 D8
Cromer Herts.............59 M3
Cromer Norfk.............106 F4
Cromford Derbys.............100 F2
Cromhall S Glos.............39 G3
Cromor W Isls.............232 f3
Cromore W Isls.............232 f3
Cromwell Notts.............102 C1
Cronberry E Ayrs.............164 C5
Crondall Hants.............30 C2
Cronton Knows.............112 C4
Crook Cumb.............138 C2
Crook Dur.............150 E7
Crookedholm E Ayrs.............163 L3
Crookes Sheff.............114 F4
Crookham Nthumb.............168 D2
Crookham W Berk.............41 K7
Crookham Village Hants.............30 C2
Crook Inn Border.............165 L4
Crooklands Cumb.............129 L3
Crook of Devon P & K.............185 L7
Cropredy Oxon.............72 F5
Cropston Leics.............87 G2
Cropthorne Worcs.............71 H5
Cropton N York.............134 B2
Cropwell Bishop Notts.............102 B5
Cropwell Butler Notts.............102 B5
Cros W Isls.............232 g1
Crosbost W Isls.............232 f3
Crosby Cumb.............147 J7
Crosby IoM.............237 c5
Crosby N Linc.............125 K7
Crosby Sefton.............111 J2
Crosby Garret Cumb.............139 G5
Crosby Ravensworth Cumb.............138 F4
Croscombe Somset.............26 E3
Cross Somset.............26 B1
Crossaig Ag & B.............172 E2
Crossapol Ag & B.............188 C7
Cross Ash Mons.............54 B4
Cross-at-Hand Kent.............33 K4
Crossbost W Isls.............232 f3
Crosscanonby Cumb.............147 J6
Crossdale Street Norfk.............106 F5
Cross Flatts C Brad.............123 G3
Crossford Fife.............176 E2
Crossford S Lans.............175 L8
Crossgatehall E Loth.............177 K5
Crossgates E Ayrs.............163 J1
Crossgates Fife.............176 F1

Cross Gates Leeds.........124 B4
Crossgates N York.........134 F3
Crossgill Lancs.............129 L6
Cross Green Leeds.........123 L4
Cross Green Suffk.........77 K4
Cross Green Suffk.........78 B4
Cross Hands Carmth.........51 H3
Crosshands E Ayrs.........163 L4
Crosshill Fife.............186 C7
Crosshill S Ayrs.............163 J7
Crosshouse E Ayrs.........163 K2
Cross Houses Shrops.........83 K3
Cross in Hand E Susx.........20 B2
Cross Inn Cerdgn.............65 L3
Cross Inn Cerdgn.............66 D2
Cross Keys Ag & B.........174 C2
Crosskeys Caerph.............37 K3
Crosskirk Highld.............230 F2
Cross Lane IoW.............17 G4
Cross Lane Head Shrops.............84 C4
Crosslee Rens.............174 D5
Crossmichael D & G.........146 C2
Cross of Jackston Abers.............216 E7
Cross o' th' hands Derbys.............100 F4
Crossroads Abers.........206 B4
Crossroads Abers.........206 E6
Cross Street Suffk.........92 E7
Crosston Angus.............196 E5
Cross Town Ches E.........113 H5
Crossway Green Worcs.............70 E2
Crossways Dorset.............14 E5
Crosswell Pembks.............64 F6
Crosthwaite Cumb.............129 J2
Croston Lancs.............121 G6
Crostwick Norfk.............92 F1
Crouch End Gt Lon.............44 F3
Croucheston Wilts.............28 B6
Crouch Hill Dorset.............14 D1
Croughton Nhants.............73 G7
Crovie Abers.............216 F2
Crowan Cnwll.............3 H4
Crowborough E Susx.............32 F6
Crowborough Warren E Susx.............32 F6
Crowcombe Somset.............25 H4
Crowdecote Derbys.............114 C7
Crowden Derbys.............114 B2
Crow Edge Barns.............114 D2
Crowell Oxon.............58 C7
Crowfield Suffk.............78 D3
Crowhill E Loth.............178 F4
Crow Hill Herefs.............54 F3
Crowhurst E Susx.............20 F3
Crowhurst Surrey.............32 D4
Crowland Lincs.............89 J2
Crowland Lincs.............78 B1
Crowlas Cnwll.............2 F5
Crowle N Linc.............125 J7
Crowle Worcs.............71 G4
Crowle Green Worcs.............71 G3
Crowmarsh Gifford Oxon.............41 L3
Crown Corner Suffk.............78 F1
Crownhill C Plym.............6 C4
Crownpits Surrey.............30 F3
Crownthorpe Norfk.............92 C3
Crowntown Cnwll.............3 H5
Crows-an-Wra Cnwll.............2 D5
Crowthorne Wokham.............42 D7
Crowton Ches W.............112 E4
Croxdale Dur.............151 G7
Croxden Staffs.............100 B5
Croxley Green Herts.............43 H2
Croxteth Lpool.............111 L3
Croxton Cambs.............75 J3
Croxton N Linc.............126 D7
Croxton Norfk.............91 K4
Croxton Norfk.............106 B6
Croxton Staffs.............99 H6
Croxton Kerrial Leics.............102 D6
Croy Highld.............213 J4
Croy N Lans.............175 J3
Croyde Devon.............23 G4

Croydon Cambs 75 K5
Croydon Gt Lon.............44 F6
Crubenmore Highld.... 203 G7
Cruckmeole Shrops 83 H2
Cruckton Shrops.........83 H2
Cruden Bay Abers 217 K6
Crudgington Wrekin 98 F8
Crudie Abers................. 216 E3
Crudwell Wilts..............39 L2
Crumlin Caerph 37 K2
Crumplehorn Cnwll......... 5 K5
Crumpsall Manch........ 113 J2
Crundale Kent...............34 E5
Crux Easton Hants 29 H1
Crwbin Carmth...............50 F3
Cryers Hill Bucks 42 E2
Crymych Pembks.............65 G2
Crynant Neath................52 C6
Crystal Palace Gt Lon....45 G5
Cuaig Highld................. 209 L3
Cuan Ag & B 181 L4
Cubert Cnwll 4 C4
Cublington Bucks...........58 D4
Cublington Herefs..........69 H6
Cuckfield W Susx...........32 B7
Cucklington Somset......27 H6
Cuckney Notts............. 115 K7
Cuddesdon Oxon...........57 L7
Cuddington Bucks..........58 C5
Cuddington Ches W 112 E7
Cuddington Heath
   Ches W......................98 C3
Cudham Gt Lon..............32 D2
Cudliptown Devon.......... 6 D1
Cudnell BCP...................15 K3
Cudworth Barns.......... 124 B8
Cudworth Somset...........13 J1
Cuffley Herts.................59 M7
Cuil Highld 191 J5
Culbokie Highld........... 212 F3
Culburnie Highld.......... 212 D6
Culcabock Highld......... 213 G5
Culcharry Highld.......... 213 K4
Culcheth Warrtn.......... 112 F3
Culdrain Abers............ 215 L7
Culduie Highld............ 209 L6
Culford Suffk.................77 J1
Culgaith Cumb............ 138 E2
Culham Oxon..................41 J2
Culkein Highld 224 C2
Culkein Drumbeg
   Highld...................... 224 D2
Culkerton Gloucs 39 L2
Cullen Moray............... 215 L2
Cullercoats N Tyne 159 J7
Cullerlie Abers............ 206 E5
Cullicudden Highld...... 213 G2
Cullingworth C Brad ... 123 G3
Cuillin Hills Highld 199 G2
Cullipool Ag & B.......... 181 L5
Cullivoe Shet.............. 235 d2
Culloden Highld........... 213 H5
Cullompton Devon 12 C2
Cullompton
   Services Devon 12 D2
Culm Davy Devon 25 H7
Culmington Shrops.......83 J6
Culmstock Devon...........25 H8
Culnacraig Highld........ 224 C7
Culnaightrie D & G...... 146 D5
Culnaknock Highld...... 209 H2
Culrain Highld............. 222 D3
Culross Fife................. 176 D2
Culroy S Ayrs............... 163 H6
Culsalmond Abers....... 216 C7
Culscadden D & G....... 145 K5
Culshabbin D & G........ 145 G5
Culswick Shet.............. 235 b6
Cultercullen Abers...... 207 H1
Cults C Aber................ 207 G5
Culverstone Green
   Kent..........................45 M7
Culverthorpe Lincs 103 G4
Culworth Nhants...........73 G5
Culzean Castle &
   Country Park
   S Ayrs...................... 163 G7
Cumbernauld N Lans... 175 K4

Cumbernauld
   Village N Lans 175 K3
Cumberworth Lincs 119 G6
Cuminestown Abers.... 216 F4
Cumledge Border 179 G6
Cummersdale Cumb... 148 D4
Cummertrees D & G ... 147 K2
Cummingston
   Moray...................... 214 E1
Cumnock E Ayrs......... 164 B5
Cumnor Oxon.................57 J7
Cumrew Cumb 148 F5
Cumrue D & G 155 J5
Cumwhinton Cumb 148 D4
Cumwhitton Cumb 148 E4
Cundall N York............ 132 F5
Cunninghamhead
   N Ayrs...................... 163 J2
Cunningsburgh Shet... 235 c7
Cupar Fife.................. 186 F4
Cupar Muir Fife.......... 186 F5
Curbar Derbys............ 114 E6
Curbridge Hants..........17 G1
Curbridge Oxon...........57 G6
Curdridge Hants...........29 K8
Curdworth Warwks.......85 L5
Curland Somset.............25 L7
Curridge W Berk 41 J6
Currie C Edin............... 177 G5
Curry Mallet Somset.....25 L6
Curry Rivel Somset.......26 B6
Curtisden Green
   Kent..........................33 J5
Curtisknowle Devon 7 H5
Cury Cnwll..................... 3 H6
Cushnie Abers............ 205 L3
Cusworth Donc........... 115 K2
Cutcloy D & G 145 J7
Cutcombe Somset 24 E4
Cuthill Highld 223 G4
Cutnall Green Worcs 70 F2
Cutsdean Gloucs...........56 C3
Cutthorpe Derbys 115 G6
Cuxham Oxon................42 A2
Cuxton Medway............46 B6
Cuxwold Lincs............ 117 K2
Cwm Denbgs............... 110 E6
Cwmafan Neath............36 B3
Cwmaman Rhondd........52 F7
Cwmbach Carmth..........50 B1
Cwmbach Powys...........68 D6
Cwmbach Rhondd........52 F7
Cwmbran Torfn............37 L2
Cwmcarn Caerph..........37 K2
Cwmcarvan Mons.........54 C6
Cwm-cou Cerdgn..........65 J6
Cwm Crawnon
   Powys........................53 H4
Cwmdare Rhondd........52 F7
Cwmdu Powys..............53 J4
Cwmdu Swans..............51 J6
Cwmduad Carmth.........65 L7
Cwmfelin Brdgnd 36 D3
Cwmfelin Myr Td..........53 H7
Cwmfelin Boeth
   Carmth......................49 K4
Cwmfelinfach Caerph....37 J3
Cwmffrwd Carmth........50 E3
Cwmgiedd Powys.........52 C5
Cwmgorse Carmth........51 K4
Cwmgwili Carmth.........51 H4
Cwmhiraeth Carmth.....65 K6
Cwm Llinau Powys.......81 J2
Cwmllynfell Neath........51 L3
Cwmmawr Carmth........51 G3
Cwmparc Rhondd.........36 E2
Cwmpengraig
   Carmth......................65 K7
Cwmtillery Blae G........53 K6
Cwm-twrch Isaf
   Powys........................52 B6
Cwm-twrch Uchaf
   Powys........................51 L4
Cwm-y-glo Gwynd...... 109 H8
Cwmystwyth Cerdgn....81 H8
Cwrtnewydd Cerdgn 66 C5
Cyfarthfa Castle
   Museum Myr Td........53 G6

Cyffylliog Denbgs..........97 G2
Cylibebyll Neath............51 L5
Cymmer Neath..............36 D2
Cymmer Rhondd...........36 F3
Cyncoed Cardif..............37 J4
Cynghordy Carmth........67 H6
Cynonville Neath..........36 C2
Cynwyd Denbgs............97 G4
Cynwyl Elfed Carmth 65 L8

D

Daccombe Devon 7 K3
Dacre Cumb................ 138 C2
Dacre N York............... 132 B7
Dacre Banks N York 132 B6
Daddry Shield Dur...... 149 M7
Dadford Bucks..............73 J6
Dadlington Leics 86 E4
Dafen Carmth................51 G5
Dagenham Gt Lon.........45 J3
Daglingworth Gloucs....55 M6
Dagnall Bucks...............59 G5
Dail bho Dheas
   W Isls...................... 232 g1
Dailly S Ayrs............... 152 F2
Dairsie Fife................. 187 G4
Dalabrog W Isls.......... 233 b8
Dalavich Ag & B.......... 182 D5
Dalbeattie D & G........ 146 E3
Dalby IoM.................... 237 b5
Dalby N York............... 133 K5
Dalcapon P & K........... 194 F5
Dalcham Highld........... 226 F7
Dalchreichart Highld ... 201 L3
Dalchruin P & K 184 F4
Dalcrue P & K 185 L2
Dalditch Devon.............12 D5
Dale Pembks.................48 D6
Dale Abbey Derbys..... 101 H5
Dalelia Highld 190 E3
Dalgarven N Ayrs....... 163 H1
Dalgety Bay Fife......... 177 G2
Dalgig E Ayrs.............. 164 B6
Dalginross P & K......... 185 G3
Dalguise P & K............ 194 F6
Dalhalvaig Highld....... 230 C5
Dalham Suffk.................77 G3
Daliburgh W Isls......... 233 b8
Dalkeith Mdloth.......... 177 K5
Dallas Moray............... 214 D4
Dallinghoo Suffk...........78 F4
Dallington E Susx 20 D2
Dallington Nhants 73 K3
Dalmally Ag & B 183 H3
Dalmary Stirlg 184 C7
Dalmellington
   E Ayrs...................... 153 K2
Dalmeny C Edin 176 F3
Dalmore Highld.......... 222 F7
Dalmuir W Duns........ 174 E4
Dalnabreck Highld...... 190 E3
Dalnacardoch P & K ... 194 B3
Dalnahaitnach
   Highld...................... 203 K2
Dalnaspidal P & K 193 K2
Dalness Highld............ 192 B6
Dalqueich P & K.......... 185 M6
Dalquhairn S Ayrs...... 153 G3
Dalreavoch Highld...... 226 D6
Dalry N Ayrs............... 174 B7
Dalrymple E Ayrs........ 163 J6
Dalserf S Lans............ 175 L7
Dalsmeran Ag & B...... 161 G6
Dalston Cumb............. 148 C5
Dalston Gt Lon.............45 G3
Dalswinton D & G....... 155 G5
Dalton D & G............... 155 K7
Dalton N York............. 132 F4
Dalton N York............. 140 E5
Dalton Nthumb........... 158 E7
Dalton-in-Furness
   Cumb....................... 128 F5
Dalton-le-Dale Dur.... 151 K7

Dalton-on-Tees
   N York...................... 141 H5
Dalton Piercy Hartpl.... 141 L2
Dalveich Stirlg............ 184 D3
Dalwhinnie Highld...... 202 F7
Dalwood Devon.............13 G3
Damerham Hants..........28 C7
Damgate Norfk..............93 J2
Damnaglaur D & G...... 144 D7
Danbury Essex..............61 J6
Danby N York.............. 142 F5
Danby Wiske N York.... 141 H7
Dandaleith Moray....... 215 G5
Danderhall Mdloth...... 177 J4
Danebridge Ches E 113 L7
Dane End Herts............60 B4
Danehill E Susx 32 D7
Dane Hills C Leic...........87 H3
Dane Street Kent..........34 E4
Danshillock Abers...... 216 D3
Danskine E Loth 178 C5
Darenth Kent................45 K5
Daresbury Halton....... 112 E5
Darfield Barns............ 115 H1
Dargate Kent................34 E3
Dargavel Rens............ 174 D4
Darite Cnwll 5 K3
Darlaston Wsall............85 H4
Darlaston Green
   Wsall........................85 H4
Darley N York.............. 132 C7
Darley Abbey C Derb ... 101 G5
Darley Bridge
   Derbys..................... 100 E1
Darley Dale Derbys 114 F8
Darley Green Solihll.....85 L8
Darleyhall Herts...........59 J4
Darley Head N York.... 132 B7
Darlingscott Warwks....72 B6
Darlington Darltn 141 H4
Darlton Notts............. 116 C6
Darnick Border........... 167 H3
Darowen Powys............81 H3
Darra Abers................ 216 E5
Darracott Devon........... 9 G2
Darracott Devon...........23 G4
Darras Hall Nthumb.... 158 E7
Darrington Wakefd.... 124 D6
Darsham Suffk...............79 J1
Darshill Somset............26 E3
Dartford Kent...............45 K5
Dartford Crossing
   Kent..........................45 K5
Dartington Devon 7 H4
Dartmoor National
   Park Devon.............. 11 G8
Dartmouth Devon 7 K5
Darton Barns............. 123 L7
Darvel E Ayrs.............. 164 B2
Darwen Bl w D........... 121 K6
Datchet W & M.............43 G5
Datchworth Herts.........59 L4
Daubhill Bolton.......... 121 K8
Daugh of
   Kinnermory
   Moray...................... 214 F6
Dauntsey Wilts.............39 M4
Dava Highld................ 214 C6
Davenham Ches W 112 F7
Davenport Stockp 113 K4
Daventry Nhants..........73 H3
Davidson's Mains
   C Edin...................... 177 G4
Davidstow Cnwll........... 8 F7
Davington D & G......... 155 M2
Davington Kent............34 D3
Daviot Abers.............. 216 E8
Daviot Highld.............. 213 H6
Daviot House Highld... 213 H6
Davoch of Grange
   Moray...................... 215 K4
Davyhulme Traffd...... 113 H3
Daw End Wsall..............85 J4
Dawesgreen Surrey......31 K3
Dawley Wrekin.............84 C2
Dawlish Devon..............12 B6
Dawlish Warren
   Devon...................... 12 C6

Daybrook Notts............ 101 L4
Daylesford Gloucs............56 E3
Deal Kent.....................35 K4
Dean Cumb 136 E3
Dean Devon 7 G3
Dean Devon 23 L2
Dean Hants..................29 K7
Dean Oxon...................57 G4
Dean Somset 26 F3
Dean Bottom Kent.........45 L6
Deanburnhaugh
    Border.................. 166 F6
Deancombe Devon.......... 7 G3
Dean Court Oxon...........57 J6
Deane Bolton.............. 121 K8
Deane Hants................29 K2
Deanhead Kirk............ 122 F7
Deanland Dorset...........27 M7
Dean Prior Devon.......... 7 H3
Deanraw Nthumb 149 L3
Deans W Loth 176 D5
Deanscales Cumb 136 F2
Deanshanger Nhants......73 L6
Deanshaugh Moray...... 215 H4
Deanston Stirlg 184 F6
Dearham Cumb 147 J2
Debach Suffk................78 F4
Debden Essex...............45 H2
Debden Essex...............60 E2
Debenham Suffk............78 E2
Deblin's Green Worcs.....70 E5
Dechmont W Loth 176 E4
Deddington Oxon...........57 J2
Dedham Essex...............62 C2
Dedworth W & M 42 F5
Deene Nhants 88 D5
Deenethorpe Nhants......88 D5
Deepcar Sheff............. 114 F3
Deeping Gate C Pete......89 G2
Deeping St James
    Lincs....................89 H2
Deeping St Nicholas
    Lincs....................89 J1
Deerhurst Gloucs...........55 K3
Defford Worcs...............71 G5
Defynnog Powys...........52 E3
Deganwy Conwy.......... 109 L5
Degnish Ag & B 182 A5
Deighton C York.......... 124 F2
Deighton N York.......... 141 J6
Deiniolen Gwynd......... 109 H8
Delabole Cnwll 8 E7
Delamere Ches W 112 E7
Delfrigs Abers............. 207 H2
Delliefure Highld......... 214 D7
Dell Quay W Susx.........18 A5
Delnabo Moray........... 204 E3
Delny Highld............... 223 G6
Delph Oldham............. 122 E8
Delves Dur................. 150 E5
Dembleby Lincs.......... 103 H5
Denaby Donc.............. 115 J2
Denbigh Denbgs.......... 110 E7
Denbrae Fife.............. 186 F4
Denbury Devon.............. 7 J3
Denby Derbys............. 101 H4
Denby Dale Kirk........... 123 J8
Denchworth Oxon.........41 G3
Dendron Cumb 128 F5
Denfield P & K............ 185 K4
Denford Nhants 88 E7
Dengie Essex...............62 B7
Denham Bucks..............43 H3
Denham Suffk...............77 H3
Denham Suffk...............92 E8
Denham Green
    Bucks 43 H3
Denhead Abers 217 J4
Denhead Fife.............. 187 G5
Denhead of Gray
    C Dund 186 F2
Denholm Border 167 J5
Denholme C Brad 123 G4
Denmead Hants 30 A8
Denmore C Aber 207 H3
Dennington Suffk..........79 G2
Denny Falk 175 L2
Dennyloanhead Falk ... 175 L3

Den of Lindores Fife... 186 D4
Denshaw Oldham 122 E7
Denside of Durris
    Abers................... 206 F6
Densole Kent................35 G6
Denston Suffk...............77 H4
Denstone Staffs 100 C4
Denstroude Kent...........34 E3
Dent Cumb 130 D3
Denton Cambs..............89 G6
Denton Darltn............ 140 F4
Denton E Susx..............19 L5
Denton Kent.................35 G5
Denton Kent.................46 A5
Denton Lincs.............. 102 E6
Denton N York............ 123 H2
Denton Nhants.............74 B3
Denton Norfk................93 G5
Denton Tamesd........... 113 L3
Denver Norfk................90 E3
Denwick Nthumb........ 169 J6
Deopham Norfk............92 C4
Deopham Green
    Norfk....................92 C4
Depden Suffk................77 H3
Deptford Gt Lon............45 G4
Deptford Wilts..............28 A4
Derby C Derb.............. 101 G5
Derby Devon.................23 J5
Derbyhaven IoM.......... 237 b7
Derculich P & K........... 194 D5
Dereham Norfk.............92 B2
Deri Caerph 53 H7
Derringstone Kent.........35 G5
Derrington Staffs 99 K7
Derry Hill Wilts.............39 L6
Derrythorpe N Linc..... 125 J4
Dersingham Norfk....... 105 H6
Dervaig Ag & B 189 K6
Derwen Denbgs.............97 G3
Derwenlas Powys.........80 F4
Derwent Valley Mills
    Derbys.................. 100 F2
Derwent Water
    Cumb 137 J3
Desborough Nhants......88 B6
Desford Leics...............86 F3
Detling Kent.................33 K2
Devauden Mons............54 C7
Devil's Bridge Cerdgn...81 G7
Devizes Wilts................40 A7
Devonport C Plym.......... 6 C5
Devonside Clacks 185 J7
Devoran Cnwll............... 4 C7
Devoran & Perran
    Cnwll....................... 3 K4
Dewarton Mdloth 177 K5
Dewlish Dorset.............14 E3
Dewsbury Kirk............ 123 K6
Dewsbury Moor
    Kirk..................... 123 J6
Deytheur Powys...........97 K8
Dibden Hants...............16 E2
Dibden Purlieu
    Hants....................16 E2
Dickleburgh Norfk........92 E6
Didbrook Gloucs...........56 B2
Didcot Oxon.................41 K3
Diddington Cambs.........75 H2
Diddlebury Shrops........83 K6
Didling W Susx.............18 A3
Didmarton Gloucs.........39 J3
Didsbury Manch 113 J3
Digby Lincs................ 103 H2
Digg Highld............... 218 C7
Diggle Oldham............ 122 F8
Digmoor Lancs............ 112 C1
Dihewyd Cerdgn...........66 C4
Dilham Norfk............. 107 G7
Dilhorne Staffs.............99 L4
Dill Hall Lancs............ 121 L4
Dillington Cambs..........75 G2
Dilston Nthumb........... 150 B3
Dilton Wilts.................27 K2
Dilton Marsh Wilts........27 J2
Dilwyn Herefs..............69 H4
Dinas Gwynd................94 E5
Dinas Cross Pembks......64 E6

Dinas-Mawddwy
    Gwynd....................81 J1
Dinas Powys V Glam 37 J6
Dinder Somset..............26 E3
Dinedor Herefs..............69 K6
Dingestow Mons...........54 C6
Dingle Lpool............... 111 K4
Dingley Nhants..............87 L6
Dingwall Highld........... 212 E3
Dinnet Abers.............. 205 K5
Dinnington N u Ty 158 F7
Dinnington Rothm....... 115 K4
Dinnington Somset 26 B8
Dinorwig Gwynd...........95 K1
Dinorwig Slate
    Landscape Gwynd....95 K1
Dinton Bucks................58 C5
Dinton Wilts.................28 A5
Dinwoodie D & G........ 155 K4
Dinworthy Devon........... 9 J2
Dipford Somset.............25 J6
Dippen Ag & B 161 K2
Dippertown Devon........10 C7
Dippin N Ayrs............. 162 D5
Dipple Moray.............. 215 H3
Dipple S Ayrs.............. 152 E2
Diptford Devon.............. 7 G4
Dipton Dur................. 150 E4
Dirleton E Loth........... 178 B2
Dirt Pot Nthumb 149 L5
Diseworth Leics.......... 101 J7
Dishforth N York......... 132 F5
Disley Ches E.............. 113 L5
Diss Norfk....................92 D7
Distington Cumb......... 136 D3
Ditchampton Wilts........28 C5
Ditcheat Somset...........26 F4
Ditchingham Norfk........93 G5
Ditchling E Susx...........19 J3
Ditherington Shrops......83 K2
Ditteridge Wilts............39 J6
Dittisham Devon............ 7 K5
Ditton Kent..................33 J2
Ditton Green Cambs......76 F3
Ditton Priors Shrops......83 L5
Dixton Mons.................54 D5
Dobcross Oldham 113 M1
Dobwalls Cnwll............... 5 K3
Doccombe Devon..........11 H7
Dochgarroch Highld 212 F6
Docking Norfk............. 105 J5
Docklow Herefs............69 L3
Dockray Cumb 137 L3
Doddinghurst Essex......60 F7
Doddington Cambs.......90 B5
Doddington Kent...........34 C4
Doddington Lincs........ 116 E7
Doddington Nthumb.... 168 E3
Doddington Shrops........84 B7
Doddiscombsleigh
    Devon....................11 K7
Dodd's Green Ches E.....98 E4
Dodford Nhants............73 H3
Dodford Worcs..............85 G8
Dodington S Glos..........39 H4
Dodington Somset.........25 J4
Dodleston Ches W 98 A1
Dodside E Rens 174 F7
Dod's Leigh Staffs....... 100 A5
Dodworth Barns 114 F1
Doe Bank Birm..............85 K4
Dogdyke Lincs............ 103 K2
Dogmersfield Hants......30 C2
Dogsthorpe C Pete........89 H4
Dolanog Powys.............82 B2
Dolbenmaen Gwynd......95 J4
Dolfach Powys..............81 K3
Dolfor Powys................82 C6
Dolgarrog Conwy........ 109 L7
Dolgellau Gwynd..........96 B8
Doll Highld................. 226 F7
Dollar Clacks.............. 185 K7
Dollarfield Clacks....... 185 K7
Dolphin Flints............ 111 H6
Dolphinholme Lancs ... 129 L8
Dolphinton S Lans...... 176 F8
Dolton Devon...............10 E3
Dolwen Conwy........... 110 B6

Dolwyddelan Conwy......96 B3
Domgay Powys.............97 L8
Doncaster Donc.......... 115 L2
Doncaster North
    Services Donc........ 125 G7
Doncaster Sheffield
    Airport Donc......... 115 M2
Donhead St Andrew
    Wilts....................27 K6
Donhead St Mary
    Wilts....................27 K6
Donibristle Fife 177 G2
Doniford Somset...........25 G3
Donington Lincs.......... 103 K5
Donington on Bain
    Lincs................... 118 C5
Donington Park
    Services Leics........ 101 J7
Donisthorpe Leics.........86 C2
Donnington Gloucs........56 D3
Donnington Shrops........83 L2
Donnington W Berk 41 J6
Donnington W Susx 18 B5
Donnington Wrekin.......84 C2
Donnington Wood
    Wrekin...................84 C2
Donyatt Somset............25 M8
Doonfoot S Ayrs.......... 163 H5
Dorback Lodge
    Highld.................. 204 D3
Dorchester Dorset.........14 D4
Dorchester-on-
    Thames Oxon.........41 L2
Dordon Warwks............86 C4
Dore Sheff................. 114 F5
Dores Highld.............. 212 F7
Dorking Surrey.............31 K2
Dormansland Surrey.....32 D5
Dormington Herefs.......69 L6
Dormston Worcs...........71 H3
Dorney Bucks...............42 F5
Dornie Highld............. 200 D1
Dornoch Highld........... 223 H4
Dornock D & G............ 147 M2
Dorrery Highld............ 230 F5
Dorridge Solhll.............85 L8
Dorrington Lincs.......... 103 H2
Dorrington Shrops........83 J3
Dorrington Shrops........99 G4
Dorsington Warwks.......71 K4
Dorstone Herefs...........69 G6
Dorton Bucks................58 B5
Douglas IoM............... 237 d6
Douglas S Lans........... 165 G4
Douglas and Angus
    C Dund 187 G2
Douglas Pier Ag & B.... 183 H7
Douglastown Angus.... 196 C6
Douglas Water
    S Lans 165 G3
Douglas West S Lans... 164 F3
Doulting Somset...........26 F3
Dounby Ork................ 234 b5
Doune Highld.............. 221 L2
Doune Stirlg.............. 184 F6
Dounepark S Ayrs....... 152 E3
Dounie Highld............ 222 D4
Dousland Devon............. 6 D3
Dove Dale Derbys....... 100 D3
Dove Holes Derbys..... 114 B6
Dovenby Cumb 147 J7
Dover Kent..................35 J6
Dover Castle Kent.........35 J6
Dovercourt Essex.........62 F2
Doverdale Worcs..........70 F2
Doveridge Derbys....... 100 C5
Doversgreen Surrey......31 L2
Dowally P & K............ 194 F6
Dowdeswell Gloucs......55 M4
Dowlais Myr Td.............53 G6
Dowland Devon............10 E2
Dowlish Wake
    Somset...................26 A8
Down Ampney
    Gloucs...................40 C2
Downderry Cnwll........... 5 L5
Downe Gt Lon..............45 H7
Downend Gloucs...........55 J2

Downend S Glos................38 F5
Downfield C Dund......186 F1
Downgate Cnwll.................6 A2
Downham Essex.............46 B2
Downham Gt Lon.............45 H5
Downham Lancs..........122 B2
Downham Market
    Norfk..........................90 E3
Down Hatherley
    Gloucs.......................55 K4
Downhead Somset.........26 E6
Downhead Somset..........27 G3
Downhill P & K...............186 A2
Downholme N York.......140 E7
Downies Abers.............207 H6
Downley Bucks.............42 D2
Down St Mary Devon....11 H4
Downside Surrey............43 J8
Down Thomas Devon.......6 D6
Downton Wilts...............28 D6
Dowsby Lincs...............103 J6
Doynton S Glos..............39 G5
Draethen Caerph.............37 K3
Draffan S Lans..............164 F1
Drakeholes Notts.........116 B4
Drakemyre N Ayrs.......174 B7
Drakes Broughton
    Worcs.........................71 G5
Draughton N York.........131 K8
Draughton Nhants...........87 L7
Drax N York.................125 G5
Draycote Warwks............72 F1
Draycott Derbys............101 H6
Draycott Gloucs..............71 L7
Draycott Somset.............26 C2
Draycott in the Clay
    Staffs.......................100 D6
Draycott in the
    Moors Staffs.............99 M4
Drayton C Port...............17 J2
Drayton Leics.................88 B5
Drayton Norfk.................92 E2
Drayton Oxon..................41 J2
Drayton Oxon..................72 E6
Drayton Somset..............26 B6
Drayton Worcs...............85 G7
Drayton Bassett
    Staffs.........................85 L4
Drayton Beauchamp
    Bucks.........................58 E5
Drayton Manor
    Resort Staffs.............85 L4
Drayton Parslow
    Bucks.........................58 D3
Drayton St Leonard
    Oxon.........................41 L2
Dreen Hill Pembks.........48 F5
Drefach Carmth...............51 G3
Drefach Carmth...............65 K6
Drefach Cerdgn...............66 C5
Dreghorn N Ayrs.........163 J2
Drellingore Kent.............35 H6
Drem E Loth................178 B3
Dresden C Stke................99 K4
Drewsteignton
    Devon........................11 H6
Driffield E R Yk............134 F7
Driffield Gloucs..............56 B7
Drift Cnwll.......................2 D5
Drigg Cumb..................136 E7
Drighlington Leeds.......123 J5
Drimnin Highld.............190 B5
Drimpton Dorset............13 K2
Drimsallie Highld.........191 J1
Dringhouses C York....124 E2
Drinkstone Suffk.............77 L3
Drinkstone Green
    Suffk...........................77 L3
Droitton Staffs.............100 A6
Droitwich Spa Worcs....70 F2
Dron P & K....................186 B4
Dronfield Derbys.........115 G5
Drongan E Ayrs............163 K5
Dronley Angus.............186 E1
Droop Dorset.................14 E2
Droxford Hants..............29 L7
Droylsden Tamesd.......113 K2
Druid Denbgs..................97 G4

Druidston Pembks..........48 E4
Druimarbin Highld.......191 L3
Druimavuic Ag & B.......191 K7
Druimdrishaig
    Ag & B.....................172 C4
Druimindarroch
    Highld......................199 L7
Drum Ag & B...............172 F3
Drum P & K.................185 L7
Drumalbin S Lans.........165 H2
Drumbeg Highld...........224 D3
Drumblade Abers..........216 B6
Drumbreddon D & G....144 C6
Drumbuie Highld..........210 B7
Drumburgh Cumb.........148 A3
Drumburn D & G...........146 F4
Drumburn D & G...........147 G3
Drumchapel C Glas.......174 F4
Drumchastle P & K.......193 L5
Drumclog S Lans..........164 C2
Drumeldrie Fife............187 G6
Drumelzier Border........165 M3
Drumfearn Highld.........199 L3
Drumfrennie Abers.......206 D5
Drumgley Angus...........196 C6
Drumguish Highld.........203 J5
Drumin Moray...............214 E7
Drumjohn D & G...........153 L3
Drumlamford S Ayrs....153 G6
Drumlasie Abers..........206 C4
Drumleaning Cumb.......148 A5
Drumlemble Ag & B......161 H5
Drumlithie Abers..........197 J1
Drummoddie D & G.....145 H6
Drummore D & G.........144 D7
Drummuir Moray..........215 J5
Drumnadrochit
    Highld......................212 D7
Drumnagorrach
    Moray.......................215 L4
Drumoak Abers............206 E5
Drumpark D & G...........154 F6
Drumruinie Highld........224 E7
Drumshang S Ayrs.......163 G6
Drumuie Highld............209 G5
Drumuillie Highld.........204 B2
Drumvaich Stirlg..........184 E6
Drunzie P & K..............186 B5
Drybeck Cumb..............138 F4
Drybridge Moray..........215 K2
Drybridge N Ayrs.........163 J3
Drybrook Gloucs............54 F4
Dryburgh Border..........167 J3
Dry Doddington
    Lincs........................102 D3
Dry Drayton Cambs.......75 L3
Drymen Stirlg...............174 E2
Drymuir Abers..............217 G5
Drynoch Highld............208 F7
Dubford Abers..............216 F2
Duchally Highld............225 J5
Ducklington Oxon..........57 G6
Duddenhoe End
    Essex.........................76 C7
Duddingston C Edin.....177 J4
Duddington Nhants........88 E4
Duddlestone Somset.....25 K7
Duddo Nthumb..............168 D2
Duddon Ches W............112 D8
Dudleston Shrops..........97 M5
Dudleston Heath
    Shrops.......................98 A5
Dudley Dudley................85 G5
Dudley N Tyne.............159 G7
Dudley Port Sandw........85 G5
Dudsbury Dorset............15 K3
Duffield Derbys............101 G4
Duffryn Neath................36 C2
Dufftown Moray............215 H6
Duffus Moray................214 E2
Dufton Cumb................139 G3
Duggleby N York..........134 D6
Duirinish Highld............210 B7
Duisdalemore
    Highld......................199 L3
Duisky Highld...............191 K2
Dukestown Blae G.........53 H6
Duke Street Suffk..........78 C6

Dukinfield Tamesd........113 L2
Dulcote Somset..............26 E3
Dulford Devon................12 D2
Dull P & K....................194 C6
Dullatur N Lans............175 K3
Dullingham Cambs.........76 F3
Dulnain Bridge
    Highld......................204 B1
Duloe Bed.......................75 H3
Duloe Cnwll......................5 K4
Dulsie Bridge
    Highld......................213 L6
Dulverton Somset..........24 E5
Dulwich Gt Lon.............45 G5
Dumbarton W Duns......174 D4
Dumbleton Gloucs..........71 H7
Dumfries D & G............155 G6
Dumgoyne Stirlg..........174 F2
Dummer Hants...............29 L3
Dumpton Kent................35 K2
Dun Angus....................197 G4
Dunalastair P & K........193 L5
Dunan Highld................209 J8
Dunan P & K................193 G5
Dunaverty Ag & B........161 H7
Dunball Somset..............25 L3
Dunbar E Loth..............178 E3
Dunbeath Highld..........227 L3
Dunbeg Ag & B............182 C2
Dunblane Stirlg............185 G6
Dunbog Fife..................186 E4
Duncanston Highld.......212 F3
Duncanstone Abers......216 B8
Dunchideock Devon......11 K7
Dunchurch Warwks........72 F1
Duncow D & G..............155 G5
Duncrievie P & K..........186 B5
Duncton W Susx............18 C3
Dundee C Dund............186 F2
Dundee Airport
    C Dund......................186 F2
Dundon Somset..............26 C5
Dundonald S Ayrs........163 J3
Dundonnell Highld........220 E4
Dundraw Cumb.............147 L5
Dundreggan Highld.......201 L3
Dundrennan D & G.......146 D5
Dundry N Som.................38 E6
Dunecht Abers..............206 E4
Dunfermline Fife..........176 F2
Dunfield Gloucs..............40 C2
Dungavel S Lans..........164 D3
Dungeness Kent.............21 L3
Dunham Massey
    Traffd.......................113 H4
Dunham-on-the-
    Hill Ches W..............112 C6
Dunham-on-Trent
    Notts........................116 D6
Dunhampton Worcs.......70 F2
Dunham Town Traffd...113 H4
Dunham
    Woodhouses
    Traffd.......................113 G4
Dunholme Lincs............117 G5
Dunino Fife..................187 J5
Dunipace Falk..............175 L2
Dunkeld P & K..............195 G7
Dunkerton BaNES..........39 G8
Dunkeswell Devon.........12 E2
Dunkeswick N York......123 L2
Dunkirk Kent..................34 E3
Dunkirk S Glos................39 H4
Dunk's Green Kent.........33 G3
Dunlappie Angus..........196 F3
Dunley Worcs.................70 E2
Dunlop E Ayrs..............174 D8
Dunmaglass Highld.......202 F2
Dunmore Falk...............176 B1
Dunnet Highld...............231 J2
Dunnichen Angus.........196 E6
Dunning P & K..............185 L4
Dunnington C York.......133 K8
Dunnington E R Yk......126 E2
Dunnington Warwks......71 J4
Dunoon Ag & B............173 K3
Dunphail Moray............214 C5
Dunragit D & G.............144 E4

Duns Border.................179 G7
Dunsby Lincs................103 J6
Dunscore D & G...........154 F5
Dunscroft Donc............124 F8
Dunsdale R & Cl..........142 D4
Dunsden Green
    Oxon.........................42 C5
Dunsdon Devon................9 J3
Dunsfold Surrey............31 G4
Dunsford Devon.............11 J6
Dunshalt Fife...............186 D5
Dunshillock Abers........217 J5
Dunsill Notts................101 J1
Dunsley N York............143 H5
Dunsley Staffs...............84 F6
Dunsmore Bucks...........58 E6
Dunsop Bridge
    Lancs.......................121 K1
Dunstable C Beds..........59 G4
Dunstall Staffs.............100 D7
Dunstan Nthumb...........169 K5
Dunster Somset.............24 F3
Duns Tew Oxon...............57 J3
Dunston Gatesd............151 G3
Dunston Lincs...............117 H8
Dunston Norfk................92 F3
Dunston Staffs...............99 L8
Dunstone Devon...............6 E5
Dunstone Devon...............7 G2
Dunsville Donc.............124 F8
Dunswell E R Yk..........126 D4
Dunsyre S Lans............176 E8
Dunterton Devon.............6 B1
Duntisbourne
    Abbots Gloucs...........55 L6
Duntisbourne
    Rouse Gloucs............55 M6
Duntish Dorset...............14 D2
Duntocher W Duns.......174 E4
Dunton Bucks.................58 D3
Dunton C Beds...............75 J5
Dunton Norfk................105 L6
Dunton Bassett Leics....87 G5
Dunton Green Kent........32 F2
Duntulm Highld............218 C6
Dunure S Ayrs..............163 G6
Dunvant Swans.............51 H6
Dunvegan Highld..........208 D5
Dunwich Suffk................79 K1
Durgan Cnwll...................3 K5
Durgates E Susx............33 H6
Durham Dur.................151 G6
Durham Cathedral
    Dur...........................151 G6
Durham Services
    Dur...........................151 H7
Durisdeer D & G...........154 F2
Durisdeermill
    D & G.......................154 F2
Durleigh Somset............25 L4
Durley Hants...................29 K7
Durley Wilts...................40 E7
Durley Street Hants......29 K7
Durlock Kent..................35 H5
Durlock Kent..................35 J2
Durness Highld.............228 F3
Durno Abers.................216 D8
Duror Highld................191 K5
Durran Ag & B..............182 D5
Durrington W Susx........18 F5
Durrington Wilts............28 D3
Dursley Gloucs...............39 H2
Dursley Cross Gloucs....55 G4
Durston Somset.............25 L5
Durweston Dorset..........15 G2
Duston Nhants................73 K3
Duthil Highld................203 L1
Dutton Ches W.............112 E5
Duxford Cambs..............76 C5
Duxford Oxon.................57 G7
Duxford IWM
    Cambs.......................76 C5
Dwygyfylchi Conwy.....109 L6
Dwyran IoA..................108 F7
Dyce C Aber.................207 G3
Dyfatty Carmth...............50 F5
Dyffryn Ardudwy
    Gwynd........................95 K7

Dyffryn Cellwen
Neath 52 D6
Dyke Lincs 103 J7
Dyke Moray 214 B3
Dykehead Angus 195 K5
Dykehead Angus 196 C4
Dykehead N Lans 176 B6
Dykehead Stirlg 184 D7
Dykelands Abers 197 H3
Dykends Angus 195 K5
Dykeside Abers 216 D5
Dykes of Gray
C Dund 186 E2
Dymchurch Kent 34 E8
Dymock Gloucs 55 G2
Dynamic Earth
C Edin 177 H4
Dyrham S Glos 39 H5
Dysart Fife 186 E8
Dyserth Denbgs 110 E5

E

Eagland Hill Lancs 120 F2
Eagle Lincs 116 E7
Eaglesfield Cumb 136 F2
Eaglesfield D & G 155 M7
Eaglesham E Rens 175 G7
Eagley Bolton 121 L7
Eakring Notts 102 A1
Ealand N Linc 125 J7
Ealing Gt Lon 44 D4
Eals Nthumb 149 H4
Eamont Bridge
Cumb 138 D2
Earby Lancs 122 D2
Earcroft Bl w D 121 K5
Eardington Shrops 84 C5
Eardisland Herefs 69 H3
Eardisley Herefs 68 F5
Eardiston Shrops 98 A7
Eardiston Worcs 70 C2
Earith Cambs 89 L8
Earlestown St Hel 112 E3
Earley Wokham 42 C6
Earlham Norfk 92 E2
Earlish Highld 208 F3
Earls Barton Nhants 74 C2
Earls Colne Essex 61 K3
Earls Common Worcs 71 G3
Earl's Croome Worcs 70 F6
Earlsdon Covtry 86 D7
Earlsferry Fife 187 H7
Earlsfield Gt Lon 44 E5
Earlsford Abers 216 F7
Earlsheaton Kirk 123 K6
Earl Shilton Leics 86 F4
Earl Soham Suffk 78 F2
Earl Sterndale
Derbys 114 C7
Earlston Border 167 J2
Earlston E Ayrs 163 K3
Earlswood Surrey 32 B4
Earlswood Warwks 85 K8
Earnley W Susx 17 M3
Earsdon N Tyne 159 H7
Earsham Norfk 93 G5
Eartham W Susx 18 C4
Easby N York 142 C5
Easdale Ag & B 181 L4
Easebourne W Susx 30 E6
Easenhall Warwks 86 F7
Eashing Surrey 30 F3
Easington Bucks 58 B6
Easington Dur 151 K6
Easington E R Yk 127 J6
Easington R & Cl 142 F4
Easington Colliery
Dur 151 K6
Easington Lane
Sundld 151 J5
Easingwold N York 133 H5
Eassie and Nevay
Angus 196 B7
East Aberthaw
V Glam 37 G6

East Allington Devon 7 H6
East Anstey Devon 24 D6
East Ardsley Leeds 123 K5
East Ashey IoW 17 H5
East Ashling W Susx 17 M2
East Ayton N York 134 F3
East Barkwith Lincs 117 K5
East Barming Kent 33 J3
East Barnby N York 143 G5
East Barnet Gt Lon 44 F2
East Barns E Loth 178 F3
East Barsham Norfk 105 L5
East Beckham
Norfk 106 E4
East Bedfont Gt Lon 43 H5
East Bergholt Suffk 78 C7
East Bilney Norfk 106 A8
East Blatchington
E Susx 20 A5
East Boldon S Tyne 151 J3
East Boldre Hants 16 D3
Eastbourne Darltn 141 H4
Eastbourne E Susx 20 C5
East Bradenham
Norfk 91 L2
East Brent Somset 25 M2
Eastbridge Suffk 79 J2
East Bridgford Notts ... 102 B4
East Buckland Devon 23 L5
East Budleigh Devon 12 D5
Eastburn C Brad 122 F2
Eastbury W Berk 41 G5
East Butterwick
N Linc 116 D1
Eastby N York 131 J8
East Calder W Loth 176 E5
East Carleton Norfk 92 E3
East Carlton Leeds 123 J2
East Carlton Nhants 88 B5
East Chaldon Dorset 14 E5
East Challow Oxon 41 G3
East Charleton
Devon 7 H7
East Chelborough
Dorset 14 A2
East Chiltington
E Susx 19 K3
East Chinnock
Somset 26 C8
East Chisenbury
Wilts 28 C2
Eastchurch Kent 47 G5
East Clandon Surrey 31 H2
East Claydon Bucks 58 C3
East Coker Somset 26 D8
Eastcombe Gloucs 55 K6
East Compton
Somset 26 E4
East Cornworthy
Devon 7 J5
Eastcote Gt Lon 43 J3
Eastcote Nhants 73 K4
Eastcote Solhll 85 L7
Eastcott Wilts 28 A1
East Cottingwith
E R Yk 125 G3
Eastcourt Wilts 40 E7
East Cowes IoW 16 F4
East Cowick E R Yk 125 G6
East Cowton N York 141 H6
East Cranmore
Somset 27 G3
East Dean E Susx 20 B6
East Dean Gloucs 54 F4
East Dean Hants 28 F6
East Dean W Susx 18 B3
East Drayton Notts 116 C6
East Dulwich Gt Lon 45 G5
East Dundry N Som 38 E7
East Ella C KuH 126 C5
Eastend Essex 46 F2
East End Hants 16 D3
East End Hants 41 H7
East End Kent 33 L6
East End Oxon 57 H5
East End Somset 26 F3
Easter Balmoral
Abers 205 G6

Easter Compton
S Glos 38 E4
Easter Dalziel Highld ... 213 H4
Eastergate W Susx 18 C5
Easterhouse C Glas 175 J5
Easter Howgate
Mdloth 177 H5
Easter Kinkell Highld 212 E4
Easter Moniack
Highld 212 E5
Eastern Green Covtry 86 C7
Easter Ord Abers 206 F4
Easter Pitkierie Fife 187 J6
Easter Skeld Shet 235 c6
Easter Softlaw
Border 168 A3
Easterton Wilts 28 A1
East Everleigh Wilts 28 D2
East Farleigh Kent 33 J3
East Farndon Nhants 87 K6
East Ferry Lincs 116 D2
Eastfield N Lans 176 B5
Eastfield N York 135 G3
East Fortune E Loth 178 C3
East Garston W Berk 41 G5
Eastgate Dur 150 B7
Eastgate Lincs 103 J8
Eastgate Norfk 106 D7
East Goscote Leics 87 J2
East Grafton Wilts 40 E7
East Grimstead Wilts 28 E5
East Grinstead
W Susx 32 D5
East Guldeford
E Susx 21 J2
East Haddon Nhants 73 J2
East Hagbourne
Oxon 41 K3
East Halton N Linc 126 E6
East Ham Gt Lon 45 H4
Easthampton Herefs 69 H2
East Hanney Oxon 41 H2
East Hanningfield
Essex 61 J7
East Hardwick
Wakefd 124 C6
East Harling Norfk 92 B6
East Harlsey N York 141 K7
East Harnham Wilts 28 C5
East Harptree BaNES 26 E1
East Harting W Susx 30 D7
East Hatch Wilts 27 L5
East Hatley Cambs 75 K4
East Hauxwell
N York 132 B2
East Haven Angus 187 J1
East Heckington
Lincs 103 K4
East Hedleyhope
Dur 150 E6
East Helmsdale
Highld 227 H5
East Hendred Oxon 41 J3
East Heslerton
N York 134 E4
East Hoathly E Susx 20 B3
East Holme Dorset 15 G5
Easthope Shrops 83 L4
Easthorpe Essex 61 L4
East Horrington
Somset 26 E3
East Horsley Surrey 31 H2
East Howe BCP 15 K4
East Huntspill
Somset 25 M3
East Ilsley W Berk 41 J4
Eastington Devon 11 H3
Eastington Gloucs 55 H6
Eastington Gloucs 56 C5
East Keal Lincs 118 E8
East Kennett Wilts 40 C6
East Keswick Leeds 124 B2
East Kilbride S Lans 175 H7
East Kirkby Lincs 118 D8
East Knighton Dorset 14 F5
East Knoyle Wilts 27 K5
East Lambrook
Somset 26 B7

Eastlands D & G 154 E7
East Langdon Kent 35 J5
East Langton Leics 87 K5
East Lavant W Susx 18 B4
East Lavington
W Susx 18 C3
East Layton N York 140 E5
Eastleach Martin
Gloucs 56 D6
Eastleach Turville
Gloucs 56 D6
East Leake Notts 101 K7
Eastleigh Devon 23 H5
Eastleigh Hants 29 J7
East Lexham Norfk 105 K8
Eastling Kent 34 C4
East Linton E Loth 178 D3
East Lockinge Oxon 41 H3
East Lound N Linc 116 C2
East Lulworth Dorset 15 G6
East Lutton N York 134 E5
East Lydford Somset 26 E5
East Malling Kent 33 J2
East Marden W Susx 30 D8
East Markham Notts 116 C6
East Martin Hants 28 B7
East Marton N York 122 D1
East Meon Hants 30 B6
East Mersea Essex 62 C5
East Midlands
Airport Leics 101 J7
East Molesey Surrey 43 J6
East Morden Dorset 15 G4
East Morton C Brad 123 G3
East Morton D & G 154 F3
East Ness N York 133 L4
Eastney C Port 17 J3
Eastnor Herefs 70 D6
East Norton Leics 87 L4
Eastoft N Linc 125 J7
East Ogwell Devon 7 J2
Easton Cambs 75 G1
Easton Devon 11 G6
Easton Dorset 14 D7
Easton Hants 29 K5
Easton Lincs 102 F7
Easton Norfk 92 D2
Easton Somset 26 D3
Easton Suffk 79 G3
Easton Wilts 39 K6
Easton Grey Wilts 39 K3
Easton-in-Gordano
N Som 38 D5
Easton Maudit
Nhants 74 C3
Easton-on-the-Hill
Nhants 88 E3
Easton Royal Wilts 40 D7
East Orchard Dorset 27 J7
East Peckham Kent 33 H4
East Pennard Somset 26 E4
East Portlemouth
Devon 7 H7
East Prawle Devon 7 H8
East Preston W Susx 18 E5
East Putford Devon 9 K2
East Quantoxhead
Somset 25 H3
East Rainton Sundld 151 H5
East Ravendale
NE Lin 118 C2
East Raynham Norfk 105 L7
Eastrea Cambs 89 K4
Eastriggs D & G 147 M2
East Rigton Leeds 124 B2
Eastrington E R Yk 125 J4
Eastrop Swindn 40 D2
East Rounton N York 141 K6
East Rudham Norfk 105 K6
East Runton Norfk 106 E4
East Ruston Norfk 107 H6
Eastry Kent 35 J4
East Saltoun E Loth 178 B5
East Sheen Gt Lon 44 D5
East Shefford W Berk 41 H5
East Stockwith Lincs 116 C3
East Stoke Dorset 15 G5
East Stoke Notts 102 C3

East Stour Dorset 27 J6
East Stourmouth
　Kent 35 H3
East Stowford Devon 23 K6
East Stratton Hants 29 K4
East Studdal Kent 35 J5
East Taphouse Cnwll 5 J3
East-the-Water
　Devon 23 G6
East Thirston
　Nthumb 158 F3
East Tilbury Thurr 46 B4
East Tisted Hants 30 B5
East Torrington
　Lincs 117 J5
East Tuddenham
　Norfk 92 C2
East Tytherley Hants 28 F5
East Tytherton Wilts 39 L5
East Village Devon 11 J4
Eastville Bristl 38 E5
Eastville Lincs 104 C2
East Walton Norfk 91 G1
East Week Devon 10 F6
Eastwell Leics 102 C6
East Wellow Hants 28 F7
East Wemyss Fife 186 E7
East Whitburn
　W Loth 176 C5
Eastwick Herts 60 C5
East Wickham
　Gt Lon 45 J5
East Williamston
　Pembks 49 J6
East Winch Norfk 91 G1
East Winterslow
　Wilts 28 E5
East Wittering
　W Susx 17 L3
East Witton N York 131 L3
Eastwood Notts 101 J3
Eastwood Sthend 46 D3
East Woodburn
　Nthumb 158 A5
East Woodhay Hants 41 H7
East Worldham
　Hants 30 C4
East Worthing
　W Susx 19 G5
East Wretham Norfk 91 K5
Eathorpe Warwks 72 E2
Eaton Ches E 113 K7
Eaton Ches W 112 E8
Eaton Leics 102 D6
Eaton Norfk 92 E3
Eaton Notts 116 B6
Eaton Oxon 57 H7
Eaton Shrops 83 K5
Eaton Bray C Beds 58 F4
Eaton Constantine
　Shrops 83 L3
Eaton Green C Beds 58 F4
Eaton Hastings Oxon 56 E7
Eaton Mascott
　Shrops 83 K3
Eaton Socon Cambs 75 H3
Eaton upon Tern
　Shrops 98 F7
Ebberston N York 134 D3
Ebbesborne Wake
　Wilts 27 M6
Ebbsfleet Kent 45 L5
Ebbw Vale Blae G 53 J6
Ebchester Dur 150 D4
Ebford Devon 12 C5
Ebley Gloucs 55 J6
Ebnal Ches W 98 C3
Ebrington Gloucs 71 L6
Ecchinswell Hants 41 J8
Ecclaw Border 178 F5
Ecclefechan D & G 155 L7
Eccles Border 168 A2
Eccles Kent 46 B7
Eccles Salfd 113 H2
Ecclesall Sheff 114 F5
Ecclesfield Sheff 115 G3
Eccleshall Staffs 99 J6
Eccleshill C Brad 123 H4

Ecclesmachan
　W Loth 176 E4
Eccles Road Norfk 92 B5
Eccleston Ches W 112 B8
Eccleston Lancs 121 G6
Eccleston St Hel 112 C3
Echt Abers 206 E4
Eckford Border 167 L4
Eckington Derbys 115 H5
Eckington Worcs 71 G6
Ecton Nhants 74 B2
Edale Derbys 114 C4
Eday Ork 234 d4
Eday Airport Ork 234 d4
Edburton W Susx 19 H4
Edderton Highld 222 F4
Eddleston Border 177 H8
Eddlewood S Lans 175 J7
Edenbridge Kent 32 D4
Edenfield Lancs 122 B6
Edenhall Cumb 138 E2
Edenham Lincs 103 H7
Eden Park Gt Lon 45 G6
Eden Project Cnwll 5 G5
Edensor Derbys 114 E7
Edentaggart Ag & B 183 K8
Edenthorpe Donc 115 L1
Edern Gwynd 94 E5
Edgbaston Birm 85 J6
Edgcott Bucks 58 B4
Edgcott Somset 24 D4
Edge Gloucs 55 J6
Edgefield Norfk 106 C5
Edgefield Green
　Norfk 106 D5
Edgerton Kirk 123 H6
Edgeworth Gloucs 55 L6
Edgmond Wrekin 99 G8
Edgton Shrops 83 H6
Edgware Gt Lon 44 D2
Edgworth Bl w D 121 L6
Edinbane Highld 208 E4
Edinburgh C Edin 177 H4
Edinburgh Airport
　C Edin 176 F4
Edinburgh Castle
　C Edin 177 H4
Edinburgh Old &
　New Town C Edin 177 H4
Edinburgh Zoo
　RZSS C Edin 177 G4
Edingale Staffs 86 B2
Edingham D & G 146 E3
Edingley Notts 102 A2
Edingthorpe Norfk 107 G6
Edingthorpe Green
　Norfk 107 G6
Edington Border 179 J7
Edington Nthumb 158 E5
Edington Somset 26 B4
Edington Wilts 27 L2
Edingworth Somset 26 A2
Edithmead Somset 25 L2
Edith Weston Rutlnd 88 D3
Edlesborough Bucks 58 F4
Edlingham Nthumb 169 G7
Edlington Lincs 118 C7
Edmondsham Dorset 15 K1
Edmondsley Dur 151 G5
Edmondthorpe Leics 102 E8
Edmonton Gt Lon 45 G2
Edmundbyers Dur 150 C5
Ednam Border 167 L2
Edradynate P & K 194 D6
Edrom Border 179 H7
Edstaston Shrops 98 D6
Edstone Warwks 71 L3
Edwalton Notts 101 L5
Edwinstowe Notts 115 L7
Edworth C Beds 75 J6
Edwyn Ralph Herefs 70 B3
Edzell Angus 196 F3
Edzell Woods Abers 197 G3
Efail-fach Neath 36 B2
Efail Isaf Rhondd 37 G4
Efailnewydd Gwynd 94 F5
Efailwen Carmth 49 K3
Efenechtyd Denbgs 97 H2

Effgill D & G 156 B4
Effingham Surrey 31 J2
Egerton Bolton 121 K7
Egerton Kent 34 B5
Eggborough N York 124 E5
Eggbuckland C Plym 6 D4
Eggesford Devon 11 G3
Eggington C Beds 58 F3
Egginton Derbys 100 E6
Eggleston Dur 140 C3
Egham Surrey 43 G6
Egleton Rutlnd 88 C3
Eglingham Nthumb 169 G5
Egloshayle Cnwll 4 F2
Egloskerry Cnwll 9 H7
Eglwysbach Conwy 109 M7
Eglwys Cross
　Wrexhm 98 C4
Eglwyswrw Pembks 65 G6
Egmanton Notts 116 B7
Egremont Cumb 136 D5
Egremont Wirral 111 K3
Egton N York 143 G6
Egton Bridge N York 143 G6
Egypt Bucks 42 F3
Eigg Highld 199 G7
Eight Ash Green
　Essex 61 M3
Eilanreach Highld 200 C2
Eilean Donan Castle
　Highld 200 D1
Eisgein W Isls 232 f3
Eishken W Isls 232 f3
Elan Valley Powys 67 J2
Elan Village Powys 67 K2
Elberton S Glos 38 E3
Elburton C Plym 6 D5
Elcombe Swindn 40 C4
Eldersfield Worcs 55 H2
Elderslie Rens 174 E5
Eldon Dur 141 G2
Elerch Cerdgn 80 F6
Elfhill Abers 206 F7
Elford Staffs 85 L2
Elgin Moray 214 F2
Elgol Highld 199 H3
Elham Kent 35 G6
Elie Fife 187 H7
Elim IoA 108 D4
Eling Hants 29 G8
Elkesley Notts 116 B6
Elkstone Gloucs 55 L5
Ella Abers 216 C3
Ellacombe Torbay 7 L3
Elland Calder 123 G6
Ellary Ag & B 172 C3
Ellastone Staffs 100 C4
Ellel Lancs 129 K7
Ellemford Border 178 F6
Ellenabeich Ag & B 181 L4
Ellenhall Staffs 99 J7
Ellen's Green Surrey 31 H4
Ellerbeck N York 141 K7
Ellerby N York 143 G4
Ellerdine Heath
　Wrekin 98 F7
Elleric Ag & B 191 K6
Ellerker E R Yk 125 L5
Ellerton E R Yk 125 G3
Ellerton N York 141 G7
Ellesborough Bucks 58 D6
Ellesmere Shrops 98 B5
Ellesmere Port
　Ches W 111 L6
Ellingham Norfk 93 H5
Ellingham Nthumb 169 H4
Ellingstring N York 132 B3
Ellington Cambs 75 H1
Ellington Nthumb 159 G4
Elliots Green Somset 27 J3
Ellisfield Hants 29 M3
Ellishader Highld 209 H2
Ellistown Leics 86 E2
Ellon Abers 217 H7
Ellonby Cumb 148 D7
Elloughton E R Yk 125 L5
Ellwood Gloucs 54 E6
Elm Cambs 89 C3

Elmbridge Worcs 70 F2
Elmdon Essex 76 C6
Elmdon Solhll 85 L6
Elmer W Susx 18 D5
Elmers End Gt Lon 45 G6
Elmer's Green Lancs 112 D1
Elmesthorpe Leics 86 F4
Elmhurst Staffs 85 K2
Elmley Castle Worcs 71 H6
Elmley Lovett Worcs 70 F1
Elmore Gloucs 55 H5
Elmore Back Gloucs 55 H5
Elm Park Gt Lon 45 K3
Elmsett Suffk 78 C5
Elmstead Market
　Essex 62 C3
Elmsted Kent 34 F5
Elmstone Kent 35 H3
Elmstone
　Hardwicke Gloucs 55 K3
Elmswell E R Yk 134 F7
Elmswell Suffk 78 B2
Elmton Derbys 115 J6
Elphin Highld 224 F6
Elphinstone E Loth 177 K4
Elrick Abers 206 F4
Elrig D & G 145 G5
Elrington Nthumb 149 L3
Elsdon Nthumb 158 B4
Elsenham Essex 60 C3
Elsfield Oxon 57 K6
Elsham N Linc 126 C7
Elsing Norfk 92 C1
Elslack N York 122 D2
Elson Hants 17 H3
Elsrickle S Lans 165 K2
Elstead Surrey 30 E3
Elsted W Susx 30 D7
Elsthorpe Lincs 103 H7
Elston Notts 102 C3
Elstow Bed 74 F5
Elstree Herts 44 D2
Elstronwick E R Yk 126 F4
Elswick Lancs 120 F3
Elswick N u Ty 151 G3
Elsworth Cambs 75 K2
Elterwater Cumb 137 K6
Eltham Gt Lon 45 H5
Eltisley Cambs 75 J3
Elton Cambs 88 F5
Elton Ches W 112 C6
Elton Derbys 100 E1
Elton Herefs 69 J1
Elton S on T 141 J4
Elton-on-the-Hill
　Notts 102 C5
Eltringham Nthumb 150 D3
Elvanfoot S Lans 165 J6
Elvaston Derbys 101 H6
Elveden Suffk 91 J7
Elvetham Heath
　Hants 30 D1
Elvington E Loth 178 A4
Elvington C York 125 G2
Elvington Kent 35 H5
Elwick Hartpl 141 K2
Elworth Ches E 99 H1
Elworthy Somset 25 G4
Ely Cambs 90 D7
Ely Cardif 37 H5
Emberton M Keyn 74 C5
Embleton Cumb 137 G2
Embleton Nthumb 169 J5
Embo Highld 223 H3
Emborough Somset 26 E2
Embo Street Highld 223 H3
Embsay N York 131 J8
Emery Down Hants 16 C2
Emley Kirk 123 K7
Emmington Oxon 58 C2
Emneth Norfk 90 C3
Emneth Hungate
　Norfk 90 D3
Empingham Rutlnd 88 D2
Empshott Hants 30 C5
Emsworth Hants 17 K2
Enborne W Berk 41 H7
Enborne Row W Berk 41 H7

Enderby Leics	87	G4
Endmoor Cumb	129	L3
Endon Staffs	99	L2
Endon Bank Staffs	99	L2
Enfield Gt Lon	60	B7
Enfield Lock Gt Lon	60	B7
Enfield Wash Gt Lon	60	B7
Enford Wilts	28	C2
Engine Common		
S Glos	39	G4
Englefield W Berk	41	L6
Englefield Green		
Surrey	43	G6
English Bicknor		
Gloucs	54	E5
Englishcombe BaNES	39	G7
English Frankton		
Shrops	98	C6
Enham Alamein		
Hants	29	G2
Enmore Somset	25	K4
Enmore Green		
Dorset	27	J6
Ennerdale Bridge		
Cumb	136	E4
Enochdhu P & K	195	G4
Ensay Ag & B	189	J6
Ensbury BCP	15	K3
Ensdon Shrops	83	H1
Enstone Oxon	57	G3
Enterkinfoot D & G	154	E2
Enville Staffs	84	E6
Eochar W Isls	233	b7
Eòlaigearraidh		
W Isls	233	b9
Eoligarry W Isls	233	b9
Eòropaidh W Isls	232	g1
Eoropie W Isls	232	g1
Epney Gloucs	55	H5
Epperstone Notts	102	A3
Epping Essex	60	D7
Epping Green Essex	60	C6
Epping Upland		
Essex	60	C6
Eppleby N York	140	F5
Epsom Surrey	44	E7
Epwell Oxon	72	D6
Epworth N Linc	116	C2
Erbistock Wrexhm	97	M4
Erdington Birm	85	K5
Eridge Green E Susx	32	F6
Erines Ag & B	172	E4
Eriska Ag & B	191	H7
Eriskay W Isls	233	c9
Eriswell Suffk	91	G7
Erith Gt Lon	45	K4
Erlestoke Wilts	27	L2
Ermington Devon	6	F5
Ernesettle C Plym	6	C4
Erpingham Norfk	106	E6
Errogie Highld	202	E2
Errol P & K	186	D3
Erskine Rens	174	E4
Erskine Bridge		
Rens	174	E4
Ervie D & G	144	B2
Erwarton Suffk	78	F7
Erwood Powys	68	C6
Eryholme N York	141	H5
Eryrys Denbgs	97	J2
Escomb Dur	140	F2
Escrick N York	124	F2
Esgairgeiliog Powys	81	G3
Esh Dur	150	F6
Esher Surrey	43	J7
Eshott Nthumb	158	F3
Esh Winning Dur	150	F6
Eskadale Highld	212	C6
Eskbank Mdloth	177	J5
Eskdale Green		
Cumb	137	G6
Eskdalemuir D & G	155	M3
Esprick Lancs	120	E3
Essendine RutInd	88	F2
Essendon Herts	59	L6
Essich Highld	213	G6
Essington Staffs	85	G3
Esslemont Abers	217	H7
Eston R & Cl	142	C4
Etal Nthumb	168	D2
Etchilhampton Wilts	40	B7
Etchingham E Susx	33	J7
Etchinghill Kent	34	F6
Etchinghill Staffs	100	B8
Eton W & M	42	F5
Eton Wick W & M	42	F5
Etruria C Stke	99	K3
Etteridge Highld	203	G6
Ettersgill Dur	139	K2
Ettiley Heath		
Ches E	99	G1
Ettingshall Wolves	85	G4
Ettington Warwks	72	C5
Etton C Pete	89	G3
Etton E R Yk	126	B2
Ettrick Border	166	D6
Ettrickbridge		
Border	166	F4
Ettrickhill Border	166	C6
Etwall Derbys	100	F6
Euston Suffk	91	K7
Euxton Lancs	121	H6
Evanton Highld	212	F2
Evedon Lincs	103	H3
Evelix Highld	223	G4
Evenjobb Powys	68	F3
Evenley Nhants	73	H7
Evenlode Gloucs	56	E3
Evenwood Dur	140	E3
Evercreech Somset	26	F4
Everingham E R Yk	125	J3
Everleigh Wilts	28	D2
Eversholt C Beds	59	G2
Evershot Dorset	14	B2
Eversley Hants	42	C7
Eversley Cross		
Hants	42	C7
Everthorpe E R Yk	125	L4
Everton C Beds	75	H4
Everton Hants	16	C4
Everton Lpool	111	K3
Everton Notts	116	B4
Evertown D & G	156	C6
Evesbatch Herefs	70	C5
Evesham Worcs	71	J5
Evington C Leic	87	J3
Ewden Village Sheff	114	F3
Ewell Surrey	44	E7
Ewell Minnis Kent	35	H6
Ewelme Oxon	41	M3
Ewen Gloucs	40	A2
Ewenny V Glam	36	D5
Ewerby Lincs	103	J3
Ewhurst Surrey	31	H4
Ewhurst Green		
E Susx	20	F2
Ewhurst Green		
Surrey	31	H4
Ewloe Flints	111	J7
Ewood Bl w D	121	K5
Eworthy Devon	10	C6
Ewshot Hants	30	D2
Ewyas Harold Herefs	54	B3
Exbourne Devon	10	E4
Exbury Hants	16	E3
Exebridge Somset	24	E6
Exelby N York	132	D3
Exeter Devon	11	L6
Exeter Airport Devon	12	C4
Exeter Services		
Devon	12	C4
Exford Somset	24	D4
Exfordsgreen Shrops	83	J3
Exhall Warwks	71	K4
Exhall Warwks	86	D6
Exlade Street Oxon	42	A4
Exminster Devon	12	B5
Exmoor National		
Park	24	D4
Exmouth Devon	12	C6
Exning Suffk	76	E2
Exton Devon	12	C5
Exton Hants	29	L7
Exton RutInd	88	D2
Exton Somset	24	E5
Exwick Devon	11	K6
Eyam Derbys	114	E6
Eydon Nhants	73	G4
Eye C Pete	89	J3
Eye Herefs	69	J2
Eye Suffk	92	D8
Eyemouth Border	179	K5
Eyeworth C Beds	75	J5
Eyhorne Street		
Kent	33	L3
Eyke Suffk	79	G4
Eynesbury Cambs	75	H3
Eynsford Kent	45	K6
Eynsham Oxon	57	H6
Eype Dorset	13	L4
Eyre Highld	208	F4
Eythorne Kent	35	H5
Eyton Herefs	69	J3
Eyton Shrops	98	C7
Eyton on Severn		
Shrops	83	L3
Eyton upon the		
Weald Moors		
Wrekin	84	B1

F

Faccombe Hants	41	H8
Faceby N York	141	L6
Fachwen Powys	82	B1
Faddiley Ches E	98	E3
Fadmoor N York	133	K2
Faerdre Swans	51	K5
Faifley W Duns	174	F4
Failand N Som	38	D6
Failford S Ayrs	163	L4
Failsworth Oldham	113	K2
Fairbourne Gwynd	80	E2
Fairburn N York	124	D5
Fairfield Derbys	114	B6
Fairfield Worcs	85	G7
Fairford Gloucs	56	D7
Fairgirth D & G	146	F4
Fair Green Norfk	90	F1
Fairhaven Lancs	120	D5
Fair Isle Shet	235	e7
Fair Isle Airport		
Shet	235	e7
Fairlands Surrey	30	F2
Fairlie N Ayrs	173	L7
Fairlight E Susx	21	G4
Fairmile Devon	12	E3
Fairmile Surrey	43	J7
Fairmilehead C Edin	177	H5
Fairnilee Border	167	G3
Fair Oak Hants	29	J7
Fairoak Staffs	99	H6
Fair Oak Green		
Hants	42	A7
Fairseat Kent	45	L7
Fairstead Essex	61	J3
Fairstead Norfk	105	G8
Fairwarp E Susx	32	E7
Fairwater Cardif	37	H5
Fairy Cross Devon	22	F6
Fakenham Norfk	105	L6
Fakenham Magna		
Suffk	91	K7
Fala Mdloth	177	L6
Fala Dam Mdloth	177	L6
Faldingworth Lincs	117	H5
Faldouët Jersey	236	e7
Falfield S Glos	39	G2
Falkenham Suffk	79	G6
Falkirk Falk	176	B3
Falkirk Wheel Falk	176	A3
Falkland Fife	186	D6
Fallburn S Lans	165	J2
Fallin Stirlg	185	H8
Fallodon Nthumb	169	J5
Fallowfield Manch	113	J3
Fallowfield Nthumb	150	B2
Falmer E Susx	19	K4
Falmouth Cnwll	3	K5
Falnash Border	156	D2
Falsgrave N York	134	F2
Falstone Nthumb	157	J5
Fanagmore Highld	228	B5
Fancott C Beds	59	G3
Fanellan Highld	212	D5
Fangdale Beck		
N York	142	C7
Fangfoss E R Yk	134	B8
Fanmore Ag & B	189	K7
Fannich Lodge		
Highld	211	K2
Fans Border	167	J2
Far Bletchley		
M Keyn	74	C7
Farcet Cambs	89	H5
Far Cotton Nhants	73	L3
Fareham Hants	17	H2
Farewell Staffs	85	J2
Faringdon Oxon	40	F2
Farington Lancs	121	H5
Farlam Cumb	148	F3
Farleigh N Som	38	D6
Farleigh Surrey	32	C2
Farleigh		
Hungerford		
Somset	39	J8
Farleigh Wallop		
Hants	29	L3
Farlesthorpe Lincs	119	G6
Farleton Cumb	129	L4
Farleton Lancs	130	B6
Farley Staffs	100	B4
Farley Wilts	28	E5
Farley Green Surrey	31	H3
Farley Hill Wokham	42	C7
Farleys End Gloucs	55	H5
Farlington C Port	17	J2
Farlington N York	133	J6
Farlow Shrops	84	B7
Farmborough BaNES	38	F7
Farmcote Gloucs	56	B3
Farmington Gloucs	56	C5
Farmoor Oxon	57	J6
Far Moor Wigan	112	D2
Farmtown Moray	215	L4
Farnborough Gt Lon	45	H7
Farnborough Hants	30	E2
Farnborough W Berk	41	H4
Farnborough Warwks	72	E5
Farnborough Park		
Hants	30	E1
Farncombe Surrey	31	G3
Farndish Bed	74	D2
Farndon Ches W	98	B2
Farndon Notts	102	C3
Farne Islands		
Nthumb	169	J2
Farnell Angus	197	G5
Farnham Dorset	27	L7
Farnham Essex	60	D3
Farnham N York	132	E7
Farnham Suffk	79	H3
Farnham Surrey	30	D3
Farnham Common		
Bucks	42	F4
Farnham Royal		
Bucks	42	F4
Farningham Kent	45	K6
Farnley Leeds	123	K4
Farnley N York	123	J2
Farnley Tyas Kirk	123	H7
Farnsfield Notts	101	M2
Farnworth Bolton	113	G1
Farnworth Halton	112	D4
Far Oakridge Gloucs	55	L7
Farr Highld	203	K5
Farr Highld	213	G7
Farr Highld	229	L3
Farraline Highld	202	E2
Farringdon Devon	12	C4
Farrington Gurney		
BaNES	26	F1
Far Sawrey Cumb	137	K7
Farsley Leeds	123	J4
Farthinghoe Nhants	73	G6
Farthingstone		
Nhants	73	H4
Fartown Kirk	123	H6
Fasnacloich Ag & B	191	K6
Fasnakyle Highld	211	L8

Fassfern Highld 191 K2
Fatfield Sundld............. 151 H4
Fauldhouse W Loth 176 C6
Faulkbourne Essex 61 J5
Faulkland Somset 27 H1
Fauls Shrops 98 E6
Faversham Kent............. 34 D3
Fawdington N York....... 132 F5
Fawdon N u Ty............. 151 G2
Fawkham Green
  Kent......................... 45 L6
Fawler Oxon.................. 57 G4
Fawley Bucks 42 C3
Fawley Hants 16 F2
Fawley W Berk 41 H4
Faxfleet E R Yk............ 125 K5
Faygate W Susx 31 K4
Fazakerley Lpool 111 K3
Fazeley Staffs 85 L3
Fearby N York 132 B4
Fearn Highld............... 223 H6
Fearnan P & K 194 B7
Fearnbeg Highld 210 B3
Fearnmore Highld....... 209 L3
Fearnoch Ag & B......... 172 F3
Featherstone Staffs.....85 G3
Featherstone
  Wakefd.................. 124 C6
Feckenham Worcs........ 71 H3
Feering Essex................ 61 L4
Feetham N York.......... 140 C7
Felbridge Surrey........... 32 C5
Felbrigg Norfk............ 106 E5
Felcourt Surrey 32 C5
Felindre Carmth 51 G2
Felindre Carmth 65 K6
Felindre Powys.............82 D7
Felindre Swans............. 51 J5
Felindre Farchog
  Pembks...................64 F6
Felinfoel Carmth 51 G5
Felingwmisaf Carmth 51 G2
Felingwmuchaf
  Carmth....................51 G1
Felixkirk N York.......... 133 G3
Felixstowe Suffk 79 G7
Felling Gatesd 151 G3
Felmersham Bed.......... 74 E3
Felmingham Norfk...... 106 F6
Felpham W Susx.......... 18 C5
Felsham Suffk............... 77 L3
Felsted Essex................ 61 G4
Feltham Gt Lon............. 43 J5
Felthamhill Surrey 43 H6
Felthorpe Norfk.......... 106 E8
Felton Herefs................ 69 L5
Felton N Som................. 38 D7
Felton Nthumb 158 F3
Felton Butler Shrops...98 B8
Feltwell Norfk............... 91 G5
Fence Lancs 122 C3
Fence Rothm 115 H4
Fencott Oxon................ 57 L5
Fendike Corner
  Lincs........................ 104 D1
Fen Ditton Cambs....... 76 C3
Fen Drayton Cambs.....75 L2
Feniscliffe Bl w D 121 K5
Feniscowles Bl w D ... 121 J5
Feniton Devon 12 E3
Feniton Court Devon....12 E3
Fenn Green Shrops......84 D6
Fenn Street Medway....46 D5
Fenny Bentley
  Derbys.................. 100 D3
Fenny Bridges Devon 12 E3
Fenny Compton
  Warwks..................72 E4
Fenny Drayton Leics...86 D4
Fenstanton Cambs......75 K2
Fen Street Norfk.........92 B4
Fenton Cambs.............. 89 K7
Fenton Cumb............... 148 E4
Fenton Lincs............... 102 E3
Fenton Lincs............... 116 D6
Fenton Notts.............. 116 C5
Fenton Nthumb 168 E3
Fenton Barns E Loth ... 178 B3

Fenwick Donc.............. 124 F7
Fenwick E Ayrs 163 L2
Fenwick Nthumb 158 D7
Fenwick Nthumb 169 G2
Feock Cnwll....................... 4 C7
Feolin Ferry Ag & B..... 171 H4
Fergushill N Ayrs 163 J2
Feriniquarrie Highld ... 208 B4
Fermain Bay Guern...... 236 d3
Fern Angus 196 D4
Ferndale Rhondd...........36 F2
Ferndown Dorset.......... 15 K3
Ferness Highld............. 214 B5
Fernham Oxon...............40 F3
Fernhill Heath Worcs....70 F3
Fernhurst W Susx 30 E5
Fernie Fife.................... 186 E4
Ferniegair S Lans 175 K7
Fernilea Highld............ 208 F7
Fernilee Derbys........... 114 A5
Fernwood Notts.......... 102 D3
Ferrensby N York 132 E7
Ferrindonald Highld... 199 K4
Ferring W Susx 18 F5
Ferrybridge
  Services Wakefd 124 D6
Ferryden Angus........... 197 H5
Ferryhill Dur............... 141 H2
Ferryhill Station Dur... 141 H2
Ferry Point Highld 223 G4
Ferryside Carmth.......... 50 D4
Fersfield Norfk...............92 C6
Fersit Highld............... 192 F2
Feshiebridge Highld ... 203 K4
Fetcham Surrey............. 31 J1
Fetlar Shet................... 235 e2
Fetterangus Abers 217 J4
Fettercairn Abers........ 197 G2
Fewston N York 132 B8
Ffairfach Carmth...........51 J2
Ffair Rhos Cerdgn........67 G2
Ffarmers Carmth..........66 E5
Ffestiniog Railway
  Gwynd.....................95 K5
Fforest Carmth.............. 51 H5
Ffostrasol Cerdgn 65 L5
Ffrith Flints...................97 L2
Ffynnongroyw Flints... 110 F5
Fickleshole Surrey 32 C2
Fiddington Somset....... 25 K4
Fiddleford Dorset......... 27 J8
Fiddlers Green Cnwll 4 C5
Field Staffs 100 A5
Field Dalling Norfk 106 B5
Field Head Leics.......... 86 F2
Fifehead Magdalen
  Dorset.....................27 H6
Fifehead Neville
  Dorset.....................14 E1
Fifehead St Quintin
  Dorset.....................14 E1
Fife Keith Moray 215 J4
Fifield Oxon.................. 56 E4
Fifield W & M.............. 42 E5
Figheldean Wilts 28 D3
Filby Norfk.................... 93 K2
Filey N York................. 135 H4
Filgrave M Keyn........... 74 C5
Filkins Oxon.................. 56 E6
Filleigh Devon.............. 23 K5
Fillingham Lincs 116 F4
Fillongley Warwks....... 86 C6
Filton S Glos................. 38 E5
Fimber E R Yk 134 D7
Finavon Angus............ 196 D5
Finberry Kent................34 D6
Fincham Norfk...............91 G3
Finchampstead
  Wokham.................42 D7
Fincharn Ag & B......... 182 C6
Finchdean Hants.......... 30 C8
Finchingfield Essex......61 G2
Finchley Gt Lon............44 F2
Findern Derbys............ 100 F6
Findhorn Moray 214 C2
Findhorn Bridge
  Highld................... 213 J8
Findochty Moray........ 215 K2

Findo Gask P & K........ 185 L4
Findon Abers 207 H6
Findon W Susx...............18 F4
Findon Mains Highld ... 212 F3
Findon Valley W Susx....18 F4
Findrack House
  Abers..................... 206 B4
Finedon Nhants............88 D8
Fingask P & K 186 C4
Fingest Bucks................42 C3
Finghall N York........... 132 B2
Fingland D & G........... 164 E6
Finglesham Kent.......... 35 J4
Fingringhoe Essex........62 B4
Finlarig Stirlg.............. 184 C1
Finmere Oxon................57 M2
Finnart P & K 193 H5
Finningham Suffk.........78 C1
Finningley Donc.......... 116 A2
Finsbay W Isls............. 232 d5
Finstall Worcs...............71 H1
Finsthwaite Cumb...... 129 H2
Finstock Oxon...............57 G5
Finstown Ork.............. 234 b6
Fintry Abers 216 E4
Fintry Stirlg................ 175 H2
Finzean Abers............. 206 B6
Fionnphort Ag & B..... 180 D3
Fionnsbhagh W Isls..... 232 d5
Firbank Cumb............. 130 C2
Firbeck Rothm 115 K4
Firby N York............... 132 D3
Firby N York............... 134 B6
Firle E Susx...................19 M4
Firsby Lincs................. 118 F8
Fir Tree Dur................ 150 E7
Fishbourne IoW............17 G4
Fishbourne W Susx 18 A5
Fishbourne Roman
  Palace W Susx...........18 A5
Fishburn Dur.............. 141 J2
Fishcross Clacks........... 185 J7
Fisherford Abers........ 216 C2
Fisherrow E Loth......... 177 K4
Fisher's Pond Hants..... 29 J7
Fisherton Highld 213 H4
Fisherton S Ayrs......... 163 H6
Fisherton de la
  Mere Wilts................27 M4
Fishery W & M.............. 42 E4
Fishguard Pembks........64 D6
Fishlake Donc............. 125 G7
Fishnish Pier Ag & B... 190 D7
Fishponds Bristl...........38 F5
Fishtoft Lincs.............. 104 B4
Fishtoft Drove Lincs ... 104 A3
Fishwick Lancs........... 121 H4
Fiskavaig Highld........ 208 E7
Fiskerton Lincs........... 117 H6
Fiskerton Notts......... 102 C3
Fittleton Wilts..............28 D2
Fittleworth W Susx......18 D2
Fitz Shrops....................98 C8
Fitzhead Somset...........25 H5
Fitzwilliam Wakefd.... 124 C7
Five Ash Down
  E Susx.....................19 M2
Five Ashes E Susx........32 F7
Fivehead Somset.......... 26 A6
Fivelanes Cnwll.............. 9 G8
Five Oak Green Kent....33 H4
Five Oaks Jersey.......... 236 c7
Five Oaks W Susx.........31 H5
Five Roads Carmth......50 F4
Flackwell Heath
  Bucks.....................42 E3
Fladbury Worcs............71 H5
Fladdabister Shet........ 235 c6
Flagg Derbys............... 114 C7
Flamborough E R Yk....135 K5
Flamborough Head
  E R Yk..................... 135 K5
Flamingo Land
  Resort N York....... 134 B4
Flamstead Herts...........59 H5
Flamstead End Herts 60 B7
Flansham W Susx..........18 C5
Flanshaw Wakefd........ 123 L6

Flasby N York 131 H7
Flash Staffs.................. 114 A7
Flashader Highld......... 208 E4
Flaunden Herts.............59 G7
Flawborough Notts...... 102 C4
Flawith N York............ 133 G6
Flax Bourton N Som.....38 D6
Flaxby N York 132 F7
Flaxley Gloucs...............55 G5
Flaxpool Somset...........25 H4
Flaxton N York 133 K6
Fleckney Leics...............87 J5
Flecknoe Warwks.........73 G2
Fledborough Notts 116 D6
Fleet Dorset..................14 C6
Fleet Hants...................30 D2
Fleet Lincs................... 104 C7
Fleet Hargate Lincs ... 104 C7
Fleet Services Hants.....30 D1
Fleetwood Lancs......... 120 D2
Fleggburgh Norfk.........93 J2
Flemingston V Glam....36 F6
Flemington S Lans 175 H6
Flempton Suffk.............77 J1
Fletchertown Cumb.... 147 L6
Fletching E Susx 19 L2
Flexbury Cnwll................ 9 G4
Flexford Surrey.............30 F2
Flimby Cumb............... 147 H7
Flimwell E Susx 33 J6
Flint Flints.................. 111 H6
Flintham Notts............ 102 C4
Flinton E R Yk............ 126 F4
Flitcham Norfk............ 105 H6
Flitch Green Essex........61 G4
Flitton C Beds...............74 F7
Flitwick C Beds.............74 F7
Flixborough N Linc..... 125 K7
Flixborough Stather
  N Linc..................... 125 K7
Flixton N York............ 135 G4
Flixton Suffk.................93 G6
Flixton Traffd............. 113 H3
Flockton Kirk.............. 123 J7
Flockton Green Kirk... 123 K7
Flodigarry Highld....... 218 C6
Flookburgh Cumb...... 129 H4
Flordon Norfk...............92 E4
Flore Nhants..................73 J3
Flowton Suffk...............78 C5
Flushing Cnwll................ 3 L4
Fluxton Devon..............12 E4
Flyford Flavell Worcs ...71 H4
Fobbing Thurr...............46 B4
Fochabers Moray........ 215 H3
Fochriw Caerph............53 H6
Fockerby N Linc.......... 125 K6
Foddington Somset...... 26 E5
Foel Powys....................81 L2
Foggathorpe E R Yk.... 125 H3
Fogo Border................ 179 G8
Fogwatt Moray 214 F3
Foindle Highld............ 228 B5
Folda Angus 195 J4
Fole Staffs................... 100 B5
Foleshill Covtry............86 D6
Folke Dorset..................26 F8
Folkestone Kent........... 35 H7
Folkestone Services
  Kent........................34 F7
Folkingham Lincs........ 103 H5
Folkington E Susx........ 20 B5
Folksworth Cambs........89 G5
Folkton N York........... 135 G4
Folla Rule Abers......... 216 D7
Follifoot N York.......... 132 E8
Folly Gate Devon......... 10 E5
Folly Hill Surrey...........30 D2
Fonthill Bishop Wilts....27 L5
Fonthill Gifford Wilts....27 L5
Fontmell Magna
  Dorset.....................27 K7
Fontmell Parva
  Dorset.....................14 E1
Fontwell W Susx...........18 C4
Foolow Derbys............ 114 D6
Forbestown Abers....... 205 H3
Forcett N York............. 140 F5

Ford Ag & B 182 C6
Ford Bucks..........................58 C6
Ford Derbys................115 H5
Ford Devon.....................22 F6
Ford Gloucs....................56 C3
Ford Nthumb................168 E2
Ford Somset..................25 H5
Ford Staffs....................100 B2
Ford W Susx...................18 D5
Ford Wilts.......................39 J5
Fordcombe Kent............32 F5
Fordell Fife...................177 G2
Forden Powys................82 E4
Ford End Essex.............61 G5
Forder Green Devon......7 H3
Fordham Cambs............76 L1
Fordham Essex..............61 L3
Fordham Norfk.............90 E4
Fordingbridge Hants...28 D8
Fordon E R Yk..............135 G4
Fordoun Abers.............197 J2
Fordstreet Essex..........61 L3
Ford Street Somset......25 J7
Fordwich Kent..............35 G3
Fordyce Abers..............216 B2
Forebridge Staffs.........99 L7
Forest Guern.................236 c4
Forest Chapel
  Ches E........................113 L6
Forest Gate Gt Lon........45 H3
Forest Green Surrey......31 J3
Forest Hall N Tyne.......151 G2
Forest Hill Gt Lon..........45 G5
Forest Hill Oxon............57 L6
Forest Lane Head
  N York.........................132 E7
Forest Mill Clacks........185 K8
Forest of Bowland
  Lancs.........................130 C8
Forest of Dean
  Gloucs.........................54 F5
Forest Row E Susx.........32 D6
Forestside W Susx.........30 C8
Forest Town Notts.......101 K1
Forfar Angus.................196 D6
Forgandenny P & K.......186 A4
Forge Hammer Torfn......37 L2
Forgie Moray................215 J4
Forgieside Moray.........215 J4
Forgue Abers.................216 B5
Formby Sefton..............111 J1
Forncett End Norfk........92 D5
Forncett St Mary
  Norfk...........................92 E5
Forncett St Peter
  Norfk...........................92 E5
Fornham All Saints
  Suffk............................77 J2
Fornham St Martin
  Suffk............................77 J2
Fornighty Highld..........213 L4
Forres Moray................214 C3
Forsbrook Staffs...........99 L4
Forse Highld.................227 M2
Forsinard Highld..........230 C6
Forss Highld.................230 F2
Fort Augustus
  Highld.........................202 B4
Forteviot P & K............185 L4
Forth S Lans.................176 C7
Forthampton Gloucs.....55 K2
Fort Hommet Guern....236 c2
Forth Rail Bridge
  C Edin.........................176 F3
Forth Road Bridge
  Fife.............................176 F3
Fortingall P & K...........194 B6
Forton Hants..................29 H3
Forton Lancs...............121 G1
Forton Shrops................83 H1
Forton Somset..............13 J2
Forton Staffs.................99 H7
Fort Richmond
  Guern.........................236 b3
Fortrie Abers...............216 C5
Fortrose Highld...........213 H3
Fortuneswell Dorset....14 D7
Fort William Highld.....191 L2

Forty Hill Gt Lon...........60 B7
Fosbury Wilts.................40 F8
Foscot Oxon...................56 E4
Fosdyke Lincs..............104 A5
Foss P & K....................194 C5
Fossebridge Gloucs......56 B5
Foster Street Essex.......60 D6
Foston Derbys..............100 D6
Foston Leics..................87 H4
Foston Lincs................102 E4
Foston N York..............133 L6
Foston on the
  Wolds E R Yk.............135 H7
Fotherby Lincs.............118 D3
Fotheringhay Nhants.....88 F5
Foula Shet....................235 a6
Foula Airport Shet......235 a6
Foulden Border............179 J7
Foulden Norfk................91 H4
Foul End Warwks...........86 B4
Foulness Island
  Essex............................47 G2
Foulridge Lancs...........122 D3
Foulsham Norfk............106 B7
Fountainhall Border....177 L8
Four Ashes Suffk...........78 B1
Four Cabots Guern.......236 c3
Four Crosses Powys......97 K8
Four Elms Kent..............32 E4
Four Forks Somset........25 K4
Four Gotes Cambs..........90 C1
Four Lanes Cnwll...........3 J4
Four Marks Hants..........30 A4
Four Mile Bridge
  IoA.............................108 C5
Four Oaks Birm.............85 K4
Four Oaks Solhll...........86 B7
Fourpenny Highld.......223 H3
Four Roads Carmth........50 F4
Fourstones Nthumb.....149 M2
Four Throws Kent..........33 K7
Fovant Wilts...................28 A5
Foveran Abers.............207 H2
Fowey Cnwll.....................5 H5
Fowlhall Kent.................33 J4
Fowlis Angus................186 E2
Fowlis Wester P & K....185 J3
Fowlmere Cambs............76 B5
Fownhope Herefs..........69 L7
Foxbar Rens.................174 E6
Foxcote Somset.............27 G1
Foxdale IoM.................237 b5
Foxearth Essex..............77 J5
Foxfield Cumb..............128 F3
Foxhole Cnwll.................4 F5
Foxholes N York..........134 F5
Foxley Norfk.................106 C7
Foxt Staffs....................100 B3
Foxton Cambs.................76 B5
Foxton Leics...................87 K5
Foxton N York..............141 K7
Foxwood Shrops............84 B7
Foy Herefs.....................54 E3
Foyers Highld...............202 D2
Foynesfield Highld......213 L4
Fraddon Cnwll.................4 E4
Fradley Staffs.................85 L2
Fradswell Staffs.............99 M6
Fraisthorpe E R Yk.......135 J7
Framfield E Susx............20 A2
Framingham Earl
  Norfk............................92 F3
Framingham Pigot
  Norfk............................92 F3
Framlingham Suffk........79 G2
Frampton Dorset...........14 C4
Frampton Lincs............104 B5
Frampton Cotterell
  S Glos...........................38 F4
Frampton Mansell
  Gloucs..........................55 L7
Frampton-on-
  Severn Gloucs............55 H6
Framsden Suffk...............78 E3
Framwellgate Moor
  Dur.............................151 G6
Franche Worcs...............84 E7
Frankby Wirral.............111 H4

Frankley Worcs...............85 H7
Frankley Services
  Worcs..........................85 H7
Frankton Warwks...........72 E1
Frant E Susx....................33 G6
Fraserburgh Abers.......217 J2
Frating Essex..................62 C4
Frating Green Essex......62 C4
Fratton C Port.................17 J3
Freathy Cnwll...................6 B5
Freckenham Suffk..........76 F1
Freckleton Lancs..........120 F5
Freeby Leics.................102 D7
Freefolk Hants................29 J2
Freeland Oxon................57 H5
Freethorpe Norfk...........93 J3
Freethorpe
  Common Norfk...........93 J3
Freiston Lincs..............104 B4
Fremington Devon.........23 H5
Fremington N York.......140 D7
Frenchay S Glos.............38 F5
Frenich P & K................194 C5
Frensham Surrey............30 D3
Freshfield Sefton.........120 C8
Freshford Wilts.............39 H7
Freshwater IoW.............16 D5
Fressingfield Suffk.......92 F7
Freston Suffk.................78 E6
Freswick Highld...........231 L3
Fretherne Gloucs..........55 G6
Frettenham Norfk.........106 F8
Freuchie Fife................186 E6
Freystrop Pembks.........49 G5
Friar Park Sandw...........85 H4
Friday Bridge Cambs.....90 C3
Friday Street Suffk.......79 H3
Fridaythorpe E R Yk....134 D7
Friendly Calder............122 F5
Friern Barnet Gt Lon......44 F2
Friesthorpe Lincs.........117 H5
Frieston Lincs..............102 F3
Frieth Bucks....................42 D3
Frilford Oxon..................41 H2
Frilsham W Berk............41 K5
Frimley Surrey................42 E8
Frindsbury Medway.......46 C6
Fring Norfk....................105 H5
Fringford Oxon...............57 L3
Frinsted Kent..................34 B4
Frinton-on-Sea
  Essex............................62 F4
Friockheim Angus........196 F6
Frisby on the
  Wreake Leics............102 B8
Friskney Lincs..............104 D2
Friston E Susx.................20 B6
Friston Suffk...................79 J3
Fritchley Derbys...........101 G3
Fritham Hants..................28 E8
Frithelstock Devon........23 G7
Frithelstock Stone
  Devon...........................23 G7
Frithville Lincs.............104 A3
Frittenden Kent..............33 K5
Frittiscombe Devon........7 J6
Fritton Norfk...................92 F5
Fritton Norfk...................93 K4
Fritwell Oxon..................57 K3
Frizinghall C Brad........123 H4
Frizington Cumb..........136 E4
Frocester Gloucs...........55 H7
Frodesley Shrops...........83 K3
Frodsham Ches W.........112 D6
Frogden Border.............168 B4
Frog End Cambs..............76 B5
Froggatt Derbys............114 E6
Froghall Staffs..............100 A3
Frogmore Devon..............7 H7
Frognall Lincs.................89 H2
Frog Pool Worcs.............70 E2
Frogwell Cnwll.................6 A3
Frolesworth Leics..........87 G5
Frome Somset.................27 H2
Frome St Quintin
  Dorset...........................14 B2
Fromes Hill Herefs........70 C5
Froncysyllte Wrexhm.....97 L4

Fron-goch Gwynd...........96 D5
Fron Isaf Wrexhm...........97 L4
Frosterley Dur..............150 C7
Froxfield Wilts................40 F6
Froxfield Green
  Hants............................30 B6
Fryern Hill Hants............29 H7
Fryerning Essex..............61 G7
Fuinary Highld..............190 C6
Fulbeck Lincs................102 F3
Fulbourn Cambs.............76 D4
Fulbrook Oxon................56 E5
Fulflood Hants................29 J5
Fulford C York...............124 F2
Fulford Somset...............25 K5
Fulford Staffs.................99 L5
Fulham Gt Lon................44 E5
Fulking W Susx...............19 H4
Fullarton N Ayrs...........163 H2
Fuller Street Essex........61 H5
Fullerton Hants..............29 G4
Fulletby Lincs...............118 D6
Fullready Warwks...........72 C5
Full Sutton E R Yk.......134 B7
Fullwood E Ayrs..........174 E7
Fulmer Bucks..................43 G4
Fulmodeston Norfk......106 B6
Fulnetby Lincs..............117 H5
Fulney Lincs..................103 L7
Fulstow Lincs...............118 D3
Fulwell Sundld..............151 J3
Fulwood Lancs.............121 H4
Fulwood Sheff..............114 F4
Fundenhall Norfk...........92 D4
Funtington W Susx........17 L2
Funtullich P & K............184 F3
Furley Devon...................13 H2
Furnace Ag & B.............182 E7
Furnace Carmth..............51 G5
Furness Vale Derbys....114 A5
Furneux Pelham
  Herts............................60 C3
Furzley Hants..................28 F7
Fyfield Essex...................60 F6
Fyfield Hants...................28 F3
Fyfield Oxon...................57 H7
Fyfield Wilts...................40 D7
Fyfield Wilts...................40 D7
Fylingthorpe N York......30 D6
Fyning W Susx................30 D6
Fyvie Abers...................216 E6

G

Gabroc Hill E Ayrs........174 E7
Gaddesby Leics...............87 K2
Gaddesden Row
  Herts............................59 H5
Gadfirth S Ayrs..............163 K5
Gaerllwyd Mons.............38 C2
Gaerwen IoA.................108 F7
Gailes N Ayrs...............163 H3
Gailey Staffs...................85 G2
Gainford Dur................140 F4
Gainsborough Lincs.....116 D4
Gainsborough Suffk......78 E6
Gainsford End Essex......77 G2
Gairloch Highld............219 J6
Gairlochy Highld..........201 J3
Gairneybridge P & K....186 B7
Gaitsgill Cumb..............148 C5
Galashiels Border........167 G3
Galgate Lancs...............129 K7
Galhampton Somset......26 F5
Gallanachbeg
  Ag & B.........................182 B2
Gallanachmore
  Ag & B.........................182 B3
Gallatown Fife..............186 E8
Galleywood Essex..........61 H7
Gallovie Highld.............202 L7
Galloway Forest
  Park............................153 J5
Gallowfauld Angus.......196 D7
Gallowhill P & K...........186 B1
Galltair Highld..............200 C8

Galmisdale Highld 199 G8
Galmpton Devon 7 G7
Galmpton Torbay 7 K5
Galphay N York 132 C5
Galston E Ayrs 163 L3
Gamblesby Cumb 149 G6
Gamlingay Cambs 75 J4
Gamlingay Great
　Heath Cambs 75 J4
Gamrie Abers 216 F2
Gamston Notts 101 L5
Gamston Notts 116 B6
Ganavan Bay Ag & B 182 B2
Ganllwyd Gwynd 96 B7
Gannachy Angus 196 F3
Ganstead E R Yk 126 E4
Ganthorpe N York 133 L5
Ganton N York 134 F4
Garbity Moray 215 H4
Garboldisham Norfk 92 B7
Garbole Highld 203 H1
Garchory Abers 205 G4
Gardeners Green
　Wokham 42 D6
Gardenstown Abers 216 F2
Garden Village Sheff ... 114 E2
Garderhouse Shet 235 c5
Gare Hill Somset 27 H4
Garelochhead
　Ag & B 173 L1
Garford Oxon 41 H2
Garforth Leeds 124 B4
Gargrave N York 131 H8
Gargunnock Stirlg 184 F8
Garlic Street Norfk 92 E6
Garlieston D & G 145 K5
Garlinge Kent 35 J2
Garlinge Green Kent 34 F4
Garlogie Abers 206 E4
Garmond Abers 216 F4
Garmouth Moray 215 H2
Garmston Shrops 83 L3
Garndolbenmaen
　Gwynd 95 J4
Garrabost W Isls 232 g2
Garrallan E Ayrs 164 B5
Garras Cnwll 3 J6
Garreg Gwynd 95 K4
Garrigill Cumb 149 J6
Garroch D & G 153 M6
Garrochtrie D & G 144 D7
Garrochty Ag & B 173 J7
Garros Highld 209 H2
Garsdale Head
　Cumb 130 E2
Garsdon Wilts 39 L3
Garshall Green Staffs 99 L5
Garsington Oxon 57 L7
Garstang Lancs 121 G2
Garston Herts 59 J7
Garston Lpool 112 B5
Gartachossan Ag & B ... 171 G6
Gartcosh N Lans 175 J5
Garth Powys 67 K5
Garth Wrexhm 97 K4
Garthamlock C Glas 175 H5
Garthmyl Powys 82 E4
Garthorpe Leics 102 D7
Garthorpe N Linc 125 K6
Garth Row Cumb 138 D7
Gartly Abers 215 L7
Gartmore Stirlg 184 C7
Gartness N Lans 175 K5
Gartness Stirlg 174 F2
Gartocharn W Duns 174 D2
Garton-on-the-
　Wolds E R Yk 134 F7
Gartymore Highld 227 H5
Garva Bridge Highld 202 E6
Garvald Border 176 F8
Garvald E Loth 178 D4
Garvan Highld 191 J2
Garvard Ag & B 171 G1
Garve Highld 212 B3
Garvellachs Ag & B 181 K5
Garvestone Norfk 92 B3
Garvock Inver 174 B4
Garway Herefs 54 C4

Garynahine W Isls 232 e2
Garyvard W Isls 232 f3
Gasper Wilts 27 H5
Gastard Wilts 39 K6
Gasthorpe Norfk 91 L7
Gaston Green Essex 60 D5
Gatcombe IoW 16 F5
Gateacre Lpool 112 B4
Gate Burton Lincs 116 D5
Gateforth N York 124 E5
Gatehead E Ayrs 163 K3
Gate Helmsley
　N York 133 L7
Gatehouse Nthumb 157 K4
Gatehouse of Fleet
　D & G 146 A4
Gateley Norfk 106 A7
Gatenby N York 132 E3
Gateshaw Border 168 B5
Gateshead Gatesd 151 G3
Gateside Angus 196 D7
Gateside E Rens 174 E6
Gateside Fife 186 C5
Gateside N Ayrs 174 C7
Gateslack D & G 154 F2
Gatley Stockp 113 J4
Gattonside Border 167 H3
Gaulby Leics 87 K4
Gauldry Fife 186 F3
Gauldswell P & K 195 K6
Gautby Lincs 117 K6
Gavinton Border 179 G7
Gawcott Bucks 58 B2
Gawsworth Ches E 113 K7
Gawthrop Cumb 130 D3
Gawthwaite Cumb 129 G3
Gaydon Warwks 72 D4
Gayhurst M Keyn 74 B5
Gayle N York 131 G2
Gayles N York 140 E5
Gayton Nhants 73 K4
Gayton Norfk 105 H8
Gayton Staffs 99 M6
Gayton le Marsh
　Lincs 118 F5
Gayton Thorpe Norfk .. 105 H8
Gaywood Norfk 105 G7
Gazeley Suffk 77 G2
Gearraidh Bhaird
　W Isls 232 f3
Gearraidh na
　h-Aibhne W Isls 232 e2
Geary Highld 208 D3
Gedding Suffk 77 L3
Geddington Nhants 88 C6
Gedling Notts 101 L4
Gedney Lincs 104 C7
Gedney Broadgate
　Lincs 104 C7
Gedney Drove End
　Lincs 104 D6
Gedney Dyke Lincs 104 C7
Gedney Hill Lincs 89 L2
Geeston Rutlnd 88 E3
Geirinis W Isls 233 b7
Geldeston Norfk 93 H5
Gellideg Myr Td 53 G6
Gellifor Denbgs 110 F8
Gelligaer Caerph 37 H2
Gellilydan Gwynd 95 M4
Gellinudd Neath 51 K5
Gellyburn P & K 195 H8
Gellywen Carmth 50 C2
Gelston D & G 146 D3
Gelston Lincs 102 E4
Gembling E R Yk 135 H7
Gentleshaw Staffs 85 J2
Georgefield D & G 156 B4
George Green Bucks 43 G4
Georgeham Devon 23 G4
Georgemas
　Junction Station
　Highld 231 H4
George Nympton
　Devon 23 L6
Georth Ork 234 b5

Gerinish W Isls 233 b7
Germansweek Devon ...10 C6
Gerrans Cnwll 4 D8
Gerrards Cross
　Bucks 43 G3
Gerrick R & Cl 142 E5
Gestingthorpe Essex 77 J6
Geuffordd Powys 82 E2
Gidea Park Gt Lon 45 K3
Giffnock E Rens 175 G6
Gifford E Loth 178 C5
Giffordtown Fife 186 E5
Giggleswick N York 130 F6
Gigha Ag & B 171 L7
Gilberdyke E R Yk 125 K5
Gilchriston E Loth 178 B5
Gilcrux Cumb 147 K7
Gildersome Leeds 123 K5
Gildingwells Rothm 115 K4
Gilesgate Moor Dur 151 H6
Gileston V Glam 36 F6
Gilfach Caerph 53 J7
Gilfach Goch Brdgnd 36 F3
Gilfachrheda Cerdgn 65 L3
Gilgarran Cumb 136 E3
Gillamoor N York 133 K2
Gillen Highld 208 D3
Gillesbie D & G 155 K4
Gilling East N York 133 J4
Gillingham Dorset 27 J4
Gillingham Medway 46 C6
Gillingham Norfk 93 J5
Gilling West N York 140 F6
Gillock Highld 231 J4
Gills Highld 231 K2
Gilmanscleuch
　Border 166 E5
Gilmerton C Edin 177 J5
Gilmerton P & K 185 J3
Gilmonby Dur 140 C5
Gilmorton Leics 87 H6
Gilsland Nthumb 149 G2
Gilston Border 177 L6
Gilston Herts 60 D5
Gilwern Mons 53 K5
Gimingham Norfk 107 G5
Gipping Suffk 78 C2
Gipsey Bridge Lincs ... 103 M3
Girdle Toll N Ayrs 163 J2
Girlsta Shet 235 c5
Girsby N York 141 J5
Girthon D & G 146 A4
Girton Cambs 76 B3
Girton Notts 116 D7
Girvan S Ayrs 152 E3
Gisburn Lancs 122 C2
Gisleham Suffk 93 K5
Gislingham Suffk 78 C1
Gissing Norfk 92 D6
Gittisham Devon 12 E3
Gladestry Powys 68 E4
Gladsmuir E Loth 177 M4
Glais S Ayrs 51 K5
Glaisdale N York 143 G6
Glamis Angus 196 C6
Glanaman Carmth 51 J3
Glandford Norfk 106 C4
Glandwr Pembks 49 K2
Glandyfi Cerdgn 80 F4
Glanllynfi Brdgnd 36 D3
Glan-rhyd Powys 52 B6
Glanton Nthumb 169 G6
Glanvilles Wootton
　Dorset 14 D2
Glan-y-don Flints 111 G5
Glapthorn Nhants 88 E5
Glapwell Derbys 115 J7
Glasbury Powys 68 D6
Glascoed Conwy 96 E3
Glascote Staffs 86 B3
Glascwm Powys 68 D3
Glasfryn Conwy 96 D3
Glasgow C Glas 175 G5
Glasgow Airport
　Rens 174 E5
Glasgow Prestwick
　Airport S Ayrs 163 J4
Glasgow Science
　Centre C Glas 175 G5

Glasinfryn Gwynd 109 H7
Glasnacardoch Bay
　Highld 199 L6
Glasnakille Highld 199 H3
Glasphein Highld 208 B4
Glassford S Lans 175 J8
Glasshouse Gloucs 55 G4
Glasshouses N York ... 132 B6
Glasslaw Abers 216 F3
Glasson Cumb 148 A3
Glassonby Cumb 149 G7
Glasson Dock Lancs ... 129 K7
Glasterlaw Angus 196 F6
Glaston Rutlnd 88 C4
Glastonbury Somset 26 D4
Glatton Cambs 89 H6
Glazebrook Warrtn 113 G3
Glazebury Warrtn 112 F3
Glazeley Shrops 84 C5
Gleaston Cumb 128 F5
Glebe Highld 202 D2
Gledhow Leeds 123 L3
Gledpark D & G 146 B5
Gledrid Shrops 97 L5
Glemsford Suffk 77 J5
Glen Achulish Highld .. 191 K5
Glenallachie Moray 215 G6
Glenancross Highld 199 K6
Glenaros House
　Ag & B 190 B7
Glen Auldyn IoM 237 d3
Glenbarr Ag & B 161 H3
Glenbarry Abers 216 B4
Glenbeg Highld 190 C4
Glenbervie Abers 197 J1
Glenboig N Lans 175 J5
Glenborrodale
　Highld 190 C4
Glenbranter Ag & B 183 G7
Glenbreck Border 165 K5
Glenbrittle Highld 198 F2
Glenbuck E Ayrs 164 E4
Glencally Angus 196 B4
Glencaple D & G 147 H2
Glencarse P & K 186 C3
Glencoe Highld 191 L5
Glencothe Border 165 L4
Glencraig Fife 186 C7
Glencrosh D & G 154 D4
Glendale Highld 208 B4
Glendaruel Ag & B 173 G2
Glendevon P & K 185 K6
Glendoe Lodge
　Highld 202 C4
Glendoick P & K 186 C3
Glenduckie Fife 186 D4
Glenegedale Ag & B ... 170 F7
Glenelg Highld 200 C2
Glenerney Moray 214 C5
Glenfarg P & K 186 B5
Glenfield Leics 87 G3
Glenfinnan Highld 191 H1
Glenfintaig Lodge
　Highld 201 K7
Glenfoot P & K 186 C4
Glenfyne Lodge
　Ag & B 183 H4
Glengarnock N Ayrs ... 174 C7
Glengolly Highld 231 G3
Glengorm Castle
　Ag & B 189 K5
Glengrasco Highld 209 G5
Glenholm Border 165 L3
Glenhoul D & G 154 A5
Glenkin Ag & B 173 K3
Glenkindie Abers 205 K3
Glenlivet Moray 214 F8
Glenlochar D & G 146 C3
Glenlomond P & K 186 C6
Glenluce D & G 144 E4
Glenmassen Ag & B ... 173 J2
Glenmavis N Lans 175 K5
Glen Maye IoM 237 b5
Glenmore Highld 209 G4
Glenmore Lodge
　Highld 204 B4
Glen Nevis House
　Highld 192 B3

Glenochil Clacks 185 H7
Glen Parva Leics......87 H4
Glenquiech Angus 196 C4
Glenralloch Ag & B.... 172 E5
Glenridding Cumb...... 137 L4
Glenrothes Fife........... 186 D7
Glenshero Lodge
  Highld.......................... 202 E6
Glenstriven Ag & B...... 173 J3
Glentham Lincs 117 G4
Glentrool D & G........... 153 H6
Glen Trool Lodge
  D & G.......................... 153 J6
Glentruim Highld 203 G6
Glentworth Lincs 116 F4
Glenuig Highld........... 190 D2
Glenvarragill Highld.. 209 G6
Glen Vine IoM 237 c5
Glenwhilly D & G 152 E7
Glespin S Lans........... 164 F4
Glewstone Herefs......54 E4
Glinton C Pete 89 H3
Glooston Leics............87 L4
Glossop Derbys 114 B3
Gloster Hill Nthumb ... 159 G2
Gloucester Gloucs....55 J4
Gloucester Services
  Gloucs 55 J5
Gloucestershire
  Airport Gloucs 55 K4
Glusburn N York....... 122 F2
Glutt Lodge Highld 227 H2
Glympton Oxon 57 H4
Glynarthen Cerdgn....65 K5
Glyn Ceiriog Wrexhm..97 J5
Glyncoch Rhondd......37 G3
Glyncorrwg Neath.....52 D7
Glynde E Susx 19 L4
Glyndyfrdwy Denbgs...97 J4
Glynneath Neath.......52 D6
Glyntawe Powys........52 D5
Glynteg Carmth 65 K6
Gnosall Staffs 99 J7
Gnosall Heath
  Staffs...........................99 J7
Goadby Leics 87 L4
Goadby Marwood
  Leics.......................... 102 C7
Goatacre Wilts...........40 A5
Goathill Dorset..........26 F7
Goathland N York...... 143 H6
Goathurst Somset......25 K5
Goat Lees Kent...........34 D5
Gobowen Shrops........97 L5
Godalming Surrey......30 F3
Goddard's Green
  Kent.............................33 L6
Godmanchester
  Cambs.........................75 J1
Godmanstone Dorset.....14 C3
Godmersham Kent.....34 E5
Godney Somset..........26 C3
Godolphin Cross
  Cnwll............................. 3 G5
Godre'r-graig Neath......51 L4
Godshill IoW 17 G6
Godstone Surrey........32 C3
Goetre Mons 53 L6
Goff's Oak Herts........60 B7
Gogar C Edin 177 G4
Goginan Cerdgn........80 F7
Golan Gwynd...........95 J4
Golant Cnwll................ 5 H5
Golberdon Cnwll.......... 5 M2
Golborne Wigan 112 E3
Golcar Kirk............... 123 G7
Goldcliff Newpt.........38 A4
Golden Green Kent......33 H4
Goldenhill C Stke.......99 J2
Golden Pot Hants......30 B3
Golders Green Gt Lon....44 E3
Goldhanger Essex.....61 L6
Goldington Bed........74 F4
Goldsborough
  N York 132 F7
Goldsborough
  N York 143 H4
Goldsithney Cnwll........ 2 F5

Goldthorpe Barns......... 115 J2
Goldworthy Devon......22 F6
Gollanfield Highld...... 213 J4
Golspie Highld 223 H2
Gomeldon Wilts.........28 D4
Gomshall Surrey........31 H2
Gonalston Notts........ 102 B3
Gonerby Hill Foot
  Lincs.......................... 102 E5
Gonfirth Shet............ 235 c4
Good Easter Essex.....60 F5
Gooderstone Norfk....91 H3
Goodleigh Devon........23 J5
Goodmanham
  E R Yk....................... 125 K2
Goodmayes Gt Lon 45 J3
Goodnestone Kent....34 D3
Goodnestone Kent....35 H4
Goodrich Herefs 54 E4
Goodrington Torbay........ 7 K4
Goodshaw Lancs....... 122 B5
Goodwick Pembks......64 C6
Goodworth Clatford
  Hants..........................29 G3
Goole E R Yk.............. 125 H5
Goom's Hill Worcs......71 H4
Goonbell Cnwll............. 3 J1
Goonhavern Cnwll........ 3 K1
Goonvrea Cnwll............ 3 J2
Goosecruives Abers 206 E8
Gooseford Devon........11 G6
Goose Green Essex......62 D3
Goose Green S Glos.....38 F5
Goose Green Wigan.... 112 E2
Gooseham Cnwll........... 9 G2
Goosey Oxon...............41 G3
Goosnargh Lancs....... 121 H3
Goostrey Ches E........ 113 H7
Gordano Services
  N Som 38 D5
Gordon Border 167 K2
Gordon Arms Hotel
  Border 166 D4
Gordonstown
  Abers......................... 216 B3
Gordonstown Abers....216 D6
Gorebridge Mdloth..... 177 K6
Gorefield Cambs.........90 B2
Gores Wilts.................40 C8
Gorey Jersey.............. 236 e7
Goring Oxon 41 L4
Goring-by-Sea
  W Susx.........................18 F5
Gorleston-on-Sea
  Norfk............................93 L3
Gorrachie Abers 216 E3
Gorran Churchtown
  Cnwll............................. 4 F7
Gorran Haven Cnwll........ 4 F7
Gorsedd Flints 111 G6
Gorseddau Slate
  Landscape Gwynd....95 K4
Gorse Hill Swindn......40 D3
Gorseinon Swans.......51 H5
Gorsgoch Cerdgn......66 C4
Gorslas Carmth.........51 H3
Gorsley Gloucs...........55 G3
Gorsley Common
  Herefs...........................54 F3
Gorstan Highld.......... 212 B2
Gorsten Ag & B.......... 181 L2
Gorsty Hill Staffs...... 100 C6
Gorthleck Highld....... 202 E2
Gorton Manch 113 K3
Gosbeck Suffk............78 D4
Gosberton Lincs....... 103 L6
Gosfield Essex............61 J3
Gosforth Cumb......... 136 E6
Gosforth N u Ty 151 G2
Gosport Hants 17 H3
Gossington Gloucs....55 H7
Gotham Notts........... 101 K6
Gotherington Gloucs....55 L2
Gotton Somset...........25 K5
Goudhurst Kent.........33 J5
Goulceby Lincs.......... 118 C5
Gourdas Abers 216 E6
Gourdie C Dund........ 186 F2

Gourdon Abers........... 197 K3
Gourock Inver 173 L3
Govan C Glas............. 174 F5
Goveton Devon............. 7 H6
Govilon Mons..............53 K5
Gowdall E R Yk.......... 124 F6
Gower Highld 212 D3
Gower Swans..............51 G7
Gowerton Swans........51 H6
Gowkhall Fife............ 176 E1
Goxhill E R Yk........... 126 F2
Goxhill N Linc 126 D6
Grabhair W Isls......... 232 f3
Graffham W Susx........18 C3
Grafham Cambs........75 H2
Grafham Surrey..........31 G3
Grafton Oxon..............56 F7
Grafton Shrops...........98 B8
Grafton Worcs.............71 H6
Grafton Flyford
  Worcs...........................71 G4
Grafton Regis Nhants....73 L5
Grafton Underwood
  Nhants.........................88 D7
Grafty Green Kent......34 B5
Graig Conwy.............. 109 M6
Graigfechan Denbgs....97 J2
Grain Medway..............46 E5
Grainsby Lincs........... 118 C2
Grainthorpe Lincs ... 118 E3
Grampound Cnwll........ 4 E6
Grampound Road
  Cnwll............................. 4 E5
Gramsdal W Isls........ 233 c6
Gramsdale W Isls...... 233 c6
Granborough Bucks....58 C3
Granby Notts............ 102 C5
Grandborough
  Warwks........................72 F2
Grand Chemins
  Jersey........................ 236 d7
Grandes Rocques
  Guern 236 c2
Grandtully P & K....... 194 E5
Grange Cumb............ 137 H4
Grange Medway..........46 D6
Grange P & K 186 D3
Grange Crossroads
  Moray......................... 215 K4
Grange Hall Moray.... 214 C3
Grangehall S Lans.... 165 J2
Grange Hill Essex.......45 H2
Grangemill Derbys.... 100 E2
Grange Moor Kirk..... 123 J7
Grangemouth Falk.... 176 C3
Grange of Lindores
  Fife............................. 186 D4
Grange-over-Sands
  Cumb.......................... 129 J4
Grangepans Falk...... 176 D3
Grange Park Nhants...73 L4
Grangetown R & Cl.... 142 C3
Grangetown Sundld.. 151 K4
Grange Villa Dur....... 151 G4
Gransmoor E R Yk.... 135 H7
Granston Pembks......64 C7
Grantchester Cambs....76 B4
Grantham Lincs........ 102 E5
Granton C Edin 177 H3
Grantown-on-Spey
  Highld........................ 214 C8
Grantshouse Border ... 179 G5
Grappenhall Warrtn.. 112 F4
Grasby Lincs............. 117 H1
Grasmere Cumb........ 137 K5
Grasscroft Oldham... 113 L1
Grassendale Lpool.... 111 L4
Grassington N York... 131 J6
Grassmoor Derbys.... 115 H7
Grassthorpe Notts.... 116 C2
Grateley Hants...........28 F3
Graveley Cambs.........75 J2
Graveley Herts...........59 L3
Gravelly Hill Birm......85 K5
Graveney Kent...........34 E3
Gravesend Kent.........46 A5
Gravir W Isls............. 232 f3
Grayingham Lincs 116 F3

Grayrigg Cumb 138 E7
Grays Thurr................45 L4
Grayshott Hants.........30 E4
Grayswood Surrey......30 E4
Greasbrough Rothm... 115 H3
Greasby Wirral.......... 111 H4
Great Abington
  Cambs..........................76 D5
Great Addington
  Nhants.........................88 D7
Great Alne Warwks......71 K3
Great Altcar Lancs 111 K1
Great Amwell Herts.....60 B5
Great Asby Cumb...... 138 F5
Great Ashfield Suffk....78 B2
Great Ayton N York... 142 C5
Great Baddow Essex....61 H6
Great Badminton
  S Glos..........................39 J4
Great Bardfield
  Essex...........................61 G2
Great Barford Bed.....75 G4
Great Barr Sandw......85 J4
Great Barrington
  Gloucs..........................56 E5
Great Barrow
  Ches W........................ 112 C7
Great Barton Suffk......77 K2
Great Barugh N York... 134 B4
Great Bavington
  Nthumb...................... 158 C6
Great Bealings Suffk....78 F5
Great Bedwyn Wilts....40 F7
Great Bentley Essex....62 D4
Great Billing Nhants....74 B3
Great Bircham Norfk... 105 J6
Great Blakenham
  Suffk............................78 D4
Great Blencow
  Cumb.......................... 138 C2
Great Bolas Wrekin....98 F7
Great Bookham
  Surrey..........................31 J1
Great Bourton Oxon....72 F5
Great Bowden Leics....87 L5
Great Bradley Suffk....76 F4
Great Braxted Essex....61 K5
Great Bricett Suffk......78 C4
Great Brickhill Bucks...58 E3
Great Bridge Sandw....85 H5
Great Bridgeford
  Staffs...........................99 K6
Great Brington
  Nhants.........................73 J2
Great Bromley Essex....62 C3
Great Broughton
  Cumb.......................... 136 E2
Great Broughton
  N York 142 C6
Great Budworth
  Ches W....................... 112 F6
Great Burdon Darltn... 141 H4
Great Burstead
  Essex...........................46 B2
Great Busby N York... 142 B6
Great Carlton Lincs... 118 E4
Great Casterton
  Rutlnd.........................88 E2
Great Chalfield Wilts....39 K7
Great Chart Kent........34 C6
Great Chatwell Staffs....84 E1
Great Chell C Stke.......99 K3
Great Chesterford
  Essex...........................76 D6
Great Cheverell Wilts....27 M1
Great Chishill Cambs...76 B6
Great Clacton Essex....62 E5
Great Clifton Cumb... 136 E2
Great Coates NE Lin.... 126 F8
Great Comberton
  Worcs...........................71 G6
Great Corby Cumb.... 148 E4
Great Cornard Suffk....77 K6
Great Cowden
  E R Yk......................... 126 F3
Great Coxwell Oxon....40 F7
Great Cransley
  Nhants.........................88 B7

Great Cressingham
Norfk..............91 J3
Great Crosthwaite
Cumb..................137 J3
Great Cubley Derbys.....100 D5
Great Cumbrae
Island N Ayrs.....173 K6
Great Dalby Leics.....87 L2
Great Denham Bed........74 E5
Great Doddington
Nhants..............74 C2
Great Dunham Norfk......91 K1
Great Dunmow Essex....61 G4
Great Durnford Wilts....28 C4
Great Easton Essex......60 F3
Great Easton Leics.........88 B5
Great Eccleston
Lancs.................120 F3
Great Edstone
N York..............133 L3
Great Ellingham
Norfk..................92 B4
Great Elm Somset............27 H2
Great Everdon
Nhants.................73 H3
Great Eversden
Cambs.................75 L4
Great Fencote
N York...............132 D2
Great Finborough
Suffk.................78 B3
Greatford Lincs..........88 F2
Great Fransham
Norfk.................91 K2
Great Gaddesden
Herts.................59 G5
Greatgate Staffs...........100 B4
Great Gidding Cambs.....89 G6
Great Givendale
E R Yk...............134 C8
Great Glemham
Suffk.................79 H3
Great Glen Leics.......87 J4
Great Gonerby Lincs....102 E5
Great Gransden
Cambs.................75 J4
Great Green Cambs....75 K5
Great Green Suffk.......77 K4
Great Habton N York....134 B4
Great Hale Lincs.........103 J4
Great Hallingbury
Essex.................60 E4
Greatham Hants.........30 C5
Greatham Hartpl...........141 L2
Greatham W Susx.......18 E3
Great Hampden
Bucks.................58 D7
Great Harrowden
Nhants.................74 C1
Great Harwood
Lancs.................121 L4
Great Haseley Oxon........57 M7
Great Hatfield E R Yk...126 F3
Great Haywood
Staffs.................100 A4
Great Heck N York......124 E6
Great Henny Essex.......77 K6
Great Hinton Wilts.......39 K8
Great Hockham
Norfk.................91 L5
Great Holland Essex.....62 E4
Great Hollands
Br For.................42 E6
Great Horkesley
Essex.................62 B2
Great Hormead
Herts.................60 C3
Great Horton C Brad....123 H4
Great Horwood
Bucks.................58 C2
Great Houghton
Barns.................115 H1
Great Houghton
Nhants.................73 L3
Great Hucklow
Derbys................114 D6
Great Kelk E R Yk........135 H7
Great Kimble Bucks......58 D6

Great Kingshill Bucks.....42 E2
Great Langdale
Cumb..................137 J6
Great Langton
N York...............141 H7
Great Leighs Essex.........61 H4
Great Limber Lincs......126 E8
Great Linford M Keyn.....74 C6
Great Livermere
Suffk.................77 K1
Great Longstone
Derbys................114 D6
Great Lumley Dur.........151 H5
Great Malvern Worcs.....70 D5
Great Maplestead
Essex.................77 J7
Great Marton Bpool......120 D4
Great Massingham
Norfk.................105 J7
Great Milton Oxon.........57 L7
Great Missenden
Bucks.................58 E7
Great Mitton Lancs.....121 K3
Great Mongeham
Kent...................35 K4
Great Moulton Norfk.....92 E5
Great Musgrave
Cumb..................139 H4
Great Ness Shrops........98 B8
Great Notley Essex........61 H4
Great Oak Mons.........54 B6
Great Oakley Essex.......62 E3
Great Oakley Nhants.....88 C6
Great Offley Herts.........59 J3
Great Ormside
Cumb..................139 G4
Great Orton Cumb.......148 B4
Great Ouseburn
N York...............133 G6
Great Oxendon
Nhants.................87 K6
Great Parndon Essex.....60 C6
Great Paxton Cambs......75 H2
Great Plumpton
Lancs.................120 E4
Great Plumstead
Norfk.................93 G2
Great Ponton Lincs.....102 F6
Great Preston Leeds.....124 B5
Great Raveley Cambs.....89 J7
Great Rissington
Gloucs................56 D5
Great Rollright Oxon......56 F2
Great Ryburgh Norfk.....106 A6
Great Ryton Shrops.......83 J3
Great Saling Essex........61 H3
Great Salkeld Cumb......148 F7
Great Sampford
Essex.................76 F7
Great Saughall
Ches W................111 K7
Great Shefford
W Berk................41 G5
Great Shelford
Cambs.................76 C4
Great Smeaton
N York...............141 H6
Great Snoring Norfk.....105 M5
Great Somerford
Wilts.................39 L4
Great Soudley
Shrops................99 G6
Great Stainton
Darltn.................141 H3
Great Stambridge
Essex.................46 E2
Great Staughton
Cambs.................75 G2
Great Steeping Lincs....118 F8
Greatstone-on-Sea
Kent...................21 L2
Great Strickland
Cumb..................138 D3
Great Stukeley
Cambs.................89 J8
Great Sturton Lincs.....117 K6
Great Swinburne
Nthumb................158 B6

Great Tew Oxon.............57 H3
Great Tey Essex............61 L3
Great Thurlow Suffk......76 F4
Great Torrington
Devon.................23 H7
Great Tosson Nthumb....158 C3
Great Totham Essex.......61 K5
Great Totham Essex.......61 L5
Great Urswick
Cumb..................129 G5
Great Wakering
Essex.................46 F3
Great Waldingfield
Suffk.................77 K5
Great Walsingham
Norfk.................105 M5
Great Waltham
Essex.................61 H5
Great Warley Essex.......45 L2
Great Washbourne
Gloucs................71 H7
Great Weeke Devon......11 G7
Great Wenham Suffk.....78 C6
Great Whittington
Nthumb................158 C7
Great Wigborough
Essex.................62 A5
Great Wilbraham
Cambs.................76 D3
Great Wishford Wilts.....28 B4
Great Witcombe
Gloucs................55 K5
Great Witley Worcs........70 D2
Great Wolford
Warwks................72 B7
Greatworth Nhants........73 G6
Great Wratting Suffk.....77 G5
Great Wymondley
Herts.................59 K3
Great Wyrley Staffs.......85 H3
Great Yarmouth
Norfk.................93 L3
Great Yeldham Essex.....77 H6
Greenburn W Loth........176 C6
Green End Herts...........60 B2
Green End Herts...........60 B4
Greenfield Ag & B........173 M1
Greenfield C Beds.........74 F7
Greenfield Flints..........111 H6
Greenfield Highld........201 J5
Greenfield Oldham.......113 M2
Greenford Gt Lon.........43 J4
Greengairs N Lans.......175 K4
Greengates C Brad.......123 J3
Greenham Somset..........25 G7
Green Hammerton
N York...............133 G7
Greenhaugh Nthumb....157 K5
Greenhead Nthumb......149 H3
Green Heath Staffs.......85 H2
Greenhill D & G............155 J6
Greenhill Falk.............175 L3
Greenhill Kent.............47 K6
Greenhill Leics............86 F2
Greenhill S Lans..........165 H3
Greenhills S Lans.........175 H7
Greenhithe Kent...........45 L5
Greenholm E Ayrs.......164 B3
Greenhouse Border......167 H5
Greenhow Hill
N York...............131 L6
Greenland Highld........231 J3
Greenland Sheff...........115 H4
Greenlaw Border.........167 L1
Greenlea D & G............155 H6
Greenloaning P & K....185 H6
Greenmount Bury.........122 B7
Greenock Inver............174 B3
Greenodd Cumb............129 G3
Green Ore Somset..........26 E2
Green Park Readg.........42 B6
Green Quarter
Cumb..................138 C6
Greenshields S Lans.....165 K2
Greenside Gatesd.........150 E3
Greenside Kirk............123 H7
Greens Norton
Nhants.................73 J4

Greenstead Green
Essex.................61 K3
Green Street Herts.........59 K7
Green Street Herts..........60 D4
Green Tye Herts.............60 C4
Greenway Somset...........25 L6
Greenwich Gt Lon..........45 G4
Greenwich
Maritime Gt Lon.....45 H4
Greet Gloucs.................56 B3
Greete Shrops................69 L1
Greetham Lincs............118 D7
Greetham Rutlnd...........88 D2
Greetland Calder...........123 G6
Greinton Somset.............26 B4
Grenaby IoM................237 b6
Grendon Nhants.............74 C3
Grendon Warwks..........86 C4
Grendon
Underwood Bucks.....58 B4
Grenoside Sheff............115 G3
Greosabhagh
W Isls.................232 e4
Gresford Wrexhm..........97 M2
Gresham Norfk.............106 E5
Greshornish Highld......208 E4
Gressenhall Norfk.........91 L1
Gressenhall Green
Norfk.................91 L1
Gressingham Lancs.....130 B5
Greta Bridge Dur........140 D5
Gretna D & G.............148 B2
Gretna Green D & G....148 B2
Gretna Services
D & G.................148 B2
Gretton Gloucs..............56 A2
Gretton Nhants..............88 C5
Gretton Shrops..............83 K4
Grewelthorpe
N York...............132 C4
Greyrigg D & G.............155 J4
Greys Green Oxon.........42 B4
Greysouthen Cumb.......136 E2
Greystoke Cumb............138 B2
Greystone Angus..........196 E7
Greywell Hants..............30 B2
Griff Warwks.................86 D5
Griffithstown Torfn.........53 L7
Grimeford Village
Lancs.................121 J7
Grimesthorpe Sheff......115 G4
Grimethorpe Barns.......124 C8
Grimister Shet.............235 d2
Grimley Worcs................70 E3
Grimmet S Ayrs............163 H7
Grimoldby Lincs...........118 E4
Grimpo Shrops...............98 A7
Grimsargh Lancs.........121 H4
Grimsby NE Lin............127 G7
Grimscote Nhants.........73 J4
Grimscott Cnwll..............9 H4
Grimshader W Isls.........232 f3
Grimsthorpe Lincs.......103 H7
Grimston Leics.............102 B7
Grimston Norfk............105 H7
Grimstone Dorset..........14 C4
Grimstone End
Suffk.................77 L2
Grindale E R Yk...........135 H5
Grindleford Derbys.......114 E6
Grindleton Lancs...........121 L2
Grindley Brook
Shrops................98 D4
Grindlow Derbys..........114 D6
Grindon Staffs............100 B2
Gringley on the Hill
Notts.................116 C4
Grinsdale Cumb...........148 C4
Grinshill Shrops.............98 D7
Grinton N York............140 D7
Griomsiadar W Isls.......232 f3
Grishipoll Ag & B........188 F4
Gristhorpe N York.........135 H3
Griston Norfk................91 L4
Gritley Ork...................234 d6
Grittenham Wilts...........40 B4
Grittleton Wilts.............39 K4
Grizebeck Cumb...........128 F3

Grizedale Cumb............ 137 K7
Groby Leics.................87 G3
Groes Conwy 110 D8
Groes-faen Rhondd.......37 G4
Groeslon Gwynd...........95 H2
Groes-Wen Caerph........37 H3
Grogarry W Isls............233 b7
Grogport Ag & B.........161 K1
Groigearraidh
   W Isls......................233 b7
Gronant Flints..............110 F5
Groombridge E Susx......32 F5
Grosebay W Isls...........232 e4
Grosmont Mons.............54 B3
Grosmont N York.........143 H6
Groton Suffk..................77 L6
Grouville Jersey...........236 e7
Grove Notts.................116 C5
Grove Oxon...................41 H3
Grove Green Kent..........33 K3
Grove Park Gt Lon........45 H5
Grovesend Swans...........51 H5
Gruinard Highld...........219 L4
Gruinart Ag & B..........170 F5
Grula Highld................208 F8
Gruline Ag & B.............190 B7
Grundisburgh Suffk........78 F4
Gruting Shet................235 c5
Grutness Shet...............235 c8
Gualachulain Highld....192 B7
Guardbridge Fife.........187 G4
Guarlford Worcs............70 E5
Guay P & K.................194 F6
Guernsey Guern...........236 c3
Guernsey Airport
   Guern.......................236 c3
Guestling Green
   E Susx........................21 G3
Guestling Thorn
   E Susx........................21 G3
Guestwick Norfk..........106 C6
Guide Bridge
   Tamesd.....................113 L3
Guilden Morden
   Cambs........................75 K5
Guilden Sutton
   Ches W.....................112 C7
Guildford Surrey...........31 G2
Guildtown P & K..........186 B2
Guilsborough
   Nhants.......................87 J8
Guilsfield Powys...........82 E2
Guiltreehill S Ayrs......163 J7
Guineaford Devon.........23 J4
Guisborough R & Cl....142 D4
Guiseley Leeds.............123 J3
Guist Norfk.................106 B7
Guiting Power
   Gloucs........................56 C3
Gullane E Loth............178 B2
Gulval Cnwll...................2 E5
Gulworthy Devon............6 C2
Gumfreston Pembks......49 J7
Gumley Leics................87 K5
Gunby Lincs................102 E7
Gundleton Hants...........29 L5
Gun Hill E Susx.............20 C3
Gunn Devon..................23 K5
Gunnerside N York......139 L7
Gunnerton Nthumb......158 A7
Gunness N Linc...........125 K7
Gunnislake Cnwll............6 C2
Gunnista Shet.............235 d6
Gunthorpe C Pete.........89 H3
Gunthorpe N Linc........116 D3
Gunthorpe Norfk.........106 B5
Gunthorpe Notts.........102 B4
Gunwalloe Cnwll.............3 H6
Gurnard IoW..................16 F4
Gurney Slade
   Somset.......................26 F2
Gurnos Powys................52 B6
Gussage All Saints
   Dorset........................15 J1
Gussage St Andrew
   Dorset........................27 L8
Gussage St Michael
   Dorset........................15 J1

Guston Kent..................35 J5
Gutcher Shet...............235 d2
Guthrie Angus.............196 F6
Guyhirn Cambs..............90 B3
Guyzance Nthumb........158 F2
Gwaenysgor Flints.......110 F5
Gwalchmai IoA............108 E6
Gwaun-Cae-
   Gurwen Carmth......51 K3
Gweek Cnwll....................3 J6
Gwenddwr Powys..........68 B6
Gwennap Cnwll...............3 J4
Gwennap Mining
   District Cnwll................3 K3
Gwernaffield Flints......111 H7
Gwernesney Mons.........54 B7
Gwernogle Carmth........66 C7
Gwernymynydd
   Flints..........................97 J1
Gwersyllt Wrexhm.........97 L2
Gwespyr Flints.............110 F5
Gwinear Cnwll................3 G4
Gwithian Cnwll...............3 G3
Gwydelwern
   Denbgs........................97 G3
Gwyddgrug Carmth........66 B7
Gwytherin Conwy..........96 D1

H

Habberley Shrops..........83 H3
Habberley Worcs............84 E7
Habergham Lancs.........122 B4
Habertoft Lincs............119 G7
Habrough NE Lin..........126 E7
Hacconby Lincs............103 J7
Haceby Lincs................103 G5
Hacheston Suffk............79 G3
Hackbridge Gt Lon........44 F6
Hackenthorpe Sheff.....115 H5
Hackford Norfk.............92 C3
Hackforth N York.........132 C2
Hackland Ork...............234 c5
Hackleton Nhants..........74 B4
Hacklinge Kent..............35 J4
Hackness N York..........134 F2
Hackney Gt Lon............45 G3
Hackthorn Lincs...........117 G5
Hackthorpe Cumb.........138 D3
Hadden Border..............168 B3
Haddenham Bucks.........58 C6
Haddenham Cambs.........90 C7
Haddington E Loth.......178 B4
Haddington Lincs.........116 E8
Haddiscoe Norfk............93 J4
Haddon Cambs...............89 G5
Hadfield Derbys...........114 A3
Hadham Ford Herts........60 C4
Hadleigh Essex..............46 D3
Hadleigh Suffk..............78 B6
Hadley Worcs................70 F2
Hadley Wrekin...............84 C2
Hadley End Staffs........100 C7
Hadley Wood Gt Lon......44 E1
Hadlow Kent..................33 H3
Hadlow Down E Susx.....20 B2
Hadnall Shrops..............98 D7
Hadrian's Wall 150 B2
Hadstock Essex..............76 D5
Hadzor Worcs.................71 G3
Haggersta Shet.............235 c5
Haggerston Nthumb.....168 F2
Haggs Falk...................175 L3
Hagley Herefs................69 L6
Hagley Worcs.................85 G7
Hagworthingham
   Lincs........................118 D7
Haile Cumb.................136 E5
Hailey Oxon...................57 G5
Hailsham E Susx............20 C4
Hail Weston Cambs........75 H3
Hainault Gt Lon............45 J2
Hainford Norfk.............106 F8
Hainton Lincs...............117 K5
Haisthorpe E R Yk.......135 H6
Hakin Pembks................48 F6

Halam Notts................102 B2
Halbeath Fife...............176 F1
Halberton Devon............24 F8
Halcro Highld...............231 J4
Hale Cumb..................129 K4
Hale Halton.................112 C5
Hale Hants....................28 D7
Hale Surrey...................30 D2
Hale Traffd.................113 H4
Hale Barns Traffd........113 H4
Hales Norfk...................93 H4
Hales Staffs..................99 G5
Halesowen Dudley.........85 G6
Hales Place Kent...........34 F3
Hale Street Kent...........33 H4
Halesworth Suffk...........93 H7
Halewood Knows..........112 C4
Halford Devon.................7 J2
Halford Warwks.............72 C5
Halfpenny Green
   Staffs........................84 E5
Halfway House
   Shrops........................83 G2
Halfway Houses Kent.....46 F5
Halifax Calder.............123 G5
Halket E Ayrs...............174 D7
Halkirk Highld.............231 G4
Halkyn Flints...............111 H7
Hall E Rens.................174 D7
Halland E Susx..............20 A3
Hallaton Leics...............87 L4
Hallatrow BaNES...........38 F8
Hallbankgate Cumb.....149 G3
Hall Dunnerdale
   Cumb........................137 H7
Hallen S Glos................38 D4
Hallgarth Dur..............151 H6
Hallglen Falk...............176 B3
Hall Green Birm............85 K7
Hallin Highld................208 D3
Halling Medway.............46 B7
Hallington Lincs...........118 D4
Hallington Nthumb.......158 C6
Halliwell Bolton............121 K7
Halloughton Notts........102 B3
Hallow Worcs.................70 E3
Hall's Green Herts.........59 L3
Hallyne Border.............166 B2
Halmore Gloucs.............55 G7
Halnaker W Susx............18 B4
Halsall Lancs...............120 E7
Halse Nhants.................73 H6
Halse Somset.................25 H5
Halsetown Cnwll.............2 E4
Halsham E R Yk...........127 G5
Halstead Essex..............61 K2
Halstead Kent................45 J7
Halstead Leics...............87 L3
Halstock Dorset.............14 A2
Haltham Lincs..............118 C8
Halton Bucks.................58 E6
Halton Halton..............112 D5
Halton Lancs................129 K6
Halton Leeds................123 L4
Halton Nthumb.............150 C2
Halton Wrexhm..............97 L4
Halton East N York.......131 K8
Halton Gill N York........131 G4
Halton Holegate
   Lincs........................118 F7
Halton Lea Gate
   Nthumb.....................149 H4
Halton Shields
   Nthumb.....................150 C2
Halton West N York......130 F8
Haltwhistle Nthumb.....149 J3
Halvergate Norfk...........93 J3
Halwell Devon.................7 H5
Halwill Devon................10 C5
Halwill Junction
   Devon........................10 C5
Ham Devon...................13 G3
Ham Gloucs...................55 G7
Ham Gt Lon...................44 D5
Ham Kent......................35 J4
Ham Somset..................25 L6
Ham Wilts.....................41 G7
Hambleden Bucks..........42 C3

Hambledon Hants..........29 M7
Hambledon Surrey..........30 F4
Hamble-le-Rice
   Hants.........................16 F2
Hambleton Lancs..........120 E3
Hambleton N York........124 E4
Hambridge Somset.........26 B6
Hambrook W Susx..........17 L2
Hameringham Lincs.....118 D7
Hamerton Cambs............89 G7
Ham Green Worcs...........71 H2
Hamilton S Lans...........175 J7
Hamilton Services
(northbound)
   S Lans.....................*175* *J6*
Hamlet Dorset................14 B2
Hammersmith Gt Lon.....44 E4
Hammerwich Staffs........85 J3
Hammoon Dorset............27 J8
Hamnavoe Shet............235 c6
Hampden Park
   E Susx........................20 C5
Hampnett Gloucs...........56 C5
Hampole Donc..............124 D7
Hampreston Dorset........15 K3
Hampstead Gt Lon..........44 E3
Hampstead Norreys
   W Berk........................41 K5
Hampsthwaite
   N York......................132 C7
Hampton Gt Lon............43 J6
Hampton Kent................47 K6
Hampton Shrops............84 D6
Hampton Swindn............40 D3
Hampton Worcs..............71 H5
Hampton Bishop
   Herefs........................69 L6
Hampton Court
   Palace Gt Lon..........44 D6
Hampton Hargate
   C Pete........................89 H5
Hampton Heath
   Ches W......................98 D3
Hampton-in-Arden
   Solhll.........................86 B7
Hampton Lovett
   Worcs........................70 F2
Hampton Lucy
   Warwks......................72 B3
Hampton Magna
   Warwks......................72 C2
Hampton Park Wilts......28 D5
Hampton Poyle Oxon.....57 J5
Hampton Vale C Pete....89 H5
Hampton Wick
   Gt Lon.......................44 D6
Hamptworth Wilts..........28 E7
Hamsey E Susx..............19 L3
Hamstall Ridware
   Staffs.......................100 C8
Hamstead Birm..............85 J5
Hamstead Marshall
   W Berk........................41 H7
Hamsterley Dur...........140 E2
Hamsterley Dur...........150 E4
Hamstreet Kent..............34 D7
Ham Street Somset........26 D4
Hamworthy BCP............15 J4
Hanbury Staffs.............100 D6
Hanbury Worcs...............71 G2
Hanchurch Staffs...........99 J4
Handa Island Highld....228 A6
Hand and Pen Devon.....12 D4
Handbridge Ches W......112 B7
Handcross W Susx.........31 L5
Handforth Ches E.........113 J5
Handley Ches W.............98 C2
Handley Derbys............101 G1
Handsworth Birm...........85 J5
Handsworth Sheff........115 H4
Hanford C Stke..............99 J5
Hanging Heaton
   Kirk..........................123 K6
Hanging Houghton
   Nhants.......................87 L8
Hanging Langford
   Wilts..........................28 B4
Hangleton Br & H..........19 H4

Hanham S Glos................38 F6
Hankelow Ches E..........98 F4
Hankerton Wilts............39 L3
Hanley C Stke................99 K3
Hanley Castle Worcs......70 E6
Hanley Child Worcs.......70 B2
Hanley Swan Worcs.......70 E6
Hanley William
  Worcs.........................70 D2
Hanlith N York............131 G7
Hanmer Wrexhm..........98 C4
Hannaford Devon..........23 J5
Hannington Hants........29 K1
Hannington Nhants.......74 B1
Hannington Swindn......40 D2
Hannington Wick
  Swindn.......................40 D2
Hanslope M Keyn...........74 B5
Hanthorpe Lincs..........103 H7
Hanwell Gt Lon.............44 D4
Hanwell Oxon...............72 E5
Hanwood Shrops..........83 J2
Hanworth Gt Lon...........43 J6
Hanworth Norfk..........106 E5
Happendon S Lans.......165 G3
Happisburgh Norfk......107 H6
Happisburgh
  Common Norfk.........107 H6
Hapsford Ches W.........112 C6
Hapton Lancs...............122 B4
Hapton Norfk................92 E4
Harberton Devon............7 H4
Harbertonford Devon......7 H5
Harbledown Kent...........34 F3
Harborne Birm..............85 H6
Harborough Magna
  Warwks......................86 F7
Harbottle Nthumb........158 B2
Harbourneford
  Devon..........................7 G4
Harburn W Loth..........176 E6
Harbury Warwks...........72 D3
Harby Leics.................102 C6
Harby Notts.................116 E7
Harcombe Devon............11 K8
Harcombe Devon............12 F4
Harcombe Bottom
  Devon.........................13 J4
Harden C Brad.............123 G3
Harden Wsall.................85 H4
Hardenhuish Wilts.........39 K5
Hardgate Abers...........206 E5
Hardgate D & G...........146 E2
Hardgate W Duns........174 F4
Hardham W Susx..........18 E3
Hardingham Norfk.........92 C3
Hardingstone Nhants....73 L3
Hardington Somset.......27 H2
Hardington
  Mandeville
  Somset.......................13 M1
Hardington Marsh
  Somset.......................13 M1
Hardington Moor
  Somset.......................26 D8
Hardisworthy Devon......22 C7
Hardley Hants..............16 E2
Hardley Street Norfk.....93 H4
Hardraw N York...........131 G2
Hardstoft Derbys.........115 H8
Hardway Hants.............17 H3
Hardway Somset...........27 G5
Hardwick Bucks............58 D4
Hardwick Cambs...........75 L3
Hardwick Derbys..........115 J8
Hardwick Nhants..........74 B1
Hardwick Norfk............92 F5
Hardwick Oxon.............57 G6
Hardwick Oxon.............57 L3
Hardwick Wsall.............85 J4
Hardwicke Gloucs.........55 H5
Hardwicke Gloucs.........55 K3
Hardy's Green Essex.....61 M4
Hare Croft C Brad........123 G4
Harefield Gt Lon...........43 H3
Hare Green Essex.........62 D3
Hare Hatch Wokham......42 D5
Harehill Derbys...........100 D5

Harehills Leeds...........123 L4
Harelaw Border...........167 H5
Harelaw D & G............156 D6
Harescombe Gloucs......55 J6
Haresfield Gloucs.........55 J6
Harestock Hants...........29 J5
Hare Street Essex.........60 C6
Hare Street Herts.........60 C3
Harewood Leeds.........123 L2
Harewood End
  Herefs.........................54 D3
Harford Devon................6 F4
Hargrave Ches W..........98 C1
Hargrave Nhants...........74 F1
Hargrave Suffk.............77 H3
Harkstead Suffk...........78 E7
Harlaston Staffs...........86 B2
Harlaxton Lincs...........102 E6
Harlech Gwynd.............95 K6
Harlech Castle
  Gwynd.........................95 K6
Harlescott Shrops.........83 K1
Harlesden Gt Lon..........44 E4
Harlesthorpe Derbys...115 J6
Harleston Devon.............7 J6
Harleston Norfk............92 F6
Harleston Suffk............78 B3
Harlestone Nhants........73 K2
Harle Syke Lancs.........122 C4
Harley Rothm..............115 G2
Harley Shrops..............83 L3
Harlington C Beds.........59 G2
Harlington Donc..........115 J2
Harlington Gt Lon.........43 H5
Harlosh Highld............208 D6
Harlow Essex................60 D6
Harlow Hill Nthumb.....150 D2
Harlthorpe E R Yk.......125 H3
Harlton Cambs..............75 L4
Harlyn Cnwll..................4 D2
Harman's Cross
  Dorset........................15 J6
Harmby N York...........131 L2
Harmer Green Herts.....59 L5
Harmer Hill Shrops.......98 C7
Harmston Lincs...........116 F8
Harnage Shrops............83 L3
Harnhill Gloucs.............56 B7
Harold Hill Gt Lon........45 K2
Haroldston West
  Pembks......................48 E4
Haroldswick Shet........235 e1
Harold Wood Gt Lon.....45 K3
Harome N York............133 K3
Harpenden Herts...........59 J3
Harpford Devon............12 E4
Harpham E R Yk.........135 H7
Harpley Norfk..............105 J7
Harpley Worcs..............70 C3
Harpole Nhants.............73 K3
Harpsdale Highld.........231 G4
Harpswell Lincs...........116 F4
Harpurhey Manch........113 K2
Harraby Cumb.............148 D4
Harracott Devon...........23 J6
Harrapool Highld.........199 K2
Harras Cumb...............136 D4
Harrietfield P & K........185 K2
Harrietsham Kent..........33 L3
Harringay Gt Lon..........44 F3
Harrington Cumb.........136 D3
Harrington Lincs..........118 E6
Harrington Nhants........87 L7
Harringworth Nhants....88 D4
Harris W Isls...............232 d4
Harrogate N York........132 D7
Harrold Bed.................74 D3
Harrow Gt Lon..............44 D3
Harrowbarrow Cnwll......6 B2
Harrowgate Village
  Darltn......................141 H4
Harrow Green Suffk......77 J4
Harrow on the Hill
  Gt Lon.......................44 D3
Harrow Weald Gt Lon....44 D2
Harston Cambs.............76 B4
Harston Leics..............102 D6
Harswell E R Yk...........125 J3

Hart Hartpl.................151 L7
Hartburn Nthumb........158 D5
Hartburn S on T..........141 K4
Hartest Suffk................77 J4
Hartfield E Susx...........32 E6
Hartford Cambs............89 J8
Hartford Ches W.........112 F6
Hartfordbridge
  Hants.........................42 C8
Hartford End Essex......61 G4
Hartforth N York.........140 F6
Hartgrove Dorset..........27 J7
Harthill Ches W............98 D2
Harthill N Lans...........176 B5
Harthill Rothm............115 J5
Harthope D & G...........165 K6
Hartington Derbys.......100 C1
Hartland Devon............22 D6
Hartland Quay Devon....22 C6
Hartlebury Worcs.........70 E1
Hartlepool Hartpl.......151 L7
Hartley Cumb.............139 H5
Hartley Kent................33 K6
Hartley Kent................45 L6
Hartley Wespall
  Hants.........................42 B8
Hartley Wintney
  Hants.........................30 C1
Hartlip Kent.................46 D7
Harton N York.............133 L6
Harton S Tyne.............151 J2
Hartpury Gloucs...........55 J3
Hartshead Kirk............123 J6
Hartshead Moor
  Services Calder......123 H5
Hartshill C Stke............99 K4
Hartshill Warwks..........86 D5
Hartshorne Derbys......100 F7
Hartwell Nhants............73 L4
Hartwith N York..........132 C6
Hartwood N Lans........175 L6
Hartwoodmyres
  Border......................166 F4
Harvel Kent..................46 A7
Harvington Worcs.........71 J5
Harvington Worcs.........84 F8
Harwell Notts..............116 B3
Harwell Oxon...............41 J3
Harwich Essex..............62 F2
Harwood Dale
  N York......................143 K7
Harworth Notts...........115 L3
Hasbury Dudley............85 G6
Hascombe Surrey..........31 G4
Haselbech Nhants.........87 K7
Haselbury Plucknett
  Somset.......................13 L1
Haseley Warwks...........72 B2
Haselor Warwks............71 K3
Hasfield Gloucs.............55 J3
Haskayne Lancs...........120 E8
Hasketon Suffk.............78 F4
Haslemere Surrey..........30 E5
Haslingden Lancs........122 B6
Haslingfield Cambs........76 B4
Haslington Ches E.........99 G2
Hassingham Norfk........93 H3
Hassocks W Susx..........19 J3
Hassop Derbys............114 E6
Haster Highld..............231 K5
Hastingleigh Kent.........34 E5
Hastings E Susx............21 G4
Hastingwood Essex......60 D6
Hastoe Herts................58 F6
Haswell Dur................151 J6
Haswell Plough Dur....151 J6
Hatch Beauchamp
  Somset.......................25 L7
Hatch End Gt Lon.........43 J3
Hatchmere Ches W.....112 D6
Hatch Warren Hants.....29 L2
Hatcliffe NE Lin..........117 K2
Hatfield Donc.............125 K6
Hatfield Herefs.............69 L3
Hatfield Herts...............59 L6
Hatfield Broad Oak
  Essex.........................60 E5
Hatfield Heath Essex....60 E5

Hatfield Peverel
  Essex.........................61 J5
Hatfield Woodhouse
  Donc........................125 G8
Hatford Oxon...............41 G2
Hatherden Hants...........29 G2
Hatherleigh Devon........10 D4
Hathern Leics.............101 J7
Hatherop Gloucs...........56 D6
Hathersage Derbys......114 E5
Hathersage Booths
  Derbys......................114 E5
Hatherton Ches E.........99 G3
Hatherton Staffs...........85 G2
Hatley St George
  Cambs........................75 K4
Hatt Cnwll......................6 B4
Hattersley Tamesd.......113 M3
Hatton Abers...............217 K6
Hatton Angus..............196 D7
Hatton Derbys.............100 E6
Hatton Gt Lon...............43 J5
Hatton Lincs...............117 K6
Hatton Shrops...............83 J5
Hatton Warrtn.............112 E5
Hatton Warwks.............72 B2
Hatton of Fintray
  Abers........................206 F3
Hatton Park Warwks......72 B2
Haugh E Ayrs..............163 L4
Haugham Lincs...........118 D5
Haughead E Duns........175 G3
Haughley Suffk.............78 B3
Haughley Green
  Suffk..........................78 B2
Haugh of Glass
  Moray.......................215 J6
Haugh of Urr D & G......146 E2
Haughs of Kinnaird
  Angus.......................197 G5
Haughton Ches E..........98 E2
Haughton Shrops..........98 B6
Haughton Staffs............99 K7
Haughton le Skerne
  Darltn......................141 H4
Haultwick Herts...........60 B4
Haunton Staffs..............86 B2
Hautes Croix Jersey....236 c6
Hauxton Cambs............76 B4
Havant Hants................17 K2
Havenstreet IoW...........17 G4
Havercroft Wakefd.......124 B7
Haverfordwest
  Pembks......................48 F4
Haverhill Suffk.............76 F5
Haverigg Cumb............128 E4
Havering-atte-
  Bower Gt Lon............45 K2
Haversham M Keyn........74 B6
Haverthwaite Cumb......129 H3
Hawyatt N Som............38 C7
Hawbush Green
  Essex.........................61 J4
Hawcoat Cumb............128 E5
Hawen Cerdgn..............65 K5
Hawes N York.............131 G2
Hawe's Green Norfk......92 F4
Hawford Worcs.............70 E3
Hawick Border............167 G6
Hawkchurch Devon.......13 J3
Hawkedon Suffk...........77 H4
Hawkeridge Wilts..........27 K2
Hawkesbury S Glos.......39 H3
Hawkesbury Upton
  S Glos........................39 H3
Hawkhead Rens...........174 F6
Hawkhurst Kent............33 K6
Hawkinge Kent.............35 G6
Hawkley Hants..............30 C5
Hawkridge Somset........24 D5
Hawkshead Cumb........137 K7
Hawkshead Hill
  Cumb........................137 K7
Hawksland S Lans......165 G2
Hawkstone Shrops........98 E6
Hawkswick N York.......131 H5
Hawksworth Leeds......123 H3

Hawksworth Notts..... 102 C4
Hawkwell Essex..............46 E2
Hawley Hants..............42 D8
Hawling Gloucs 56 B4
Hawnby N York..........133 H2
Haworth C Brad............122 F3
Hawstead Suffk..............77 J3
Hawthorn Dur 151 K5
Hawthorn Hill Lincs.....103 K2
Hawton Notts...............102 C3
Haxby C York 133 J7
Haxey N Linc.................116 C2
Haydock St Hel............112 E3
Haydon Bridge
  Nthumb 149 L3
Haydon Wick Swindn.....40 C3
Hayes Gt Lon 43 J4
Hayes Gt Lon 45 H6
Hayes End Gt Lon.........43 H4
Hayfield Ag & B 182 F3
Hayfield Derbys............114 B4
Hayhillock Angus..........196 F6
Hayle Cnwll........................2 F4
Hayle Port Cnwll...............2 F4
Hayley Green Dudley.....85 G6
Hayling Island Hants.....17 K3
Hayne Devon 11 H7
Haynes C Beds 75 G6
Haynes Church End
  C Beds.................74 F6
Haynes West End
  C Beds.................74 F6
Hay-on-Wye Powys........68 E6
Hayscastle Pembks..........48 F3
Hayscastle Cross
  Pembks................48 F3
Hay Street Herts............60 C3
Hayton Cumb 147 K6
Hayton Cumb 148 E4
Hayton E R Yk................125 J2
Hayton Notts..................116 B5
Haytor Vale Devon 7 H1
Haytown Devon 9 K3
Haywards Heath
  W Susx.................19 J2
Haywood Donc 124 E7
Hazelbank S Lans 165 G1
Hazelbury Bryan
  Dorset.................14 E2
Hazeleigh Essex..............61 K7
Hazel Grove Stockp......113 L4
Hazelton Walls Fife......186 E3
Hazelwood Derbys 101 G4
Hazlemere Bucks............42 E2
Hazlerigg N u Ty............159 G7
Hazleton Gloucs..............56 B4
Heacham Norfk.............105 G5
Headbourne Worthy
  Hants..................29 J5
Headcorn Kent................33 L4
Headingley Leeds 123 K4
Headington Oxon 57 K6
Headlam Dur 140 F4
Headlesscross
  N Lans.................176 B6
Headless Cross
  Worcs..................71 J2
Headley Hants 30 D4
Headley Hants 41 K7
Headley Surrey...............31 K1
Headley Down Hants.....30 D4
Headon Notts...............116 C6
Heads Nook Cumb.......148 E4
Heage Derbys................101 G3
Healaugh N York 124 D2
Healaugh N York 140 C7
Heald Green Stockp......113 J4
Heale Somset..................25 K7
Heale Somset..................26 B6
Healey N York...............132 B4
Healeyfield Dur.............150 D5
Healing NE Lin 126 F7
Heamoor Cnwll..................2 E5
Heanor Derbys..............101 H3
Heanton
  Punchardon
  Devon................23 H4
Heapham Lincs..............116 E4

Heart of Scotland
  Services N Lans 176 B5
Heasley Mill Devon......24 B5
Heaste Highld...............199 K2
Heath Derbys 115 H7
Heath Wakefd...............123 L6
Heath and Reach
  C Beds.................58 F3
Heathcote Derbys.......100 D1
Heather Leics.................86 E2
Heathfield E Susx 20 C2
Heathfield Somset..........25 J6
Heath Green Worcs........71 J1
Heath Hall D & G 155 H6
Heath Hayes &
  Wimblebury
  Staffs.................85 H2
Heath Hill Shrops 84 D2
Heathrow Airport
  Gt Lon.................43 H5
Heathton Shrops..........84 E5
Heath Town Wolves......85 G4
Heatley Warrtn 113 G4
Heaton C Brad 123 H4
Heaton N u Ty 151 G2
Heaton Staffs................113 L8
Heaton Chapel
  Stockp.................113 K3
Heaton Mersey
  Stockp.................113 K4
Heaton Norris
  Stockp.................113 K4
Heaton's Bridge
  Lancs.................120 E7
Heaverham Kent............33 G2
Heaviley Stockp...........113 K4
Heavitree Devon............12 B4
Hebburn S Tyne............151 H3
Hebden N York..............131 J6
Hebden Bridge
  Calder.................122 E5
Hebing End Herts...........60 A4
Hebron Carmth...............49 K3
Hebron Nthumb............158 F4
Heckfield Hants 42 B7
Heckfield Green
  Suffk...................92 E7
Heckfordbridge
  Essex..................61 M4
Heckington Lincs.........103 J4
Heckmondwike Kirk.....123 J5
Heddington Wilts..........39 M6
Heddon-on-the-
  Wall Nthumb...........150 E2
Hedenham Norfk............93 G5
Hedge End Hants 29 J8
Hedgerley Bucks.............42 F3
Hedging Somset.............25 L5
Hedley on the Hill
  Nthumb...............150 D3
Hednesford Staffs..........85 H2
Hedon E R Yk.................126 F5
Hedsor Bucks..................42 E3
Heeley Sheff..................115 G5
Heglibister Shet 235 c5
Heighington Darltn......141 G3
Heighington Lincs.......117 G7
Heightington Worcs.......70 D1
Heiton Border...............167 L4
Hele Devon 12 C2
Hele Devon 23 H3
Helensburgh Ag & B 174 B2
Helenton S Ayrs 163 K3
Helford Cnwll....................3 K6
Helford Passage
  Cnwll....................3 K6
Helhoughton Norfk.......105 K7
Helions Bumpstead
  Essex..................76 F6
Helland Cnwll...................5 G2
Hellescott Cnwll...............9 H6
Hellesdon Norfk..............92 E2
Hellidon Nhants..............73 G3
Hellifield N York 131 G7
Hellingly E Susx 20 C4
Helmdon Nhants............73 H5
Helme Kirk 123 G7
Hellmingham Suffk.........78 E3

Helmsdale Highld 227 H5
Helmshore Lancs..........122 B6
Helmsley N York 133 J3
Helperby N York 133 G5
Helperthorpe N York.....134 E5
Helpringham Lincs........103 J4
Helpston C Pete.............89 G3
Helsby Ches W 112 C6
Helston Cnwll....................3 H5
Helstone Cnwll..................8 E8
Helton Cumb 138 D3
Hemel Hempstead
  Herts...................59 H6
Hemerdon Devon.............6 E4
Hemingbrough
  N York.................125 G4
Hemingby Lincs.............118 C6
Hemingford Abbots
  Cambs.................75 K1
Hemingford Grey
  Cambs.................75 K1
Hemingstone Suffk........78 D4
Hemington Leics 101 J6
Hemington Nhants..........88 F6
Hemington Somset..........27 G2
Hemley Suffk..................79 G6
Hemlington Middsb......142 B4
Hempnall Norfk...............92 F5
Hempnall Green
  Norfk...................92 F5
Hempriggs Moray.........214 D2
Hempstead Essex..........76 F6
Hempstead Medway......46 C6
Hempstead Norfk.........106 D5
Hempstead Norfk.........107 J6
Hempton Norfk.............105 L6
Hempton Oxon 57 H2
Hemsby Norfk...............107 K8
Hemswell Lincs.............116 E4
Hemswell Cliff Lincs 116 F4
Hemsworth Wakefd.....124 C7
Hemyock Devon.............25 H8
Henbury Bristl...............38 E5
Hendon Gt Lon..............44 E3
Hendon Sundld.............151 K4
Hendredenny Caerph 37 H3
Hendy Carmth................51 H5
Henfield W Susx.............19 G3
Hengoed Caerph............37 J2
Hengoed Powys..............68 E4
Hengrave Suffk...............77 J2
Henham Essex................60 E3
Heniarth Powys..............82 C2
Henlade Somset.............25 L6
Henley Dorset................14 D2
Henley Somset...............26 B5
Henley Suffk..................78 E4
Henley W Susx...............30 E6
Henley Green Covtry.....86 D6
Henley-in-Arden
  Warwks...............71 L2
Henley-on-Thames
  Oxon..................42 C4
Henley's Down
  E Susx.................20 E3
Henllan Cerdgn..............65 K6
Henllan Denbgs............110 E7
Henllys Torfn..................37 K3
Henlow C Beds...............75 H6
Henlow Camp C Beds....75 H7
Hennock Devon..............11 J8
Henny Street Essex........77 K6
Henryd Conwy..............109 L6
Henry's Moat
  (Castell Hendre)
  Pembks...............49 H3
Hensall N York..............124 F5
Henshaw Nthumb.........149 J3
Hensingham Cumb........136 D4
Henstead Suffk...............93 K6
Hensting Hants...............29 J6
Henstridge Somset.........27 G7
Henstridge Ash
  Somset................27 G7
Henton Oxon.................58 C7
Henton Somset...............26 C3
Henwick Worcs................70 E4
Henwood Cnwll................5 L2

Heol-y-Cyw Brdgnd........36 E4
Hepple Nthumb.............158 C2
Hepscott Nthumb.........158 F5
Heptonstall Calder 122 E5
Hepworth Kirk...............114 D1
Hepworth Suffk..............92 B8
Herbrandston
  Pembks................48 E6
Hereford Herefs 69 K6
Hereson Kent..................35 K2
Heribusta Highld...........218 B7
Heriot Border................177 L7
Hermiston C Edin..........177 G4
Hermitage Border 156 E3
Hermitage Dorset..........14 C2
Hermitage W Berk..........41 J5
Hermon Carmth..............65 K7
Hermon Pembks.............65 K6
Herne Kent.....................47 K6
Herne Bay Kent..............47 K6
Herne Hill Gt Lon............44 F5
Herne Pound Kent..........33 H3
Hernhill Kent 34 E3
Herodsfoot Cnwll.............5 K4
Heronsford S Ayrs 152 D5
Herriard Hants 30 A3
Herringfleet Suffk...........93 K4
Herringswell Suffk..........77 G1
Herringthorpe
  Rothm.................115 J3
Herrington Sundld........151 J4
Hersden Kent..................35 G3
Hersham Surrey.............43 J7
Herstmonceux
  E Susx.................20 D3
Herston Dorset..............15 J6
Herston Ork..................234 c7
Hertford Herts................60 B5
Hertford Heath Herts.....60 B5
Hertingfordbury
  Herts...................60 A5
Hesketh Bank Lancs.....120 F5
Hesketh Lane Lancs......121 J3
Hesket Newmarket
  Cumb.................148 C7
Hesleden Dur 151 K7
Heslington C York..........124 F1
Hessay C York 133 H8
Hessenford Cnwll.............5 L4
Hessett Suffk..................77 L3
Hessle E R Yk 126 C5
Hessle Wakefd...............124 C6
Hest Bank Lancs...........129 K6
Heston Gt Lon................43 J5
Heston Services
  Gt Lon.................43 J5
Hestwall Ork.................234 b5
Heswall Wirral...............111 J5
Hethe Oxon....................57 L3
Hethersett Norfk.............92 D3
Hethersgill Cumb..........148 E2
Hett Dur.......................151 G7
Hetton N York...............131 H7
Hetton-le-Hole
  Sundld................151 J5
Heugh Nthumb.............158 D7
Heughhead Abers 205 J3
Heugh Head Border 179 H6
Heveningham Suffk........93 G8
Hever Kent......................32 E4
Heversham Cumb.........129 K3
Hevingham Norfk..........106 E7
Hewas Water Cnwll..........4 F6
Hewelsfield Gloucs........54 E7
Hewish Somset..............13 K2
Hewood Dorset..............13 J2
Hexham Nthumb..........150 B3
Hextable Kent.................45 K6
Hexthorpe Donc...........115 K2
Hexton Herts..................59 J2
Hexworthy Cnwll.............9 K8
Hexworthy Devon............6 F2
Heybridge Essex.............61 G7
Heybridge Essex.............61 K6
Heybrook Bay Devon 6 D6
Heydon Cambs...............76 B6
Heydon Norfk...............106 D6
Heydour Lincs...............103 H4

Heylipoll Ag & B 188 C7
Heylor Shet 235 c3
Heysham Lancs 129 J7
Heyshott W Susx 18 B3
Heytesbury Wilts 27 L3
Heythrop Oxon 57 G3
Heywood Rochdl 122 C7
Heywood Wilts 27 K2
Hibaldstow N Linc 116 F2
Hickleton Donc 115 J1
Hickling Norfk 107 J7
Hickling Notts 102 B6
Hickling Green
  Norfk 107 J7
Hickstead W Susx 31 L7
Hidcote Bartrim
  Gloucs 71 L6
Hidcote Boyce
  Gloucs 71 L6
High Ackworth
  Wakefd 124 C6
Higham Barns 114 F1
Higham Derbys 101 H2
Higham Kent 33 G4
Higham Kent 46 B5
Higham Lancs 122 B3
Higham Suffk 77 H2
Higham Suffk 78 B7
Higham Ferrers
  Nhants 74 D2
Higham Gobion
  C Beds 59 J2
Higham Hill Gt Lon 45 G3
Higham on the Hill
  Leics 86 E4
Highams Park Gt Lon ... 45 H2
High Ardwell D & G ... 144 C6
High Auldgirth D & G.. 154 F5
High Bankhill Cumb ... 148 F6
High Barnet Gt Lon 44 E2
High Beach Essex 60 C7
High Bentham
  N York 130 C5
High Bickington
  Devon 23 J7
High Biggins Cumb ... 130 B4
High Blantyre S Lans ... 175 J6
High Bonnybridge
  Falk 175 L3
High Bray Devon 23 L5
Highbridge Somset 25 L3
Highbrook W Susx 32 C7
High Brooms Kent 33 G5
Highburton Kirk 123 J7
Highbury Gt Lon 44 F3
Highbury Somset 27 G2
High Callerton E R Yk.. 133 L8
Highclere Hants 41 H8
Highcliffe BCP 16 B4
High Coniscliffe
  Darltn 141 G4
High Crosby Cumb 148 E3
High Cross E Ayrs 163 K1
High Cross Hants 30 B6
High Cross Herts 60 B4
High Cross Warwks 71 L2
High Drummore
  D & G 144 D7
High Easter Essex 60 F5
High Ellington
  N York 132 B3
Higher Ansty Dorset ... 14 E2
Higher Bartle Lancs .. 121 G4
Higher
  Bockhampton
  Dorset 14 D4
Higher Brixham
  Torbay 7 L5
High Ercall Wrekin 98 E8
Higher Chillington
  Somset 13 K1
Higher Folds Wigan .. 113 G2
Higher Gabwell
  Devon 7 L3
Higher Heysham
  Lancs 129 J7
Higher Irlam Salfd .. 113 G3

Higher Kinnerton
  Flints 97 L1
Higher Muddiford
  Devon 23 J4
Higher Penwortham
  Lancs 121 G5
Higher Prestacott
  Devon 9 K5
Higher Town Cnwll 4 C6
Higher Town Cnwll 4 F4
Higher Town IoS 2 b1
Higher Walton
  Lancs 121 H5
Higher Walton
  Warrtn 112 E4
Higher Wambrook
  Somset 13 H2
Higher Waterston
  Dorset 14 D4
Higher Wheelton
  Lancs 121 J6
Higher Whitley
  Ches W 112 F5
Higher Wincham
  Ches W 113 G6
Higher Wraxhall
  Dorset 14 B3
Higher Wych Ches W... 98 C4
High Etherley Dur 140 E2
Highfield Gatesd 150 E3
Highfield N Ayrs 174 C7
Highfields
  Caldecote Cambs 75 L3
High Garrett Essex 61 J3
Highgate Gt Lon 44 F3
Highgate Kent 33 K6
High Grantley N York.. 132 C5
High Green Norfk 92 D3
High Green Norfk 92 E5
High Green Sheff 115 G3
High Halden Kent 34 B7
High Halstow
  Medway 46 C5
High Ham Somset 26 B5
High Harrington
  Cumb 136 D3
High Harrogate
  N York 132 D7
High Hatton Shrops ... 98 E7
High Hauxley
  Nthumb 159 G2
High Hawsker
  N York 143 J5
High Hesket Cumb 148 E6
High Hoyland Barns .. 123 K8
High Hurstwood
  E Susx 32 E7
High Hutton N York... 134 B5
High Ireby Cumb 147 M7
High Kilburn N York.. 133 H4
High Lands Dur 140 E3
Highlane Derbys 115 H5
High Lane Stockp 113 L4
High Lanes Cnwll 3 G4
Highleadon Gloucs 55 H4
High Legh Ches E 113 G5
Highleigh W Susx 18 A6
High Leven S on T 141 K5
Highley Shrops 84 D6
High Littleton BaNES... 38 F8
High Lorton Cumb 137 G3
High Marnham
  Notts 116 D7
High Melton Donc 115 K2
High Mickley Nthumb.. 150 D3
Highmoor Oxon 42 B4
Highmoor Cross
  Oxon 42 B4
Highnam Gloucs 55 H4
High Newport
  Sundld 151 J4
High Newton Cumb .. 129 J3
High Newton-by-
  the-Sea Nthumb 169 J4
High Nibthwaite
  Cumb 129 G2
High Offley Staffs 99 H7
High Ongar Essex 60 E7

High Onn Staffs 84 E1
High Park Corner
  Essex 62 C4
High Pennyvenie
  E Ayrs 163 L7
High Pittington Dur ... 151 H6
High Roding Essex 60 F4
High Salvington
  W Susx 18 F4
High Spen Gatesd 150 E3
Highsted Kent 34 B3
High Street Cnwll 4 F5
Highstreet Kent 34 E3
Highstreet Green
  Surrey 31 G4
Hightae D & G 155 J6
Highter's Heath Birm .. 85 J7
Hightown Sefton 111 J2
Hightown Green
  Suffk 77 L4
High Toynton Lincs 118 C7
High Valleyfield Fife .. 176 D2
Highweek Devon 7 J2
Highwood Essex 61 G7
Highwood W Susx 31 J5
Highwood Hill Gt Lon.. 44 E2
Highwoods Essex 62 B3
Highworth Swindn 40 D2
High Wray Cumb 137 K7
High Wych Herts 60 D5
High Wycombe
  Bucks 42 E2
Hilborough Norfk 91 J4
Hilcott Wilts 40 C8
Hildenborough Kent.... 32 F4
Hilden Park Kent 33 G4
Hildersham Cambs 76 D5
Hilderstone Staffs 99 L5
Hilderthorpe E R Yk... 135 J6
Hilgay Norfk 90 E4
Hill S Glos 38 F2
Hill Warwks 72 F2
Hillam N York 124 D5
Hill Brow Hants 30 C6
Hillbutts Dorset 15 J3
Hill Chorlton Staffs..... 99 H5
Hillclifflane Derbys ... 100 F3
Hill Common Somset... 25 H6
Hilldyke Lincs 104 B3
Hillend Fife 176 F2
Hill End Fife 185 L7
Hillend Mdloth 177 H5
Hillend N Lans 175 L5
Hillesden Bucks 58 B3
Hillesley Gloucs 39 H3
Hillfarrance Somset 25 J6
Hill Green Kent 46 D7
Hillhead Abers 216 B7
Hill Head Hants 17 G2
Hillhead S Lans 165 J2
Hillhead of Cocklaw
  Abers 217 K5
Hilliclay Highld 231 H3
Hillingdon Gt Lon 43 H4
Hillington C Glas 174 F5
Hillington Norfk 105 H7
Hillmorton Warwks 87 G8
Hill of Beath Fife 176 F1
Hill of Fearn Highld... 223 H5
Hillowton D & G 146 D3
Hill Ridware Staffs 100 B8
Hillside Abers 207 H5
Hillside Angus 197 H4
Hill Side Kirk 123 H6
Hills Town Derbys 115 J7
Hillstreet Hants 29 G7
Hillswick Shet 235 c3
Hill Top Sandw 85 H5
Hill Top Wakefd 123 L7
Hillwell Shet 235 c8
Hilmarton Wilts 40 A5
Hilperton Wilts 39 K8
Hilsea C Port 17 J2
Hilston E R Yk 127 G4
Hilton Border 179 H7
Hilton Cambs 75 K2
Hilton Cumb 139 G3

Hilton Derbys 100 E6
Hilton Dorset 14 E2
Hilton Dur 140 F3
Hilton S on T 141 K5
Hilton Shrops 84 D4
Hilton of Cadboll
  Highld 223 J6
Hilton Park
  Services Staffs 85 G3
Himbleton Worcs 71 G3
Himley Staffs 84 F5
Hincaster Cumb 129 L3
Hinchley Wood
  Surrey 44 D6
Hinckley Leics 86 E5
Hinderclay Suffk 92 B7
Hinderwell N York 143 G4
Hindhead Surrey 30 D4
Hindhead Tunnel
  Surrey 30 E4
Hindley Wigan 112 F1
Hindlip Worcs 70 F3
Hindolveston Norfk ... 106 C6
Hindon Wilts 27 K5
Hindringham Norfk ... 106 B5
Hingham Norfk 92 B3
Hinstock Shrops 99 G7
Hintlesham Suffk 78 C5
Hinton Herefs 69 G6
Hinton Nhants 73 G4
Hinton S Glos 39 G5
Hinton Shrops 83 H2
Hinton Ampner
  Hants 29 L6
Hinton Blewett
  BaNES 26 E1
Hinton
  Charterhouse
  BaNES 39 H8
Hinton-in-the-
  Hedges Nhants........ 73 H6
Hinton Martell
  Dorset 15 J2
Hinton on the
  Green Worcs 71 H6
Hinton Parva Swindn.. 40 E4
Hinton St George
  Somset 26 B8
Hinton St Mary
  Dorset 27 H7
Hinton Waldrist
  Oxon 57 G7
Hints Staffs 85 L3
Hinwick Bed 74 D3
Hinxhill Kent 34 D6
Hinxton Cambs 76 C5
Hinxworth Herts 75 J6
Hipperholme Calder ... 123 H5
Hipswell N York 140 F7
Hirn Abers 206 D5
Hirnant Powys 97 G7
Hirst Nthumb 159 G5
Hirst Courtney
  N York 124 F5
Hirwaun Rhondd 52 E6
Hiscott Devon 23 J6
Histon Cambs 76 B2
Hitcham Suffk 78 B4
Hitcham Causeway
  Suffk 78 B4
Hitchin Herts 59 K3
Hither Green Gt Lon .. 45 H5
Hittisleigh Devon 11 H5
Hive E R Yk 125 J4
Hixon Staffs 100 A7
Hoaden Kent 35 H3
Hoar Cross Staffs 100 C7
Hoarwithy Herefs 54 D3
Hoath Kent 47 K7
Hobarris Shrops 82 F7
Hobkirk Border 167 J7
Hobson Dur 150 F4
Hoby Leics 102 A8
Hockering Norfk 92 C2
Hockerton Notts 102 B2
Hockley Essex 46 D2
Hockley Heath Solhll .. 85 L8
Hockliffe C Beds 58 F3

Hockwold cum
Wilton Norfk..........**91** G6
Hockworthy Devon......**25** G7
Hoddesdon Herts........**60** B6
Hoddlesden Bl w D....**121** L6
Hoddom Cross
D & G.....................**155** L7
Hoddom Mains
D & G.....................**155** K7
Hodgeston Pembks.....**49** H7
Hodnet Shrops...........**98** E6
Hodsock Notts.........**115** L4
Hodsoll Street Kent....**45** M7
Hodson Swindn..........**40** D4
Hodthorpe Derbys.....**115** K6
Hoe Norfk.................**92** B1
Hogben's Hill Kent......**34** D4
Hoggeston Bucks.......**58** D3
Hoggrill's End
Warwks.....................**86** B5
Hoghton Lancs.........**121** J5
Hognaston Derbys.....**100** E3
Hogsthorpe Lincs.....**119** H6
Holbeach Lincs.........**104** B7
Holbeach Bank
Lincs.......................**104** B6
Holbeach Clough
Lincs.......................**104** B6
Holbeach Drove
Lincs.........................**89** K2
Holbeach Hurn Lincs..**104** C6
Holbeach St Johns
Lincs.......................**104** B8
Holbeach St Mark's
Lincs.......................**104** B6
Holbeach St
Matthew Lincs.......**104** C6
Holbeck Notts.........**115** K6
Holberrow Green
Worcs.......................**71** H3
Holbeton Devon..........**6** F5
Holborn Gt Lon...........**44** F4
Holbrook Derbys.......**101** G4
Holbrook Suffk...........**78** E6
Holbrooks Covtry......**86** D6
Holbury Hants............**16** E2
Holcombe Devon........**12** B7
Holcombe Somset......**26** F2
Holcombe Rogus
Devon......................**25** G7
Holcot Nhants............**73** L1
Holden Lancs...........**122** B1
Holdenby Nhants.......**73** K2
Holder's Green Essex..**61** G3
Holdgate Shrops.......**83** L5
Holdingham Lincs.....**103** H3
Holditch Dorset..........**13** J2
Holemoor Devon........**10** B4
Holford Somset..........**25** J3
Holgate C York.........**124** E1
Holker Cumb.............**129** H4
Holkham Norfk.........**105** L4
Hollacombe Devon........**9** K4
Holland Fen Lincs.....**103** L3
Holland-on-Sea
Essex......................**62** E5
Hollandstoun Ork.....**234** e3
Hollee D & G.............**148** A2
Hollesley Suffk...........**79** H5
Hollicombe Torbay.......**7** K4
Hollingbourne Kent....**33** L3
Hollington Br & H.......**19** J4
Hollingdon Bucks.......**58** E3
Hollington Derbys.....**100** E5
Hollington Staffs.......**100** B5
Hollingworth Tamesd..**114** A3
Hollinsclough Staffs..**114** B7
Hollins End Sheff.....**115** G5
Hollins Green
Warrtn....................**113** G4
Hollinswood Wrekin....**84** C2
Hollocombe Devon......**10** F3
Holloway Derbys.......**100** F2
Holloway Gt Lon..........**44** F3
Hollowell Nhants.......**73** K1
Hollowmoor Heath
Ches W....................**112** C7
Hollows D & G..........**156** C6

Hollybush Caerph.......**53** J7
Hollybush E Ayrs......**163** K6
Hollybush Herefs........**70** D6
Hollym E R Yk..........**127** H5
Holmbridge Kirk.......**114** C1
Holmbury St Mary
Surrey.......................**31** J3
Holmbush Cnwll...........**5** G5
Holmcroft Staffs........**99** K7
Holme Cambs.............**89** H6
Holme Cumb.............**129** L4
Holme Kirk..............**114** C1
Holme N York..........**132** E3
Holme Notts............**102** D2
Holme Chapel Lancs..**122** C5
Holme Hale Norfk.......**91** K3
Holme Lacy Herefs......**69** L7
Holme Marsh Herefs....**69** G4
Holme next the Sea
Norfk......................**105** H4
Holme on the Wolds
E R Yk....................**126** B2
Holme Pierrepont
Notts.......................**101** L5
Holmer Herefs............**69** K6
Holmer Green Bucks....**42** E2
Holme St Cuthbert
Cumb......................**147** J5
Holmes Chapel
Ches E....................**113** H7
Holmesfield Derbys...**114** F6
Holmeswood Lancs...**120** F6
Holmethorpe Surrey....**32** B3
Holme upon
Spalding Moor
E R Yk....................**125** J3
Holmewood Derbys...**115** H7
Holmfirth Kirk.........**123** H8
Holmhead E Ayrs......**164** B5
Holmpton E R Yk......**127** J5
Holmrook Cumb........**136** E2
Holmside Dur...........**150** F5
Holne Devon................**7** G3
Holnicote Somset.......**24** E3
Holsworthy Devon........**9** J4
Holsworthy Beacon
Devon........................**9** K3
Holt Dorset................**15** J2
Holt Norfk...............**106** C5
Holt Wilts.................**39** K7
Holt Worcs................**70** E3
Holt Wrexhm..............**98** B2
Holtby C York..........**133** K8
Holt End Worcs..........**71** J1
Holt Heath Worcs.......**70** E2
Holton Oxon..............**57** L6
Holton Somset...........**27** G6
Holton Suffk.............**93** J7
Holton cum
Beckering Lincs......**117** J5
Holton le Clay Lincs...**118** C2
Holton le Moor
Lincs......................**117** H3
Holton St Mary Suffk..**78** C6
Holwell Dorset...........**14** D1
Holwell Herts.............**59** K2
Holwell Leics...........**102** B7
Holwell Oxon.............**56** E6
Holwick Dur.............**139** K2
Holybourne Hants.......**30** B4
Holyhead IoA............**108** C5
Holy Island IoA.........**108** C5
Holy Island Nthumb...**169** H2
Holy Island Nthumb...**169** H2
Holymoorside
Derbys....................**115** G7
Holyport W & M..........**42** E5
Holystone Nthumb....**158** B2
Holytown N Lans.......**175** K6
Holywell C Beds.........**59** G5
Holywell Cambs..........**75** L1
Holywell Cnwll............**4** B4
Holywell Dorset..........**14** B1
Holywell Flints.........**111** H6
Holywell Green
Calder....................**123** G6
Holywell Lake
Somset.....................**25** H7

Holywell Row Suffk.....**91** G7
Holywood D & G........**155** G6
Holywood Village
D & G.....................**155** G6
Homer Shrops............**84** B3
Homersfield Suffk.......**93** G6
Homington Wilts.........**28** C6
Honeybourne Worcs....**71** K5
Honeychurch Devon....**10** F4
Honeystreet Wilts.......**40** C7
Honey Tye Suffk.........**77** L7
Honiley Warwks..........**86** B8
Honing Norfk............**107** G6
Honingham Norfk.......**92** D2
Honington Lincs.......**102** F4
Honington Suffk.........**91** K8
Honington Warwks......**72** C6
Honiton Devon...........**12** F3
Honley Kirk.............**123** H7
Hooe C Plym................**6** D5
Hooe E Susx...............**20** E4
Hoo Green Ches E......**113** G5
Hoohill Bpool............**120** D3
Hook E R Yk............**125** H5
Hook Gt Lon..............**44** D7
Hook Hants................**30** B1
Hook Pembks.............**49** G5
Hook Wilts.................**40** B4
Hooke Dorset.............**14** A3
Hook Green Kent........**33** H6
Hook Norton Oxon......**57** G2
Hookway Devon..........**11** K5
Hooley Surrey............**32** B3
Hoo St Werburgh
Medway....................**46** C5
Hooton Levitt Rothm...**115** K3
Hooton Pagnell
Donc......................**124** D8
Hooton Roberts
Rothm....................**115** J3
Hope Derbys.............**114** D5
Hope Devon.................**7** G7
Hope Flints................**97** L2
Hope Staffs..............**100** C2
Hope Bagot Shrops.....**83** L8
Hope Bowdler
Shrops.....................**83** J5
Hopehouse Border....**166** D6
Hopeman Moray........**214** E1
Hope Mansell Herefs...**54** F4
Hopesay Shrops..........**83** H6
Hope under
Dinmore Herefs......**69** K4
Hopgrove C York......**133** K8
Hopperton N York....**132** F7
Hopstone Shrops........**84** D5
Hopton Derbys.........**100** E2
Hopton Staffs.............**99** L7
Hopton Suffk.............**92** B7
Hopton Cangeford
Shrops.....................**83** K7
Hopton Castle
Shrops.....................**83** G7
Hoptonheath Shrops....**83** H7
Hopton on Sea Norfk...**93** L4
Hopton Wafers
Shrops.....................**84** B7
Hopwas Staffs............**85** L3
Hopwood Worcs..........**85** J7
Horam E Susx.............**20** C3
Horbling Lincs..........**103** J5
Horbury Wakefd........**123** K6
Horden Dur..............**151** K6
Hordle Hants.............**16** C4
Hordley Shrops...........**98** B6
Horfield Bristl...........**38** E5
Horham Suffk.............**92** E8
Horkesley Heath
Essex......................**62** B3
Horkstow N Linc......**126** B6
Horley Oxon...............**72** E5
Horley Surrey............**32** B5
Hornblotton Green
Somset.....................**26** E5
Hornby Lancs...........**130** B5
Hornby N York.........**132** C2

Hornby N York.........**141** J6
Horncastle Lincs.......**118** C7
Hornchurch Gt Lon......**45** K3
Horncliffe Nthumb....**179** J7
Horndean Border......**179** J8
Horndean Hants.........**30** B8
Horndon Devon..........**10** D8
Horndon on the Hill
Thurr......................**46** A4
Horne Surrey..............**32** C4
Horner Somset...........**24** D3
Horning Norfk..........**107** H8
Horninghold Leics......**88** B4
Horninglow Staffs.....**100** E7
Horningsea Cambs......**76** C3
Horningsham Wilts......**27** J3
Horningtoft Norfk.....**105** M7
Horns Cross Devon......**22** F6
Hornsea E R Yk........**126** F2
Hornsey Gt Lon...........**44** F3
Hornton Oxon............**72** E5
Horrabridge Devon........**6** D2
Horringer Suffk...........**77** J3
Horrocksford Lancs...**121** L2
Horsebridge Devon.......**6** B2
Horsebridge E Susx....**20** C4
Horsebridge Hants......**29** G5
Horsehay Wrekin........**84** C3
Horseheath Cambs......**76** E5
Horsehouse N York...**131** K4
Horsell Surrey............**43** G8
Horseman's Green
Wrexhm.....................**98** C4
Horsey Norfk...........**107** K7
Horsey Somset...........**25** L4
Horsford Norfk...........**92** E1
Horsforth Leeds.......**123** J3
Horsham W Susx.........**31** K5
Horsham Worcs...........**70** D3
Horsham St Faith
Norfk........................**92** E1
Horsington Lincs.......**117** K7
Horsington Somset......**27** G6
Horsley Derbys.........**101** G4
Horsley Gloucs...........**39** J4
Horsley Nthumb........**150** D2
Horsley Nthumb........**157** M7
Horsleycross Street
Essex......................**62** D3
Horsleyhill Border.....**167** H5
Horsley Woodhouse
Derbys....................**101** H4
Horsmonden Kent.......**33** J5
Horspath Oxon...........**57** L6
Horstead Norfk.........**106** F8
Horsted Keynes
W Susx.....................**32** C7
Horton Bucks.............**58** F4
Horton Dorset............**15** J2
Horton Lancs...........**122** C1
Horton Nhants...........**74** B4
Horton S Glos.............**39** H4
Horton Somset...........**25** L7
Horton Staffs.............**99** L2
Horton Swans............**50** F7
Horton W & M.............**43** G5
Horton Wilts..............**40** B7
Horton Wrekin...........**84** C1
Horton-cum-
Studley Oxon..........**57** L5
Horton Green
Ches W......................**98** C3
Horton-in-
Ribblesdale
N York....................**130** F5
Horton Kirby Kent......**45** K6
Horwich Bolton........**121** J7
Horwood Devon..........**23** H6
Hoscote Border.........**166** F6
Hose Leics...............**102** B6
Hosh P & K..............**185** H3
Hoswick Shet...........**235** c7
Hotham E R Yk.........**125** L4
Hothfield Kent...........**34** C5
Hoton Leics.............**101** L7
Hough Ches E............**99** G3
Hougham Lincs.........**102** E4
Hough Green Halton...**112** C4

Hough-on-the-Hill
Lincs........................... 102 F3
Houghton Cambs............75 K1
Houghton Hants 29 G5
Houghton Pembks 49 G6
Houghton W Susx............18 D4
Houghton Conquest
C Beds......................74 F6
Houghton Green
E Susx........................21 H2
Houghton-le-
Spring Sundld......... 151 H5
Houghton on the
Hill Leics.................87 J3
Houghton Regis
C Beds.......................59 G4
Houghton St Giles
Norfk....................... 105 L5
Hound Green Hants........42 B8
Houndslow Border........ 178 D8
Houndwood Border....... 179 H5
Hounslow Gt Lon...........43 J5
Househill Highld........... 213 L4
Houses Hill Kirk........... 123 J6
Housieside Abers......... 207 G1
Houston Rens............... 174 D5
Houstry Highld............. 227 K2
Houton Ork...............234 b6
Hove Br & H...................19 J5
Hoveringham Notts..... 102 B3
Hoveton Norfk............. 107 G8
Hovingham N York....... 133 K4
How Caple Herefs..........54 E3
Howden E R Yk............ 125 H5
Howden-le-Wear
Dur......................... 150 E7
Howe Highld................ 231 K3
Howe N York................ 132 E4
Howe Norfk....................92 F4
Howe Green Essex..........61 J7
Howegreen Essex..........61 K7
Howell Lincs................ 103 J4
Howe of Teuchar
Abers...................... 216 E5
Howes D & G.............. 147 L2
Howe Street Essex..........61 H5
Howe Street Essex..........77 G7
Howey Powys.................68 B3
Howgate Cumb............ 136 D3
Howgate Mdloth........... 177 H6
Howick Nthumb............ 169 K5
Howlett End Essex..........76 E7
Howley Somset.............13 H1
How Mill Cumb............ 148 E4
Howmore W Isls........... 233 b7
Hownam Border.......... 168 B5
Howsham N Linc.......... 117 H2
Howsham N York........... 133 L6
Howtel Nthumb........... 168 D3
How Wood Herts...........59 J7
Howwood Rens........... 174 D6
Hoxa Ork...................234 c7
Hoxne Suffk...................92 E7
Hoy Ork......................234 b7
Hoylake Wirral............ 111 H4
Hoyland Barns............ 115 G2
Hoylandswaine
Barns...................... 114 G2
Hubberston Pembks......48 E6
Huby N York................. 123 K2
Huby N York................. 133 J6
Hucclecote Gloucs........55 K4
Hucking Kent................33 L2
Hucknall Notts............ 101 K3
Huddersfield Kirk........ 123 H7
Huddington Worcs........71 G3
Hudswell N York.......... 140 E7
Huggate E R Yk........... 134 D7
Hughenden Valley
Bucks.......................42 E2
Hughley Shrops...........83 L4
Hugh Town IoS 2 b2
Huish Devon.................10 D3
Huish Wilts...................40 C7
Huish Champflower
Somset.....................25 G5
Huish Episcopi
Somset.....................26 B6

Hùisinis W Isls............. 232 d3
Huisinish W Isls........... 232 d3
Hulcott Bucks................58 D5
Hulham Devon...............12 C5
Hulland Derbys........... 100 E3
Hulland Ward
Derbys.................... 100 E3
Hullavington Wilts........39 K4
Hullbridge Essex 46 D2
Hull, Kingston upon
C KuH...................... 126 D5
Hulme Manch.............. 113 J3
Hulme Staffs..................99 L4
Hulme Warrtn.............. 112 E4
Hulme End Staffs........ 100 C2
Hulme Walfield
Ches E..................... 113 J7
Hulton Lane Ends
Bolton..................... 113 G1
Hulverstone IoW...........16 E5
Hulver Street Suffk........93 K6
Humber Bridge
N Linc...................... 126 C5
Humberside Airport
N Linc...................... 126 D7
Humberston NE Lin...... 118 D1
Humberstone C Leic......87 J3
Humbie E Loth............. 178 B5
Humbleton E R Yk....... 126 F4
Humby Lincs................ 103 G6
Hume Border............... 167 L2
Humshaugh
Nthumb................... 158 A7
Huna Highld................ 231 L2
Huncote Leics...............87 G4
Hundalee Border......... 167 K5
Hunderthwaite Dur..... 140 C3
Hundleby Lincs........... 118 E7
Hundleton Pembks........49 G7
Hundon Suffk................77 G5
Hundred House
Powys.......................68 C4
Hungarton Leics...........87 K3
Hungerford Somset.......25 G4
Hungerford W Berk........41 G6
Hungerford
Newtown W Berk.......41 G6
Hungerstone Herefs......69 J7
Hunmanby N York....... 135 H4
Hunningham Warwks 72 D2
Hunsbury Hill Nhants ...73 K3
Hunsdon Herts.............60 C5
Hunsingore N York...... 132 F8
Hunslet Leeds............. 123 L4
Hunsonby Cumb.......... 149 G7
Hunstanton Norfk....... 105 G4
Hunstanworth Dur...... 150 B5
Hunsterson Ches E........99 G4
Hunston Suffk...............77 L2
Hunston W Susx............18 B5
Hunstrete BaNES...........38 F7
Hunsworth Kirk........... 123 J5
Hunter's Quay
Ag & B..................... 173 K3
Huntham Somset..........25 M6
Hunthill Lodge
Angus...................... 196 D3
Huntingdon Cambs........89 J8
Huntingfield Suffk.........93 G8
Huntington C York....... 133 J7
Huntington Ches W...... 112 B8
Huntington E Loth....... 178 B4
Huntington Herefs.........68 E4
Huntington Staffs.........85 H2
Huntingtowerfield
P & K...................... 185 M3
Huntley Gloucs.............55 G4
Huntly Abers............... 215 L6
Hunton Kent.................33 J4
Hunton N York............. 132 B2
Huntscott Somset..........24 E3
Huntsham Devon..........24 F7
Huntshaw Devon..........23 H6
Huntspill Somset..........25 L3
Huntstile Somset..........25 K5
Huntworth Somset........25 L4
Hunwick Dur............... 140 F2
Hunworth Norfk......... 106 C5

Hurdcott Wilts...............28 D5
Hurdsfield Ches E........ 113 L6
Hurley W & M................42 D4
Hurley Warwks..............86 B4
Hurley Common
Warwks......................86 B4
Hurlford E Ayrs........... 163 L3
Hurn BCP......................15 L3
Hursley Hants................29 H6
Hurst Wokham..............42 C5
Hurstbourne Priors
Hants........................29 H3
Hurstbourne Tarrant
Hants........................29 G2
Hurst Green E Susx........33 J7
Hurst Green Essex..........62 C5
Hurst Green Lancs....... 121 K3
Hurst Green Surrey........32 D3
Hurst Hill Dudley...........85 G5
Hurstpierpoint
W Susx.......................19 J3
Hurstwood Lancs........ 122 C4
Hurtiso Ork...............234 c6
Hurworth-on-Tees
Darltn...................... 141 H5
Hurworth Place
Darltn...................... 141 H5
Husbands Bosworth
Leics........................87 J6
Husborne Crawley
C Beds.......................74 D7
Husthwaite N York....... 133 H4
Huthwaite Notts.......... 101 J2
Huttoft Lincs............... 119 G6
Hutton Border............. 179 J7
Hutton E R Yk.............. 134 F8
Hutton Essex.................45 M2
Hutton Lancs............... 121 G5
Hutton N Som................37 M8
Hutton Buscel
N York...................... 134 F3
Hutton Conyers
N York...................... 132 E5
Hutton Cranswick
E R Yk...................... 126 C1
Hutton End Cumb........ 148 D7
Hutton Henry Dur....... 151 K7
Hutton-le-Hole
N York...................... 133 L2
Hutton Lowcross
R & Cl...................... 142 D4
Hutton Magna Dur...... 140 E5
Hutton Roof Cumb....... 130 B4
Hutton Roof Cumb....... 148 C7
Hutton Rudby N York.... 141 K6
Hutton Sessay
N York...................... 133 G4
Hutton Wandesley
N York...................... 124 D1
Huxham Devon..............12 B3
Huxley Ches W...............98 D1
Huyton Knows............. 112 C4
Hycemoor Cumb......... 128 D2
Hyde Tamesd.............. 113 L3
Hyde Heath Bucks.........58 F7
Hyde Lea Staffs............99 K8
Hylands Estate Essex..... 61 G7
Hyndford Bridge
S Lans...................... 165 H2
Hynish Ag & B............. 188 C8
Hyssington Powys.........82 F5
Hythe Essex..................62 B3
Hythe Hants..................16 E2
Hythe Kent....................34 F7
Hythe End W & M..........43 G6

I

Ibberton Dorset.............14 E2
Ible Derbys.................. 100 E2
Ibsley Hants..................15 L1
Ibstock Leics.................86 E2
Ibstone Bucks...............42 C2
Ibthorpe Hants..............29 G2
Iburndale N York.......... 143 H5
Ibworth Hants...............29 K1

Ichrachan Ag & B......... 182 E2
Ickburgh Norfk..............91 J4
Ickenham Gt Lon...........43 H3
Ickford Bucks................57 M6
Ickham Kent..................35 G3
Ickleford Herts..............59 K2
Icklesham E Susx...........21 H3
Ickleton Cambs..............76 C5
Icklingham Suffk...........91 H8
Ickornshaw N York...... 122 E2
Ickwell Green C Beds.....75 G5
Icomb Gloucs................56 E4
Idbury Oxon..................56 E4
Iddesleigh Devon..........10 E3
Ide Devon.....................11 K6
Ideford Devon.................7 K1
Ide Hill Kent.................32 E3
Iden E Susx...................21 H2
Iden Green Kent............33 J5
Iden Green Kent............33 K6
Idle C Brad................. 123 H3
Idless Cnwll 4 C6
Idlicote Warwks............72 C5
Idmiston Wilts...............28 D4
Idole Carmth.................50 E3
Idridgehay Derbys....... 100 F3
Idrigill Highld.............. 208 F2
Idstone Oxon.................40 E4
Iffley Oxon....................57 K7
Ifield W Susx.................31 L4
Ifold W Susx..................31 G5
Iford BCP......................15 L4
Iford E Susx...................19 L4
Ifton Mons...................38 C3
Ightfield Shrops............98 E5
Ightham Kent................33 G2
Ilam Staffs.................. 100 C3
Ilchester Somset...........26 D6
Ilderton Nthumb......... 168 F5
Ilford Gt Lon.................45 H3
Ilford Somset................26 A7
Ilfracombe Devon.........23 H2
Ilkeston Derbys........... 101 J4
Ilketshall St Andrew
Suffk........................93 H6
Ilketshall St
Margaret Suffk..........93 H6
Ilkley C Brad............... 123 G2
Illand Cnwll.....................5 L1
Illey Dudley...................85 H7
Illogan Cnwll 3 H3
Illston on the Hill
Leics........................87 K4
Ilmer Bucks...................58 C6
Ilmington Warwks..........72 B5
Ilminster Somset...........26 A8
Ilsington Devon...............7 H2
Ilston Swans..................51 H7
Ilton N York................. 132 B4
Ilton Somset.................25 M7
Imachar N Ayrs........... 161 G2
Immingham NE Lin...... 126 F7
Immingham Dock
NE Lin...................... 126 F7
Impington Cambs..........76 C2
Ince Ches W................. 112 C6
Ince Blundell Sefton.... 111 K2
Ince-in-Makerfield
Wigan..................... 112 E1
Inchbae Lodge
Highld...................... 221 K7
Inchbare Angus........... 196 F4
Inchberry Moray......... 215 G3
Incheril Highld............ 211 G3
Inchinnan Rens........... 174 E5
Inchlaggan Highld....... 201 J5
Inchmichael P & K 186 D3
Inchmore Highld......... 212 E5
Inchnadamph Highld... 224 F4
Inchture P & K............. 186 D2
Inchyra P & K.............. 186 C4
Indian Queens Cnwll 4 E4
Ingatestone Essex.........61 G7
Ingbirchworth Barns... 114 E2
Ingestre Staffs..............99 L7
Ingham Lincs............... 116 F5
Ingham Norfk.............. 107 H7
Ingham Suffk.................77 J1

Ingham Corner
Norfk.........................107 H6
Ingleby Derbys.............101 G6
Ingleby Arncliffe
N York 141 K6
Ingleby Barwick
S on T.......................141 K4
Ingleby Greenhow
N York 142 C6
Ingleigh Green
Devon.........................10 E4
Inglesbatch BaNES......39 G7
Inglesham Swindn 56 D7
Ingleston D & G..........147 G2
Ingleton Dur 140 F3
Ingleton N York..........130 D5
Inglewhite Lancs 121 H3
Ingoe Nthumb............158 C7
Ingol Lancs 121 G4
Ingoldisthorpe
Norfk........................105 G6
Ingoldmells Lincs 119 H7
Ingoldsby Lincs 103 G6
Ingram Nthumb..........168 F6
Ingrave Essex 45 M2
Ingrow C Brad............122 F3
Ings Cumb 138 C7
Ingst S Glos.................38 E3
Ingthorpe RutInd.........88 E2
Ingworth Norfk...........106 E6
Inkberrow Worcs 71 H3
Inkersall Green
Derbys.....................115 H6
Inkhorn Abers.............217 H6
Inkpen W Berk 41 G7
Inkstack HighId...........231 J2
Innellan Ag & B...........173 K4
Innerleithen Border 166 E3
Innerleven Fife 186 F7
Innermessan D & G......144 C3
Innerwick E Loth 178 F4
Innesmill Moray 215 G2
Insch Abers 216 C8
Insh HighId 203 J5
Inshes HighId.............213 G5
Inskip Lancs 120 F3
Instow Devon 23 G5
Intake Sheff 115 H5
Inver Abers 204 F6
Inver HighId 223 J5
Inver P & K.................194 F7
Inverailort HighId........190 F1
Inveralligin HighId......210 C3
Inverallochy Abers.......217 K2
Inveran HighId 222 D2
Inveraray Ag & B.........182 F5
Inverarish HighId 209 J7
Inverarity Angus..........196 D7
Inverarnan Stirlg.........183 K4
Inverarnie HighId........213 G7
Inverasdale HighId......219 J4
Inverbeg Ag & B 183 K7
Inverbervie Abers........197 K2
Inverboyndie Abers 216 C2
Invercreran Lodge
Ag & B 191 K6
Inverdruie HighId........203 L3
Inveresk E Loth 177 K4
Inveresragan Ag & B....182 E1
Inverey Abers...............204 D7
Inverfarigaig HighId.....202 D2
Inverfolla Ag & B.........191 J7
Invergarry HighId........201 L5
Invergeldie P & K.........184 F2
Invergloy HighId 201 K7
Invergordon HighId......222 F7
Invergowrie P & K........186 F2
Inverguseran HighId 200 B4
Inverhadden P & K.......193 L5
Inverie HighId.............200 B5
Inverinan Ag & B.........182 E4
Inverinate HighId 200 E2
Inverkeilor Angus........197 G6
Inverkeithing Fife 176 F2
Inverkeithny Abers......216 C5
Inverkip Inver 173 L4
Inverkirkaig HighId.....224 C4
Inverlael HighId 220 F4

Inverlair HighId............192 E1
Inverliever Lodge
Ag & B 182 C6
Inverlochy Ag & B........183 H2
Invermark Angus........196 D1
Invermoriston
HighId......................202 C3
Invernaver HighId.......229 L4
Inverneill Ag & B.........172 E3
Inverness HighId.........213 G5
Inverness Airport
HighId......................213 J4
Invernettie Abers.........217 L5
Invernoaden Ag & B.....183 G7
Inveroran Hotel
Ag & B 192 D7
Inverquharity Angus....196 C5
Inverquhomery
Abers........................217 J5
Inverroy HighId 201 K8
Inversanda HighId......191 J4
Invershiel HighId........200 E2
Invershin HighId 222 D3
Invershore HighId........231 J8
Inversnaid Hotel
Stirlg........................183 K5
Inverugie Abers...........217 L5
Inveruglas Ag & B........183 K5
Inveruglass HighId......203 J5
Inverurie Abers...........206 E2
Inwardleigh Devon.......10 E5
Inworth Essex..............61 L4
Iochdar W Isls.............233 b7
Iona Ag & B.................180 D3
Iping W Susx 30 D6
iPort Logistics Park
Donc........................115 L2
Ipplepen Devon 7 J3
Ipsden Oxon 41 M4
Ipstones Staffs 100 A3
Ipswich Suffk 78 E5
Irby Wirral 111 J5
Irby in the Marsh
Lincs........................118 F8
Irby upon Humber
NE Lin......................117 K1
Irchester Nhants 74 D2
Ireby Cumb.................147 M7
Ireby Lancs 130 C4
Ireleth Cumb 128 F4
Ireshopeburn Dur 149 L7
Irlam Salfd 113 G3
Irnham Lincs 103 G7
Iron Acton S Glos..........39 G4
Ironbridge Wrekin.......84 C3
Ironbridge Gorge
Wrekin.......................84 C3
Ironmacannie D & G....154 B6
Ironville Derbys...........101 H3
Irstead Norfk..............107 H7
Irthington Cumb.........148 E3
Irthlingborough
Nhants.......................74 D1
Irton N York................134 F3
Irvine N Ayrs...............163 H2
Isauld HighId 230 E3
Isbister Shet.................235 c2
Isbister Shet.................235 d4
Isfield E Susx 19 L3
Isham Nhants 88 C8
Isington Hants.............30 C3
Islay Ag & B 171 G6
Islay Airport Ag & B.....170 F7
Isle Abbotts Somset......26 A7
Isle Brewers Somset......26 A7
Isleham Cambs.............90 F8
Isle of Dogs Gt Lon......45 G4
Isle of Grain Medway....46 E5
Isle of Lewis W Isls......232 f2
Isle of Man IoM..........237 c4
Isle of Man
Ronaldsway
Airport IoM..............237 b7
Isle of Mull Ag & B......181 J1
Isle of Purbeck
Dorset........................15 J5
Isle of Sheppey Kent....46 F6
Isle of Skye HighId......208 F6

Isle of Thanet Kent.........35 J2
Isle of Walney Cumb....128 E6
Isle of Whithorn
D & G.......................145 K7
Isle of Wight IoW..........17 G5
Isleornsay HighId 199 L3
Isles of Scilly IoS............2 b1
Isles of Scilly St
Mary's Airport
IoS..............................2 b2
Islesteps D & G............155 G7
Islet Village Guern.......236 d2
Isleworth Gt Lon..........44 D5
Isley Walton Leics 101 H7
Islibhig W Isls..............232 d3
Islington Gt Lon 44 F3
Islip Nhants.................88 E7
Islip Oxon 57 K5
Islivig W Isls................232 d3
Isombridge Wrekin.......83 L2
Istead Rise Kent...........45 M6
Itchen Abbas Hants......29 K5
Itchen Stoke Hants.......29 K5
Itchingfield W Susx......31 J5
Itteringham Norfk........106 D6
Itton Mons 38 C2
Itton Common Mons......38 C2
Ivegill Cumb.................148 D6
Iver Bucks 43 G4
Iver Heath Bucks..........43 G4
Iveston Dur 150 E5
Ivinghoe Bucks............58 F5
Ivinghoe Aston
Bucks.........................58 F4
Ivington Herefs............69 J3
Ivybridge Devon 6 F5
Ivychurch Kent.............21 K1
Ivy Hatch Kent..............33 G3
Iwade Kent....................46 E6
Iwerne Courtney
Dorset........................27 K8
Iwerne Minster
Dorset........................27 K8
Ixworth Suffk...............77 L1
Ixworth Thorpe Suffk......91 K8

Jack-in-the-Green
Devon........................12 C4
Jackton S Lans 175 G2
Jacobstow Cnwll............9 G5
Jacobstowe Devon........10 E4
Jameston Pembks 49 H7
Jamestown HighId........212 D3
Jamestown W Duns......174 D3
Janetstown HighId 227 L3
Jardine Hall D & G.......155 J5
Jarrow S Tyne..............151 H3
Jasper's Green Essex......61 H3
Jawcraig Falk..............175 L4
Jaywick Essex...............62 D5
Jedburgh Border 167 K5
Jeffreyston Pembks.......49 J6
Jemimaville HighId 213 H2
Jerbourg Guern...........236 d4
Jersey Jersey...............236 c6
Jersey Airport Jersey...236 b7
Jesmond N u Ty...........151 G2
Jevington E Susx...........20 B5
Jockey End Herts..........59 H5
Jodrell Bank Ches E......113 H7
Johnby Cumb...............148 D7
John Lennon
Airport Lpool............112 B5
John o' Groats
HighId......................231 L2
Johnshaven Abers 197 J3
Johnston Pembks..........48 F5
Johnstone D & G...........155 M3
Johnstone Rens............174 D5
Johnstonebridge
D & G.......................155 J4
Johnstown Carmth.......50 E2
Johnstown Wrexhm......97 L4
Joppa C Edin................177 J4

Joppa Cerdgn................66 D2
Joppa S Ayrs 163 K5
Jordanston Pembks.......64 C7
Joyden's Wood Kent......45 K5
Juniper Nthumb...........150 B3
Juniper Green
C Edin.......................177 G5
Jura Ag & B.................171 J2
Jurassic Coast Devon....13 H4
Jurby IoM....................237 c2

K

Kaber Cumb..................139 H5
Kaimend S Lans 165 J1
Kames Ag & B 173 G4
Kames E Ayrs 164 D4
Kea Cnwll 4 C7
Keadby N Linc..............125 K7
Keal Cotes Lincs 104 B1
Kearsley Bolton............113 H1
Kearsney Kent................35 H6
Kearstwick Cumb.........130 B4
Kedington Suffk............77 G5
Kedleston Derbys.........100 F4
Keelby Lincs 126 E8
Keele Staffs 99 J4
Keele Services Staffs......99 J4
Keelham C Brad 123 G4
Keeston Pembks............48 F4
Keevil Wilts...................39 L8
Kegworth Leics 101 J7
Kehelland Cnwll..............3 G3
Keig Abers....................206 B2
Keighley C Brad...........122 F3
Keilarsbrae Clacks.......185 J8
Keillour P & K..............185 K3
Keiloch Abers...............204 E6
Keils Ag & B.................171 K5
Keinton Mandeville
Somset.......................26 D5
Keir Mill D & G............154 E4
Keisley Cumb...............139 G3
Keiss HighId.................231 L4
Keith Moray 215 J4
Keithick P & K..............195 K8
Keithock Angus............196 F4
Keithtown HighId 212 E3
Kelbrook Lancs............122 D2
Kelby Lincs...................103 G4
Keld N York 139 K6
Kelfield N York.............124 F3
Kelham Notts...............102 C2
Kelhead D & G..............147 K2
Kellamergh Lancs.........120 E5
Kellas Angus................187 G1
Kellas Moray 214 E4
Kellaton Devon 7 J7
Kelling Norfk................106 C4
Kellington N York.........124 E5
Kelloe Dur 151 J7
Kelloholm D & G 164 E6
Kells Cumb...................136 D4
Kelly Devon 9 K8
Kelmarsh Nhants..........87 K7
Kelmscott Oxon............56 E7
Kelsale Suffk.................79 H2
Kelsall Ches W..............112 D7
Kelshall Herts................75 K7
Kelsick Cumb...............147 L5
Kelso Border.................167 L3
Kelstedge Derbys..........115 G8
Kelstern Lincs 118 C4
Kelston BaNES...............39 G6
Keltneyburn P & K.......194 B6
Kelton D & G.................155 H7
Kelty Fife.....................186 B8
Kelvedon Essex..............61 K4
Kelvedon Hatch
Essex.........................60 F7
Kelvinhead N Lans........175 K3
Kelynack Cnwll 2 C5
Kemback Fife...............187 G4
Kemberton Shrops........84 D3
Kemble Gloucs..............39 M2
Kemerton Worcs...........71 G6

Kemeys Commander
Mons.............................53 M6
Kemnay Abers..............206 E3
Kempley Gloucs..............54 F3
Kempley Green
Gloucs...........................55 G3
Kempsey Worcs.............70 F5
Kempsford Gloucs......40 D2
Kempshott Hants..........29 L2
Kempston Bed..............74 F5
Kempton Shrops..........83 G6
Kemp Town Br & H......19 J5
Kemsing Kent.................32 F2
Kenardington Kent.....34 C7
Kenchester Herefs.......69 J6
Kencot Oxon...................56 E6
Kendal Cumb.............129 L2
Kenfig Brdgnd..............36 C4
Kenfig Hill Brdgnd.......36 C4
Kenilworth Warwks......72 C1
Kenley Gt Lon................32 B2
Kenley Shrops...............83 L4
Kenmore Highld..........210 B3
Kenmore P & K...........194 B7
Kenn Devon...................11 L7
Kenn N Som...................38 B6
Kennacraig Ag & B....172 D5
Kennall Vale Cnwll.........3 J4
Kennerleigh Devon.....11 J4
Kennet Clacks..............176 C1
Kennethmont Abers....215 L8
Kennett Cambs...............77 G2
Kennford Devon...........11 L7
Kenninghall Norfk.........92 C6
Kennington Kent...........34 D5
Kennington Oxon...........57 K7
Kennington Lees
Kent...............................34 D5
Kennoway Fife..............186 F6
Kenny Somset................25 L7
Kenny Hill Suffk............90 F7
Kennythorpe N York...134 C6
Kenovay Ag & B...........188 C6
Kensaleyre Highld.......208 F4
Kensington Gt Lon........44 E4
Kensington Palace
Gt Lon...........................44 E4
Kensworth Common
C Beds...........................59 G4
Kentallen Highld.........191 K5
Kentchurch Herefs.......54 B3
Kentford Suffk................77 G2
Kentisbeare Devon......12 D2
Kentisbury Devon.........23 K3
Kentish Town Gt Lon....44 F3
Kentmere Cumb..........138 C6
Kenton Devon................12 B5
Kenton Gt Lon................44 D3
Kenton N u Ty..............150 F2
Kenton Suffk..................78 E2
Kenton Bankfoot
N u Ty..........................150 F2
Kentra Highld................190 D3
Kentsboro Hants............28 F4
Kent's Green Gloucs......55 H4
Kent's Oak Hants...........28 F6
Kenwyn Cnwll..................4 C6
Keoldale Highld...........228 F3
Keppoch Highld............200 D1
Kepwick N York............133 G2
Keresley Covtry.............86 D6
Kerrera Ag & B.............182 B2
Kerry Powys....................82 D5
Kerrycroy Ag & B.........173 J6
Kersall Notts.................116 B8
Kersbrook Devon...........12 D5
Kersey Suffk....................78 B5
Kershader W Isls..........232 f3
Kerswell Devon..............12 D2
Kerswell Green
Worcs............................70 F5
Kesgrave Suffk................78 F5
Kessingland Suffk..........93 L6
Kestle Cnwll......................4 F6
Kestle Mill Cnwll.............4 D4
Keston Gt Lon................45 H7
Keswick Cumb...............137 J3

Keswick Norfk................92 E3
Kettering Nhants............88 C7
Ketteringham Norfk......92 E3
Kettins P & K.................195 K8
Kettlebaston Suffk........77 L4
Kettlebridge Fife..........186 E6
Kettlebrook Staffs.........86 B3
Kettleburgh Suffk..........78 F3
Kettlebrook D & G........155 K6
Kettleshulme Ches E....113 M5
Kettlesing N York..........132 C7
Kettlesing Bottom
N York..........................132 C7
Kettlestone Norfk.......106 A6
Kettlethorpe Lincs......116 D6
Kettletoft Ork...............234 d4
Kettlewell N York.........131 H5
Ketton Rutlnd.................88 E3
Kew Gt Lon.....................44 D5
Kew Royal Botanic
Gardens Gt Lon............44 D5
Kewstoke N Som...........37 M7
Kexby C York..................125 G1
Kexby Lincs...................116 E4
Key Green Ches E.........113 K8
Keyham Leics..................87 J3
Keyhaven Hants.............16 C4
Keyingham E R Yk........127 G5
Keymer W Susx...............19 J3
Keynsham BaNES..........38 F6
Keysoe Bed.....................74 F3
Keysoe Row Bed...........74 F3
Keyston Cambs...............88 F7
Keyworth Notts............101 L6
Kibblesworth Gatesd...151 G4
Kibworth
Beauchamp Leics........87 K5
Kibworth Harcourt
Leics..............................87 K5
Kidbrooke Gt Lon..........45 H5
Kidderminster Worcs....84 E7
Kidlington Oxon.............57 J5
Kidmore End Oxon........42 B5
Kidsdale D & G..............145 J7
Kidsgrove Staffs............99 J2
Kidwelly Carmth.............50 E4
Kiel Crofts Ag & B.........191 H8
Kielder Nthumb............157 G4
Kielder Forest N York....157 G5
Kiells Ag & B..................171 H5
Kilbarchan Rens..........174 D5
Kilbeg Highld...............199 K4
Kilberry Ag & B.............172 C5
Kilbirnie N Ayrs...........174 C7
Kilbride Ag & B.............172 C3
Kilbride Ag & B.............173 H5
Kilbuiack Moray...........214 D3
Kilburn Derbys..............101 G4
Kilburn Gt Lon................44 E4
Kilburn N York..............133 H4
Kilby Leics.......................87 J4
Kilchamaig Ag & B.......172 D6
Kilchattan Ag & B.........173 J7
Kilchattan Ag & B.........180 E7
Kilcheran Ag & B..........191 G8
Kilchoan Highld...........189 L4
Kilchoman Ag & B........170 D5
Kilchrenan Ag & B.......182 E3
Kilconquhar Fife..........187 H6
Kilcot Gloucs...................55 G3
Kilcoy Highld................212 E4
Kilcreggan Ag & B........173 L3
Kildale N York...............142 D5
Kildalloig Ag & B..........161 J5
Kildary Highld...............223 G6
Kildavaig Ag & B...........173 G5
Kildavanan Ag & B........173 H5
Kildonan Highld...........227 G4
Kildonan Lodge
Highld...........................226 F4
Kildonnan Highld.........199 G7
Kildrochet House
D & G...........................144 C4
Kildrummy Abers..........205 K2
Kildwick N York............122 F2
Kilfinan Ag & B.............172 F3
Kilfinnan Highld...........201 K6

Kilgetty Pembks.............49 J6
Kilgrammie S Ayrs.......152 F2
Kilgwrrwg Common
Mons............................38 C2
Kilham E R Yk...............135 G6
Kilkenneth Ag & B........188 B7
Kilkenzie Ag & B...........161 H4
Kilkerran Ag & B...........161 J5
Kilkhampton Cnwll..........9 H3
Killamarsh Derbys.......115 J5
Killay Swans...................51 H6
Killearn Stirlg...............174 F2
Killen Highld.................213 G3
Killerby Darltn..............140 F3
Killerton Devon..............12 C3
Killichonan P & K.........193 J5
Killiechonate Highld....192 D1
Killiechronan Ag & B....190 B7
Killiecrankie P & K.......194 E4
Killilan Highld...............210 E7
Killimster Highld..........231 K4
Killin Stirlg....................184 C2
Killinghall N York.........132 D7
Killington Cumb...........130 C2
Killington Lake
Services Cumb............130 B2
Killingworth N Tyne.....159 G7
Killochyett Border........167 G1
Kilmacolm Inver...........174 C4
Kilmahog Stirlg.............184 D5
Kilmahumaig Ag & B....182 A8
Kilmaluag Highld.........218 C6
Kilmany Fife.................186 F3
Kilmarnock E Ayrs.......163 K2
Kilmartin Ag & B..........182 B7
Kilmaurs E Ayrs...........163 K2
Kilmelford Ag & B........182 B5
Kilmersdon Somset......27 G2
Kilmeston Hants............29 L6
Kilmichael Ag & B........161 H5
Kilmichael Glassary
Ag & B..........................182 B8
Kilmichael of
Inverlussa
Ag & B..........................172 D2
Kilmington Devon..........13 H3
Kilmington Wilts.............27 H4
Kilmorack Highld.........212 D5
Kilmore Ag & B.............182 C3
Kilmore Highld.............199 K4
Kilmory Ag & B.............182 C4
Kilmory Highld.............190 B3
Kilmory N Ayrs.............162 B5
Kilmuir Highld..............208 D5
Kilmuir Highld..............213 G4
Kilmuir Highld..............218 B7
Kilmuir Highld..............223 G6
Kilmun Ag & B..............173 K3
Kilnave Ag & B.............170 F4
Kilncadzow S Lans.......176 B8
Kilndown Kent................33 J6
Kilninver Ag & B...........182 B3
Kilnsea E R Yk...............127 J7
Kilnsey N York..............131 H6
Kilnwick E R Yk............126 C1
Kiloran Ag & B.............180 E7
Kilpatrick N Ayrs.........162 A4
Kilpeck Herefs................54 C3
Kilpin E R Yk..................125 J5
Kilrenny Fife.................187 J6
Kilsby Nhants.................73 H1
Kilspindie P & K...........186 C3
Kilstay D & G................144 D7
Kilsyth N Lans...............175 J3
Kiltarlity Highld............212 D6
Kilton R & Cl.................142 E4
Kilton Thorpe
R & Cl...........................142 E4
Kilvaxter Highld...........218 B7
Kilve Somset....................25 J3
Kilvington Notts............102 D4
Kilwinning N Ayrs.........163 H2
Kimberley Norfk.............92 C3
Kimberley Notts............101 J4
Kimberworth Rothm.....115 H3
Kimblesworth Dur.......151 G5
Kimbolton Cambs..........75 G2
Kimbolton Herefs...........69 K3

Kimcote Leics.................87 H6
Kimmeridge Dorset......15 H6
Kimpton Hants................28 F3
Kimpton Herts.................59 K4
Kinbrace Highld...........226 F3
Kinbuck Stirlg...............185 G6
Kincaple Fife.................187 G4
Kincardine Fife.............176 C2
Kincardine Highld.........222 E4
Kincardine Bridge
Fife...............................176 C2
Kincardine O'Neil
Abers...........................206 B5
Kinclaven P & K............195 J8
Kincorth C Aber.............207 H5
Kincorth House
Moray...........................214 C3
Kincraig Highld.............203 K4
Kincraigie P & K............194 F6
Kindallachan P & K......194 F6
Kinerarach Ag & B........172 B7
Kineton Gloucs................56 C3
Kineton Warwks..............72 D4
Kinfauns P & K..............186 C3
Kingarth Ag & B............173 J6
Kingcausie Abers.........207 G5
Kingcoed Mons..............54 B6
Kingerby Lincs..............117 H3
Kingham Oxon................56 E3
Kingholm Quay
D & G...........................155 G7
Kinghorn Fife................177 H2
Kinglassie Fife..............186 D7
Kingoodie P & K............186 E2
Kingsand Cnwll................6 C5
Kingsbarns Fife............187 K5
Kingsbridge Devon.........7 H6
Kingsbridge Somset......24 F4
King's Bromley Staffs....85 K1
Kingsburgh Highld.......208 F4
Kingsbury Gt Lon..........44 D3
Kingsbury Warwks.........86 B4
Kingsbury Episcopi
Somset..........................26 B7
King's Caple Herefs......54 E3
Kingsclere Hants............41 K8
King's Cliffe Nhants......88 E4
Kings Clipstone
Notts............................115 L8
Kingscote Gloucs...........39 J2
Kingscott Devon.............23 H7
King's Coughton
Warwks..........................71 J3
Kingscross N Ayrs........162 D4
Kingsdon Somset...........26 D6
Kingsdown Kent.............35 K5
Kingsdown Swindn........40 D3
Kingsdown Wilts.............39 J6
Kingseat Abers.............207 G2
Kingseat Fife.................176 F1
Kingsey Bucks................58 C6
Kingsfold W Susx...........31 K4
Kingsford C Aber..........206 F4
Kingsford E Ayrs..........174 E8
Kingsgate Kent...............35 K1
Kingshall Street
Suffk..............................77 K3
King's Heath Birm.........85 J7
Kings Hill Kent...............33 H3
King's Hill Wsall............85 H4
Kings House Hotel
Highld...........................192 D5
Kingshurst Solhll............85 L6
Kingskerswell Devon......7 K3
Kingskettle Fife............186 E5
Kingsland Herefs...........69 J3
Kingsland IoA...............108 C5
Kings Langley Herts.......59 H7
Kingsley Ches W...........112 D6
Kingsley Hants................30 C4
Kingsley Staffs..............100 A3
Kingsley Green
W Susx............................30 E5
Kingsley Park Nhants....73 L3
King's Lynn Norfk.........104 F8
Kings Meaburn
Cumb...........................138 E3
King's Mills Guern.......236 c3

Kingsmuir Angus 196 D6
Kings Muir Border 166 C2
Kingsmuir Fife 187 J5
Kingsnorth Kent 34 D6
King's Norton Birm 85 J7
King's Norton Leics 87 K4
Kings Nympton
Devon 23 L7
King's Pyon Herefs 69 J4
Kings Ripton Cambs ... 89 J7
King's Somborne
Hants 29 G5
King's Stag Dorset 14 D1
King's Stanley Gloucs ... 55 J7
King's Sutton Nhants ... 72 F7
Kingstanding Birm 85 J4
Kingsteignton Devon ... 7 K2
Kingsteps Highld 213 L3
Kingsthorne Herefs 54 D2
Kingsthorpe Nhants 73 L2
Kingston Cambs 75 L4
Kingston Cnwll 6 A2
Kingston Devon 6 F6
Kingston Dorset 14 E1
Kingston Dorset 15 H6
Kingston E Loth 178 C3
Kingston IoW 16 F6
Kingston Kent 35 G4
Kingston Bagpuize
Oxon 57 H7
Kingston Blount
Oxon 58 C7
Kingston by Sea
W Susx 19 H4
Kingston Deverill
Wilts 27 J4
Kingstone Herefs 69 H7
Kingstone Somset 26 B8
Kingstone Staffs 100 B6
Kingston Lacy Dorset ... 15 J3
Kingston Lisle Oxon ... 40 F3
Kingston near
Lewes E Susx 19 K4
Kingston on Soar
Notts 101 J6
Kingston on Spey
Moray 215 H2
Kingston Russell
Dorset 14 B4
Kingston St Mary
Somset 25 K5
Kingston Seymour
N Som 38 B6
Kingston upon Hull
C KuH 126 D5
Kingston upon
Thames Gt Lon 44 D6
King's Walden Herts 59 K4
Kingswear Devon 7 K5
Kingswells C Aber 207 G4
Kings Weston Bristl ... 38 D5
Kingswinford Dudley ... 84 F5
Kingswood Bucks 58 B4
Kingswood C KuH 126 D4
Kingswood Gloucs 39 H3
Kingswood S Glos 38 F5
Kingswood Somset 25 H4
Kingswood Surrey 31 L1
Kingswood Warwks 71 L1
Kingswood
Common Staffs 84 E3
Kings Worthy Hants ... 29 J5
Kingthorpe Lincs 117 J6
Kington Herefs 68 F3
Kington S Glos 38 F3
Kington Worcs 71 H4
Kington Langley
Wilts 39 L5
Kington Magna
Dorset 27 H6
Kington St Michael
Wilts 39 K5
Kingussie Highld 203 H5
Kingweston Somset 26 D5
Kinharrachie Abers ... 217 H7
Kinharvie D & G 147 G2
Kinkell Bridge P & K ... 185 J4
Kinknockie Abers 217 J6

Kinleith C Edin 177 G5
Kinlet Shrops 84 C7
Kinloch Highld 198 F5
Kinloch Highld 225 H2
Kinloch Highld 229 H5
Kinloch P & K 195 J7
Kinlochard Stirlg 184 B6
Kinlochbervie
Highld 228 C4
Kinlocheil Highld 191 J1
Kinlochewe Highld ... 210 F3
Kinloch Hourn
Highld 200 E4
Kinlochlaggan
Highld 202 E7
Kinlochleven Highld ... 192 C4
Kinlochmoidart
Highld 190 E2
Kinlochnanuagh
Highld 200 B8
Kinloch Rannoch
P & K 193 L5
Kinloss Moray 214 C3
Kinmel Bay Conwy 110 D5
Kinmuck Abers 206 F2
Kinmundy Abers 207 G2
Kinnabus Ag & B 160 B2
Kinnadie Abers 217 H5
Kinnaird P & K 194 F5
Kinneff Abers 197 K2
Kinnelhead D & G 155 H2
Kinnell Angus 196 F6
Kinnerley Shrops 97 M7
Kinnersley Herefs 69 G5
Kinnersley Worcs 70 F5
Kinnerton Powys 68 E2
Kinnesswood
P & K 186 C6
Kinnordy Angus 196 B5
Kinoulton Notts 102 B6
Kinross P & K 186 B6
Kinrossie P & K 186 C2
Kinross Services
P & K 186 B6
Kinsham Herefs 69 G2
Kinsham Worcs 71 G7
Kinsley Wakefd 124 C7
Kinson BCP 15 K3
Kintail Highld 200 F2
Kintbury W Berk 41 G6
Kintessack Moray 214 B3
Kintillo P & K 186 B4
Kinton Herefs 83 H8
Kinton Shrops 98 A8
Kintore Abers 206 E3
Kintour Ag & B 171 H7
Kintra Ag & B 170 F8
Kintra Ag & B 180 D3
Kintraw Ag & B 182 B6
Kintyre Ag & B 161 J2
Kinveachy Highld 203 L2
Kinver Staffs 84 E6
Kippax Leeds 124 C4
Kippen Stirlg 184 E7
Kippford D & G 146 E4
Kipping's Cross Kent ... 33 H5
Kirbister Ork 234 b6
Kirby Bedon Norfk 93 G3
Kirby Bellars Leics ... 102 B8
Kirby Cane Norfk 93 H5
Kirby Cross Essex 62 E4
Kirby Grindalythe
N York 134 D6
Kirby Hill N York 132 F5
Kirby Hill N York 140 E6
Kirby Knowle N York ... 133 G3
Kirby-le-Soken
Essex 62 F4
Kirby Misperton
N York 134 B4
Kirby Muxloe Leics 87 G3
Kirby Underdale
E R Yk 134 C7
Kirby Wiske N York ... 132 E3
Kirdford W Susx 31 G6
Kirk Highld 231 K4
Kirkabister Shet 235 d6
Kirkandrews D & G ... 146 A5

Kirkandrews upon
Eden Cumb 148 C4
Kirkbampton Cumb ... 148 B4
Kirkbean D & G 147 G3
Kirk Bramwith Donc ... 124 F7
Kirkbride Cumb 147 M4
Kirkbuddo Angus 196 E7
Kirkburn Border 166 D2
Kirkburn E R Yk 134 F7
Kirkburton Kirk 123 J7
Kirkby Knows 111 L2
Kirkby Lincs 117 H3
Kirkby N York 142 C6
Kirkby Fleetham
N York 141 G7
Kirkby Green Lincs ... 103 H2
Kirkby-in-Ashfield
Notts 101 J2
Kirkby-in-Furness
Cumb 128 F3
Kirkby la Thorpe
Lincs 103 J4
Kirkby Lonsdale
Cumb 130 B4
Kirkby Malham
N York 131 G2
Kirkby Mallory Leics ... 86 F4
Kirkby Malzeard
N York 132 C5
Kirkbymoorside
N York 133 L3
Kirkby on Bain Lincs ... 118 C8
Kirkby Overblow
N York 123 L2
Kirkby Stephen
Cumb 139 H5
Kirkby Thore Cumb ... 138 F3
Kirkby Underwood
Lincs 103 H6
Kirkby Wharf N York ... 124 D3
Kirkcaldy Fife 186 D8
Kirkcambeck Cumb ... 148 F2
Kirkchrist D & G 146 B5
Kirkcolm D & G 144 B2
Kirkconnel D & G 164 E6
Kirkconnell D & G ... 147 G2
Kirkcowan D & G 145 G3
Kirkcudbright D & G ... 146 B5
Kirkdale Lpool 111 K3
Kirk Deighton
N York 124 B1
Kirk Ella E R Yk 126 C5
Kirkfieldbank S Lans ... 165 G2
Kirkgunzeon D & G ... 146 F2
Kirk Hallam Derbys ... 101 J4
Kirkham Lancs 120 F4
Kirkham N York 134 B6
Kirkhamgate Wakefd ... 123 K6
Kirk Hammerton
N York 133 G7
Kirkhaugh Nthumb ... 149 H5
Kirkheaton Kirk 123 H6
Kirkheaton Nthumb ... 158 C6
Kirkhill Highld 212 E5
Kirkhope S Lans 165 J7
Kirkibost Highld 199 H2
Kirkinch P & K 195 L7
Kirkinner D & G 145 J5
Kirkintilloch E Duns ... 175 H4
Kirk Ireton Derbys ... 100 E3
Kirkland Cumb 136 E4
Kirkland D & G 154 E4
Kirkland D & G 155 H4
Kirkland D & G 164 E6
Kirk Langley Derbys ... 100 F5
Kirkleatham R & Cl ... 142 D3
Kirklevington S on T ... 141 K5
Kirkley Suffk 93 L5
Kirklington N York ... 132 D4
Kirklington Notts 102 B2
Kirklinton Cumb 148 D2
Kirkliston C Edin 176 F4
Kirkmabreck D & G ... 145 K4
Kirkmaiden D & G ... 144 D7
Kirk Merrington Dur ... 141 G2
Kirk Michael IoM 237 c4
Kirkmichael P & K ... 195 H4
Kirkmichael S Ayrs ... 163 K4

Kirkmuirhill S Lans ... 164 F2
Kirknewton Nthumb ... 168 D4
Kirknewton W Loth ... 176 F5
Kirkney Abers 215 L7
Kirk of Shotts
N Lans 175 L5
Kirkoswald Cumb 148 F6
Kirkoswald S Ayrs ... 163 G7
Kirkpatrick D & G ... 154 F4
Kirkpatrick Durham
D & G 154 D7
Kirkpatrick-
Fleming D & G 156 B7
Kirk Sandall Donc ... 124 F8
Kirksanton Cumb 128 D4
Kirk Smeaton N York ... 124 D7
Kirkstall Leeds 123 K4
Kirkstead Lincs 103 K1
Kirkstile Abers 215 L7
Kirkstile D & G 156 C4
Kirkstyle Highld 231 L2
Kirkthorpe Wakefd ... 124 B4
Kirkton Abers 206 C1
Kirkton D & G 155 G6
Kirkton Fife 186 F3
Kirkton Highld 210 C8
Kirkton Highld 210 D6
Kirkton P & K 185 K4
Kirkton Manor
Border 166 C2
Kirkton of Airlie
Angus 195 L6
Kirkton of
Auchterhouse
Angus 196 B8
Kirkton of Barevan
Highld 213 K5
Kirkton of Collace
P & K 186 C2
Kirkton of Durris
Abers 206 E6
Kirkton of
Glenbuchat
Abers 205 J3
Kirkton of Glenisla
Angus 195 K4
Kirkton of
Kingoldrum
Angus 196 B5
Kirkton of Lethendy
P & K 195 H7
Kirkton of Logie
Buchan Abers 217 J7
Kirkton of
Maryculter Abers ... 207 G5
Kirkton of Menmuir
Angus 196 E4
Kirkton of Monikie
Angus 196 E8
Kirkton of Rayne
Abers 216 D7
Kirkton of Skene
Abers 206 F4
Kirkton of Tealing
Angus 196 C8
Kirkton of Tough
Abers 206 C3
Kirktown Abers 217 J2
Kirktown Abers 217 K4
Kirktown of Alvah
Abers 216 D3
Kirktown of Bourtie
Abers 206 E4
Kirktown of
Deskford Moray 215 L3
Kirktown of
Fetteresso Abers ... 206 F7
Kirktown of
Mortlach Moray 215 H6
Kirktown of Slains
Abers 217 K8
Kirkurd Border 165 M1
Kirkwall Ork 234 c6
Kirkwall Airport Ork ... 234 c6
Kirkwhelpington
Nthumb 158 C5
Kirk Yetholm Border ... 168 C4
Kirmington N Linc ... 126 D7

Kirmond le Mire
Lincs.............................117 K3
Kirn Ag & B.....................173 K3
Kirriemuir Angus...........196 C5
Kirstead Green Norfk....93 G4
Kirtlebridge D & G.......155 M7
Kirtling Cambs.................77 G3
Kirtling Green Cambs....76 F4
Kirtlington Oxon.............57 J4
Kirtomy Highld.............229 M3
Kirton Lincs...................104 A5
Kirton Notts..................116 B7
Kirton Suffk....................78 F6
Kirtonhill W Duns.......174 D4
Kirton in Lindsey
N Linc..........................116 F2
Kirwaugh D & G...........145 J4
Kishorn Highld.............210 C6
Kislingbury Nhants........73 K3
Kitt Green Wigan.........112 D1
Kittisford Somset...........25 G6
Kitt's Green Birm..........85 L6
Kittybrewster
C Aber.........................207 H4
Kivernoll Herefs.............54 C2
Kiveton Park Rothm....115 J5
Knaith Lincs.................116 D5
Knap Corner Dorset.......27 J6
Knaphill Surrey...............42 F8
Knapp Somset..................25 L6
Knapton C York............124 E1
Knapton N York...........134 D4
Knapton Norfk..............107 G5
Knapwell Cambs............75 K2
Knaresborough
N York.........................132 E7
Knarsdale Nthumb........149 H4
Knaven Abers.................217 G5
Knayton N York............132 F2
Knebworth Herts...........59 L4
Knedlington E R Yk......125 H5
Kneesall Notts..............116 B8
Kneeton Notts...............102 B4
Knelston Swans..............50 F7
Knenhall Staffs...............99 L5
Knightcote Warwks........72 E4
Knightley Staffs..............99 J7
Knighton C Leic.............87 H4
Knighton Dorset.............14 C1
Knighton Powys.............68 F1
Knighton Somset............25 J3
Knighton Staffs...............99 G4
Knighton Staffs...............99 H6
Knighton on Teme
Worcs.............................70 B1
Knightwick Worcs...........70 D4
Knill Herefs......................68 F3
Knipoch Ag & B............182 B3
Knipton Leics................102 D6
Kniveton Derbys...........100 E3
Knock Cumb..................138 F2
Knock Highld.................199 K4
Knock Moray.................215 L4
Knock W Isls.................232 g2
Knockally Highld...........227 K3
Knockan Highld.............224 F6
Knockando Moray..........214 F6
Knockbain Highld.........212 E5
Knockbain Highld.........212 F3
Knock Castle N Ayrs....173 L5
Knockdee Highld...........231 H4
Knockdow Ag & B........173 J4
Knockdown Wilts...........39 J3
Knockeen S Ayrs..........153 G3
Knockenkelly N Ayrs....162 D4
Knockentiber E Ayrs....163 K2
Knockholt Kent.............32 E2
Knockholt Pound
Kent.............................32 E2
Knockin Shrops...............97 M7
Knockinlaw E Ayrs........163 K2
Knocknain D & G..........144 B3
Knockrome Ag & B......171 K4
Knocksharry IoM..........237 b4
Knocksheen D & G.......153 M5
Knockvennie
Smithy D & G..............154 D7
Knodishall Suffk.............79 J3

Knodishall Common
Suffk.............................79 J3
Knole Somset..................26 C6
Knolls Green Ches E.....113 J5
Knolton Wrexhm............98 B5
Knook Wilts.....................27 L3
Knossington Leics...........88 B2
Knott End-on-Sea
Lancs...........................120 E2
Knotting Bed...................74 E2
Knotting Green Bed.......74 E3
Knottingley Wakefd....124 D5
Knotty Ash Lpool.........112 B3
Knowbury Shrops...........83 L7
Knowe D & G.................153 G7
Knowehead D & G........154 A4
Knoweside S Ayrs........163 G6
Knowes of Elrick
Abers...........................216 B4
Knowle Bristl..................38 E6
Knowle Devon..................11 H5
Knowle Devon..................12 C2
Knowle Devon..................12 D6
Knowle Devon..................23 H4
Knowle Shrops................83 L8
Knowle Solhll..................85 L7
Knowle Somset...............24 E3
Knowlefield Cumb........148 D4
Knowle Green Lancs....121 J3
Knowle St Giles
Somset...........................13 J1
Knowl Hill W & M..........42 D4
Knowsley Knows...........112 C3
Knowsley Safari
Knows..........................112 C3
Knowstone Devon...........24 C6
Knox Bridge Kent...........33 K5
Knoydart Highld...........200 C5
Knucklas Powys..............82 F8
Knuston Nhants..............74 D2
Knutsford Ches E..........113 H5
Knutsford Services
Ches E.........................113 G6
Krumlin Calder.............122 F6
Kuggar Cnwll.....................3 J7
Kyleakin Highld............200 B1
Kyle of Lochalsh
Highld.........................210 B8
Kylerhea Highld............200 B2
Kylesku Highld..............224 F2
Kylesmorar Highld.......200 C6
Kyles Scalpay W Isls...232 e4
Kylestrome Highld.......224 F2
Kynnersley Wrekin........84 C1
Kyrewood Worcs............69 L2

L

La Bellieuse Guern........236 d3
Lacasaigh W Isls...........232 f3
Lacasdal W Isls.............232 f2
Laceby NE Lin...............117 K1
Lacey Green Bucks........58 D7
Lach Dennis Ches W....113 G6
Lackford Suffk.................77 H1
Lackford Green Suffk....77 H1
Lacock Wilts.....................39 K6
Ladbroke Warwks............72 E3
Laddingford Kent............33 J4
Ladock Cnwll......................4 D5
Lady Ork.........................234 d4
Ladybank Fife................186 E5
Ladygill S Lans..............165 H4
Lady Hall Cumb............128 E3
Ladykirk Border............179 J8
Ladywood Birm...............85 J6
Ladywood Worcs.............70 F3
La Fontenelle Guern.....236 e1
La Fosse Guern.............236 d4
Lag D & G......................154 F5
Laga Highld...................190 D4
Lagavulin Ag & B..........160 C1
Lagg N Ayrs..................162 B5
Laggan Highld...............201 L6
Laggan Highld...............202 F6
Lagganlia Highld...........203 K5

La Greve Guern.............236 d2
La Grève de Lecq
Jersey..........................236 b5
La Hougue Bie
Jersey..........................236 d7
La Houguette Guern.....236 b3
Laid Highld.....................228 F4
Laide Highld...................219 L3
Laig Highld.....................199 G7
Laigh Clunch E Ayrs....174 E8
Laigh Fenwick
E Ayrs..........................163 L2
Laigh Glenmuir
E Ayrs..........................164 C5
Laighstonehall
S Lans..........................175 J7
Laindon Essex..................46 B3
Lairg Highld...................225 M7
Laisterdyke C Brad......123 J4
Lake IoW..........................17 H5
Lake Wilts........................28 C4
Lake District Cumb......137 H5
Lake District
National Park
Cumb...........................137 H5
Lakenham Norfk.............92 F3
Lakenheath Suffk............91 G6
Lakes End Norfk............90 D4
Laleston Brdgnd............36 D4
Lamarsh Essex................77 K7
Lamas Norfk..................106 F7
Lambden Border...........167 L2
Lamberhurst Kent..........33 H6
Lamberhurst Down
Kent.............................33 H6
Lamberton Border........179 K6
Lambeth Gt Lon..............44 F4
Lambfair Green Suffk....77 G4
Lambley Notts...............101 M4
Lambley Nthumb...........149 H4
Lambourn W Berk...........40 F5
Lambourne End
Essex............................45 J2
Lambs Green W Susx.....31 L4
Lamerton Devon................6 C1
Lamesley Gatesd...........151 G4
Lamington S Lans.........165 J3
Lamlash N Ayrs.............162 C3
Lamonby Cumb.............148 D7
Lamorna Cnwll.................2 E6
Lamorran Cnwll................4 D7
Lampeter Cerdgn............66 D5
Lampeter Velfrey
Pembks..........................49 K5
Lamphey Pembks............49 H7
Lamplugh Cumb.............136 F3
Lamport Nhants..............87 L8
Lamyatt Somset...............26 F4
Lanark S Lans................165 G2
Lancaster Lancs............129 K7
Lancaster Services
Lancs...........................121 G1
Lanchester Dur.............150 F5
Lancing W Susx..............19 G5
L'Ancresse Guern.........236 d1
Landbeach Cambs...........76 C2
Landcross Devon.............23 G6
Landerberry Abers........206 E4
Landford Wilts................28 E7
Land-hallow Highld......227 L2
Landimore Swans...........50 F6
Landkey Devon................23 J5
Landore Swans.................51 J6
Landrake Cnwll.................6 B4
Land's End Airport
Cnwll...............................2 C5
Landulph Cnwll.................6 C4
Lane Cnwll..........................4 C4
Laneast Cnwll....................9 G7
Lane End Bucks..............42 D3
Lane End Kent.................45 L5
Lane End Wilts................27 J3
Lane Ends Derbys.........100 E5
Laneham Notts..............116 D6
Lane Head Dur..............140 E5
Lane Head Wsall............85 H4
Lane Side Lancs............122 B6

Langal Highld.................190 E3
Langaller Somset.............25 K6
Langar Notts..................102 B5
Langbank Rens..............174 D4
Langbar N York..............123 G1
Langcliffe N York..........130 F6
Langdale End N York...134 E2
Langdon Hills Essex.......46 B3
Langdown Hants..............16 E2
Langdyke Fife................186 E6
Langenhoe Essex.............62 B4
Langford C Beds..............75 H6
Langford Devon................12 D2
Langford Essex................61 K6
Langford Notts..............102 D2
Langford Oxon.................56 E7
Langford Budville
Somset...........................25 H6
Langham Essex................62 B2
Langham Norfk.............106 B4
Langham Rutlnd..............88 B2
Langham Suffk................77 L1
Langho Lancs.................121 K4
Langholm D & G............156 C5
Langland Swans..............51 H7
Langlee Border..............167 H3
Langley Hants..................16 F3
Langley Herts..................59 K4
Langley Kent....................33 K3
Langley Nthumb............149 L3
Langley Slough................43 G5
Langley Somset...............25 G5
Langley W Susx...............30 D5
Langley Warwks..............71 L3
Langley Burrell Wilts.....39 L5
Langley Green Essex.....61 L4
Langley Marsh
Somset...........................25 G5
Langley Mill Derbys.....101 H3
Langley Park Dur..........150 F6
Langley Street Norfk......93 H3
Langley Upper
Green Essex...................76 C7
Langney E Susx................20 D5
Langold Notts.................115 L4
Langore Cnwll....................9 J7
Langport Somset.............26 B6
Langrick Lincs................103 L3
Langridge BaNES............39 H6
Langrigg Cumb..............147 K5
Langrish Hants.................30 B6
Langsett Barns..............114 E2
Langside P & K..............185 G5
Langstone Hants..............17 K2
Langthorne N York........132 C2
Langthorpe N York.......132 F6
Langthwaite N York......140 C6
Langtoft E R Yk.............134 F6
Langtoft Lincs..................89 G2
Langton Dur...................140 F4
Langton Lincs.................118 C7
Langton Lincs.................118 E5
Langton N York.............134 C6
Langton by Wragby
Lincs............................117 J6
Langton Green Kent......32 F5
Langton Herring
Dorset...........................14 C6
Langton Matravers
Dorset...........................15 J6
Langtree Devon...............10 C2
Langwathby Cumb........148 F7
Langwell Highld.............224 E7
Langwell House
Highld.........................227 K4
Langwith Derbys...........115 K7
Langwith Junction
Derbys.........................115 K7
Langworth Lincs............117 H6
Lanhydrock Cnwll.............5 H3
Lanivet Cnwll....................5 G3
Lanlivery Cnwll.................5 G4
Lanner Cnwll......................3 J4
Lanreath Cnwll.................5 H4
Lansallos Cnwll................5 J5
Lanteglos Cnwll................8 E2
Lanteglos Highway
Cnwll...............................5 J5

Lanton Border 167 J5
Lanton Nthumb 168 D3
La Passee Guern 236 d2
Lapford Devon 11 H3
Laphroaig Ag & B. 160 C1
Lapley Staffs 84 F2
La Pulente Jersey 236 a7
Lapworth Warwks 71 L1
Larachbeg Highld 190 E6
Larbert Falk 176 B3
Largie Abers 216 B7
Largiemore Ag & B 172 F2
Largoward Fife 187 H5
Largs N Ayrs 173 L6
Largybeg N Ayrs 162 D5
Largymore N Ayrs 162 D4
Larkfield Inver 173 L4
Larkfield Kent 33 J2
Larkhall S Lans 175 K7
Larkhill Wilts 28 C3
Larling Norfk 91 L5
La Rocque Jersey 236 e8
La Rousaillerie
  Guern 236 d2
Lartington Dur 140 C4
Lasham Hants 30 A3
Lasswade Mdloth 177 J5
Lastingham N York 133 L2
Latchford Warrtn 112 F4
Latchingdon Essex 61 L7
Latchley Cnwll 6 B2
Lathbury M Keyn 74 C5
Latheron Highld 227 L2
Latheronwheel
  Highld 227 L3
Lathones Fife 187 H5
Latimer Bucks 59 G7
Latteridge S Glos 38 F4
Lattiford Somset 27 G6
Latton Wilts 40 C2
Lauder Border 178 C8
Laugharne Carmth 50 C4
Laughterton Lincs 116 D6
Laughton E Susx 20 A3
Laughton Leics 87 J5
Laughton Lincs 103 H6
Laughton Lincs 116 D3
Laughton Common
  Rothm 115 K4
Laughton-en-le-
  Morthen Rothm 115 K4
Launcells Cnwll 9 J7
Launton Oxon 57 L4
Laurencekirk Abers 197 H3
Laurieston D & G 146 B3
Laurieston Falk 176 B3
Lavendon M Keyn 74 D4
Lavenham Suffk 77 K5
Lavernock V Glam 37 J6
Laversdale Cumb 148 E3
Laverstock Wilts 28 D5
Laverstoke Hants 29 J2
Laverton Gloucs 71 J7
Laverton N York 132 C5
Laverton Somset 27 H2
La Villette Guern 236 d4
Lavister Wrexhm 98 A2
Law S Lans 175 L7
Lawers P & K 193 L7
Lawford Essex 62 C2
Lawford Somset 25 H4
Law Hill S Lans 175 L7
Lawhitton Cnwll 9 J7
Lawkland N York 130 E6
Lawley Wrekin 84 C2
Lawrence Weston
  Bristl 38 D5
Lawrenny Pembks 49 H6
Lawshall Suffk 77 K4
Laxay W Isls 232 f3
Laxdale W Isls 232 f2
Laxey IoM 237 d4
Laxfield Suffk 93 G8
Laxford Bridge
  Highld 228 C6
Laxo Shet 235 d4
Laxton E R Yk 125 J5
Laxton Nhants 88 D4

Laxton Notts 116 B7
Laycock C Brad 122 F3
Layer Breton Essex 61 M4
Layer-de-la-Haye
  Essex 62 A4
Layer Marney Essex 61 L4
Layham Suffk 78 B6
Laymore Dorset 13 K2
Laytham E R Yk 125 H3
Lazonby Cumb 148 F6
Lea Derbys 101 G2
Lea Herefs 54 F4
Lea Lincs 116 D4
Lea Shrops 83 G5
Lea Wilts 39 L3
Leachkin Highld 212 F5
Leadburn Border 177 H7
Leadenham Lincs 102 F3
Leaden Roding
  Essex 60 F5
Leadgate Dur 150 E5
Leadhills S Lans 165 G6
Leafield Oxon 56 F5
Leagrave Luton 59 H4
Leake Common
  Side Lincs 104 C3
Lealholm N York 142 F5
Lealt Highld 209 H3
Lea Marston Warwks 86 B5
Leamington
  Hastings Warwks 72 F2
Leamington Spa
  Warwks 72 D2
Leap Cross E Susx 20 C4
Learney Abers 206 C5
Leasgill Cumb 129 K3
Leasingham Lincs 103 H3
Leasingthorne Dur 141 G2
Leatherhead Surrey 31 K1
Leathley N York 123 J2
Leaton Shrops 98 C8
Leaveland Kent 34 D4
Leavenheath Suffk 77 L6
Leavening N York 134 C6
Leaves Green Gt Lon 45 H7
Lebberston N York 135 G3
Le Bigard Guern 236 c4
Le Bourg Guern 236 c4
Le Bourg Jersey 236 e8
Lechlade on
  Thames Gloucs 56 E7
Lecht Gruinart
  Ag & B 170 E5
Leck Lancs 130 C4
Leckbuie P & K 193 L7
Leckford Hants 29 G4
Leckhampstead
  Bucks 73 K6
Leckhampstead
  W Berk 41 H5
Leckhampstead
  Thicket W Berk 41 H5
Leckhampton Gloucs 55 L4
Leckmelm Highld 220 F4
Leconfield E R Yk 126 C2
Ledaig Ag & B 191 H8
Ledburn Bucks 58 E4
Ledbury Herefs 70 C6
Ledgemoor Herefs 69 H4
Ledmore Highld 224 F6
Ledsham Leeds 124 C4
Ledston Leeds 124 C5
Ledwell Oxon 57 H3
Lee Devon 23 H3
Lee Gt Lon 45 H5
Leebotwood Shrops 83 J4
Lee Brockhurst
  Shrops 98 D6
Leece Cumb 128 F5
Lee Chapel Essex 46 B3
Lee Clump Bucks 58 E6
Leeds Kent 33 L3
Leeds Leeds 123 K4
Leeds Bradford
  Airport Leeds 123 J3
Leeds Castle Kent 33 L3
Leeds Skelton Lake
  Services Leeds 123 L4

Leedstown Cnwll 3 G4
Leek Staffs 99 M2
Leek Wootton
  Warwks 72 C2
Lee Mill Devon 6 E5
Leeming N York 132 D2
Leeming Bar N York 132 D2
Leeming Bar Rest
  Area N York 132 D2
Lee-on-the-Solent
  Hants 17 G3
Lees Derbys 100 E5
Lees Oldham 113 L4
Lees Green Derbys 100 E5
Leesthorpe Leics 87 L2
Leeswood Flints 97 K1
Leetown P & K 186 C3
Leftwich Ches W 112 F6
Legbourne Lincs 118 E5
Legerwood Border 167 J2
Legoland W & M 42 F5
Le Gron Guern 236 c3
Legsby Lincs 117 J4
Le Haguais Jersey 236 d8
Le Hocq Jersey 236 d8
Leicester C Leic 87 H3
Leicester Forest
  East Services
  Leics 87 G3
Leigh Dorset 14 C2
Leigh Gloucs 55 K3
Leigh Kent 32 F4
Leigh Surrey 31 L3
Leigh Wigan 112 F2
Leigh Wilts 40 D3
Leigh Worcs 70 D4
Leigh Beck Essex 46 D4
Leigh Delamere
  Wilts 39 K5
Leigh Delamere
  Services Wilts 39 K5
Leigh Green Kent 34 B7
Leigh Knoweglass
  S Lans 175 H7
Leigh-on-Sea Sthend 46 D3
Leigh Park Dorset 15 J3
Leigh Park Hants 17 K2
Leigh Sinton Worcs 70 D4
Leighswood Wsall 85 J3
Leighterton Gloucs 39 J3
Leighton Powys 82 E3
Leighton Shrops 84 B3
Leighton
  Bromswold
  Cambs 89 G7
Leighton Buzzard
  C Beds 58 F3
Leigh upon Mendip
  Somset 27 G3
Leigh Woods N Som 38 E6
Leinthall Earls
  Herefs 69 J2
Leinthall Starkes
  Herefs 69 J1
Leintwardine Herefs 83 H8
Leire Leics 87 G5
Leiston Suffk 79 J3
Leith C Edin 177 H3
Leitholm Border 168 B1
Lelant Cnwll 2 F4
Lelley E R Yk 126 F4
Lempitlaw Border 168 B3
Lemreway W Isls 232 f3
Lemsford Herts 59 L5
Lenchwick Worcs 71 J5
Lendalfoot S Ayrs 152 D4
Lendrick Stirlg 184 C6
Lendrum Terrace
  Abers 217 L6
Lenham Kent 34 B4
Lenham Heath Kent 34 B5
Lenie Highld 202 D1
Lennel Border 168 C2
Lennox Plunton
  D & G 146 A5
Lennoxtown E Duns 175 H3
Lent Bucks 42 F4
Lenton C Nott 101 K5

Lenton Lincs 103 G6
Lenwade Norfk 106 D8
Lenzie E Duns 175 H4
Leochel-Cushnie
  Abers 205 L4
Leominster Herefs 69 K3
Leonard Stanley
  Gloucs 55 J7
Leoville Jersey 236 b6
Lephin Highld 208 B4
Leppington N York 134 B7
Lepton Kirk 123 J7
Lerags Ag & B 182 B3
L'Erée Guern 236 b3
Lerryn Cnwll 5 J4
Lerwick Shet 235 d6
Les Arquêts Guern 236 b3
Lesbury Nthumb 169 J6
Les Hubits Guern 236 d3
Leslie Abers 206 B1
Leslie Fife 186 D6
Lesmahagow S Lans 164 F2
Les Lohiers Guern 236 c3
Les Murchez Guern 236 c4
Lesnewth Cnwll 8 F6
Les Nicolles Guern 236 c4
Les Quartiers Guern 236 d2
Les Quennevais
  Jersey 236 b7
Les Sages Guern 236 b3
Lessingham Norfk 107 H6
Lessonhall Cumb 147 L5
Les Villets Guern 236 c4
Leswalt D & G 144 B3
L'Etacq Jersey 236 a6
Letchmore Heath
  Herts 43 J2
Letchworth Garden
  City Herts 59 L2
Letcombe Bassett
  Oxon 41 G4
Letcombe Regis
  Oxon 41 G3
Letham Angus 196 E6
Letham Border 167 K7
Letham Falk 176 B2
Letham Fife 186 E4
Letham Grange
  Angus 197 G7
Lethenty Abers 206 B2
Lethenty Abers 216 F6
Letheringham Suffk 78 F3
Letheringsett Norfk 106 C5
Letterewe Highld 219 L7
Letterfearn Highld 200 D2
Letterfinlay Lodge
  Hotel Highld 201 K6
Letters Highld 220 F4
Lettershaw S Lans 165 H5
Letterston Pembks 48 F2
Lettoch Highld 204 C2
Lettoch Highld 214 D7
Letton Herefs 69 G5
Letty Green Herts 59 M5
Letwell Rothm 115 K4
Leuchars Fife 187 G3
Leumrabhagh W Isls 232 f3
Leurbost W Isls 232 f3
Levan Inver 173 L3
Levedale Staffs 84 F1
Leven E R Yk 126 D2
Leven Fife 186 F7
Levens Cumb 129 K3
Levens Green Herts 60 B4
Levenshulme Manch 113 K3
Levenwick Shet 235 c7
Leverburgh W Isls 232 d5
Leverington Cambs 90 C2
Leverstock Green
  Herts 59 H6
Leverton Lincs 104 C3
Le Villocq Guern 236 c2
Levington Suffk 78 F6
Levisham N York 134 C2
Lew Oxon 56 F6
Lewannick Cnwll 9 H8
Lewdown Devon 10 D7
Lewes E Susx 19 L5

Leweston Pembks..........48 F3
Lewisham Gt Lon..........45 G5
Lewiston Highld........212 D8
Lewistown Brdgnd.........36 E3
Lewknor Oxon..........42 B2
Lewson Street Kent........34 C3
Lewtrenchard Devon......10 C7
Lexden Essex..........62 A3
Lexworthy Somset........25 K4
Leybourne Kent..........33 H2
Leyburn N York..........131 L2
Leygreen Herts..........59 K3
Ley Hill Bucks..........59 G7
Leyland Lancs..........121 H6
Leylodge Abers..........206 E3
Leys Abers..........217 J4
Leys P & K..........195 K8
Leysdown-on-Sea
  Kent..........47 G6
Leysmill Angus..........196 F6
Leys of Cossans
  Angus..........196 C6
Leysters Herefs..........69 L2
Leyton Gt Lon..........45 G3
Leytonstone Gt Lon......45 H3
Lezant Cnwll..........5 M1
Lhanbryde Moray........215 G3
Libanus Powys..........52 F3
Libberton S Lans..........165 J2
Liberton C Edin..........177 J4
Lichfield Staffs..........85 K2
Lickey Worcs..........85 H8
Lickey End Worcs........85 H8
Lickfold W Susx..........30 F6
Liddesdale Highld......190 F4
Liddington Swindn......40 E4
Lidgate Suffk..........77 G3
Lidlington C Beds..........74 E6
Liff Angus..........186 E2
Lifford Birm..........85 J7
Lifton Devon..........9 K7
Liftondown Devon........9 K7
Lighthorne Warwks........72 D4
Lighthorne Heath
  Warwks..........72 D4
Lightwater Surrey..........42 F7
Lightwater
  Valley Family
  Adventure Park
  N York..........132 D4
Lightwood C Stke..........99 L4
Lilbourne Nhants........87 H7
Lilleshall Wrekin........84 D1
Lilley Herts..........59 J3
Lilliesleaf Border........167 H4
Lillingstone Dayrell
  Bucks..........73 K6
Lillingstone Lovell
  Bucks..........73 K6
Lillington Dorset..........26 F8
Lilliput BCP..........15 K4
Lilstock Somset..........25 J3
Limbury Luton..........59 H3
Limekilnburn S Lans..175 J7
Limekilns Fife..........176 E2
Limerigg Falk..........176 B4
Limerstone IoW..........16 E6
Lime Street Worcs........55 J2
Limington Somset........26 D6
Limmerhaugh E Ayrs..164 C4
Limpenhoe Norfk........93 H3
Limpley Stoke Wilts......39 H7
Limpsfield Surrey..........32 D3
Limpsfield Chart
  Surrey..........32 D3
Linby Notts..........101 K3
Linchmere W Susx........30 E5
Lincluden D & G..........155 G6
Lincoln Lincs..........116 F7
Lincomb Worcs..........70 E2
Lindale Cumb..........129 J4
Lindal in Furness
  Cumb..........128 F4
Lindfield W Susx..........32 C7
Lindford Hants..........30 D4
Lindley Kirk..........123 G6
Lindores Fife..........186 D4
Lindridge Worcs..........70 C2

Lindsell Essex..........61 G3
Lindsey Suffk..........77 L5
Lindsey Tye Suffk........78 B5
Lingdale R & Cl..........142 E4
Lingen Herefs..........69 G2
Lingfield Surrey..........32 C4
Lingfield Common
  Surrey..........32 C4
Lingwood Norfk..........93 H2
Liniclate W Isls..........233 b7
Linicro Highld..........218 B7
Linkend Worcs..........55 J2
Linkenholt Hants..........41 G8
Linkinhorne Cnwll..........5 L2
Linktown Fife..........177 J1
Linkwood Moray........214 F3
Linley Shrops..........83 G5
Linley Green Herefs......70 C4
Linlithgow W Loth......176 D3
Linsidemore Highld......222 D2
Linslade C Beds..........58 E3
Linstead Parva
  Suffk..........93 G7
Linstock Cumb..........148 D4
Linthurst Worcs..........85 H8
Linthwaite Kirk..........123 G7
Lintlaw Border..........179 H6
Lintmill Moray..........215 L2
Linton Border..........168 B4
Linton Cambs..........76 E5
Linton Derbys..........86 C1
Linton Herefs..........54 F3
Linton Kent..........33 K3
Linton Leeds..........124 B2
Linton N York..........131 J6
Linton Hill Herefs........54 F3
Linton-on-Ouse
  N York..........133 G7
Linwood Lincs..........117 J4
Linwood Rens..........174 E5
Lionacleit W Isls..........233 b7
Lional W Isls..........232 g1
Liphook Hants..........30 D5
Liscard Wirral..........111 J3
Liscombe Somset........24 D5
Liskeard Cnwll..........5 K3
Lismore Ag & B..........191 G7
Liss Hants..........30 C5
Lissett E R Yk..........135 H7
Lissington Lincs..........117 J5
Lisvane Cardif..........37 J4
Liswerry Newpt..........37 M3
Litcham Norfk..........105 L8
Litchborough Nhants....73 J4
Litchfield Hants..........29 J2
Litherland Sefton......111 K2
Litlington Cambs........75 K6
Litlington E Susx..........20 B5
Little Abington
  Cambs..........76 D5
Little Addington
  Nhants..........88 D8
Little Airies D & G..........145 J5
Little Alne Warwks......71 K3
Little Altcar Sefton......111 J1
Little Amwell Herts......60 B5
Little Aston Staffs........85 K4
Little Ayton N York......142 C5
Little Baddow Essex......61 J6
Little Badminton
  S Glos..........39 J4
Little Bampton
  Cumb..........148 A4
Little Bardfield Essex....61 G2
Little Barford Bed........75 H3
Little Barningham
  Norfk..........106 D5
Little Barrington
  Gloucs..........56 D5
Little Barrow
  Ches W..........112 C7
Little Bavington
  Nthumb..........158 C6
Little Bedwyn Wilts......40 F7
Little Bentley Essex......62 D3
Little Berkhamsted
  Herts..........59 M6
Little Billing Nhants......74 B3

Little Billington
  C Beds..........58 F4
Little Birch Herefs........54 D2
Little Blakenham
  Suffk..........78 D5
Little Blencow Cumb...148 E7
Little Bloxwich Wsall.....85 H3
Little Bognor W Susx......31 G7
Little Bollington
  Ches E..........113 G4
Little Bookham
  Surrey..........31 J1
Littleborough Notts......116 D5
Littleborough Rochdl...122 D7
Littlebourne Kent..........35 G3
Little Bourton Oxon......72 F5
Little Braxted Essex......61 K5
Little Brechin Angus....196 F4
Littlebredy Dorset..........14 B5
Little Brickhill
  M Keyn..........58 E2
Little Brington
  Nhants..........73 J2
Little Bromley Essex....62 C3
Little Budworth
  Ches W..........112 E7
Littleburn Highld........212 F4
Little Burstead Essex.....46 A2
Littlebury Essex..........76 D6
Littlebury Green
  Essex..........76 C6
Little Bytham Lincs......103 G8
Little Carlton Lincs......118 E4
Little Casterton
  Rutlnd..........88 E2
Little Cawthorpe
  Lincs..........118 E5
Little Chalfont Bucks....43 G2
Little Chart Kent..........34 C5
Little Chesterford
  Essex..........76 D6
Little Cheverell Wilts.....27 M2
Little Chishill Cambs......76 B6
Little Clacton Essex......62 E4
Little Clifton Cumb......136 E2
Little Coates NE Lin....127 G8
Little Comberton
  Worcs..........71 G5
Little Common
  E Susx..........20 E4
Little Compton
  Warwks..........56 E3
Little Cornard Suffk......77 K6
Little Cowarne
  Herefs..........69 L4
Little Coxwell Oxon......40 F2
Little Crakehall
  N York..........132 C2
Little Cressingham
  Norfk..........91 K4
Little Crosby Sefton....111 K2
Little Cubley Derbys....100 D5
Little Dalby Leics........87 L2
Littledean Gloucs..........54 F5
Little Dewchurch
  Herefs..........54 D2
Little Ditton Cambs......76 F3
Little Downham
  Cambs..........90 D6
Little Driffield E R Yk...134 F7
Little Dunham Norfk.....91 K2
Little Dunkeld P & K....195 G7
Little Dunmow Essex....61 G4
Little Durnford Wilts......28 C5
Little Easton Essex......61 G4
Little Eaton Derbys......101 G4
Little Ellingham
  Norfk..........92 B4
Little Everdon Nhants....73 H3
Little Eversden
  Cambs..........75 L4
Little Faringdon
  Oxon..........56 E7
Little Fencote N York...132 D2
Little Fenton N York.....124 D4
Littleferry Highld........223 H3
Little Fransham
  Norfk..........91 K2

Little Gaddesden
  Herts..........59 G5
Little Glemham Suffk.....79 H3
Little Gorsley Herefs......55 G3
Little Gransden
  Cambs..........75 J4
Little Green Somset......27 G2
Little Hadham Herts......60 C4
Little Hale Lincs..........103 J4
Little Hallam Derbys....101 J4
Little Hallingbury
  Essex..........60 D4
Littleham Devon..........12 D6
Littleham Devon..........23 G6
Littlehampton
  W Susx..........18 D5
Little Harrowden
  Nhants..........74 C1
Little Haseley Oxon......57 M7
Little Haven Pembks......48 E5
Littlehaven W Susx......31 K5
Little Hay Staffs..........85 K3
Little Haywood
  Staffs..........100 A7
Littlehempston
  Devon..........7 J4
Little Hereford
  Herefs..........69 K2
Little Horkesley
  Essex..........62 A2
Little Hormead Herts....60 C3
Little Horsted E Susx....19 M3
Little Horton
  C Brad..........123 H4
Little Horwood Bucks...58 C2
Little Houghton
  Barns..........115 H1
Little Houghton
  Nhants..........74 B3
Little Hucklow
  Derbys..........114 D5
Little Hutton N York.....133 G4
Little Irchester
  Nhants..........74 C2
Little Keyford Somset...27 H3
Little Kimble Bucks......58 D6
Little Kineton
  Warwks..........72 D4
Little Kingshill Bucks....58 E7
Little Knox D & G........146 E3
Little Langdale Cumb...137 J6
Little Langford Wilts......28 B4
Little Leigh Ches W......112 F6
Little Leighs Essex......61 H5
Little Lever Bolton......121 L8
Little Linford M Keyn....74 B5
Little Load Somset......26 C6
Little London Cambs......90 B4
Little London E Susx......20 C2
Little London Hants......29 G5
Little London Hants......41 L8
Little Longstone
  Derbys..........114 D6
Little Maplestead
  Essex..........77 J2
Little Marcle Herefs......70 C7
Little Marlow Bucks......42 E3
Little Massingham
  Norfk..........105 J7
Little Melton Norfk......92 E3
Littlemill Abers..........205 H6
Littlemill Highld..........213 L4
Little Mill Mons..........53 L7
Little Milton Oxon..........57 L7
Little Missenden
  Bucks..........58 F7
Littlemore Oxon..........57 K7
Little Musgrave
  Cumb..........139 H5
Little Ness Shrops........98 B8
Little Newcastle
  Pembks..........49 G2
Little Newsham Dur...140 E4
Little Norton Somset.....26 C7
Little Oakley Essex......62 F3
Little Oakley Nhants......88 C6
Little Orton Cumb......148 C4
Littleover C Derb........101 G5

Little Packington
Warwks..........................86 B6
Little Paxton Cambs......75 H3
Little Petherick
Cnwll.................................4 E2
Little Plumstead
Norfk................................93 G2
Little Ponton Lincs......102 F6
Littleport Cambs............90 E6
Little Preston
Nhants.............................73 H4
Littler Ches W..............112 F7
Little Raveley Cambs....89 J7
Little Reedness
E R Yk...........................125 J6
Little Ribston N York...132 F8
Little Rissington
Gloucs.............................56 D4
Little Rollright Oxon......56 F3
Little Ryburgh Norfk....106 A6
Little Salkeld Cumb.....148 F7
Little Sampford
Essex...............................76 F7
Little Saughall
Ches W............................111 K7
Little Saxham Suffk........77 H2
Little Scatwell
Highld............................212 B3
Little Shelford
Cambs..............................76 C4
Little Singleton
Lancs.............................120 E3
Little Skipwith
N York............................125 G3
Little Smeaton
N York............................124 D6
Little Snoring Norfk....106 A6
Little Sodbury S Glos....39 H4
Little Somborne
Hants...............................29 G5
Little Somerford
Wilts................................39 L4
Little Soudley Shrops....99 G6
Little Stainton Darltn..141 J3
Little Stanney
Ches W............................112 B6
Little Staughton Bed....75 G3
Little Steeping Lincs...118 F8
Little Stoke Staffs..........99 K6
Littlestone-on-Sea
Kent................................21 L2
Little Stonham Suffk.....78 D3
Little Stretton Leics......87 J4
Little Stretton Shrops...83 J5
Little Strickland
Cumb.............................138 E4
Little Stukeley
Cambs..............................89 H7
Little Sugnall Staffs......99 J6
Little Swinburne
Nthumb..........................158 B6
Little Sypland D & G...146 C4
Little Tew Oxon..............57 G3
Little Tey Essex..............61 L4
Little Thetford Cambs....90 D7
Little Thorpe Dur.........151 K6
Littlethorpe Leics..........87 G4
Littlethorpe N York......132 E5
Little Thurlow Suffk......76 F4
Little Thurrock Thurr.....45 L4
Littleton Ches W...........112 C7
Littleton D & G............146 B4
Littleton Hants..............29 J5
Littleton Somset............26 C5
Littleton Surrey.............43 H6
Littleton Drew Wilts......39 J4
Littleton of Airlie
Angus............................196 B6
Littleton-on-Severn
S Glos..............................38 E3
Littleton Panell Wilts....27 M1
Little Torrington
Devon..............................10 D2
Littletown Dur..............151 H6
Little Town Lancs.........121 K4
Little Urswick Cumb....128 F5
Little Wakering
Essex...............................46 F3

Little Walden Essex........76 D6
Little Waldingfield
Suffk................................77 K5
Little Walsingham
Norfk.............................105 M5
Little Waltham Essex.....61 H5
Little Weighton
E R Yk...........................126 B4
Little Wenlock
Wrekin.............................84 B3
Little Weston Somset.....26 F6
Little Whitefield IoW.....17 H4
Littlewick Green
W & M..............................42 D4
Little Wilbraham
Cambs..............................76 D3
Little Witcombe
Gloucs.............................55 K5
Little Witley Worcs........70 D2
Little Wittenham
Oxon................................41 K2
Little Wolford
Warwks............................72 C7
Little Woodcote
Gt Lon..............................44 F7
Littleworth Oxon.............40 F2
Littleworth Staffs............99 L1
Littleworth Worcs...........70 F4
Little Wymington
Bed..................................74 D2
Little Wymondley
Herts................................59 K3
Little Wyrley Staffs.........85 H3
Little Yeldham Essex......77 H6
Littley Green Essex.........61 H4
Litton Derbys................114 D6
Litton N York................131 G5
Litton Somset.................26 E1
Litton Cheney Dorset.....14 A4
Liurbost W Isls..............232 f3
Liverpool Lpool.............111 K4
Liversedge Kirk............123 J5
Liverton Devon.................7 J2
Liverton R & Cl.............142 F4
Livingston W Loth........176 E5
Livingston Village
W Loth............................176 E5
Lixwm Flints.................111 G7
Lizard Cnwll......................3 J8
Llanaelhaearn Gwynd....95 G4
Llanafan Cerdgn.............80 F8
Llanafan-Fawr
Powys..............................67 L4
Llanallgo IoA................109 G4
Llanarmon Dyffryn
Ceiriog Wrexhm...........97 J6
Llanarmon-yn-Ial
Denbgs.............................97 J2
Llanarth Cerdgn.............65 L3
Llanarth Mons................54 B5
Llanarthne Carmth.........51 G2
Llanasa Flints...............110 F5
Llanbadarn Fawr
Cerdgn.............................80 E7
Llanbadarn Fynydd
Powys..............................82 C7
Llanbadoc Mons.............54 B7
Llanbeder Newpt............38 B3
Llanbedr Gwynd.............95 K6
Llanbedr Powys...............53 K4
Llanbedr-Dyffryn-
Clwyd Denbgs..............97 H2
Llanbedrgoch IoA........109 G5
Llanbedrog Gwynd..........94 F6
Llanbedr-y-Cennin
Conwy.............................109 L7
Llanberis Gwynd.............95 K1
Llanbethêry V Glam.......37 G6
Llanbister Powys............82 C8
Llanblethian V Glam......36 F5
Llanboidy Carmth............49 L3
Llanbradach Caerph........37 J3
Llanbrynmair Powys.......81 J3
Llancadle V Glam............37 G6
Llancarfan V Glam..........37 G6
Llancloudy Herefs...........54 D4
Llandaff Cardif................37 J5
Llandanwg Gwynd...........95 K6

Llanddaniel Fab IoA...109 G7
Llanddarog Carmth........51 G3
Llanddeiniol Cerdgn......66 D1
Llanddeiniolen
Gwynd............................109 H7
Llandderfel Gwynd..........96 F5
Llanddeusant IoA.........108 D4
Llanddew Powys..............53 G2
Llanddewi Swans............50 F7
Llanddewi Brefi
Cerdgn.............................66 F4
Llanddewi
Rhydderch Mons........53 M5
Llanddewi Velfrey
Pembks............................49 K4
Llanddewi
Ystradenni Powys.......68 C2
Llanddoged Conwy.......109 M8
Llanddona IoA...............109 H5
Llanddowror Carmth.......50 B3
Llanddulas Conwy........110 C6
Llanddwywe Gwynd........95 K7
Llanddyfnan IoA............109 G5
Llandefaelog-Tre'r-
Graig Powys................53 H3
Llandefalle Powys...........68 C7
Llandegfan IoA..............109 H6
Llandegla Denbgs............97 J3
Llandegley Powys............68 D2
Llandegveth Mons...........37 M2
Llandeilo Carmth.............51 J2
Llandeilo Graban
Powys..............................68 C5
Llandeloy Pembks...........48 E3
Llandenny Mons..............54 B7
Llandevaud Newpt..........38 B3
Llandevenny Mons..........38 B3
Llandinam Powys.............82 B5
Llandissilio Pembks.........49 J3
Llandogo Mons................54 D7
Llandough V Glam..........36 F6
Llandough V Glam..........37 J5
Llandovery Carmth..........67 G7
Llandow V Glam.............36 E5
Llandre Carmth...............66 F6
Llandre Cerdgn................80 E6
Llandre Isaf Pembks.......49 J2
Llandrillo Denbgs............97 G5
Llandrillo-yn-Rhôs
Conwy............................110 B5
Llandrindod Wells
Powys..............................68 B3
Llandrinio Powys.............97 L8
Llandudno Conwy.........109 L5
Llandudno Junction
Conwy............................109 M6
Llandulas Powys..............67 J6
Llandwrog Gwynd...........95 H2
Llandybie Carmth............51 J3
Llandyfaelog Carmth......50 E3
Llandyfriog Cerdgn.........65 K6
Llandygai Gwynd...........109 H7
Llandygwydd Cerdgn......65 H5
Llandyrnog Denbgs.......110 F8
Llandyssil Powys.............82 E4
Llandysul Cerdgn............65 L6
Llanedeyrn Cardif............37 K4
Llaneglwys Powys...........68 B6
Llanegryn Gwynd............80 D3
Llanegwad Carmth..........51 G2
Llaneilian IoA................108 F7
Llanelian-yn-Rhôs
Conwy............................110 B6
Llanelidan Denbgs...........97 H3
Llanelieu Powys...............68 D7
Llanellen Mons................53 L5
Llanelli Carmth................51 G5
Llanelltyd Gwynd............96 A8
Llanelwedd Powys...........68 B4
Llanenddwyn Gwynd.......95 K7
Llanengan Gwynd............94 E6
Llanerchymedd IoA.......108 E5
Llanerfyl Powys...............82 B2
Llanfachraeth IoA.........108 D5
Llanfachreth Gwynd........96 B7
Llanfaelog IoA...............108 D6
Llanfaelrhys Gwynd.........94 D6
Llanfaethlu IoA..............108 D4

Llanfair Gwynd................95 K6
Llanfair Caereinion
Powys..............................82 C3
Llanfair Clydogau
Cerdgn.............................66 E4
Llanfair Dyffryn
Clwyd Denbgs..............97 H2
Llanfairfechan
Conwy............................109 K6
Llanfairpwllgwyngyll
IoA................................109 G6
Llanfair Talhaiarn
Conwy............................110 C7
Llanfair Waterdine
Shrops.............................82 E7
Llanfairynghornwy
IoA................................108 D4
Llanfair-yn-
Neubwll IoA...............108 C6
Llanfallteg Carmth..........49 K4
Llanfallteg West
Carmth.............................49 K4
Llanfarian Cerdgn............80 D7
Llanfechain Powys...........97 J7
Llanfechell IoA...............108 E3
Llanferres Denbgs...........97 J1
Llan Ffestiniog
Gwynd..............................96 A4
Llanfihangel-ar-
arth Carmth................66 B6
Llanfihangel Glyn
Myfyr Conwy...............96 F3
Llanfihangel Nant
Bran Powys.................67 K7
Llanfihangel
Rhydithon Powys........68 D2
Llanfihangel Rogiet
Mons...............................38 C3
Llanfihangel-y-
Creuddyn Cerdgn.......80 F7
Llanfihangel-yng-
Ngwynfa Powys..........82 C1
Llanfihangel yn
Nhowyn IoA..............108 D6
Llanfilo Powys.................53 H2
Llanfoist Mons................53 L5
Llanfor Gwynd.................96 E5
Llanfrechfa Torfn............37 L2
Llanfrynach Powys...........53 G3
Llanfwrog Denbgs............97 H2
Llanfwrog IoA................108 C5
Llanfyllin Powys..............97 H8
Llanfynydd Carmth..........66 D8
Llanfynydd Flints............97 L2
Llanfyrnach Pembks........49 L2
Llangadfan Powys............81 L2
Llangadog Carmth............66 F8
Llangadwaladr IoA.......108 E7
Llangaffo IoA.................108 F7
Llangammarch
Wells Powys................67 K5
Llangan V Glam...............36 F5
Llangarron Herefs...........54 D4
Llangathen Carmth..........51 H2
Llangattock Powys...........53 K4
Llangattock
Lingoed Mons.............54 A4
Llangedwyn Powys...........97 J7
Llangefni IoA.................108 F6
Llangeinor Brdgnd..........36 E3
Llangeitho Cerdgn...........66 E3
Llangeler Carmth.............65 L6
Llangelynin Gwynd..........80 D3
Llangennech Carmth........51 H5
Llangennith Swans..........50 E7
Llangenny Powys..............53 K4
Llangernyw Conwy.........110 B7
Llangian Gwynd...............94 E6
Llangloffan Pembks.........64 C7
Llanglydwen Carmth........49 K3
Llangoed IoA.................109 J5
Llangollen Denbgs...........97 K4
Llangolman Pembks.........49 J3
Llangors Powys................53 H3
Llangower Gwynd............96 D6
Llangranog Cerdgn..........65 K4
Llangristiolus IoA..........108 F6
Llangrove Herefs.............54 D4
Llangunllo Powys..............68 E1

Llangunnor Carmth	50 E2
Llangurig Powys	81 K7
Llangwm Conwy	96 F4
Llangwm Mons	54 B7
Llangwm Pembks	49 G5
Llangwnnadl Gwynd	94 D6
Llangwyryfon Cerdgn	66 D1
Llangybi Cerdgn	66 E4
Llangybi Gwynd	95 G4
Llangybi Mons	38 A2
Llangyndeyrn Carmth	50 F3
Llangynhafal Denbgs	110 F8
Llangynidr Powys	53 J4
Llangynin Carmth	50 B2
Llangynog Carmth	50 D3
Llangynog Powys	97 G7
Llangynwyd Brdgnd	36 D3
Llanhamlach Powys	53 H3
Llanharan Rhondd	36 F4
Llanharry Rhondd	36 F4
Llanhennock Mons	38 A2
Llanhilleth Blae G	53 K7
Llanidloes Powys	81 K6
Llaniestyn Gwynd	94 E5
Llanigon Powys	68 E6
Llanilar Cerdgn	80 E8
Llanilid Rhondd	36 F4
Llanina Cerdgn	65 L3
Llanishen Cardif	37 J4
Llanishen Mons	54 C7
Llanllechid Gwynd	109 J7
Llanllowell Mons	54 B7
Llanllugan Powys	82 B3
Llanllwch Carmth	50 E2
Llanllwchaiarn Powys	82 C5
Llanllwni Carmth	66 C6
Llanllyfni Gwynd	95 H3
Llanmadoc Swans	50 F6
Llanmaes V Glam	36 F6
Llanmartin Newpt	38 B3
Llanmiloe Carmth	50 B4
Llannefydd Conwy	110 D7
Llannon Carmth	51 G4
Llannor Gwynd	94 F5
Llanon Cerdgn	66 C2
Llanover Mons	53 L6
Llanpumsaint Carmth	65 L8
Llanrhaeadr-ym-Mochnant Powys	97 H7
Llanrhian Pembks	48 D2
Llanrhidian Swans	50 F6
Llanrhychwyn Conwy	96 B1
Llanrhyddlad IoA	108 D4
Llanrhystud Cerdgn	66 C1
Llanrug Gwynd	109 G8
Llanrumney Cardif	37 K4
Llanrwst Conwy	96 C1
Llansadurnen Carmth	50 C4
Llansadwrn Carmth	66 F7
Llansadwrn IoA	109 H6
Llansaint Carmth	50 E4
Llansamlet Swans	51 K6
Llansanffraid Glan Conwy Conwy	110 A6
Llansannan Conwy	110 C7
Llansantffraed Powys	53 H4
Llansantffraed-Cwmdeuddwr Powys	67 L2
Llansantffraid-in-Elvel Powys	68 C4
Llansantffraid Cerdgn	66 C2
Llansantffraid-ym-Mechain Powys	97 K7
Llansawel Carmth	66 E7
Llansilin Powys	97 K6
Llansoy Mons	54 C7
Llanspyddid Powys	52 F3
Llanstadwell Pembks	48 F6
Llansteffan Carmth	50 D4
Llantarnam Torfn	37 L2
Llanteg Pembks	49 K5
Llanthewy Skirrid Mons	53 M5
Llanthony Mons	53 L3
Llantilio-Crossenny Mons	54 B5
Llantilio Pertholey Mons	53 L5
Llantrisant Mons	38 B2
Llantrisant Rhondd	37 G4
Llantrithyd V Glam	37 G6
Llantwit Fardre Rhondd	37 G4
Llantwit Major V Glam	36 F6
Llanuwchllyn Gwynd	96 D6
Llanvaches Newpt	38 B3
Llanvair Discoed Mons	38 C3
Llanvapley Mons	54 A5
Llanvetherine Mons	54 A5
Llanvihangel Crucorney Mons	53 L4
Llanwddyn Powys	96 F8
Llanwenog Cerdgn	66 C5
Llanwern Newpt	38 A3
Llanwinio Carmth	50 C1
Llanwnda Gwynd	95 H2
Llanwnda Pembks	64 C6
Llanwnnen Cerdgn	66 C5
Llanwnog Powys	82 B5
Llanwrda Carmth	66 F7
Llanwrin Powys	81 H3
Llanwrthwl Powys	67 L2
Llanwrtyd Wells Powys	67 J5
Llanwyddelan Powys	82 C4
Llanyblodwel Shrops	97 K7
Llanybri Carmth	50 D3
Llanybydder Carmth	66 C5
Llanycefn Pembks	49 J3
Llanychaer Pembks	64 D7
Llanymawddwy Gwynd	96 D8
Llanymynech Powys	97 K7
Llanynghenedl IoA	108 D5
Llanynys Denbgs	110 F8
Llanyre Powys	68 B3
Llanystumdwy Gwynd	95 H5
Llanywern Powys	53 H3
Llawhaden Pembks	49 H4
Llawryglyn Powys	81 K5
Llay Wrexhm	97 M2
Llechrhyd Caerph	53 H6
Llechryd Cerdgn	65 H5
Lledrod Cerdgn	66 E1
Llithfaen Gwynd	94 F4
Lloc Flints	111 G6
Llowes Powys	68 D6
Llwydcoed Rhondd	52 F6
Llwydiarth Powys	82 B1
Llwyncelyn Cerdgn	66 C3
Llwyndafydd Cerdgn	65 K4
Llwyngwril Gwynd	80 D2
Llwynmawr Wrexhm	97 K5
Llwynypia Rhondd	36 F2
Llynclys Shrops	97 L7
Llynfaes IoA	108 E5
Llŷn Peninsula Gwynd	94 E5
Llysfaen Conwy	110 B6
Llyswen Powys	68 C6
Llysworney V Glam	36 E5
Llys-y-frân Pembks	49 H3
Llywel Powys	52 D3
Loan Border	176 C3
Loanhead Mdloth	177 J5
Loaningfoot D & G	147 G4
Loans S Ayrs	163 J3
Lobhillcross Devon	10 C7
Lochailort Highld	200 B8
Lochaline Highld	190 D7
Lochans D & G	144 C4
Locharbriggs D & G	155 H6
Lochavich Ag & B	182 D4
Lochawe Ag & B	183 G2
Loch Baghasdail W Isls	233 c8
Lochboisdale W Isls	233 c8
Lochbuie Ag & B	181 J3
Lochcarron Highld	210 D6
Lochdon Ag & B	181 L2
Lochdonhead Ag & B	181 L2
Lochead Ag & B	172 D3
Lochearnhead Stirlg	184 D3
Lochee C Dund	186 F2
Loch Eil Highld	191 L2
Locheilside Station Highld	191 K1
Lochend Highld	212 F6
Locheport W Isls	233 c6
Loch Euphort W Isls	233 c6
Lochfoot D & G	154 F7
Lochgair Ag & B	172 F1
Lochgelly Fife	186 C8
Lochgilphead Ag & B	172 E2
Lochgoilhead Ag & B	183 H6
Lochieheads Fife	186 D5
Lochill Moray	215 G2
Lochindorb Lodge Highld	214 B7
Lochinver Highld	224 D4
Loch Lomond and The Trossachs National Park	184 A5
Loch Loyal Lodge Highld	229 J6
Lochluichart Highld	211 L2
Lochmaben D & G	155 J5
Lochmaddy W Isls	233 c6
Loch nam Madadh W Isls	233 c6
Loch Ness Highld	202 E1
Lochore Fife	186 C7
Loch Portain W Isls	233 c6
Lochranza N Ayrs	172 F7
Loch Sgioport W Isls	233 c7
Lochside Abers	197 H4
Lochside D & G	155 G6
Lochside Highld	213 J4
Lochskipport W Isls	233 c7
Lochslin Highld	223 J5
Lochton S Ayrs	152 F6
Lochty Angus	196 E4
Lochty Fife	187 H5
Lochuisge Highld	190 F5
Lochwinnoch Rens	174 C6
Lochwood D & G	155 J3
Lockengate Cnwll	5 G4
Lockerbie D & G	155 K5
Lockeridge Wilts	40 C6
Lockerley Hants	28 F6
Locking N Som	38 A8
Locking Stumps Warrtn	112 F3
Lockington E R Yk	126 B2
Lockleywood Shrops	99 G6
Locksbottom Gt Lon	45 H6
Locks Heath Hants	17 G2
Lockton N York	134 C2
Loddington Leics	87 L3
Loddington Nhants	88 B7
Loddiswell Devon	7 G6
Loddon Norfk	93 H4
Lode Cambs	76 D3
Lode Heath Solhll	85 L7
Loders Dorset	13 L4
Lodsworth W Susx	30 F6
Lofthouse Leeds	123 L5
Lofthouse N York	131 L5
Lofthouse Gate Wakefd	123 L5
Loftus R & Cl	142 F4
Logan E Ayrs	164 C5
Loganlea W Loth	176 C6
Loggerheads Staffs	99 G5
Logie Angus	197 H4
Logie Fife	186 F4
Logie Moray	214 C4
Logie Coldstone Abers	205 K4
Logie Newton Abers	216 C6
Logie Pert Angus	197 G4
Logierait P & K	194 F6
Logierieve Abers	217 H8
Login Carmth	49 K3
Lolworth Cambs	75 L2
Lonbain Highld	209 L4
Londesborough E R Yk	125 K2
London Gt Lon	45 G4
London Apprentice Cnwll	4 F6
London Ashford Airport Kent	21 L2
London City Airport Gt Lon	45 H4
London Colney Herts	59 K7
Londonderry N York	132 D2
London Gateway Services Gt Lon	44 D2
London Gatwick Airport W Susx	32 B5
London Heathrow Airport Gt Lon	43 H5
London Luton Airport Luton	59 J4
London Oxford Airport Oxon	57 J5
London Southend Airport Essex	46 E3
London Stansted Airport Essex	60 E4
Londonthorpe Lincs	102 F5
London Zoo ZSL Gt Lon	44 F4
Londubh Highld	219 K5
Lonemore Highld	219 J6
Long Ashton N Som	38 D6
Long Bank Worcs	84 D8
Long Bennington Lincs	102 D4
Longbenton N Tyne	151 G2
Longborough Gloucs	56 D3
Long Bredy Dorset	14 B4
Longbridge Birm	85 J6
Longbridge Deverill Wilts	27 K4
Long Buckby Nhants	73 J2
Longburton Dorset	26 F8
Long Clawson Leics	102 B6
Longcliffe Derbys	100 E2
Longcombe Devon	7 J4
Long Compton Staffs	99 J7
Long Compton Warwks	56 F2
Longcot Oxon	40 F3
Long Crendon Bucks	58 B6
Long Crichel Dorset	15 J1
Longden Shrops	83 J3
Long Ditton Surrey	44 D6
Longdon Staffs	85 J2
Longdon Worcs	70 E7
Longdon Green Staffs	85 J2
Longdon upon Tern Wrekin	84 B1
Longdown Devon	11 K6
Longdowns Cnwll	3 J4
Long Duckmanton Derbys	115 H7
Long Eaton Derbys	101 J5
Longfield Kent	45 L6
Longford Covtry	86 D6
Longford Derbys	100 E5
Longford Gloucs	55 J4
Longford Shrops	98 F5
Longford Wrekin	99 G8
Longforgan P & K	186 E2
Longformacus Border	178 E6
Longframlington Nthumb	158 E3
Long Green Ches W	112 C7
Longham Dorset	15 K3
Longham Norfk	91 L1
Long Hanborough Oxon	57 H5
Longhaven Abers	217 L6
Longhirst Nthumb	158 F4
Longhope Gloucs	55 G4
Longhope Ork	234 b7
Longhorsley Nthumb	158 E4
Longhoughton Nthumb	169 J6

Long Itchington
Warwks.................**72** E2
Longlane Derbys..........**100** E5
Long Lawford
Warwks..................**86** F7
Longleat Wilts.................**27** J3
Longlevens Gloucs........**55** J4
Longleys P & K..............**195** L7
Long Load Somset..........**26** C6
Longmanhill Abers.......**216** E2
Long Marston Herts.......**58** E5
Long Marston N York....**124** D1
Long Marston
Warwks...................**71** L5
Long Marton Cumb.......**138** F3
Long Melford Suffk.........**77** J5
Longmoor Camp
Hants.....................**30** C5
Longmorn Moray...........**214** F3
Longmoss Ches E............**113** K6
Long Newnton
Gloucs....................**39** K3
Longnewton Border......**167** J4
Long Newton N Loth.....**178** B5
Longnewton S on T........**141** J4
Longney Gloucs..............**55** H5
Longniddry E Loth........**177** L3
Longnor Shrops............**83** J4
Longnor Staffs..............**114** C8
Longparish Hants............**29** H3
Long Preston N York.....**130** F7
Longridge Lancs.............**121** J3
Longridge W Loth.........**176** C5
Longriggend N Lans......**175** L4
Long Riston E R Yk......**126** E3
Longrock Cnwll.................**2** E5
Longsdon Staffs.............**99** L2
Longside Abers.............**217** K5
Longstanton Cambs......**76** B2
Longstock Hants.............**29** G4
Longstowe Cambs..........**75** K4
Long Stratton Norfk.....**92** E5
Long Street M Keyn......**74** B5
Longstreet Wilts............**28** C2
Long Sutton Hants.........**30** C3
Long Sutton Lincs.........**104** C7
Long Sutton Somset.......**26** C6
Longthorpe C Pete........**89** H4
Long Thurlow Suffk......**78** B2
Longthwaite Cumb.......**138** B3
Longton Lancs...............**121** G5
Longtown Cumb............**148** C2
Longtown Herefs...........**53** L3
Longueville Jersey........**236** d7
Longville in the
Dale Shrops..............**83** K5
Long Waste Wrekin.......**84** B1
Long Whatton Leics.....**101** J7
Longwick Bucks.............**58** C6
Long Wittenham
Oxon.......................**41** K2
Longwitton Nthumb.....**158** D4
Longwood D & G..........**146** C3
Longworth Oxon............**57** G7
Longyester E Loth.........**178** C5
Lonmay Abers...............**217** J3
Lonmore Highld............**208** D5
Looe Cnwll........................**5** K5
Loose Kent......................**33** K3
Loosley Row Bucks........**58** D7
Lootcherbrae Abers....**216** C4
Lopen Somset..................**26** B8
Loppington Shrops.........**98** C6
Lordshill C Sotn..............**29** H7
Lords Wood Medway......**46** C7
Lornty P & K...................**195** J6
Loscoe Derbys................**101** H3
Losgaintir W Isls...........**232** d4
Lossiemouth Moray......**214** F1
Lostock Gralam
Ches W....................**113** G6
Lostock Green
Ches W....................**113** G6
Lostwithiel Cnwll..............**5** H4
Lothbeg Highld..............**227** G6
Lothersdale N York......**122** E2
Lothmore Highld...........**227** G6
Loudwater Bucks...........**42** E3

Loudwater Herts.............**43** H2
Loughborough Leics.....**101** K8
Loughor Swans...............**51** H6
Loughton Essex..............**45** H2
Loughton M Keyn..........**74** B6
Lound Lincs....................**103** H8
Lound Notts...................**116** B4
Lound Suffk.....................**93** K4
Lount Leics.....................**101** G8
Louth Lincs....................**118** D4
Lover Wilts......................**28** E7
Loversall Donc...............**115** L2
Loveston Pembks............**49** J5
Lovington Somset...........**26** E5
Low Ackworth
Wakefd...................**124** C6
Low Barbeth D & G.......**144** B2
Low Bentham
N York...................**130** C5
Low Biggins Cumb.......**130** B4
Low Borrowbridge
Cumb......................**138** E6
Low Bradfield Sheff......**114** E3
Low Bradley N York.....**122** F2
Low Burnham N Linc....**116** C2
Lowca Cumb....................**136** D3
Low Catton E R Yk.......**133** L8
Low Crosby Cumb.........**148** D3
Lowdham Notts.............**102** A3
Low Dinsdale Darltn....**141** J5
Lower Aisholt
Somset....................**25** J4
Lower Ansty Dorset........**14** E2
Lower Apperley
Gloucs.....................**55** J3
Lower Arboll Highld....**223** J5
Lower Ashton Devon......**11** J7
Lower Assendon
Oxon.......................**42** C4
Lower Badcall
Highld....................**228** B6
Lower Bartle Lancs.......**121** G4
Lower Basildon
W Berk....................**41** L5
Lower Beeding
W Susx.....................**31** L6
Lower Benefield
Nhants.....................**88** E5
Lower Bentley Worcs.....**71** H2
Lower Boddington
Nhants.....................**72** F4
Lower Bourne Surrey......**30** D3
Lower Brailes
Warwks....................**72** C6
Lower Breakish
Highld....................**199** L2
Lower Broadheath
Worcs......................**70** E1
Lower Broxwood
Herefs......................**69** G4
Lower Bullingham
Herefs......................**69** K6
Lower Burgate Hants......**28** D7
Lower Caldecote
C Beds......................**75** H5
Lower Chapel Powys.....**68** B7
Lower Chicksgrove
Wilts........................**27** L5
Lower Chute Wilts..........**28** F2
Lower Clapton
Gt Lon.....................**45** G3
Lower Clent Worcs.........**85** G7
Lower
Cumberworth
Kirk........................**123** J8
Lower Darwen
Bl w D.....................**121** K5
Lower Dean Bed.............**74** F2
Lower Diabaig
Highld....................**210** C3
Lower Dicker E Susx......**20** B4
Lower Down Shrops........**83** G6
Lower Dunsforth
N York...................**133** G6
Lower Egleton
Herefs......................**70** B5
Lower End M Keyn........**74** D6
Lower Eythorne Kent....**35** H5

Lower Failand N Som....**38** D5
Lower Farringdon
Hants......................**30** B4
Lower Feltham
Gt Lon....................**43** H6
Lower Froyle Hants........**30** C3
Lower Gabwell
Devon........................**7** L2
Lower Gledfield
Highld....................**222** D4
Lower Godney
Somset....................**26** C3
Lower Gornal Dudley....**85** G5
Lower Gravenhurst
C Beds......................**75** G7
Lower Green Kent...........**32** F5
Lower Green Kent...........**33** G5
Lower Halstow Kent.......**46** E6
Lower Hamworthy
BCP..........................**15** J4
Lower Hardres Kent........**34** F4
Lower Hartwell
Bucks.......................**58** C5
Lower Hergest
Herefs......................**68** F4
Lower Heyford Oxon......**57** J3
Lower Heysham
Lancs.....................**129** J7
Lower Houses Kirk.......**123** H7
Lower Irlam Salfd.........**113** G3
Lower Killeyan
Ag & B...................**160** A2
Lower Langford
N Som......................**38** C7
Lower Largo Fife..........**187** G6
Lower Leigh Staffs........**100** A5
Lower Loxhore
Devon.......................**23** K4
Lower Lydbrook
Gloucs......................**54** E5
Lower Lye Herefs............**69** H2
Lower Machen
Newpt.......................**37** K3
Lower Merridge
Somset....................**25** J4
Lower Middleton
Cheney Nhants..........**73** G6
Lower Moor Worcs.........**71** H5
Lower Morton S Glos......**38** F3
Lower Nazeing Essex.....**60** C6
Lower Oddington
Gloucs......................**56** E3
Lower Penarth
V Glam.....................**37** J6
Lower Penn Staffs..........**84** F4
Lower Peover
Ches E......................**113** H6
Lower Place Rochdl......**122** D7
Lower Quinton
Warwks....................**71** L5
Lower Raydon Suffk......**78** C6
Lower Roadwater
Somset....................**25** G4
Lower Seagry Wilts........**39** L4
Lower Shelton
C Beds......................**74** E6
Lower Shiplake Oxon....**42** C4
Lower Shuckburgh
Warwks....................**72** F3
Lower Slaughter
Gloucs......................**56** D4
Lower Standen Kent......**35** H6
Lower Stanton St
Quintin Wilts...........**39** L4
Lower Stoke Medway......**46** D5
Lower Stondon
C Beds......................**75** H7
Lower Stone Gloucs......**38** F2
Lower Stow Bedon
Norfk.......................**91** L5
Lower Street Norfk.......**106** F5
Lower Street Suffk.........**78** D4
Lower Swanwick
Hants.......................**16** F1
Lower Swell Gloucs.......**56** D3
Lower Tasburgh
Norfk.......................**92** E4
Lower Tean Staffs.........**100** A5

Lower Town Devon...........**7** G2
Lower Town Pembks......**64** D6
Lower Upham Hants.......**29** K7
Lower Weare Somset.......**26** B2
Lower Welson Herefs......**68** F4
Lower Westmancote
Worcs......................**71** G6
Lower Whatley
Somset....................**27** H3
Lower Whitley
Ches W...................**112** E5
Lower Wield Hants..........**29** M4
Lower Willingdon
E Susx.....................**20** C5
Lower Withington
Ches E.....................**113** J7
Lower Woodford
Wilts........................**28** C4
Lower Wraxall
Dorset......................**14** B3
Lowesby Leics.................**87** K3
Lowestoft Suffk...............**93** L5
Loweswater Cumb........**137** G3
Low Etherley Dur.........**140** F2
Low Fell Gatesd...........**151** G3
Lowfield Heath
W Susx.....................**31** L4
Low Gartachorrans
Stirlg.....................**174** E2
Low Grantley N York....**132** C5
Low Ham Somset............**26** B5
Low Harrogate
N York...................**132** D7
Low Hesket Cumb.........**148** E5
Low Hutton N York.......**134** B6
Lowick Nhants................**88** E7
Lowick Nthumb.............**168** F2
Lowick Green Cumb.....**129** G3
Low Lorton Cumb.........**137** G3
Low Marnham
Notts......................**116** D7
Low Mill N York............**142** E7
Low Moorsley
Sundld...................**151** H5
Low Moresby Cumb......**136** D3
Low Newton Cumb........**129** J3
Low Row Cumb..............**149** G3
Low Row N York...........**140** B7
Low Salchrie D & G......**144** B2
Low Santon N Linc........**125** L7
Lowsonford Warwks.......**71** L2
Low Tharston Norfk......**92** E4
Lowther Cumb...............**138** D3
Lowthorpe E R Yk.........**135** G7
Lowton Somset................**25** J7
Lowton Common
Wigan.....................**112** F3
Low Torry Fife..............**176** D2
Low Worsall N York......**141** J5
Low Wray Cumb.............**137** K6
Loxbeare Devon..............**11** L2
Loxhill Surrey.................**31** G4
Loxhore Devon................**23** K4
Loxley Warwks................**72** C4
Loxton N Som.................**26** A1
Loxwood W Susx.............**31** H5
Lubenham Leics..............**87** K6
Luccombe Somset...........**24** E3
Luccombe Village
IoW...........................**17** H6
Lucker Nthumb..............**169** H4
Luckett Cnwll....................**6** B2
Lucking Street Essex......**77** J7
Luckington Wilts............**39** J4
Lucklawhill Fife............**187** G3
Luckwell Bridge
Somset....................**24** E4
Lucton Herefs..................**69** J2
Ludag W Isls..................**233** b9
Ludborough Lincs.........**118** D3
Ludbrook Devon................**6** F5
Ludchurch Pembks.........**49** K5
Luddenden Calder.........**122** F5
Luddenden Foot
Calder....................**122** F5
Luddesdown Kent...........**46** A6
Luddington N Linc........**125** J7
Luddington Warwks.......**71** L4

Luddington in the
  Brook Nhants 89 G6
Ludford Lincs 117 K4
Ludford Shrops 83 K8
Ludgershall Bucks 58 A4
Ludgershall Wilts 28 E2
Ludgvan Cnwll 2 E5
Ludham Norfk 107 H8
Ludlow Shrops 83 K7
Ludney Somset 26 B8
Ludwell Wilts 27 K6
Ludworth Dur 151 J6
Luffness E Loth 178 B3
Lugar E Ayrs 164 C5
Luggate Burn E Loth 178 D4
Luggiebank N Lans 175 K4
Lugton E Ayrs 174 D7
Lugwardine Herefs 69 K6
Luib Highld 209 J8
Luing Ag & B 181 L5
Lulham Herefs 69 H6
Lullington Derbys 86 B2
Lullington Somset 27 H2
Lulsgate Bottom
  N Som 38 D7
Lulsley Worcs 70 D4
Lumb Calder 122 F6
Lumby N York 124 D4
Lumphanan Abers 206 B4
Lumphinnans Fife 186 C8
Lumsden Abers 205 K2
Lunan Angus 197 H6
Lunanhead Angus 196 D6
Luncarty P & K 186 A2
Lund E R Yk 126 B2
Lund N York 125 G4
Lundie Angus 186 E1
Lundin Links Fife 187 G6
Lundin Mill Fife 187 G6
Lundy Devon 22 B3
Lunga Ag & B 181 L5
Lunna Shet 235 d4
Lunsford Kent 33 J2
Lunsford's Cross
  E Susx 20 E4
Lunt Sefton 111 K2
Luppitt Devon 12 F2
Lupset Wakefd 123 L6
Lupton Cumb 129 L4
Lurgashall W Susx 30 F6
Lurley Devon 11 L2
Luscombe Devon 7 J4
Luskentyre W Isls 232 d4
Luss Ag & B 183 L8
Lussagiven Ag & B 171 L2
Lusta Highld 208 D3
Lustleigh Devon 11 H8
Luston Herefs 69 J2
Luthermuir Abers 197 G3
Luthrie Fife 186 E4
Luton Devon 7 K1
Luton Devon 12 D2
Luton Luton 59 H4
Luton Medway 46 C6
Luton Airport Luton 59 J4
Lutterworth Leics 87 G6
Lutton Devon 6 E4
Lutton Devon 7 G4
Lutton Lincs 104 C7
Lutton Nhants 89 G6
Luxborough Somset 24 F4
Luxulyan Cnwll 5 G4
Luxulyan Valley Cnwll 5 G4
Lybster Highld 231 J7
Lydbury North
  Shrops 83 G6
Lydd Kent 21 K2
Lydd Airport Kent 21 L2
Lydden Kent 35 H5
Lydden Kent 35 K2
Lyddington Rutlnd 88 C4
Lydeard St
  Lawrence Somset 25 H5
Lyde Green S Glos 39 G5
Lydford Devon 10 D7
Lydford on Fosse
  Somset 26 E5
Lydgate Calder 122 D5

Lydham Shrops 83 G5
Lydiard Millicent
  Wilts 40 C3
Lydiard Tregoze
  Swindn 40 C4
Lydiate Sefton 111 K2
Lydiate Ash Worcs 85 H7
Lydlinch Dorset 27 H8
Lydney Gloucs 54 F7
Lydstep Pembks 49 J7
Lye Dudley 85 G6
Lye Green E Susx 32 F6
Lye Green Warwks 71 L2
Lye's Green Wilts 27 J3
Lyford Oxon 41 H2
Lymbridge Green
  Kent 34 F6
Lyme Regis Dorset 13 J4
Lyminge Kent 34 F6
Lymington Hants 16 C4
Lyminster W Susx 18 D5
Lymm Warrtn 113 G4
Lymm Services
  Warrtn 112 F4
Lympne Kent 34 F7
Lympsham Somset 25 M1
Lympstone Devon 12 C5
Lynchat Highld 203 J5
Lynch Green Norfk 92 D3
Lyndhurst Hants 16 C2
Lyndon Rutlnd 88 C3
Lyndon Green Birm 85 K6
Lyne Border 166 B2
Lyne Surrey 43 G7
Lyneal Shrops 98 C6
Lyneham Oxon 56 F4
Lyneham Wilts 40 A5
Lynemouth Nthumb 159 H4
Lyne of Skene Abers 206 E4
Lyness Ork 234 b7
Lyng Norfk 106 C8
Lyng Somset 25 M5
Lynmouth Devon 23 L2
Lynsted Kent 34 C3
Lynton Devon 23 L2
Lyon's Gate Dorset 14 C2
Lyonshall Herefs 69 G4
Lytchett Matravers
  Dorset 15 H4
Lytchett Minster
  Dorset 15 H4
Lyth Highld 231 K3
Lytham Lancs 120 E5
Lytham St Annes
  Lancs 120 D5
Lythe N York 143 H5
Lythmore Highld 230 F3

M

Maaruig W Isls 232 e4
Mabe Burnthouse
  Cnwll 3 K4
Mablethorpe Lincs 119 G4
Macclesfield Ches E 113 K6
Macduff Abers 216 D2
Macharioch Ag & B 161 J7
Machen Caerph 37 K3
Machrie N Ayrs 162 A3
Machrihanish Ag & B 161 G5
Machrins Ag & B 180 E8
Machroes Gwynd 94 F7
Machynlleth Powys 81 G4
Machynys Carmth 51 G5
Mackworth Derbys 100 F5
Macmerry E Loth 177 L4
Madderty P & K 185 K3
Maddiston Falk 176 C3
Madeley Staffs 99 H4
Madeley Wrekin 84 C3
Madingley Cambs 76 B3
Madley Herefs 69 H6
Madresfield Worcs 70 E5
Madron Cnwll 2 E5
Maenclochog
  Pembks 49 J3

Maendy V Glam 36 F5
Maentwrog Gwynd 95 L4
Maen-y-groes
  Cerdgn 65 L3
Maer Staffs 99 H5
Maerdy Conwy 96 F4
Maerdy Rhondd 36 F2
Maesbrook Shrops 97 L7
Maesbury Shrops 97 L7
Maesbury Marsh
  Shrops 97 L7
Maesllyn Cerdgn 65 K5
Maesteg Brdgnd 36 D3
Maesybont Carmth 51 H3
Maesycwmmer
  Caerph 37 J2
Maggieknockater
  Moray 215 H5
Magham Down
  E Susx 20 C4
Maghull Sefton 111 K2
Magna Park Leics 87 G6
Magor Mons 38 B3
Magor Services
  Mons 38 B3
Maidenbower W Susx 32 B6
Maiden Bradley Wilts 27 J4
Maidencombe Torbay 7 L3
Maidenhayne Devon 13 H4
Maiden Head N Som 38 E6
Maidenhead W & M 42 E4
Maiden Newton
  Dorset 14 B3
Maidens S Ayrs 163 G7
Maiden's Green
  Br For 42 E5
Maiden Wells
  Pembks 49 G7
Maidford Nhants 73 H4
Maids Moreton
  Bucks 73 K7
Maidstone Kent 33 K3
Maidstone Services
  Kent 33 L3
Maidwell Nhants 87 L7
Mail Shet 235 d6
Maindee Newpt 37 L3
Mainland Ork 234 c6
Mainland Shet 235 c5
Mainsforth Dur 141 H2
Mains of Balhall
  Angus 196 E4
Mains of
  Balnakettle
  Abers 197 G2
Mains of Dalvey
  Highld 214 D7
Mains of Haulkerton
  Abers 197 H2
Mains of Lesmoir
  Abers 215 K8
Mains of Melgunds
  Angus 196 E5
Mainsriddle D & G 147 G4
Mainstone Shrops 82 F6
Maisemore Gloucs 55 J4
Major's Green Worcs 85 K7
Malborough Devon 7 G7
Maldon Essex 61 K6
Malham N York 131 G6
Maligar Highld 209 G2
Mallaig Highld 199 L6
Mallaigvaig Highld 199 L5
Malleny Mills
  C Edin 177 G5
Malltraeth IoA 108 E7
Mallwyd Gwynd 81 J2
Malmesbury Wilts 39 L3
Malmsmead Devon 24 C2
Malpas Ches W 98 C3
Malpas Cnwll 4 D7
Malpas Newpt 37 L3
Maltby Rothm 115 K3
Maltby S on T 141 L4
Maltby le Marsh
  Lincs 118 F5
Maltman's Hill Kent 34 B6
Malton N York 134 C5

Malvern Worcs 70 D5
Malvern Hills 70 D5
Malvern Link Worcs 70 E5
Malvern Wells Worcs 70 D6
Mamble Worcs 70 C1
Mamhilad Mons 53 L7
Manaccan Cnwll 3 K6
Manafon Powys 82 C3
Mànais W Isls 232 d5
Manaton Devon 11 H8
Manby Lincs 118 E4
Mancetter Warwks 86 D4
Manchester Manch 113 J3
Manchester Airport
  Manch 113 J5
Mancot Flints 111 K7
Mandally Highld 201 L5
Manea Cambs 90 C5
Maney Birm 85 K4
Manfield N York 140 F4
Mangersta W Isls 232 d2
Mangotsfield S Glos 38 F5
Mangurstadh W Isls 232 d2
Manish W Isls 232 d5
Manley Ches W 112 D7
Manmoel Caerph 53 J7
Mannal Ag & B 188 C7
Manningford
  Bohune Wilts 40 C8
Manningford Bruce
  Wilts 40 C8
Manningham C Brad 123 H4
Mannings Heath
  W Susx 31 K5
Mannington Dorset 15 K2
Manningtree Essex 62 D2
Mannofield C Aber 207 H4
Manorbier Pembks 49 H7
Manorbier Newton
  Pembks 49 H7
Manorhill Border 167 K3
Manorowen Pembks 64 C7
Manor Park Gt Lon 45 H3
Mansell Gamage
  Herefs 69 H5
Mansell Lacy Herefs 69 H5
Mansfield E Ayrs 164 C6
Mansfield Notts 101 K1
Mansfield
  Woodhouse
  Notts 115 K8
Manston Dorset 27 J7
Manston Kent 35 J2
Manston Leeds 124 B4
Manswood Dorset 15 J2
Manthorpe Lincs 88 F1
Manton N Linc 116 F2
Manton Rutlnd 88 C3
Manton Wilts 40 D6
Manuden Essex 60 D3
Maperton Somset 26 F6
Maplebeck Notts 102 B1
Mapledurham Oxon 42 A5
Mapledurwell Hants 30 B2
Maplehurst W Susx 31 K6
Maplescombe Kent 45 K7
Mapleton Derbys 100 D3
Mapperley Derbys 101 H4
Mapperley Park
  C Nott 101 L4
Mapperton Dorset 13 L3
Mappleborough
  Green Warwks 71 J2
Mappleton E R Yk 126 F2
Mapplewell Barns 123 L7
Mappowder Dorset 14 E2
Màraig W Isls 232 e4
Marazion Cnwll 2 F5
Marbhig W Isls 232 f3
Marbury Ches E 98 E4
March Cambs 89 B4
March S Lans 165 J6
Marcham Oxon 41 J2
Marchamley Shrops 98 E6
Marchington Staffs 100 C6
Marchwiel Wrexhm 98 A3
Marchwood Hants 16 D1
Marcross V Glam 36 E6

Marden Herefs.....69 K5
Marden Kent.....33 J4
Marden Wilts.....40 C8
Marden Thorn Kent.....33 K5
Mardy Mons.....53 L5
Mareham le Fen
  Lincs.....103 L1
Mareham on the
  Hill Lincs.....118 C7
Marehill W Susx.....18 E3
Maresfield E Susx.....19 M2
Marfleet C KuH.....126 E5
Marford Wrexhm.....98 A2
Margam Neath.....36 B3
Margaret Marsh
  Dorset.....27 J7
Margaretting Essex.....61 G7
Margaretting Tye
  Essex.....61 G7
Margate Kent.....35 K1
Margnaheglish
  N Ayrs.....162 D3
Margrie D & G.....145 M5
Margrove Park
  R & Cl.....142 E4
Marham Norfk.....91 G2
Marhamchurch Cnwll.....9 G4
Marham Park Suffk.....77 J2
Marholm C Pete.....89 G3
Mariansleigh Devon.....24 B6
Marine Town Kent.....46 F5
Marionburgh Abers.....206 D4
Marishader Highld.....209 H2
Maristow Devon.....6 C3
Marjoriebanks D & G.....155 J5
Mark Somset.....26 B2
Markbeech Kent.....32 E5
Markby Lincs.....119 G5
Mark Cross E Susx.....33 G6
Market Bosworth
  Leics.....86 E3
Market Deeping
  Lincs.....89 G2
Market Drayton
  Shrops.....98 F5
Market Harborough
  Leics.....87 K6
Market Lavington
  Wilts.....28 A1
Market Overton
  Rutlnd.....88 C1
Market Rasen Lincs.....117 J4
Market Stainton
  Lincs.....118 B5
Market Warsop Notts..115 K7
Market Weighton
  E R Yk.....125 K3
Market Weston Suffk...92 B7
Markfield Leics.....86 F2
Markham Caerph.....53 J7
Markham Moor
  Notts.....116 B6
Markinch Fife.....186 E6
Markington N York.....132 D6
Markle E Loth.....178 C3
Marksbury BaNES.....38 F7
Marks Tey Essex.....61 L4
Markyate Herts.....59 H5
Marlborough Wilts.....40 D6
Marlcliff Warwks.....71 K4
Marldon Devon.....7 K3
Marlesford Suffk.....79 G3
Marlingford Norfk.....92 D2
Marloes Pembks.....48 D5
Marlow Bucks.....42 D3
Marlow Bottom
  Bucks.....42 D3
Marlpit Hill Kent.....32 D4
Marnhull Dorset.....27 H7
Marple Stockp.....113 L4
Marr Donc.....115 K1
Marrick N York.....140 D7
Marsden Kirk.....122 F7
Marsden S Tyne.....151 J3
Marshalswick Herts...59 K6
Marsham Norfk.....106 E7
Marsh Baldon Oxon...57 K7
Marshborough Kent...35 J3

Marshbrook Shrops.....83 J5
Marshchapel Lincs.....118 E2
Marsh Farm Luton.....59 H3
Marshfield Newpt.....37 K4
Marshfield S Glos.....39 H5
Marshgate Cnwll.....8 F6
Marsh Gibbon Bucks...57 M4
Marsh Green Devon.....12 D4
Marsh Green Kent.....32 D4
Marshland St
  James Norfk.....90 D2
Marsh Lane Derbys.....115 H5
Marsh Street Somset...24 F3
Marshwood Dorset.....13 J3
Marske N York.....140 D6
Marske-by-the-Sea
  R & Cl.....142 D3
Marston Herefs.....69 G3
Marston Lincs.....102 E4
Marston Oxon.....57 K6
Marston Staffs.....99 L6
Marston Wilts.....27 L1
Marston Green Solhll...85 L6
Marston Magna
  Somset.....26 E6
Marston Meysey
  Wilts.....40 C2
Marston
  Montgomery
  Derbys.....100 C5
Marston Moretaine
  C Beds.....74 E6
Marston on Dove
  Derbys.....100 E6
Marston St
  Lawrence Nhants...73 G6
Marston Trussell
  Nhants.....87 K6
Marstow Herefs.....54 D4
Marsworth Bucks.....58 F5
Marten Wilts.....40 F7
Martham Norfk.....107 J8
Martin Hants.....28 B7
Martin Kent.....35 J5
Martin Lincs.....103 J1
Martinhoe Devon.....23 L2
Martin Hussingtree
  Worcs.....70 F7
Martinstown Dorset...14 C5
Martlesham Suffk.....78 F5
Martlesham Heath
  Suffk.....78 F5
Martletwy Pembks.....49 H5
Martley Worcs.....70 D3
Martock Somset.....26 C7
Marton Ches E.....113 J7
Marton E R Yk.....126 F3
Marton Lincs.....116 D5
Marton Middsb.....142 B4
Marton N York.....134 B3
Marton Shrops.....82 F3
Marton Warwks.....72 E2
Marton-cum-
  Grafton N York.....132 F6
Marton-le-Moor
  N York.....132 E5
Martyr Worthy Hants...29 K5
Marvig W Isls.....232 f3
Marwell Zoo Hants.....29 J6
Marwick Ork.....234 b5
Marwood Devon.....23 H4
Marybank Highld.....212 D4
Maryburgh Highld.....212 E3
Marygold Border.....179 G6
Maryhill C Glas.....175 G4
Marykirk Abers.....197 H3
Marylebone Gt Lon...44 F4
Marylebone Wigan...121 H8
Marypark Moray.....214 F6
Maryport Cumb.....147 H7
Maryport D & G.....144 D7
Marystow Devon.....10 C7
Mary Tavy Devon.....6 D1
Maryton Angus.....196 C5
Maryton Angus.....197 H5
Marywell Abers.....206 B6
Marywell Abers.....207 H5
Marywell Angus.....197 G7

Masham N York.....132 C4
Masongill N York.....130 C4
Mastin Moor Derbys...115 J6
Matching Green
  Essex.....60 E5
Matching Tye Essex...60 E5
Matfen Nthumb.....158 C7
Matfield Kent.....33 H5
Mathern Mons.....38 D3
Mathon Herefs.....70 D5
Mathry Pembks.....48 E2
Matlask Norfk.....106 D5
Matlock Derbys.....100 F1
Matlock Bath
  Derbys.....100 F2
Matson Gloucs.....55 J5
Mattersey Notts.....116 B4
Mattingley Hants.....42 B8
Mattishall Norfk.....92 C2
Mattishall Burgh
  Norfk.....92 C2
Mauchline E Ayrs.....163 L4
Maud Abers.....217 H5
Maufant Jersey.....236 d6
Maugersbury Gloucs...56 D3
Maughold IoM.....237 e3
Mauld Highld.....212 C6
Maulden C Beds.....74 F6
Maulds Meaburn
  Cumb.....138 F4
Maunby N York.....132 E3
Maundown Somset.....25 G5
Mautby Norfk.....93 K2
Mavesyn Ridware
  Staffs.....85 J1
Mavis Enderby Lincs...118 E7
Mawbray Cumb.....147 J5
Mawdesley Lancs.....121 G7
Mawdlam Brdgnd.....36 C4
Mawgan Cnwll.....3 J6
Mawgan Porth Cnwll...4 D3
Mawla Cnwll.....3 J3
Mawnan Cnwll.....3 K5
Mawnan Smith Cnwll...3 K5
Mawsley Nhants.....88 B7
Maxey C Pete.....89 G2
Maxstoke Warwks.....86 B6
Maxton Border.....167 J4
Maxton Kent.....35 J6
Maxwelltown D & G...155 G6
Maxworthy Cnwll.....9 H6
May Bank Staffs.....99 J3
Maybole S Ayrs.....163 H7
Maybury Surrey.....43 G8
Mayfield E Susx.....33 G7
Mayfield Mdloth.....177 K5
Mayfield Staffs.....100 D4
Mayford Surrey.....31 G1
May Hill Gloucs.....55 G4
Mayland Essex.....61 L7
Maylandsea Essex.....61 L7
Maynard's Green
  E Susx.....20 C3
Maypole Birm.....85 J7
Maypole Green Norfk...93 J4
Maypole Green Suffk...77 K3
Meadgate BaNES.....39 G8
Meadle Bucks.....58 D6
Meadowfield Dur.....151 G6
Meadwell Devon.....9 K8
Mealabost W Isls.....232 g2
Meanwood Leeds.....123 K3
Meare Somset.....26 C3
Meare Green Somset...25 L6
Meare Green Somset...25 M6
Mearns E Rens.....174 F7
Mears Ashby Nhants....74 B2
Measham Leics.....86 D2
Meath Green Surrey...32 B4
Meathop Cumb.....129 J4
Meavaig W Isls.....232 d2
Meavy Devon.....6 E4
Medbourne Leics.....88 B5
Meddon Devon.....9 H2
Meden Vale Notts.....115 L7
Medmenham Bucks...42 D4
Medomsley Dur.....150 E4
Medstead Hants.....30 A4

Medway Services
  Medway.....46 D7
Meerbrook Staffs.....99 M1
Meesden Herts.....60 C2
Meeth Devon.....10 E3
Meeting House Hill
  Norfk.....107 G6
Meidrim Carmth.....50 C2
Meifod Powys.....82 D2
Meigle P & K.....195 L7
Meikle Carco D & G...164 F6
Meikle Earnock
  S Lans.....175 J7
Meikle Ferry Highld...223 G4
Meikle Kilmory
  Ag & B.....173 H6
Meikle Obney P & K...195 G8
Meikleour P & K.....195 J7
Meikle Wartle Abers...216 D7
Meinciau Carmth.....50 F4
Meir C Stke.....99 L4
Melbost W Isls.....232 g2
Melbourn Cambs.....75 L5
Melbourne Derbys.....101 G7
Melbourne E R Yk.....125 H2
Melbourne Essex.....61 H6
Melbury Abbas
  Dorset.....27 K7
Melbury Bubb Dorset...14 B2
Melbury Osmond
  Dorset.....14 B2
Melchbourne Bed.....74 E2
Melcombe Bingham
  Dorset.....14 E2
Meldon Devon.....10 E6
Meldon Nthumb.....158 E6
Meldreth Cambs.....75 L5
Meldrum Stirlg.....184 F7
Melfort Ag & B.....182 B5
Meliden Denbgs.....110 E5
Melin-y-wig Denbgs....97 G3
Melkinthorpe Cumb...138 D3
Melkridge Nthumb.....149 J3
Melksham Wilts.....39 K7
Melling Lancs.....130 B5
Melling Sefton.....111 L2
Mellis Suffk.....92 C8
Mellon Charles
  Highld.....219 K3
Mellon Udrigle
  Highld.....219 K3
Mellor Lancs.....121 J4
Mellor Stockp.....113 M4
Mellor Brook Lancs...121 J4
Mells Somset.....27 G2
Melmerby Cumb.....149 G7
Melmerby N York.....131 K3
Melmerby N York.....132 E4
Melness Highld.....229 J3
Melplash Dorset.....13 L3
Melrose Border.....167 H3
Melsetter Ork.....234 b7
Melsonby N York.....140 F5
Meltham Kirk.....123 G7
Melton E R Yk.....126 B5
Melton Suffk.....79 G4
Melton Constable
  Norfk.....106 C6
Melton Mowbray
  Leics.....102 C8
Melton Ross N Linc...126 D7
Melvaig Highld.....219 H4
Melverley Shrops.....83 G1
Melvich Highld.....230 C3
Membury Devon.....13 H2
Membury Services
  W Berk.....40 F5
Memsie Abers.....217 H2
Memus Angus.....196 C5
Menai Bridge IoA.....109 H6
Mendham Suffk.....92 F6
Mendip Hills.....26 D2
Mendlesham Suffk.....78 D2
Mendlesham Green
  Suffk.....78 D2
Menheniot Cnwll.....5 L4
Mennock D & G.....164 F7
Menston C Brad.....123 H2

Menstrie Clacks............ 185 H7
Mentmore Bucks............58 E4
Meoble Highld 200 C7
Meole Brace Shrops......83 J2
Meonstoke Hants 29 L7
Meopham Kent 45 M6
Mepal Cambs 90 B7
Meppershall C Beds.....75 G7
Mere Ches E 113 C6
Mere Wilts......................27 J5
Mere Brow Lancs......... 120 F6
Mereclough Lancs....... 122 C4
Mere Green Birm...........85 K4
Mereworth Kent 33 H3
Meriden Solhll 86 B6
Merkadale Highld 208 F7
Merley BCP 15 J3
Merrion Pembks 48 F7
Merriott Somset 26 C8
Merrow Surrey 31 G2
Merry Hill Herts 43 J2
Merryhill Wolves 84 F4
Merrymeet Cnwll 5 L3
Mersea Island Essex....62 B5
Mersey Gateway
   Bridge Halton 112 D5
Mersham Kent...............34 E6
Merstham Surrey..........32 B3
Merston W Susx 18 B5
Merstone IoW................17 G5
Merthyr Cynog
   Powys......................67 L6
Merthyr Mawr
   Brdgnd....................36 D5
Merthyr Tydfil Myr Td ...53 G6
Merthyr Vale Myr Td.....53 G7
Merton Devon 10 D3
Merton Gt Lon...............44 E6
Merton Norfk 91 K4
Merton Oxon 57 L4
Meshaw Devon 24 B7
Messing Essex 61 L4
Messingham N Linc..... 116 E2
Metfield Suffk................93 G7
Metherell Cnwll 6 B3
Metheringham
   Lincs......................103 H1
Methil Fife...................186 F7
Methilhill Fife 186 F7
Methley Leeds 124 B5
Methlick Abers............217 G6
Methven P & K............185 L3
Methwold Norfk............91 G4
Methwold Hythe
   Norfk.......................91 G4
Mettingham Suffk........93 H5
Metton Norfk 106 E5
Mevagissey Cnwll 4 F6
Mexborough Donc 115 J2
Mey Highld 231 K2
Meysey Hampton
   Gloucs....................56 C7
Miabhaig W Isls..........232 d2
Michaelchurch
   Herefs.....................54 D3
Michaelchurch
   Escley Herefs..........69 G7
Michaelstone-y-
   Fedw Newpt............37 K4
Michaelston-le-Pit
   V Glam....................37 J5
Michaelstow Cnwll.........5 G1
Michaelwood
   Services Gloucs 39 G2
Micheldever Hants.......29 K4
Micheldever Station
   Hants......................29 K3
Michelmersh Hants......29 G6
Mickfield Suffk..............78 D3
Micklebring Donc....... 115 K3
Mickleby N York 143 G5
Micklefield Leeds 124 C4
Mickleham Surrey 31 K2
Micklecover C Derb.....100 F5
Mickleton Dur............140 B3
Mickleton Gloucs.........71 L5
Mickle Trafford
   Ches W....................112 C7

Mickley N York..............132 C4
Mickley Square
   Nthumb...................150 D3
Mid Ardlaw Abers 217 H2
Midbea Ork..................234 c4
Mid Beltie Abers.........206 C5
Mid Calder W Loth......176 E5
Mid Clyth Highld 231 K7
Mid Culbeuchly
   Abers......................216 C3
Middle Aston Oxon 57 J3
Middle Barton Oxon 57 H3
Middlebie D & G 155 L6
Middlebridge P & K 194 D3
Middle Chinnock
   Somset....................26 C8
Middle Claydon
   Bucks......................58 B3
Middlecroft Derbys.....115 H6
Middleham N York.......131 L3
Middle Handley
   Derbys....................115 H6
Middlehill Wilts............39 J6
Middlehope Shrops......83 K5
Middle Kames
   Ag & B...................172 F1
Middle Littleton
   Worcs......................71 J5
Middlemarsh Dorset.....14 C2
Middle Mayfield
   Staffs.....................100 C4
Middle Rasen Lincs 117 H4
Middle Rocombe
   Devon........................7 K2
Middlesbrough
   Middsb....................141 L4
Middleshaw Cumb........129 L2
Middlesmoor N York....131 K5
Middle Stoke
   Medway....................46 D5
Middleton Dur 141 G2
Middlestown Wakefd ...123 K6
Middlethird Border 167 K2
Middleton Ag & B 188 B7
Middleton Derbys 100 F2
Middleton Derbys 114 D8
Middleton Essex 77 K6
Middleton Hants 29 H3
Middleton Herefs 69 K1
Middleton Leeds 123 L5
Middleton N York........123 G2
Middleton N York........134 B3
Middleton Nhants 88 B5
Middleton Norfk 90 F1
Middleton Nthumb......158 D5
Middleton P & K 186 B6
Middleton Rochdl 113 K1
Middleton Shrops 83 K7
Middleton Suffk 79 J2
Middleton Swans..........50 E7
Middleton Warwks.........85 L4
Middleton Cheney
   Nhants......................73 G6
Middleton-in-
   Teesdale Dur..........139 L3
Middleton Moor
   Suffk.......................79 J2
Middleton One Row
   Darltn....................141 J5
Middleton-on-Sea
   W Susx....................18 C5
Middleton on the
   Hill Herefs..............69 K2
Middleton on the
   Wolds E R Yk..........125 L2
Middleton Park
   C Aber....................207 H3
Middleton
   Quernhow N York...132 E4
Middleton St
   George Darltn........141 J5
Middleton Scriven
   Shrops....................84 C6
Middleton Stoney
   Oxon.......................57 K4
Middleton Tyas
   N York....................141 G6
Middle Town IoS 2 a2

Middletown Powys........82 F2
Middle Tysoe Warwks ...72 D5
Middle Wallop Hants 28 F4
Middlewich Ches E.......113 G7
Middle Winterslow
   Wilts........................28 E5
Middlewood Cnwll 5 L2
Middle Woodford
   Wilts........................28 C4
Middlewood Green
   Suffk.......................78 D3
Middlezoy Somset 26 B5
Midford BaNES 39 H7
Midgham W Berk 41 K6
Midgley Calder 122 F5
Midgley Wakefd 123 K7
Midhopestones
   Sheff......................114 E2
Midhurst W Susx..........30 E6
Mid Lavant W Susx 18 B4
Midlem Border 167 H4
Mid Mains Highld........212 C6
Midpark Ag & B 173 H6
Midsomer Norton
   BaNES.....................26 F1
Midtown Highld...........229 J4
Mid Yell Shet..............235 d3
Migdale Highld 222 E3
Migvie Abers...............205 K4
Milborne Port
   Somset....................26 F7
Milborne St Andrew
   Dorset......................14 F3
Milborne Wick
   Somset....................26 F7
Milbourne Nthumb 158 E6
Milbourne Wilts............39 L3
Milburn Cumb..............138 F2
Milbury Heath S Glos ...38 F3
Milby N York...............132 F6
Milcombe Oxon............72 E7
Milden Suffk.................77 L5
Mildenhall Suffk 91 G8
Mildenhall Wilts............40 E6
Mileham Norfk 105 L8
Mile Oak Br & H 19 H4
Milesmark Fife............176 E2
Miles Platting
   Manch....................113 J2
Mile Town Kent 46 F5
Milfield Nthumb 168 D3
Milford Derbys 101 G4
Milford Devon 22 C6
Milford Staffs...............99 L7
Milford Surrey 30 F3
Milford Haven
   Pembks....................48 F6
Milford on Sea Hants...16 C4
Milkwall Gloucs 54 E6
Millais Jersey..............236 a5
Milland W Susx.............30 D5
Mill Bank Calder 122 F6
Millbeck Cumb 137 H3
Millbreck Abers...........217 J5
Millbridge Surrey 30 D3
Millbrook C Beds..........74 E6
Millbrook C Sotn..........29 G8
Millbrook Cnwll 6 B5
Millbrook Jersey..........236 c7
Mill Brow Stockp........113 L4
Millbuie Abers.............206 F4
Millbuie Highld 212 E4
Millcorner E Susx 21 G2
Millcraig Highld...........222 E7
Milldale Staffs............100 C2
Mill End Bucks.............42 C4
Mill End Herts..............60 B2
Millerhill Mdloth 177 J4
Miller's Dale Derbys....114 C6
Millerston C Glas........175 H5
Mill Green Cambs.........76 F5
Mill Green Essex...........61 G7
Mill Green Lincs...........103 L7
Mill Green Norfk...........77 L6
Mill Green Suffk...........78 B3
Mill Green Suffk...........78 D3
Millhalf Herefs..............68 F5
Millheugh S Lans 175 K7
Mill Hill Gt Lon.............44 E2

Millhouse Ag & B 173 G4
Millhousebridge
   D & G.....................155 K5
Millhouse Green
   Barns.....................114 E2
Millhouses Sheff.........115 G5
Milliken Park Rens 174 D6
Millington E R Yk.........125 J1
Millmeece Staffs..........99 J5
Mill of Drummond
   P & K.....................185 H4
Mill of Haldane
   W Duns...................174 D2
Millom Cumb...............128 E4
Millport N Ayrs 173 K7
Mill Street Suffk...........78 C1
Millthrop Cumb 130 C2
Milltimber C Aber 207 G5
Milltown Abers............205 G4
Milltown Abers............205 K3
Milltown D & G...........156 C6
Milltown Devon 23 J4
Milltown Highld...........209 L5
Milltown of
   Auchindoun
   Moray.....................215 H6
Milltown of
   Campfield Abers.....206 C5
Milltown of
   Edinvillie Moray......215 G6
Milltown of
   Rothiemay Moray....215 L5
Milnathort P & K 186 B6
Milngavie E Duns 175 G4
Milnrow Rochdl 122 D7
Milnthorpe Cumb 129 K3
Milovaig Highld 208 B4
Milson Shrops...............84 B8
Milstead Kent 34 B3
Milston Wilts................28 D3
Milthorpe Nhants.........73 H5
Milton C Stke 99 K3
Milton Cambs...............76 C2
Milton Cumb...............148 F3
Milton D & G...............144 F4
Milton D & G...............154 E7
Milton Derbys 100 F7
Milton Highld 212 D7
Milton Highld 212 E4
Milton Highld 223 G6
Milton Highld 231 L5
Milton Inver...............174 C5
Milton Kent..................46 A5
Milton Moray..............204 E2
Milton Moray..............215 L2
Milton N Som 37 M7
Milton Notts...............116 B6
Milton Oxon.................41 J3
Milton Oxon.................72 F7
Milton P & K 195 G4
Milton Pembks.............49 H6
Milton Somset..............26 C6
Milton Stirlg...............184 B6
Milton W Duns............174 D4
Milton Abbas Dorset 14 F3
Milton Abbot Devon......9 K8
Milton Bridge
   Mdloth....................177 H5
Milton Bryan C Beds....58 F3
Milton Clevedon
   Somset....................26 F4
Milton Combe Devon......6 D3
Milton Damerel
   Devon........................9 K3
Milton Ernest Bed......74 E4
Milton Green Ches W ...98 C2
Milton Hill Oxon...........41 J3
Milton Keynes
   M Keyn....................74 C6
Milton Lilbourne
   Wilts........................40 D7
Milton Malsor
   Nhants......................73 K4
Milton Morenish
   P & K.....................184 D1
Milton of
   Auchinhove
   Abers......................206 B5

Milton of Balgonie
Fife.....................**186** E7
Milton of Buchanan
Stirlg................**174** E1
Milton of Campsie
E Duns..............**175** H3
Milton of Finavon
Angus...............**196** D5
Milton of Leys
Highld...............**213** G6
Milton of Murtle
C Aber..............**207** G5
Milton on Stour
Dorset.................**27** J5
Milton Regis Kent **46** E6
Milton-under-
Wychwood Oxon **56** E4
Milverton Somerset **25** H6
Milverton Warwks.......**72** C2
Milwich Staffs................**99** L6
Minard Ag & B..............**182** D7
Minchinhampton
Gloucs................**55** K7
Minehead Somerset.........**24** F3
Minera Wrexhm...........**97** L3
Minety Wilts.................**40** A3
Minffordd Gwynd...........**95** K5
Mingarrypark Highld ...**190** D3
Miningsby Lincs **118** D8
Minions Cnwll...................**5** L2
Minishant S Ayrs..........**163** J6
Minllyn Gwynd................**81** J2
Minnigaff D & G **145** J2
Minnonie Abers **216** E3
Minskip N York **132** F6
Minstead Hants.............**16** C1
Minsted W Susx............**30** D7
Minster Kent..................**35** J2
Minsterley Shrops **83** G3
Minster Lovell Oxon **56** F5
Minster-on-Sea
Kent...................**46** F5
Minsterworth Gloucs....**55** H5
Minterne Magna
Dorset................**14** C2
Minting Lincs **117** K6
Mintlaw Abers..............**217** J5
Minto Border................**167** H5
Minton Shrops...............**83** H5
Mirehouse Cumb **136** D4
Mireland Highld............**231** K4
Mirfield Kirk.................**123** J6
Miserden Gloucs............**55** L6
Miskin Rhondd................**37** G4
Misson Notts................**116** B3
Misterton Notts.............**116** C3
Misterton Somerset **13** L2
Mistley Essex..................**62** D2
Mitcham Gt Lon.............**44** F6
Mitcheldean Gloucs......**54** F4
Mitchell Cnwll.................**4** D5
Mitchellslacks D & G...**155** G3
Mitchel Troy Mons..........**54** C6
Mitford Nthumb **158** F5
Mithian Cnwll...................**3** J2
Mixbury Oxon................**73** H7
Mobberley Ches E........**113** H5
Mobberley Staffs..........**100** A4
Mochdre Powys.............**82** B5
Mochrum D & G............**145** H5
Mockbeggar Kent..........**33** J4
Mockerkin Cumb...........**136** F3
Modbury Devon...............**6** F5
Moddershall Staffs........**99** L5
Moelfre IoA **109** G4
Moelfre Powys...............**97** J6
Moffat D & G................**155** J2
Moggerhanger
C Beds..................**75** G5
Moira Leics..................**86** C1
Molash Kent..................**34** D4
Mol-chlach Highld **199** G3
Mold Flints..................**111** H8
Moldgreen Kirk............**123** H7
Molehill Green
Essex...................**60** E3
Molescroft E R Yk........**126** C3
Molesworth Cambs.........**88** F7

Moll Highld **209** J7
Molland Devon...............**24** C5
Mollington Ches W........**111** L7
Mollington Oxon............**72** F5
Mollinsburn N Lans.......**175** J4
Mondynes Abers............**197** J1
Monewden Suffk.............**78** F3
Moneydie P & K **185** M2
Moniaive D & G..............**154** D4
Monifieth Angus............**187** H2
Monikie Angus...............**196** E8
Monimail Fife................**186** E5
Monken Hadley
Gt Lon.................**44** E1
Monk Fryston
N York **124** D5
Monkhide Herefs............**70** B5
Monkhill Cumb..............**148** C3
Monkhopton Shrops.......**84** B5
Monkland Herefs............**69** J3
Monkleigh Devon............**23** G7
Monknash V Glam...........**36** E6
Monkokehampton
Devon..................**10** E4
Monkseaton N Tyne **159** H7
Monks Eleigh Suffk.......**77** L5
Monk's Gate W Susx......**31** K6
Monks Heath
Ches E................**113** J6
Monk Sherborne
Hants..................**29** L1
Monksilver Somerset......**25** G4
Monks Kirby Warwks.....**86** F6
Monk Soham Suffk..........**78** E2
Monks Risborough
Bucks..................**58** D6
Monksthorpe Lincs **118** F7
Monk Street Essex.........**60** F3
Monkswood Mons...........**53** M7
Monkton Devon..............**12** F2
Monkton Kent................**47** M6
Monkton S Ayrs.............**163** J4
Monkton S Tyne **151** H3
Monkton Combe
BaNES.................**39** H7
Monkton Deverill
Wilts....................**27** J4
Monkton Farleigh
Wilts....................**39** J7
Monkton Heathfield
Somerset..............**25** K6
Monkton Wyld
Dorset.................**13** J3
Monkwearmouth
Sundld...............**151** J4
Monkwood Hants............**30** A5
Monmore Green
Wolves.................**85** G4
Monmouth Mons............**54** D5
Monnington on Wye
Herefs.................**69** G5
Monreith D & G............**145** H6
Montacute Somerset........**26** D7
Montford Shrops............**83** H1
Montford Bridge
Shrops.................**83** H1
Montgarrie Abers..........**206** B2
Montgomery Powys........**82** E4
Montrose Angus............**197** H5
Mont Saint Guern........**236** b3
Monxton Hants...............**28** F3
Monyash Derbys...........**114** D7
Monymusk Abers...........**206** D3
Monzie P & K................**185** H3
Moodiesburn
N Lans.................**175** J4
Moonzie Fife................**186** E4
Moor Allerton
Leeds.................**123** L3
Moorby Lincs................**118** D8
Moor Crichel Dorset.......**15** J2
Moordown BCP................**15** K4
Moore Halton................**112** E5
Moor End Calder...........**122** F5
Moorends Donc.............**125** G7
Moorhead C Brad **123** H3
Moorhouse Cumb **148** B4
Moorhouse Notts **116** C7

Moorhouse Bank
Surrey..................**32** D3
Moorlinch Somset **26** B4
Moor Monkton
N York **133** H7
Moorsholm R & Cl **142** E4
Moorside Dorset............**27** H7
Moorswater Cnwll.............**5** K3
Moorthorpe
Wakefd................**124** C7
Moortown Leeds...........**123** K3
Moortown Lincs **117** H2
Morangie Highld **223** G5
Morar Highld **199** L6
Morborne Cambs............**89** G5
Morchard Bishop
Devon..................**11** H4
Morcombelake
Dorset..................**13** K4
Morcott Rutlnd...............**88** D4
Morda Shrops.................**97** L6
Morden Dorset................**15** H4
Morden Gt Lon...............**44** E6
Mordiford Herefs............**69** L6
Mordon Dur..................**141** H2
More Shrops...................**83** G5
Morebath Devon.............**24** E6
Morebattle Border........**168** B4
Morecambe Lancs.........**129** J6
Moredon Swindn............**40** C3
Morefield Highld **220** E3
Morehall Kent................**35** G7
Moreleigh Devon.............**7** H5
Morenish P & K **184** D1
Morestead Hants.............**29** K6
Moreton Dorset..............**14** F4
Moreton Essex................**60** E6
Moreton Herefs...............**69** K2
Moreton Oxon................**58** B6
Moreton Wirral.............**111** J4
Moreton Corbet
Shrops.................**98** E7
Moreton Hall Suffk.......**77** K2
Moretonhampstead
Devon..................**11** H7
Moreton-in-Marsh
Gloucs.................**56** D2
Moreton Jeffries
Herefs.................**69** L5
Moreton Morrell
Warwks................**72** C4
Moreton on Lugg
Herefs.................**69** K5
Moreton Pinkney
Nhants.................**73** H5
Moreton Say Shrops......**98** F5
Moreton Valence
Gloucs.................**55** H6
Morfa Nefyn Gwynd.......**94** E4
Morham E Loth............**178** C4
Morland Cumb..............**138** E3
Morley Ches E...............**113** J5
Morley Derbys...............**101** H4
Morley Leeds................**123** K5
Morley Green
Ches E................**113** J5
Morley St Botolph
Norfk...................**92** C4
Morningside C Edin......**177** H4
Morningside N Lans......**175** L7
Morningthorpe
Norfk...................**92** F5
Morpeth Nthumb...........**158** F5
Morphie Abers...............**197** H4
Morrey Staffs................**100** C8
Morriston Swans............**51** J6
Morston Norfk..............**106** B4
Mortehoe Devon.............**23** G3
Morthen Rothm............**115** J4
Mortimer W Berk............**41** M7
Mortimer West End
Hants..................**41** M7
Mortlake Gt Lon.............**44** E5
Morton Cumb................**148** C4
Morton Derbys...............**101** H1
Morton Lincs................**103** H7
Morton Lincs................**116** D3
Morton Notts................**102** B3

Morton Shrops...............**97** L7
Morton-on-Swale
N York **132** E2
Morton on the Hill
Norfk...................**92** D1
Morvah Cnwll...................**2** D4
Morvich Highld **200** E2
Morville Shrops...............**84** C5
Morwenstow Cnwll **9** G2
Mosborough Sheff **115** H5
Moscow E Ayrs **163** L2
Moseley Birm..................**85** J6
Moseley Wolves...............**85** G4
Moseley Worcs................**70** E3
Moss Ag & B..................**188** B7
Moss Donc...................**124** F7
Mossat Abers................**205** K2
Mossbank Shet..............**235** d4
Moss Bank St Hel **112** D3
Mossbay Cumb..............**136** D2
Mossblown S Ayrs **163** K4
Mossburnford
Border.................**167** K6
Mossdale D & G.............**154** B7
Mossdale E Ayrs............**153** K2
Moss Edge Lancs..........**120** F2
Mossend N Lans............**175** K6
Mossley Tamesd............**113** L2
Mosspaul Inn Border.....**156** D3
Moss-side Highld..........**213** K4
Mosstodloch Moray.......**215** H3
Mossyard D & G.............**145** L5
Mossy Lea Lancs..........**121** H7
Mosterton Dorset.............**13** L2
Moston Manch...............**113** K2
Mostyn Flints................**111** G5
Motcombe Dorset............**27** J6
Mothecombe Devon..........**6** F6
Motherby Cumb.............**138** B2
Motherwell N Lans........**175** K6
Motspur Park Gt Lon......**44** E6
Mottingham Gt Lon.........**45** H5
Mottisfont Hants.............**28** F6
Mottistone Hants.............**28** F6
Mottistone IoW..............**16** E6
Mottram in
Longdendale
Tamesd...............**113** M3
Mottram St Andrew
Ches E................**113** K5
Mouilpied Guern...........**236** c3
Mouldsworth
Ches W...............**112** D7
Moulin P & K................**194** E4
Moulsecoomb
Br & H..................**19** J4
Moulsford Oxon.............**41** L4
Moulsoe M Keyn.............**74** C6
Moultavie Highld...........**222** E7
Moulton Ches W............**112** F7
Moulton Lincs...............**104** A7
Moulton N York..............**141** G6
Moulton Nhants..............**73** L2
Moulton Suffk................**77** G2
Moulton V Glam..............**37** G6
Moulton Chapel
Lincs..................**103** M8
Moulton St Mary
Norfk...................**93** H3
Moulton Seas End
Lincs..................**104** A6
Mount Cnwll.....................**5** J3
Mountain C Brad............**123** G4
Mountain Ash
Rhondd................**53** G7
Mountain Cross
Border.................**176** F8
Mount Ambrose
Cnwll....................**3** J3
Mount Bures Essex.........**61** L2
Mountfield E Susx..........**20** E2
Mountgerald Highld.......**212** E3
Mount Hawke Cnwll.........**3** J2
Mountjoy Cnwll...............**4** D4
Mount Lothian
Mdloth.................**177** H6
Mountnessing Essex......**60** F8
Mounton Mons................**38** D2

Mount Pleasant
Derbys.......................... 101 G3
Mount Pleasant
Suffk........................... 77 G5
Mountsorrel Leics 87 H2
Mount Tabor Calder 122 F5
Mousehole Cnwll.............. 2 E6
Mouswald D & G........ 155 J7
Mow Cop Ches E............. 99 J2
Mowhaugh Border 168 B5
Mowmacre Hill
C Leic.........................87 H3
Mowsley Leics 87 J5
Moy Highld 202 C8
Moy Highld 213 J7
Moyle Highld 200 D2
Moylegrove Pembks....... 64 F5
Muasdale Ag & B 161 H2
Muchalls Abers 207 G6
Much Birch Herefs......54 D3
Much Cowarne
Herefs........................70 B5
Much Dewchurch
Herefs....................... 54 C2
Muchelney Somset......... 26 B6
Muchelney Ham
Somset........................26 C6
Much Hadham Herts......60 C4
Much Hoole Lancs 120 F6
Muchlarnick Cnwll 5 K5
Much Marcle Herefs......54 F2
Much Wenlock
Shrops.........................84 B4
Muck Highld 189 K1
Muckleburgh
Military
Collection Norfk..... 106 D4
Mucklestone Staffs........99 G5
Muckton Lincs 118 E5
Muddiford Devon............23 J4
Muddles Green
E Susx 20 B3
Mudeford BCP................16 A4
Mudford Somset............26 E7
Mudford Sock
Somset.........................26 E7
Mugdock Stirlg............. 175 G3
Mugeary Highld............ 209 G6
Mugginton Derbys........ 100 F4
Muirden Abers 216 D4
Muirdrum Angus......... 196 F8
Muiresk Abers 216 D5
Muirhead Angus.......... 186 E1
Muirhead Fife.............. 186 E6
Muirhead N Lans......... 175 J4
Muirhouses Falk.......... 176 D3
Muirkirk E Ayrs........... 164 D4
Muirmill Stirlg.............. 175 J2
Muir of Fowlis Abers... 206 B3
Muir of Miltonduff
Moray........................ 214 E3
Muir of Ord Highld 212 E4
Muirshearlich Highld... 192 B1
Muirtack Abers 217 J6
Muirton P & K............. 185 J5
Muirton Mains
Highld........................ 212 C4
Muirton of Ardblair
P & K......................... 195 J7
Muker N York 139 K7
Mulbarton Norfk...........92 E4
Mulben Moray 215 H4
Mull Ag & B................. 181 J1
Mullardoch Highld....... 211 K7
Mullion Cnwll................... 3 H7
Mullion Cove Cnwll.......... 3 H7
Mumby Lincs 119 G6
Munderfield Row
Herefs.........................70 B4
Munderfield Stocks
Herefs.........................70 B4
Mundesley Norfk.......... 107 G5
Mundford Norfk...........91 H5
Mundham Norfk...........93 G4
Mundon Essex..............61 K7
Mungrisdale Cumb....... 137 K2
Munlochy Highld.......... 213 G4
Munnoch N Ayrs 174 B8

Munsley Herefs 70 B6
Munslow Shrops 83 K6
Murchington Devon......11 G7
Murcott Oxon.................57 L5
Murkle Highld.............. 231 H2
Murlaggan Highld........ 200 F6
Murroes Angus........... 187 G1
Murrow Cambs..............89 L3
Mursley Bucks..............58 D3
Murston Kent................46 F7
Murthill Angus............ 196 D5
Murthly P & K.............. 195 H8
Murton C York 133 K8
Murton Cumb............... 139 G3
Murton Dur................. 151 J5
Murton Nthumb 179 K8
Musbury Devon 13 H4
Musselburgh E Loth 177 K4
Muston Leics............... 102 D5
Muston N York 135 H4
Muswell Hill Gt Lon.......44 F3
Mutehill D & G............ 146 C5
Mutford Suffk...............93 K6
Muthill P & K............... 185 H4
Mybster Highld............ 231 H5
Myddfai Carmth............52 B3
Myddle Shrops..............98 C7
Mydroilyn Cerdgn.........66 B4
Myland Essex................62 B3
Mylor Cnwll...................... 4 C8
Mylor Bridge Cnwll........ 4 C8
Mynachlog ddu
Pembks.......................49 K2
Mynydd-bach Mons 38 C2
Mynydd-Bach Swans 51 J6
Mynyddgarreg
Carmth.......................50 E4
Mynydd Isa Flints 111 J8
Myrebird Abers 206 E5
Myredykes Border 157 G3
Mytchett Surrey 30 E1
Mytholm Calder.......... 122 E5
Mytholmroyd Calder... 122 F5
Myton-on-Swale
N York 132 F6

N

Naast Highld 219 J5
Na Buirgh W Isls......... 232 d4
Naburn C York............ 124 F2
Nackington Kent............34 F4
Nacton Suffk.................78 F6
Nafferton E R Yk......... 135 G7
Nailsbourne Somset......25 K5
Nailsea N Som 38 C6
Nailstone Leics.............86 E3
Nailsworth Gloucs.........55 J7
Nairn Highld 213 K3
Nannerch Flints........... 111 G7
Nanpantan Leics......... 101 K8
Nanpean Cnwll................ 4 F5
Nanstallon Cnwll............. 5 G3
Nanternis Cerdgn..........65 L3
Nantgaredig Carmth......50 F2
Nantglyn Denbgs..........96 F1

Nantlle Valley Slate
Landscape Gwynd......95 J2
Nantmel Powys.............68 B2
Nantmor Gwynd............95 K4
Nant Peris Gwynd..........95 K2
Nantwich Ches E............98 F3
Nantyglo Blae G............53 J6
Nant-y-moel Brdgnd......36 E2
Naphill Bucks................42 D2
Napton on the Hill
Warwks.......................72 F3
Narberth Pembks...........49 J4
Narborough Leics..........87 G4
Narborough Norfk..........91 H2
Nasareth Gwynd............95 H3
Naseby Nhants..............87 K7
Nash Bucks....................73 L7
Nash Newpt...................37 M4
Nash Shrops..................69 L1
Nassington Nhants........88 F4

Nateby Cumb................ 139 H6
Nateby Lancs 120 F2
National Memorial
Arboretum
Staffs...........................85 L1
National Space
Centre C Leic............87 H3
Natland Cumb............. 129 L2
Naughton Suffk.............78 B5
Naunton Gloucs.............56 C4
Naunton Worcs..............70 F6
Naunton
Beauchamp
Worcs.........................71 G4
Navenby Lincs 103 G2
Navestock Essex...........45 K1
Navestock Side
Essex..........................60 E8
Navidale Highld........... 227 J5
Navity Highld............... 213 J2
Nawton N York............ 133 K3
Nayland Suffk...............77 L7
Nazeing Essex...............60 C6
Neap Shet................... 235 d5
Near Cotton Staffs...... 100 B4
Near Sawrey Cumb 137 K7
Neasden Gt Lon............44 E3
Neasham Darltn.......... 141 H5
Neath Neath.................51 L6
Neatham Hants.............30 C4
Neatishead Norfk........ 107 H7
Nebo Cerdgn.................66 D2
Nebo Conwy..................96 C2
Nebo Gwynd..................95 H3
Nebo IoA..................... 108 F4
Necton Norfk................91 K2
Nedd Highld 224 D3
Nedging Suffk................78 B5
Nedging Tye Suffk.........78 B4
Needham Norfk..............92 F6
Needham Market
Suffk...........................78 C4
Needingworth Cambs....75 L1
Neen Savage Shrops......84 C7
Neen Sollars Shrops......84 B8
Neenton Shrops..............84 B6
Nefyn Gwynd.................94 E4
Neilston E Rens........... 174 E6
Nelson Caerph...............37 H2
Nelson Lancs............... 122 C3
Nemphlar S Lans......... 165 G1
Nempnett Thrubwell
BaNES.........................38 D7
Nenthead Cumb........... 149 K6
Nenthorn Border......... 167 K2
Nerabus Ag & B........... 170 E7
Nercwys Flints..............97 K1
Nerston S Lans........... 175 H6
Nesbit Nthumb............ 168 E3
Nesfield N York........... 123 G1
Nesscliffe Shrops..........98 B8
Neston Ches W............ 111 J6
Neston Wilts.................39 K6
Netchwood Shrops........84 B5
Nether Abington
S Lans........................ 165 H5
Nether Alderley
Ches E........................ 113 J6
Netheravon Wilts..........28 D2
Nether Blainslie
Border....................... 167 H2
Netherbrae Abers........ 216 F3
Nether Broughton
Leics......................... 102 B7
Netherburn S Lans...... 175 L8
Netherbury Dorset........13 L3
Netherby N York......... 123 L2
Nether Cerne Dorset....14 C3
Nethercleuch D & G... 155 K5
Nether Compton
Dorset..........................26 E7
Nether Crimond
Abers......................... 206 F2
Nether Dallachy
Moray........................ 215 H2
Netherend Gloucs..........54 E7
Netherfield E Susx........20 E2
Netherfield Notts........ 101 L4

Nether Fingland
S Lans........................ 165 H7
Netherhampton
Wilts...........................28 C5
Nether Handwick
Angus........................ 196 B7
Nether Haugh
Rothm........................ 115 H3
Netherhay Dorset..........13 K2
Nether Headon
Notts......................... 116 C6
Nether Heage
Derbys....................... 101 G3
Nether Heyford
Nhants.........................73 J3
Nether Kellet Lancs 129 K6
Nether Kinmundy
Abers......................... 217 K5
Nether Langwith
Notts......................... 115 K7
Netherley Abers........... 207 G6
Netherley Lpool......... 112 C4
Nethermill D & G........ 155 H5
Nethermuir Abers 217 G5
Netherne-on-the-
Hill Surrey..................32 B3
Netheroyd Hill Kirk..... 123 H6
Nether Padley
Derbys....................... 114 E6
Nether Poppleton
C York....................... 133 J8
Netherseal Derbys.........86 C2
Nether Silton N York... 133 G2
Nether Stowey
Somset.........................25 J4
Netherthird E Ayrs...... 164 B5
Netherthong Kirk........ 123 H8
Netherton Angus......... 196 E5
Netherton Devon............ 7 K2
Netherton Dudley..........85 G6
Netherton Kirk............ 123 H7
Netherton N Lans........ 175 K7
Netherton Nthumb...... 168 E7
Netherton P & K.......... 195 J6
Netherton Sefton........ 111 K2
Netherton Stirlg.......... 175 G3
Netherton Wakefd...... 123 K6
Nethertown Cumb....... 136 D5
Nethertown Highld...... 231 L1
Nethertown Staffs...... 100 C8
Netherurd Border....... 165 L1
Nether Wallop Hants....28 F4
Nether Wasdale
Cumb......................... 136 F6
Nether Westcote
Gloucs.........................56 E4
Nether Whitacre
Warwks........................86 B5
Nether Whitecleuch
S Lans........................ 165 G5
Nether Winchendon
Bucks..........................58 B5
Netherwitton
Nthumb...................... 158 D4
Nethy Bridge Highld 204 B2
Netley Hants.................16 F2
Netley Marsh Hants......29 G8
Nettlebed Oxon.............42 B3
Nettlebridge Somset......26 F2
Nettlecombe Dorset......13 M4
Nettleden Herts............59 G6
Nettleham Lincs.......... 117 G6
Nettlestead Kent...........33 H3
Nettlestead Green
Kent............................33 H3
Nettlestone IoW...........17 H4
Nettlesworth Dur........ 151 G5
Nettleton Lincs............ 117 J2
Nettleton Wilts.............39 J5
Netton Wilts.................28 C4
Nevern Pembks..............64 F6
Nevill Holt Leics...........88 B5
New Abbey D & G 147 G2
New Aberdour
Abers......................... 217 G2
New Addington
Gt Lon.........................45 G7
Newall Leeds 123 J2

New Alresford Hants......29 L5
New Alyth P & K.........195 K6
Newark C Pete..........89 H4
Newark Ork............234 e4
Newark-on-Trent
  Notts.................102 D2
New Arley Warwks....86 C5
Newarthill N Lans......175 K6
New Ash Green Kent....45 L6
New Balderton
  Notts.................102 D3
New Barn Kent.........45 L6
New Barnet Gt Lon........44 F2
Newbattle Mdloth........177 J5
New Bewick Nthumb.....169 G5
Newbie D & G............147 L3
Newbiggin Cumb........138 C2
Newbiggin Cumb........138 F2
Newbiggin Cumb........148 F5
Newbiggin Dur...........139 K2
Newbiggin N York.......131 J3
Newbiggin-by-the-
  Sea Nthumb...........159 H5
Newbigging Angus.......187 H1
Newbigging Angus.......195 L7
Newbigging Angus.......196 C8
Newbigging S Lans.......165 K1
Newbiggin-on-
  Lune Cumb...........139 G6
New Bilton Warwks....86 F7
Newbold Derbys.........115 G6
Newbold on Avon
  Warwks................86 F7
Newbold on Stour
  Warwks................72 B5
Newbold Pacey
  Warwks................72 C3
Newbold Verdon
  Leics..................86 F3
New Bolingbroke
  Lincs.................104 A2
Newborough C Pete.....89 H3
Newborough IoA.......108 E2
Newborough Staffs......100 C7
New Boultham Lincs....116 F7
Newbourne Suffk.......78 F6
New Bradwell
  M Keyn................74 B6
New Brampton
  Derbys................115 G7
New Brancepeth
  Dur..................151 G6
Newbridge C Edin......176 F4
Newbridge Caerph.......37 K2
Newbridge Cnwll..........2 D5
Newbridge D & G.......155 G6
Newbridge Hants........28 F7
Newbridge IoW...........16 E5
Newbridge Green
  Worcs.................70 E6
Newbridge-on-Wye
  Powys.................67 L3
New Brighton Wirral...111 J3
Newbrough Nthumb....149 L2
New Buckenham
  Norfk..................92 C5
Newbuildings Devon......11 J4
Newburgh Abers........207 J1
Newburgh Abers........217 H3
Newburgh Fife..........186 D4
Newburgh Lancs.........121 G7
Newburn N u Ty........150 F2
Newbury Somset........27 G2
Newbury W Berk........41 J6
Newbury Park Gt Lon....45 J3
Newby Cumb...........138 E3
Newby Lancs...........122 B2
Newby N York..........130 D5
Newby N York..........134 F2
Newby N York..........142 B5
Newby Bridge Cumb...129 H3
Newby East Cumb......148 E4
New Byth Abers........216 F4
Newby West Cumb......148 C4
Newcastle Mons........54 C5
Newcastle Shrops........82 E6
Newcastle Airport
  Nthumb...............158 F7

Newcastle Emlyn
  Carmth................65 J6
Newcastle Great
  Park N u Ty..........158 F7
Newcastleton
  Border.................156 E5
Newcastle-under-
  Lyme Staffs............99 J4
Newcastle upon
  Tyne N u Ty.........151 G3
Newchapel Pembks......65 H6
Newchapel Surrey........32 C5
Newchurch IoW..........17 G5
Newchurch Kent..........34 E7
Newchurch Mons........38 C2
Newchurch Powys........68 E4
Newchurch Staffs......100 D7
New Costessey Norfk...92 E2
Newcraighall C Edin....177 J4
New Crofton Wakefd...124 B6
New Cross Gt Lon.......45 G5
New Cross Somset......26 B7
New Cumnock
  E Ayrs................164 C6
New Deer Abers.......217 G5
New Denham Bucks....43 H4
Newdigate Surrey.......31 K3
New Duston Nhants.....73 K3
New Earswick C York..133 J7
New Edlington Donc...115 K2
New Elgin Moray.......204 F3
New Ellerby E R Yk....126 E3
Newell Green Br For....42 E6
New Eltham Gt Lon.....45 H5
New End Worcs..........71 J3
Newenden Kent..........33 L7
New England C Pete.....89 H4
Newent Gloucs..........55 G3
New Ferry Wirral......111 K4
Newfield Dur..........150 F7
Newfield Highld.......223 H6
New Fletton C Pete.....89 H4
New Forest
  National Park.......16 C2
Newgale Pembks........48 E3
New Galloway D & G...154 B6
Newgate Street
  Herts..................59 M6
New Gilston Fife.......187 G5
New Grimsby IoS.........2 a1
Newhall Ches E.........98 E4
New Hartley Nthumb...159 H6
Newhaven C Edin......177 H3
Newhaven E Susx.......19 L5
New Haw Surrey.........43 H7
New Hedges Pembks....49 J6
New Holland N Linc...126 D5
Newholm N York.......143 H5
New Houghton
  Derbys................115 J7
New Houghton
  Norfk.................105 J6
Newhouse N Lans......175 L6
New Hutton Cumb.....130 B2
Newick E Susx..........19 L2
Newington Kent.........35 G6
Newington Kent.........46 E6
Newington Oxon........41 L2
New Inn Carmth........66 B6
New Inn Torfn..........53 L7
New Invention
  Shrops................82 F7
New Lanark S Lans....165 G2
New Lanark Village
  S Lans..............165 G2
Newland C KuH........126 D4
Newland Gloucs.........54 D6
Newland N York.......125 G5
Newland Somset........24 C4
Newland Worcs..........70 E5
Newlandrig Mdloth....177 K6
Newlands Border......156 E4
Newlands Nthumb.....150 D4
Newlands of
  Dundurcas Moray...215 G4
New Langholm D & G..156 D6
New Leake Lincs.......104 C2
New Leeds Abers......217 J4

New Lodge Barns.......123 L8
New Longton
  Lancs.................121 G5
New Luce D & G.......144 E3
Newlyn Cnwll............2 E5
Newmachar Abers......207 G2
Newmains N Lans......175 L6
New Malden Gt Lon....44 E6
Newman's Green
  Suffk...................77 K5
Newmarket Suffk.......76 F2
Newmarket W Isls....232 f2
New Marske R & Cl...142 D3
New Marston Oxon......57 K6
New Mill Abers........206 E8
Newmill Border.......167 G7
New Mill Cnwll...........2 E4
Newmill Moray........215 K4
Newmillerdam
  Wakefd...............123 L7
Newmill of
  Inshewan Angus....196 C4
Newmills C Edin.......177 G5
New Mills Derbys......113 M4
Newmills Fife..........176 D2
Newmills Mons..........54 D6
New Mills Powys........82 C4
Newmiln P & K.........186 B2
Newmilns E Ayrs......164 B2
New Milton Hants.......16 B4
New Mistley Essex......62 D2
New Moat Pembks......49 H3
Newney Green Essex....61 G6
Newnham Hants.........30 B2
Newnham Herts.........75 J6
Newnham Kent..........34 C3
Newnham Nhants.......73 H3
Newnham Bridge
  Worcs.................70 B2
Newnham on
  Severn Gloucs........55 G5
New Ollerton Notts....116 A7
New Oscott Birm.......85 K5
New Pitsligo Abers....217 G3
Newport Cnwll...........9 J7
Newport E R Yk.......125 K4
Newport Essex.........76 D7
Newport Gloucs.........39 G2
Newport Highld.......227 K4
Newport IoW...........16 F5
Newport Newpt.........37 L3
Newport Pembks........64 E6
Newport Wrekin........99 H8
Newport-on-Tay
  Fife..................187 G2
Newport Pagnell
  M Keyn................74 C5
Newport Pagnell
  Services M Keyn....74 C5
New Prestwick
  S Ayrs................163 J4
New Quay Cerdgn......65 L3
Newquay Cnwll..........4 C4
Newquay Zoo Cnwll....4 C4
New Rackheath
  Norfk..................93 G2
New Radnor Powys.....68 E3
New Ridley Nthumb...150 D3
New Romney Kent......21 L2
New Rossington
  Donc.................115 L2
New Sauchie Clacks...185 J7
Newseat Abers........216 D7
Newsham Lancs........121 G4
Newsham N York......132 E3
Newsham N York......140 E5
Newsham Nthumb.....159 H6
New Sharlston
  Wakefd...............124 B6
Newsholme E R Yk....125 H5
New Silksworth
  Sundld................151 J4
Newsome Kirk.........123 H7
New Somerby Lincs....102 F5
Newstead Border......167 H3
Newstead Notts.......101 K3
Newstead Nthumb.....169 H4

New Stevenston
  N Lans................175 K6
New Swanage Dorset....15 J6
Newthorpe Notts......101 J4
New Thundersley
  Essex..................46 C3
Newton Ag & B........182 F7
Newton Border........167 J5
Newton Brdgnd.........36 C5
Newton C Beds.........75 J5
Newton Cambs.........76 B5
Newton Cambs.........90 B1
Newton Ches W........98 D1
Newton Ches W.......112 B7
Newton Cumb.........128 F5
Newton Derbys........101 H2
Newton Herefs........53 M2
Newton Herefs........69 K4
Newton Highld........212 F4
Newton Highld........213 H5
Newton Highld........213 J2
Newton Highld........231 L5
Newton Lincs.........103 H5
Newton Mdloth........177 J4
Newton Moray........214 E2
Newton Moray........215 H2
Newton Nhants........88 C6
Newton Norfk..........91 J1
Newton Notts.........102 B4
Newton Nthumb.......150 C3
Newton S Lans........165 H3
Newton S Lans........175 H6
Newton Sandw.........85 J5
Newton Staffs........100 B7
Newton Suffk..........77 K6
Newton W Loth.......176 E3
Newton Warwks........87 G7
Newton Abbot Devon....7 K2
Newton Arlosh
  Cumb.................147 L4
Newton Aycliffe Dur...141 G3
Newton Bewley
  Hartpl................141 K2
Newton
  Blossomville
  M Keyn................74 D4
Newton Bromswold
  Nhants................74 D2
Newton Burgoland
  Leics..................86 D2
Newton by Toft Lincs...117 H4
Newton Ferrers
  Devon...................6 E6
Newton Ferry W Isls...232 c5
Newton Flotman
  Norfk..................92 E4
Newtongrange
  Mdloth................177 J5
Newton Green Mons...38 D3
Newton Harcourt
  Leics..................87 J4
Newton Heath
  Manch................113 K2
Newtonhill Abers.....207 G6
Newton-in-
  Bowland Lancs.....121 K1
Newton Kyme
  N York...............124 C2
Newton-le-Willows
  N York...............132 C2
Newton-le-Willows
  St Hel................112 E3
Newtonloan Mdloth....177 J5
Newton Longville
  Bucks..................58 D2
Newton Mearns
  E Rens................174 F7
Newtonmill Angus.....196 F4
Newtonmore Highld...203 H5
Newton Morrell
  N York...............141 G5
Newton of
  Balcanquhal
  P & K.................186 B5
Newton of
  Balcormo Fife......187 H6
Newton of Belltrees
  Rens.................174 D6

Newton-on-Ayr
S Ayrs 163 J5
Newton-on-Ouse
N York 133 H7
Newton-on-Rawcliffe N York 134 C2
Newton-on-the-Moor Nthumb 158 F2
Newton on Trent
Lincs 116 D6
Newton Poppleford
Devon 12 E4
Newton Purcell Oxon 57 L3
Newton Regis
Warwks 86 C3
Newton Reigny
Cumb 138 C2
Newton St Cyres
Devon 11 K5
Newton St Faith
Norfk 92 F1
Newton St Loe
BaNES 39 G7
Newton St Petrock
Devon 9 K3
Newton Solney
Derbys 100 F7
Newton Stacey Hants 29 H4
Newton Stewart
D & G 145 J3
Newton Tony Wilts 28 E4
Newton Tracey Devon 23 H6
Newton under
Roseberry R & Cl ... 142 C5
Newton upon
Derwent E R Yk 125 H2
Newton Valence
Hants 30 B5
Newton Wamphray
D & G 155 K3
Newton with Scales
Lancs 120 F4
Newtown BCP 15 K4
Newtown Cumb 147 J5
Newtown Cumb 148 E3
Newtown D & G 164 F7
Newtown Devon 12 D3
Newtown Devon 24 B6
New Town E Susx 19 M2
Newtown Gloucs 54 F7
Newtown Hants 29 L8
Newtown Herefs 70 B5
Newtown Highld 202 B4
Newtown IoW 16 E4
Newtown Nthumb 168 F4
Newtown Powys 82 C5
Newtown Shrops 98 C6
Newtown Somset 25 L8
Newtown Staffs 99 K1
Newtown Wigan 112 E1
Newtown Worcs 70 F4
Newtown Linford
Leics 87 G2
Newtown St
Boswells Border 167 J3
New Tredegar Caerph ... 53 H7
New Trows S Lans 164 F2
Newtyle Angus 195 L7
New Walsoken
Cambs 90 C2
New Waltham NE Lin ... 118 C1
New Winton E Loth 177 L4
Newyork Ag & B 182 D5
New York Lincs 103 L2
New York N Tyne 159 H7
Neyland Pembks 49 G6
Nicholashayne Devon ... 25 H7
Nicholaston Swans 51 G7
Nidd N York 132 D7
Nigg C Aber 207 H5
Nigg Highld 223 H6
Nigg Ferry Highld 223 H7
Ninebanks Nthumb 149 K4
Nine Elms Swindn 40 C3
Ninfield E Susx 20 E3
Ningwood IoW 16 E5
Nisbet Border 167 K4
Nisbet Hill Border 179 G7

Niton IoW 17 F6
Nitshill C Glas 174 F6
Nocton Lincs 117 H8
Noke Oxon 57 K5
Nolton Pembks 48 E4
Nolton Haven
Pembks 48 E4
No Man's Heath
Ches W 98 D3
No Man's Heath
Warwks 86 C2
Nomansland Devon 11 J3
Nomansland Wilts 28 E7
Noneley Shrops 98 C6
Nonington Kent 35 H4
Nook Cumb 129 L3
Norbiton Gt Lon 44 D6
Norbury Ches E 98 E3
Norbury Derbys 100 C4
Norbury Gt Lon 44 F6
Norbury Shrops 83 G5
Norbury Staffs 99 H7
Norchard Worcs 70 F2
Nordelph Norfk 90 D4
Nordley Shrops 84 C4
Norfolk Broads Norfk ... 93 K2
Norham Nthumb 179 J8
Norley Ches W 112 E6
Norleywood Hants 16 D3
Normanby Lincs 117 G4
Normanby N Linc 125 K7
Normanby N York 134 B3
Normanby R & Cl 142 C4
Normanby le Wold
Lincs 117 J3
Normandy Surrey 30 F2
Norman's Green
Devon 12 D2
Normanton C Derb 101 G5
Normanton Leics 102 D4
Normanton Notts 102 B2
Normanton Wakefd ... 124 B6
Normanton le
Heath Leics 86 D2
Normanton on
Cliffe Lincs 102 F4
Normanton on Soar
Notts 101 K7
Normanton on the
Wolds Notts 101 L6
Normanton on Trent
Notts 116 C7
Norris Green Lpool 111 L3
Norris Hill Leics 86 D1
Norristhorpe Kirk 123 J6
Northall Bucks 58 F4
Northallerton N York ... 141 J7
Northam C Sotn 29 H8
Northam Devon 23 G5
Northampton Nhants ... 73 L3
Northampton Worcs 70 E2
Northampton
Services Nhants 73 K3
North Anston Rothm ... 115 K5
North Ascot Br For 42 E6
North Aston Oxon 57 J3
Northaw Herts 59 L7
Northay Somset 13 H1
North Baddesley
Hants 29 H7
North Ballachulish
Highld 191 L4
North Barrow Somset ... 26 E5
North Barsham
Norfk 105 L5
Northbay W Isls 233 b9
North Benfleet Essex 46 C3
North Berwick E Loth ... 178 C2
North Boarhunt
Hants 17 H1
Northborough C Pete ... 89 H3
Northbourne Kent 35 J4
North Bovey Devon 11 H7
North Bradley Wilts 27 J1
North Brentor Devon ... 10 C8
North Brewham
Somset 27 G4
Northbrook Hants 29 K4

North Buckland
Devon 23 G4
North Burlingham
Norfk 93 H2
North Cadbury
Somset 26 F6
North Carlton Lincs 116 F6
North Carlton Notts 115 L4
North Cave E R Yk 125 K4
North Cerney Gloucs 56 A6
North Chailey E Susx ... 19 K2
Northchapel W Susx 30 F5
North Charford
Hants 28 D7
North Charlton
Nthumb 169 H5
North Cheam Gt Lon 44 E6
North Cheriton
Somset 27 G6
North Chideock
Dorset 13 K4
Northchurch Herts 58 F6
North Cliffe E R Yk 125 K3
North Clifton Notts 116 D6
North Cockerington
Lincs 118 E4
North Connel Ag & B .. 182 C1
North Cornelly
Brdgnd 36 C4
North Cotes Lincs 118 E2
Northcott Devon 9 J6
Northcourt Oxon 57 J7
North Cove Suffk 93 K5
North Cowton
N York 141 G6
North Crawley
M Keyn 74 D5
North Creake Norfk 105 K5
North Curry Somset 25 L6
North Dalton E R Yk ... 125 L1
North Deighton
N York 124 B1
Northdown Kent 35 K2
North Downs 34 B4
North Duffield
N York 125 G3
North Elmham Norfk ... 106 B7
North Elmsall
Wakefd 124 D7
North End C Port 17 J3
North End Essex 61 G4
North End Hants 28 C7
North End Nhants 74 D2
North End W Susx 18 D5
Northend Warwks 72 E4
Northenden Manch 113 J4
North Erradale
Highld 219 H5
North Evington
C Leic 87 J3
North Fambridge
Essex 61 K7
North Ferriby E R Yk .. 126 B5
Northfield Birm 85 H7
Northfield C Aber 207 G4
Northfield E R Yk 126 C5
Northfields Lincs 88 E2
Northfleet Kent 45 M5
North Frodingham
E R Yk 135 H8
North Gorley Hants 15 M1
North Green Suffk 79 G3
North Greetwell
Lincs 117 G6
North Grimston
N York 134 C6
North Hayling Hants ... 17 K2
North Hill Cnwll 5 L1
North Hillingdon
Gt Lon 43 H4
North Hinksey
Village Oxon 57 J6
North Holmwood
Surrey 31 K3
North Huish Devon 7 G5
North Hykeham
Lincs 116 F7
Northiam E Susx 21 G2

Northill C Beds 75 G5
Northington Hants 29 K4
North Kelsey Lincs 117 H2
North Kessock
Highld 213 G5
North Killingholme
N Linc 126 E6
North Kilvington
N York 132 F3
North Kilworth Leics 87 H6
North Kyme Lincs 103 J3
North Landing
E R Yk 135 K5
Northlands Lincs 104 B2
Northleach Gloucs 56 C5
North Lee Bucks 58 D6
Northleigh Devon 12 F3
North Leigh Oxon 57 H5
North Leverton with
Habblesthorpe
Notts 116 C5
Northlew Devon 10 D5
North Littleton
Worcs 71 J5
North Lopham Norfk 92 C6
North Luffenham
Rutlnd 88 D3
North Marden
W Susx 30 D7
North Marston Bucks ... 58 C4
North Middleton
Mdloth 177 K6
North Millbrex
Abers 216 F5
North Milmain
D & G 144 C4
North Molton Devon 24 B5
Northmoor Oxon 57 H7
North Moreton Oxon 41 K3
Northmuir Angus 196 C5
North Mundham
W Susx 18 B5
North Muskham
Notts 102 D2
North Newbald
E R Yk 125 L3
North Newington
Oxon 72 E6
North Newton Wilts 40 C8
North Newton
Somset 25 L5
Northney Hants 17 K2
North Nibley Gloucs 39 H2
Northolt Gt Lon 43 J4
Northolt Airport
Gt Lon 43 H4
Northop Flints 111 H7
Northop Hall Flints 111 J7
North Ormesby
Middsb 142 B4
North Ormsby Lincs ... 118 C3
Northorpe Kirk 123 J6
Northorpe Lincs 103 K5
Northorpe Lincs 116 E3
North Otterington
N York 132 E2
North Owersby Lincs ... 117 H3
Northowram Calder 123 G5
North Perrott Somset ... 13 L1
North Petherton
Somset 25 L5
North Petherwin
Cnwll 9 H6
North Pickenham
Norfk 91 J3
North Piddle Worcs 71 G4
North Poorton
Dorset 13 M3
Northport Dorset 15 H5
North Queensferry
Fife 176 F3
North Rauceby
Lincs 103 G3
Northrepps Norfk 106 F5
North Reston Lincs 118 E5
North Rigton N York ... 123 K1
North Rode Ches E 113 K7
North Roe Shet 235 c3

North Ronaldsay
Ork 234 e3
North Ronaldsay
Airport Ork 234 e3
North Runcton Norfk...... 90 F1
North Scarle Lincs 116 D7
North Shian Ag & B.... 191 H7
North Shields
N Tyne 151 J2
North Shoebury
Sthend.................... 46 F3
North Shore Bpool 120 D3
North Side C Pete........ 89 K4
North Somercotes
Lincs 118 F3
North Stainley
N York 132 D4
North Stifford Thurr...... 45 L4
North Stoke BaNES........ 39 G6
North Stoke Oxon........ 41 L3
North Stoke W Susx........ 18 D4
Northstowe Cambs........ 76 B2
North Street Kent........ 34 D3
North Street W Berk 41 M6
North Sunderland
Nthumb 169 J3
North Tamerton
Cnwll 9 J5
North Tawton Devon...... 10 F4
North Third Stirlg 175 K1
North Thoresby
Lincs 118 D2
North Tolsta W Isls...... 232 g2
Northton W Isls 232 d5
North Town Devon........ 10 D3
North Town Somset........ 26 E3
North Town W & M 42 E4
North Tuddenham
Norfk...................... 92 C2
North Uist W Isls.......... 233 b6
Northumberland
National Park
Nthumb 157 K5
North Walsham
Norfk.................... 107 G6
North Waltham
Hants...................... 29 K3
North Warnborough
Hants...................... 30 B2
North Weald
Bassett Essex 60 D7
North Wheatley
Notts 116 C4
Northwich Ches W 112 F6
Northwick Worcs........ 70 E3
North Widcombe
BaNES..................... 38 E8
North Willingham
Lincs 117 K4
North Wingfield
Derbys.................. 115 H8
North Witham Lincs...... 102 F7
Northwold Norfk.......... 91 H4
Northwood C Stke........ 99 K3
Northwood Gt Lon........ 43 H3
Northwood IoW.......... 16 F4
Northwood Shrops........ 98 C6
Northwood Green
Gloucs.................... 55 G5
North Wootton
Dorset.................... 26 F8
North Wootton
Norfk.................... 105 G7
North Wootton
Somset.................... 26 E3
North Wraxall Wilts...... 39 J5
North York Moors
National Park 142 F6
Norton Donc.............. 124 E7
Norton E Susx............ 19 M5
Norton Gloucs............ 55 J3
Norton Halton............ 112 D5
Norton Nhants............ 73 H2
Norton Notts............. 115 L6
Norton Powys............. 68 F2
Norton S on T............ 141 K3
Norton Sheff............. 115 G5
Norton Shrops........... 84 D4

Norton Suffk.............. 77 L2
Norton Swans............. 51 H7
Norton W Susx............ 18 C4
Norton Wilts.............. 39 K4
Norton Worcs............. 70 F4
Norton Worcs............. 71 J5
Norton Bavant Wilts...... 27 K3
Norton Canes Staffs...... 85 H2
Norton Canes
Services Staffs........... 85 H3
Norton Canon
Herefs.................... 69 H5
Norton Disney Lincs 102 E2
Norton Fitzwarren
Somset.................... 25 J6
Norton Green IoW........ 16 D5
Norton Hawkfield
BaNES.................... 38 E7
Norton Heath Essex 60 F6
Norton in Hales
Shrops.................... 99 G5
Norton-Juxta-
Twycross Leics........ 86 D3
Norton-le-Clay
N York 132 F5
Norton-le-Moors
C Stke.................... 99 K3
Norton Lindsey
Warwks.................... 72 B2
Norton Little Green
Suffk.................... 77 L2
Norton Malreward
BaNES.................... 38 E7
Norton-on-Derwent
N York 134 C5
Norton St Philip
Somset.................... 27 H1
Norton Subcourse
Norfk.................... 93 J4
Norton sub Hamdon
Somset.................... 26 C7
Norwell Notts............ 102 C1
Norwell Woodhouse
Notts.................... 116 B8
Norwich Norfk............ 92 F2
Norwich Airport
Norfk.................... 92 E2
Norwick Shet............ 235 e1
Norwood Clacks.......... 185 J8
Norwood Green
Gt Lon.................... 43 J5
Norwood Hill Surrey...... 31 L3
Norwoodside Cambs...... 90 B4
Noss Mayo Devon.......... 6 E6
Nosterfield N York...... 132 D4
Nostie Highld.......... 210 D8
Notgrove Gloucs.......... 56 C4
Nottage Brdgnd.......... 36 C5
Nottingham C Nott...... 101 L5
Notton Wakefd.......... 123 L7
Notton Wilts............. 39 K6
Noutard's Green
Worcs.................... 70 E2
Nuffield Oxon............ 42 A3
Nunburnholme
E R Yk.................... 125 K2
Nuneaton Warwks........ 86 D5
Nunhead Gt Lon.......... 45 G5
Nun Monkton N York.... 133 H7
Nunney Somset............ 27 G3
Nunnington N York...... 133 K4
Nunsthorpe NE Lin 127 G8
Nunthorpe C York...... 124 F1
Nunthorpe Middsb...... 142 C4
Nunthorpe Village
Middsb.................. 142 C5
Nunton Wilts............. 28 D6
Nunwick N York.......... 132 E5
Nursling Hants............ 29 G7
Nutbourne W Susx........ 17 L2
Nutbourne W Susx........ 18 E3
Nutfield Surrey.......... 32 B3
Nuthall Notts............ 101 K4
Nuthampstead Herts...... 76 B7
Nuthurst W Susx.......... 31 K6
Nutley E Susx............ 32 D7
Nuttall Bury............. 122 B7
Nybster Highld.......... 231 L3

Nyetimber W Susx.......... 18 B6
Nyewood W Susx.......... 30 D6
Nymans W Susx............ 31 L5
Nymet Rowland
Devon.................... 11 G4
Nymet Tracey Devon...... 11 G5
Nympsfield Gloucs........ 55 J7
Nynehead Somset.......... 25 H6
Nyton W Susx............. 18 C5

O

Oadby Leics.............. 87 J4
Oad Street Kent.......... 34 B3
Oakamoor Staffs........ 100 B4
Oakbank W Loth........ 176 E5
Oak Cross Devon.......... 10 D5
Oakdale Caerph.......... 37 J2
Oake Somset.............. 25 J6
Oaken Staffs............. 84 F3
Oakenclough Lancs 121 H2
Oakengates Wrekin........ 84 C2
Oakenshaw Dur.......... 150 F7
Oakenshaw Kirk........ 123 H5
Oakford Cerdgn.......... 66 B3
Oakford Devon............ 24 E6
Oakham Rutlnd........... 88 C2
Oakhanger Hants.......... 30 C4
Oakhill Somset............ 26 F3
Oakington Cambs........ 76 B2
Oaklands Herts............ 59 L4
Oakle Street Gloucs...... 55 H4
Oakley Bed............... 74 E4
Oakley Bucks............. 57 M5
Oakley Fife.............. 176 D1
Oakley Hants............. 29 K2
Oakley Suffk............. 92 E7
Oakridge Lynch
Gloucs.................... 55 K7
Oaksey Wilts............. 39 M2
Oakthorpe Leics.......... 86 D2
Oakwood C Derb.......... 101 G5
Oakworth C Brad........ 122 F3
Oare Kent................. 34 D3
Oare Somset.............. 24 C3
Oare Wilts............... 40 D7
Oasby Lincs............. 103 G5
Oath Somset.............. 26 B6
Oathlaw Angus.......... 196 D5
Oatlands Park Surrey...... 43 H7
Oban Ag & B............. 182 B2
Oban Airport Ag & B... 182 C1
Obley Shrops............. 83 G7
Obney P & K............. 195 G8
Oborne Dorset............ 26 F7
Occold Suffk............. 78 D1
Occumster Highld........ 231 J7
Ochiltree E Ayrs........ 163 L5
Ockbrook Derbys........ 101 H5
Ocker Hill Sandw........ 85 H5
Ockham Surrey............ 31 H1
Ockle Highld............ 190 B3
Ockley Surrey............ 31 J4
Ocle Pychard Herefs...... 69 L5
Odcombe Somset.......... 26 D7
Odd Down BaNES........ 39 H7
Oddingley Worcs.......... 71 G3
Oddington Oxon.......... 57 K5
Odell Bed................ 74 D3
Odiham Hants............. 30 C2
Odsal C Brad............ 123 H5
Odsey Cambs............. 75 K6
Odstock Wilts............ 28 D6
Odstone Leics............ 86 E3
Offchurch Warwks........ 72 D2
Offenham Worcs.......... 71 J5
Offerton Stockp........ 113 K4
Offham E Susx............ 19 L3
Offham Kent.............. 33 H2
Offham W Susx............ 18 D4
Offord Cluny Cambs...... 75 J2
Offord D'Arcy Cambs...... 75 J2
Offton Suffk............. 78 C5
Offwell Devon............ 12 F3
Ogbourne Maizey
Wilts.................... 40 D6

Ogbourne St
Andrew Wilts............ 40 D6
Ogbourne St
George Wilts............ 40 D5
Ogle Nthumb............ 158 E6
Oglet Lpool............. 112 C5
Ogmore V Glam.......... 36 D5
Ogmore-by-Sea
V Glam.................... 36 D5
Ogmore Vale Brdgnd...... 36 E3
Okeford Fitzpaine
Dorset.................... 14 F1
Okehampton Devon........ 10 E5
Oker Side Derbys........ 100 F1
Okewood Hill Surrey 31 J4
Old Nhants.............. 87 L8
Old Aberdeen
C Aber.................. 207 H4
Old Alresford Hants........ 29 L5
Oldany Highld.......... 224 D2
Old Arley Warwks 86 C5
Old Auchenbrack
D & G................... 154 D3
Old Basford C Nott...... 101 K4
Old Basing Hants.......... 30 A2
Old Beetley Norfk...... 106 A8
Oldberrow Warwks........ 71 K2
Old Bewick Nthumb...... 169 G5
Old Bolingbroke
Lincs.................... 118 E8
Old Boxted Essex........ 62 B2
Old Bramhope
Leeds.................... 123 J2
Old Brampton
Derbys.................. 115 G6
Old Bridge of Urr
D & G................... 146 D2
Old Buckenham
Norfk.................... 92 C5
Old Burghclere
Hants.................... 41 J8
Oldbury Sandw............ 85 H5
Oldbury Shrops............ 84 C5
Oldbury Warwks............ 86 C5
Oldbury-on-Severn
S Glos.................... 38 E2
Oldbury on the Hill
Gloucs.................... 39 J3
Old Byland N York........ 133 H3
Old Cantley Donc........ 115 L2
Oldcastle Mons........... 53 L3
Old Catton Norfk.......... 92 F2
Old Clee NE Lin.......... 127 G8
Old Cleeve Somset........ 25 G3
Old Colwyn Conwy 110 B6
Oldcotes Notts.......... 115 L4
Old Coulsdon Gt Lon...... 32 B2
Old Dailly S Ayrs........ 152 F3
Old Dalby Leics.......... 102 A7
Old Deer Abers.......... 217 J5
Old Edlington Donc...... 115 K3
Old Ellerby E R Yk........ 126 E3
Old Felixstowe Suffk...... 79 G7
Oldfield Worcs.......... 70 E2
Old Fletton C Pete........ 89 H4
Oldford Somset............ 27 H2
Old Forge Herefs........ 54 E4
Old Grimsby IoS............ 2 a1
Old Hall Green Herts...... 60 B4
Oldham Oldham.......... 113 L1
Oldhamstocks E Loth... 178 F4
Old Harlow Essex........ 60 D5
Old Hunstanton
Norfk.................... 105 G4
Old Hurst Cambs........ 89 K7
Old Hutton Cumb........ 130 B2
Old Inns Services
N Lans.................. 175 K3
Old Kilpatrick
W Duns.................. 174 E4
Old Knebworth Herts...... 59 L4
Old Lakenham Norfk...... 92 F3
Oldland S Glos........... 38 F6
Old Langho Lancs...... 121 K4
Old Leake Lincs.......... 104 C3
Old Malton N York...... 134 C4
Oldmeldrum Abers...... 216 F8
Oldmill Cnwll.............. 5 F8

Old Milverton
Warwks..................72 C2
Oldmixon N Som.......37 M8
Old Newton Suffk......78 C3
Old Portlethen
Abers....................207 H6
Old Radford C Nott....101 K4
Old Radnor Powys......68 E3
Old Rayne Abers.......216 D8
Old Romney Kent.......21 K2
Old Shoreham
W Susx..................19 G4
Oldshoremore Highld..228 C4
Old Sodbury S Glos....39 H4
Old Somerby Lincs....102 F5
Oldstead N York.......133 H4
Old Stratford Nhants...73 L6
Old Struan P & K......194 C4
Old Swinford Dudley...84 F6
Old Thirsk N York.....132 F3
Old Town Cumb.........130 B3
Old Town E Susx.......20 C5
Old Town IoS...........2 b2
Old Trafford Traffd...113 J3
Oldwall Cumb..........148 E3
Oldwalls Swans........50 F6
Old Warden C Beds.....75 G5
Old Weston Cambs......89 G7
Old Wick Highld......231 L5
Old Windsor W & M.....43 G5
Old Wives Lees Kent...34 E4
Old Woking Surrey.....43 G8
Olgrinmore Highld....231 G5
Olive Green Staffs...100 C8
Oliver's Battery
Hants....................29 J6
Ollaberry Shet........235 c3
Ollach Highld.........209 H6
Ollerton Ches E.......113 H6
Ollerton Notts........116 A7
Ollerton Shrops.......98 F7
Olney M Keyn..........74 C4
Olrig House Highld...231 H3
Olton Solhll..........85 K6
Olveston S Glos.......38 E3
Ombersley Worcs.......70 E2
Ompton Notts.........116 B7
Onchan IoM............237 d5
Onecote Staffs.......100 B2
Onibury Shrops........83 J7
Onich Highld.........191 K4
Onllwyn Neath.........52 C6
Onneley Staffs........99 H4
Onslow Green Essex....61 G4
Onslow Village
Surrey...................31 G2
Onston Ches W........112 E6
Opinan Highld........219 H6
Orbliston Moray......215 G3
Orbost Highld........208 D5
Orby Lincs...........119 G7
Orchard Portman
Somset...................25 K6
Orcheston Wilts.......28 B3
Orcop Herefs..........54 C3
Orcop Hill Herefs.....54 C3
Ord Abers.............216 C3
Ordhead Abers........206 C3
Ordie Abers..........205 K5
Ordiequish Moray.....215 H3
Ordsall Notts........116 B5
Ore E Susx............21 G4
Orford Suffk..........79 J4
Orford Warrtn........112 E4
Organford Dorset......15 H4
Orkney Islands Ork....234 c6
Orkney Neolithic
Ork....................234 b6
Orlestone Kent........34 D7
Orleton Herefs........69 J2
Orleton Worcs.........70 C2
Orlingbury Nhants.....74 C1
Ormesby R & Cl.......142 C4
Ormesby St
Margaret Norfk.......93 K1
Ormesby St Michael
Norfk....................93 K1
Ormiscaig Highld.....219 K4

Ormiston E Loth......177 L4
Ormsaigmore Highld...189 L4
Ormsary Ag & B.......172 C4
Ormskirk Lancs.......120 F8
Oronsay Ag & B.......171 G2
Orphir Ork...........234 b6
Orpington Gt Lon......45 J6
Orrell Sefton........111 K3
Orrell Wigan.........112 D2
Orroland D & G.......146 D5
Orsett Thurr..........45 M4
Orslow Staffs.........84 E1
Orston Notts.........102 C4
Orton Cumb...........138 F5
Orton Nhants..........88 B7
Orton Staffs..........84 F4
Orton Longueville
C Pete...................89 H4
Orton-on-the-Hill
Leics....................86 C3
Orton Waterville
C Pete...................89 H4
Orwell Cambs..........75 L4
Osbaldeston Lancs....121 J4
Osbaldwick C York....124 F1
Osbaston Leics........86 E3
Osbaston Shrops.......97 L7
Osborne IoW...........17 G4
Osbournby Lincs......103 H5
Oscroft Ches W.......112 D7
Ose Highld...........208 E6
Osgathorpe Leics.....101 H8
Osgodby Lincs........117 H3
Osgodby N York.......124 F4
Osgodby N York.......135 G3
Oskaig Highld........209 H6
Oskamull Ag & B......189 L7
Osmaston Derbys......100 D4
Osmington Dorset......14 D5
Osmington Mills
Dorset...................14 E6
Osmondthorpe
Leeds...................123 L4
Osmotherley N York...141 K7
Osney Oxon............57 J6
Ospringe Kent.........34 D3
Ossett Wakefd.......123 K6
Ossington Notts......116 C8
Osterley Gt Lon.......44 D5
Oswaldkirk N York....133 K4
Oswaldtwistle Lancs..121 L5
Oswestry Shrops.......97 L6
Otairnis W Isls......232 c5
Otford Kent...........32 F2
Otham Kent............33 K3
Othery Somset.........26 B5
Otley Leeds..........123 J2
Otley Suffk...........78 E4
Otterbourne Hants.....29 J6
Otterburn N York.....131 G7
Otterburn Nthumb.....157 M4
Otter Ferry Ag & B...172 F2
Otterham Cnwll........8 F6
Otterhampton
Somset...................25 K3
Otternish W Isls......232 c5
Ottershaw Surrey......43 G7
Otterswick Shet......235 d3
Otterton Devon........12 E5
Ottery St Mary Devon...12 E4
Ottinge Kent..........34 F6
Ottringham E R Yk....127 G5
Oughterside Cumb.....147 K6
Oughtibridge Sheff...114 F3
Oughtrington Warrtn..113 G4
Oulston N York.......133 H5
Oulton Cumb..........147 M5
Oulton Norfk.........106 D6
Oulton Staffs.........99 K5
Oulton Suffk..........93 L5
Oulton Broad Suffk....93 L5
Oulton Street Norfk..106 D6
Oundle Nhants.........88 F6
Ousdale Highld.......230 F8
Ousby Cumb...........149 G7
Ousden Suffk..........77 G3
Ousefleet E R Yk.....125 K6
Ouston Dur...........151 G4

Outgate Cumb.........137 K7
Outhgill Cumb........139 H6
Outhill Warwks........71 K2
Outlane Kirk.........123 G6
Out Rawcliffe Lancs..120 E3
Out Skerries Shet....235 e4
Outwell Norfk.........90 D3
Outwood Surrey........32 B4
Outwoods Staffs.......99 H8
Ouzlewell Green
Leeds...................123 L5
Ovenden Calder......123 G5
Over Cambs............75 L1
Over Ches W..........112 F7
Overbury Worcs........71 G6
Overcombe Dorset......14 D6
Over Compton
Dorset...................26 E7
Over Haddon Derbys...114 D7
Over Hulton Bolton...113 G1
Over Kellet Lancs....129 L5
Over Kiddington
Oxon.....................57 H4
Overleigh Somset......26 C4
Over Norton Oxon......56 F3
Over Peover Ches E...113 H6
Overpool Ches W......111 L6
Overscaig Highld.....225 J4
Overseal Derbys.......86 C1
Over Silton N York...133 G2
Oversland Kent........34 E3
Overstone Nhants......74 B2
Over Stowey Somset....25 J4
Overstrand Norfk.....106 F4
Over Stratton
Somset...................26 B7
Overthorpe Nhants.....72 F6
Overton C Aber.......207 G3
Overton Hants.........29 K2
Overton Lancs........129 J7
Overton N York.......133 H7
Overton Shrops........69 K1
Overton Swans.........50 F7
Overton Wakefd......123 K7
Overton Wrexhm........98 A4
Overtown N Lans......175 L7
Over Wallop Hants.....28 F4
Over Whitacre
Warwks...................86 B5
Over Worton Oxon......57 H3
Oving Bucks...........58 C4
Oving W Susx..........18 B5
Ovingdean Br & H......19 K5
Ovingham Nthumb.....150 D3
Ovington Dur.........140 E4
Ovington Essex........77 H6
Ovington Hants........29 K5
Ovington Norfk........91 K3
Ovington Nthumb.....150 D3
Ower Hants............28 F7
Owermoigne Dorset.....14 E5
Owlerton Sheff.......115 G4
Owlsmoor Br For.......42 D7
Owlswick Bucks........58 C6
Owmby Lincs..........117 G4
Owmby Lincs..........117 H1
Owslebury Hants.......29 K6
Owston Donc..........124 F7
Owston Leics..........87 L3
Owston Ferry N Linc..116 D2
Owstwick E R Yk......127 G4
Owthorne E R Yk......127 H5
Owthorpe Notts.......102 A5
Owton Manor Hartpl...141 L2
Oxborough Norfk.......91 G3
Oxcombe Lincs........118 D6
Oxenholme Cumb.......129 L2
Oxenhope C Brad......122 F4
Oxen Park Cumb.......129 G3
Oxenpill Somset.......26 C3
Oxenton Gloucs........55 L2
Oxenwood Wilts........40 F8
Oxford Oxon...........57 K6
Oxford Airport Oxon....57 J5
Oxford Services
Oxon.....................57 L6
Oxgangs C Edin......177 H4
Oxhey Herts...........43 J2

Oxhill Dur...........150 F4
Oxhill Warwks.........72 C5
Oxley Wolves..........84 F3
Oxley Green Essex.....61 L5
Oxlode Cambs..........90 C6
Oxnam Border.........167 L5
Oxnead Norfk.........106 F7
Oxshott Surrey........43 J7
Oxspring Barns.......114 F2
Oxted Surrey..........32 D3
Oxton Border.........178 B7
Oxton N York.........124 D2
Oxton Notts..........101 M3
Oxton Wirral.........111 J4
Oxwich Swans..........51 G7
Oxwich Green Swans....50 F7
Oykel Bridge Highld..221 K2
Oyne Abers...........206 D1
Oystermouth Swans.....51 H7

P

Pabail W Isls........232 g2
Packington Leics......86 D1
Packmoor C Stke.......99 K2
Padanaram Angus......196 C6
Padbury Bucks.........58 B2
Paddington Gt Lon.....44 F4
Paddlesworth Kent.....35 G6
Paddlesworth Kent.....46 B7
Paddock Wood Kent.....33 H4
Padiham Lancs........122 B4
Padside N York.......132 B7
Padstow Cnwll..........4 E2
Padworth W Berk.......41 L7
Pagham W Susx.........18 B6
Paglesham Essex.......46 F2
Paignton Torbay.......7 K4
Pailton Warwks........86 F6
Painscastle Powys.....68 D5
Painshawfield
Nthumb..................150 D3
Painsthorpe
E R Yk..................134 C7
Painswick Gloucs......55 K6
Painter's Forstal
Kent.....................34 D3
Paisley Rens.........174 E5
Pakefield Suffk.......93 L5
Pakenham Suffk........77 L2
Paley Street W & M....42 E5
Palfrey Wsall.........85 H4
Palgrave Suffk........92 D7
Pallington Dorset.....14 E4
Palmarsh Kent.........34 F7
Palmerston E Ayrs....163 L5
Palnackie D & G......146 E4
Palnure D & G........145 J3
Palterton Derbys.....115 J7
Pamber End Hants......41 L8
Pamber Green Hants....41 L8
Pamber Heath Hants....41 L7
Pamington Gloucs......55 L2
Pamphill Dorset.......15 J3
Pampisford Cambs......76 C5
Panbride Angus.......187 J1
Pancrasweek Devon......9 H4
Pandy Mons............53 M4
Pandy Wrexhm..........97 M2
Pandy Tudur Conwy....110 B8
Panfield Essex........61 H3
Pangbourne W Berk.....41 M5
Pangdean W Susx.......19 J4
Pannal N York.......123 L1
Pannal Ash N York....132 D8
Pant Shrops...........97 L7
Pantasaph Flints.....111 G6
Pant-ffrwyth Brdgnd...36 E4
Pant Glas Gwynd.......95 H3
Pantglas Powys........81 G4
Panton Lincs.........117 K5
Pantside Caerph.......37 K2
Pant-y-dwr Powys......81 L8
Pantymwyn Flints.....111 H8
Panxworth Norfk.......93 H2
Papa Stour Shet......235 b5

Papa Stour Airport
Shet......................... 235 b5
Papa Westray Ork...... 234 c3
Papa Westray
  Airport Ork................ 234 c3
Papcastle Cumb.......... 136 F2
Papigoe Highld............ 231 L5
Papple E Loth................ 178 D4
Papplewick Notts......... 101 K3
Papworth Everard
  Cambs........................75 K3
Papworth St Agnes
  Cambs........................75 J2
Par Cnwll.......................5 G5
Parbold Lancs............. 121 G7
Parbrook Somset........26 E4
Parc Gwynd..................96 D5
Parc Seymour Newpt 38 B3
Pardshaw Cumb......... 136 F3
Parham Suffk...............79 G3
Park D & G................... 154 F4
Park Nthumb............... 149 H3
Park Corner Oxon.......42 B3
Parkend Gloucs............54 E6
Parker's Green Kent 33 G4
Parkeston Essex...........62 F2
Parkeston Quay
  Essex...........................62 F2
Park Farm Kent............34 D6
Parkgate Ches W........ 111 J6
Parkgate D & G.......... 155 H4
Park Gate Hants..........17 G2
Park Gate Leeds......... 123 J3
Parkgate Surrey...........31 K3
Parkhall W Duns......... 174 E4
Parkham Devon............22 F6
Parkmill Swans.............51 G7
Park Royal Gt Lon........44 D4
Parkside Dur.............. 151 K5
Parkside N Lans......... 175 L6
Parkstone BCP.............15 J4
Park Street Herts.........59 J6
Parracombe Devon......23 L3
Parson Drove Cambs....89 L2
Parson's Heath Essex....62 B3
Partick C Glas............. 174 F5
Partington Traffd....... 113 G3
Partney Lincs.............. 118 F7
Parton Cumb.............. 136 D3
Partridge Green
  W Susx.........................19 G2
Parwich Derbys......... 100 D2
Passenham Nhants......73 L6
Paston C Pete...............89 H3
Paston Norfk............. 107 G5
Patcham Br & H...........19 J4
Patching W Susx...........18 E4
Patchway S Glos..........38 E4
Pateley Bridge
  N York...................... 132 B6
Pathhead Fife............. 186 E8
Pathhead Mdloth....... 177 K5
Path of Condie
  P & K......................... 185 M5
Patna E Ayrs.............. 163 K7
Patney Wilts.................40 B8
Patrick IoM................ 237 b5
Patrick Brompton
  N York....................... 132 C2
Patricroft Salfd.......... 113 H2
Patrington E R Yk....... 127 H6
Patrington Haven
  E R Yk........................ 127 H6
Patrixbourne Kent......35 G4
Patterdale Cumb........ 137 L4
Pattingham Staffs........84 E4
Pattishall Nhants.........73 J4
Pattiswick Green
  Essex...........................61 K3
Paul Cnwll.......................2 E5
Paulerspury Nhants....73 K5
Paull E R Yk................ 126 E5
Paulton BaNES............26 F1
Paultons Park Hants....28 F7
Pauperhaugh
  Nthumb...................... 158 D3
Pavenham Bed............74 E4
Pawlett Somset............25 L3

Paxford Gloucs 71 L6
Paxton Border............ 179 J7
Payhembury Devon......12 E3
Paythorne Lancs........ 122 C1
Peacehaven E Susx......19 L5
Peak District
  National Park 114 D3
Peak Forest Derbys.... 114 C5
Peakirk C Pete..............89 H3
Peasedown St John
  BaNES..........................39 G8
Peasemore W Berk......41 J5
Peasenhall Suffk.........79 H2
Pease Pottage
  W Susx.........................31 L5
Pease Pottage
  Services W Susx...........31 L5
Peaslake Surrey 31 H3
Peasley Cross St Hel... 112 D3
Peasmarsh E Susx........21 H2
Peathill Abers............. 217 H2
Peat Inn Fife.............. 187 G5
Peatling Magna
  Leics...........................87 H5
Peatling Parva Leics 87 H5
Pebmarsh Essex...........77 J7
Pebsham E Susx...........20 F4
Pebworth Worcs...........71 K5
Pecket Well Calder..... 122 E5
Peckforton Ches E........98 D2
Peckham Gt Lon...........45 G5
Peckleton Leics............86 F4
Pedlinge Kent...............34 F7
Pedmore Dudley...........85 G6
Pedwell Somset...........26 B4
Peebles Border........... 166 C2
Peel IoM..................... 237 b4
Peene Kent...................35 G6
Pegsdon C Beds............59 J2
Pegswood Nthumb..... 159 G5
Pegwell Kent...............35 K2
Peinchorran Highld.... 209 H7
Peinlich Highld.......... 208 F3
Peldon Essex................62 B5
Pelsall Wsall................85 H3
Pelton Dur................. 151 G4
Pelynt Cnwll..................5 K5
Pemberton Carmth......51 G5
Pemberton Wigan...... 112 D2
Pembrey Carmth..........50 E5
Pembridge Herefs........69 H3
Pembroke Pembks........49 G7
Pembroke Dock
  Pembks........................49 G6
Pembrokeshire
  Coast National
  Park Pembks..........48 E4
Pembury Kent..............33 G5
Pen-allt Herefs.............54 E3
Penallt Mons................54 D6
Penally Pembks.............49 J7
Penarth V Glam............37 J6
Pen-bont
  Rhydybeddau
  Cerdgn........................80 F6
Penbryn Cerdgn...........65 J4
Pencader Carmth..........66 B7
Pencaitland E Loth..... 177 L5
Pencarnisiog IoA....... 108 D6
Pencarreg Carmth........66 C5
Pencelli Powys.............53 H3
Penclawdd Swans.......51 G6
Pencoed Brdgnd...........36 E4
Pencombe Herefs.........69 L4
Pencraig Herefs............54 E4
Pencraig Powys.............97 G6
Pendeen Cnwll...............2 C4
Penderyn Rhondd........52 E6
Pendine Carmth...........50 B4
Pendlebury Salfd....... 113 H2
Pendleton Lancs......... 121 L3
Pendock Worcs.............55 H2
Pendoggett Cnwll..........8 D8
Pendomer Somset.......13 M1
Pendoylan V Glam........37 G5
Penegoes Powys...........81 G4
Pen-ffordd Pembks......49 J3
Pengam Caerph............37 J2

Pengam Cardif.............37 K5
Penge Gt Lon................45 G6
Pengelly Cnwll................8 E7
Penhallow Cnwll.............3 K2
Penhalvean Cnwll...........3 J4
Penhill Swindn.............40 D3
Penhow Newpt.............38 B3
Penicuik Mdloth......... 177 H6
Penifiler Highld.......... 209 G6
Peninver Ag & B......... 161 J4
Penistone Barns........ 114 E2
Penkill S Ayrs............. 152 F3
Penkridge Staffs...........85 G2
Penley Wrexhm............98 B4
Penllyn V Glam.............36 F5
Penmachno Conwy......96 C3
Penmaen Caerph.........37 J2
Penmaen Swans...........51 G7
Penmaenmawr
  Conwy...................... 109 K6
Penmaenpool Gwynd ...95 M8
Penmark V Glam...........37 G6
Penmynydd IoA.......... 109 G6
Pennal Gwynd..............80 F4
Pennan Abers.............. 216 F2
Pennant Powys............81 J4
Pennar Pembks.............49 G6
Pennerley Shrops.........83 G4
Pennines.................... 122 E4
Pennington Cumb...... 128 F4
Pennorth Powys...........53 H3
Penn Street Bucks........42 F2
Penny Bridge Cumb... 129 G3
Pennycross Ag & B...... 181 G3
Pennyghael Ag & B..... 181 H3
Pennyglen S Ayrs....... 163 H7
Pennymoor Devon.......11 K3
Pennywell Sundld...... 151 J4
Penparc Cerdgn............65 H5
Penperlleni Mons.........53 L6
Penpoll Cnwll..................5 J5
Penponds Cnwll.............3 H4
Penpont D & G........... 154 E4
Pen-rhiw Pembks........65 H6
Penrhiwceiber
  Rhondd.......................37 G2
Pen Rhiwfawr Neath....51 L4
Penrhiwllan Cerdgn.....65 K6
Penrhiwpal Cerdgn......65 K5
Penrhos Gwynd............94 F5
Penrhos Mons..............54 B5
Penrhyn Bay Conwy... 110 A5
Penrhyn-coch
  Cerdgn........................80 E6
Penrhyndeudraeth
  Gwynd........................95 K5
Penrhyn Slate
  Landscape Gwynd.. 109 J7
Penrice Swans..............50 F7
Penrioch N Ayrs......... 161 L1
Penrith Cumb.............. 138 D2
Penrose Cnwll................4 D2
Penruddock Cumb...... 138 B2
Penryn Cnwll..................3 K4
Pensarn Conwy.......... 110 C5
Pensax Worcs...............70 C2
Penselwood Somset.....27 H5
Pensford BaNES............38 F7
Pensham Worcs............71 G5
Penshaw Sundld......... 151 H4
Penshurst Kent.............32 F4
Pensilva Cnwll.................5 L2
Pensnett Dudley...........85 G5
Pentewan Cnwll..............4 F6
Pentir Gwynd.............. 109 H7
Pentire Cnwll..................4 C4
Pentlow Essex..............77 J5
Pentney Norfk..............91 G2
Pentonbridge Cumb... 156 D6
Penton Mewsey
  Hants..........................29 G3
Pentraeth IoA............. 109 G6
Pentre Mons................54 B7
Pentre Rhondd.............36 F2
Pentre Shrops...............98 A8
Pentrebach Myr Td......52 E7
Pentre-bach Powys......52 B2
Pentre Berw IoA......... 108 F6

Pentrecelyn Denbgs.....97 J2
Pentre-celyn Powys.....81 J3
Pentre-chwyth
  Swans.........................51 J6
Pentre-cwrt Carmth....65 L6
Pentredwr Denbgs.......97 J3
Pentrefelin Gwynd.......95 J5
Pentrefoelas Conwy.....96 D3
Pentregat Cerdgn.........65 K4
Pentre-Gwenlais
  Carmth........................51 H3
Pentre Hodrey
  Shrops........................83 G7
Pentre Llanrhaeadr
  Denbgs..................... 110 F8
Pentre Meyrick
  V Glam........................36 E5
Pentre-tafarn-y-
  fedw Conwy..............96 C1
Pentrich Derbys.......... 101 G3
Pentridge Dorset.........28 B7
Pentwyn Cardif............37 J4
Pen-twyn Mons............54 D6
Pentwynmaur Caerph...37 J2
Pentyrch Cardif............37 H4
Penwithick Cnwll...........5 G5
Penybanc Carmth.........51 H2
Penybont Powys...........68 C2
Pen-y-bont Powys........97 K7
Penybontfawr Powys....97 G7
Pen-y-bryn Pembks......65 G6
Penycae Wrexhm..........97 L4
Pen-y-clawdd Mons.....54 C6
Pen-y-coedcae
  Rhondd.......................37 G3
Penycwm Pembks.........48 E3
Pen-y-felin Flints........ 111 H2
Penyffordd Flints..........97 L1
Pen-y-Garnedd
  Powys.........................97 H7
Pen-y-graig Gwynd......94 D5
Penygraig Rhondd........36 F3
Penygroes Carmth........51 H3
Penygroes Gwynd.........95 H2
Pen-y-Mynydd
  Carmth........................50 F5
Penymynydd Flints.......97 L1
Penysarn IoA.............. 108 F4
Pen-y-stryt Denbgs......97 K2
Penywaun Rhondd........52 F6
Penzance Cnwll...............2 E5
Peopleton Worcs..........71 G4
Peplow Shrops..............98 F7
Perceton N Ayrs.......... 163 J2
Percyhorner Abers..... 217 H2
Perelle Guern............. 236 b3
Perham Down Wilts......28 E2
Periton Somset.............24 E3
Perivale Gt Lon.............44 D4
Perkins Village
  Devon.........................12 D4
Perlethorpe Notts...... 115 M7
Perranarworthal
  Cnwll............................3 K4
Perranporth Cnwll.........3 K1
Perranuthnoe Cnwll......2 F5
Perranwell Cnwll............3 K4
Perranzabuloe Cnwll.....3 K2
Perry Birm...................85 J5
Perry Cambs.................75 G2
Perry Barr Birm............85 J5
Perry Green Wilts.........39 L3
Pershall Staffs..............99 J6
Pershore Worcs............71 G5
Pertenhall Bed.............74 F2
Perth P & K................. 186 B3
Perthy Shrops...............98 A5
Perton Herefs...............69 L6
Perton Staffs................84 F4
Peterborough C Pete....89 H4
Peterborough
  Services Cambs......89 G4
Peterchurch Herefs......69 G6
Peterculter C Aber...... 206 F5
Peterhead Abers........ 217 L5
Peterlee Dur............... 151 K6
Petersfield Hants..........30 C6
Peter's Green Herts......59 J4

Petersham Gt Lon..........44 D5
Peters Marland
  Devon..................10 C3
Peterstone
  Wentlooge Newpt.....37 K4
Peterston-super-
  Ely V Glam.............37 G5
Peterstow Herefs..........54 E3
Peter Tavy Devon...........6 D1
Petham Kent..............34 F4
Petherwin Gate
  Cnwll....................9 H6
Petrockstow Devon.......10 D3
Pett E Susx...............21 H3
Pettaugh Suffk...........78 E3
Petterden Angus........196 C7
Pettinain S Lans.........165 J2
Pettistree Suffk..........79 G4
Petton Devon.............24 F6
Petts Wood Gt Lon.......45 J6
Pettycur Fife............177 H2
Pettymuk Abers.........207 G1
Petworth W Susx.........31 G6
Pevensey E Susx..........20 D5
Pevensey Bay E Susx....20 D5
Pewsey Wilts.............40 D7
Pewsham Wilts...........39 L6
Phepson Worcs...........71 G3
Philham Devon...........22 D6
Philiphaugh Border....166 F4
Phillack Cnwll.............2 F4
Philleigh Cnwll............4 D7
Philpstoun W Loth.....176 E3
Phoenix Green Hants....30 C1
Pibsbury Somset........26 C6
Pickburn Donc..........115 K1
Pickering N York........134 C3
Pickford Covtry..........86 C6
Pickhill N York...........132 E3
Picklescott Shrops.......83 J4
Pickmere Ches E........113 G6
Pickney Somset..........25 J5
Pickwell Leics............87 L2
Pickworth Lincs........103 H5
Pickworth Rutlnd........88 E2
Picton Ches W..........112 B7
Picton N York...........141 K5
Piddinghoe E Susx......19 L5
Piddington Nhants......74 B4
Piddington Oxon........57 M5
Piddlehinton Dorset....14 D3
Piddletrenthide
  Dorset.................14 D3
Pidley Cambs............89 K7
Piercebridge Darltn...140 F4
Pierowall Ork...........234 c3
Pilgrims Hatch Essex...45 L2
Pilham Lincs............116 E3
Pillaton Cnwll.............6 A3
Pillerton Hersey
  Warwks..................72 C5
Pillerton Priors
  Warwks..................72 C5
Pilley Barns............115 G2
Pilley Hants..............16 D3
Pillgwenlly Newpt.......37 L3
Pilling Lancs............120 E2
Pilning S Glos...........38 D4
Pilsbury Derbys.........114 C8
Pilsdon Dorset...........13 K3
Pilsley Derbys...........101 H1
Pilsley Derbys..........114 E7
Pilson Green Norfk......93 H2
Piltdown E Susx.........19 L2
Pilton Devon.............23 J5
Pilton Nhants............88 E6
Pilton Rutlnd.............88 D3
Pilton Somset............26 E3
Pimlico Herts............59 H6
Pimperne Dorset........15 G1
Pinchbeck Lincs........103 L7
Pin Green Herts..........59 L3
Pinhoe Devon............12 C4
Pinley Green Warwks...72 B2
Pinminnoch S Ayrs....152 E4
Pinmore S Ayrs.........152 E4
Pinn Devon..............12 E5
Pinner Gt Lon............43 J3

Pinner Green Gt Lon....43 J3
Pinvin Worcs.............71 G5
Pinwherry S Ayrs......152 E5
Pinxton Derbys.........101 J2
Pipe and Lyde Herefs...69 K5
Pipe Aston Herefs.......69 J1
Pipe Gate Shrops........99 G4
Piperdam Angus........186 E1
Piperhill Highld........213 K4
Pipewell Nhants.........88 B6
Pirbright Surrey..........30 F1
Pirnie Border...........167 K4
Pirnmill N Ayrs.........161 L1
Pirton Herts.............59 J2
Pishill Oxon..............42 B3
Pistyll Gwynd.............94 F4
Pitblae Abers...........217 J2
Pitcairngreen P & K...185 M3
Pitcalnie Highld........223 H6
Pitcaple Abers.........206 D1
Pitcarity Angus........196 B4
Pitchcombe Gloucs.....55 J6
Pitchcott Bucks..........58 C4
Pitchford Shrops.........83 K3
Pitch Green Bucks.......58 C7
Pitchroy Moray.........214 E6
Pitcombe Somset........26 F5
Pitcox E Loth...........178 E4
Pitfichie Abers.........206 D3
Pitglassie Abers........216 D5
Pitgrudy Highld.........223 H3
Pitlessie Fife...........186 E5
Pitlochry P & K.........194 E5
Pitmachie Abers........216 C8
Pitmain Highld.........203 H5
Pitmedden Abers.......217 G8
Pitmedden Garden
  Abers.................217 G8
Pitminster Somset.......25 K7
Pitmuies Angus........196 F6
Pitmunie Abers.........206 C3
Pitney Somset............26 C5
Pitroddie P & K.........186 C3
Pitscottie Fife..........187 G5
Pitsea Essex..............46 C3
Pitsford Nhants..........73 L2
Pitstone Bucks...........58 F5
Pittarrow Abers........197 H2
Pittentrail Highld......226 C7
Pittenweem Fife........187 J6
Pitteuchar Fife.........186 D7
Pittodrie House
  Hotel Abers...........206 D1
Pitton Wilts..............28 E5
Pittulie Abers..........217 H2
Pity Me Dur.............151 G5
Pixham Surrey...........31 K2
Plains N Lans...........175 L5
Plaish Shrops............83 K4
Plaistow Gt Lon..........45 H4
Plaistow W Susx.........31 G5
Plaitford Hants..........28 F7
Plawsworth Dur........151 G5
Plaxtol Kent..............33 G3
Playden E Susx...........21 H2
Playford Suffk...........78 F5
Play Hatch Oxon.........42 C5
Playing Place Cnwll......4 C7
Playley Green Gloucs...55 H2
Plealey Shrops...........83 H3
Plean Stirlg.............175 L2
Pleasance Fife..........186 D5
Pleasington Bl w D....121 J5
Pleasley Derbys........115 J8
Pleasurewood Hills
  Suffk...................93 L4
Pleinheaume Guern...236 d2
Plemont Jersey.........236 a5
Plemstall Ches W.......112 C7
Pleshey Essex............61 G5
Plockton Highld........210 C7
Plowden Shrops.........83 H6
Pluckley Kent............34 B5
Pluckley Thorne Kent...34 B5
Plumbland Cumb.......147 K6
Plumley Ches E.........113 G6
Plumpton Cumb........148 E2
Plumpton E Susx........19 K3

Plumpton Nhants........73 H5
Plumpton Green
  E Susx..................19 K3
Plumstead Gt Lon.......45 J4
Plumstead Norfk.......106 D5
Plumtree Notts.........101 L6
Plungar Leics...........102 C5
Plurenden Kent..........34 C7
Plush Dorset.............14 D3
Plwmp Cerdgn...........65 K4
Plymouth C Plym..........6 C5
Plympton C Plym..........6 D5
Plymstock C Plym.........6 D5
Plymtree Devon..........12 D2
Pockley N York.........133 K3
Pocklington E R Yk....125 J2
Podimore Somset........26 D6
Podington Bed...........74 D3
Podmore Staffs..........99 H5
Pointon Lincs...........103 J6
Pokesdown BCP..........15 L4
Polbain Highld.........224 B6
Polbathic Cnwll............6 A4
Polbeth W Loth........176 D5
Poldark Mine Cnwll......3 H5
Polebrook Nhants........88 F6
Polegate E Susx..........20 C5
Polesden Lacey
  Surrey..................31 J2
Polesworth Warwks....86 C3
Polglass Highld........224 C6
Polgooth Cnwll............4 F5
Polgown D & G..........154 C2
Poling W Susx............18 E5
Poling Corner
  W Susx..................18 E5
Polkerris Cnwll............5 H5
Pollington E R Yk......124 F6
Polloch Highld.........190 F3
Pollok C Glas............174 F6
Pollokshaws C Glas...175 G6
Pollokshields C Glas...175 G5
Polmassick Cnwll.........4 F6
Polmont Falk............176 C3
Polnish Highld..........200 B8
Polperro Cnwll............5 K5
Polruan Cnwll.............5 H5
Polstead Suffk............78 B6
Poltalloch Ag & B......182 B7
Poltimore Devon........12 C3
Polton Mdloth.........177 J5
Polwarth Border.......178 F7
Polyphant Cnwll..........9 H7
Polzeath Cnwll............4 E1
Pomathorn Mdloth....177 H6
Pondersbridge
  Cambs..................89 J5
Ponders End Gt Lon....45 G2
Ponsanooth Cnwll........3 K4
Ponsworthy Devon.......7 G2
Pont Abraham
  Services Carmth......51 H4
Pontac Jersey..........236 e8
Pontantwn Carmth......50 F3
Pontardawe Neath......51 K5
Pontarddulais Swans...51 H5
Pont-ar-gothi
  Carmth.................51 G2
Pontarsais Carmth......66 B8
Pontblyddyn Flints....97 L1
Pontcysyllte
  Aqueduct Wrexhm....97 L4
Pontefract Wakefd....124 C6
Ponteland Nthumb....158 F7
Ponterwyd Cerdgn......81 G7
Pontesbury Shrops......83 H3
Pontesford Shrops......83 H3
Pontfadog Wrexhm.....97 K5
Pontfaen Pembks........64 E7
Pont-faen Powys........67 L7
Pontgarreg Cerdgn......65 K4
Pont Henri Carmth......50 F4
Ponthir Torfn............37 M2
Ponthirwaun Cerdgn...65 J5
Pontllanfraith
  Caerph.................37 J2
Pontlliw Swans..........51 H5
Pontllyfni Gwynd.......95 G3

Pontlottyn Caerph......53 H6
Pontnêddféchan
  Neath..................52 D6
Pontnewydd Torfn.....37 L2
Pontrhydfendigaid
  Cerdgn.................67 G2
Pontrhydyfen Neath...36 C2
Pont-rhyd-y-groes
  Cerdgn.................81 G8
Pontrilas Herefs.........54 B3
Pont Robert Powys.....82 C2
Pontsian Cerdgn.........66 B5
Pontsticill Myr Td......53 G5
Pontwelly Carmth......65 L6
Pontyates Carmth.......50 F4
Pontyberem Carmth....51 G4
Pontybodkin Flints.....97 L2
Pontyclun Rhondd......37 G4
Pontycymer Brdgnd....36 D3
Pontymister Caerph....37 K3
Pont-y-pant Conwy.....96 B2
Pontypool Torfn........53 L7
Pontypridd Rhondd....37 G3
Pontywaun Caerph.....37 K2
Pool Cnwll................3 H3
Poole BCP................15 J4
Poole Keynes Gloucs...39 M2
Poolewe Highld........219 K5
Pooley Bridge Cumb...138 C3
Poolfold Staffs..........99 K1
Poolhill Gloucs..........55 G3
Pool in Wharfedale
  Leeds.................123 J2
Pool of Muckhart
  Clacks.................185 L7
Pool Street Essex........77 H6
Poplar Gt Lon............45 G4
Porchfield IoW...........16 F4
Poringland Norfk.......92 F3
Porkellis Cnwll............3 J5
Porlock Somset..........24 D3
Porlock Weir Somset...24 D2
Portachoillan Ag & B...172 C6
Port-an-Eorna
  Highld................210 B7
Port Appin Ag & B.....191 H7
Port Askaig Ag & B....171 H5
Portavadie Ag & B......172 F4
Port Bannatyne
  Ag & B.................173 J5
Portbury N Som.........38 D5
Port Carlisle Cumb....147 M3
Port Charlotte
  Ag & B.................170 E6
Portchester Hants......17 H2
Port Driseach
  Ag & B.................173 G4
Port Ellen Ag & B.....160 C1
Port Elphinstone
  Abers..................206 E2
Portencalzie D & G....152 B7
Portencross N Ayrs....173 K8
Port Erin IoM..........237 a6
Portesham Dorset......14 B5
Portessie Moray.......215 K2
Port Eynon Swans......50 F7
Portfield Gate
  Pembks.................48 F4
Portgate Devon.........10 B7
Port Gaverne Cnwll......8 D8
Port Glasgow Inver....174 C4
Portgordon Moray....215 J2
Portgower Highld.....227 H5
Porth Cnwll...............4 C4
Porth Rhondd............36 F3
Porthallow Cnwll........3 K6
Porthallow Cnwll........5 K5
Porthcawl Brdgnd......36 C5
Porthcothan Cnwll.......4 D2
Porthcurno Cnwll........2 C6
Port Henderson
  Highld................219 H6
Porthgain Pembks......46 A7
Porthgwarra Cnwll......2 C6
Porthill Staffs...........99 J3
Porthkerry V Glam......37 G6
Porthleven Cnwll........3 H6
Porthmadog Gwynd....95 K5

Porthmadog Gwynd.......95 K5
Porth Navas Cnwll..............3 K5
Porthoustock Cnwll...........3 K6
Porthpean Cnwll...................5 G5
Porthtowan Cnwll................3 J2
Porthyrhyd Carmth.........51 G3
Portincaple Ag & B.......183 J8
Portinfer Jersey.............236 a5
Portington E R Yk........125 J4
Portinnisherrich
Ag & B.........................182 D5
Portinscale Cumb.......137 H3
Port Isaac Cnwll.................8 D8
Portishead N Som.........38 C5
Portknockie Moray.....215 K2
Portland Dorset..............14 D7
Portlethen Abers.........207 H6
Portling D & G..............146 F4
Portloe Cnwll.....................4 E7
Port Logan D & G.........144 D6
Portmahomack
Highld..........................223 K5
Port Mary D & G...........146 D6
Portmeirion Gwynd......95 K5
Portmellon Cnwll..............4 F6
Port Mòr Highld.........189 K1
Portnacroish
Ag & B.........................191 H6
Portnaguran W Isls.....232 g2
Portnahaven Ag & B...170 D7
Portnalong Highld.......208 E7
Portnancon Highld.....228 F4
Port nan Giùran
W Isls............................232 g2
Port nan Long
W Isls............................232 c5
Port Nis W Isls.............232 g1
Portobello C Edin........177 J4
Portobello Wolves........85 G4
Port of Menteith
Stirlg.............................184 D6
Port of Ness W Isls......232 g1
Porton Wilts.....................28 D4
Portpatrick D & G........144 B4
Port Quin Cnwll.................8 C8
Port Ramsay Ag & B....191 H7
Portreath Cnwll..................3 H3
Portreath Harbour
Cnwll................................3 H3
Portree Highld..............209 G5
Port Righ Ag & B.........161 K2
Port St Mary IoM.........237 b7
Portscatho Cnwll.............4 D8
Portsea C Port................17 J3
Portskerra Highld........230 C3
Portskewett Mons........38 D3
Portslade Br & H...........19 H4
Portslade-by-Sea
Br & H............................19 H5
Portslogan D & G........144 B3
Portsmouth C Port........17 J3
Portsmouth Calder.......122 D5
Portsmouth Historic
Dockyard C Port.........17 J3
Port Soderick IoM.......237 c6
Portsonachan Hotel
Ag & B.........................182 F3
Portsoy Abers..............216 B2
Port Sunlight
Wirral...........................111 K5
Portswood C Sotn........29 H8
Port Talbot Neath.........36 B3
Port Tennant Swans.....51 K6
Portuairk Highld.........189 K3
Portway Sandw..............85 H6
Portway Worcs...............85 J8
Port Wemyss
Ag & B.........................170 D7
Port William D & G.....145 H6
Portwrinkle Cnwll...........6 A5
Portyerrock D & G.......145 K7
Poslingford Suffk..........77 H5
Posso Border................166 B3
Postbridge Devon..........10 F8
Postcombe Oxon...........58 B7
Postling Kent..................34 F6
Postwick Norfk..............93 G2
Potarch Abers..............206 B6

Potten End Herts..........59 G6
Potter Brompton
N York..........................134 F4
Potterhanworth
Lincs............................117 H7
Potterhanworth
Booths Lincs.............117 H7
Potter Heigham
Norfk............................107 J8
Potterne Wilts...............39 M8
Potterne Wick Wilts......39 M8
Potters Bar Herts..........59 L7
Potters Corner Kent......34 D5
Potters Crouch Herts....59 J6
Potters Green Covtry....86 D6
Potters Marston
Leics..............................87 G4
Potterspury Nhants........73 L6
Potter Street Essex........60 D6
Potterton Abers...........207 H3
Potto N York.................141 L6
Potton C Beds................75 J5
Pott Shrigley
Ches E..........................113 L5
Poughill Cnwll..................9 G4
Poughill Devon...............11 K3
Poulner Hants................15 M2
Poulshot Wilts...............39 L7
Poulton Gloucs..............56 C7
Poulton Wirral..............111 J4
Poulton-le-Fylde
Lancs............................120 D3
Poundbury Dorset..........14 D4
Poundffald Swans.........51 H6
Pound Green E Susx.......20 B2
Pound Green Suffk........77 G4
Pound Hill W Susx.........32 B5
Poundon Bucks..............57 M3
Poundsgate Devon..........7 G2
Poundstock Cnwll...........9 G5
Pouton D & G...............145 K5
Povey Cross Surrey.......31 L3
Powburn Nthumb.........168 F6
Powderham Devon.........12 C5
Powerstock Dorset.........13 M3
Powfoot D & G.............147 K2
Powick Worcs.................70 E4
Powmill P & K...............185 L7
Poxwell Dorset...............14 E5
Poyle Slough..................43 G5
Poynings W Susx...........19 H4
Poyntington Dorset........26 F7
Poynton Ches E............113 L5
Poynton Green
Wrekin...........................98 E8
Praa Sands Cnwll............3 G5
Praze-an-Beeble
Cnwll................................3 H4
Prees Shrops..................98 D5
Preesall Lancs...............120 E2
Prees Green Shrops........98 E6
Prees Heath Shrops.......98 D5
Prees Higher Heath
Shrops...........................98 E5
Pren-gwyn Cerdgn........65 L5
Prenteg Gwynd..............95 K4
Prescot Knows..............112 C3
Prescott Devon...............25 H8
Presnerb Angus............195 J3
Prestatyn Denbgs........110 E5
Prestbury Ches E..........113 K6
Prestbury Gloucs...........55 L4
Presteigne Powys..........69 G2
Prestleigh Somset.........26 F4
Preston Border.............179 G6
Preston Br & H...............19 J4
Preston Devon.................7 K2
Preston Dorset...............14 D5
Preston E R Yk..............126 F4
Preston Gloucs...............56 B7
Preston Herts.................59 K3
Preston Kent..................34 D3
Preston Kent..................35 H3
Preston Lancs...............121 H4
Preston Nthumb...........169 H4
Preston Rutlnd...............88 C3
Preston Somset..............25 H4
Preston Torbay................7 K4

Preston Wilts..................40 B5
Preston Bagot
Warwks..........................71 L2
Preston Bissett
Bucks..............................58 A3
Preston Bowyer
Somset...........................25 H6
Preston Brockhurst
Shrops...........................98 D7
Preston Brook
Halton..........................112 E5
Preston Candover
Hants..............................29 L3
Preston Capes
Nhants............................73 H4
Preston Green
Warwks..........................71 L2
Preston Gubbals
Shrops...........................98 C8
Preston on Stour
Warwks..........................72 B4
Preston on the Hill
Halton..........................112 E5
Preston on Wye
Herefs............................69 H6
Prestonpans E Loth.....177 K4
Preston Patrick
Cumb............................129 L3
Preston Plucknett
Somset...........................26 D7
Preston St Mary
Suffk..............................77 L4
Preston-under-
Scar N York..................131 K2
Preston upon the
Weald Moors
Wrekin...........................84 C1
Preston Wynne
Herefs............................69 L5
Prestwich Bury.............113 J1
Prestwick S Ayrs..........163 J4
Prestwick Airport
S Ayrs...........................163 J4
Prestwood Bucks..........58 E7
Prickwillow Cambs.......90 E6
Priddy Somset................26 D2
Priest Hutton Lancs.....129 L5
Priestland E Ayrs.........164 B2
Priest Weston
Shrops...........................82 F4
Primrosehill Border.....179 G6
Primrose Hill Dudley....85 G6
Primsidemill Border....168 B4
Prince of Wales
Bridge Mons..................38 D3
Princes Risborough
Bucks..............................58 D7
Princethorpe Warwks....72 E1
Princetown Devon...........6 E2
Priors Hardwick
Warwks..........................72 F4
Priorslee Wrekin............84 C2
Priors Marston
Warwks..........................72 F3
Priors Norton Gloucs....55 K3
Priors Park Gloucs.........55 K2
Priston BaNES................39 G7
Prittlewell Sthend.........46 E3
Privett Hants..................30 B6
Prixford Devon................23 J4
Probus Cnwll.....................4 E6
Prora E Loth.................178 C3
Prospect Cumb.............147 K6
Prospidnick Cnwll...........3 H5
Protstonhill Abers........216 F2
Prudhoe Nthumb.........150 D3
Pubil P & K...................193 G7
Publow BaNES................38 F7
Puckeridge Herts...........60 C4
Puckington Somset........26 B7
Pucklechurch S Glos.....39 G5
Puddington Ches W.....111 K6
Puddington Devon..........11 J3
Puddletown Dorset........14 E4
Pudsey Leeds................123 J4
Pulborough W Susx........18 E3
Pulford Ches W..............98 A2
Pulham Dorset...............14 D2

Pulham Market
Norfk..............................92 E6
Pulham St Mary
Norfk..............................92 E6
Pulloxhill C Beds...........74 F7
Pulverbatch Shrops.......83 H3
Pumpherston W Loth...176 E4
Pumsaint Carmth...........66 E6
Puncheston Pembks.......49 G2
Puncknowle Dorset........14 A5
Punnett's Town
E Susx.............................20 C2
Purbrook Hants...............17 J2
Purfleet-on-
Thames Thurr...............45 K4
Puriton Somset...............25 L3
Purleigh Essex...............61 K7
Purley Gt Lon..................44 F7
Purley on Thames
W Berk............................42 A5
Purse Caundle
Dorset.............................27 G7
Purtington Somset.........13 K2
Purton Gloucs................54 F6
Purton Gloucs................55 G7
Purton Wilts...................40 C3
Purton Stoke Wilts........40 C3
Pury End Nhants............73 K5
Pusey Oxon.....................41 G2
Putley Herefs..................70 B6
Putley Green Herefs......70 B6
Putney Gt Lon.................44 E5
Puttenham Surrey..........30 F2
Puxley Nhants................73 L6
Puxton N Som.................38 B7
Pwll Carmth...................50 F5
Pwll-glâs Denbgs...........97 H2
Pwllgloyw Powys...........68 B7
Pwllheli Gwynd..............94 F5
Pwllmeyric Mons............38 D2
Pwll-trap Carmth...........50 C3
Pwll-y-glaw Neath.........36 C2
Pye Bridge Derbys.......101 H3
Pyecombe W Susx..........19 J3
Pyle Brdgnd....................36 C4
Pyleigh Somset...............25 H5
Pylle Somset...................26 E4
Pymoor Cambs...............90 C6
Pymore Dorset................13 L4
Pyrford Surrey................43 H8
Pyrton Oxon....................42 B2
Pytchley Nhants..............88 C8
Pyworthy Devon...............9 J4

Q

Quadring Lincs.............103 L6
Quadring Eaudike
Lincs............................103 L5
Quainton Bucks..............58 C4
Quantock Hills
Somset...........................25 J4
Quarff Shet...................235 c6
Quarley Hants................28 F3
Quarndon Derbys.........101 G4
Quarrier's Village
Inver.............................174 C5
Quarrington Lincs........103 H4
Quarrington Hill
Dur...............................151 H7
Quarry Bank Dudley.....85 G6
Quarrywood Moray......214 E2
Quarter N Ayrs.............173 L6
Quarter S Lans..............175 J7
Quatford Shrops............84 D5
Quatt Shrops..................84 D6
Quebec Dur...................150 F6
Quedgeley Gloucs..........55 J5
Queen Adeladie
Cambs............................90 E7
Queenborough Kent.......46 E5
Queen Camel Somset....26 E6
Queen Charlton
BaNES.............................38 F7
Queen Elizabeth
Forest Park Stirlg....184 D6

Queen Elizabeth II
Bridge Thurr 45 L5
Queenhill Worcs 70 F6
Queen Oak Dorset........27 H5
Queen's Bower IoW 17 H5
Queensbury C Brad..... 123 G4
Queensferry Flints........ 111 K7
Queensferry
  Crossing Fife........... 176 F3
Queenslie C Glas......... 175 H5
Queen's Park Bed 74 F4
Queen's Park Essex 46 A2
Queen's Park Nhants 73 L3
Queenzieburn
  N Lans 175 J3
Quendon Essex 60 E3
Queniborough Leics....87 J2
Quenington Gloucs 56 C7
Queslett Birm............85 J4
Quethiock Cnwll 5 L3
Quidenham Norfk........92 B6
Quidhampton Wilts....28 C5
Quinton Nhants 73 L4
Quintrell Downs
  Cnwll 4 D4
Quixwood Border......... 179 G5
Quoig P & K 185 H3
Quorn Leics 87 H1
Quothquan S Lans ... 165 J2
Quoyburray Ork 234 c6
Quoyloo Ork............. 234 b5

R

Raasay Highld 209 J5
Rachan Mill Border...... 165 L3
Rachub Gwynd............ 109 J7
Rackenford Devon.......24 D7
Rackham W Susx...........18 E3
Rackheath Norfk.........93 G2
Racks D & G 155 H7
Rackwick Ork............. 234 a7
Radbourne Derbys 100 F5
Radcliffe Bury 113 H1
Radcliffe on Trent
  Notts 101 M5
Radclive Bucks 73 J7
Raddery Highld............ 213 H3
Radernie Fife.............. 187 G5
Radford Covtry 86 D7
Radford Semele
  Warwks..................72 D2
Radlett Herts 59 K7
Radley Oxon 57 K7
Radley Green Essex......60 F6
Radnage Bucks...........42 C2
Radstock BaNES..........27 G1
Radstone Nhants.......73 H6
Radway Warwks 72 D5
Radwell Bed..............74 E3
Radwell Herts.............75 J7
Radwinter Essex..........76 E6
Radyr Cardif 37 H4
Rafford Moray............ 214 C3
RAF Museum
  Cosford Shrops 84 E3
RAF Museum
  London Gt Lon......44 E3
Ragdale Leics 102 A8
Raglan Mons 54 B6
Ragnall Notts............. 116 D6
Raigbeg Highld 213 J8
Rainbow Hill Worcs......70 F4
Rainford St Hel 112 C2
Rainham Gt Lon...........45 K4
Rainham Medway........46 D6
Rainhill St Hel 112 C4
Rainhill Stoops
  St Hel 112 D4
Rainow Ches E............ 113 L6
Rainton N York............. 132 L2
Rainworth Notts......... 101 L2
Rait P & K 186 D3
Raithby Lincs 118 D5
Raithby Lincs 118 E7
Rake Hants 30 D5

Ralia Highld 203 H5
Ramasaig Highld......... 208 B5
Rame Cnwll 3 J4
Rame Cnwll 6 B6
Rampisham Dorset 14 B3
Rampside Cumb 128 F6
Rampton Cambs..........76 B2
Rampton Notts.......... 116 D5
Ramsbottom Bury....... 122 B6
Ramsbury Wilts...........40 F6
Ramscraigs Highld 227 K3
Ramsdean Hants 30 B6
Ramsdell Hants..........41 L8
Ramsden Oxon............57 G5
Ramsden Bellhouse
  Essex......................46 B2
Ramsden Heath
  Essex......................46 B2
Ramsey Cambs............89 K6
Ramsey Essex..............62 E2
Ramsey IoM 237 e3
Ramsey Forty Foot
  Cambs......................89 K6
Ramsey Heights
  Cambs......................89 J6
Ramsey Island
  Pembks 48 B3
Ramsey Mereside
  Cambs......................89 K5
Ramsey St Mary's
  Cambs......................89 J6
Ramsgate Kent...........35 K2
Ramsgill N York........... 131 L5
Ramshope Nthumb..... 157 J2
Ramshorn Staffs........ 100 B4
Ramsnest Common
  Surrey 30 F5
Ranby Lincs 118 B5
Ranby Notts............. 116 A5
Rand Lincs 117 J5
Randwick Gloucs 55 J6
Ranfurly Rens........... 174 D5
Rangemore Staffs 100 D7
Rangeworthy S Glos ...39 G3
Rankinston E Ayrs 163 L6
Rannoch Station
  P & K 193 G5
Ranscombe Somset 24 E3
Ranskill Notts........... 116 A4
Ranton Staffs............99 J7
Ranton Green Staffs....99 J7
Ranworth Norfk.........93 H1
Raploch Stirlg............ 185 G7
Rapness Ork 234 c4
Rascarrel D & G 146 D5
Rashfield Ag & B........ 173 K2
Rashwood Worcs..........71 G2
Raskelf N York........... 133 G5
Rastrick Calder......... 123 H6
Ratagan Highld......... 200 E2
Ratby Leics 87 G3
Ratcliffe Culey Leics...86 D4
Ratcliffe on Soar
  Notts 101 J6
Ratcliffe on the
  Wreake Leics..........87 J1
Rathen Abers 217 J3
Rathillet Fife.............. 186 F3
Rathmell N York......... 130 F7
Ratho C Edin............ 176 F4
Ratho Station C Edin... 176 F4
Rathven Moray.......... 215 K2
Ratley Warwks 72 E5
Ratling Kent...............35 H4
Ratlinghope Shrops 83 H4
Rattar Highld............ 231 J2
Rattery Devon............. 7 H4
Rattlesden Suffk..........77 L3
Ratton Village E Susx...20 C5
Rattray P & K 195 J7
Raunds Nhants..........88 E8
Ravenfield Rothm...... 115 J3
Ravenglass Cumb 136 F7
Raveningham Norfk.....93 H4
Ravenscar N York....... 143 K6
Ravenscraig N Lans ... 175 K0
Ravensden Bed............74 F4
Ravenshead Notts..... 101 K2

Ravensthorpe Kirk...... 123 J6
Ravensthorpe Nhants.....73 J1
Ravenstone Leics........86 E2
Ravenstone M Keyn......74 B4
Ravenstonedale
  Cumb 139 G6
Ravenstruther
  S Lans 165 H1
Ravensworth N York ... 140 E5
Rawcliffe C York......... 133 J8
Rawcliffe E R Yk........ 125 G6
Rawdon Leeds............ 123 J3
Rawling Street Kent....34 B3
Rawmarsh Rothm...... 115 H3
Rawreth Essex............46 C2
Rawridge Devon..........12 F2
Rawtenstall Lancs 122 B6
Raydon Suffk..............78 C6
Rayleigh Essex............46 D2
Rayne Essex................61 H4
Raynes Park Gt Lon....44 E6
Reach Cambs 76 E2
Read Lancs 122 B4
Reading Readg............42 B5
Reading Services
  W Berk...................42 A6
Reading Street Kent....34 B8
Reading Street Kent....35 K2
Reagill Cumb............. 138 E4
Rearquhar Highld...... 223 G3
Rearsby Leics.............87 J2
Reawla Cnwll 3 G4
Reay Highld.............. 230 D3
Reculver Kent.............47 L6
Red Ball Devon............25 H7
Redberth Pembks 49 J6
Redbourn Herts...........59 J5
Redbourne N Linc....... 116 F2
Redbrook Gloucs........54 D6
Redbrook Wrexhm.......98 D4
Redbrook Street
  Kent.......................34 C7
Redburn Highld.......... 213 L5
Redcar R & Cl............ 142 D3
Redcastle D & G......... 146 E2
Redcastle Highld........ 212 F4
Redding Falk............. 176 C3
Reddingmuirhead
  Falk...................... 176 C3
Reddish Stockp......... 113 K3
Redditch Worcs...........71 J2
Rede Suffk.................77 J4
Redenhall Norfk.........92 F6
Redesmouth
  Nthumb................ 157 L5
Redford Abers 197 J3
Redford Angus.......... 196 F7
Redford W Susx..........30 E6
Redfordgreen
  Border................... 166 E6
Redgate Rhondd.........36 F3
Redgorton P & K........ 186 A2
Redgrave Suffk...........92 C7
Redhill Abers 206 E4
Red Hill BCP 15 K4
Redhill Herts.............59 M2
Redhill N Som.............38 D7
Redhill Surrey............32 B3
Redisham Suffk..........93 J6
Redland Bristl............38 E5
Redland Ork............. 234 b5
Redlingfield Suffk........78 E1
Redlingfield Green
  Suffk.......................78 E1
Red Lodge Suffk..........77 G1
Redlynch Somset 27 G5
Redlynch Wilts...........28 D7
Redmarley Worcs........70 D2
Redmarley D'Abitot
  Gloucs...................55 H2
Redmarshall S on T...... 141 J3
Redmile Leics............ 102 D5
Redmire N York......... 131 K6
Redmyre Abers........... 197 J2
Rednal Shrops............98 A6
Redpath Border......... 167 J3
Red Point Highld....... 219 H7
Red Roses Carmth......49 L6

Red Row Nthumb 159 G3
Redruth Cnwll 3 J3
Redstone P & K 186 C1
Red Street Staffs..........99 J3
Red Wharf Bay IoA 109 G5
Redwick Newpt............38 B4
Redwick S Glos............38 D3
Redworth Darltn 141 G3
Reed Herts.................75 L7
Reedham Norfk...........93 J3
Reedness E R Yk........ 125 J6
Reeds Holme Lancs ... 122 B5
Reepham Lincs........... 117 H6
Reepham Norfk......... 106 D7
Reeth N York 140 C7
Reeves Green Solhll....86 C7
Regil N Som................38 D7
Reiff Highld............... 224 B5
Reigate Surrey.............31 L2
Reighton N York......... 135 H4
Reinigeadal W Isls 232 e4
Reisque Abers 207 G2
Reiss Highld.............. 231 L5
Relubbus Cnwll 2 F5
Relugas Moray........... 214 B5
Remenham Wokham 42 C4
Remenham Hill
  Wokham.................42 C4
Rempstone Notts 101 L7
Rendcomb Gloucs 56 A6
Rendham Suffk............79 H2
Rendlesham Suffk.......79 G4
Renfrew Rens........... 174 F5
Renhold Bed..............74 F4
Renishaw Derbys 115 J6
Rennington Nthumb... 169 J5
Renton W Duns........ 174 D3
Renwick Cumb......... 149 G6
Repps Norfk..............93 J1
Repton Derbys.......... 100 F6
Reraig Highld............ 210 C8
Resaurie Highld......... 213 H5
Resipole Burn
  Highld.................. 190 E4
Reskadinnick Cnwll 3 H3
Resolis Highld............ 213 G2
Resolven Neath..........52 C7
Rest and be
  thankful Ag & B...... 183 J6
Reston Border........... 179 H6
Reswallie Angus....... 196 E6
Retford Notts........... 116 B5
Rettendon Common
  Essex......................61 J7
Rettendon Village
  Essex......................46 C2
Revesby Lincs........... 103 M1
Rewe Devon...............12 B3
Rew Street IoW...........16 F4
Reymerston Norfk......92 B3
Reynalton Pembks......49 J5
Reynoldston Swans....50 F7
Rezare Cnwll 6 A1
Rhandirmwyn
  Carmth...................67 H5
Rhayader Powys.........67 L2
Rheindown Highld...... 212 D5
Rhenigidale W Isls..... 232 e4
Rhes-y-cae Flints...... 111 G7
Rhewl Denbgs............97 H1
Rhewl Denbgs............97 J4
Rhicarn Highld.......... 224 D4
Rhiconich Highld...... 228 C5
Rhicullen Highld........ 222 F6
Rhigos Rhondd...........52 E6
Rhives Highld............ 223 H2
Rhiwbina Cardif 37 J4
Rhiwderyn Newpt.......37 K3
Rhiwlas Gwynd......... 109 H7
Rhoden Green Kent.....33 H4
Rhodes Minnis Kent....34 F6
Rhodiad-y-brenin
  Pembks..................48 C3
Rhonehouse D & G.... 146 C3
Rhoose V Glam..........37 G6
Rhos Carmth..............65 L7
Rhos Neath................51 L5
Rhoscolyn IoA 108 C6

Rhoscrowther
Pembks 48 F6
Rhosesmor Flints 111 H7
Rhosgoch Powys 68 D5
Rhoshill Pembks 65 H6
Rhoshirwaun Gwynd 94 D6
Rhoslefain Gwynd 80 D3
Rhosllanerchrugog
Wrexhm 97 L3
Rhosmeirch IoA 108 F6
Rhosneigr IoA 108 D6
Rhosnesni Wrexhm 97 M3
Rhôs-on-Sea Conwy ...110 B5
Rhossili Swans 50 E7
Rhostryfan Gwynd 95 H2
Rhostyllen Wrexhm 97 L3
Rhosybol IoA 108 F4
Rhos-y-gwaliau
Gwynd 96 E5
Rhosymedre Wrexhm....97 L4
RHS Garden Harlow
Carr N York 132 D8
RHS Garden Wisley
Surrey 43 H8
Rhu Ag & B 174 B2
Rhuallt Denbgs 110 F6
Rhubodach Ag & B 173 H4
Rhuddlan Denbgs 110 E6
Rhue Highld 220 E3
Rhunahaorine
Ag & B 172 C8
Rhyd Gwynd 95 L4
Rhydargaeau Carmth 50 F1
Rhydcymerau Carmth.....66 D6
Rhyd-Ddu Gwynd............95 K3
Rhydlewis Cerdgn 65 K5
Rhydowen Cerdgn 66 B5
Rhyd-uchaf Gwynd 96 D5
Rhyd-y-clafdy
Gwynd 94 F5
Rhyd-y-foel Conwy 110 C6
Rhydyfro Neath 51 K4
Rhyd-y-groes
Gwynd 109 H7
Rhyd-y-pennau
Cerdgn 80 E6
Rhyl Denbgs 110 D5
Rhymney Caerph 53 H6
Rhynd P & K 186 B4
Rhynie Abers 215 L8
Rhynie Highld 223 J5
Ribbesford Worcs 84 D8
Ribbleton Lancs 121 H4
Ribchester Lancs 121 J4
Riby Lincs 126 F8
Riccall N York 124 F3
Riccarton Border 156 F3
Riccarton E Ayrs 163 K3
Richards Castle
Herefs 69 J1
Richmond Gt Lon 44 D5
Richmond N York 140 F6
Richmond Sheff 115 H4
Rickerscote Staffs 99 L7
Rickford N Som 38 C8
Rickham Devon 7 H7
Rickinghall Suffk 92 C7
Rickling Green Essex.....60 E3
Rickmansworth
Herts 43 H2
Riddell Border 167 H4
Riddlecombe Devon 10 F3
Riddlesden C Brad.........123 G3
Ridge Dorset 15 H5
Ridge Herts 59 K7
Ridge Wilts 27 L5
Ridge Lane Warwks 86 C4
Ridgeway Derbys 115 H5
Ridgewell Essex 77 G6
Ridgewood E Susx 19 M2
Ridgmont C Beds 74 E7
Riding Mill Nthumb 150 C3
Ridlington Norfk 107 H6
Ridlington RutInd...........88 B3
Ridsdale Nthumb 158 A5
Rievaulx N York 133 J3
Rigg D & G 148 B2
Riggend N Lans 175 K4

Righoul Highld 213 K4
Rigsby Lincs 118 F6
Rigside S Lans 165 G3
Riley Green Lancs 121 J5
Rilla Mill Cnwll 5 L2
Rillington N York 134 D5
Rimington Lancs 122 B2
Rimpton Somset 26 E6
Rimswell E R Yk 127 H5
Rinaston Pembks 49 G3
Rindleford Shrops 84 D4
Ringford D & G 146 C4
Ringland Norfk 92 D2
Ringmer E Susx 19 L3
Ringmore Devon 6 F6
Ringmore Devon 7 L2
Ringorm Moray 215 G5
Ringsfield Suffk 93 J5
Ringsfield Corner
Suffk 93 J6
Ringshall Herts 59 G5
Ringshall Suffk 78 C4
Ringshall Stocks
Suffk 78 C4
Ringstead Nhants 88 E7
Ringstead Norfk 105 H4
Ringwood Hants 15 L2
Ringwould Kent 35 K5
Rinmore Abers 205 J3
Ripe E Susx 20 B4
Ripley Derbys 101 H3
Ripley Hants 15 M3
Ripley N York 132 D7
Ripley Surrey 31 H1
Riplington Hants 30 A6
Ripon N York 132 D5
Rippingale Lincs 103 H6
Ripple Kent 35 J5
Ripple Worcs 70 F6
Ripponden Calder 122 F6
Risabus Ag & B 160 B2
Risbury Herefs 69 K4
Risby Suffk 77 H2
Risca Caerph 37 K3
Rise E R Yk 126 E3
Risegate Lincs 103 K6
Riseley Bed 74 F3
Riseley Wokham 42 B7
Rishangles Suffk 78 E2
Rishton Lancs 121 L4
Rishworth Calder 122 F6
Risley Derbys 101 J5
Risley Warrtn 112 F3
Risplith N York 132 C5
River Kent 35 J6
River W Susx 30 F6
Riverford Highld............212 E4
Riverhead Kent 32 F3
Rivington Lancs 121 J7
Rivington Services
Lancs 121 J7
Roade Nhants 73 L4
Roadmeetings
S Lans 176 B7
Roadside E Ayrs 164 B5
Roadside Highld 231 H4
Roadwater Somset 25 G4
Roag Highld 208 D5
Roan of Craigoch
S Ayrs 153 G2
Roath Cardif 37 J5
Roberton Border 166 F6
Roberton S Lans 165 H4
Robertsbridge E Susx....20 E2
Robertstown Kirk 123 J6
Robeston Wathen
Pembks 49 J4
Robgill Tower D & G ...155 M7
Robin Hood's Bay
N York 143 K6
Roborough Devon 6 D4
Roborough Devon 10 E2
Robroyston C Glas 175 H5
Roby Knows 112 B4
Rocester Staffs 100 C5
Roch Pembks 48 E3
Rochdale Rochdl 122 D7
Roche Cnwll 4 F4

Rochester Medway 46 C6
Rochester Nthumb 157 L3
Rochford Essex 46 E3
Rochford Worcs 70 B2
Rock Cnwll 4 E2
Rock Nthumb 169 J5
Rock Worcs 70 D1
Rockbeare Devon 12 C4
Rockbourne Hants 28 C7
Rockcliffe Cumb 148 C3
Rockcliffe D & G 146 E4
Rockend Torbay 7 L4
Rock Ferry Wirral 111 K4
Rockfield Highld 223 K5
Rockfield Mons 54 C5
Rockford Devon 24 B2
Rockhampton S Glos.......38 F2
Rockhill Shrops 82 F7
Rockingham Nhants 88 C5
Rockland All Saints
Norfk 92 B4
Rockland St Mary
Norfk 93 G3
Rockland St Peter
Norfk 92 B4
Rockley Notts 116 B6
Rockliffe Lancs 122 C6
Rockville Ag & B 173 L1
Rockwell End Bucks 42 D3
Rodborough Gloucs 55 J6
Rodbourne Swindn 40 C4
Rodbourne Wilts 39 L4
Rodden Dorset 14 B5
Rode Somset 27 J2
Rode Heath Ches E..........99 J2
Rodel W Isls 232 d5
Roden Wrekin 83 L1
Rodhuish Somset 24 F4
Rodington Wrekin...........83 L1
Rodington Heath
Wrekin 83 L1
Rodley Gloucs 55 H5
Rodley Leeds 123 J3
Rodmarton Gloucs 39 L2
Rodmell E Susx 19 L4
Rodmersham Kent 34 B3
Rodmersham Green
Kent 34 B3
Rodney Stoke
Somset 26 C2
Rodsley Derbys 100 D4
Roecliffe N York 132 E6
Roe Green Herts 59 K6
Roe Green Herts 75 K7
Roehampton Gt Lon 44 E5
Roffey W Susx 31 K5
Rogart Highld 223 G2
Rogate W Susx 30 D6
Rogerstone Newpt 37 L3
Roghadal W Isls 232 d5
Rogiet Mons 38 C3
Roke Oxon 41 L2
Roker Sundld 151 J3
Rollesby Norfk 93 J1
Rolleston Leics 87 K4
Rolleston Notts 102 C3
Rolleston on Dove
Staffs 100 E6
Rolston E R Yk 126 F2
Rolvenden Kent 33 L6
Rolvenden Layne
Kent 33 L7
Romaldkirk Dur 140 C3
Romanby N York 132 E2
Romanno Bridge
Border 177 G8
Romansleigh Devon 24 B7
Romesdal Highld............208 F4
Romford Dorset 15 K1
Romford Gt Lon 45 K3
Romiley Stockp 113 L4
Romsey Cambs 76 C3
Romsey Hants 29 G6
Romsley Shrops 84 D6
Romsley Worcs 85 G7
Rona Highld 209 K3
Ronachan Ag & B 172 C7
Rookhope Dur 150 B6

Rookley IoW 17 G5
Rooks Bridge Somset 26 A2
Rooks Nest Somset 25 H5
Rookwith N York 132 C3
Roos E R Yk 127 G4
Roothams Green
Bed 75 G3
Ropley Hants 29 M5
Ropley Dean Hants 29 L5
Ropsley Lincs 103 G5
Rora Abers 217 K4
Rorrington Shrops 82 F4
Rosarie Moray 215 J4
Rose Cnwll 3 K1
Rose Ash Devon 24 C6
Rosebank S Lans 175 L7
Rosebush Pembks 49 J2
Rosedale Abbey
N York 142 F7
Rose Green Essex 61 L3
Rose Green Suffk 77 L5
Rose Green Suffk 77 L6
Rose Green W Susx 18 B5
Rosehall Highld 225 K7
Rosehearty Abers 217 H2
Rose Hill Lancs 122 C4
Roseisle Moray 214 E2
Roselands E Susx 20 C5
Rosemarket Pembks 49 G5
Rosemarkie Highld 213 H3
Rosemary Lane
Devon 25 J7
Rosemount P & K 195 J7
Rosenannon Cnwll 4 E3
Rosewell Mdloth 177 J6
Roseworth S on T 141 K3
Rosgill Cumb 138 D4
Roskhill Highld 208 D5
Rosley Cumb 148 B6
Roslin Mdloth 177 H5
Rosliston Derbys 86 B1
Rosneath Ag & B 174 B2
Ross D & G 146 B6
Rossett Wrexhm 98 A2
Rossett Green
N York 132 D8
Rossington Donc 115 L2
Ross-on-Wye Herefs.......54 E4
Roster Highld 231 J7
Rostherne Ches E 113 H5
Rosthwaite Cumb 137 H4
Roston Derbys 100 C4
Rosyth Fife 176 F2
Rothbury Nthumb 158 D2
Rotherby Leics 87 J1
Rotherfield E Susx 32 F7
Rotherfield Greys
Oxon 42 B4
Rotherfield Peppard
Oxon 42 B4
Rotherham Rothm 115 H3
Rothersthorpe
Nhants 73 K3
Rotherwick Hants 30 B1
Rothes Moray 215 G4
Rothesay Ag & B 173 J5
Rothiebrisbane
Abers 216 E6
Rothiemurchus
Lodge Highld 204 B4
Rothienorman Abers... 216 D7
Rothley Leics 87 H2
Rothmaise Abers 216 D7
Rothwell Leeds 123 L5
Rothwell Lincs 117 J2
Rothwell Nhants 88 B7
Rottal Lodge Angus 196 B3
Rottingdean Br & H.........19 K5
Rottington Cumb 136 D5
Roucan D & G 155 H6
Rougham Norfk 105 K7
Rougham Suffk 77 K3
Rough Common
Kent 34 F3
Roughpark Abers 205 H3
Roughton Lincs 118 C8
Roughton Norfk 106 F5
Roughton Shrops 84 D4

Roundbush Green
Essex................60 F5
Round Green Luton........59 J4
Roundham Somset.......13 K1
Roundhay Leeds.........123 L3
Rounds Green Sandw.....85 H5
Roundswell Devon........23 H5
Roundway Wilts...........40 A7
Roundhill Angus.......196 C6
Rousay Ork.............234 c4
Rousdon Devon..........13 H4
Rousham Oxon...........57 J3
Rous Lench Worcs.........71 H4
Routenburn N Ayrs....173 L6
Routh E R Yk...........126 D3
Row Cumb..............129 K2
Rowanburn D & G......156 D6
Rowardennan Stirlg....183 L7
Rowarth Derbys.........114 A4
Rowberrow Somset.......38 C8
Rowde Wilts.............39 L7
Rowen Conwy...........109 L6
Rowfoot Nthumb.......149 H3
Rowhedge Essex.........62 B4
Rowington Warwks.......72 B2
Rowland Derbys.........114 E6
Rowland's Castle
Hants...............17 K1
Rowlands Gill Gatesd..150 E4
Rowledge Surrey.........30 D3
Rowley Dur.............150 D5
Rowley Regis Sandw.....85 H6
Rowlstone Herefs........54 A3
Rowly Surrey.............31 H4
Rowner Hants...........17 H3
Rowney Green Worcs....71 J1
Rownhams Hants.........29 G7
Rownhams Services
Hants...............29 H7
Rowrah Cumb..........136 E4
Rowsham Bucks.........58 D4
Rowsley Derbys.........114 E7
Rowston Lincs..........103 H2
Rowton Ches W.........112 C8
Rowton Wrekin..........98 E8
Roxburgh Border.......167 L4
Roxby N Linc...........125 L6
Roxton Bed.............75 G4
Roxwell Essex............61 G6
Royal Botanic
Garden
Edinburgh C Edin....177 H4
Royal Leamington
Spa Warwks...........72 D2
Royal Sutton
Coldfield Birm.........85 K4
Royal Tunbridge
Wells Kent.............33 G5
Royal Wootton
Bassett Wilts...........40 B4
Royal Yacht
Britannia C Edin....177 H3
Roy Bridge Highld......192 D1
Roydon Essex............60 C6
Roydon Norfk............92 D7
Roydon Norfk...........105 H7
Roydon Hamlet
Essex...............60 C6
Royston Barns.........124 B7
Royston Herts...........75 L6
Royton Oldham.......122 D8
Rozel Jersey............236 e6
Ruabon Wrexhm........97 L4
Ruaig Ag & B..........188 D6
Ruan Lanihorne
Cnwll................4 D7
Ruan Major Cnwll........3 J7
Ruan Minor Cnwll........3 J7
Ruardean Gloucs........54 F4
Ruardean Hill Gloucs....54 F5
Ruardean Woodside
Gloucs..............54 F5
Rubery Birm............85 H7
Rubha Ban W Isls.....233 c9
Ruckhall Herefs.........69 J6
Ruckinge Kent...........34 D7
Ruckley Shrops..........83 K4
Rudby N York...........141 L6

Rudchester Nthumb.....150 E2
Ruddington Notts........101 L6
Rudge Somset...........27 J2
Rudgeway S Glos.........38 F3
Rudgwick W Susx.........31 H5
Rudheath Ches W........112 F6
Rudley Green Essex......61 K7
Rudloe Wilts.............39 J6
Rudry Caerph............37 J3
Rudston E R Yk.........135 H6
Rudyard Staffs............99 L2
Ruecastle Border........167 J5
Rufford Lancs...........120 F7
Rufford Abbey Notts....115 M8
Rufforth C York.........124 D1
Rugby Warwks............87 G7
Rugby Services
Warwks..............87 G7
Rugeley Staffs..........100 B8
Ruigh'riabhach
Highld...............220 D3
Ruisgarry W Isls........232 c5
Ruishton Somset.........25 K6
Ruisigearraidh
W Isls...............232 c5
Ruislip Gt Lon...........43 H3
Rùm Highld.............198 F5
Rumbach Moray.........215 J4
Rumbling Bridge
P & K...............185 L7
Rumburgh Suffk..........93 H7
Rumford Cnwll............4 D2
Rumford Falk...........176 C3
Rumney Cardif...........37 K5
Runcorn Halton.........112 D5
Runcton W Susx..........18 B5
Runcton Holme
Norfk...............90 E2
Runfold Surrey...........30 E3
Runhall Norfk............92 C3
Runham Norfk............93 K2
Runnington Somset......25 H6
Runswick N York.......143 G4
Runtaleave Angus.......195 L3
Runwell Essex............46 C2
Ruscombe Wokham.......42 D5
Rush Green Essex........62 E5
Rush Green Gt Lon........45 K3
Rush Green Warrtn......113 G4
Rushlake Green
E Susx..............20 D3
Rushmere Suffk..........93 K6
Rushmoor Surrey........30 E4
Rushock Worcs...........70 F1
Rusholme Manch........113 J3
Rushton Nhants...........88 B6
Rushton Spencer
Staffs...............113 L8
Rushwick Worcs..........70 E4
Rushyford Dur..........141 G2
Ruskie Stirlg............184 D7
Ruskington Lincs.......103 H3
Rusland Cross Cumb...129 H2
Rusper W Susx............31 K4
Ruspidge Gloucs.........54 F5
Russell's Water Oxon....42 B3
Russ Hill Surrey.........31 L4
Rusthall Kent............32 F5
Rustington W Susx.......18 E5
Ruston N York..........134 E3
Ruston Parva
E R Yk.............135 G6
Ruswarp N York.........143 H5
Rutherford Border......167 K4
Rutherglen S Lans......175 H6
Ruthernbridge Cnwll......4 F3
Ruthin Denbgs...........97 H2
Ruthrieston C Aber....207 H4

Ruthven Abers..........215 L5
Ruthven Angus..........195 L6
Ruthven Highld.........203 H5
Ruthven Highld.........213 J7
Ruthvoes Cnwll............4 E4
Ruthwell D & G.........147 J2
Ruyton-XI-Towns
Shrops..............98 B7
Ryal Nthumb...........158 C7
Ryall Dorset.............13 K4
Ryall Worcs..............70 F6
Ryarsh Kent.............33 H2
Rydal Cumb............137 K6
Ryde IoW................17 H4
Rye E Susx..............21 H2
Rye Foreign E Susx.......21 H2
Rye Street Worcs.........70 D7
Ryhall Rutlnd.............88 F2
Ryhill Wakefd...........124 B7
Ryhope Sundld..........151 K4
Ryland Lincs............117 G5
Rylands Notts...........101 K5
Rylstone N York.........131 H7
Ryme Intrinseca
Dorset..............14 B1
Ryther N York...........124 E3
Ryton Gatesd...........150 E3
Ryton Shrops............84 D3
Ryton-on-
Dunsmore
Warwks..............86 E8
RZSS Edinburgh
Zoo C Edin..........177 G4

S

Sabden Lancs..........122 B3
Sacombe Herts...........60 B4
Sacriston Dur..........151 G5
Sadberge Darltn.........141 H4
Saddell Ag & B.........161 K3
Saddington Leics.........87 J5
Saddlebow Norfk.........90 E1
Saddlescombe
W Susx.............19 H4
Saffron Walden
Essex...............76 D6
Sageston Pembks.........49 H6
Saham Hills Norfk........91 K3
Saham Toney Norfk......91 K3
Saighton Ches W.........98 C1
St Abbs Border.........179 J5
St Agnes Border.......178 E5
St Agnes Cnwll............3 J2
St Agnes IoS.............2 a2
St Agnes Mining
District Cnwll..........3 J2
St Albans Herts..........59 J6
St Allen Cnwll.............4 C5
St Andrew Guern.......236 c3
St Andrews Fife........187 H4
St Andrews Botanic
Garden Fife..........187 H4
St Andrews Major
V Glam.............37 H6
St Andrews Well
Dorset..............13 L4
St Anne's Lancs.........120 D5
St Ann's D & G..........155 J4
St Ann's Chapel
Cnwll.................6 B2
St Ann's Chapel
Devon................6 F6
St Anthony-in-
Meneage Cnwll........3 K6
St Anthony's Hill
E Susx.............20 D5
St Arvans Mons...........38 D2
St Asaph Denbgs........110 E6
St Athan V Glam.........36 F6
St Aubin Jersey........236 b7
St Austell Cnwll...........4 F5
St Bees Cumb...........136 D5
St Blazey Cnwll............5 G5
St Boswells Border......167 J3
St Brelade Jersey.......236 b7

St Brelade's Bay
Jersey.............236 b7
St Breward Cnwll...........5 H1
St Briavels Gloucs.......54 E6
St Brides Major
V Glam.............36 D5
St Brides-super-Ely
V Glam.............37 H5
St Brides
Wentlooge Newpt....37 L4
St Budeaux C Plym........6 C4
Saintbury Gloucs..........71 K6
St Buryan Cnwll...........2 D6
St Catherines Ag & B...183 G6
St Chloe Gloucs..........55 J7
St Clears Carmth.........50 C3
St Cleer Cnwll.............5 K3
St Clement Cnwll...........4 D6
St Clement Jersey......236 e8
St Clether Cnwll...........9 G7
St Colmac Ag & B.......173 H5
St Columb Major
Cnwll................4 E3
St Columb Minor
Cnwll................4 D4
St Columb Road
Cnwll................4 E4
St Combs Abers........217 K2
St Cross South
Elmham Suffk........93 G6
St Cyrus Abers.........197 J4
St David's P & K.......185 K4
St Davids Pembks.......48 C3
St Davids Cathedral
Pembks.............48 C3
St Day Cnwll..............3 J3
St Dennis Cnwll...........4 E4
St Dogmaels Pembks....65 G5
St Dominick Cnwll.........6 B3
St Donats V Glam........36 E6
St Endellion Cnwll.........4 F1
St Enoder Cnwll...........4 D4
St Erme Cnwll.............4 D6
St Erney Cnwll.............6 B4
St Erth Cnwll..............2 F4
St Erth Praze Cnwll.......3 G4
St Ervan Cnwll.............4 D2
St Eval Cnwll.............4 D3
St Ewe Cnwll.............4 F6
St Fagans Cardif.........37 H5
St Fagans National
Museum of
History Cardif........37 H5
St Fergus Abers........217 K4
St Fillans P & K.........184 F3
St Florence Pembks......49 J7
St Gennys Cnwll...........8 F5
St George Conwy.......110 D6
St Georges N Som........38 B7
St George's V Glam......37 H5
St Germans Cnwll..........6 A4
St Giles in the
Wood Devon.........23 H7
St Giles-on-the-
Heath Devon...........9 K6
St Harmon Powys........81 L8
St Helen Auckland
Dur................140 F2
St Helen's E Susx........21 G4
St Helens IoW...........17 J5
St Helens St Hel.........112 D3
St Helier Gt Lon..........44 E6
St Helier Jersey........236 d7
St Hilary Cnwll............2 F5
St Hilary V Glam.........36 F5
St Ippolyts Herts.........59 K3
St Ishmael's Pembks....48 C6
St Issey Cnwll.............4 E2
St Ive Cnwll..............5 L3
St Ives Cambs...........75 K1
St Ives Cnwll.............2 F3
St James's End
Nhants..............73 L3
St James South
Elmham Suffk........93 G7
St Jidgey Cnwll............4 E3
St John Cnwll.............6 B5
St John Jersey.........236 c5

St John's E Susx 32 E6
St John's IoM 237 b5
St John's Kent 32 F3
St Johns Surrey 43 G8
St Johns Worcs 70 E4
St John's Chapel Devon 23 H5
St John's Chapel Dur 149 M7
St John's Fen End Norfk 90 D2
St John's Kirk S Lans ...165 J3
St John's Town of Dalry D & G 154 B6
St John's Wood Gt Lon 44 F4
St Judes IoM 237 d3
St Just Cnwll 2 C5
St Just-in-Roseland Cnwll 4 D8
St Just Mining District Cnwll 2 D5
St Katherines Abers 216 E7
St Keverne Cnwll 3 K6
St Kew Cnwll 5 G1
St Kew Highway Cnwll 5 G2
St Keyne Cnwll 5 K4
St Lawrence Essex 62 A6
St Lawrence IoW 17 G6
St Lawrence Jersey 236 c6
St Lawrence Kent 35 K2
St Lawrence Bay Essex 61 M6
St Leonards Bucks 58 E6
St Leonards Dorset 15 L2
St Leonards E Susx 20 F4
St Levan Cnwll 2 C6
St Lythans V Glam 37 H6
St Mabyn Cnwll 5 G2
St Madoes P & K 186 C3
St Margarets Herefs 69 G7
St Margarets Herts 60 B5
St Margaret's at Cliffe Kent 35 K5
St Margaret's Hope Ork 234 c7
St Margaret South Elmham Suffk 93 G6
St Marks IoM 237 c6
St Martin Cnwll 3 J6
St Martin Cnwll 5 K5
St Martin Guern 236 d3
St Martin Jersey 236 e6
St Martin's IoS 2 b1
St Martin's P & K 186 B2
St Martin's Shrops 97 L5
St Mary Jersey 236 b6
St Mary Bourne Hants 29 H2
St Marychurch Torbay 7 L3
St Mary Church V Glam 36 F6
St Mary Cray Gt Lon 45 J6
St Mary in the Marsh Kent 21 L1
St Mary's IoS 2 b1
St Mary's Ork 234 c6
St Mary's Bay Kent 21 L1
St Mary's Hoo Medway 46 D5
St Mary's Platt Kent 33 G2
St Maughans Green Mons 54 C5
St Mawes Cnwll 3 L5
St Mawgan Cnwll 4 D3
St Mellion Cnwll 6 B3
St Mellons Cardif 37 K4
St Merryn Cnwll 4 D2
St Michael Caerhays Cnwll 4 F7
St Michael Church Somset 25 L5
St Michael Penkevil Cnwll 4 D7
St Michaels Kent 34 B7
St Michaels Worcs 69 L2

St Michael's Mount Cnwll 2 F5
St Michael's on Wyre Lancs 120 F3
St Minver Cnwll 4 F1
St Monans Fife 187 H6
St Neot Cnwll 5 J3
St Neots Cambs 75 H3
St Newlyn East Cnwll 4 C5
St Nicholas Pembks 64 C7
St Nicholas V Glam 37 H5
St Nicholas-at-Wade Kent 47 L6
St Ninians Stirlg 185 G8
St Olaves Norfk 93 J4
St Osyth Essex 62 D5
St Ouen Jersey 236 b6
St Owen's Cross Herefs 54 D3
St Paul's Cray Gt Lon 45 J6
St Paul's Walden Herts 59 K4
St Peter Jersey 236 b6
St Peter Port Guern 236 d3
St Peter's Guern 236 b3
St Peter's Kent 35 K2
St Peter's Hill Cambs 89 J8
St Pinnock Cnwll 5 J3
St Quivox S Ayrs 163 J5
St Sampson Guern 236 d2
St Saviour Guern 236 c3
St Saviour Jersey 236 d7
St Stephen Cnwll 4 E5
St Stephens Cnwll 6 B4
St Stephens Cnwll 9 J7
St Teath Cnwll 8 E8
St Thomas Devon 11 K6
St Tudy Cnwll 5 G1
St Twynnells Pembks 48 F7
St Veep Cnwll 5 J5
St Vigeans Angus 197 G7
St Wenn Cnwll 4 F3
St Weonards Herefs 54 D3
Salcombe Devon 7 H7
Salcombe Regis Devon 12 F5
Salcott-cum-Virley Essex 61 M5
Sale Traffd 113 H3
Saleby Lincs 118 F5
Sale Green Worcs 71 G3
Salehurst E Susx 20 F2
Salem Cerdgn 80 F6
Salen Ag & B 190 C7
Salen Highld 190 D4
Salford C Beds 74 D6
Salford Oxon 56 F3
Salford Salfd 113 J3
Salford Priors Warwks 71 J4
Salfords Surrey 32 B4
Salhouse Norfk 93 G1
Saline Fife 185 L8
Salisbury Wilts 28 C5
Salisbury Plain Wilts 28 B3
Salkeld Dykes Cumb 148 F7
Sallachy Highld 225 L6
Salle Norfk 106 D7
Salmonby Lincs 118 D6
Salperton Gloucs 56 B4
Salsburgh N Lans 175 L5
Salt Staffs 99 L6
Saltaire C Brad 123 H3
Saltaire C Brad 123 H3
Saltash Cnwll 6 B4
Saltburn Highld 223 G7
Saltburn-by-the-Sea R & Cl 142 E3
Saltby Leics 102 D7
Saltcoats N Ayrs 163 G2
Saltcotes Lancs 120 E5
Saltdean Br & H 19 K5
Salterbeck Cumb 136 D3
Salterforth Lancs 122 D2
Salterswall Ches W 112 F7
Salterton Wilts 28 C4
Saltfleet Lincs 118 F3

Saltfleetby All Saints Lincs 118 F4
Saltfleetby St Clement Lincs 118 F3
Saltfleetby St Peter Lincs 118 F4
Saltford BaNES 39 G6
Salthouse Norfk 106 C4
Saltley Birm 85 K6
Saltmarshe E R Yk 125 J5
Saltney Flints 111 L8
Salton N York 133 L4
Saltrens Devon 23 G6
Saltwood Kent 34 F7
Salvington W Susx 18 F5
Salwarpe Worcs 70 F3
Salway Ash Dorset 13 L3
Sambourne Warwks 71 J3
Sambrook Wrekin 99 G7
Sampford Arundel Somset 25 H7
Sampford Brett Somset 25 H4
Sampford Courtenay Devon 10 F5
Sampford Moor Somset 25 H7
Sampford Peverell Devon 25 G8
Sampford Spiney Devon 6 D2
Samsonlane Ork 234 d5
Samuelston E Loth 178 B4
Sanaigmore Ag & B 170 E4
Sancreed Cnwll 2 D5
Sancton E R Yk 125 L3
Sandaig Highld 199 L5
Sandal Magna Wakefd 123 L6
Sanday Ork 234 d4
Sanday Airport Ork 234 d4
Sandbach Ches E 99 H1
Sandbach Services Ches E 99 H1
Sandbank Ag & B 173 K3
Sandbanks BCP 15 K5
Sandend Abers 216 B2
Sanderstead Gt Lon 45 G7
Sandford Cumb 139 G4
Sandford Devon 11 J4
Sandford Dorset 15 H5
Sandford Hants 15 M3
Sandford IoW 17 G6
Sandford N Som 38 B8
Sandford S Lans 164 E2
Sandford-on-Thames Oxon 57 K7
Sandford Orcas Dorset 26 F7
Sandford St Martin Oxon 57 H3
Sandgate Kent 35 G7
Sandhaven Abers 217 H2
Sandhead D & G 144 D5
Sand Hills Leeds 124 B3
Sandhills Oxon 57 K6
Sandhills Surrey 30 F4
Sandhoe Nthumb 150 B2
Sandhole Ag & B 182 E7
Sand Hole E R Yk 125 J3
Sandholme E R Yk 125 J4
Sandhurst Br For 42 D7
Sandhurst Gloucs 55 J4
Sandhurst Kent 33 K7
Sandhutton N York 132 F3
Sand Hutton N York 133 L7
Sandiacre Derbys 101 J5
Sandilands Lincs 119 G5
Sandleheath Hants 28 C7
Sandleigh Oxon 57 J7
Sandley Dorset 27 H6
Sandness Shet 235 b5
Sandon Essex 61 H6
Sandon Herts 75 L6
Sandon Staffs 99 L6
Sandon Bank Staffs 99 L6
Sandown IoW 17 H5
Sandplace Cnwll 5 K4

Sandridge Herts 59 K6
Sandringham Norfk 105 H6
Sandsend N York 143 H5
Sandtoft N Linc 125 H8
Sandway Kent 34 B5
Sandwich Kent 35 J3
Sandwick Shet 235 c7
Sandwick W Isls 232 g2
Sandwith Cumb 136 D4
Sandy C Beds 75 H5
Sandyford D & G 155 L4
Sandygate Devon 7 K2
Sandygate IoM 237 d3
Sandyhills D & G 146 F4
Sandylands Lancs 129 J6
Sandy Lane Wilts 39 L6
Sandy Park Devon 11 G6
Sangobeg Highld 228 F3
Sangomore Highld 228 F3
Sankyn's Green Worcs 70 E2
Sanna Highld 189 K3
Sanndabhaig W Isls 232 g2
Sannox N Ayrs 162 C1
Sanquhar D & G 164 F7
Santon Bridge Cumb 136 F6
Santon Downham Suffk 91 J6
Sapcote Leics 86 F5
Sapey Common Herefs 70 C2
Sapiston Suffk 91 K7
Sapley Cambs 89 J8
Sapperton Gloucs 55 L7
Sapperton Lincs 103 G5
Saracen's Head Lincs 104 B6
Sarclet Highld 231 L6
Sarisbury Hants 17 G2
Sarn Powys 82 E5
Sarnau Cerdgn 65 K4
Sarnau Powys 82 E1
Sarn Mellteyrn Gwynd 94 D6
Sarn Park Services Brdgnd 36 D4
Saron Carmth 51 H3
Saron Gwynd 109 G2
Sarratt Herts 59 H7
Sarre Kent 47 L6
Sarsden Oxon 56 F4
Satley Dur 150 E6
Satterleigh Devon 23 L6
Satterthwaite Cumb 129 H2
Sauchen Abers 206 D3
Saucher P & K 186 C2
Sauchieburn Abers 197 G3
Saul Gloucs 55 H6
Saundby Notts 116 C4
Saundersfoot Pembks 49 K6
Saunderton Bucks 58 C7
Saunton Devon 23 G4
Sausthorpe Lincs 118 E7
Savile Town Kirk 123 K6
Sawbridge Warwks 73 G2
Sawbridgeworth Herts 60 D5
Sawdon N York 134 E3
Sawley Derbys 101 J6
Sawley Lancs 122 B2
Sawley N York 132 C6
Sawston Cambs 76 C5
Sawtry Cambs 89 H6
Saxby Leics 102 D8
Saxby Lincs 117 G4
Saxby All Saints N Linc 126 B7
Saxelbye Leics 102 B7
Saxham Street Suffk 78 C3
Saxilby Lincs 116 E6
Saxlingham Norfk 106 B5
Saxlingham Green Norfk 92 F4
Saxlingham Nethergate Norfk 92 F4
Saxlingham Thorpe Norfk 92 E4

Saxmundham Suffk........79 H2
Saxondale Notts 102 B4
Saxon Street Cambs 76 F3
Saxtead Suffk................78 F2
Saxtead Green Suffk.......78 F2
Saxtead Little Green
Suffk...............................78 F2
Saxthorpe Norfk 106 D6
Saxton N York 124 D3
Sayers Common
W Susx........................19 H3
Scackleton N York....... 133 K5
Scadabay W Isls 232 e4
Scadabhagh W Isls ... 232 e4
Scafell Pike Cumb 137 H5
Scaftworth Notts 116 A3
Scagglethorpe
N York 134 C5
Scalasaig Ag & B....... 180 E8
Scalby E R Yk 125 K5
Scalby N York 134 F2
Scaldwell Nhants.........73 L1
Scaleby Cumb 148 D3
Scalebyhill Cumb....... 148 D3
Scales Cumb................ 129 G5
Scales Cumb................ 137 K2
Scalford Leics............. 102 C7
Scaling N York 142 F4
Scalloway Shet 235 c6
Scalpay Highld 209 J7
Scalpay W Isls 232 e4
Scamblesby Lincs...... 118 C5
Scamodale Highld 191 G2
Scampston N York..... 134 D4
Scampton Lincs 116 F5
Scaniport Highld........ 212 F6
Scapegoat Hill Kirk .. 123 G7
Scarba Ag & B 181 K6
Scarborough N York .. 135 G2
Scarcewater Cnwll 4 E5
Scarcliffe Derbys 115 J7
Scarcroft Leeds.......... 124 B3
Scarfskerry Highld..... 231 J2
Scarinish Ag & B 188 D7
Scarning Norfk............. 91 L2
Scarrington Notts 102 B4
Scartho NE Lin 118 C1
Scatsta Airport Shet.... 235 c4
Scaur D & G.................. 146 E4
Scawby N Linc............. 116 F1
Scawsby Donc 115 K1
Scawthorpe Donc...... 115 K1
Scawton N York.......... 133 H3
Scayne's Hill W Susx.... 19 K2
Scethrog Powys............ 53 H3
Scholar Green
Ches E..........................99 J2
Scholes Kirk................ 123 H8
Scholes Leeds............. 124 B3
Scholes Rothm........... 115 H3
Scholes Wigan 112 L1
Scissett Kirk............... 123 K7
Scleddau Pembks........ 64 C7
Scofton Notts 115 M5
Scole Norfk.................... 92 D7
Scone P & K 186 B3
Sconser Highld 209 H7
Scoonie Fife 186 F6
Scopwick Lincs 103 H2
Scoraig Highld 220 C3
Scorborough E R Yk... 126 C2
Scorrier Cnwll 3 J3
Scorton Lancs............. 121 G2
Scorton N York 141 G7
Scotby Cumb............... 148 D4
Scotch Corner
N York 140 F6
Scotch Corner Rest
Area N York 140 F6
Scotforth Lancs.......... 129 K7
Scothern Lincs 117 G6
Scotlandwell P & K... 186 C6
Scotscalder Station
Highld....................... 231 G4
Scot's Gap Nthumb ... 158 C5
Scotsmill Abers.......... 206 B2
Scotstoun C Glas 174 F5

Scotswood N u Ty 150 F3
Scotter Lincs............... 116 E2
Scotterthorpe Lincs... 116 E2
Scottish Seabird
Centre E Loth............ 178 C2
Scotton Lincs.............. 116 E2
Scotton N York............ 132 E7
Scotton N York............ 140 F7
Scoulton Norfk............. 92 B4
Scourie Highld............ 228 B6
Scourie More Highld ... 228 B6
Scousburgh Shet........ 235 c7
Scrabster Highld........ 231 G2
Scraesburgh Border ... 167 K5
Scrane End Lincs........ 104 C4
Scraptoft Leics............ 87 J3
Scratby Norfk................ 93 K1
Scrayingham N York... 133 L7
Scredington Lincs....... 103 H4
Scremby Lincs............. 118 F7
Scremerston Nthumb... 179 L8
Screveton Notts......... 102 B4
Scriven N York............ 132 E7
Scrooby Notts............. 115 M4
Scropton Derbys........ 100 D6
Scrub Hill Lincs.......... 103 L2
Scruton N York 132 D2
Scullomie Highld 229 J4
Sculthorpe Norfk....... 105 L6
Scunthorpe N Linc..... 125 K7
Seaborough Dorset.....13 K2
Seabridge Staffs...........99 J4
Seabrook Kent 35 G7
Seaburn Sundld 151 J3
Seacombe Wirral........ 111 K4
Seacroft Leeds............ 123 L4
Seafield W Loth.......... 176 D5
Seaford E Susx.............. 20 A6
Seaforth Sefton 111 K3
Seagrave Leics............ 101 L8
Seaham Dur 151 K5
Seahouses Nthumb.... 169 J3
Seal Kent......................32 F2
Sealand Flints............. 111 K7
Seale Surrey..................30 E2
Seamer N York............. 134 F3
Seamer N York............. 142 B5
Seamill N Ayrs 173 L8
Sea Palling Norfk....... 107 J6
Searby Lincs................ 117 H1
Seasalter Kent...............47 H6
Seascale Cumb............ 136 E6
Seathwaite Cumb....... 137 H7
Seatoller Cumb........... 137 H4
Seaton Cnwll................... 5 L5
Seaton Cumb............... 136 E2
Seaton Devon..............13 G4
Seaton E R Yk............. 126 E2
Seaton Kent 35 G3
Seaton Nthumb.......... 159 H6
Seaton Rutlnd..............88 C4
Seaton Carew Hartpl... 142 B2
Seaton Delaval
Nthumb..................... 159 H6
Seaton Ross E R Yk.... 125 J3
Seaton Sluice
Nthumb..................... 159 H6
Seatown Dorset...........13 K4
Seatown Moray 214 F1
Seave Green N York ... 142 C7
Seaview IoW 17 J4
Seaville Cumb............. 147 K4
Seavington St Mary
Somset.......................26 B7
Seavington St
Michael Somset 26 B7
Sebastopol Torfn.........37 L2
Sebergham Cumb....... 148 C6
Seckington Warwks.....86 C3
Second Severn
Crossing Mons..........38 D3
Sedbergh Cumb.......... 130 C2
Sedbury Gloucs...........38 D2
Sedbusk N York 131 G2
Sedgeberrow Worcs.....71 H6
Sedgebrook Lincs 102 D5
Sedgefield Dur........... 141 J2
Sedgeford Norfk......... 105 H5

Sedgehill Wilts..............27 K5
Sedgemoor
Services Somset......26 A2
Sedgley Dudley............85 G5
Sedgley Park Bury 113 J2
Sedgwick Cumb.......... 129 L3
Sedlescombe E Susx ...20 F3
Sedrup Bucks................58 D5
Seend Wilts 39 L7
Seend Cleeve Wilts.....39 L7
Seer Green Bucks.........42 F3
Seething Norfk..............93 G4
Sefton Sefton 111 K2
Seighford Staffs...........99 K7
Seion Gwynd 109 H7
Seisdon Staffs..............84 E4
Selattyn Shrops...........97 K5
Selborne Hants 30 C5
Selby N York................ 124 F4
Selham W Susx..............30 F7
Selhurst Gt Lon............45 G6
Selkirk Border 167 G4
Sellack Herefs 54 E3
Sellafield Station
Cumb......................... 136 E6
Sellafirth Shet 235 d2
Sellindge Kent..............34 E6
Selling Kent 34 D4
Sells Green Wilts.........39 L7
Selly Oak Birm 85 J6
Selmeston E Susx........20 B4
Selsdon Gt Lon 45 G7
Selsey W Susx...............18 B6
Selside N York............. 130 E4
Selsley Gloucs..............55 J7
Selsted Kent.................35 G5
Selston Notts 101 J2
Selworthy Somset........24 E3
Semer Suffk..................78 B5
Semington Wilts..........39 K7
Semley Wilts.................27 K6
Send Surrey..................31 G1
Senghenydd Caerph... 37 H3
Sennen Cnwll.................. 2 C6
Sennen Cove Cnwll........ 2 C6
Sennybridge Powys.....52 E3
Sessay N York............. 133 G4
Setchey Norfk...............90 F2
Seton Mains E Loth.... 177 L4
Settle N York............... 130 F6
Settrington N York..... 134 C5
Sevenhampton
Gloucs.......................56 B4
Sevenhampton
Swindn.......................40 E3
Seven Kings Gt Lon.....45 J3
Sevenoaks Kent...........32 F3
Sevenoaks Weald
Kent...........................32 F3
Seven Sisters Neath....52 C6
Severn Beach S Glos... 38 D4
Severn Bridge S Glos... 38 E3
Severn Stoke Worcs.....70 F5
Severn View
Services S Glos........38 E3
Sevington Kent 34 D6
Sewards End Essex......76 E6
Sewell C Beds...............59 G4
Sewerby E R Yk 135 J3
Seworgan Cnwll.............. 3 J5
Sewstern Leics........... 102 E7
Sgalpaigh W Isls........ 232 e4
Sgiogarstaigh W Isls.. 232 g1
Shabbington Bucks.....58 A6
Shackerstone Leics.....86 D3
Shackleford Surrey......30 F3
Shader W Isls 232 f1
Shadforth Dur............. 151 H6
Shadingfield Suffk......93 J6
Shadoxhurst Kent........34 C6
Shadwell Leeds........... 123 L3
Shadwell Norfk............91 L6
Shaftenhoe End
Herts..........................76 B6
Shaftesbury Dorset.....27 K6
Shafton Barns............ 124 B7
Shakerley Wigan........ 113 G2
Shalbourne Wilts.........40 F7

Shalden Hants 30 B3
Shaldon Devon.............. 7 L2
Shalfleet IoW...............16 E5
Shalford Essex.............61 H3
Shalford Surrey...........31 G3
Shalford Green
Essex..........................61 H3
Shalmsford Street
Kent...........................34 E4
Shalstone Bucks..........73 J7
Shamley Green
Surrey.......................31 G3
Shandford Angus....... 196 D4
Shandon Ag & B 174 B2
Shandwick Highld...... 223 J6
Shangton Leics............87 K4
Shanklin IoW 17 H6
Shantron Ag & B 174 C2
Shap Cumb.................. 138 E4
Shapinsay Ork............ 234 c5
Shapwick Dorset.........15 H3
Shapwick Somset........26 B4
Shard End Birm............85 L5
Shardlow Derbys........ 101 H6
Shareshill Staffs.........85 G3
Sharlston Wakefd...... 124 B6
Sharmans Cross
Solhll..........................85 K7
Sharnbrook Bed..........74 E3
Sharnford Leics...........86 F5
Sharoe Green Lancs... 121 G4
Sharow N York............ 132 E5
Sharpenhoe C Beds.....59 H2
Sharperton Nthumb... 158 B2
Sharpness Gloucs........54 F7
Sharrington Norfk..... 106 C5
Shatterford Worcs......84 E7
Shaugh Prior Devon...... 6 D3
Shavington Ches E......99 G3
Shaw Oldham 122 D8
Shaw Swindn..............40 C4
Shaw W Berk 41 J6
Shaw Wilts...................39 K7
Shawbirch Wrekin......84 B2
Shawbost W Isls 232 e2
Shawbury Shrops........98 E7
Shawell Leics...............87 G7
Shawford Hants...........29 J6
Shawhead D & G......... 154 F6
Shaw Mills N York 132 C6
Shawsburn S Lans..... 175 K7
Shearington D & G..... 147 H2
Shearsby Leics............87 J5
Shearston Somset.......25 L5
Shebbear Devon..........10 C3
Shebdon Staffs............99 H7
Shebster Highld.......... 230 E3
Shedfield Hants...........29 K8
Sheen Staffs............... 100 C1
Sheepridge Kirk......... 123 H6
Sheepscar Leeds........ 123 L4
Sheepscombe Gloucs... 55 K6
Sheepstor Devon.......... 6 E3
Sheepwash Devon.......10 C4
Sheepy Magna Leics...86 D3
Sheepy Parva Leics....86 D3
Sheering Essex............60 E5
Sheerness Kent...........46 F5
Sheerwater Surrey......43 G7
Sheet Hants.................30 C6
Sheffield Sheff &........ 115 G4
Sheffield Park &
Garden E Susx..........19 L2
Shefford C Beds...........75 G6
Sheigra Highld............ 228 B4
Sheinton Shrops..........83 L3
Shelderton Shrops.....83 H7
Sheldon Birm..............85 L6
Sheldon Derbys.......... 114 D7
Sheldon Devon............12 E2
Sheldwich Kent...........34 D4
Shelfanger Norfk.........92 D6
Shelford Notts............ 102 A4
Shelley Kirk................. 123 J7
Shelley Suffk................78 B6
Shellingford Oxon......40 F2
Shellow Bowells
Essex..........................60 F6

Shelsley
Beauchamp
Worcs....................70 D2
Shelsley Walsh
Worcs....................70 C2
Shelton Bed 74 F2
Shelton Norfk 92 F5
Shelton Notts.........102 C4
Shelton Lock
C Derb 101 G6
Shelton Under
Harley Staffs..........99 J5
Shelve Shrops 83 G4
Shelwick Herefs 69 K6
Shenfield Essex 45 L2
Shenington Oxon.......72 D6
Shenley Herts..........59 K7
Shenley Brook End
M Keyn 74 B7
Shenley Church End
M Keyn 74 B7
Shenmore Herefs 69 H6
Shennanton D & G .. 145 H3
Shenstone Staffs........85 K3
Shenstone Worcs.......84 F8
Shenton Leics..........86 E4
Shenval Moray........214 F7
Shephall Herts.........59 L4
Shepherd's Bush
Gt Lon..................44 E4
Shepherdswell Kent....35 H5
Shepley Kirk..........123 J8
Shepperton Surrey......43 H6
Shepreth Cambs.......76 B5
Shepshed Leics.......101 J8
Shepton
Beauchamp
Somset 26 B7
Shepton Mallet
Somset 26 F3
Shepton Montague
Somset 27 G5
Shepway Kent 33 K3
Sheraton Dur.........151 K7
Sherborne Dorset......26 F7
Sherborne Gloucs.......56 D5
Sherborne Somset......26 E1
Sherborne St John
Hants....................29 L1
Sherbourne Warwks 72 C3
Sherburn Dur.........151 H6
Sherburn N York 134 E4
Sherburn Hill Dur 151 H6
Sherburn in Elmet
N York 124 D4
Shere Surrey............31 H2
Shereford Norfk 105 L6
Sherfield English
Hants....................28 F6
Sherfield on
Loddon Hants..........42 B8
Sherford Devon 7 H6
Sheriffhales Shrops 84 D2
Sheriff Hutton
N York 133 K6
Sheringham Norfk 106 E4
Sherington M Keyn....74 C5
Shernborne Norfk 105 H6
Sherrington Wilts......27 L4
Sherston Wilts.........39 J3
Sherwood C Nott 101 K4
Sherwood Forest
Notts 101 L1
Shetland Islands
Shet....................235 c5
Shettleston C Glas...175 H5
Shevington Wigan 121 H8
Shevington Vale
Wigan 121 G8
Sheviock Cnwll..........6 B5
Shibden Head
C Brad 123 G5
Shide IoW 16 F5
Shidlaw Nthumb 168 B2
Shiel Bridge Highld ..200 E2
Shieldaig Highld.......210 C4
Shieldhill D & G 155 H5
Shieldhill Falk 176 B3

Shieldhill House
Hotel S Lans.........165 J2
Shields N Lans 175 K7
Shielfoot Highld 190 D3
Shielhill Angus 196 C5
Shielhill Inver.........173 L4
Shifnal Shrops 84 D2
Shilbottle Nthumb ...169 J7
Shildon Dur...........141 G3
Shillford E Rens........174 E6
Shillingford Devon 24 F6
Shillingford Oxon......41 L2
Shillingford Abbot
Devon 11 K6
Shillingford St
George Devon.........11 K7
Shillingstone Dorset...14 F1
Shillington C Beds......75 G7
Shilton Oxon 56 E6
Shilton Warwks 86 E6
Shimpling Norfk 92 D6
Shimpling Suffk 77 J4
Shimpling Street
Suffk....................77 K4
Shincliffe Dur.........151 H6
Shiney Row Sundld....151 H4
Shinfield Wokham 42 B6
Shinness Highld 225 L5
Shipbourne Kent 33 G3
Shipdham Norfk.........91 L3
Shipham Somset........38 C8
Shiphay Torbay 7 K3
Shiplake Oxon 42 C5
Shipley C Brad 123 H3
Shipley W Susx 31 J6
Shipley Bridge
Surrey 32 B5
Shipmeadow Suffk.....93 H5
Shippon Oxon 41 J2
Shipston-on-Stour
Warwks 72 B6
Shipton Gloucs.........56 B4
Shipton N York.......133 H7
Shipton Shrops.........83 L5
Shipton Bellinger
Hants....................28 E3
Shipton Gorge
Dorset 13 L4
Shipton Green
W Susx 17 L3
Shipton Moyne
Gloucs 39 K3
Shipton-on-
Cherwell Oxon 57 J5
Shiptonthorpe
E R Yk 125 K2
Shipton-under-
Wychwood Oxon 56 F4
Shirburn Oxon 42 B2
Shirdley Hill Lancs ..120 E7
Shirebrook Derbys ...115 K7
Shiregreen Sheff 115 G3
Shirehampton Bristl...38 D5
Shiremoor N Tyne ...159 H7
Shirenewton Mons.....38 C2
Shireoaks Notts 115 K5
Shirland Derbys 101 H2
Shirley C Sotn 29 H8
Shirley Derbys 100 E4
Shirley Gt Lon 45 G6
Shirley Solhll 85 K7
Shirrell Heath Hants ..29 L8
Shirwell Devon 23 J4
Shiskine N Ayrs 162 B4
Shobdon Herefs........69 H3
Shobrooke Devon 11 K5
Shoby Leics 102 B7
Shocklach Ches W......98 C3
Shoeburyness Sthend...46 F3
Sholden Kent 35 K4
Sholing C Sotn 16 F1
Shop Cnwll...............9 G2
Shoreditch Gt Lon.....45 G4
Shoreditch Somset.....25 K6
Shoreham Kent.........45 K7
Shoreham-by-Sea
W Susx 19 H5
Shorley Hants 29 L6

Shorne Kent..........46 B6
Shortgate E Susx......20 A3
Short Heath Birm.....85 K5
Short Heath Wsall.....85 H4
Shortlanesend Cnwll....4 C6
Shortlees E Ayrs 163 K3
Shorwell IoW 16 F5
Shoscombe BaNES.....27 G1
Shotesham Norfk.......92 F4
Shotgate Essex 46 C2
Shotley Suffk............78 F7
Shotley Bridge Dur...150 D4
Shotley Gate Suffk.....78 F7
Shottenden Kent 34 D4
Shottery Warwks........71 L4
Shotteswell Warwks ...72 E5
Shottisham Suffk.......79 G5
Shottlegate Derbys ..100 F3
Shotton Dur...........151 K6
Shotton Flints 111 J7
Shotton Colliery Dur..151 J6
Shotts N Lans.........176 B6
Shotwick Ches W......111 K6
Shougle Moray 214 F4
Shouldham Norfk......90 F2
Shouldham Thorpe
Norfk....................90 F2
Shoulton Worcs.........70 E3
Shrawardine Shrops....83 H1
Shrawley Worcs.........70 E2
Shrewley Warwks.......72 B2
Shrewsbury Shrops.....83 J2
Shrewton Wilts..........28 B3
Shripney W Susx......18 C5
Shrivenham Oxon......40 E3
Shropham Norfk........92 B5
Shroton Dorset..........27 K8
Shrub End Essex........62 A4
Shucknall Herefs.......69 L6
Shudy Camps Cambs..76 E5
Shuna Ag & B.........181 M5
Shurdington Gloucs....55 L4
Shurlock Row W & M...42 D5
Shurrery Highld 230 F4
Shurrery Lodge
Highld.................230 F4
Shurton Somset........25 J3
Shustoke Warwks......86 B5
Shute Devon 11 K5
Shute Devon 13 G3
Shutford Oxon 72 E6
Shut Heath Staffs......99 K7
Shuthonger Gloucs....70 F7
Shutlanger Nhants 73 K4
Shuttington Warwks...86 B3
Shuttlewood Derbys ..115 J6
Shuttleworth Bury....122 B6
Siabost W Isls........232 e2
Siadar W Isls..........232 f1
Sibbertoft Nhants......87 K6
Sibford Ferris Oxon...72 D6
Sibford Gower Oxon...72 D6
Sible Hedingham
Essex....................77 H7
Sibley's Green Essex ..60 F3
Sibsey Lincs...........104 B3
Sibson Cambs 89 G4
Sibson Leics............86 D4
Sibster Highld 231 K5
Sibthorpe Notts 102 C4
Sibthorpe Notts 116 B6
Sibton Suffk............79 H1
Sicklesmere Suffk......77 K3
Sicklinghall N York..124 B2
Sidbury Devon 12 E4
Sidbury Shrops.........84 C6
Sidcot N Som 38 B8
Sidcup Gt Lon..........45 J5
Siddington Ches E ...113 J7
Siddington Gloucs.....56 B7
Sidestrand Norfk 106 F4
Sidford Devon 12 E4
Sidlesham W Susx.....18 B6
Sidley E Susx...........20 F4
Sidmouth Devon 12 E5
Sigglesthorne E R Yk..126 E2
Signingstone V Glam...36 F6
Silchester Hants 41 L7

Sileby Leics.............87 H1
Silecroft Cumb.......128 D3
Silfield Norfk............92 D4
Silkstone Barns 114 F1
Silkstone Common
Barns..................114 F1
Silk Willoughby
Lincs..................103 H4
Silloth Cumb..........147 K4
Silpho N York 134 E2
Silsden C Brad 122 F2
Silsoe C Beds 74 F7
Silton Dorset...........27 H5
Silverburn Mdloth ...177 G6
Silverdale Lancs......129 K4
Silverdale Staffs........99 J3
Silver End Essex........61 K4
Silverford Abers.......216 E2
Silver Jubilee
Bridge Halton 112 D5
Silverstone Nhants....73 J5
Silverton Devon 12 B2
Silvington Shrops 84 B7
Simonburn Nthumb ..157 L7
Simonsbath Somset...24 B4
Simonstone Lancs....122 B4
Simprim Border 168 C1
Simpson M Keyn.......74 C7
Simpson Cross
Pembks 48 F3
Sinclair's Hill Border ..179 G7
Sinclairston E Ayrs..163 L6
Sinderby N York 132 E3
Sinderland Green
Traffd.................113 G4
Sindlesham Wokham...42 C6
Sinfin C Derb 101 G6
Singleton Kent..........34 D6
Singleton Lancs 120 E3
Singleton W Susx......18 B3
Singlewell Kent 46 A6
Sinnahard Abers......205 K3
Sinnington N York ...134 B3
Sinton Worcs............70 E3
Sinton Worcs............70 E3
Sinton Green Worcs...70 E3
Sissinghurst Kent......33 K5
Siston S Glos 39 G5
Sithney Cnwll.............3 H5
Sittingbourne Kent....34 B3
Six Ashes Shrops 84 E5
Sixhills Lincs..........117 K4
Six Mile Bottom
Cambs...................76 E3
Sixpenny Handley
Dorset 27 M7
Six Rues Jersey......236 c6
Skaill Ork..............234 d6
Skara Brae Ork.......234 b5
Skares E Ayrs 164 B6
Skateraw Abers.......207 G6
Skateraw E Loth 178 F4
Skeabost Highld 208 F5
Skeeby N York 140 F5
Skeffington Leics......87 L3
Skeffling E R Yk 127 K4
Skegby Notts 101 J1
Skegby Notts 116 C7
Skegness Lincs 119 H8
Skelbo Highld 223 H3
Skelbo Street Highld..223 H3
Skelbrooke Donc 124 D7
Skeldyke Lincs........104 B4
Skellingthorpe Lincs ..116 F6
Skellow Donc 124 E7
Skelmanthorpe Kirk ..123 J7
Skelmersdale Lancs...112 C1
Skelmorlie N Ayrs....173 L5
Skelpick Highld 229 L4
Skelston D & G 154 E5
Skelton C York 133 J7
Skelton Cumb.........148 D7
Skelton E R Yk.......125 H5
Skelton R & Cl.......142 E4
Skelton on Ure
N York 132 E5
Skelwith Bridge
Cumb..................137 K6

Skendleby Lincs............ 118 F7
Skene House Abers..... 206 E4
Skenfrith Mons..............54 C4
Skerne E R Yk...............135 G7
Skerray Highld............. 229 K3
Skerricha Highld........... 228 C5
Skerton Lancs...............129 K6
Sketchley Leics..............86 E5
Sketty Swans.................51 J4
Skewsby N York.............133 K5
Skiall Highld..................230 E3
Skidby E R Yk...............126 C4
Skigersta W Isls........... 232 g1
Skilgate Somset.............24 F6
Skillington Lincs........... 102 E7
Skinburness Cumb...... 147 K4
Skinflats Falk................176 B2
Skinidin Highld............. 208 C5
Skipness Ag & B........... 172 F6
Skipper's Bridge
  D & G......................... 156 C5
Skipsea E R Yk.............135 J8
Skipton N York..............122 E1
Skipton-on-Swale
  N York....................... 132 E4
Skipwith N York............125 G3
Skirbeck Lincs...............104 B4
Skirlaugh E R Yk..........126 E3
Skirling Border..............165 L2
Skirmett Bucks...............42 C3
Skirpenbeck E R Yk...... 134 B7
Skirwith Cumb...............149 G7
Skirza Highld.................231 L2
Skokholm Island
  Pembks........................48 C6
Skomer Island
  Pembks........................48 C5
Skulamus Highld........... 199 K2
Skye Green Essex..........61 L4
Skye of Curr Highld...... 204 B1
Slack Calder..................122 E5
Slackbuie Highld............213 G6
Slacks of
  Cairnbanno
  Abers.......................... 216 F5
Slad Gloucs...................55 K6
Slade Devon...................23 H3
Slade Green Gt Lon........45 K5
Slade Hooton Rothm.... 115 K4
Slaggyford Nthumb........149 H4
Slaidburn Lancs............130 D8
Slaithwaite Kirk............123 G7
Slaley Nthumb...............150 B4
Slamannan Falk.............176 B4
Slapton Bucks.................58 F4
Slapton Devon..................7 J6
Slapton Nhants...............73 J5
Slaugham W Susx...........31 L5
Slaughterford Wilts........39 J5
Slawston Leics................87 L5
Sleaford Hants................30 D4
Sleaford Lincs................103 H4
Sleagill Cumb................138 E4
Sleapford Wrekin............84 B1
Sleasdairidh Highld...... 222 E3
Sledmere E R Yk............134 E6
Sleetbeck Cumb.............156 E6
Sleights N York..............143 H5
Slickly Highld.................231 K3
Sliddery N Ayrs..............162 B5
Sligachan Highld........... 209 G7
Sligrachan Ag & B.........173 K1
Slimbridge Gloucs..........55 H7
Slindon Staffs.................99 J6
Slindon W Susx...............18 C4
Slinfold W Susx...............31 J5
Slingsby N York..............133 L4
Slip End C Beds...............59 H4
Slip End Herts.................75 K6
Slipton Nhants................88 D7
Slitting Mill Staffs.........100 B8
Slochd Highld................ 203 K1
Slockavullin Ag & B..... 182 B7
Sloncombe Devon...........11 H7
Sloothby Lincs................119 G7
Slough Slough.................43 G4
Slough Green
  Somset.........................25 L7

Slumbay Highld............. 210 D6
Slyfield Surrey...............31 G2
Slyne Lancs...................129 K6
Smailholm Border......... 167 K3
Smallburgh Norfk..........107 G7
Smallburn E Ayrs...........164 D4
Small Dole W Susx..........19 G3
Smalley Derbys...............101 H4
Smallfield Surrey............32 B5
Small Heath Birm............85 K6
Small Hythe Kent............34 B8
Smallridge Devon............13 H3
Smallthorne C Stke..........99 K3
Smallworth Norfk...........92 B7
Smannell Hants...............29 G2
Smarden Kent..................34 B6
Smarden Bell Kent...........34 B6
Smart's Hill Kent..............32 F5
Smeatharpe Devon...........12 F1
Smeeth Kent....................34 E6
Smeeton Westerby
  Leics...........................87 K5
Smerral Highld...............227 L2
Smestow Staffs................84 F5
Smethwick Sandw............85 H6
Smirisary Highld.............190 D2
Smisby Derbys................101 G8
Smithfield Cumb.............148 D3
Smith's Green Essex.........76 F6
Smithstown Highld..........219 J6
Smithton Highld............. 213 H5
Smoo Highld...................228 F3
Smythe's Green
  Essex...........................61 L4
Snade D & G...................154 E5
Snailbeach Shrops............83 G3
Snailwell Cambs.............76 F2
Snainton N York.............134 E3
Snaith E R Yk.................124 F6
Snape N York..................132 D3
Snape Suffk.....................79 H3
Snape Street Suffk...........79 H3
Snaresbrook Gt Lon.........45 H3
Snarestone Leics.............86 D2
Snarford Lincs.................117 H5
Snargate Kent..................34 D8
Snave Kent......................34 D8
Sneaton N York...............143 J5
Snelland Lincs.................117 H5
Snelston Derbys..............100 D4
Snetterton Norfk..............92 B5
Snettisham Norfk............105 G5
Snitter Nthumb...............158 C2
Snitterby Lincs................117 G3
Snitterfield Warwks..........72 B3
Snitton Shrops.................83 L7
Snodland Kent..................46 B7
Snowdon Gwynd...............95 K2
Snowdonia National
  Park............................96 C6
Snow End Herts...............60 C2
Snowshill Gloucs..............71 K7
Soake Hants....................17 J1
Soay Highld....................199 G3
Soberton Hants................29 L7
Soberton Heath
  Hants...........................29 L8
Sockburn Darltn.............141 J6
Soham Cambs..................90 E8
Solas W Isls................... 232 c5
Soldridge Hants...............29 M4
Sole Street Kent...............34 E5
Sole Street Kent...............46 A6
Solihull Solhll.................85 L7
Sollas W Isls.................. 232 c5
Sollers Dilwyn
  Herefs...........................69 H4
Sollers Hope Herefs..........54 E2
Solva Pembks...................48 D3
Solwaybank D & G..........156 B6
Somerby Leics.................87 L2
Somerby Lincs................117 H1
Somercotes Derbys..........101 H2
Somerford BCP................15 M4
Somerford Keynes
  Gloucs.........................40 A2
Somerley W Susx.............17 M3
Somerleyton Suffk...........93 K4

Somersal Herbert
  Derbys.........................100 C5
Somersby Lincs...............118 D6
Somersham Cambs..........89 L7
Somersham Suffk.............78 C5
Somerton Oxon................57 J3
Somerton Somset.............26 C5
Somerton Suffk................77 J4
Sompting W Susx.............19 G5
Sonning Wokham.............42 C5
Sonning Common
  Oxon...........................42 B4
Sopley Hants...................15 M3
Sopwell Herts..................59 J6
Sopworth Wilts................39 J3
Sorbie D & G..................145 J5
Sordale Highld............... 231 G3
Sorisdale Ag & B.............189 H4
Sorn E Ayrs.....................164 B4
Sornhill E Ayrs................163 M3
Sortat Highld................. 231 K3
Sotby Lincs.....................117 K5
Sotterley Suffk.................93 J6
Soughton Flints...............111 H7
Soulbury Bucks.................58 E3
Soulby Cumb...................139 H5
Souldern Oxon.................57 K2
Souldrop Bed...................74 E3
Sound Ches E...................98 F3
Sound Muir Moray...........215 H4
Soundwell S Glos.............38 F5
Sourton Devon.................10 D6
Soutergate Cumb.............128 F3
South Acre Norfk..............91 J2
South Alkham Kent...........35 H6
Southall Gt Lon................43 J4
South Allington
  Devon............................7 J7
South Alloa Falk.............185 J8
Southam Gloucs...............55 L3
Southam Warwks.............72 E3
South Ambersham
  W Susx..........................30 E7
Southampton C Sotn........29 H8
Southampton
  Airport Hants................29 J7
South Anston
  Rothm........................115 K5
South Ashford Kent...........34 D6
South Baddesley
  Hants...........................16 D3
South Bank C York..........124 F1
South Barrow
  Somset.........................26 E5
South Beddington
  Gt Lon..........................44 F7
South Benfleet Essex........46 C3
Southborough Gt Lon........45 H6
Southborough Kent...........33 G5
Southbourne BCP.............15 L4
Southbourne W Susx.........17 L2
South Bramwith
  Donc...........................124 F7
South Brent Devon............7 G4
South Brewham
  Somset.........................27 G4
South Broomhill
  Nthumb.......................159 G3
Southburgh Norfk............92 B3
South Burlingham
  Norfk...........................93 H3
Southburn E R Yk............134 F8
South Cadbury
  Somset.........................26 F6
South Carlton Lincs..........116 F6
South Carlton
  Notts...........................115 L5
South Cave E R Yk..........125 L4
South Cerney Gloucs........40 B2
South Chailey E Susx........19 K3
South Charlton
  Nthumb.......................169 H5
South Cheriton
  Somset.........................27 G6
South Church Dur............140 F2
Southchurch Sthend..........46 E3
South Cliffe E R Yk..........125 L4
South Clifton Notts..........116 D7

South Cockerington
  Lincs...........................118 E4
South Cornelly
  Brdgnd..........................36 C4
Southcott Cnwll.................9 G5
Southcott Devon...............11 H8
Southcourt Bucks..............58 D5
South Cove Suffk..............93 K7
South Creake Norfk.........105 K5
South Croxton Leics..........87 K2
South Dalton E R Yk........126 B2
South Darenth Kent..........45 K6
South Dell W Isls............ 232 g1
South Downs
  National Park................19 K4
South Duffield
  N York.........................125 G4
South Earlswood
  Surrey...........................32 B4
Southease E Susx..............19 L5
South Elkington
  Lincs...........................118 D4
South Elmsall
  Wakefd........................124 D7
Southend Ag & B.............161 H7
Southend Airport
  Essex............................46 E3
Southend-on-Sea
  Sthend...........................46 E3
Southerndown
  V Glam..........................36 D5
Southerness D & G...........147 G4
South Erradale
  Highld.........................219 H7
Southerton Devon.............12 D4
Southery Norfk.................90 E5
South Fambridge
  Essex............................46 E2
South Ferriby N Linc........126 B6
South Field E R Yk...........126 C5
Southfield Falk................175 L4
Southfleet Kent.................45 L5
Southgate Gt Lon..............44 F2
Southgate Swans..............51 G7
South Gorley Hants..........15 M1
South Gosforth
  N u Ty.........................151 G2
South Green Essex............46 B2
South Green Kent..............33 L2
South Green Norfk............92 C2
South Gyle C Edin...........177 G4
South Hanningfield
  Essex............................61 H8
South Harting
  W Susx..........................30 C7
South Hayling Hants.........17 K3
South Heath Bucks............58 E7
South Heighton
  E Susx..........................19 L5
South Hetton Dur............151 J6
South Hiendley
  Wakefd........................124 B7
South Hill Cnwll.................5 M2
South Hinksey Oxon..........57 K7
South Holmwood
  Surrey...........................31 K3
South Hornchurch
  Gt Lon..........................45 K4
South Huish Devon............7 G7
South Hykeham
  Lincs...........................116 F8
South Hylton Sundld........151 J4
Southill C Beds.................75 H6
Southington Hants............29 J2
South Kelsey Lincs...........117 H2
South Kessock
  Highld.........................213 G5
South Killingholme
  N Linc.........................126 E7
South Kilvington
  N York.........................132 F3
South Kilworth Leics..........87 H6
South Kirkby Wakefd.......124 C7
South Kyme Lincs............103 K3
Southleigh Devon.............12 F4
South Leigh Oxon.............57 H6
South Leverton
  Notts...........................116 C5

South Littleton
Worcs................71 J5
South Lopham Norfk....92 C7
South Luffenham
Rutlnd..............88 D3
South Lynn Norfk.......104 F8
South Malling E Susx.....19 L4
South Marston
Swindn.............40 D3
South Merstham
Surrey.............32 B3
South Milford N York...124 D4
South Milton Devon.....7 G7
South Mimms Herts......59 L7
South Mimms
Services Herts.........59 L7
Southminster Essex......62 A7
South Molton Devon......23 L6
South Moor Dur.........150 F5
Southmoor Oxon.........41 H2
South Moreton Oxon......41 K3
Southmuir Angus........196 C5
South Mundham
W Susx.............18 B5
South Newbald
E R Yk.............125 L4
South Newington
Oxon...............57 H2
South Newsham
Nthumb............159 H6
South Newton Wilts.....28 C4
South Nitshill
C Glas.............174 F6
South Normanton
Derbys.............101 H2
South Norwood
Gt Lon.............45 G6
South Ockendon
Thurr..............45 L4
Southoe Cambs...........75 H2
Southolt Suffk..........78 E2
South Ormsby Lincs.....118 E6
Southorpe C Pete........88 F3
South Otterington
N York.............132 E3
Southover Dorset........14 C4
South Owersby
Lincs..............117 H3
Southowram Calder......123 G5
South Park Surrey.......31 L2
South Perrott Dorset.....13 L2
South Petherton
Somset.............26 B7
South Petherwin
Cnwll..............9 J8
South Pickenham
Norfk..............91 J3
South Pill Cnwll.........6 B4
South Pool Devon.........7 H7
South Poorton
Dorset.............13 M3
Southport Sefton.......120 D6
South Queensferry
C Edin.............176 F3
South Raceby Lincs....103 G4
South Raynham
Norfk..............105 L7
South Reddish
Stockp.............113 K3
Southrepps Norfk.......106 F5
South Reston Lincs.....118 E5
Southrey Lincs..........117 J7
South Ronaldsay
Ork................234 c7
Southrop Gloucs.........56 D7
Southrope Hants.........30 A3
South Runcton Norfk.....90 F2
South Scarle Notts.....116 D8
Southsea C Port.........17 J3
South Shian Ag & B.....191 H7
South Shields S Tyne...151 J2
South Shore Bpool......120 D4
Southside Dur..........140 E2
South Stainley
N York.............132 D6
South Stifford Thurr.....45 L4
South Stoke BaNES.......39 H7
South Stoke Oxon........41 L4

South Stoke W Susx......18 D4
South Street Kent.......34 E3
South Street Kent.......47 J6
South Tarbrax S Lans...176 D7
South Tawton Devon......10 F6
South Tehidy Cnwll......3 H3
South Thoresby
Lincs..............118 E6
Southtown Norfk.........93 L3
South Uist W Isls......233 c8
Southwaite Cumb.......148 D6
Southwaite
Services Cumb........148 D6
South Walsham
Norfk..............93 H2
Southwark Gt Lon........44 F4
South Warnborough
Hants..............30 B3
Southwater W Susx.......31 J6
Southway C Plym.........6 C4
South Weald Essex.......45 L2
Southwell Notts........102 B2
South Weston Oxon.......42 B2
South Wheatley
Notts.............116 C4
Southwick Hants.........17 J2
Southwick Nhants........88 E5
Southwick Sundld......151 J4
Southwick W Susx.......19 H5
Southwick Wilts........27 J1
South Widcombe
BaNES..............38 E8
South Wigston Leics....87 H4
South Willingham
Lincs.............117 K5
South Wingfield
Derbys............101 G2
South Witham Lincs....102 F8
Southwold Suffk........93 K7
South Woodham
Ferrers Essex.......61 J7
South Wootton
Norfk.............105 G7
South Wraxall Wilts.....39 J7
South Zeal Devon........10 F6
Sovereign Harbour
E Susx.............20 D5
Sowerby Calder........122 F6
Sowerby N York........132 F4
Sowerby Bridge
Calder............122 F5
Sowood Calder.........123 G6
Sowton Devon...........6 D3
Sowton Devon...........12 C4
Soyland Town Calder...122 F6
Spain's End Essex.......76 F6
Spalding Lincs.........103 L7
Spaldington E R Yk.....125 H4
Spaldwick Cambs.........89 G8
Spalford Notts.........116 D7
Spanby Lincs...........103 H5
Sparham Norfk..........106 C8
Spark Bridge Cumb......129 G3
Sparkford Somset........26 E6
Sparkhill Birm..........85 K6
Sparkwell Devon.........6 E4
Sparrowpit Derbys......114 C5
Sparrows Green
E Susx.............33 H6
Sparsholt Hants.........29 H5
Sparsholt Oxon..........41 G3
Spaunton N York........133 L2
Spaxton Somset..........25 K4
Spean Bridge Highld....201 K8
Spearywell Hants........28 F6
Speen Bucks............58 D7
Speen W Berk...........41 J6
Speeton N York.........135 J5
Speke Lpool...........112 C5
Speldhurst Kent.........32 F5
Spellbrook Herts........60 D4
Spencers Wood
Wokham.............42 B6
Spen Green Ches E.......99 J1
Spennithorne
N York.............131 L2
Spennymoor Dur........151 G7
Spetchley Worcs.........70 F4

Spetisbury Dorset.......15 G3
Spexhall Suffk..........93 H7
Spey Bay Moray........215 H2
Speybridge Highld......204 C1
Speyview Moray........215 G6
Spilsby Lincs..........118 E7
Spinkhill Derbys.......115 J5
Spinningdale Highld....222 F4
Spital Wirral..........111 K5
Spital Hill Donc.......115 L3
Spittal E Loth.........178 B3
Spittal Highld.........231 H5
Spittal Nthumb.........179 L7
Spittal Pembks..........49 G3
Spittalfield P & K.....195 H7
Spittal of
Glenmuick Abers....205 G7
Spittal of Glenshee
P & K..............195 H3
Spittal-on-Rule
Border.............167 J5
Spixworth Norfk.........92 F1
Splatt Devon............10 E4
Splayne's Green
E Susx.............19 L2
Splott Cardif...........37 J5
Spofforth N York.......124 B1
Spondon C Derb........101 H5
Spooner Row Norfk......92 D4
Sporle Norfk............91 J2
Spott E Loth..........178 E4
Spottiswoode
Border.............178 D7
Spratton Nhants.........73 K1
Spreakley Surrey........30 D3
Spreyton Devon..........11 G5
Spriddlestone Devon......6 D5
Spridlington Lincs.....117 G5
Springburn C Glas......175 G5
Springfield D & G.....148 B2
Springfield Essex.......61 H6
Springfield Fife.......186 E5
Springholm D & G......154 E7
Springside N Ayrs......163 J2
Springthorpe Lincs.....116 E4
Springwell Sundld......151 H4
Sproatley E R Yk.......126 F4
Sproston Green
Ches W.............113 G7
Sprotbrough Donc......115 K2
Sproughton Suffk........78 D5
Sprouston Border.......168 A3
Sprowston Norfk.........92 F2
Sproxton Leics........102 D7
Sproxton N York........133 J3
Spurstow Ches E.........98 D2
Spyway Dorset...........14 A4
Stableford Shrops.......84 D4
Stacey Bank Sheff......114 F4
Stackhouse N York......130 F6
Stackpole Pembks........49 G7
Stackpole Elidor
Pembks.............49 G7
Staddiscombe
C Plym..............6 D5
Stadhampton Oxon........57 L7
Stadhlaigearraidh
W Isls............233 b7
Staffield Cumb.........148 F6
Staffin Highld.........218 D7
Stafford Staffs.........99 L7
Stafford Services
(northbound)
Staffs.............99 K6
Stafford Services
(southbound)
Staffs.............99 K6
Stagsden Bed............74 E5
Stainburn Cumb.........136 E2
Stainby Lincs..........102 E7
Staincross Barns.......123 L7
Staindrop Dur..........140 E3
Staines-upon-
Thames Surrey.......43 G6
Stainforth Donc........124 F7
Stainforth N York......130 F6
Staining Lancs.........120 D4
Stainland Calder.......123 G6

Stainsacre N York......143 J5
Stainton Cumb..........129 L3
Stainton Cumb..........138 C2
Stainton Donc..........115 K3
Stainton Dur...........140 D4
Stainton Middsb........141 L4
Stainton by
Langworth Lincs....117 H6
Staintondale N York....143 K7
Stainton le Vale
Lincs..............117 K3
Stainton with
Adgarley Cumb......128 F5
Stair E Ayrs..........163 K5
Stairhaven D & G.......144 E4
Staithes N York........143 G4
Stakes Hants............17 K2
Stalbridge Dorset.......27 G7
Stalbridge Weston
Dorset.............27 G7
Stalham Norfk..........107 H7
Stalisfield Green
Kent...............34 C4
Stallen Dorset..........26 E7
Stallingborough
NE Lin.............126 F7
Stalmine Lancs.........120 E2
Stalybridge Tamesd....113 L2
Stambourne Essex........77 G6
Stambourne Green
Essex..............77 G6
Stamford Lincs..........88 E3
Stamford Nthumb.......169 J5
Stamford Bridge
Ches W............112 C7
Stamford Bridge
E R Yk............133 L7
Stamfordham
Nthumb............158 D7
Stamford Hill Gt Lon....45 G3
Stanbridge C Beds.......58 F3
Stanbury C Brad.......122 F3
Stand N Lans..........175 K5
Standburn Falk.........176 C4
Standeford Staffs.......85 G3
Standen Kent............33 L5
Standerwick Somset......27 J2
Standford Hants.........30 D4
Standingstone
Cumb..............147 J7
Standish Wigan.........121 H7
Standlake Oxon..........57 H7
Standon Hants...........29 H6
Standon Herts...........60 C4
Standon Staffs..........99 J5
Stane N Lans...........176 B6
Stanfield Norfk........105 M7
Stanford C Beds.........75 H6
Stanford Kent...........34 F6
Stanford Bishop
Herefs.............70 C4
Stanford Bridge
Worcs..............70 C2
Stanford Dingley
W Berk.............41 L6
Stanford in the Vale
Oxon...............41 G2
Stanford le Hope
Thurr..............46 B4
Stanford on Avon
Nhants.............87 H7
Stanford on Soar
Notts.............101 K7
Stanford on Teme
Worcs..............70 C2
Stanfree Derbys........115 J6
Stanghow R & Cl.......142 E4
Stanground C Pete.......89 H4
Stanhoe Norfk..........105 J5
Stanhope Border.......165 L4
Stanhope Dur..........150 C6
Stanhope Kent...........34 D6
Stanion Nhants..........88 D6
Stanley Derbys.........101 H4
Stanley Dur...........150 F4
Stanley P & K..........186 B2
Stanley Staffs..........99 L3
Stanley Crook Dur......150 E7

Stanley Pontlarge
Gloucs 55 M3
Stanmer Br & H...............19 K4
Stanmore Gt Lon..........44 D2
Stanmore Hants............29 J5
Stannersburn
Nthumb 157 J5
Stanningfield Suffk........77 K3
Stannington Nthumb.....158 F6
Stannington Sheff.........114 F4
Stannington Station
Nthumb 158 F5
Stansbatch Herefs..........69 G3
Stansfield Suffk..............77 H4
Stanstead Suffk..............77 J5
Stanstead Abbotts
Herts.........................60 C5
Stansted Kent.................45 L7
Stansted Airport
Essex.........................60 E4
**Stansted
Mountfitchet**
Essex.........................60 E3
Stanton Gloucs 71 J7
Stanton Nthumb 158 E4
Stanton Staffs..............100 C4
Stanton Suffk.................91 L8
Stanton by Bridge
Derbys......................101 G6
Stanton by Dale
Derbys......................101 J5
Stanton Drew BaNES......38 E7
Stanton Fitzwarren
Swindn 40 D3
Stanton Harcourt
Oxon.........................57 H6
Stanton in Peak
Derbys.....................114 E8
Stanton Lacy Shrops......83 K7
Stanton Lees Derbys 114 E8
Stanton Long Shrops.....83 L5
**Stanton-on-the-
Wolds** Notts 101 M6
Stanton Prior BaNES......39 G7
Stanton St Bernard
Wilts.........................40 C7
Stanton St John
Oxon.........................57 L6
Stanton St Quintin
Wilts.........................39 K4
Stanton Street Suffk......77 L2
**Stanton under
Bardon** Leics.............86 F2
**Stanton upon Hine
Heath** Shrops...........98 E7
Stanton Wick BaNES......38 E7
Stanway Essex...............61 M3
Stanway Gloucs..............56 B2
Stanwell Surrey..............43 H5
Stanwick Nhants............74 E1
Stanwix Cumb..............148 D4
Staoinebrig W Isls.........233 b8
Stape N York.................143 G7
Stapeley Ches E...............99 G3
Stapenhill Staffs...........100 E7
Staple Kent.....................35 H4
Staple Cross Devon.........25 G7
Staplecross E Susx..........20 F2
Staplefield W Susx 32 B7
Staple Fitzpaine
Somset.......................25 K7
Stapleford Cambs..........76 C4
Stapleford Herts.............60 A5
Stapleford Leics............102 D8
Stapleford Lincs............102 E2
Stapleford Notts............101 J5
Stapleford Wilts..............28 B4
Stapleford Abbotts
Essex.........................45 K2
Staplegrove Somset.......25 K6
Staplehay Somset...........25 K6
Staplehurst Kent............33 K5
Staplers IoW.................17 G4
Staplestreet Kent...........34 E3
Stapleton Herefs.............69 G2
Stapleton Leics...............86 E4
Stapleton N York............141 G5
Stapleton Shrops.............83 J3

Stapleton Somset 26 C7
Stapley Somset...............25 J8
Staploe Bed....................75 G3
Staplow Herefs................70 C6
Star Fife.........................186 E6
Star Pembks.....................65 H7
Star Somset....................38 C8
Starbeck N York.............132 E7
Starbotton N York..........131 H5
Starcross Devon..............12 C6
Stareton Warwks............72 D1
Starlings Green
Essex.........................60 D2
Starston Norfk................92 F6
Startforth Dur................140 D4
Startley Wilts..................39 L4
Statenborough Kent........35 J4
Statham Warrtn.............112 F4
Stathe Somset.................26 A5
Stathern Leics...............102 C6
Staunton Gloucs..............54 D5
Staunton Gloucs..............55 H3
Staunton on Arrow
Herefs.......................69 G3
Staunton on Wye
Herefs.......................69 G5
Staveley Cumb...............138 C7
Staveley Derbys.............115 H6
Staveley N York.............132 E6
**Staveley-in-
Cartmel** Cumb 129 H3
Staverton Devon 7 J3
Staverton Gloucs.............55 K4
Staverton Nhants............73 G3
Staverton Wilts................39 J7
Stawell Somset................26 A4
Stawley Somset...............25 G6
Staxigoe Highld.............231 L5
Staxton N York..............134 F4
Staynall Lancs...............120 E2
Stean N York..................131 K5
Stearsby N York.............133 J5
Steart Somset..................25 L3
Stebbing Essex................61 G3
Stechford Birm................85 K6
Stedham W Susx..............30 E6
Steelend Fife..................185 L8
Steele Road Border......156 F4
Steen's Bridge
Herefs.......................69 K3
Steep Hants....................30 C6
Steep Lane Calder........122 F5
Steeple Essex..................61 M7
Steeple Ashton Wilts......27 K1
Steeple Aston Oxon........57 J3
Steeple Bumpstead
Essex.........................76 F6
Steeple Claydon
Bucks........................58 B3
Steeple Gidding
Cambs.......................89 G7
Steeple Langford
Wilts.........................28 B4
Steeple Morden
Cambs.......................75 K6
Steeton C Brad..............122 F2
Stein Highld...................208 D3
Stelling Minnis Kent 34 F5
Stembridge Somset.........26 B7
Stenalees Cnwll 4 F4
Stenhouse D & G............154 D4
Stenhousemuir Falk.......176 B2
Stenness Ork.................234 b6
Stenscholl Highld...........218 D7
Stenson Fields
Derbys......................101 G6
Stenton E Loth...............178 D4
Steòrnabhagh
W Isls......................232 f2
Stepaside Pembks............49 K6
Stepford D & G..............154 E5
Stepney Gt Lon................45 G4
Steppingley C Beds.........74 E7
Stepps N Lans...............175 H5
Sternfield Suffk................79 H3
Stert Wilts........................40 B8
Stetchworth Cambs.........76 F3
Stevenage Herts..............59 L3

Stevenston N Ayrs.........163 H2
Steventon Hants.............29 K2
Steventon Oxon..............41 J3
Steventon End Essex......76 E6
Stevington Bed................74 E4
Stewartby Bed.................74 E6
Stewartfield S Lans.......175 H7
Stewarton Ag & B..........161 H5
Stewarton E Ayrs...........163 K1
Stewkley Bucks...............58 D3
Stewley Somset................25 L7
Steyning W Susx..............19 G4
Steynton Pembks..............48 F6
Stibb Cnwll........................9 G3
Stibbard Norfk................106 B6
Stibb Cross Devon...........10 C2
Stibb Green Wilts............40 E7
Stibbington Cambs...........88 F4
Stichill Border................167 L2
Sticker Cnwll......................4 F5
Stickford Lincs...............104 B1
Sticklepath Devon............10 F6
Stickney Lincs................104 B2
Stiffkey Norfk.................106 A4
Stifford Clays Thurr........45 L4
Stilligarry W Isls............233 b7
Stillingfleet N York.......124 F3
Stillington N York..........133 J6
Stillington S on T..........141 J3
Stilton Cambs...................89 H5
Stinchcombe Gloucs.........55 G7
Stinsford Dorset..............14 D4
Stiperstones Shrops........83 G4
Stirchley Wrekin...............84 C3
Stirling Abers.................217 L6
Stirling Stirlg.................185 G8
Stirling Castle
Stirlg.......................185 G8
Stirling Services
Stirlg.......................175 L1
Stirtloe Cambs.................75 H2
Stirton N York................131 H8
Stisted Essex....................61 J3
Stithians Cnwll..................3 J4
Stivichall Covtry..............86 D7
Stixwould Lincs..............117 K7
St Michaels Fife............187 G3
Stoak Ches W..................112 B6
Stobo Border..................166 B2
Stoborough Dorset..........15 H5
Stobs Castle Border......167 H7
Stobswood Nthumb........158 F3
Stock Essex......................61 H7
Stock N Som.....................38 C7
Stockbridge Hants...........29 G4
Stockbridge W Susx........18 B5
Stockbriggs S Lans........164 F3
Stockbury Kent................46 D7
Stockcross W Berk..........41 H6
Stockerston Leics............88 B4
Stock Green Worcs..........71 H3
Stocking Herefs................54 F2
Stockingford
Warwks......................86 D5
Stocking Pelham
Herts.........................60 D3
Stockland Devon..............13 G2
Stockland Bristol
Somset.......................25 K3
Stockleigh English
Devon........................11 K4
Stockleigh Pomeroy
Devon........................11 K4
Stockley Wilts..................39 M6
Stocklinch Somset...........26 B7
Stockport Stockp............113 K4
Stocksbridge Sheff........114 E2
Stocksfield Nthumb........150 D3
Stockton Herefs...............69 K3
Stockton Norfk.................93 H5
Stockton Shrops...............84 C4
Stockton Warwks.............72 E2
Stockton Wilts..................27 M4
Stockton Wrekin...............84 D1
Stockton Brook
Staffs.........................99 K3
Stockton Heath
Warrtn.....................112 E4

Stockton-on-Tees
S on T.....................141 K4
Stockton on Teme
Worcs........................70 C2
**Stockton on the
Forest** C York...........133 K7
Stockwell End
Wolves......................84 F4
Stockwood Bristl.............38 F6
Stockwood Dorset............14 B2
Stock Wood Worcs...........71 H3
Stodmarsh Kent...............35 G3
Stody Norfk....................106 C5
Stoer Highld..................224 C3
Stoford Somset................26 E8
Stoford Wilts...................28 B4
Stogumber Somset...........25 H4
Stogursey Somset.............25 J3
Stoke Covtry.....................86 D7
Stoke Devon....................22 C6
Stoke Hants.....................17 K3
Stoke Hants.....................29 H2
Stoke Medway...................46 D5
Stoke Abbott Dorset........13 L3
Stoke Albany Nhants........88 B5
Stoke Ash Suffk...............78 D1
Stoke Bardolph
Notts.......................101 M4
Stoke Bliss Worcs............70 B2
Stoke Bruerne
Nhants......................73 L4
Stoke-by-Clare Suffk......77 G5
Stoke-by-Nayland
Suffk.........................78 B7
Stoke Canon Devon..........12 B3
Stoke Charity Hants.........29 J4
Stoke Climsland
Cnwll..........................6 A2
Stoke Cross Herefs...........70 B4
Stoke D'Abernon
Surrey.......................43 J8
Stoke Doyle Nhants.........88 E6
Stoke Dry Rutlnd.............88 C4
Stoke Edith Herefs...........69 L6
Stoke Farthing Wilts........28 B6
Stoke Ferry Norfk............91 G4
Stoke Fleming Devon.........7 K6
Stokeford Dorset..............15 G5
Stoke Gabriel Devon..........7 J4
Stoke Gifford S Glos........38 F4
Stoke Golding Leics.........86 E4
Stoke Goldington
M Keyn.....................74 B5
Stokeham Notts..............116 C6
Stoke Hammond
Bucks........................58 E3
Stoke Holy Cross
Norfk........................92 F3
Stokeinteignhead
Devon..........................7 L2
Stoke Lacy Herefs............70 B5
Stoke Lyne Oxon..............57 K3
Stoke Mandeville
Bucks........................58 D6
Stokenchurch Bucks.........42 C2
Stoke Newington
Gt Lon......................45 G3
Stokenham Devon..............7 J7
Stoke-on-Trent
C Stke.......................99 K3
Stoke Orchard
Gloucs.......................55 K3
Stoke Poges Bucks...........42 F4
Stoke Prior Herefs...........69 K3
Stoke Prior Worcs............71 G2
Stoke Rivers Devon..........23 K4
Stoke Rochford
Lincs.......................102 F6
Stoke Row Oxon...............42 B4
Stoke St Gregory
Somset.......................25 M6
Stoke St Mary
Somset.......................25 K6
Stoke St Michael
Somset.......................26 F3
**Stoke St
Milborough**
Shrops.......................83 L6

Stokesby Norfk 93 J2
Stokesley N York 142 B5
Stoke sub Hamdon
Somset 26 C7
Stoke Talmage Oxon 58 B7
Stoke Trister Somset 27 H5
Stoke upon Tern
Shrops 98 F6
Stolford Somset 25 K3
Stondon Massey
Essex 60 F7
Stone Bucks 58 C5
Stone Gloucs 39 G2
Stone Rothm 115 K4
Stone Staffs 99 K5
Stone Worcs 84 F7
Stone Allerton
Somset 26 B2
Ston Easton Somset 26 F2
Stonebridge N Som 38 B7
Stonebridge Warwks 86 B6
Stonebroom Derbys 101 H2
Stone Cross Kent 35 J4
Stonecrouch Kent 33 J6
Stoneferry C KuH 126 D4
Stonefield Castle
Hotel Ag & B 172 E4
Stonegate E Susx 33 H7
Stonegrave N York 133 K4
Stonehaven Abers 207 G7
Stonehenge Wilts 28 C3
Stonehouse C Plym 6 C5
Stonehouse Gloucs 55 J6
Stonehouse S Lans 175 K8
Stone in Oxney Kent 21 J1
Stoneleigh Warwks 86 D8
Stonesby Leics 102 D7
Stonesfield Oxon 57 H4
Stones Green Essex 62 E3
Stone Street Kent 33 G3
Stone Street Suffk 93 H6
Stonewells Moray 215 G2
Stoneybridge W Isls 233 b8
Stoneyburn W Loth 176 D5
Stoneygate C Leic 87 H3
Stoneykirk D & G 144 C4
Stoney Middleton
Derbys 114 E6
Stoney Stanton Leics 86 F4
Stoney Stoke Somset 27 G5
Stoney Stratton
Somset 26 F4
Stoneywood C Aber 207 G3
Stoneywood Falk 175 L2
Stonham Aspal Suffk ... 78 D3
Stonnall Staffs 85 J3
Stonor Oxon 42 B3
Stonton Wyville
Leics 87 K4
Stonybreck Shet 235 e7
Stony Houghton
Derbys 115 J7
Stony Stratford
M Keyn 73 L6
Stoodleigh Devon 23 K5
Stoodleigh Devon 24 E7
Stopham W Susx 18 D2
Stopsley Luton 59 J3
Stornoway W Isls 232 f2
Stornoway Airport
W Isls 232 g2
Storrington W Susx 18 E3
Storth Cumb 129 K4
Storwood E R Yk 125 H2
Stotfield Moray 214 F1
Stotfold C Beds 75 J7
Stottesdon Shrops 84 C6
Stoughton Leics 87 J3
Stoughton Surrey 31 G2
Stoughton W Susx 17 L1
Stoulton Worcs 70 F4
Stourbridge Dudley 84 F6
Stourhead Wilts 27 H5
Stourpaine Dorset 15 G1
Stourport-on-
Severn Worcs 70 E1
Stour Provost Dorset 27 H6
Stour Row Dorset 27 J7

Stourton Staffs 84 F6
Stourton Warwks 72 C6
Stourton Wilts 27 H5
Stourton Caundle
Dorset 27 G7
Stove Shet 235 c7
Stoven Suffk 93 J6
Stow Border 167 G1
Stow Lincs 116 E5
Stow Bardolph Norfk 90 F3
Stow Bedon Norfk 91 L4
Stowbridge Norfk 90 E3
Stow-cum-Quy
Cambs 76 D3
Stowe Shrops 82 F8
Stowe-by-Chartley
Staffs 100 A6
Stowell Somset 27 G6
Stowey BaNES 38 E7
Stowford Devon 10 C7
Stowford Devon 12 E4
Stowlangtoft Suffk 77 L2
Stow Longa Cambs 75 G1
Stow Maries Essex 61 K7
Stowmarket Suffk 78 C3
Stow-on-the-Wold
Gloucs 56 D3
Stowting Kent 34 F6
Stowupland Suffk 78 C3
Straad Ag & B 173 H6
Straanruie Highld 204 B3
Strachan Abers 206 D6
Strachur Ag & B 182 F6
Stradbroke Suffk 92 F8
Stradishall Suffk 77 H4
Stradsett Norfk 90 F3
Stragglethorpe
Lincs 102 E3
Straiton Mdloth 177 H5
Straiton S Ayrs 153 H2
Straloch Abers 207 G2
Straloch P & K 195 G4
Stramshall Staffs 100 B5
Strang IoM 237 c5
Strangeways Salfd 113 J2
Strangford Herefs 54 E3
Stranraer D & G 144 C3
Stratfield Mortimer
W Berk 42 A7
Stratfield Saye Hants 42 B7
Stratfield Turgis
Hants 42 B7
Stratford Gt Lon 45 H3
Stratford St Andrew
Suffk 79 H3
Stratford St Mary
Suffk 78 C7
Stratford sub Castle
Wilts 28 C5
Stratford Tony Wilts 28 C6
Stratford-upon-
Avon Warwks 72 B4
Strath Highld 219 J5
Strathan Highld 224 D4
Strathan Highld 229 J3
Strathaven S Lans 164 D1
Strathblane Stirlg 175 G3
Strathcanaird Highld .. 220 F2
Strathcarron Highld ... 210 E6
Strathcoil Ag & B 181 K2
Strathdon Abers 205 H3
Strathkinness Fife 187 G4
Strathloanhead
W Loth 176 C4
Strathmashie House
Highld 202 F6
Strathmiglo Fife 186 C5
Strathpeffer Highld ... 212 D3
Strathtay P & K 194 E5
Strathwhillan
N Ayrs 162 D3
Strathy Highld 230 B3
Strathy Inn Highld 230 B3
Strathyre Stirlg 184 C4
Stratton Cnwll 9 G4
Stratton Dorset 14 C4
Stratton Gloucs 56 A7
Stratton Audley Oxon ... 57 L3

Stratton-on-the-
Fosse Somset 26 F2
Stratton St
Margaret Swindn 40 D3
Stratton St Michael
Norfk 92 E5
Stratton Strawless
Norfk 106 F7
Streat E Susx 19 K3
Streatham Gt Lon 44 F5
Streatley C Beds 59 H3
Streatley W Berk 41 L4
Street Devon 12 F5
Street Somset 26 C4
Street Ashton
Warwks 86 F6
Street Dinas Shrops 97 M5
Street End Kent 34 F4
Street End W Susx 18 A5
Streethay Staffs 85 K2
Streetlam N York 141 H7
Streetly End Cambs 76 E5
Street on the Fosse
Somset 26 F4
Strelitz P & K 186 C1
Strelley Notts 101 J4
Strensall C York 133 K7
Strensham Services
(northbound)
Worcs 70 F6
Strensham Services
(southbound)
Worcs 70 F6
Stretcholt Somset 25 L3
Strete Devon 7 J6
Stretford Traffd 113 H3
Strethall Essex 76 C6
Stretham Cambs 90 D8
Strettington W Susx 18 B4
Stretton Derbys 101 H1
Stretton Rutlnd 88 D1
Stretton Staffs 84 F2
Stretton Staffs 100 E7
Stretton Warrtn 112 F5
Stretton Grandison
Herefs 70 B5
Stretton-on-
Dunsmore
Warwks 86 E8
Stretton on Fosse
Warwks 72 B6
Stretton Sugwas
Herefs 69 J6
Stretton under
Fosse Warwks 86 F7
Stretton Westwood
Shrops 83 L4
Strichen Abers 217 H4
Stringston Somset 25 J3
Strixton Nhants 74 C3
Stroat Gloucs 38 E2
Strollamus Highld 209 J8
Stroma Highld 231 L1
Stromeferry Highld ... 210 D7
Stromness Ork 234 b6
Stronaba Highld 201 J8
Stronachlachar
Stirlg 183 L5
Stronafian Ag & B 173 H3
Stronchrubie Highld .. 224 F5
Strone Ag & B 173 L3
Strone Highld 192 B1
Strone Highld 212 E8
Stronmilchan Ag & B . 183 G2
Stronsay Ork 234 d5
Stronsay Airport
Ork 234 d5
Strontian Highld 191 G4
Strood Medway 46 B6
Stroud Gloucs 55 J6
Stroud Hants 30 B6
Stroud Green Gloucs 55 J6
Stroxton Lincs 102 E6
Struan Highld 208 D3
Struan P & K 194 C4
Strumpshaw Norfk 93 H3
Strutherhill S Lans 175 K7
Struthers Fife 186 F5

Struy Highld 212 B6
Stuartfield Abers 217 H5
Stubbington Hants 17 G2
Stubbins Lancs 122 B6
Stubton Lincs 102 E3
Stuckton Hants 28 D8
Studham C Beds 59 G5
Studland Dorset 15 J6
Studlands Park Suffk ... 76 F2
Studley Warwks 71 J2
Studley Wilts 39 L6
Studley Common
Warwks 71 J2
Studley Roger
N York 132 D5
Studley Royal N York . 132 D5
Studley Royal Park
& Fountains
Abbey N York 132 D5
Stuntney Cambs 90 D7
Sturmer Essex 77 G5
Sturminster
Common Dorset 27 H8
Sturminster
Marshall Dorset 15 H3
Sturminster Newton
Dorset 27 H8
Sturry Kent 35 G3
Sturton N Linc 116 F2
Sturton by Stow
Lincs 116 E5
Sturton le Steeple
Notts 116 C5
Stuston Suffk 92 D7
Stutton N York 124 D3
Stutton Suffk 78 D7
Styal Ches E 113 J5
Stynie Moray 215 H3
Styrrup Notts 115 L4
Succoth Ag & B 183 K6
Suckley Worcs 70 C4
Sudborough Nhants 88 D6
Sudbourne Suffk 79 J4
Sudbrook Lincs 102 F4
Sudbrook Mons 38 D3
Sudbrooke Lincs 117 G6
Sudbury Derbys 100 D6
Sudbury Gt Lon 44 D3
Sudbury Suffk 77 K6
Suffield N York 134 F2
Suffield Norfk 106 F6
Sugnall Staffs 99 H6
Sugwas Pool Herefs 69 J6
Suisnish Highld 199 J3
Sulby IoM 237 d3
Sulgrave Nhants 73 G5
Sulham W Berk 41 M5
Sulhamstead W Berk .. 41 M6
Sullom Shet 235 c4
Sullom Voe Shet 235 c4
Sully V Glam 37 J6
Sumburgh Airport
Shet 235 c8
Summerbridge
N York 132 C6
Summercourt Cnwll 4 D5
Summerfield Norfk 105 J5
Summerhill Pembks 49 K6
Summerhouse
Darltn 140 F4
Summersdale W Susx .. 18 A4
Summerseat Bury 122 B7
Summertown Oxon 57 K6
Sunbury-on-
Thames Surrey 43 J6
Sundaywell D & G 154 E5
Sunderland Ag & B 170 E5
Sunderland Cumb 147 L2
Sunderland Lancs 129 J7
Sunderland Sundld 151 J4
Sunderland Bridge
Dur 151 G7
Sundhope Border 166 E4
Sundon Park Luton 59 H3
Sundridge Kent 32 E3
Sunningdale W & M 42 F6
Sunninghill W & M 42 F6
Sunningwell Oxon 57 J7

Sunniside Dur 150 E7
Sunniside Gatesd......... 150 F3
Sunnyhill C Derb 101 G6
Sunnyhurst Bl w D........ 121 K6
Sunnylaw Stirlg............ 185 G7
Sunnymead Oxon 57 J6
Surbiton Gt Lon 44 D6
Surfleet Lincs 103 L6
Surlingham Norfk.........93 G3
Surrex Essex 61 L4
Sustead Norfk............. 106 E5
Susworth Lincs............ 116 D2
Sutcombe Devon 9 J3
Sutcombemill Devon....... 9 J3
Sutterby Lincs.............. 118 E6
Sutterton Lincs............ 103 M5
Sutton C Beds 75 J5
Sutton C Pete 89 G4
Sutton Cambs 90 C7
Sutton Devon 7 G7
Sutton E Susx 20 A5
Sutton Gt Lon 44 E7
Sutton Kent...................35 J5
Sutton N York.............. 124 D5
Sutton Norfk 107 H7
Sutton Notts............... 102 C5
Sutton Oxon 57 H6
Sutton Shrops 83 K2
Sutton Shrops 84 D6
Sutton Staffs................99 H7
Sutton Suffk 79 G5
Sutton W Susx...............18 D3
Sutton-at-Hone
  Kent............................45 K6
Sutton Bassett
  Nhants.........................87 L5
Sutton Benger Wilts......39 L5
Sutton Bonington
  Notts.......................... 101 J7
Sutton Bridge Lincs 104 D7
Sutton Cheney Leics 86 E4
Sutton Coldfield
  Birm...........................85 K4
Sutton Courtenay
  Oxon...........................41 J2
Sutton cum Lound
  Notts.......................... 116 B5
Sutton Green Surrey......31 G1
Sutton Heath Suffk 79 G5
Sutton Howgrave
  N York 132 D4
Sutton-in-Ashfield
  Notts.......................... 101 J1
Sutton-in-Craven
  N York 122 F2
Sutton Maddock
  Shrops........................84 C3
Sutton Mallet Somset....26 A4
Sutton Mandeville
  Wilts..........................27 M5
Sutton Montis
  Somset........................26 F6
Sutton-on-Hull
  C KuH........................ 126 E4
Sutton on Sea Lincs 119 G5
Sutton-on-the-
  Forest N York 133 J6
Sutton on the Hill
  Derbys....................... 100 E5
Sutton on Trent
  Notts.......................... 116 D7
Sutton St Edmund
  Lincs...........................89 L2
Sutton St James
  Lincs......................... 104 C8
Sutton St Nicholas
  Herefs.........................69 K5
Sutton Scotney
  Hants..........................29 J4
Sutton-under-
  Brailes Warwks 72 C6
Sutton-under-
  Whitestonecliffe
  N York 133 G3
Sutton upon
  Derwent E R Yk....... 125 G2
Sutton Valence Kent......33 L4
Sutton Veny Wilts 27 K3

Sutton Waldron
  Dorset.........................27 K7
Sutton Weaver
  Ches W...................... 112 D5
Sutton Wick BaNES......38 E8
Sutton Wick Oxon 41 J2
Swaby Lincs................. 118 E6
Swadlincote Derbys..... 100 F8
Swaffham Norfk............91 J2
Swaffham Bulbeck
  Cambs.........................76 D3
Swaffham Prior
  Cambs.........................76 E2
Swafield Norfk............ 107 G6
Swainby N York 141 L6
Swainsthorpe Norfk 92 F4
Swainswick BaNES.......39 H6
Swalcliffe Oxon............72 E6
Swalecliffe Kent 47 J6
Swallow Lincs.............. 117 K2
Swallow Beck Lincs 116 F7
Swallowcliffe Wilts......27 L6
Swallowfield Wokham....42 B7
Swanage Dorset...........15 J6
Swanbourne Bucks......58 D3
Swan Green Ches W 113 G6
Swanland E R Yk 126 B5
Swanley Kent...............45 K6
Swanley Village Kent 45 K6
Swanmore Hants..........29 L7
Swannington Leics......86 E1
Swannington Norfk..... 106 D8
Swanpool Lincs........... 116 F7
Swanscombe Kent........45 L5
Swansea Swans.............51 J6
Swansea Airport
  Swans.........................51 H7
Swansea West
  Services Swans........51 J5
Swanton Abbot
  Norfk......................... 106 F7
Swanton Morley
  Norfk...........................92 B1
Swanton Novers
  Norfk......................... 106 B6
Swan Village Sandw......85 H5
Swanwick Derbys........ 101 H2
Swanwick Hants...........17 G1
Swarby Lincs............... 103 H4
Swardeston Norfk........92 E3
Swarkestone Derbys... 101 G6
Swarland Nthumb...... 158 F2
Swarraton Hants..........29 K4
Swarthmoor Cumb..... 129 G4
Swaton Lincs.............. 103 J5
Swavesey Cambs..........75 L2
Sway Hants...................16 C3
Swayfield Lincs........... 103 G7
Swaythling C Sotn........29 H7
Sweetham Devon..........11 K5
Sweethaws E Susx........32 E7
Sweets Cnwll.................. 8 F5
Sweetshouse Cnwll........ 5 H4
Swefling Suffk...............79 H2
Swepstone Leics...........86 D2
Swerford Oxon.............57 G2
Swettenham Ches E..... 113 J7
Swilland Suffk...............78 E4
Swillington Leeds....... 124 B4
Swimbridge Devon........23 K5
Swimbridge
  Newland Devon.........23 J5
Swinbrook Oxon...........56 F5
Swincliffe N York 132 C7
Swinderby Lincs......... 116 E8
Swindon Gloucs............55 L3
Swindon Staffs..............84 F5
Swindon Swindn...........40 D4
Swine E R Yk 126 E4
Swinefleet E R Yk....... 125 H6
Swineshead Bed...........74 F2
Swineshead Lincs........ 103 L4
Swiney Highld............. 227 M2
Swinford Leics.............87 H7
Swingfield Minnis
  Kent...........................35 G6
Swingfield Street
  Kent...........................35 H6

Swingleton Green
  Suffk...........................77 L5
Swinhoe Nthumb........ 169 J4
Swinithwaite N York... 131 K2
Swinside Cumb............ 137 H3
Swinstead Lincs.......... 103 G7
Swinton Border 179 H8
Swinton N York.......... 132 C4
Swinton N York.......... 134 B5
Swinton Rothm........... 115 J2
Swinton Salfd.............. 113 H2
Swiss Valley Carmth......51 G5
Swithland Leics............87 G2
Swordale Highld......... 212 E2
Swordland Highld...... 200 B6
Swordly Highld........... 229 L3
Swynnerton Staffs........99 J5
Swyre Dorset................13 M5
Sychtyn Powys..............81 L3
Syde Gloucs...................55 L5
Sydenham Gt Lon.........45 G5
Sydenham Oxon............58 B7
Sydenham Damerel
  Devon........................... 6 B2
Syderstone Norfk 105 K6
Sydling St Nicholas
  Dorset........................14 C3
Sydmonton Hants.........41 J8
Syerston Notts............ 102 C3
Sykehouse Donc......... 124 F6
Symbister Shet 235 d4
Symington S Ayrs 163 J3
Symington S Lans...... 165 J3
Symondsbury Dorset....13 K4
Symonds Yat (West)
  Herefs.........................54 E5
Syre Highld................. 229 L6
Syreford Gloucs............56 B4
Syresham Nhants.........73 J6
Syston Leics.................87 J2
Syston Lincs............... 102 F4
Sytchampton Worcs.....70 E2
Sywell Nhants...............74 B2

T

Tackley Oxon................57 J4
Tacolneston Norfk........92 D4
Tadcaster N York........ 124 D2
Taddington Derbys..... 114 C7
Tadley Hants.................41 L7
Tadlow Cambs...............75 K5
Tadmarton Oxon...........72 E6
Tadpole Swindn............40 C3
Tadworth Surrey..........44 E8
Taff's Well Cardif..........37 H4
Taibach Neath...............36 B3
Tain Highld................. 223 G5
Tain Highld................. 231 J3
Takeley Essex...............60 F4
Takeley Street Essex 60 E4
Talaton Devon...............12 D3
Talbenny Pembks..........48 E5
Talbot Village BCP........15 K4
Taleford Devon.............12 E3
Talerddig Powys............81 K4
Talgarreg Cerdgn..........65 L4
Talgarth Powys.............68 D7
Talisker Highld........... 208 E7
Talke Staffs...................99 J3
Talke Pits Staffs............99 J3
Talkin Cumb............... 148 F4
Talladale Highld.......... 219 L7
Talla Linnfoots
  Border...................... 165 M5
Tallaminnock S Ayrs ... 153 J3
Tallarn Green
  Wrexhm......................98 C4
Tallentire Cumb.......... 147 K7
Talley Carmth...............66 E7
Tallington Lincs............88 F2
Talmine Highld........... 229 J3
Talog Carmth................50 D1
Talsarn Cerdgn............66 D4
Talsarnau Gwynd..........95 K5
Talskiddy Cnwll.............. 4 E3

Talwrn IoA................... 109 G6
Tal-y-bont Cerdgn........80 E5
Tal-y-Bont Conwy...... 109 L7
Talybont Gwynd............95 K7
Tal-y-bont Gwynd...... 109 J7
Talybont-on-Usk
  Powys.........................53 H4
Tal-y-Cafn Conwy...... 109 M7
Tal-y-coed Mons..........54 B5
Talysarn Gwynd............95 H2
Tamar Valley Mining
  District Devon........... 6 C3
Tamerton Foliot
  C Plym........................ 6 C4
Tamworth Staffs...........86 B3
Tamworth Services
  Warwks......................86 B4
Tandridge Surrey..........32 C3
Tanfield Dur............... 150 F4
Tanfield Lea Dur......... 150 F4
Tangasdale W Isls 233 b9
Tangley Hants...............28 F2
Tangmere W Susx........18 B4
Tankerness Ork........... 234 c6
Tankersley Barns........ 115 G2
Tankerton Kent 47 J6
Tannach Highld........... 231 K6
Tannachie Abers......... 206 E8
Tannadice Angus........ 196 D5
Tanner's Green
  Worcs.........................85 J8
Tannington Suffk..........78 F2
Tannochside N Lans.... 175 J6
Tansley Derbys........... 100 F1
Tansor Nhants..............88 F5
Tantobie Dur.............. 150 F4
Tanworth in Arden
  Warwks......................71 K1
Tan-y-groes Cerdgn......65 J5
Taobh Tuath W Isls.... 232 d5
Taplow Bucks...............42 E4
Tarbert Ag & B........... 172 B7
Tarbert Ag & B........... 172 E5
Tarbert W Isls............ 232 e4
Tarbet Ag & B............ 183 K6
Tarbet Highld............. 200 B6
Tarbet Highld............. 228 B5
Tarbolton S Ayrs........ 163 K4
Tarbrax S Lans........... 176 D7
Tardebigge Worcs........71 H2
Tarfside Angus........... 196 D1
Tarland Abers............. 205 K4
Tarleton Lancs............ 120 F6
Tarlton Gloucs..............55 L7
Tarnock Somset...........26 B2
Tarporley Ches W....... 112 D8
Tarrant Crawford
  Dorset........................15 H2
Tarrant Gunville
  Dorset........................27 L8
Tarrant Hinton
  Dorset........................15 H1
Tarrant Keyneston
  Dorset........................15 H2
Tarrant Launceston
  Dorset........................15 H1
Tarrant Monkton
  Dorset........................15 H2
Tarrant Rawston
  Dorset........................15 H2
Tarrant Rushton
  Dorset........................15 H2
Tarring Neville
  E Susx.........................19 L5
Tarrington Herefs.........70 B6
Tarskavaig Highld...... 199 J4
Tarves Abers............... 217 G7
Tarvin Ches W............ 112 C7
Tasburgh Norfk............92 E4
Tatenhill Staffs.......... 100 D7
Tathwell Lincs............ 118 D5
Tatsfield Surrey...........32 D2
Tattenhall Ches W........98 C2
Tatterford Norfk......... 105 K6
Tattersett Norfk......... 105 K6
Tattershall Lincs........ 103 K2
Tattershall Thorpe
  Lincs......................... 103 L1

Tattingstone Suffk............78 D6
Tattingstone White
 Horse Suffk...............78 D6
Tatton Park Ches E...... 113 H5
Tatworth Somset.............13 J2
Tauchers Moray 215 J4
Taunton Somset..............25 K6
Taunton Deane
 Services Somset 25 J7
Taverham Norfk..............92 E2
Tavernspite Pembks......49 K5
Tavistock Devon.............. 6 C2
Tavistock Devon.............. 6 C2
Taw Green Devon.............10 F5
Tawstock Devon..............23 J5
Taxal Derbys................. 114 A5
Tay Bridge C Dund...... 187 G2
Taychreggan Hotel
 Ag & B...................... 182 F3
Tay Forest Park
 P & K........................ 194 C4
Tayinloan Ag & B.......... 161 H1
Taynton Gloucs..............55 G4
Taynton Oxon.................56 E5
Taynuilt Ag & B............ 182 E2
Tayport Fife.................. 187 G2
Tayvallich Ag & B......... 172 C2
Tealby Lincs................. 117 J4
Tealing Angus.............. 196 C8
Team Valley Gatesd..... 151 G3
Teangue Highld............ 199 K4
Teanord Highld............ 212 F2
Tebay Cumb.................. 138 E6
Tebay Services
 Cumb.......................... 138 E6
Tebworth C Beds...........59 G3
Tedburn St Mary
 Devon..........................11 J6
Teddington Gloucs.........55 L2
Teddington Gt Lon.........44 D6
Tedstone Delamere
 Herefs.........................70 C3
Tedstone Wafer
 Herefs.........................70 C3
Teesside
 International
 Airport S on T........ 141 J5
Teeton Nhants................73 K1
Teffont Evias Wilts.........27 M5
Teffont Magna Wilts......27 M5
Tegryn Pembks...............65 H7
Teigh Rutlnd...................88 C1
Teigngrace Devon........... 7 K2
Teignmouth Devon..........12 B7
Teindside Border......... 166 F7
Telford Wrekin................84 C2
Telford Services
 Shrops.........................84 D2
Tellisford Somset...........27 J1
Telscombe E Susx...........19 L5
Tempar P & K............... 193 L5
Templand D & G........... 155 J5
Temple Cnwll.................. 5 J2
Temple Bar Cerdgn........66 C4
Temple Cloud BaNES......38 F8
Templecombe
 Somset........................27 G6
Temple Grafton
 Warwks........................71 K4
Temple Guiting
 Gloucs.........................56 C3
Temple Hirst N York..... 124 F5
Temple Normanton
 Derbys....................... 115 H7
Temple of Fiddes
 Abers......................... 206 F8
Temple Sowerby
 Cumb.......................... 138 E2
Templeton Devon............11 K3
Templeton Pembks.........49 J5
Templetown Dur........... 150 E5
Tempsford C Beds...........75 H4
Tenbury Wells Worcs.....69 L2
Tenby Pembks.................49 J7
Tendring Essex...............62 D3
Tendring Green
 Essex...........................62 D3

Tendring Heath
 Essex...........................62 D3
Ten Mile Bank Norfk......90 E4
Tenterden Kent..............34 B7
Terling Essex..................61 J5
Ternhill Shrops...............98 F6
Terregles D & G............ 155 G6
Terrington N York........ 133 K5
Terrington St
 Clement Norfk......... 104 E7
Terrington St John
 Norfk...........................90 D2
Teston Kent...................33 J3
Testwood Hants..............29 G8
Tetbury Gloucs...............39 K2
Tetchill Shrops...............98 B6
Tetcott Devon.................. 9 J5
Tetford Lincs................ 118 D6
Tetney Lincs................. 118 D2
Tetsworth Oxon..............58 B7
Tettenhall Wolves..........84 F4
Tettenhall Wood
 Wolves.........................84 F4
Teversal Notts.............. 101 J1
Teversham Cambs..........76 C3
Teviothead Border....... 156 D2
Tewin Herts...................59 L5
Tewkesbury Gloucs........55 K2
Teynham Kent................34 C3
Thackley C Brad........... 123 H3
Thainstone Abers......... 206 E2
Thakeham W Susx..........18 F3
Thame Oxon...................58 B6
Thames Ditton
 Surrey..........................44 D6
Thamesmead Gt Lon......45 J4
Thamesport Medway......46 E5
Thanington Kent............34 F4
Thankerton S Lans...... 165 J2
Tharston Norfk...............92 E5
Thatcham W Berk...........41 K6
Thaxted Essex................60 F2
Theakston N York........ 132 D3
Thealby N Linc............. 125 K6
Theale Somset................26 C3
Theale W Berk................41 M6
Thearne E R Yk............ 126 D3
The Beeches Gloucs.......56 B7
Theberton Suffk.............79 J2
The Braes Highld......... 209 H7
The Bridge Kent.............45 K5
The Broads................... 93 K2
The Brunt E Loth......... 178 E4
The Bungalow IoM....... 237 d4
The Burf Worcs...............70 E2
The City Bucks...............42 C2
The Common Wilts........28 E5
Theddingworth Leics.....87 J6
Theddlethorpe All
 Saints Lincs............ 118 F4
Theddlethorpe St
 Helen Lincs............. 119 G4
The Deep C Kuh........... 126 D5
The Den N Ayrs............ 174 C7
The Forstal Kent............34 D6
The Green Cumb.......... 128 E3
The Green Essex............61 J4
The Green N York......... 143 G6
The Green Wilts.............27 K5
The Hill Cumb.............. 128 E3
The Lee Bucks................58 E6
The Lhen IoM............... 237 d2
Thelnetham Suffk..........92 B7
The Lochs Moray.......... 215 G2
Thelveton Norfk.............92 E7
Thelwall Warrtn........... 112 F4
Themelthorpe Norfk.... 106 C7
The Middles Dur.......... 150 F5
The Moor Kent...............33 K7
The Mumbles Swans......51 J7
The Murray S Lans...... 175 H7
The Neuk Abers........... 206 D5
Thenford Nhants............73 G6
The Reddings Gloucs.....55 K4
Therfield Herts..............75 L6
The Ross P & K............ 185 G3
The Spring Warwks........86 C8
The Stocks Kent.............21 H1

The Strand Wilts............39 L8
Thetford Norfk...............91 K6
Thetford Forest
 Park...........................91 J5
Theydon Bois Essex.......60 D7
Thickwood Wilts............39 J5
Thimbleby Lincs........... 118 C7
Thimbleby N York........ 141 K7
Thingwall Wirral.......... 111 J5
Thirkleby N York.......... 133 G4
Thirlby N York.............. 133 G3
Thirlestane Border...... 178 C8
Thirn N York................ 132 C3
Thirsk N York............... 132 F3
Thistleton Lancs.......... 120 E3
Thistleton Rutlnd........ 102 E8
Thistley Green Suffk......90 F7
Thixendale N York....... 134 C7
Thockrington
 Nthumb..................... 158 B6
Tholomas Drove
 Cambs.........................90 B3
Tholthorpe N York....... 133 G6
Thomastown Abers...... 216 B6
Thompson Norfk............91 K4
Thomshill Moray.......... 214 F3
Thongsbridge Kirk...... 123 H8
Thoralby N York........... 131 J3
Thoresway Lincs.......... 117 K3
Thorganby Lincs.......... 117 K3
Thorganby N York........ 125 G3
Thorgill N York............ 142 E7
Thorington Suffk...........93 J8
Thorington Street
 Suffk...........................78 B7
Thorlby N York............. 131 H8
Thorley Herts.................60 D4
Thorley Street IoW........16 D5
Thormanby N York....... 133 G5
Thornaby-on-Tees
 S on T....................... 141 K4
Thornage Norfk............ 106 C5
Thornborough Bucks.....73 L7
Thornborough
 N York....................... 132 D4
Thornbury C Brad........ 123 J4
Thornbury Devon........... 9 K3
Thornbury Herefs..........70 B3
Thornbury S Glos..........38 F3
Thornby Nhants.............87 J7
Thorncliff Staffs.......... 100 A2
Thorncombe Dorset...... 13 J2
Thorndon Suffk..............78 D1
Thorndon Cross
 Devon..........................10 D6
Thorne Donc................ 125 G7
Thorner Leeds.............. 124 B3
Thorne St Margaret
 Somset........................25 H7
Thorney C Pete..............89 K3
Thorney Notts.............. 116 E6
Thorney Somset.............26 B6
Thorney Hill Hants........16 A3
Thorney Island
 W Susx........................17 L2
Thornfalcon Somset......25 L6
Thornford Dorset...........26 E8
Thorngrafton
 Nthumb..................... 149 K2
Thorngumbald
 E R Yk....................... 126 F5
Thornham Norfk.......... 105 H4
Thornham Magna
 Suffk...........................78 D1
Thornham Parva
 Suffk...........................92 D8
Thornhaugh C Pete........88 F4
Thornhill C Sotn............29 J8
Thornhill Cumb............ 136 D5
Thornhill D & G........... 154 F3
Thornhill Derbys.......... 114 D5
Thornhill Kirk.............. 123 K6
Thornhill Stirlg........... 184 F7
Thornholme E R Yk...... 135 H6
Thornicombe Dorset..... 15 G2
Thornington Nthumb... 168 D3
Thornley Dur............... 150 E7
Thornley Dur............... 151 J6

Thornliebank E Rens ... 174 F6
Thorns Suffk...................77 G4
Thornsett Derbys......... 114 A4
Thornthwaite Cumb..... 137 H3
Thornthwaite N York ... 132 B7
Thornton Angus........... 196 C6
Thornton Bucks.............73 L7
Thornton C Brad.......... 123 G4
Thornton E R Yk.......... 125 H2
Thornton Fife.............. 186 E7
Thornton Lancs........... 120 D3
Thornton Leics..............86 F3
Thornton Middsb........ 141 L4
Thornton Nthumb........ 179 K8
Thornton Curtis
 N Linc....................... 126 D6
Thorntonhall S Lans.... 175 G7
Thornton Heath
 Gt Lon........................44 F6
Thornton Hough
 Wirral........................ 111 J5
Thornton-in-
 Craven N York.......... 122 D2
Thornton in
 Lonsdale N York...... 130 D5
Thornton-le-Beans
 N York....................... 132 F2
Thornton-le-Clay
 N York....................... 133 L6
Thornton-le-Dale
 N York....................... 134 C3
Thornton le Moor
 Lincs......................... 117 H3
Thornton-le-Moor
 N York....................... 132 F2
Thornton-le-Moors
 Ches W...................... 112 C6
Thornton-le-Street
 N York....................... 132 F3
Thorntonloch E Loth... 178 F4
Thornton Rust
 N York....................... 131 H2
Thornton Steward
 N York....................... 132 B3
Thornton Watlass
 N York....................... 132 C3
Thornydykes Border.... 178 D8
Thornythwaite
 Cumb......................... 137 L3
Thoroton Notts............ 102 C4
Thorp Arch Leeds........ 124 C2
Thorpe Derbys............. 100 D3
Thorpe E R Yk.............. 126 B2
Thorpe N York.............. 131 J6
Thorpe Notts............... 102 C3
Thorpe Surrey................43 G6
Thorpe Abbotts
 Norfk...........................92 E7
Thorpe Arnold Leics.... 102 C7
Thorpe Audlin
 Wakefd....................... 124 D7
Thorpe Bassett
 N York....................... 134 D5
Thorpe Bay Sthend........46 E3
Thorpe by Water
 Rutlnd.........................88 C4
Thorpe Constantine
 Staffs..........................86 C2
Thorpe End Norfk..........93 G2
Thorpe Green Essex......62 E4
Thorpe Green Suffk.......77 L4
Thorpe Hesley
 Rothm........................ 115 G3
Thorpe in Balne
 Donc......................... 124 F7
Thorpe Langton
 Leics...........................87 L5
Thorpe Lea Surrey.........43 G6
Thorpe-le-Soken
 Essex...........................62 E4
Thorpe le Street
 E R Yk....................... 125 K2
Thorpe Malsor
 Nhants........................88 B7
Thorpe Mandeville
 Nhants........................73 G5
Thorpe Market
 Norfk......................... 106 F5

Thorpe Marriot
Norfk.................................92 E1
Thorpe Morieux
Suffk.................................77 L4
Thorpeness Suffk..........79 K3
Thorpe on the Hill
Lincs..............................116 E7
Thorpe Park Resort
Surrey..............................43 G6
Thorpe St Andrew
Norfk.................................92 F2
Thorpe St Peter
Lincs..............................104 D1
Thorpe Salvin Rothm... 115 K5
Thorpe Satchville
Leics.................................87 K2
Thorpe Thewles
S on T............................141 J3
Thorpe Tilney Lincs.....103 J2
Thorpe Underwood
N York............................133 G7
Thorpe Waterville
Nhants...............................88 E7
Thorpe Willoughby
N York............................124 E4
Thorrington Essex........62 C4
Thorverton Devon.........11 L4
Thrandeston Suffk........92 D7
Thrapston Nhants............88 E7
Threapwood Ches W......98 C4
Threapwood Staffs.......100 B4
Threave S Ayrs.............163 J7
Three Bridges
W Susx..............................32 B5
Three Chimneys
Kent..................................33 L5
Three Cocks Powys......68 D6
Three Crosses Swans....51 H6
Three Cups Corner
E Susx..............................20 D2
Threekingham Lincs.....103 H5
Three Leg Cross
E Susx..............................33 H6
Three Legged Cross
Dorset..............................15 K2
Three Mile Cross
Wokham...........................42 B6
Threemilestone
Cnwll..................................3 K3
Threemiletown
W Loth............................176 B3
Three Oaks E Susx........21 G3
Threlkeld Cumb.............137 J3
Threshers Bush
Essex................................60 D6
Threshfield N York.......131 J6
Thrigby Norfk..................93 K2
Thrintoft N York...........132 D2
Thriplow Cambs.............76 B5
Throcking Herts.............60 B3
Throckley N u Ty...........150 E2
Throckmorton Worcs.....71 H4
Throop BCP......................15 L4
Thropton Nthumb.........158 C2
Throsk Stirlg..................176 B1
Throughgate D & G......154 F5
Throwleigh Devon..........11 G6
Throwley Forstal
Kent..................................34 C4
Thrumpton Notts..........101 J6
Thrumster Highld..........231 L6
Thrunscoe NE Lin.........127 H8
Thrupp Gloucs.................55 K7
Thrussington Leics.........87 J1
Thruxton Hants...............28 F3
Thruxton Herefs.............69 J7
Thrybergh Rothm..........115 J3
Thulston Derbys............101 H6
Thundersley Essex.........46 C3
Thurcaston Leics.............87 H2
Thurcroft Rothm...........115 J4
Thurgarton Norfk.........106 E5
Thurgarton Notts..........102 B3
Thurgoland Barns.........114 F2
Thurlaston Leics.............87 G4
Thurlaston Warwks........72 F1
Thurlbear Somset...........25 K7
Thurlby Lincs...................89 G1

Thurlby Lincs..................102 E1
Thurlby Lincs..................119 G6
Thurleigh Bed.................74 F3
Thurlestone Devon...........7 G7
Thurloxton Somset........25 L5
Thurlstone Barns..........114 E2
Thurlton Norfk.................93 J4
Thurmaston Leics...........87 H2
Thurnby Leics..................87 J3
Thurne Norfk...................93 J1
Thurnham Kent...............33 K2
Thurning Nhants.............88 F6
Thurning Norfk..............106 C6
Thurnscoe Barns...........115 J1
Thurrock Services
Thurr.............................45 L4
Thursby Cumb................148 B5
Thursford Norfk.............106 B5
Thursley Surrey..............30 E4
Thurso Highld................231 G2
Thurstaston Wirral........111 H5
Thurston Suffk................77 K2
Thurstonfield Cumb.......148 B4
Thurstonland Kirk.........123 H7
Thurton Norfk..................93 G4
Thurvaston Derbys........100 E5
Thuxton Norfk.................92 B3
Thwaite N York..............139 K7
Thwaite Suffk..................78 D2
Thwaite Head Cumb......129 H2
Thwaite St Mary
Norfk................................93 G4
Thwing E R Yk...............135 G5
Tibbermore P & K.........185 L3
Tibbers D & G...............154 E3
Tibberton Gloucs............55 H4
Tibberton Worcs.............70 F3
Tibberton Wrekin............99 G7
Tibenham Norfk..............92 D5
Tibshelf Derbys..............101 H1
Tibshelf Services
Derbys............................101 H1
Tibthorpe E R Yk..........134 E7
Ticehurst E Susx.............33 H7
Tichborne Hants.............29 L5
Tickencote Rutlnd...........88 E2
Tickenham N Som...........38 C6
Tickhill Donc.................115 L3
Ticklerton Shrops...........83 J5
Ticknall Derbys..............101 G7
Tickton E R Yk..............126 D3
Tidcombe Wilts...............40 F8
Tiddington Oxon.............57 M6
Tiddington Warwks........72 B4
Tidebrook E Susx............33 G7
Tideford Cnwll..................6 A4
Tidenham Gloucs............38 E2
Tideswell Derbys...........114 D6
Tidmarsh W Berk............41 M5
Tidmington Warwks........72 C6
Tidworth Wilts................28 E2
Tiers Cross Pembks........48 F5
Tiffield Nhants................73 K4
Tigerton Angus..............196 E4
Tigh a' Ghearraidh
W Isls............................233 b6
Tigharry W Isls..............233 b6
Tighnabruaich
Ag & B...........................173 G4
Tigley Devon.....................7 H4
Tilbrook Cambs...............74 F2
Tilbury Thurr...................45 M5
Tile Cross Birm...............85 L6
Tile Hill Covtry................86 C7
Tilehurst Readg..............42 A5
Tilford Surrey..................30 E3
Tilgate W Susx................31 L4
Tilham Street Somset.....26 E4
Tillicoultry Clacks..........185 J7
Tillietudlem S Lans........164 F1
Tillingham Essex.............62 B7
Tillington Herefs.............69 J5
Tillington W Susx............30 F6
Tillington Common
Herefs..............................69 J5
Tillybirloch Abers..........206 D4
Tillyfourie Abers...........206 C3
Tillygreig Abers.............207 G2

Tillyrie P & K.................186 B6
Tilmanstone Kent...........35 J4
Tilney All Saints
Norfk..............................104 F8
Tilney High End
Norfk..............................104 E8
Tilney St Lawrence
Norfk................................90 D2
Tilshead Wilts..................28 B2
Tilstock Shrops................98 D5
Tilston Ches W................98 C3
Tilstone Fearnall
Ches W.............................98 E1
Tilsworth C Beds.............59 G3
Tilton on the Hill
Leics.................................87 L3
Tiltups End Gloucs..........39 J2
Timberland Lincs...........103 J2
Timbersbrook
Ches E............................113 K8
Timberscombe
Somset..............................24 E3
Timble N York................132 B8
Timpanheck D & G........156 B7
Timperley Traffd...........113 H4
Timsbury BaNES.............38 F8
Timsbury Hants...............29 G6
Timsgarry W Isls...........232 d2
Timsgearraidh
W Isls............................232 d2
Timworth Suffk...............77 J2
Timworth Green
Suffk................................77 J2
Tincleton Dorset.............14 E4
Tindale Cumb.................149 G3
Tingewick Bucks.............58 A2
Tingrith C Beds...............59 G2
Tingwall Airport
Shet.................................235 c6
Tingwell Ork..................234 c5
Tinhay Devon.....................9 K7
Tinsley Sheff..................115 H4
Tinsley Green W Susx.....32 B5
Tintagel Cnwll...................8 E7
Tintern Mons...................54 D7
Tintinhull Somset............26 D7
Tintwistle Derbys..........114 A3
Tinwald D & G...............155 H5
Tinwell Rutlnd.................88 E3
Tipton Sandw..................85 G5
Tipton Green Sandw.......85 G5
Tipton St John
Devon................................12 E4
Tiptree Essex...................61 L5
Tiptree Heath Essex........61 L5
Tirabad Powys.................67 J6
Tiree Ag & B..................188 D7
Tiree Airport Ag & B... 188 C7
Tiretigan Ag & B...........172 C6
Tirley Gloucs...................55 J3
Tiroran Ag & B..............181 G2
Tirphil Caerph.................53 H7
Tirril Cumb....................138 D2
Tisbury Wilts....................27 L5
Tissington Derbys..........100 D3
Titchberry Devon.............22 C6
Titchfield Hants...............17 G2
Titchmarsh Nhants..........88 E7
Titchwell Norfk...............105 J4
Tithby Notts...................102 B5
Tithebarn Devon.............12 C4
Titley Herefs....................69 G3
Titsey Surrey....................32 D3
Titson Cnwll......................9 H5
Tittensor Staffs................99 K5
Tittleshall Norfk.............105 L7
Titton Worcs.....................70 E1
Tiverton Ches W..............98 D1
Tiverton Devon.................24 E8
Tivetshall St
Margaret Norfk............92 E6
Tivetshall St Mary
Norfk................................92 E6
Tixall Staffs......................99 L7
Tixover Rutlnd..................88 E4
Toab Shet........................235 c8
Tobermory Ag & B.........189 L5
Toberonochy Ag & B.....181 L5

Tobha Mòr W Isls..........233 b7
Tocher Abers..................216 D7
Tochieneal Moray..........215 L2
Tockenham Wilts.............40 B4
Tockholes Bl w D...........121 K6
Tockington S Glos...........38 E3
Tockwith N York............133 G8
Todber Dorset..................27 J7
Toddington C Beds..........59 G3
Toddington Gloucs..........56 B2
Toddington
Services C Beds.............59 G3
Todenham Gloucs............72 B7
Todhills Angus...............196 C8
Todhills Rest Area
Cumb.............................148 C3
Todmorden Calder.........122 D5
Todwick Rothm..............115 J5
Toft Cambs.......................75 L4
Toft Lincs.........................88 F1
Toft Shet.........................235 c3
Toft Hill Dur...................140 E2
Toft Monks Norfk............93 J4
Toft next Newton
Lincs..............................117 H4
Toftrees Norfk................105 L6
Togston Nthumb.............159 G2
Tokavaig Highld.............199 J3
Tokers Green Oxon..........42 B5
Tolastadh bho
Thuath W Isls..............232 g2
Tolland Somset................25 H5
Tollard Royal Wilts..........27 L7
Toll Bar Donc................124 E8
Toller Fratrum
Dorset..............................14 B3
Toller Porcorum
Dorset..............................14 B3
Tollerton N York............133 H6
Tollerton Notts..............101 L5
Tollesbury Essex..............62 A6
Tolleshunt D'Arcy
Essex................................61 L5
Tolleshunt Knights
Essex................................61 L5
Tolleshunt Major
Essex................................61 L5
Toll of Birness Abers......217 J7
Tolpuddle Dorset.............14 E4
Tolworth Gt Lon..............44 D6
Tomatin Highld...............213 J8
Tomchrasky Highld.........201 K3
Tomdoun Highld.............201 H5
Tomich Highld.................211 L8
Tomich Highld.................212 E5
Tomich Highld.................222 F7
Tomich Highld.................226 A7
Tomintoul Moray............204 E2
Tomnacross Highld.........212 D6
Tomnavoulin Moray........204 F1
Tonbridge Kent...............33 G4
Tondu Brdgnd...................36 D4
Tonedale Somset.............25 H6
Tong C Brad...................123 J4
Tong Kent.........................34 C4
Tong Shrops.....................84 E3
Tong W Isls....................232 g2
Tonge Leics.....................101 H7
Tongham Surrey...............30 E2
Tongland D & G.............146 C4
Tong Norton Shrops........84 E2
Tongue Highld................229 J4
Tongwynlais Cardif..........37 H4
Tonmawr Neath...............36 C2
Tonna Neath.....................52 B7
Tonwell Herts...................60 B5
Tonypandy Rhondd..........36 F3
Tonyrefail Rhondd............36 F3
Toot Baldon Oxon............57 K7
Toot Hill Essex................60 E7
Toothill Swindn................40 C4
Tooting Gt Lon.................44 F5
Tooting Bec Gt Lon..........44 F5
Topcliffe N York.............132 F4
Topcroft Norfk.................92 F5
Topcroft Street Norfk......92 F5
Toppesfield Essex............77 G6
Toprow Norfk...................92 E4

Topsham Devon................12 C5
Torbeg N Ayrs 162 A4
Torboll Highld 223 G2
Torbreck Highld 213 G6
Torbryan Devon...................7 J3
Torcastle Highld 192 B2
Torcross Devon....................7 J7
Tore Highld.....................212 F4
Torinturk Ag & B 172 D5
Torksey Lincs 116 D5
Torlundy Highld 192 B2
Tormarton S Glos...........39 H5
Tormore N Ayrs 161 M3
Tornagrain Highld..........213 J4
Tornaveen Abers 206 C4
Torness Highld 212 E8
Toronto Dur 140 F2
Torpenhow Cumb 147 L6
Torphichen W Loth 176 C4
Torphins Abers 206 C5
Torpoint Cnwll 6 C5
Torquay Torbay 7 L3
Torquhan Border 177 L8
Torran Highld 209 J5
Torrance E Duns 175 H4
Torranyard N Ayrs..........163 J1
Torridon Highld 210 D3
Torridon House
   Highld.........................210 D3
Torrin Highld 199 J2
Torrisdale Ag & B...........161 K3
Torrisdale Highld 229 K3
Torrish Highld 227 G5
Torrisholme Lancs 129 K6
Torrobull Highld 226 A7
Torry C Aber 207 H4
Torryburn Fife 176 D2
Torteval Guern................236 b4
Torthorwald D & G 155 H6
Tortington W Susx 18 D5
Torton Worcs...................84 E8
Tortworth S Glos.............39 G2
Torvaig Highld.................209 H5
Torver Cumb 137 J7
Torwood Falk 175 L2
Torwoodlee Border 167 G2
Torworth Notts...............116 A4
Toscaig Highld 209 L6
Toseland Cambs 75 J3
Tosside Lancs 130 E7
Tostock Suffk...................77 L2
Totaig Highld 208 C4
Tote Highld.....................208 F5
Tote Highld.....................209 H3
Totland IoW......................16 D5
Totley Sheff 114 F5
Totley Brook Sheff 114 F5
Totnes Devon.....................7 J4
Toton Notts....................101 J5
Totronald Ag & B 188 F5
Totscore Highld 208 F2
Tottenham Gt Lon............45 G3
Tottenhill Norfk...............90 F2
Totteridge Gt Lon............44 E2
Totternhoe C Beds...........59 G4
Tottington Bury 122 B7
Totton Hants...................29 G8
Toulton Somset................25 J5
Toulvaddie Highld...........223 J5
Tovil Kent........................33 K3
Toward Ag & B 173 K5
Toward Quay Ag & B 173 J5
Towcester Nhants............73 K5
Towednack Cnwll...............2 E4
Tower of London
   Gt Lon............................45 G4
Towersey Oxon................58 B6
Towie Abers 205 K3
Tow Law Dur...................150 E6
Town End Cambs 90 B4
Townend W Duns 174 D3
Townhead D & G 114 D2
Townhead D & G 155 H4
Townhead of
   Greenlaw D & G.........146 C3
Townhill Fife 176 F1
Town Littleworth
   E Susx 19 L3

Townshend Cnwll 3 G5
Town Street Suffk..........91 H6
Town Yetholm
   Border 168 B4
Towthorpe E York 133 K7
Towton N York.................124 D3
Towyn Conwy 110 D5
Toxteth Lpool 111 K4
Toynton All Saints
   Lincs...........................118 E8
Toy's Hill Kent.................32 E3
Trabboch E Ayrs.............163 K5
Trabbochburn
   E Ayrs..........................163 L5
Tradespark Highld 213 K3
Trafford Park Traffd 113 H3
Trallong Powys 52 E3
Tranent E Loth................177 L4
Tranmere Wirral 111 J4
Trantelbeg Highld 230 C5
Trantlemore Highld 230 C5
Trap Carmth.....................51 J2
Traprain E Loth...............178 D4
Traquair Border 166 E3
Trawden Lancs 122 D3
Trawsfynydd Gwynd........96 A5
Trealaw Rhondd 36 F3
Treales Lancs 120 F4
Trearddur Bay IoA 108 C5
Trebetherick Cnwll............4 E1
Treborough Somset..........24 F4
Trebullett Cnwll.................5 M1
Treburley Cnwll 6 A1
Trecastle Powys...............52 D3
Trecwn Pembks................64 D7
Trecynon Rhondd 52 F7
Tredegar Blae G 53 H6
Tredington Gloucs 55 K3
Tredington Warwks 72 C5
Tredunnock Mons 38 B2
Treen Cnwll........................2 D6
Treeton Rothm 115 H4
Trefasser Pembks.............64 C6
Trefecca Powys.................53 H2
Trefechan Myr Td.............53 G6
Trefeglwys Powys............81 L5
Treffgarne Pembks..........49 G3
Treffgarne Owen
   Pembks 48 E3
Trefilan Cerdgn 66 D3
Trefin Pembks...................64 B7
Trefnant Denbgs.............110 E7
Trefonen Shrops...............97 K6
Trefor Gwynd...................94 F4
Treforest Rhondd.............37 G3
Trefriw Conwy 109 L8
Tregadillett Cnwll 9 H7
Tregare Mons 54 B6
Tregaron Cerdgn 66 F3
Tregarth Gwynd 109 H7
Tregeare Cnwll 9 H7
Tregeiriog Wrexhm...........97 J5
Tregele IoA 108 D3
Treglemais Pembks..........48 D2
Tregonetha Cnwll 4 E3
Tregonning &
   Gwinear Mining
   District Cnwll 3 G5
Tregony Cnwll 4 E6
Tregorrick Cnwll 4 F5
Tregoyd Powys.................68 E6
Tre-groes Cerdgn 65 L5
Tregynon Powys................82 C4
Tre-gynwr Carmth 50 E2
Trehafod Rhondd..............37 G3
Trehan Cnwll......................6 B4
Treharris Myr Td..............37 H2
Treherbert Rhondd...........52 E7
Trekenner Cnwll.................6 A1
Treknow Cnwll 8 D7
Trelawnyd Flints.............110 F5
Trelech Carmth.................65 J7
Treleddyd-fawr
   Pembks 48 C2
Trelewis Myr Td................37 H2
Trelights Cnwll 8 C8
Trelill Cnwll 5 G1
Trellech Mons 54 D6

Trelogan Flints 110 F5
Tremadog Gwynd.............95 K4
Tremail Cnwll......................8 F7
Tremain Cerdgn................65 H5
Tremaine Cnwll 9 G6
Tremar Cnwll 5 K3
Trematon Cnwll 6 B4
Tremeirchion
   Denbgs 110 F6
Trenance Cnwll 4 D3
Trenance Cnwll 4 E2
Trench Wrekin...................84 C2
Trenear Cnwll.....................3 H5
Treneglos Cnwll 9 G7
Trent Dorset 26 E7
Trentham C Stke...............99 K4
Trentishoe Devon.............23 K2
Trent Vale C Stke.............99 K4
Treoes V Glam..................36 E5
Treorchy Rhondd..............36 E2
Trequite Cnwll 5 G1
Trerhyngyll V Glam..........36 F5
Trerulefoot Cnwll...............5 M4
Tresaith Cerdgn................65 J4
Tresco IoS 2 a1
Trescowe Cnwll 3 G5
Tresean Cnwll 4 D3
Tresham Gloucs................39 H3
Treshnish Isles
   Ag & B 189 G7
Tresillian Cnwll 4 D6
Treskinnick Cross
   Cnwll..............................9 G5
Tresmeer Cnwll 9 G7
Tresparrett Cnwll 8 F6
Tressait P & K 194 C4
Tresta Shet 235 c5
Tresta Shet 235 e3
Treswell Notts 116 C5
Tre Taliesin Cerdgn..........80 E5
Trethewey Cnwll 8 E6
Trethewey Cnwll 8 E6
Trethurgy Cnwll 5 G5
Tretire Herefs..................54 D4
Tretower Powys 53 J4
Treuddyn Flints 97 K2
Trevalga Cnwll 8 E6
Trevalyn Wrexhm.............98 B2
Trevarrian Cnwll................4 D3
Treveal Cnwll.....................4 C4
Treveighan Cnwll 8 E8
Trevellas Downs
   Cnwll..............................3 J2
Trevelmond Cnwll 5 K3
Treverva Cnwll 3 K5
Trevescan Cnwll 2 C6
Treviscoe Cnwll 4 E5
Trevone Cnwll 4 D2
Trevor Wrexhm.................97 L4
Trewalder Cnwll 8 E7
Trewarmett Cnwll 8 E7
Trewavas Mining
   District Cnwll 3 G6
Trewen Cnwll 9 H7
Trewint Cnwll 9 G8
Trewithian Cnwll 4 D7
Trewoon Cnwll 4 F5
Treyford W Susx.............30 D7
Trimdon Dur 151 J7
Trimdon Colliery
   Dur 151 J7
Trimdon Grange
   Dur 151 J7
Trimingham Norfk..........107 G5
Trimley St Martin
   Suffk..............................78 F6
Trimley St Mary
   Suffk..............................79 G7
Trimsaran Carmth............50 F5
Trimstone Devon..............23 H3
Trinafour P & K 194 B4
Tring Herts 58 F5
Trinity Angus 196 F4
Trinity Jersey 236 d6
Trinity Gask P & K 185 K4
Triscombe Somset...........25 J4
Trislaig Highld.................191 L2
Trispen Cnwll 4 D5

Tritlington Nthumb 158 F4
Trochry P & K 194 F7
Troedyraur Cerdgn 65 K5
Troedyrhiw Myr Td...........53 G7
Trois Bois Jersey 236 c6
Troon Cnwll 3 H4
Troon S Ayrs 163 H3
Tropical World
   Leeds Leeds 123 L3
Trossachs Stirlg..............184 B5
Trossachs Pier Stirlg...184 B6
Troston Suffk....................91 K8
Trotshill Worcs.................70 F4
Trottiscliffe Kent.............33 H2
Trotton W Susx 30 D6
Troutbeck Cumb..............137 L6
Troutbeck Bridge
   Cumb 137 L7
Troway Derbys 115 H5
Trowbridge Wilts 39 J8
Trowell Notts 101 J4
Trowle Services
   Notts 101 J4
Trowle Common
   Wilts 39 J8
Trowse Newton
   Norfk.............................92 F3
Trudoxhill Somset 27 H3
Trull Somset.....................25 K6
Trumpan Highld...............208 C3
Trumpet Herefs................70 B6
Trumpington Cambs.........76 C4
Trunch Norfk...................107 G5
Truro Cnwll 4 C6
Trusham Devon 11 K7
Trusley Derbys 100 E5
Trusthorpe Lincs 119 G5
Trysull Staffs 84 F5
Tubney Oxon....................57 H7
Tuckenhay Devon...............7 J5
Tuckhill Shrops.................84 E6
Tuckingmill Cnwll 3 H3
Tuckingmill Wilts 27 L5
Tuckton BCP....................15 L4
Tuddenham Suffk...............77 G1
Tuddenham St
   Martin Suffk..................78 E5
Tudeley Kent....................33 G7
Tudhoe Dur 151 G7
Tudweiliog Gwynd 94 D5
Tuffley Gloucs..................55 J5
Tufton Hants....................29 J3
Tufton Pembks.................49 H2
Tugby Leics.......................87 L4
Tugford Shrops.................83 L6
Tughall Nthumb 169 J4
Tullibody Clacks...............185 H7
Tullich Abers 205 J6
Tullich Highld 212 F8
Tullich Highld 223 J6
Tulliemet P & K 194 F5
Tulloch Abers...................216 F7
Tullochgorm
   Ag & B 182 D7
Tulloch Station
   Highld..........................192 F1
Tullymurdoch P & K........195 J5
Tullynessle Abers 206 B2
Tulse Hill Gt Lon..............44 F5
Tumble Carmth.................51 G3
Tumby Lincs 103 L1
Tumby Woodside
   Lincs...........................103 L2
Tummel Bridge
   P & K 194 B5
Tunbridge Wells
   Kent.............................33 J5
Tundergarth D & G..........155 L6
Tunga W Isls 232 g2
Tunley BaNES..................39 G8
Tunstall E R Yk 127 H4
Tunstall Kent....................34 B3
Tunstall Lancs 130 B5
Tunstall N York 140 F5
Tunstall Norfk 93 J2
Tunstall Staffs..................99 H6
Tunstall Suffk 79 H4
Tunstall Sundld 151 J4

Tunstead Derbys 114 C6
Tunstead Norfk.............. 107 G7
Tunstead Milton
Derbys.................. 114 B5
Tupsley Herefs.............. 69 K6
Turgis Green Hants........ 42 B8
Turkdean Gloucs 56 C4
Tur Langton Leics........ 87 K5
Turleigh Wilts 39 J7
Turnastone Herefs 69 G7
Turnberry S Ayrs 152 E2
Turnditch Derbys 100 F3
Turners Hill W Susx.......32 C6
Turnhouse C Edin......... 177 G4
Turnworth Dorset.......... 14 F2
Turriff Abers................ 216 D4
Turton Bottoms
Bl w D.................... 121 L7
Turves Cambs...............89 L4
Turvey Bed 74 D4
Turville Bucks 42 C3
Turweston Bucks 73 H6
Tushielaw Inn
Border.................. 166 D5
Tutbury Staffs 100 E6
Tutshill Gloucs 38 D2
Tuttington Norfk......... 106 F6
Tuxford Notts 116 C7
Twatt Ork................... 234 b5
Twatt Shet.................. 235 c5
Twechar E Duns........... 175 J3
Tweedbank Border 167 H3
Tweedmouth
Nthumb 179 K7
Tweedsmuir Border 165 L4
Twelveheads Cnwll........... 3 K3
Twemlow Green
Ches E 113 H7
Twenty Lincs 103 J7
Twerton BaNES...........39 G7
Twickenham Gt Lon......44 D5
Twigworth Gloucs 55 J4
Twineham W Susx..........19 H2
Twinstead Essex............77 J6
Twitchen Devon............24 C5
Two Dales Derbys 114 F8
Two Gates Staffs...........86 B4
Two Waters Herts.........59 H6
Twycross Leics...............86 D3
Twycross Zoo Leics........86 C3
Twyford Bucks 58 A3
Twyford Hants 29 J6
Twyford Leics................87 K2
Twyford Norfk............ 106 B7
Twyford Wokham 42 C5
Twynholm D & G 146 B4
Twyning Gloucs 70 F6
Twynllanan Carmth........51 L2
Twywell Nhants 88 D7
Tyberton Herefs 69 H6
Tyburn Birm 85 K5
Tycroes Carmth.............51 H4
Tycrwyn Powys 97 H8
Tydd Gote Lincs.......... 104 D8
Tydd St Giles Cambs.......90 B1
Tydd St Mary Lincs....... 104 C8
Tye Green Essex...........76 E7
Tyldesley Wigan.......... 113 G2
Tyler Hill Kent...............34 F3
Tylorstown Rhondd.........36 F2
Ty-nant Conwy...............96 F4
Tyndrum Stirlg............ 183 K2
Ty'n-dwr Denbgs 97 K4
Tynemouth N Tyne....... 151 J2
Tyne Tunnel S Tyne..... 151 H2
Tyningham E Loth....... 178 D3
Tynron D & G............. 154 E4
Tynygraig Cerdgn.........66 F1
Ty'n-y-Groes
Conwy 109 L7
Tyrie Abers................ 217 H2
Tyringham M Keyn.......74 C5
Tyseley Birm.................85 K6
Tythegston Brdgnd 36 D5
Tytherington Ches E..... 113 K6
Tytherington S Glos.......38 F3
Tytherington Wilts 27 K3
Tytherleigh Devon 13 H2

Tytherton Lucas
Wilts......................39 L5
Tywardreath Cnwll 5 H5
Tywyn Gwynd..............80 D4

U

Ubbeston Green
Suffk......................79 G1
Ubley BaNES.................38 D8
Uckfield E Susx.............19 M2
Uckinghall Worcs 70 F6
Uckington Gloucs 55 K3
Uddingston S Lans 175 J6
Uddington S Lans 165 G3
Udimore E Susx.............21 G2
Udny Green Abers....... 207 G1
Udny Station Abers...... 207 G1
Uffculme Devon 25 G8
Uffington Lincs...............88 F3
Uffington Oxon...............40 F3
Uffington Shrops...........83 K2
Ufford C Pete 89 G3
Ufford Suffk..................79 G4
Ufton Warwks...............72 E3
Ufton Nervet W Berk 41 M6
Ugadale Ag & B 161 K4
Ugborough Devon 7 G5
Uggeshall Suffk.............93 J7
Ugglebarnby N York.... 143 H5
Ughill Sheff 114 E4
Ugley Essex...................60 E3
Ugley Green Essex........60 E3
Ugthorpe N York 143 G5
Uibhist A Deas
W Isls.................... 233 c8
Uibhist A Tuath
W Isls.................... 233 b6
Uig Ag & B.................. 188 F5
Uig Highld 208 C4
Uig Highld 208 F2
Uig W Isls.................. 232 d2
Uigshader Highld........ 209 G5
Uisken Ag & B 180 E4
Ulbster Highld............ 231 K7
Ulceby Lincs 118 F6
Ulceby N Linc 126 D7
Ulceby Skitter
N Linc 126 E7
Ulcombe Kent...............33 L4
Uldale Cumb............... 147 M7
Uley Gloucs 55 H7
Ulgham Nthumb 159 G4
Ullapool Highld........... 220 E3
Ullenhall Warwks...........71 K2
Ulleskelf N York......... 124 D3
Ullesthorpe Leics.........87 G6
Ulley Rothm 115 J4
Ullingswick Herefs........69 L4
Ullock Cumb............... 136 E3
Ullswater Cumb........... 138 B3
Ullswater 'Steamers'
Cumb................... 137 L4
Ulpha Cumb............... 128 E2
Ulrome E R Yk............ 135 J7
Ulsta Shet.................. 235 d3
Ulva Ag & B................ 189 K7
Ulverley Green
Solhll......................85 K6
Ulverston Cumb 129 G4
Ulwell Dorset...............15 J6
Ulzieside D & G 164 F7
Umberleigh Devon 23 K6
Unapool Highld........... 224 F2
Underbarrow Cumb..... 129 K2
Under Burnmouth
Border.................. 156 E5
Undercliffe C Brad...... 123 J4
Underdale Shrops........83 K2
Underriver Kent............32 F3
Underwood Notts....... 101 J3
Undy Mons....................38 C3
Union Mills IoM........... 237 c5
Unst Shet................... 235 d1
Unstone Derbys.......... 115 G6
Upavon Wilts...............28 C1

Upchurch Kent...............46 D6
Upcott Devon 24 B5
Up Exe Devon 12 B2
Upgate Norfk 106 D8
Uphall Dorset................14 B2
Uphall W Loth............. 176 E4
Upham Devon 11 K3
Upham Hants 29 K7
Uphampton Herefs........69 H2
Uphampton Worcs 70 E2
Uphill N Som 37 L8
Up Holland Lancs 112 D1
Uplawmoor E Rens..... 174 E7
Upleadon Gloucs...........55 H3
Upleatham R & Cl 142 D4
Uploders Dorset............13 L4
Uplowman Devon 24 F7
Uplyme Devon...............13 H4
Up Marden W Susx........30 D8
Upminster Gt Lon.........45 K3
Up Mudford Somset......26 E7
Up Nately Hants 30 B2
Upottery Devon 12 F2
Upper Affcot Shrops......83 J6
Upper Arley Worcs 84 D7
Upper Badcall
Highld.................. 228 B7
Upper Basildon
W Berk...................41 L5
Upper Beeding
W Susx...................19 G4
Upper Benefield
Nhants...................88 E5
Upper Bentley Worcs ... 71 H2
Upper Bighouse
Highld.................. 230 C4
Upper Boddington
Nhants...................72 F4
Upper Brailes
Warwks...................72 C6
Upper Broadheath
Worcs.....................70 E4
Upper Broughton
Notts 102 B7
Upper Bucklebury
W Berk...................41 K6
Upper Burgate
Hants.....................28 D7
Upperby Cumb 148 D4
Upper Caldecote
C Beds....................75 H5
Upper Chapel Powys......67 L6
Upper Chicksgrove
Wilts......................27 L5
Upper Chute Wilts.........28 F2
Upper Clapton
Gt Lon...................45 G3
Upper Clatford Hants....29 G3
Upper Cound
Shrops...................83 K3
Upper
Cumberworth
Kirk..................... 123 J8
Upper Dallachy
Moray................... 215 H2
Upper Deal Kent...........35 K4
Upper Dean Bed...........74 F2
Upper Denby Kirk....... 114 E1
Upper Dicker E Susx......20 B4
Upper Dounreay
Highld.................. 230 E3
Upper Dovercourt
Essex.....................62 F2
Upper Drumbane
Stirlg 184 E6
Upper Dunsforth
N York 133 G6
Upper Eashing
Surrey....................30 F3
Upper Eathie Highld 213 J2
Upper Egleton
Herefs....................70 B5
Upper Elkstone
Staffs................... 100 B2
Upper Ellastone
Staffs................... 100 C4
Upper Farringdon
Hants.....................30 B4

Upper Framilode
Gloucs....................55 H6
Upcott Devon 24 B5
Upper Froyle
Hants.....................30 C3
Upperglen Highld....... 208 E4
Upper Godney
Somset...................26 C3
Upper Gravenhurst
C Beds....................75 G7
Upper Green W Berk......41 G7
Upper Grove
Common Herefs 54 E3
Upper Hale Surrey........30 D2
Upper Halliford
Surrey....................43 H6
Upper Hambleton
Rutlnd....................88 C3
Upper Harbledown
Kent......................34 F3
Upper Hartfield
E Susx 32 E6
Upper Hatherley
Gloucs....................55 L4
Upper Heaton Kirk...... 123 H6
Upper Helmsley
N York 133 L7
Upper Hergest
Herefs....................68 F4
Upper Heyford
Nhants...................73 J3
Upper Heyford Oxon.....57 J3
Upper Hill Herefs 69 J4
Upper Hopton Kirk 123 J6
Upper Hulme Staffs..... 100 A1
Upper Inglesham
Swindn 40 D2
Upper Killay Swans.......51 H6
Upper Kinchrackine
Ag & B................. 183 G2
Upper Knockando
Moray................... 214 E5
Upper Lambourn
W Berk...................40 F4
Upper Landywood
Staffs.....................85 H3
Upper Langford
N Som....................38 C7
Upper Langwith
Derbys.................. 115 K7
Upper Largo Fife........ 187 G6
Upper Layham Suffk.....78 C6
Upper Leigh Staffs...... 100 A5
Upper Lochton
Abers................... 206 D6
Upper Longdon
Staffs.....................85 J2
Upper Lybster
Highld.................. 231 J7
Upper Lydbrook
Gloucs....................54 E5
Upper Lye Herefs.........69 H2
Uppermill Oldham....... 113 M1
Upper Milton Worcs 84 E8
Upper Minety Wilts.......40 A3
Upper Mulben
Moray................... 215 H4
Upper Netchwood
Shrops...................83 L5
Upper Nobut Staffs..... 100 B5
Upper Norwood
W Susx...................18 C3
Upper Oddington
Gloucs....................56 E3
Upper Poppleton
C York 133 H8
Upper Ratley Hants......28 F6
Upper Rissington
Gloucs....................56 D4
Upper Rochford
Worcs.....................70 B2
Upper Ruscoe
D & G................... 145 L3
Upper Sapey Herefs 70 C2
Upper Seagry Wilts.......39 L4
Upper Shelton
C Beds....................74 E5
Upper Sheringham
Norfk.................... 106 D4

Upper Skelmorlie
N Ayrs......................... 173 L5
Upper Slaughter
Gloucs.........................56 D4
Upper Soudley
Gloucs.........................54 F6
Upper Standen Kent......35 H6
Upper Stoke Norfk......92 F3
Upper Stondon
C Beds.........................75 G7
Upper Stowe Nhants......73 J3
Upper Street Hants......28 D7
Upper Street Norfk......93 H1
Upper Street Norfk......107 G8
Upper Street Suffk......77 H4
Upper Street Suffk......78 D4
Upper Sundon
C Beds.........................59 H3
Upper Swell Gloucs......56 D3
Upper Tean Staffs......100 A5
Upperthong Kirk.........123 H8
Upperton W Susx.........30 F6
Upper Town Herefs......69 L5
Uppertown Highld......231 L1
Upper Town N Som.......38 D7
Upper Town Suffk......77 K2
Upper Tumble
Carmth........................51 G3
Upper Tysoe Warwks......72 D5
Upper Victoria
Angus.........................187 J1
Upper Wardington
Oxon...........................72 F5
Upper Welland
Worcs.........................70 D6
Upper Wellingham
E Susx........................19 L3
Upper Weybread
Suffk..........................92 F7
Upper Wield Hants......29 L4
Upper Winchendon
Bucks.........................58 C5
Upper Woodford
Wilts..........................28 C4
Upper Wraxall
Wilts..........................39 J5
Uppingham Rutlnd......88 C4
Uppington Shrops.......83 L2
Upsall N York............133 G3
Upsettlington
Border........................168 C1
Upshire Essex...........60 C7
Up Somborne
Hants.........................29 H5
Upstreet Kent...........35 G3
Upton Bucks.............58 C5
Upton C Pete............89 G4
Upton Cambs............89 H7
Upton Ches W...........112 B7
Upton Cnwll.............5 L2
Upton Devon.............7 G7
Upton Devon.............12 E2
Upton Dorset............14 E5
Upton Dorset............15 J4
Upton Halton............112 C4
Upton Hants.............29 G1
Upton Hants.............29 G7
Upton Leics.............86 D4
Upton Lincs.............116 E4
Upton Norfk.............93 H2
Upton Notts.............102 B2
Upton Notts.............116 C6
Upton Oxon..............41 K3
Upton Slough............43 G5
Upton Somset............24 F5
Upton Somset............26 C6
Upton Wakefd............124 D7
Upton Wirral.............111 J4
Upton Bishop Herefs......54 F3
Upton Cheyney
S Glos........................39 G6
Upton Cressett
Shrops........................84 B5
Upton Grey Hants.......30 B2
Upton Hellions
Devon.........................11 J4
Upton Lovell Wilts......27 L4
Upton Magna Shrops......83 K2

Upton Noble Somset......27 G4
Upton Pyne Devon.......11 L5
Upton St Leonards
Gloucs.........................55 K5
Upton Scudamore
Wilts..........................27 K2
Upton Snodsbury
Worcs.........................71 G4
Upton-upon-Severn
Worcs.........................70 F6
Upton Warren Worcs......71 G2
Upwaltham W Susx......18 C3
Upwell Norfk.............90 C3
Upwood Cambs...........89 J6
Urchfont Wilts..........40 B8
Urmston Traffd.........113 H3
Urquhart Moray..........215 G2
Urquhart Castle
Highld........................212 E8
Urra N York..............142 C6
Urray Highld.............212 D4
Ury Abers.................207 G2
Uryside Abers...........206 E2
Usan Angus...............197 H5
Ushaw Moor Dur..........151 G6
Usk Mons.................54 B7
Usselby Lincs...........117 H3
Usworth Sundld.........151 H4
Utkinton Ches W.........112 D7
Utley C Brad.............122 F3
Uton Devon...............11 J5
Utterby Lincs............118 D3
Uttoxeter Staffs........100 C6
Uxbridge Gt Lon.........43 H4
Uyeasound Shet..........235 d2
Uzmaston Pembks.........49 G5

V

Vale Guern..............236 d2
Valley IoA...............108 C5
Valtos Highld............209 H2
Valtos W Isls............232 d2
Vange Essex..............46 B3
Vatsetter Shet...........235 d3
Vatten Highld............208 D5
Vaynor Myr Td............53 G6
Vazon Bay Guern..........236 b3
Veensgarth Shet..........235 c6
Velindre Powys...........68 D7
Venngreen Devon..........9 K3
Venn Ottery Devon........12 D4
Ventnor IoW..............17 G6
Venton Devon.............6 E4
Vernham Dean
Hants.........................29 G1
Vernham Street
Hants.........................41 G8
Verwood Dorset...........15 K2
Veryan Cnwll.............4 E7
Vickerstown Cumb.........128 E5
Victoria Cnwll...........4 F4
Vidlin Shet...............235 d4
Viewfield Moray..........215 G3
Viewpark N Lans..........175 J6
Vigo Kent................45 M7
Village de Putron
Guern........................236 d3
Ville la Bas Jersey......236 a5
Villiaze Guern...........236 c3
Vines Cross E Susx........20 C3
Virginia Water
Surrey........................43 G6
Virginstow Devon.........9 K6
Vobster Somset...........27 G2
Voe Shet..................235 c4
Vowchurch Herefs........69 G7

W

Waberthwaite Cumb......128 D2
Wackerfield Dur.........140 E3
Wacton Norfk............92 E5
Wadborough Worcs........70 F5

Waddesdon Bucks.........58 C5
Waddesdon Manor
Bucks.........................58 B5
Waddeton Devon..........7 K4
Waddingham Lincs........117 G3
Waddington Lancs........121 L2
Waddington Lincs........116 F8
Waddon Gt Lon...........44 F7
Wadebridge Cnwll........4 F2
Wadeford Somset.........13 H1
Wadenhoe Nhants.........88 E6
Wadesmill Herts.........60 B4
Wadhurst E Susx.........33 H6
Wadshelf Derbys..........114 F7
Wadworth Donc...........115 K3
Wainfleet All Saints
Lincs.........................104 D2
Wainfleet St Mary
Lincs.........................104 D2
Wainhouse Corner
Cnwll........................9 G5
Wainscott Medway........46 C6
Wainstalls Calder........122 F5
Waitby Cumb.............139 H5
Waithe Lincs.............118 C2
Wakefield Wakefd........123 L6
Wake Green Birm.........85 K6
Wakehurst W Susx........32 C6
Wakerley Nhants.........88 D4
Wakes Colne Essex.......61 L3
Walberswick Suffk.......93 K8
Walberton W Susx........18 C4
Walbutt D & G............146 D2
Walcombe Somset.........26 D3
Walcot Lincs.............103 H5
Walcot Shrops...........83 L2
Walcot Swindn............40 D4
Walcote Leics............87 H6
Walcot Green Norfk......92 D7
Walcott Lincs............103 J2
Walcott Norfk............107 H6
Walden Stubbs
N York........................124 E6
Walderslade Medway......46 C7
Walderton W Susx........17 L1
Walditch Dorset..........13 L4
Waldridge Dur............151 G5
Waldringfield Suffk......79 G5
Waldron E Susx...........20 B2
Wales Rothm.............115 J5
Wales Somset.............26 E6
Walesby Lincs............117 J3
Walesby Notts............116 B7
Walford Herefs...........54 E4
Walford Herefs...........83 H8
Walford Heath
Shrops........................98 C8
Walgherton Ches E.......99 G3
Walgrave Nhants.........74 B1
Walkden Salfd............113 G2
Walker N u Ty.............151 H3
Walkerburn Border.......166 E3
Walkeringham
Notts........................116 C3
Walkerith Lincs..........116 C3
Walkern Herts............59 M3
Walker's Heath Birm......85 J7
Walkerton Fife..........186 D6
Walkford BCP.............16 B4
Walkhampton Devon........6 D2
Walkington E R Yk........126 B3
Walkley Sheff............115 G4
Walk Mill Lancs..........122 C5
Walkwood Worcs..........71 J2
Wall Nthumb..............150 A2
Wall Staffs..............85 K3
Wallacetown S Ayrs......153 G2
Wallacetown S Ayrs......163 J5
Wallands Park E Susx......19 L4
Wallasey Wirral.........111 J3
**Wallasey
(Kingsway)
Tunnel** Wirral.............111 K4
Wall Heath Dudley.......84 F5
Wallingford Oxon........41 L3
Wallington Gt Lon........44 F6
Wallington Hants.........17 H2
Wallington Herts.........75 K7

Wallington Heath
Wsall.........................85 H3
Wallisdown BCP...........15 K4
Walliswood Surrey........31 J4
Walls Shet................235 b5
Wallsend N Tyne..........151 H2
Wallyford E Loth.........177 K4
Walmer Kent..............35 K5
Walmer Bridge
Lancs........................121 G5
Walmley Birm.............85 K5
Walmley Ash Birm.........85 K5
Walpole Suffk............93 H8
Walpole Cross Keys
Norfk........................104 E8
Walpole Highway
Norfk........................90 D2
Walpole St Andrew
Norfk........................104 D8
Walpole St Peter
Norfk........................90 C1
Walsall Wsall............85 H4
Walsden Calder...........122 D6
Walsgrave on Sowe
Covtry.......................86 E7
Walsham le Willows
Suffk.........................78 B1
Walshford N York.........132 F3
Walsoken Norfk...........90 C2
Walston S Lans...........165 K1
Walsworth Herts.........59 K3
Walter's Ash Bucks.......42 D2
Waltham Kent.............34 E5
Waltham NE Lin...........118 C2
Waltham Abbey
Essex........................60 C7
Waltham Chase
Hants.........................29 K7
Waltham Cross Herts......60 B7
**Waltham on the
Wolds** Leics...............102 D7
**Waltham St
Lawrence** W & M...........42 D5
Walthamstow Gt Lon......45 G3
Walton C Pete............89 H3
Walton Cumb..............148 F3
Walton Derbys............115 G7
Walton Leeds.............124 C2
Walton Leics.............87 H6
Walton M Keyn............74 C7
Walton Powys.............68 F3
Walton Somset............26 C4
Walton Suffk.............79 G7
Walton W Susx............17 M2
Walton Wakefd............123 L6
Walton Wrekin............98 E8
Walton Cardiff
Gloucs........................55 K2
Walton East Pembks......49 H3
Walton Highway
Norfk........................90 C2
Walton-in-Gordano
N Som........................38 B5
Walton-le-Dale
Lancs........................121 H5
Walton-on-Thames
Surrey........................43 J6
Walton-on-the-Hill
Staffs........................99 L7
Walton-on-the-Hill
Surrey........................31 L1
**Walton-on-the-
Naze** Essex.................62 F4
**Walton on the
Wolds** Leics...............101 L8
Walton-on-Trent
Derbys.......................100 E8
Walton Park N Som.......38 B6
Walton West Pembks......48 E5
Walworth Darltn..........141 G4
Walworth Gt Lon..........45 G4
Walwyn's Castle
Pembks.......................48 E5
Wambrook Somset.........13 H2
Wanborough Surrey.......30 F2
Wanborough Swindn......40 E4
Wandsworth Gt Lon.......44 E5
Wangford Suffk..........93 K7

Wanlip Leics................87 H2
Wanlockhead D & G..... 165 G6
Wannock E Susx............20 C5
Wansford C Pete............88 F4
Wansford E R Yk......... 135 G7
Wanshurst Green
 Kent...........................33 K4
Wanstead Gt Lon............45 H3
Wanstrow Somset............27 G3
Wanswell Gloucs............55 G7
Wantage Oxon................41 H3
Wappenbury Warwks.......72 E2
Wappenham Nhants 73 J5
Warbleton E Susx............20 C3
Warborough Oxon............41 L2
Warboys Cambs...............89 K7
Warbreck Bpool 120 D3
Warbstow Cnwll............... 9 G6
Warburton Traffd 113 G4
Warcop Cumb 139 H4
Warden Nthumb............ 150 A2
Ward End Birm...............85 K5
Wardington Oxon............72 F5
Wardle Ches E.................98 E2
Wardle Rochdl............ 122 D6
Wardley Gatesd............ 151 H3
Wardley Rutlnd...............88 B4
Wardlow Derbys............ 114 D6
Wardy Hill Cambs............90 C6
Ware Herts 60 B5
Wareham Dorset..............15 H5
Warehorne Kent.............34 D7
Warenford Nthumb 169 H4
Wareside Herts...............60 C5
Waresley Cambs..............75 J4
Warfield Br For...............42 E6
Warfleet Devon............... 7 K6
Wargrave Wokham..........42 C5
Warham Norfk............ 105 M4
Wark Nthumb............... 157 L6
Wark Nthumb............... 168 C2
Warkleigh Devon............23 K6
Warkton Nhants..............88 C7
Warkworth Nhants 72 F6
Warkworth Nthumb 159 G2
Warlaby N York............ 132 E2
Warleggan Cnwll 5 J3
Warley Town Calder 122 F5
Warlingham Surrey..........32 C2
Warmfield Wakefd...... 124 B6
Warmingham Ches E......99 G1
Warmington Nhants........88 F5
Warmington Warwks.......72 E5
Warminster Wilts............27 K3
Warmley S Glos...............38 F5
Warmsworth Donc 115 K2
Warmwell Dorset...........14 E5
Warner Bros. Studio
 Tour London
 Herts............................59 H7
Warnford Hants...............29 L6
Warnham W Susx............31 J5
Warningcamp
 W Susx.......................18 D4
Warninglid W Susx.........31 L6
Warren Ches E............. 113 K7
Warren Pembks...............48 F7
Warrenhill S Lans 165 J2
Warren Row
 W & M.........................42 D4
Warren Street Kent........34 C4
Warrington M Keyn........74 C4
Warrington Warrtn...... 112 E4
Warriston C Edin......... 177 H4
Warsash Hants................16 F2
Warslow Staffs............ 100 C2
Warter E R Yk.............. 125 K1
Warthermaske
 N York...................... 132 C4
Warthill N York............ 133 K7
Wartling E Susx..............20 D4
Wartnaby Leics............ 102 B7
Warton Lancs............... 120 E5
Warton Lancs............... 129 K5
Warton Warwks..............86 C3
Warwick Warwks.............72 C1
Warwick Bridge
 Cumb......................... 148 E4

Warwick Castle
 Warwks........................72 C2
Warwick Services
 Warwks........................72 D3
Wasbister Ork 234 c4
Wasdale Head Cumb ... 137 G5
Washaway Cnwll 5 G2
Washbourne Devon......... 7 J5
Washbrook Suffk............78 D6
Washfield Devon.............11 L2
Washford Somset............25 G3
Washford Pyne
 Devon.........................11 J3
Washingborough
 Lincs........................ 117 G7
Washington Sundld 151 H4
Washington W Susx 18 F3
Washington
 Services Gatesd...... 151 G4
Washwood Heath
 Birm...........................85 K5
Wasperton Warwks 72 C3
Wass N York................ 133 H4
Wast Water Cumb........ 137 G6
Watchet Somset..............25 G3
Watchfield Oxon.............40 E3
Watchgate Cumb.......... 138 D7
Water Devon...................11 H8
Waterbeach Cambs.........76 C2
Waterbeach W Susx........18 B4
Waterbeck D & G......... 155 M6
Water End E R Yk......... 125 J3
Waterfall Staffs............ 100 B3
Waterfoot Ag & B........ 161 K3
Waterfoot E Rens........ 175 G7
Waterfoot Lancs.......... 122 C6
Waterford Herts..............60 A5
Waterheads Border...... 177 H7
Waterhouses Staffs 100 B3
Wateringbury Kent.........33 H3
Waterloo Highld 199 K2
Waterloo N Lans 175 L7
Waterloo P & K........... 195 G8
Waterloo Pembks...........49 G6
Waterloo Sefton.......... 111 K2
Waterlooville Hants........17 J1
Watermead Bucks.......... 58 D5
Watermillock Cumb 138 C3
Water Newton
 Cambs.........................89 G4
Water Orton Warwks.....85 L5
Waterperry Oxon............57 L6
Waterrow Somset...........25 G6
Watersfield W Susx........18 D3
Waterside Bl w D.......... 121 K5
Waterside E Ayrs......... 163 K7
Waterside E Ayrs......... 163 L2
Waterside E Duns 175 J4
Waterstein Highld....... 208 B5
Waterstock Oxon............57 M6
Waterston Pembks.........48 F6
Water Stratford
 Bucks.........................73 J7
Waters Upton Wrekin....98 F8
Watford Herts................43 J2
Watford Nhants..............73 H2
Watford Gap
 Services Nhants........73 H2
Wath N York................ 132 B6
Wath N York................ 132 E4
Wath upon Dearne
 Rothm....................... 115 H2
Watlington Norfk...........90 E2
Watlington Oxon.............42 B2
Watten Highld.............. 231 J5
Wattisfield Suffk............92 B8
Wattisham Suffk.............78 B4
Watton Dorset................13 L4
Watton E R Yk.............. 126 C1
Watton Norfk.................91 K4
Watton-at-Stone
 Herts..........................60 A4
Wattston N Lans.......... 175 K4
Wattsville Caerph...........37 J3
Waulkmill Abers.......... 206 C6
Waunarlwydd Swans......51 H6
Waunfawr Cerdgn..........80 E6
Waunfawr Gwynd..........95 J2

Wavendon M Keyn........74 C6
Waverbridge Cumb 147 L5
Waverley Rothm.......... 115 H4
Waverton Ches W 112 C8
Waverton Cumb........... 147 L5
Wawne E R Yk.............. 126 D3
Waxham Norfk............ 107 J7
Wayford Somset.............13 K2
Waytown Dorset.............13 L3
Way Village Devon..........11 K3
Weacombe Somset.........25 H4
Weald Oxon....................56 F7
Wealdstone Gt Lon........44 D3
Weardley Leeds............ 123 K2
Weare Somset................26 B2
Weare Giffard Devon......23 G6
Wearhead Dur............. 149 L6
Wearne Somset..............26 B5
Weasenham All
 Saints Norfk............ 105 K7
Weasenham St
 Peter Norfk............. 105 K7
Weaste Salfd............... 113 J2
Weaverham Ches W..... 112 E6
Weaverthorpe
 N York...................... 134 E5
Webheath Worcs............71 H2
Wedderlairs Abers...... 216 F7
Weddington Warwks......86 D5
Wedhampton Wilts.........40 B8
Wedmore Somset...........26 C2
Wednesbury Sandw........85 H4
Wednesfield Wolves.......85 G4
Weedon Bucks................58 D4
Weedon Bec Nhants......73 J3
Weedon Lois Nhants......73 H5
Weeford Staffs...............85 K3
Weeke Hants..................29 J5
Weekley Nhants..............88 C7
Week St Mary Cnwll....... 9 H5
Weel E R Yk.................. 126 D3
Weeley Essex..................62 D4
Weeley Heath Essex......62 D4
Weem P & K................ 194 D6
Weethley Warwks...........71 J4
Weeting Norfk................91 H5
Weeton E R Yk.............. 127 H6
Weeton Lancs............... 120 E4
Weeton N York............ 123 K2
Weetwood Leeds.......... 123 K3
Weir Lancs................... 122 C5
Weir Quay Devon............ 6 C3
Weisdale Shet.............. 235 c5
Welborne Norfk.............92 C2
Welbourn Lincs............ 102 F2
Welburn N York........... 133 L6
Welbury N York........... 141 J6
Welby Lincs................. 102 F5
Welcombe Devon...........22 C7
Weldon Nhants..............88 D5
Welford Nhants..............87 J7
Welford W Berk.............41 H5
Welford-on-Avon
 Warwks........................71 K4
Welham Leics.................87 L5
Welham Notts.............. 116 B5
Welham Green Herts......59 L6
Well Hants....................30 C3
Well Lincs................... 118 F6
Well N York................. 132 D3
Welland Worcs...............70 E6
Wellbank Angus........... 196 D8
Wellesbourne
 Warwks........................72 C4
Well Head Herts.............59 K3
Welling Gt Lon................45 J5
Wellingborough
 Nhants.........................74 C2
Wellingham Norfk....... 105 L7
Wellingore Lincs.......... 103 G2
Wellington Cumb......... 136 F6
Wellington Herefs..........69 K5
Wellington Somset.........25 H7
Wellington Wrekin.........84 B2
Wellington Heath
 Herefs..........................70 C6
Wellow BaNES................39 H5
Wellow IoW...................16 E5

Wellow Notts............... 116 A7
Wells Somset.................26 D3
Wells-next-the-Sea
 Norfk......................... 105 L4
Wellstye Green Essex.....61 G4
Welltree P & K............. 185 K3
Wellwood Fife............. 176 E2
Welney Norfk.................90 D5
Welshampton Shrops 98 C5
Welsh Frankton
 Shrops........................98 A6
Welsh Newton
 Herefs..........................54 D4
Welshpool Powys...........82 E3
Welsh St Donats
 V Glam........................36 F5
Welton Cumb............... 148 C6
Welton E R Yk.............. 126 B5
Welton Lincs................ 117 G5
Welton Nhants...............73 H2
Welton le Marsh
 Lincs......................... 119 G7
Welton le Wold
 Lincs......................... 118 C4
Welwick E R Yk............ 127 H6
Welwyn Herts................59 L5
Welwyn Garden City
 Herts..........................59 L5
Wem Shrops..................98 D6
Wembdon Somset..........25 L4
Wembley Gt Lon............44 D3
Wembury Devon............. 6 D6
Wemworthy Devon....... 10 F3
Wemyss Bay Inver....... 173 L4
Wendens Ambo
 Essex..........................76 D7
Wendlebury Oxon..........57 K4
Wendling Norfk..............91 L2
Wendover Bucks............58 E6
Wendron Cnwll............... 3 H5
Wendron Mining
 District Cnwll............... 3 J5
Wendy Cambs................75 K5
Wenhaston Suffk...........93 J7
Wennington Cambs........89 J7
Wennington Gt Lon.......45 K4
Wennington Lancs....... 130 C5
Wensley Derbys........... 100 E1
Wensley N York........... 131 K2
Wentbridge Wakefd.... 124 D6
Wentnor Shrops............83 H5
Wentworth Cambs.........90 C7
Wentworth Rothm...... 115 G2
Wenvoe V Glam..............37 H6
Weobley Herefs..............69 H4
Wepham W Susx............18 E4
Wereham Norfk..............90 F3
Werrington C Pete..........89 H3
Werrington Cnwll........... 9 J7
Wervin Ches W............ 112 B6
Wesham Lancs............. 120 F4
Wessington Derbys...... 101 G2
West Acre Norfk.............91 H1
West Alvington
 Devon........................ 7 G6
West Anstey Devon........24 D6
West Ashby Lincs......... 118 C6
West Ashling W Susx.....17 M2
West Ashton Wilts.........27 K1
West Auckland Dur..... 140 F3
West Ayton N York....... 134 F3
West Bagborough
 Somset.........................25 J5
West Bank Halton........ 112 D5
West Barkwith Lincs.... 117 K5
West Barnby N York.... 143 G5
West Barns E Loth...... 178 E3
West Barsham
 Norfk......................... 105 L5
West Bay Dorset.............13 L4
West Beckham
 Norfk......................... 106 D5
West Bedfont Surrey......43 H5
Westbere Kent...............35 G3
West Bergholt Essex......62 A3
West Bexington
 Dorset........................13 M5
West Bilney Norfk..........91 G1

West Blatchington
Br & H 19 J4
West Boldon S Tyne 151 J3
Westborough Lincs .. 102 D4
Westbourne BCP 15 K4
Westbourne W Susx....17 L2
West Bowling C Brad... 123 H4
West Bradenham
Norfk 91 K2
West Bradford Lancs... 121 L2
West Bradley Somset....26 E4
West Bretton Wakefd... 123 K7
West Bridgford
Notts 101 L5
West Bromwich
Sandw 85 H5
Westbrook Kent..........35 J2
Westbrook W Berk.......41 H6
West Buckland
Devon...............23 K5
West Buckland
Somset...............25 J7
West Burrafirth Shet... 235 b5
West Burton N York... 131 J3
Westbury Bucks..........73 J7
Westbury Shrops..........83 G2
Westbury Wilts...........27 K2
Westbury Leigh Wilts...27 K2
**Westbury-on-
Severn** Gloucs 55 G5
Westbury-on-Trym
Bristl 38 E5
**Westbury-sub-
Mendip** Somset 26 D2
West Butterwick
N Linc...............116 D1
Westby Lancs 120 E4
West Byfleet Surrey 43 H7
West Cairngaan
D & G...............144 D8
West Caister Norfk......93 K2
West Calder W Loth... 176 D5
West Camel Somset 26 E6
West Chaldon Dorset ...14 E5
West Challow Oxon....41 G3
West Charleton
Devon...............7 H7
West Chiltington
W Susx...............18 E3
West Chinnock
Somset...............26 C8
West Clandon Surrey......31 H2
West Cliffe Kent..........35 J5
Westcliff-on-Sea
Sthend...............46 E3
West Coker Somset......26 D8
Westcombe Somset 27 G4
West Compton
Somset...............26 E3
**West Compton
Abbas** Dorset 14 B4
Westcote Gloucs 56 E4
Westcote Barton
Oxon...............57 H3
Westcott Bucks..........58 B5
Westcott Devon..........12 C2
Westcott Surrey..........31 J2
West Cottingwith
N York...............125 G3
Westcourt Wilts..........40 E7
West Cowick E R Yk... 124 F6
West Cross Swans......51 H7
West Curthwaite
Cumb...............148 B5
Westdean E Susx.........20 B5
West Dean W Susx......18 B3
West Dean Wilts..........28 E6
West Deeping Lincs...89 G2
West Derby Lpool......111 L3
West Dereham Norfk...90 F4
West Down Devon......23 H3
Westdowns Cnwll 8 E7
West Drayton Gt Lon...43 H4
West Drayton Notts... 116 B6
West Dunnet Highld... 231 J2
West Ella E R Yk........ 126 C5
West End Bed...........74 E4
West End Hants..........29 J8

West End N Som..........38 C6
West End Norfk..........93 K2
West End Surrey..........42 F7
West End Surrey..........43 J7
West End Wilts..........27 M6
West End Green
Hants...............42 A7
Wester Aberchalder
Highld...............202 E2
Wester Balblair
Highld...............212 D5
Westerdale Highld...... 231 G5
Westerdale N York...... 142 E6
Westerfield Suffk..........78 E5
Westergate W Susx......18 C5
Wester Hailes C Edin... 177 G4
Westerham Kent..........32 B3
Westerhope N u Ty...... 150 F2
Westerland Devon 7 K4
Westerleigh S Glos......39 G4
Western Isles W Isls... 232 d5
Wester Ochiltree
W Loth...............176 D4
Wester Pitkierie Fife... 187 J6
Wester Ross Highld..... 220 C5
Westerton of Rossie
Angus...............197 G5
Westerwick Shet 235 c6
West Farleigh Kent......33 J3
West Farndon Nhants...73 G4
West Felton Shrops......97 M7
Westfield BaNES 26 F2
Westfield Cumb...........136 D2
Westfield E Susx..........21 G3
Westfield Highld........ 230 F3
Westfield N Lans........ 175 J4
Westfield Norfk..........92 B2
Westfield Surrey..........31 G1
Westfield W Loth........ 176 C4
Westfields Herefs..........69 K6
**Westfields of
Rattray** P & K....... 195 J6
Westgate Dur............150 A7
Westgate N Linc........ 125 J8
Westgate-on-Sea
Kent...............35 J2
West Grafton Wilts........40 E7
West Green Hants..........30 C1
West Grimstead
Wilts...............28 E6
West Grinstead
W Susx...............31 K6
West Haddlesey
N York...............124 E5
West Haddon
Nhants...............73 J1
West Hagbourne
Oxon...............41 K3
West Hagley Worcs......84 F7
Westhall Suffk..........93 J7
West Hallam Derbys... 101 H4
West Halton N Linc.... 125 L6
Westham Dorset 14 C6
Westham E Susx..........20 D5
West Ham Gt Lon........45 H4
Westham Somset..........26 B3
Westhampnett
W Susx...............18 B4
West Handley
Derbys...............115 H6
West Hanney Oxon......41 H2
West Hanningfield
Essex...............61 H7
West Harptree
BaNES...............38 E8
West Harting W Susx....30 C7
West Hatch Somset......25 L7
West Hatch Wilts..........27 L5
West Haven Angus... 187 J1
Westhay Somset..........26 C3
West Heath Birm..........85 J7
West Helmsdale
Highld...............227 H5
West Hendred Oxon......41 H3
West Heslerton
N York...............134 E4
West Hewish N Som......38 B7

Westhide Herefs..........69 L5
Westhill Abers 206 F4
West Hill Devon..........12 D4
Westhill Highld..........213 H5
West Hoathly W Susx...32 C6
West Holme Dorset......15 G5
Westhope Herefs..........69 J4
Westhope Shrops..........83 J6
West Horndon Essex....45 M3
Westhorpe Lincs........ 103 L6
Westhorpe Suffk..........78 C2
West Horrington
Somset...............26 E3
West Horsley Surrey......31 H2
West Hougham Kent......35 H6
Westhoughton
Bolton...............112 F1
Westhouse N York...... 130 D5
Westhouses Derbys...... 101 H2
West Howe BCP..........15 K4
Westhumble Surrey......31 K2
West Huntingtower
P & K...............185 M3
West Huntspill
Somset...............25 L3
West Hythe Kent..........34 F7
West Ilsley W Berk......41 J4
West Itchenor
W Susx...............17 L3
West Kennett Wilts......40 C6
West Kilbride N Ayrs... 173 L8
West Kingsdown
Kent...............45 L7
West Kington Wilts........39 J5
West Kirby Wirral......111 H4
West Knapton
N York...............134 D4
West Knighton
Dorset...............14 D5
West Knoyle Wilts........27 K5
Westlake Devon 6 F5
West Lambrook
Somset...............26 B7
West Langdon Kent......35 J5
West Lavington
W Susx...............30 E7
West Lavington Wilts....28 A2
West Layton N York... 140 E5
West Leake Notts........ 101 K7
Westleigh Devon..........23 G5
Westleigh Devon..........25 G7
West Leigh Somset......25 H5
Westleton Suffk..........79 J2
West Lexham Norfk......91 J1
Westley Suffk..........77 J2
Westley Waterless
Cambs...............76 E3
West Lilling N York.... 133 K6
Westlington Bucks......58 C6
West Linton Border...... 176 F7
Westlinton Cumb........ 148 D3
West Littleton S Glos....39 H5
West Lockinge Oxon....41 H3
West Lulworth
Dorset...............14 F6
West Lutton N York.... 134 E5
West Lydford Somset...26 E5
West Lyng Somset..........25 L5
West Lynn Norfk........ 104 F7
West Malling Kent........33 H2
West Malvern Worcs......70 D5
West Marden W Susx...30 C8
West Markham
Notts...............116 B6
Westmarsh Kent..........35 H3
West Marsh NE Lin.... 127 G8
West Marton N York... 122 D1
West Melbury Dorset....27 K7
West Meon Hants..........29 M6
West Mersea Essex......62 B5
Westmeston E Susx......19 K3
**West Midland Safari
Park** Worcs...........84 E7
Westmill Herts..........60 B3
West Milton Dorset......13 L3
Westminster Gt Lon......44 F4
*Westminster Abbey
& Palace* Gt Lon......44 F4

West Molesey Surrey......43 J6
West Monkton
Somset...............25 K5
West Moors Dorset......15 K2
West Morden Dorset......15 G4
West Morriston
Border...............167 J2
West Mudford
Somset...............26 E7
Westmuir Angus........ 196 B5
West Ness N York...... 133 L4
Westnewton Cumb...... 147 K6
West Newton E R Yk... 126 F3
West Newton Norfk... 105 H6
West Newton Somset...25 L5
West Norwood
Gt Lon...............44 F5
Westoe S Tyne........151 J2
West Ogwell Devon 7 J2
Weston BaNES..........39 G6
Weston Ches E..........99 G3
Weston Devon..........12 E3
Weston Devon..........12 F5
Weston Hants..........30 B6
Weston Herts..........59 L3
Weston Lincs..........103 M7
Weston N York........ 123 H2
Weston Nhants..........73 H5
Weston Notts..........116 C7
Weston Shrops..........83 L5
Weston Shrops..........97 L6
Weston Staffs..........99 L6
Weston W Berk..........41 H5
Weston Beggard
Herefs...............69 L6
Westonbirt Gloucs......39 J3
Weston by Welland
Nhants...............87 L5
Weston Colville
Cambs...............76 E4
Weston Corbett
Hants...............30 B3
Weston Coyney
C Stke...............99 L4
Weston Favell
Nhants...............73 L3
Weston Green Cambs...76 E4
Weston Heath Shrops...84 D2
Westoning C Beds......59 G2
Weston-in-Gordano
N Som...............38 C5
Weston Jones Staffs...99 H7
Weston Longville
Norfk...............92 D1
Weston Lullingfields
Shrops...............98 B7
**Weston-on-the-
Green** Oxon........57 K4
Weston Park Staffs......84 E2
Weston Patrick
Hants...............30 B3
Weston Rhyn Shrops...97 L5
Weston-sub-Edge
Gloucs...............71 K6
**Weston-super-
Mare** N Som..........37 L7
Weston Turville
Bucks...............58 D6
**Weston-under-
Lizard** Staffs..........84 E2
**Weston under
Penyard** Herefs......54 F4
**Weston-under-
Redcastle** Shrops......98 C6
**Weston under
Wetherley**
Warwks...............72 D1
Weston Underwood
Derbys...............100 F4
Weston Underwood
M Keyn...............74 C4
Weston-upon-Trent
Derbys...............101 H4
Westonzoyland
Somset...............25 M4
West Orchard Dorset....27 J7
West Overton Wilts......40 C6
Westow N York........ 134 B6

West Park Abers........... 206 E5
West Parley Dorset 15 K3
West Peckham Kent.....33 H3
West Pelton Dur...... 151 G4
West Pennard
    Somset....................26 D4
West Pentire Cnwll 4 B4
West Porlock Somset 24 D3
Westport Somset........26 B7
West Putford Devon...... 9 K2
West Quantoxhead
    Somset....................25 H3
Westquarter Falk........ 176 B3
West Rainton Dur 151 H5
West Rasen Lincs........ 117 H4
Westray Ork................. 234 c3
Westray Airport Ork... 234 c3
West Raynham
    Norfk..................... 105 L7
Westrigg W Loth........ 176 B5
Westrop Swindn 40 D2
West Rounton
    N York..................... 141 K6
West Row Suffk...........90 F7
West Rudham Norfk 105 K6
West Runton Norfk 106 E4
Westruther Border 178 D7
Westry Cambs.............90 B4
West Saltoun E Loth..... 178 B5
West Sandford Devon....11 J4
West Sandwick Shet ... 235 d3
West Scrafton
    N York..................... 131 K3
West Stafford Dorset.....14 D4
West Stockwith
    Notts..................... 116 C3
West Stoke W Susx......17 M2
West Stour Dorset........27 H6
West Stourmouth
    Kent.........................35 H3
West Stow Suffk...........77 J1
West Stowell Wilts.......40 C7
West Street Suffk 78 B1
West Tanfield N York... 132 D4
West Taphouse Cnwll..... 5 J3
West Tarbert Ag & B... 172 E5
West Tarring W Susx 18 F5
West Thirston
    Nthumb 158 F3
West Thorney W Susx....17 L3
West Thorpe Notts..... 101 L7
West Thurrock Thurr....45 L4
West Tilbury Thurr........46 A4
West Tisted Hants........29 M5
West Torrington
    Lincs..................... 117 J5
West Town Hants 17 K3
West Town N Som 38 C6
West Tytherley Hants....28 F5
West Walton Norfk.......90 C2
Westward Cambs........ 148 B6
Westward Ho! Devon.....23 G5
Westwell Kent 34 D5
Westwell Oxon............56 E6
Westwell Leacon
    Kent.........................34 C5
West Wellow Hants.......28 F7
West Wembury
    Devon..................... 6 D6
West Wemyss Fife...... 186 E7
Westwick Cambs.........76 B2
West Wickham
    Cambs.....................76 E5
West Wickham
    Gt Lon.....................45 G6
West Williamston
    Pembks....................49 H6
West Winch Norfk.......90 F1
West Winterslow
    Wilts........................28 E5
West Wittering
    W Susx....................17 L3
West Witton N York.... 131 K2
Westwood Devon........12 C3
Westwood Kent...........35 K2
Westwood Wilts...........39 J8
West Woodburn
    Nthumb 157 M5

West Woodhay
    W Berk.....................41 H7
Westwoodside
    N Linc................... 116 C2
West Worldham
    Hants......................30 C4
West Worthing
    W Susx....................18 F5
West Wratting
    Cambs.....................76 E4
West Wylam
    Nthumb 150 E3
Wetheral Cumb........ 148 E4
Wetherby Leeds 124 B2
Wetherby Services
    N York................... 124 C1
Wetherden Suffk..........78 B3
Wetheringsett Suffk 78 D2
Wethersfield Essex......61 H2
Wetherup Street
    Suffk.......................78 D2
Wetley Rocks Staffs......99 L3
Wettenhall Ches E........98 F1
Wetton Staffs............ 100 C2
Wetwang E R Yk........ 134 E7
Wetwood Staffs...........99 H5
Wexcombe Wilts..........40 F8
Weybourne Norfk 106 D4
Weybourne Surrey........30 D2
Weybread Suffk...........92 F7
Weybread Street
    Suffk.......................92 F7
Weybridge Surrey........43 H7
Weycroft Devon...........13 H3
Weydale Highld......... 231 H3
Weyhill Hants.............28 F3
Weymouth Dorset........14 D6
Whaddon Bucks..........74 B7
Whaddon Cambs.........75 L5
Whaddon Gloucs.........55 J5
Whaddon Wilts...........28 D6
Whaddon Wilts...........39 K7
Whaley Derbys........... 115 K7
Whaley Bridge
    Derbys................... 114 A5
Whaley Thorns
    Derbys................... 115 K7
Whaligoe Highld....... 231 K7
Whalley Lancs........... 121 L4
Whalsay Shet........... 235 d4
Whalton Nthumb 158 E6
Whaplode Lincs........ 104 A7
Whaplode Drove
    Lincs......................89 K2
Wharf Warwks............72 E4
Wharfe N York........... 130 E5
Wharles Lancs........... 120 F4
Wharley End C Beds....74 D5
Wharncliffe Side
    Sheff..................... 114 F3
Wharram-le-Street
    N York................... 134 D6
Wharton Ches W....... 112 F7
Wharton Herefs..........69 K4
Whashton N York....... 140 E6
Whasset Cumb.......... 129 L4
Whatcote Warwks........72 C5
Whateley Warwks........86 B4
Whatfield Suffk...........78 B5
Whatley Somset..........13 J2
Whatley Somset..........27 G3
Whatley's End S Glos....38 F4
Whatlington E Susx......20 F3
Whatton-in-the-
    Vale Notts............. 102 C5
Whauphill D & G........ 145 J5
Wheal Peevor Cnwll 3 J3
Wheatacre Norfk........93 K5
Wheathampstead
    Herts......................59 K5
Wheatley Hants..........30 C4
Wheatley Oxon...........57 L6
Wheatley Hill Dur...... 151 J6
Wheatley Hills Donc.... 115 L1
Wheaton Aston
    Staffs......................84 F2
Wheddon Cross
    Somset....................24 E4

Wheeler's Green
    Wokham...................42 C6
Wheelock Ches E..........99 H2
Wheelton Lancs........ 121 J6
Wheldrake C York...... 125 G2
Whelford Gloucs..........56 D7
Whelpley Hill Bucks.....59 G6
Whempstead Herts......60 A4
Whenby N York......... 133 K5
Whepstead Suffk.........77 J3
Wherstead Suffk..........78 E6
Wherwell Hants..........29 H3
Wheston Derbys....... 114 C6
Whetsted Kent...........33 H4
Whetstone Gt Lon.......44 E2
Whetstone Leics.........87 G4
Whicham Cumb........ 128 D3
Whichford Warwks......72 C7
Whickham Gatesd..... 150 F3
Whiddon Down
    Devon.....................11 G6
Whigstreet Angus..... 196 D7
Whilton Nhants..........73 J2
Whimple Devon..........12 D3
Whimpwell Green
    Norfk..................... 107 H6
Whinburgh Norfk........92 B2
Whinnieliggate
    D & G.................... 146 C4
Whinnyfold Abers...... 217 K7
Whippingham IoW.......17 G4
Whipsnade C Beds.......59 G4
Whipsnade Zoo ZSL
    C Beds....................59 G4
Whipton Devon...........12 B4
Whisby Lincs............ 116 E7
Whissendine Rutlnd.....88 B2
Whissonsett Norfk..... 105 L7
Whistlefield Ag & B... 183 J8
Whistlefield Inn
    Ag & B................... 183 G8
Whistley Green
    Wokham...................42 C5
Whiston Knows 112 C3
Whiston Nhants..........74 B3
Whiston Rothm......... 115 H4
Whiston Staffs............84 F2
Whiston Staffs.......... 100 B3
Whitbeck Cumb........ 128 D3
Whitbourne Herefs......70 D3
Whitburn S Tyne 151 J3
Whitburn W Loth...... 176 C5
Whitby N York.......... 143 J5
Whitchester Border ... 178 F6
Whitchurch BaNES......38 F6
Whitchurch Bucks......58 D4
Whitchurch Cardif......37 J4
Whitchurch Devon 6 D2
Whitchurch Hants......29 J2
Whitchurch Herefs......54 D4
Whitchurch Oxon.......41 M5
Whitchurch Pembks....48 D3
Whitchurch Shrops....98 D4
Whitchurch
    Canonicorum
    Dorset....................13 K4
Whitchurch Hill
    Oxon......................41 M5
Whitcombe Dorset......14 D5
Whitcot Shrops...........83 H5
Whitcott Keysett
    Shrops....................82 F6
Whiteacre Heath
    Warwks...................86 B5
White Ball Somset.......25 H7
Whitebridge Highld... 202 D3
Whitebrook Mons........54 D6
Whitebushes Surrey.....32 B4
Whitecairns Abers..... 207 H2
Whitechapel Gt Lon.....45 G4
White Chapel Lancs... 121 H3
White Colne Essex......61 L3
Whitecraig E Loth..... 177 K4
Whitecrook D & G..... 144 E4
White Cross Cnwll........ 3 H6
Whitecross Falk....... 176 C3
Whiteface Highld...... 222 F4
Whitefarland N Ayrs ... 161 L2

Whitefaulds S Ayrs...... 163 H7
Whitefield Bury......... 113 J1
Whitefield Somset......25 G5
Whiteford Abers....... 206 D1
Whitegate Ches W..... 112 F7
Whitehall Ork............ 234 d5
Whitehaven Cumb..... 136 D4
Whitehill Hants..........30 C5
Whitehills Abers....... 216 C2
Whitehouse Abers 206 C3
Whitehouse Ag & B... 172 D6
Whitehouse
    Common Birm..........85 K4
Whitekirk E Loth........ 178 D3
White Lackington
    Dorset....................14 D3
Whitelackington
    Somset....................26 B7
White Ladies Aston
    Worcs.....................71 G4
Whiteleaf Bucks..........58 D6
Whiteley Hants...........17 G1
Whiteley Bank IoW......17 G6
Whitemire Moray...... 214 B4
Whitemoor C Nott..... 101 K4
Whitemoor Cnwll......... 4 F4
Whiteness Shet......... 235 c6
White Notley Essex......61 J4
Whiteparish Wilts........28 E6
White Pit Lincs.......... 118 E6
Whiterashes Abers 206 F2
White Roding Essex.....60 E5
Whiterow Highld....... 231 L5
Whiterow Moray....... 214 C3
Whiteshill Gloucs........55 J6
Whitesmith E Susx......20 B3
Whitestaunton
    Somset....................13 H1
Whitestone Warwks....86 E5
Whitestone Cross
    Devon.....................11 K6
White Waltham
    W & M......................42 D5
Whitewell Lancs........ 121 K2
Whitfield C Dund...... 187 G2
Whitfield Kent............35 J5
Whitfield Nhants.........73 H6
Whitfield Nthumb..... 149 K4
Whitfield S Glos.........38 F3
Whitford Devon...........13 G4
Whitford Flints......... 111 G5
Whitgift E R Yk......... 125 J6
Whitgreave Staffs.......99 K6
Whithorn D & G........ 145 J6
Whiting Bay N Ayrs... 162 D4
Whitkirk Leeds.......... 124 B4
Whitland Carmth.........49 L4
Whitlaw Border 167 G6
Whitletts S Ayrs........ 163 J5
Whitley N York.......... 124 E6
Whitley Readg...........42 B6
Whitley Sheff........... 115 G3
Whitley Wilts..............39 K6
Whitley Bay N Tyne... 159 J7
Whitley Chapel
    Nthumb 150 B4
Whitley Lower Kirk... 123 J6
Whitminster Gloucs.....55 H6
Whitmore Staffs..........99 J4
Whitnage Devon.........25 G7
Whitnash Warwks........72 D2
Whitney-on-Wye
    Herefs.....................68 F5
Whitsbury Hants.........28 C7
Whitsome Border 179 H7
Whitson Newpt...........38 B4
Whitstable Kent..........47 J6
Whitstone Cnwll........... 9 H5
Whittingham
    Nthumb 168 F6
Whittingslow Shrops....83 H5
Whittington Derbys... 115 G6
Whittington Gloucs.....56 A4
Whittington Lancs..... 130 B4
Whittington Norfk......91 G4
Whittington Shrops....97 L6
Whittington Staffs......84 F6
Whittington Staffs......85 L2

Whittington Warwks 86 C4
Whittington Worcs 70 F4
Whittlebury Nhants 73 K5
Whittle-le-Woods
  Lancs 121 H6
Whittlesey Cambs 89 J4
Whittlesford Cambs 76 C5
Whitton N Linc 125 L5
Whitton Nthumb 158 D3
Whitton Powys 68 F2
Whitton S on T 141 J3
Whitton Shrops 83 L8
Whittonstall Nthumb.... 150 D4
Whitway Hants 41 J8
Whitwell Derbys 115 K6
Whitwell Herts 59 K4
Whitwell IoW 17 G6
Whitwell N York 141 G7
Whitwell Rutlnd..........88 D2
Whitwell-on-the-
  Hill N York 133 L6
Whitwell Street
  Norfk 106 D7
Whitwick Leics 86 E1
Whitworth Lancs 122 D6
Whixall Shrops 98 D5
Whixley N York 133 G7
Whorlton Dur 140 E4
Whyle Herefs 69 L3
Whyteleafe Surrey.......32 C2
Wibsey C Brad.......... 123 H4
Wibtoft Warwks..........86 F6
Wichelstowe Swindn....40 C4
Wichenford Worcs.......70 D3
Wichling Kent..........34 B4
Wick BCP 15 L4
Wick Highld 231 L5
Wick S Glos..............39 G5
Wick V Glam 36 E6
Wick W Susx 18 D5
Wick Worcs 71 G5
Wicken Cambs 76 E1
Wicken Nhants.........73 L6
Wicken Bonhunt
  Essex....................60 D2
Wickenby Lincs 117 H5
Wicken Green
  Village Norfk 105 K6
Wickersley Rothm...... 115 J3
Wicker Street Green
  Suffk 77 L6
Wickford Essex 46 C2
Wickham Hants..........17 H1
Wickham W Berk 41 H6
Wickham Bishops
  Essex....................61 K5
Wickhambreaux
  Kent.....................35 G3
Wickhambrook Suffk....77 H4
Wickhamford Worcs.....71 J6
Wickham Green
  Suffk.....................78 D2
Wickham Market
  Suffk.....................79 G4
Wickhampton Norfk 93 J3
Wickham St Paul
  Essex.....................77 J7
Wickham Skeith
  Suffk.....................78 C2
Wickham Street
  Suffk.....................78 C1
Wick John o' Groats
  Airport Highld........ 231 L5
Wicklewood Norfk 92 C3
Wickmere Norfk....... 106 E5
Wick St Lawrence
  N Som.....................38 A7
Wicksteed Park
  Nhants..................88 C7
Wickwar S Glos..........39 G3
Widdington Essex 60 E2
Widdrington
  Nthumb 159 G3
Widdrington Station
  Nthumb 159 G4
Widecombe in the
  Moor Devon 7 G1
Widegates Cnwll..........5 L4

Widemouth Bay
  Cnwll 9 G4
Wideopen N Tyne...... 159 G7
Widford Essex 61 H6
Widford Herts............60 C5
Widmer End Bucks......42 E2
Widmerpool Notts 101 M6
Widmore Gt Lon 45 H6
Widnes Halton 112 D4
Widworthy Devon 13 G3
Wigan Wigan 112 E1
Wigborough Somset....26 C2
Wiggaton Devon 12 E4
Wiggenhall St
  Germans Norfk 90 E2
Wiggenhall St Mary
  Magdalen Norfk........90 E2
Wiggenhall St Mary
  the Virgin Norfk 90 E2
Wigginton C York...... 133 J7
Wigginton Herts.........58 F6
Wigginton Oxon.........57 H2
Wigginton Staffs.........86 B3
Wigglesworth
  N York 130 F7
Wiggonby Cumb....... 148 B4
Wighill N York......... 124 D2
Wighton Norfk......... 105 M4
Wightwick Wolves 84 F4
Wigley Hants............29 G7
Wigmore Herefs.........69 H2
Wigmore Medway 46 D6
Wigsley Notts 116 E7
Wigsthorpe Nhants 88 F6
Wigston Leics 87 H4
Wigston Fields Leics......87 H4
Wigston Parva
  Leics.....................86 F5
Wigthorpe Notts....... 115 L5
Wigtoft Lincs 103 L5
Wigton Cumb 148 A5
Wigtown D & G......... 145 J4
Wike Leeds 123 L3
Wilbarston Nhants.......88 B5
Wilberfoss E R Yk...... 125 H1
Wilburton Cambs 90 C7
Wilby Nhants............74 C2
Wilby Norfk..............92 B5
Wilby Suffk..............78 F1
Wilcot Wilts.............40 C7
Wilcott Shrops..........98 B8
Wildboarclough
  Ches E.................. 113 M7
Wilden Bed..............75 G4
Wilden Worcs............84 E8
Wildmanbridge
  S Lans.................. 175 L7
Wildmill Brdgnd 36 D4
Wildmoor Worcs.........85 G7
Wildsworth Lincs...... 116 D3
Wilford C Nott........ 101 K5
Wilkesley Ches E.........98 F4
Wilkhaven Highld...... 223 K4
Wilkieston W Loth 176 F5
Willand Devon 12 D1
Willaston Ches E 99 G3
Willaston Ches W...... 111 K6
Willen M Keyn...........74 C6
Willenhall Covtry.......86 D7
Willenhall Wsall.........85 H4
Willerby E R Yk....... 126 C4
Willerby N York 134 F4
Willersey Gloucs 71 K6
Willersley Herefs........68 F5
Willesborough Kent 34 D6
Willesborough Lees
  Kent....................34 D6
Willesden Gt Lon........44 E3
Willesley Wilts 39 J3
Willett Somset 25 H5
Willey Shrops 84 C4
Willey Warwks...........86 F6
Willey Green Surrey......30 F2
Williamscot Oxon........72 F5
Willian Herts............59 L2
Willingale Essex 60 F6
Willingdon E Susx 20 C5
Willingham Cambs......76 B1

Willingham by Stow
  Lincs................... 116 E5
Willingham St Mary
  Suffk.....................93 J6
Willington Bed...........75 G4
Willington Derbys 100 F6
Willington Dur 150 F7
Willington Kent..........33 K3
Willington N Tyne 151 H2
Willington Warwks.......72 C6
Willitoft E R Yk........ 125 H4
Williton Somset..........25 G3
Willoughby Lincs 119 G6
Willoughby Warwks.....73 G2
Willoughby-on-
  the-Wolds Notts..... 101 M7
Willoughby
  Waterleys Leics......87 H5
Willoughton Lincs 116 F3
Willows Green Essex......61 H4
Willtown Somset.........26 B6
Wilmcote Warwks.......71 L3
Wilmington Devon 13 G3
Wilmington E Susx 20 B5
Wilmington Kent.........45 K5
Wilmslow Ches E 113 J5
Wilpshire Lancs........ 121 K4
Wilsden C Brad........ 123 G3
Wilsford Lincs......... 103 G4
Wilsford Wilts 28 C4
Wilsford Wilts 40 C8
Wilshaw Kirk........... 123 G8
Wilsill N York......... 132 B6
Wilson Leics.......... 101 H7
Wilsontown S Lans.... 176 C7
Wilstead Bed 74 F5
Wilsthorpe Lincs.........88 F2
Wilstone Herts..........58 E5
Wilton Herefs............54 E3
Wilton N York......... 134 D3
Wilton R & Cl.......... 142 C4
Wilton Wilts.............28 C5
Wilton Wilts.............40 E7
Wilton Dean Border.... 167 G6
Wimbish Green
  Essex....................76 E7
Wimbledon Gt Lon......44 E6
Wimblington Cambs.....90 B5
Wimboldsley Ches W.. 113 G8
Wimborne Minster
  Dorset.................15 J3
Wimborne St Giles
  Dorset..................28 B8
Wimbotsham Norfk......90 E3
Wimpole Cambs 75 L4
Wimpstone Warwks......72 B5
Wincanton Somset.......27 G5
Winchburgh W Loth 176 E4
Winchcombe Gloucs.....56 A3
Winchelsea E Susx 21 H3
Winchester Hants........29 J5
Winchester
  Services Hants........29 K4
Winchet Hill Kent........33 J5
Winchfield Hants.........30 C1
Winchmore Hill
  Bucks...................42 F2
Winchmore Hill
  Gt Lon..................44 F2
Wincle Ches E 113 L7
Wincobank Sheff...... 115 G3
Windermere Cumb 137 L7
Windermere Jetty
  Museum Cumb 137 L7
Winderton Warwks.......72 D6
Windhill Highld........ 212 E5
Windlesham Surrey 42 F7
Windmill Cnwll............4 D2
Windmill Hill E Susx 20 D4
Windmill Hill Somset....25 L7
Windrush Gloucs.........56 D5
Windsole Abers........ 216 B3
Windsor W & M..........42 F5
Windsor Castle
  W & M..................42 F5
Windsoredge Gloucs.....55 J7
Windsor Green Suffk.....77 K4
Windygates Fife 186 E7

Wineham W Susx.........31 L7
Winestead E R Yk...... 127 G5
Winfarthing Norfk.......92 D6
Winford IoW.............17 G5
Winford N Som 38 D7
Winforton Herefs.........68 F5
Winfrith Newburgh
  Dorset..................14 F5
Wing Bucks..............58 E4
Wing Rutlnd.............88 C3
Wingate Dur 151 J7
Wingerworth Derbys ... 115 G2
Wingfield C Beds 59 G3
Wingfield Suffk 92 F7
Wingfield Wilts..........27 J1
Wingham Kent...........35 H3
Wingrave Bucks..........58 E4
Winkburn Notts 102 B2
Winkfield Br For..........42 E6
Winkfield Row Br For....42 E6
Winkhill Staffs......... 100 B3
Winkleigh Devon.........10 F4
Winksley N York 132 C2
Winlaton Gatesd 150 F3
Winless Highld......... 231 K5
Winmarleigh Lancs 120 F2
Winnall Hants............29 J5
Winnersh Wokham......42 C6
Winnington Ches W.... 112 F6
Winscombe N Som.......38 B8
Winsford Ches W 112 F6
Winsford Somset.........24 E4
Winsham Somset.........13 J2
Winshill Staffs......... 100 F7
Winshwen Swans.........51 K6
Winskill Cumb......... 149 G2
Winsley Wilts 39 J7
Winslow Bucks 58 C3
Winson Gloucs 56 C6
Winsor Hants............28 F8
Winster Cumb 129 J2
Winster Derbys........ 100 E1
Winston Dur 140 E4
Winston Suffk 78 E3
Winstone Gloucs 55 L6
Winswell Devon..........10 D3
Winterborne Came
  Dorset.................14 D5
Winterborne
  Clenston Dorset.......14 F2
Winterborne
  Houghton Dorset......14 F2
Winterborne
  Kingston Dorset.......15 G3
Winterborne
  Monkton Dorset.......14 D5
Winterborne
  Stickland Dorset.......14 F2
Winterborne
  Whitechurch
  Dorset.................14 F2
Winterborne
  Zelston Dorset..........15 G3
Winterbourne S Glos.....38 F4
Winterbourne
  W Berk..................41 J6
Winterbourne
  Abbas Dorset...........14 C4
Winterbourne
  Bassett Wilts..........40 C5
Winterbourne
  Dauntsey Wilts........28 D4
Winterbourne Earls
  Wilts....................28 D5
Winterbourne
  Gunner Wilts..........28 D4
Winterbourne
  Monkton Wilts.........40 C6
Winterbourne
  Steepleton Dorset.....14 C4
Winterbourne Stoke
  Wilts....................28 B3
Winterburn N York 131 H7
Winteringham
  N Linc................. 125 L5
Winterley Ches E........99 H2
Winterslow Wilts........28 E5
Winterton N Linc...... 125 L6

Winterton-on-Sea
Norfk 107 K8
Winthorpe Notts 102 D2
Winton BCP 15 K4
Winton Cumb 139 H5
Wintringham Cambs....75 H3
Wintringham N York 134 D5
Winwick Cambs....89 G7
Winwick Nhants 87 J8
Winwick Warrtn 112 E3
Wirksworth Derbys 100 F2
Wirral 111 J4
Wirswall Ches E 98 D4
Wisbech Cambs....90 C2
Wisbech St Mary
Cambs....90 B2
Wisborough Green
W Susx....31 H6
Wiseman's Bridge
Pembks....49 K6
Wiseton Notts.... 116 B4
Wishaw N Lans 175 L7
Wishaw Warwks....85 L5
Wispington Lincs....117 K6
Wissett Suffk....93 H7
Wissington Suffk 62 A2
Wistanstow Shrops 83 H6
Wistanswick Shrops....98 F6
Wistaston Ches E.... 99 G2
Wistaston Green
Ches E....99 G2
Wiston Pembks....49 H4
Wiston S Lans 165 J3
Wiston W Susx....18 F3
Wistow Cambs....89 K7
Wistow N York 124 F4
Wiswell Lancs.... 121 L3
Witcham Cambs....90 C7
Witchampton Dorset....15 J2
Witchford Cambs....90 C7
Witcombe Somset 26 C6
Witham Essex....61 K5
Witham Friary
Somset....27 H3
Witham on the Hill
Lincs....88 F1
Witham St Hughs
Lincs....102 E1
Withcall Lincs....118 C5
Withdean Br & H....19 J4
Witherenden Hill
E Susx....33 H7
Witheridge Devon....11 J3
Witherley Leics....86 D4
Withern Lincs....118 F5
Withernsea E R Yk....127 H5
Withernwick E R Yk....126 F3
Withersdale Street
Suffk....92 F7
Withersfield Suffk....76 F5
Witherslack Cumb....129 J3
Withiel Cnwll.... 4 F3
Withiel Florey
Somset....24 F5
Withington Gloucs....56 B5
Withington Herefs....69 L5
Withington Manch.... 113 J3
Withington Shrops....83 L2
Withington Staffs.... 100 B5
Withleigh Devon....11 K3
Withnell Lancs.... 121 J6
Withybed Green
Worcs....85 H8
Withybrook Warwks....86 E6
Withycombe Somset....24 F3
Withyham E Susx....32 E6
Withypool Somset....24 D4
Withywood Bristl....38 E6
Witley Surrey....30 F4
Witnesham Suffk....78 E4
Witney Oxon....57 G6
Wittering C Pete....88 F3
Wittersham Kent....21 H1
Witton Birm....85 J5
Witton Norfk....93 G2
Witton Norfk.... 107 H6
Witton Gilbert Dur.... 151 G5
Witton le Wear Dur.... 140 E2

Witton Park Dur 140 F2
Wiveliscombe
Somset....25 G5
Wivelrod Hants 30 A4
Wivelsfield E Susx 19 K2
Wivelsfield Green
E Susx....19 K2
Wivenhoe Essex....62 C4
Wiveton Norfk 106 C4
Wix Essex....62 E3
Wixams Bed....74 F5
Wixford Warwks....71 K4
Wixoe Suffk....77 G6
Woburn C Beds....58 F2
Woburn Safari Park
C Beds....74 D7
Woburn Sands
M Keyn....74 D7
Woking Surrey....43 G8
Wokingham Wokham ...42 D6
Woldingham Surrey....32 C3
Wold Newton E R Yk.... 135 G5
Wold Newton NE Lin.... 118 C3
Wolfclyde S Lans 165 K3
Wolferton Norfk 105 G6
Wolfhill P & K 186 B2
Wolf's Castle Pembks 49 G3
Wolfsdale Pembks....48 F3
Wollaston Dudley....84 F6
Wollaston Nhants....74 C2
Wollaston Shrops....83 G2
Wollaton C Nott.... 101 K4
Wollaton Hall C Nott.... 101 K5
Wollerton Shrops....98 F6
Wollescote Dudley....85 G6
Wolseley Bridge
Staffs.... 100 A7
Wolsingham Dur.... 150 D7
Wolstanton Staffs....99 J3
Wolston Warwks....86 E7
Wolvercote Oxon....57 J6
Wolverhampton
Wolves....85 G4
Wolverhampton
Halfpenny Green
Airport Staffs....84 E5
Wolverley Worcs....84 E7
Wolverton Hants....41 K8
Wolverton M Keyn....74 B6
Wolverton Warwks....72 B3
Wolverton Wilts....27 H5
Wolvesnewton Mons....54 C7
Wolvey Warwks....86 E6
Wolvey Heath
Warwks....86 E5
Wolviston S on T.... 141 K3
Wombleton N York.... 133 K3
Wombourne Staffs....84 F5
Wombwell Barns.... 115 H2
Womenswold Kent....35 G5
Womersley N York.... 124 E6
Wonersh Surrey....31 G3
Wonford Devon....12 B4
Wonston Dorset....14 E2
Wonston Hants....29 J4
Wooburn Bucks....42 E3
Wooburn Green
Bucks....42 E3
Woodacott Devon.... 9 K4
Woodall Rothm.... 115 J5
Woodall Services
Rothm.... 115 J5
Woodbastwick Norfk....93 G1
Wood Bevington
Warwks....71 J4
Woodborough Notts....101 M3
Woodborough Wilts....40 C7
Woodbridge Suffk....78 F5
Woodbury Devon....12 C5
Woodbury Salterton
Devon....12 C5
Woodchester Gloucs....55 J7
Woodchurch Kent....34 C7
Woodcombe Somset....24 E3
Woodcote Gt Lon....44 F7
Woodcote Oxon....41 M4
Woodcote Wrekin....84 D1
Woodcroft Gloucs....38 D2

Wood Dalling Norfk 106 C6
Woodditton Cambs 76 F3
Woodeaton Oxon....57 K5
Wood End Gt Lon....43 J4
Wood End Herts....60 B3
Woodend Highld.... 190 F4
Woodend Nhants....73 H5
Woodend W Loth.... 176 C4
Woodend W Susx....17 M2
Wood End Warwks....71 K1
Wood End Wolves....85 G4
Wood Enderby Lincs.... 118 C8
Woodfalls Wilts....28 D7
Woodford Cnwll.... 9 G3
Woodford Gloucs....39 G2
Woodford Gt Lon....45 H2
Woodford Nhants....88 D7
Woodford Stockp.... 113 K5
Woodford Bridge
Gt Lon....45 H2
Woodford Green
Gt Lon....45 H2
Woodford Halse
Nhants....73 G4
Woodford Wells
Gt Lon....45 H2
Woodgate Birm....85 H6
Woodgate Devon....25 H7
Woodgate W Susx....18 C5
Woodgate Worcs....71 H2
Wood Green Gt Lon....44 F2
Woodgreen Hants....28 D7
Woodhall N York.... 131 J2
Woodhall Spa Lincs.... 117 K8
Woodham Bucks....58 B4
Woodham Surrey....43 H7
Woodham Ferrers
Essex....61 J7
Woodham Mortimer
Essex....61 K6
Woodham Walter
Essex....61 K6
Wood Hayes Wolves....85 G3
Woodhead Abers.... 216 E6
Woodhill Shrops....84 D6
Woodhill Somset....26 A6
Woodhorn Nthumb.... 159 H4
Woodhouse Leeds.... 123 K4
Woodhouse Leics....87 G1
Woodhouse Sheff.... 115 H4
Woodhouse Wakefd.... 124 B6
Woodhouse Eaves
Leics....87 G2
Woodhouselee
Mdloth.... 177 H5
Woodhouselees
D & G.... 156 D6
Woodhouses Oldham.... 113 K2
Woodhouses Staffs.... 100 D8
Woodhurst Cambs....89 K7
Woodingdean
Br & H....19 K5
Woodkirk Leeds.... 123 K5
Woodland Abers.... 207 G2
Woodland Devon.... 6 F5
Woodland Devon.... 7 J3
Woodland Dur.... 140 D2
Woodland S Ayrs.... 152 E3
Woodlands Donc.... 124 E8
Woodlands Dorset....15 K2
Woodlands Hants....16 C1
Woodlands N York.... 132 E8
Woodlands of
Durris Abers.... 206 E6
Woodlands Park
W & M....42 E5
Woodland View
Sheff.... 114 F4
Woodleigh Devon.... 7 H6
Woodley Wokham....42 C5
Woodmancote
Gloucs....39 H2
Woodmancote
Gloucs....55 L3
Woodmancote
Gloucs....56 A6
Woodmancote
W Susx....17 L2

Woodmancote
W Susx....19 H3
Woodmancott Hants....29 K3
Woodmansey E R Yk.... 126 C3
Woodmansgreen
W Susx....30 E6
Woodmansterne
Surrey....32 B2
Woodmanton Devon....12 C5
Woodnesborough
Kent....35 J4
Woodnewton Nhants....88 F5
Wood Norton Norfk.... 106 B6
Woodplumpton
Lancs.... 121 G4
Woodrising Norfk....92 B3
Wood's Corner
E Susx....20 D2
Woodseaves Staffs....99 H7
Woodsetts Rothm.... 115 K5
Woodsford Dorset....14 E4
Wood's Green E Susx....33 H6
Woodside Br For....42 F6
Woodside Fife.... 187 G5
Woodside Gt Lon....45 G6
Woodside P & K.... 195 K8
Woodstock Oxon....57 H5
Woodston C Pete....89 H4
Wood Street Norfk.... 107 H7
Wood Street Village
Surrey....30 F2
Woodton Norfk....93 G5
Woodtown Devon....22 F6
Woodville Derbys.... 100 F8
Wood Walton Cambs....89 J7
Woofferton Shrops....69 K2
Wookey Somset....26 D3
Wookey Hole Somset....26 D2
Wool Dorset....14 F5
Woolacombe Devon....23 G3
Woolage Green Kent....35 H5
Woolaston Gloucs....54 E7
Woolaston Common
Gloucs....54 E7
Woolavington
Somset....25 M3
Woolbeding W Susx....30 E6
Woolbrook Devon....12 E5
Wooler Nthumb.... 168 E4
Woolfardisworthy
Devon....11 J3
Woolfardisworthy
Devon....22 E7
Woolfords S Lans.... 176 D6
Woolhampton
W Berk....41 L6
Woolhope Herefs....69 L7
Woolland Dorset....14 E2
Woolley BaNES....39 H6
Woolley Cambs....89 G8
Woolley Wakefd.... 123 L7
Woolley Edge
Services Wakefd 123 K7
Woolmere Green
Worcs....71 G2
Woolmer Green
Herts....59 L4
Woolminstone
Somset....13 K2
Woolpit Suffk....77 L3
Woolstaston Shrops....83 J4
Woolsthorpe by
Belvoir Lincs.... 102 D5
Woolsthorpe-by-
Colsterworth
Lincs.... 102 F7
Woolston C Soth....16 E1
Woolston Shrops....97 L7
Woolston Somset....25 H4
Woolston Somset....26 F5
Woolston Warrtn.... 112 F4
Woolstone Gloucs....55 L3
Woolstone M Keyn....74 C6
Woolstone Oxon....40 F3
Woolston Green
Devon.... 7 H3
Woolton Lpool.... 112 B4
Woolton Hill Hants....41 H7

Woolverstone Suffk......78 E6
Woolverton Somset......27 H2
Woolwich Gt Lon............45 H4
Woonton Herefs............69 G4
Woore Shrops..................99 G4
Wootten Green Suffk.....92 F8
Wootton Bed..................74 E5
Wootton Kent..................35 G5
Wootton N Linc............126 D7
Wootton Nhants............73 L3
Wootton Oxon................57 H4
Wootton Oxon................57 J7
Wootton Staffs............100 C4
Wootton Bassett
Wilts..............................40 B4
Wootton Bridge
IoW................................17 G4
Wootton Courtenay
Somset..........................24 E3
Wootton Fitzpaine
Dorset............................13 J4
Wootton Rivers Wilts.....40 D7
Wootton St
Lawrence Hants........29 L2
Wootton Wawen
Warwks..........................71 L2
Worcester Worcs..........70 F4
Worcester Park
Gt Lon............................44 E6
Wordsley Dudley............84 F6
Worfield Shrops............84 D4
Workington Cumb......136 D2
Worksop Notts............115 L5
Worlaby N Linc............126 C7
Worlds End Hants........29 M8
Worlds End W Susx........19 J2
Worle N Som..................38 A7
Worleston Ches E..........98 F2
Worlingham Suffk..........93 J5
Worlington Devon..........11 H3
Worlington Suffk............91 G8
Worlingworth Suffk........78 F2
Wormbridge Herefs........54 B2
Wormegay Norfk............90 F2
Wormelow Tump
Herefs............................54 C3
Wormhill Derbys..........114 C6
Wormingford Essex......61 M2
Worminghall Bucks......57 M6
Wormington Gloucs......71 J7
Wormit Fife..................186 F3
Wormleighton
Warwks..........................72 F4
Wormley Herts..............60 B6
Wormley Surrey..............30 F4
Wormshill Kent..............34 B3
Wormsley Herefs............69 H5
Worplesdon Surrey........30 F2
Worrall Sheff................114 F3
Worsbrough Barns......115 G2
Worsbrough Bridge
Barns..........................115 G2
Worsbrough Dale
Barns..........................115 G2
Worsley Salfd..............113 H2
Worstead Norfk............107 G7
Worsthorne Lancs........122 C4
Worston Devon................6 E5
Worston Lancs............122 B3
Worth Kent....................35 J4
Wortham Suffk..............92 C7
Worthen Shrops............83 G3
Worthenbury
Wrexhm..........................98 B4
Worthing Norfk............106 B8
Worthing W Susx............18 F5
Worthington Leics......101 H7
Worth Matravers
Dorset............................15 H6
Wortley Barns..............114 F2
Wortley Leeds..............123 K4
Worton N York............131 H2
Worton Wilts..................39 L8
Wortwell Norfk..............92 F6
Wotton-under-
Edge Gloucs................39 H2
Wotton Underwood
Bucks............................58 B5

Woughton on the
Green M Keyn............74 C6
Wouldham Kent............46 B7
Wrabness Essex............62 E2
Wrafton Devon..............23 H4
Wragby Lincs..............117 J6
Wragby Wakefd............124 C6
Wrangaton Devon............7 G4
Wrangle Lincs..............104 C3
Wrangway Somset..........25 H7
Wrantage Somset..........25 L6
Wrawby N Linc............126 C8
Wraxall N Som................38 C6
Wraxall Somset..............26 E4
Wray Lancs..................130 B6
Wraysbury W & M..........43 G5
Wrayton Lancs............130 C5
Wrea Green Lancs........120 E4
Wreay Cumb................148 D5
Wrecclesham
Surrey............................30 D3
Wrekenton Gatesd......151 G3
Wrelton N York............134 B3
Wrenbury Ches E............98 E3
Wreningham Norfk..........92 E4
Wrentham Suffk..............93 K6
Wrentnall Shrops............83 H3
Wressle E R Yk............125 G4
Wressle N Linc............126 B8
Wrestlingworth
C Beds............................75 J5
Wretton Norfk................91 G4
Wrexham Wrexhm..........97 M3
Wrexham Industrial
Estate Wrexhm..........98 B3
Wribbenhall Worcs........84 E7
Wrinehill Staffs..............99 H3
Wrington N Som............38 C7
Writhlington BaNES......27 G1
Writtle Essex..................61 G6
Wrockwardine
Wrekin............................84 B2
Wroot N Linc................116 B2
Wrose C Brad..............123 H3
Wrotham Kent................33 G2
Wroughton Swindn........40 C4
Wroxall IoW....................17 G6
Wroxall Warwks..............72 B1
Wroxeter Shrops............83 L2
Wroxham Norfk............107 G8
Wroxton Oxon................72 E6
Wyaston Derbys............100 D4
Wyberton Lincs............104 A4
Wyboston Bed................75 H3
Wybunbury Ches E..........99 G3
Wychbold Worcs............71 G2
Wychnor Staffs..............85 L1
Wyck Rissington
Gloucs............................56 D4
Wycliffe Dur................140 E4
Wycoller Lancs............122 D3
Wycomb Leics............102 C7
Wycombe Marsh
Bucks............................42 E3
Wyddial Herts................60 B2
Wye Kent........................34 E5
Wyke C Brad................123 H5
Wyke Dorset..................27 H6
Wyke Champflower
Somset..........................26 F4
Wykeham N York..........134 E3
Wyken Covtry..................86 D7
Wyken Shrops................84 D4
Wyke Regis Dorset........14 C6
Wykey Shrops..................98 B7
Wylam Nthumb............150 E3
Wylde Green Birm..........85 K5
Wylye Wilts....................28 A4
Wymeswold Leics........101 L7
Wymington Bed..............74 D2
Wymondham Leics......102 D8
Wymondham Norfk........92 D3
Wynford Eagle
Dorset............................14 B3
Wyre Piddle Worcs........71 G5
Wysall Notts................101 L6
Wythall Worcs................85 J7
Wytham Oxon................57 J6

Wythenshawe
Manch........................113 J4
Wyton Cambs................89 K8
Wyton E R Yk..............126 E4
Wyverstone Suffk..........78 C2
Wyverstone Street
Suffk..............................78 B2

Y

Yaddlethorpe N Linc....116 E1
Yafforth N York............141 H7
Yalberton Torbay..............7 K4
Yalding Kent..................33 J3
Yanwath Cumb............138 D2
Yanworth Gloucs............56 B5
Yapham E R Yk............125 J1
Yapton W Susx..............18 D5
Yarborough N Som..........38 B8
Yarburgh Lincs............118 E3
Yarcombe Devon............13 G2
Yard Devon....................24 B6
Yardley Birm..................85 K6
Yardley Gobion
Nhants............................73 L5
Yardley Hastings
Nhants............................74 C3
Yardley Wood Birm........85 K7
Yarkhill Herefs................69 L6
Yarley Somset................26 D3
Yarlington Somset..........26 F5
Yarm S on T..................141 K5
Yarmouth IoW................16 D4
Yarnbrook Wilts..............27 K1
Yarnfield Staffs..............99 K6
Yarnscombe Devon........23 J6
Yarnton Oxon................57 J5
Yarpole Herefs................69 J2
Yarrow Border..............166 E4
Yarrow Feus Border......166 E4
Yarrowford Border......166 F4
Yarwell Nhants..............88 F4
Yate S Glos....................39 G4
Yateley Hants................42 D7
Yatesbury Wilts..............40 B6
Yattendon W Berk..........41 K5
Yatton Herefs................69 H2
Yatton N Som................38 B7
Yatton Keynell Wilts......39 K5
Yaverland IoW................17 H5
Yaxham Norfk................92 B2
Yaxley Cambs................89 H5
Yaxley Suffk..................92 D8
Yazor Herefs..................69 H5
Yeading Gt Lon..............43 J4
Yeadon Leeds..............123 J3
Yealand Conyers
Lancs..........................129 K5
Yealand Redmayne
Lancs..........................129 K4
Yealmpton Devon............6 E5
Yearsley N York............133 J5
Yeaton Shrops................98 B8
Yeaveley Derbys..........100 D4
Yeavering Nthumb........168 D4
Yedingham N York........134 D4
Yelford Oxon..................57 G6
Yell Shet......................235 d3
Yelling Cambs................75 J3
Yelvertoft Nhants............87 H7
Yelverton Devon..............6 D3
Yelverton Norfk..............93 G3
Yenston Somset..............27 G7
Yeoford Devon................11 H5
Yeolmbridge Cnwll..........9 J7
Yeovil Somset................26 D7
Yeovil Marsh Somset....26 D7
Yeovilton Somset..........26 D6
Yesnaby Ork................234 b5
Yetminster Dorset..........14 B1
Yettington Devon............12 D5
Yetts o'Muckhart
Clacks........................185 L6
Yew Tree Sandw............85 H4
Y Felinheli Gwynd........109 G7
Y Ferwig Cerdgn............65 G5

Y Ffôr Gwynd..................95 G5
Yielden Bed....................74 E2
Yieldshields S Lans......176 B7
Yiewsley Gt Lon............43 H4
Ynys Gwynd..................95 K5
Ynysboeth Rhondd........37 G2
Ynysddu Caerph............37 J2
Ynyshir Rhondd..............36 F3
Ynystawe Swans............51 K5
Ynysybwl Rhondd..........37 G2
Yockleton Shrops............83 H2
Yokefleet E R Yk..........125 J5
Yoker C Glas................174 F5
York C York..................124 F1
Yorkletts Kent................34 E3
Yorkley Gloucs................54 F6
Yorkshire Dales
National Park......131 G4
York Town Surrey............42 E7
Youlgreave Derbys......114 E8
Youlthorpe E R Yk........134 B7
Youlton N York............133 G6
Yoxall Staffs................100 C8
Yoxford Suffk..................79 H2
Y Rhiw Gwynd................94 D6
Ysbyty Ifan Conwy........96 C3
Ysbyty Ystwyth
Cerdgn............................67 G1
Ysceifiog Flints............111 G7
Ystalyfera Neath............52 B6
Ystrad Rhondd................36 F2
Ystrad Aeron Cerdgn......66 C4
Ystradfellte Powys..........52 E5
Ystradgynlais Powys......52 C6
Ystrad Meurig
Cerdgn............................66 F2
Ystrad Mynach
Caerph............................37 H2
Ystradowen V Glam........36 F5
Ythanbank Abers..........217 G7
Ythanwells Abers..........216 C6
Ythsie Abers................217 G7

Z

Zeal Monachorum
Devon............................11 G4
Zeals Wilts......................27 H5
Zelah Cnwll......................4 C5
Zennor Cnwll....................2 E4
Zouch Notts................101 J7
ZSL London Zoo
Gt Lon............................44 F4
ZSL Whipsnade Zoo
C Beds............................59 G4

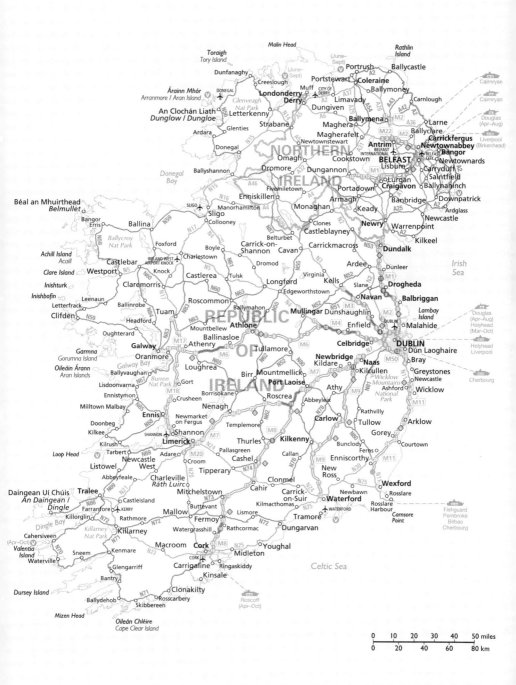

Ireland

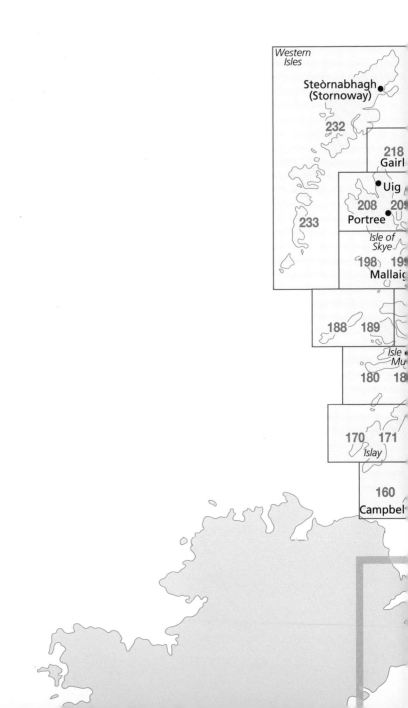

Western
Isles

Steòrnabhagh
(Stornoway)

232

218
Gairl

Uig

208   20
233   Portree

Isle of
Skye

198   19
Mallaic

188   189

Isle
Mu

180   18

170   171
Islay

160
Campbel